THE
ROUND
BARN

—

A BIOGRAPHY
OF AN AMERICAN FARM

JACQUELINE DOUGAN JACKSON

Beloit College PRESS

Beloit College Press
Beloit, Wisconsin

© Jacqueline Dougan Jackson 2011
www.roundbarnstories.com

First published 2011
Manufactured in the United States of America
ISBN: 978-1-884941-18-4

Design by Jeremy Schmidt
Artwork and cover by Megan Trever Ryan

Cover photos: The barn as seen from the cow yard;
W.J. Dougan with Marie of Sarnia

To Grampa

In Fulfillment of a Promise

CONTENTS
VOLUME ONE

Book Two: The Milkhouse

Book Three: Milk Routes

VOLUME TWO will contain
Book Four: The Big House
Book Five: Crops and Hybrid Seed Corn
Book Six: Ron's Home Place and American Breeders Service

VOLUME THREE will contain
Book Seven: Neighbors, Town, and County
Book Eight: State, Nation, and the World

TO THE READERS OF
THE ROUND BARN

This is the first of three volumes about the Dougan farm near Beloit, Wisconsin. Volume I, divided into three books, is organized around the milk business aspects of the farm: the cows and barns, milk processing, distribution. It contains stories, accounts, history—the Table of Contents will indicate to you its scope. Volume II, also with stories and accounts, continues with general farming aspects: crops, the hired help, life in the big farm house and the little house, the acquirement of two more farms, and the growth of the hybrid seed corn business. Volume III moves out to the farm's relationship with neighbors, Turtle Township, the town of Beloit, Rock County, the state of Wisconsin, and the rest of the world. It contains a history of the growth of artificial insemination and American Breeders Service—personally acquired—and the ending of this small but significant family farm and business enterprise.

The material is related through the eyes of Jackie, myself, who lived through much of this time, but it is not a personal memoir. It is a collective biography. The entire work chronicles an inestimable way of life that in this land has waned and is now either vastly changed or has ended.

There is a wealth of material connected with this farm through its years of activity—from W.J.'s buying of the farm in 1906, to his son Ronald's retirement from the milk business in 1967, and finally from the hybrid seed corn business, and active farming, in 1972. The material has come from hundreds of people and sources. A number of the stories have already been published in *Stories from the Round Barn* (Northwestern University Press, 1997) and *More Stories from the Round Barn* (Northwestern University Press, 2002); those stories were all originally part of *The Round Barn*, and have now (sometimes slightly altered) been reunited with their parent work. They join many more stories, histories and oral histories, biographies and autobiographies, letters, diaries, essays, magazine and newspaper articles, school assignments, science and technology, scribbled notes, and what I call "accounts," with the stories forming the glue for all the informational material—though much of that material has stories within it. And everything bears on the telling of the farm's overall history.

The farm was an unusual one in that its founder, my grandfather, had a philosophy that he painted on his silo, and lived by. Over the years he, and my father after him, hired a diversity of help—local people (often Turtle Township neighbors), university students, men around the country found by advertising in *Hoard's Dairyman*, and a number of foreign workers. These latter escalated in the post World War II years, when there were two Scandinavians on the farm every six months, through the American Scandinavian Foundation. There were also a number of handicapped workers; W.J.'s deafness gave him a special feel for the handicapped, and my father, growing up in the household, followed that lead as a natural course. In the teen years of the century the farm was on the cutting edge of alfalfa development, and then hybrid seed corn and artificial insemination in the thirties and forties. Both my grandfather and father stayed in close touch with the University of Wisconsin, and methods of scientific farming from other sources as well.

Over the seventy years of the farm's history, it produced many documents: personal, business, and other. These documents have come from many places: the attic and spare room at my parents' house at the farm (Chez Nous) have been cornucopias, for over the years they became repositories not only for the direct family's materials, but also for relatives' papers, books, photographs, and furniture which had a way of accumulating there. My grandparents' papers, including boxes of my Uncle Trever's papers, were moved from the dairy farm's Big House to my grandparents' house in town when Grampa retired, and then to my parents' catch-all room when Grama died. Trever himself, his son my cousin Jerry, and my brother Craig, contributed many documents. Papers, including ledgers, also came from my parents' home offices, the dairy office, business files, even the round barn itself. My grandparents' letters to my father when he was in college were mixed in with kids' drawings and unsorted family papers brought up from the Little House when our family made the move a mile up Colley Road in 1938, to Chez Nous, and stored in the attic of our remodeled farmhouse. No one had looked over these materials until my mother alerted me to their existence. When I continued searching, I found more papers and letters stashed in boxes, photo albums, scrap books, work baskets, the backs (and cracks) of drawers, behind pictures, on closet shelves, or merely loose in peculiar places. I'm grateful that so many, however unlikely, have been preserved.

Readers may wonder why there is so much. I suggest several reasons. Ours was a literate and educated family. Grampa and Grama were both college graduates at a time when the terminal degree was eighth grade, and this was true also of my maternal grandparents. Both my parents had college degrees. Everyone was a reader and letter writer. Grampa and Grama wrote voluminously to their sons in college, worrying over their spending and their moral development, but the letters also contained news of farm and family activities. And because of Grampa's deafness, many things were written to him that would ordinarily have been spoken and lost. Grampa himself often wrote out what he wanted to discuss with his son, or someone else, the next day. And obviously, we were all inveterate savers. Much also was preserved merely by chance.

In addition, meticulous files were kept in the business. Every cow was documented, every milk route, all plantings—including where, dates, and conditions. All business transactions were filed, all government correspondence.

To add to this richness, beginning in 1967 I sought out people who had to do with the farm, and were willing to tell me about it. Some supplied photos and letters. My parents were partners in this, and it enriched their old age. I'm sorry I didn't get to certain key people before they died—although some had died before I was born, or before I was old enough, or savvy enough, to know what I was wanting to do. (One former employee, a Turtle Township man, refused to tell me a certain story which I'm sure reflected badly on my grandfather. I tried several times to weasel it out of him, but he was adamant. This is too bad, for with so many considering Grampa a saint, it would have been good to have a few more negative bits to relate than I have.)

Everything in these pages is directly connected with the farm. And everything is as accurate as I have been able to make it. I would say that this book is true, but with these qualifications: history and memory are always in the present. People's memories are selective and faulty, including my own, and even change from year to year. I've often had different sources who don't agree on the same set of "facts"; in these cases I've taken the more likely or, if equally so, the more interesting. When there are gaps that have needed filling, I've supplied what would have been most likely, given the people and the times. The "accounts" are as factual as I've been able to make them, including the history, science, technology, and people. These have been aided by actual documents of the time. However, though I have included much on many subjects—corn, artificial breeding, the history of farming in general—much has been left out. Treatment of some important subjects has been omitted entirely, except by oblique reference, such as soils, pesticides, and an orderly discussion of the development of alfalfa.

When it comes to the actual stories, I have been more free. They fit the genre of "creative non-fiction." Many are "true" all the way through, sometimes even to the major conversation—an example is my grandfather's "Begone, laddie," at the Janesville 4-H Fair. That climaxing sentence is still seared on my brother's brain. Mostly, details and conversation have been added, but always within a framework of actuality. Every story has its basis in a real occurrence. The interpretation of a situation is sometimes that of my source, but is often my own, and could well be wrong and is certainly only a partial picture. I've tried not to give in too often to my raconteur father's lifelong advice, "Never ruin a good story for the facts."

My mother is not adequately depicted in these pages. Her influence on everything, especially on the people herein, was tremendous. She was my grandfather's confidante and often his secretary. But mainly she was busy with her work in the music world, and raising her children to be musicians and dancers and artists and writers and scholars, as well as honorable people. Stories involving her are plentiful, but most are not directly connected with farm activities, and so are omitted.

A final story about my father, who had been supplying material and reading and critiquing this work over many, many years: When it appeared the book was going to be published, he (at age 90) asked me, "Now just how soon will this book be out?"

—Jackie: "Well, I haven't finished it yet, and that'll take at least a year, and then it will take them at least a year to edit and publish it—"

—Ron, shaking his head ruefully: "I'm afraid it's going to be a posthumous book."

—Jackie: "Oh, come on, Dad, you can manage to live a few more years!"

—Ron, quick as a flash: "I didn't mean me!"

ABOUT THE NOW

When I was a kid at the Little House on the dairy, my dad one noon pulled down the dining room curtains so that "I can see my cows!" From then on, we all enjoyed watching cows as we chewed our cuds, and as they, in their pasture, did also.

The Round Barn stories essentially end when my father retired in 1972. Though I haven't written about it, I am aware of what has happened in agriculture since that time. One of agribusiness's giants, Archer Daniels Midland, is a few miles from my home. Nearer is a CAFO (Concentrated Animal Feeding Operation) where weaned piglets arrive to be fattened for market, and never put snout to soil. The fate of most present-day cows is to be fed antibiotics, milked around the clock, and allowed only a few years of production before being sent to slaughter. I know of genetic splicing, its virtues and dangers: the problems of monoculture; ethanol; the swallowing of arable land; the mining of ancient waters. The dangers in our air, soil, oceans. Our over-processed diets that produce obesity and diabetes. I've read the books of those prominent in environment and agriculture. They have written knowledgeably about what is happening in our world. But these subjects are beyond the scope of this book.

However, there are exciting movements that run counter the direction of the recent past — movements for sustainable agriculture, for organic and healthy foods, for humaneness in the treatment of animals, for the preservation of both farmland and our necessary wildernesses. They recognize saving diversity is essential, and that loving and caring for its thin skin of soil makes life on our planet possible.

I am hopeful that the Round Barn volumes might serve as a touchstone for values worth honoring, recovering, and making prominent once again. These values have not vanished entirely. Against the tide of ever-bigger agriculture, innumerable family farms across the country strive to maintain ways of life that my grandfather would recognize and honor. His values, so eloquently stated on the silo at the heart of his farm, can be relevant to our lives today, and to our current attitudes toward farming. I am grateful that I grew up on wholesome food in a healthy atmosphere, and was able, for the most part, to raise my children that way. Might it be the same for my grandchildren, and for the generations to come. It is not an impossible dream.

American farming on the Fourth of July, c.1919, when tractors were the most advanced development in agricultural technology. This one is a Yankee, made by the American Tractor Corporation of Peoria, Illinois.

ACKNOWLEDGMENTS

I wish to thank the many people who have talked or written to me over the years, sharing their knowledge about the farm and the people who participated in its life. Many contributed pictures, clippings and other materials. A number have died since the collecting of material was begun. Some, like my Dougan grandparents, died before this work was begun in this form, but their contributions, and their lives, are the foundation of *The Round Barn*. A number of the living, and those who, like my parents, died while this work was in progress, have critiqued parts of the manuscript, including their own sections, thus keeping a brake on any tendency to fictionalize. There are surely contributors I've missed in this listing. I am grateful to all who have so generously helped me put together this work.

The family comes first: Eunice and Wesson Dougan, Ronald and Vera Dougan, Trever and Bernice Dougan, Jerry Dougan, Joan Dougan Schmidt, Karl Schmidt, Jeremy Schmidt, Pat Dougan Dalvit, Lewis Dalvit, Craig Dougan, Jackie Dalvit Guthrie, Stephanie Dalvit McPhillips, Damaris Jackson, Megan Jackson Ryan, Gillian Jackson Ferranto, Elspeth Jackson DeBow, Paul Campagna, and June Campagna Schaffer. Eloise Marston Schnaitter has been the richest non-family source, and supplied many details of Esther's story.

Others who participated in the stories or have told their own stories include Walter Abbott, Allen Adams, Arthur Adams, Hugh Alberts, Pat and Ralph Anderson, Lyall Bacon, Bob Babcock, Anthony Bannister, David Bartlett, Ada Beadle, Bill Behling, Oscar and Marian Berg, Theodore Booth-Clibborn, Al Bowen, Quentin Bowen, Earl and Geneva Bown, Floyd Brewer, Phyllis Bruyere, Helen Burnette, Fred Buschner, Anna Marie Calland, Ernie Capps, Georgia Clary, David Collins, Scottie Cook, Al Cox, Mrs. Gustave Dahlstrom, Jean Maxworthy Davis, Mathias Dietrick, Robert Fey, Ralph Flagler, Erv and Olive Fonda, Ron and Georgie Freitag, Bob and Evelyn George, Alfred Gerue, Gulbrand and Solveig Gjestvang, Dan Goldsmith, Lowrey Greenburg, Copeland Greene, Amos and Isabelle Grundahl, Russell and

Mary Adair Gunderson, Benny Harder, Robert Hart, Dorothy Bach Haugan, Paul Herreid, Phil Higley, John Holmes, Jean and Phil Holmes, Red and Loretta Holmes, Sally Holmes, Julia Hornbostel, Lloyd Hornbostel, Jim Howard, Jesse Hunt, Margaret Weiland Ikeman, Rodney Jennings, Florence and Justin Johnson, Howard Johnson, Raymond and Berniece Jorgenson, Bernard and Grace Kassilke, Charles Kellor, Mark Kellor, Jr., Dan Kelley, Glen Kinderman, Don King, Marie Knilans, Richard Knilans, Harlan Koch, Milton Koenecke, Omer Koopman, John Kopp, Marge Kopp, Lawrence Langklotz, Nils Lang-Ree, Lester L. Larson, George Lentell, C.E. Loomis, Dorothy Kirk Lueken, Neil Manley, Clair Mathews, Homer Mathews, Bob Maxworthy, Dolores McCormick, Polly Kirk Mersky, Howard Milner, Norman Neal, Roscoe Ocker, Stanley Otis, David Orlin, Sandy Parker, Norman Peebles, Ed Pfaff, Jerry Pfaff, Dick Post, Orland Potts, Larry Raymer, Cleo Reinfeldt, Lester Richardson, Katie Weiland Russell, Fay Sims, Oscar Skogen, Lester and Mildred Stam, Irene Sommers, John Sullivan, Helen Tapp, George and Elsie Tscharner, Russel Ullius, Fannie Veihman, Fred Veihman, Harry Vogts, Otto Waggershauser, Gary Wallace, Betty Beadle Wallace, Bridget Walsh, Jim Walsh, Dick Walsh, Robert Walton, Robert Weiland, Harry Wellnitz, Harlan Whitmore, Helen Wallace Wildermuth.

I owe thanks to many people for sharing their technical expertise; most of those listed here have also gone over portions of the manuscript: Paul Doby, DVM, retired Illinois State Veterinarian; Walter Johnson, DVM; J.J. Smith, DVM and his wife LaVerne (tantamount to DVM); Professors R.J. Lambert, D.A. Miller, and Joseph Tobias at the University of Illinois; Professors Norman Neal, William Tracy, and Hugh Iltis of the University of Wisconsin; Professor Luke Snell of Southern Illinois University, Edwardsville; Professor Richard Dimond, University of Illinois Springfield, and Lloyd Hornbostel; also Dr. David Bartlett, Dr. Lester L. Larson, Dr. Robert Walton, Dr. John Sullivan, Phil Higley, Robert Woodward, Mathias Dietrick, Harlan Koch, Fred Buschner, and Neil Manley, all of American Breeders Service; Mary Schroeder of the United Methodist Church, Wisconsin Annual Conference. Gillian Ferranto has generously contributed her knowledge of chemistry, nutrition, farming, and milk.

Those who have supported and critiqued during the writing process include: John and Peg Knoepfle, Carol Manley, Gary Smith, Karl Schmidt, Phil Kendall, David Bartlett, Paul Doby, Walter Johnson, LaVerne and JJ Smith, Jean Ladendorf, Michele Woolsey, Sue Anders, Lloyd and Julia Hornbostel, Rodd Whelpley, Yosh Golden, Martha Miller, Christy Cameron, Jeanne

Handy, Pat Martin, Larry Wright, Brian Jackson, Amy Spies, Anita Stienstra, the members of the Brainchild Writing Collective, Bill Furry, Eva and Chad Walsh, Alison Walsh Sackett, Carol Dell, Sandy Costa, Robert McElroy, Berniece Rabe, Chomingwen Pond, Ethan Lewis, Barbara Burkhardt, Barbara Olson, and my daughters Damaris Jackson, Megan Ryan, Gillian Ferranto, and Elspeth DeBow. Professor Richard Dimond helped with retrieving memories. Sangamon State University (now University of Illinois Springfield) granted me three sabbaticals. A number of the above people have helped me with the researching, transcribing of tapes, typing, word processing, and proofing, as did Betty Bradley, Ruth Vogel, Marian Levin, Lola Lucas, Charla Stone, Dorothy Ford, Annette Hunsaker, and Wendy Baylor. Proofing for the present volume was contributed by Julie Low, Amy Spies, Posy Flatt, Peg Knoepfle, Nancy Flood, Pat Martin, and Hannah Kay. Further thanks go to Elle DeBow for helping me to adapt my manuscripts to current technology.

I have had much help in gathering and preparing photographs, from, among others, Paul Kerr of the Beloit Historical Society, Steve Larson of *Hoard's Dairyman*, James Quillen, Wesley Nelson, Beverly Jorgenson Soper, Steve Truesdale, Jerome Dougan, Craig Dougan, Pat Dougan Dalvit, Eloise Schnaitter, Marie Knilans, Howard Milner, Shirley Bauer, Freila Bennett, Susan Kelly, Carol Patterson, David Luebke, Dorothy Lueken, Cheryl Martingilio, Carol Hanson, Phyllis Bruyere, George Lentell, Benny Harder, John Kopp, Ariel Amend, Penny Van Kampen, Nils Lang-Ree., Celia Wesle, Megan Ryan, Roland Klose. Very special thanks go my techno-wizard Mitch Hopper, who has taken apparently impossibly damaged photos and repaired them via computer. He even added a few small cows to an aerial view, and produced a CD and DVD gallery of thousands of Dougan farm pictures and who also has created and is maintaining my personal web site. I owe many thanks to my daughter Megan for graphics, photography enhancement, and art work. She has also designed a website for the Round Barn books, which can be found at *www.roundbarnstories.com*.

A thank-you is due to my grandparents and parents for creating documents, letters, photographs, and other source material, and never throwing anything out. I'm also grateful for their colorful lives. I'm indebted to my brother Craig Dougan for his excellent memory and for the diaries he kept throughout his teens, and to my first cousin Jerry Dougan for all his assistance in supplying and critiquing family materials. Thanks go to Ed Grutzner who in his memoir, *Tell Me a Story, Grandpa* (2003), devoted a chapter to working on the Dougan farm. From it I lifted valuable details.

A number of these stories were first published in the *Beloit Daily News* at the invitation of editor Bill Behling, associate editor Larry Raymer, and Minnie Mills Enking. Others have appeared in *Brainchild, At the Edges of Our Comfort, American Farm Youth, The Alchemist Review, The Writer's Barbeque, FOCUS/midwest, TriQuarterly,* and *TriQuarterlyOnline. Stories from the Round Barn* was read over Wisconsin Public Radio's Chapter A Day by Karl Schmidt, and *More Stories* by Jim Fleming. *Stories* has been read onto disk for the visually impaired by the Milwaukee (Wisconsin) Public Library, and used by CTB McGraw-Hill.

A special thanks goes to Steven A. Larson, editor of *Hoard's Dairyman*, for permission to reprint material originally published in that magazine.

I appreciate my alma mater, Beloit College, for sponsoring this work through The Beloit College Press, plus Jason Hughes, Tim McKearn, and Ron Nief who have facilitated this. Again, my appreciation goes always to my writing mentors: Professor Chad Walsh of Beloit College, Professor Roy Cowden, Director of the Hopwood Program, University of Michigan, and Professor William Perlmutter, Academic Vice President of St. John's University, Minnesota.

For this completed *The Round Barn, Volume I,* I have been rich in experienced editors. As mentioned above, Mitch Hopper has been my technical editor, and Megan Jackson Ryan my graphics artist and editor. Rodd Whelpley, former editor at *Illinois Issues* (University of Illinois Springfield) contributed valuable preliminary work on the text. Roland Klose, former editor of *Illinois Times*, now an editor for *The Commercial Appeal*, Memphis, has worked with me most closely (and patiently) here in Springfield. He's dug into research I could never have managed or thought of, as well as discussing with me topics I skimmed or hadn't considered. Freelance author and editor of prize-winning books, Jeremy Schmidt (who, being family, takes a personal as well as professional interest), designed the book, did further careful editing, and has seen this volume into production. Professor Tom McBride is my Beloit College Press editor. Overseeing the entire project, and never giving up on it, is the one who first accepted *The Round Barn*, my unequalled editor Reginald Gibbons of Northwestern University. I am grateful to you all.

PROLOGUE

There is the land. In the center of the land are the farm buildings. In the center of the buildings is the round barn. In the center of the barn rises a tall concrete silo. On the side of the silo are printed these words:

> The Aims of This Farm
> 1. Good Crops
> 2. Proper Storage
> 3. Profitable Live Stock
> 4. A Stable Market
> 5. Life as well as a Living
>   W.J. Dougan

The inside silo of the round barn, showing W.J. Dougan's "The Aims of This Farm."

Jackie could read these words before she could read. She said, "What do they say?" and her older sisters read them to her, or a hired man, or whoever was there. She learned them by heart without trying. She did not ask what the words meant.

W.J. Dougan is Grampa. He had the words lettered there, inside the barn

Jackie Dougan, twelve, helping with the haying.

on the silo, when he had just built the round barn. That was 1911, when Daddy was nine years old. Jackie sees these words every day. Sometimes twenty times, on a day when she and Craig and the others are playing hide-and-seek in the barn. Sometimes not for several days in a row. But add up the times she has seen them, and the days of her life, and they will come out even.

––––––––

Jackie is fifteen. She sits on the arm of Grampa's easy chair. She rumples his thinning hair and shapes it into a kewpie-doll twist. This is a ritual, with all the grandchildren, ever since they were little. Grampa laughs with his stomach, silently.

An idea strikes Jackie. She takes a pencil and paper. These are always near Grampa, for Grampa is deaf. They are always near Jackie, too, for Jackie writes things down. Maybe she has this habit from writing for Grampa all her life. Being his ears. She writes, "Grampa, I am going to write you a book. I am going to call it 'The Round Barn.'"

Grampa studies the paper. He takes a long time to ponder it. Then he nods slowly. "The Round Barn," he says. "Yes, the round barn will have a lot to say." He crinkles all over his face and laughs silently. He is pleased, she can tell.

"I can write," says Jackie to herself, "what the round barn sees. Not just what I know it sees. But what Grampa knows it sees. And Daddy. The milkmen. The cows. All of us! For the round barn is in the middle of us all, and it sees everything. It is the center."

Jackie thinks, here are the circles of the book. She draws a picture, starting with the silo and going out to the barn, and beyond.

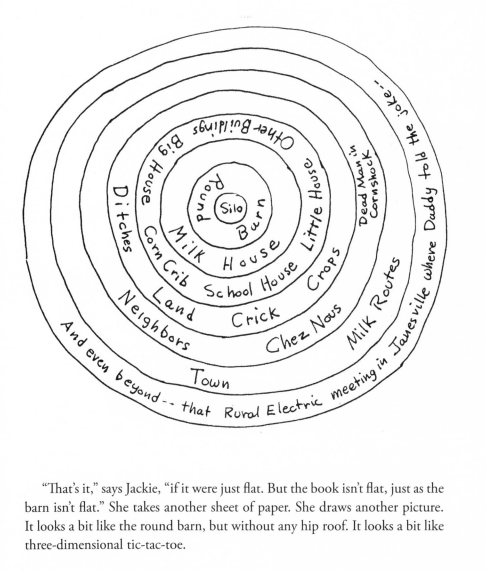

"That's it," says Jackie, "if it were just flat. But the book isn't flat, just as the barn isn't flat." She takes another sheet of paper. She draws another picture. It looks a bit like the round barn, but without any hip roof. It looks a bit like three-dimensional tic-tac-toe.

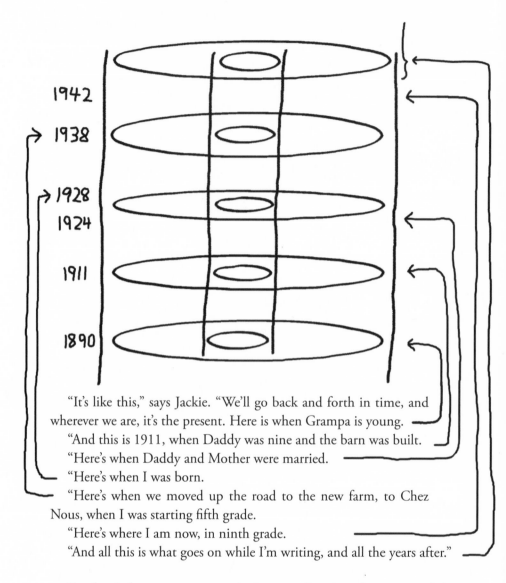

1942

1938

1928
1924

1911

1890

"It's like this," says Jackie. "We'll go back and forth in time, and wherever we are, it's the present. Here is when Grampa is young.

"And this is 1911, when Daddy was nine and the barn was built.

"Here's when Daddy and Mother were married.

"Here's when I was born.

"Here's when we moved up the road to the new farm, to Chez Nous, when I was starting fifth grade.

"Here's where I am now, in ninth grade.

"And all this is what goes on while I'm writing, and all the years after."

For the circles go out, concentric, in space. But they also go up and down in time. Like an onion. But not like an onion completely, for onion parts are too cleanly separated. They pop apart. It's more like elm wood. Elm logs can hardly be split, for the fibers interpenetrate, ring from ring, and bind all the circles together.

The story, the farm, Jackie decides, is like a log of elm wood. Everything, in all directions, in all dimensions, is bound together.

XXII   THE ROUND BARN

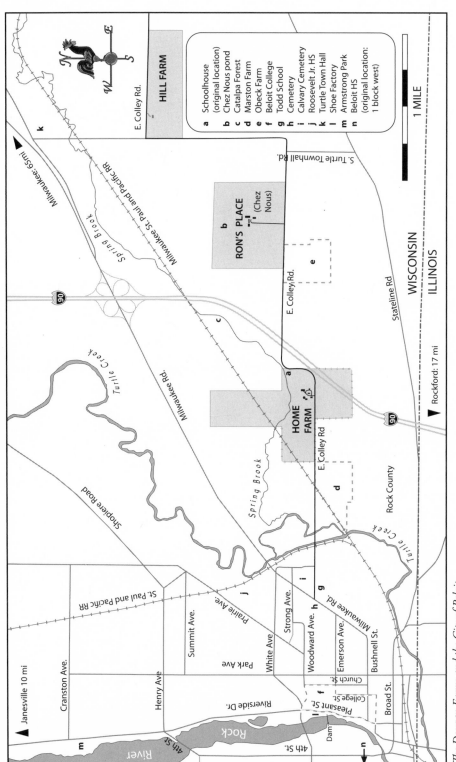

The Dougan Farms and the City of Beloit.

The Dougan Dairy Farm as it appeared by 1960.

Megan Trever Ryan

Chez Nous, the home farm of Ronald and Vera, who remodelled the old farmhouse and moved here in 1938.

FAMILY

Here is the family you'll meet in these pages.

Grampa: Wesson Joseph Dougan, 1868-1949

Grampa was generally called "Daddy Dougan" by farm people and the community. He began his career as a Methodist minister but left because of deafness. At fourteen he took over the work of the family farm—his father was injured—so he was unable to start high school till his father's death and the sale of the farm in 1887. He attended Wayland Academy in Beaver Dam and the University of Wisconsin. In 1906 he bought the Colley farm, began peddling milk in Beloit in 1907, and built the round barn in 1911. His mother, Delcyetta, bore him when she was forty-five. He had three older sisters, Della (of Mason City, Iowa), Ida, and Lillian. Ida married James Croft and lived in Beloit; they adopted a daughter, Hazel. After James's death, Lillian moved in with Ida. Grampa also had second cousins, Jennie and Nelly Needham, as well as a niece and nephew, the Bosworths—the "rich relatives" of Elgin, Illinois. The youngest of their four daughters was Betsy.

Grama: Eunice Trever Dougan, 1869-1959

Eunice came from England at six months, with eight siblings; two more were born in Wisconsin. She graduated from Lawrence College and taught for two years before marriage. Her oldest brother, George, was a conservative Methodist minister of some distinction; her youngest, Albert Augustus, became a beloved professor at Lawrence, wrote an ancient history textbook still in use, and has had a hall named after him. Uncle Bert was the Dougan kids' and grandkids' favorite, and Grama's sister Ria, nine when she came to the States, was the favorite aunt. Rose, the youngest, was epileptic and probably mildly retarded. Eunice was called "Mother Dougan" by the help who lived at the Big House.

Wesson and Eunice's Children

The first child, Esther (1900) bled to death at a botched birth (the drunk doctor cut the cord too close to the body). They had two sons, Ronald (1902-96) and Trever (1904-83). Esther (1909-76) was a foster daughter. All three attended the District 12 school (with occasional stints at a town school) and Beloit High School. Ronald went to Northwestern for three years; spent a year in France and married (in 1924) Vera Wardner (1895-1988) of Chicago, who was in France doing the same type of social work; returned to Beloit and took his senior year at Beloit College. He then went into business with his father. Trever attended the University of Wisconsin, married Bernice (Binney) Marion (1905-94), worked for United Airlines for many years, and eventually owned a Chicago blueprint firm.

Ronald and Vera's Children

Ronald and Vera had four children. Joan (1925) married Karl Schmidt and they produced Peter, Jeremy, Katie, Dan, and Tom. Patricia (1926) married Lewis Dalvit and had Jackie Jo and Stephanie. Jacqueline (1928) married Robert Jackson. They had four daughters: Damaris, Megan, Gillian, and Elspeth. Craig (1930) married Carol Glad who had two sons; Craig fathered Cynthia Sue and Trever. After Carol's death he married Barbara McDonald who had three children, thus making a family of seven children.

Trever and Binney's Children

Trever and Binney had two children. Jerry (1932) married Deborah Greabell and had Scott, Patrick, and Dan. Karla (1937) married John Pendexter and had Leslie, Jay, and Geoff.

Esther's Child

Esther had one son, Russell, born in 1926. He was killed in the Korean War, 1951. Russell married and had a son, Rusty.

BOOK ONE
THE SILO
THE BARN

Megan Jackson

1 ⚔ OWL

Ronald is nine. It's fall, 1911, and the round barn is new. He comes running up the gravel incline onto the barn floor. He has a stone in his hand. He sees overhead a small brown barn owl on a rafter. He flings his stone at the owl.

Ronald Dougan, about eight, in front of the Big House.

To his astonishment, he hits the owl. The bird plummets to the new barn floor, its wings thrashing in a frenzy of death.

Ronald stands aghast. He bursts into tears. He rushes down the ramp. He crouches in the hidey place in the middle of the lilac bush on the front lawn. His eyes don't see the sun dappled, heart-shaped lilac leaves. His eyes see nothing but the flopping, flailing owl.

2 ⚔ HAYLOFT

Jackie races up the ramp of the round barn to the barn floor, springs onto an extended ladder placed against a cliff of hay, and scrambles up. From the top rung she carefully squirms over the sloping lip of green till she's a safe distance from the edge, then springs and sinks across the hay to flop down with her nose against one of the little windows spaced under the eaves. Below her is the gravel area between the round barn, the milkhouse, and the Big House. In the center, leaning on the elm tree with his face buried in the crook of his arm, is her brother, Craig. He's six, two years younger than she is. She can hear his muffled shout: "Niney-eight, niney-nine, *one hunnert*, here I come, ready or not!" He turns, looks all around, then wanders off between the icehouse and the tool house.

Jackie considers running in free, but that's too easy when only two are playing. She rolls over on her back in the new, sweet-smelling hay.

The loft is so full that hay reaches to the very top of the walls. Right over her head the roof rafters arch up, like the spokes of an umbrella or the brown gills of a mushroom, springing toward the dusty dimness of the center. The fat concrete silo is like the white stem of the mushroom; it rises from the cow barn, from below the cow barn, comes up through the barn floor, and continues through the loft to the roof. Its final few feet before the peak are made of wood, golden brown with age, and topped with a circle of little glassed windows that let light from the barn into the silo. From inside the silo you can look up and see this odd little floorless room, its ceiling a pointed cap where all the barn beams converge.

In the loft, part way up the beams, is a fretwork of lighter rafters lacing the beams together. Sparrows and pigeons balance their nests on these rafters; the straw sticks out untidily. Jackie listens to the chirping and cooing and the rush of wings. Cobwebs festoon all the rafters, great strands and streamers and ropes of cobwebs, made by generations of spiders. Old webs can't blow away in the round barn. They only grow thicker and heavier with dust.

The round barn, ramp, and side barn, around 1914.

Above her head, a little way up the slope of the roof, is the metal track for the hayfork. It circles the loft, bolted to each beam. During haying, the track has a thick-rollered trolley hanging from it, and the hayfork is fastened to the trolley. She loves to watch the fork in operation. It swings out over a loaded wagon that's been pulled up onto the barn floor by a team or tractor. It drops, crunching into the hay, and a farmhand helps embed its four great teeth firmly. On command, the horses hitched up outside start to walk, the rope they are pulling strains, the fork lifts. It grips an island of hay in its gigantic two-toothed jaws, a hill torn up by the roots. It carries it to the roof, shedding wisps, swings it sideways with a swish, and running on the track in a wide curve carries it to the spot where it's to be dropped. Up in the mow, another farmhand trips the trailing rope, the jaws unclamp, and the island falls with a *schlunk*. The men in the mow attack it with pitchforks and distribute it evenly while the fork rolls back for another bite. At each drop, the dust motes, thickly visible in the sunbeams that stream through the little windows, go crazy.

Jackie wonders what it would be like to climb along that track, like Daddy and Uncle Trever did once when they were little. The barn was new, and so full of hay that they could reach up and grasp the track. They'd pulled themselves onto it and, leaning backwards, inched along, reaching from brace to brace, past the safety of the hay beneath them, past the edge of the cliff and out over the barn floor thirty feet below. They'd inched all the way to the start of the track at the barn doors and then sat down and swung their legs. Grama had found them there and screamed. She'd ordered them down instantly, but they couldn't get down in an instant. They had to inch back. Grama couldn't bear to watch. She ordered them to report to the kitchen as soon as they were down. But Daddy and Trever hadn't reported; they'd gone behind the horse barn and thrown horse apples at the sparrows till suppertime.

Daddy hadn't been so lucky with the chute. Jackie looks over to where the chute is, alongside the silo, but there's so much hay its top is hidden. She crawls over and finds the hole, a deep black well with a square of light from the cow barn at the bottom. She can see the cement floor. It's like looking through the wrong end of a spyglass. This is the chute Daddy fell down when he was twelve, and even though he landed on a small mound of hay, he broke both his heels. His heels are still strange, with little spurs behind. "Like a bird claw," says Daddy. "I can perch on a twig and clamp from both directions and never fall off."

A pitchfork is stuck upright beside the chute. Jackie runs her fingers along its polished handle, pulls it out, and tries the weight of the hay on its tines. She pitches a pancake of hay into the chute and watches it fall as slowly as Alice down the rabbit hole. It makes the chute dark, until it breaks into the

Grampa — W.J. — standing by the wall of hay in the hayloft.

light and lands like a feather on the cow barn floor.

She crawls to the edge of the hay cliff and lies on her stomach, waiting for Craig to come seeking her. On the vast barn floor is where Daddy and Trever had their pulleys. Daddy'd said they'd taken hammers, nails, jackknives, empty spools, and string up onto the barn floor. They'd notched the spools. They'd constructed an ever more elaborate system of pulleys with the string and spools, some strings stretching for long distances. Some went horizontally, some vertically, some diagonally, till the barn floor was a web—from silo to doors to granaries to grain mill.

"We started," Daddy'd said, "with a primary loop fastened to the flywheel of the corn sheller. When we turned on the sheller it set all the strings and spools rotating. What a grand and satisfying sight! And open to myriad permutations. But after a hired man or two tangled with our strings, we were ordered to dismantle our cats-cradles after every session. And we weren't allowed to take spools or string or nails into the hay, for cows are dumb. They'll swallow anything."

These school kids, in 1955, are ogling at the size and structure of the upper barn.

She and Craig have been saving spools from Grama's sewing, ever since Daddy told them about the pulleys.

She's not so eager to try his and Trever's elevator, where they put a rope around a pulley up in the rafters, and on one end tied a gunny sack full of grain, slightly heavier than the weight of one boy. At the other end they made a loop, for sitting in. Then they'd pull the sack up to the top, and as it came down it would pull one of them up. The one at the bottom would let out a little grain, and the boy up top would come down again. "Really educational," Daddy'd said. "A regular Otis elevator!" But Jackie's doubtful—what if the sack fell off or spilled? You'd be one big splat.

She's not so sure about their rope swing, either, where they'd fly from the top of the hay bank right out the barn doors, and then in again.

"If we didn't make it back, it would just oscillate, and we'd eventually make it to the floor," Daddy'd said.

She hears a crunch, too heavy for Craig's bare feet. Grampa comes up beside the feed bin and starts to sort through the pile of old gunny sacks stacked there. He holds them up one after another. He makes a little crooning noise, like humming to himself and clearing his throat at the same time, like a chicken prowling around the woodpile. He can't hear the little song he makes.

He's standing under the old fashioned printing on the silo, under THE AIMS OF THIS FARM. How could he have signed his name? The letters are big, and high over his head.

"Hello, W.J. Dougan," says Jackie conversationally. "Hello, Wesson Joseph." She looks around for a way to get Grampa's attention. There's nothing to throw except the pitchfork, and she would never do that. Accidents happen with pitchforks. She doesn't like to think about the neighbor who threw a pitchfork up into his haymow and it hit a beam and bounced back and killed him.

She feels in a pocket and finds loose corn. It's often there, for she likes to jumble it in her fingers or worry a kernel with her teeth. She's learned these habits from Daddy and Grampa. She throws the corn at Grampa and it peppers his back. He looks up. His face registers huge astonishment. She puts her finger to her lips and points to the barn door. Grampa understands. He laughs silently. Grampa always laughs silently; it's on account of his deafness.

He picks up a gunny sack. He looks up at her, down at the sack. She gets his idea. She motions a question out the door. Grampa looks. "Quick, cubby, he's coming!" he shouts, loudly, because he can't hear himself.

She eases carefully onto the ladder, then scrambles down. Grampa holds open the gunny sack. She dives in and he closes it with a bit of twine. She can hear his breathing as he ties, and through a hole, she can see the arm of his blue work shirt. Then the arm moves, and she glimpses her brother coming into the barn. He's drinking a half-pint of chocolate milk.

She lies still. The sack smells strongly of grain, and the dust makes her hold her breath to keep from sneezing. She prickles all over from the hay in her clothing and the oat spears stuck in the sack. The loose burlap weave allows a dim light to filter through.

Craig asks out loud, "Grampa, have you seen Jackie?" Through the hole she watches him spell her name on his fingers and look inquiring. She can talk to Grampa with the finger alphabet, too. It was the first thing she learned after learning to read; her sisters taught her. Grampa was greatly pleased when she spelled her first word to him. Before that he'd only pretended to read when she made her hand go. She still can't spell lickety-split like Grama and Daddy. Neither can Craig.

Grampa is playing dumb. He looks puzzled at Craig's spelling.

H-I-D-E A-N-D S-E-E-K, spells Craig.

Grampa's face lights up. He motions toward the loft. "Have you looked in the hay?"

Craig is impatient. He shakes his head. D-I-D Y-O-U S-E-E H-E-R?

Grampa begins to laugh silently. Jackie laughs silently, too. The sack jiggles. Craig grabs at it.

"Hi!" Grampa shouts. "Leave my sack of potatoes alone!"

Jackie rolls and lurches away. Craig's hands beat on her. His chocolate milk spills through the sack.

"You're it!" cries Craig.

The twine parts; the sack bursts open. Jackie stumbles out running and heads for the barn doors.

"I tagged you!" shrills Craig. "You're it!"

"Inside the sack! It doesn't count!" Jackie races down the ramp and reaches the tree. "Home free!"

Craig, looking injured, walks down the incline.

Grampa stands in the doorway, laughing and waving the gunny sack like a semaphore.

3 ⊰ BOOTS

It's summer. The round barn was finished last fall, and now the silo in its center is being filled for the first time.

Ronald, who is ten, watches. The horses pull the wagons of cornstalks onto the loft floor. The stalks are in bundles, piled in rows on the wagons. Two hired men, Percy Werner and Jack Ward, stand on the bundles and sling them to the loader. Grampa is the loader; he cuts the twine and feeds stalks, leaves, ears, into a trough with a belt rotating the length of it. The belt carries the stalks into the blades of the chopper. A fan blows the chopped stalks up a long tube into the top of the silo, where the silage then rains down, gradually filling up the great concrete cylinder. The chopper-blower is powered by a twenty-five-horsepower gasoline motor.

Inside the silo is a man with a silage pitchfork. He's not a regular farmhand but an itinerant who wanted work, and W.J. hired him. Extra hands are often needed in the summer. His job is to spread the silage clear to the edges so that air spaces are eliminated and the silage will ferment properly. Ronald knows it's the fermentation of the sugary juices in the stalks that preserves the silage, and also gives it the sharp, sweet-sour taste that cows like.

The worker got into the silo by climbing up the wooden ventilation chute alongside it. There's a narrow gap in the silo's concrete from top to bottom; the metal reinforcing rods continue right through the gap and form rungs. Inside the silo the worker has a pile of wooden shutters that just fit the gap. As the silo fills, he fits a shutter into the gap and plasters the edges airtight with clay. Then the silage won't spill out the opening, nor will air get in. Ronald's early-morning job was to fill a bucket with clay from the crick bank and lug it to the barn. His job now is to be sure a second bucket is always ready.

Ronald watches the stalks moving along the belt into the chopper. He watches the knives grab them, and the brief battle that reduces them to bits. It's a noisy process: the motor, the grinding whirl of the chopper and fan blades, the shooshy rattle as the silage is both blown and blasted up the tube.

His eyes follow the tube to where it bends at the top of the silo and the end of it disappears through one of the little windows of the wooden superstructure. He's curious to view the complete trip, to see the silage falling down on the inside.

Through its narrow door on the barn floor, he slides into the ventilator chute and climbs the rungs. He climbs past the most recently placed shutter and now can see the silage pouring down from far above. He climbs a little higher to get a better view.

Something is not right. The silage isn't spread out as it should be. There's a mound of it, a small pyramid which is steadily growing as the silage rains down. Is the man with the silage fork behind the pyramid, bent over? He watches a moment and sees no movement. But then he spots something—a pair of boots sticking out from under the pyramid. He skins down the rungs as fast as he can and emerges, screeching, onto the barn floor. He screams over the noise of the machinery. "Stop! Stop! He's buried up there! You're burying him in silage!" He pounds his father's arm. "Stop! Stop!"

The men stop the machinery. Jack and Percy crowd into the shaft and disappear up it. Ronald follows on their heels. He's in time to see them haul the worker out from under the silage by his boots. They pump his chest and the man gasps and turns from blue to red. He's still alive; Ronald has saved his life. They pull out the last shutter, turn the man on his stomach, and thread him between the rungs out into the shaft. Percy above and Jack below lower him down the narrow column. Out on the barn floor, they prop him up against the hay. When he recovers sufficiently, Grampa fires him. It takes him a while to recover, though, for besides being nearly suffocated he's dead drunk.

At supper that night, referring to both the action of the silage and the action of the whiskey, Percy says to Ronald, "If you hadn't noticed him, we'd have had a twice-pickled farmhand!"

The next spring, when Jack is pitching down silage, he uncovers the empty bottle.

4 ⚔ EARLY DOUGANS

Grampa as a boy lives on a farm near Lowell, Wisconsin. His father, Arthur, was called "Square" Dougan. Perhaps this was because he supposedly owned a 640-acre piece of land, a section, called a square. This is unlikely, for the standard free-holder's parcel offered at the time his father, John Dougan, Sr., arrived in Wisconsin, in 1845, would have been 160 acres, making his son's share a mere 80 acres. Perhaps it was square in shape. Or he might have been called this because of his honesty, but Daddy, Jackie's informant, isn't sure—it could merely be, Daddy says, that he was an Irish blockhead. Or, maybe "Square" was the local pronunciation of "Squire." Grampa's mother has the interesting name of Delcyetta.

Some history is known about the Dougan family before Lowell. Arthur's father, John (born 1796, Jackie's great-great-grandfather) lived in County Armaugh, in the north of Ireland, Ulster. His father, the senior Arthur Dougan, was married to Sarah Buchanan, whose sister, Maria, was the wife of Samuel McGibney. They were all Protestants, known now as Scots-Irish, then as Ulster-Scots—all of Celtic stock. The McGibney branch was Presbyterian, the Dougans, Methodists, converted by John Wesley. The families most likely emigrated to America for the reasons most Europeans did: political turmoil and poverty behind, the prospect of free land and prosperity ahead. The McGibneys preceded the Dougan departure by a generation; no doubt Maria Buchanan McGibney urged everyone to come, and kept them aware of what was happening in upper New York state as to family matters and work situations.

The senior Arthur Dougan and Sarah Buchanan Dougan never left Ulster. But their son John, surely hearing tales of the boundless land in America from his McGibney relatives, went on ahead of his siblings, perhaps to test the waters. He was one of a large number of Ulster Scots-Irish who came to America in the last half of the eighteenth and first half of the nineteenth centuries, many of whom entered the country at Philadelphia. That is where John disembarked in 1819, according to his much later naturalization papers. A ship's passenger list from Ulster names a John Dougan for 1817, which also fits the time frame. If this latter is the correct date, John's departure could have been spurred by an economic depression. 1816 was a year of severe crop failure all over Europe because of cold; we now know this was caused by blockage of the sun's rays by particles in the air from a remote volcanic eruption.

John's first stop, instead of going north, was McConnelsburgh in south central Pennsylvania, an area where many Ulster immigrants gathered. It's likely that he had to work off an indenture there, for he probably borrowed to pay for his passage. The records indicate he taught school. Once free, after about four years, he had choices. He might have stayed in Pennsylvania, or gone into the piedmont of Virginia and the Carolinas as many Scots-Irish immigrants did, or he could strike out on his own, following his original intentions, to upstate New York.

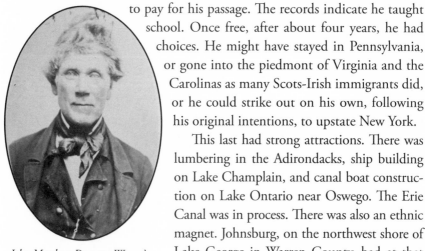

This last had strong attractions. There was lumbering in the Adirondacks, ship building on Lake Champlain, and canal boat construction on Lake Ontario near Oswego. The Erie Canal was in process. There was also an ethnic magnet. Johnsburg, on the northwest shore of Lake George in Warren County, had at that time no Presbyterian or Catholic churches, but a Methodist one, with parishioners with Scotch-Irish names. One of these was McGibney, John's aunt and uncle, the family which had been established in New York for a generation—Mariah and Samuel's children were John's first cousins. He may well have had his cousin Elizabeth in mind when he arrived in America, and chafed at his long stay in Pennsylvania. So with the pull of economics, an ethnically congenial community, and a twenty-three-year-old plum ripe for the picking, John headed north.

John Matthew Dougan, Wesson's grandfather, emigrated from northern Ireland about 1817.

By the next year he was living in Warren County near Lake George, courting his cousin. Difference of religion was not a problem. The dourest of the dour Presbyterian ills had never got much beyond Nova Scotia and Newfoundland in North America. The liberal Presbyterians, having been filtered by the 18th Century evangelistic influences, managed to come to the U.S., where they thrived separately and independently with the other isolated and similarly "liberated" rural Protestant communities. There was a gravitational cohesion that characterized virtually all rural immigrant settlements in early

America. Hence the strict Presbyterianism of the Ulster McGibneys had been tempered by the less restricted life in the new world; there was now little difference between Elizabeth's family's faith and John Dougan's Methodism.

John found Elizabeth more than receptive to his wooing. If there was any problem, it must have been that someone raised the question about the close blood ties, for her tart response—recorded in a letter—was that she was going to marry John Dougan no matter what anybody said, she'd marry him if she had to live in a tree. Apparently her father Samuel had few misgivings—her marriage dowry was three cows, three loads of furniture, and three silk dresses. The couple was married in Washington County in 1824 and went to live seventy miles away.

John found plenty of work. The Erie Canal, begun in its middle near Rome, New York, where the terrain presented no obstacles of locks or granite ridges, was progressing in both directions; it was completed in late 1825. There were feeder canals, Champlain, Oswego. Strong backs were needed for clearing the land, and for the now more difficult canal work. And there was construction work in the developments along the canal—docks, warehouses—and in the communities springing up nearby. Along with that, he was home-

Elizabeth McGibney Dougan, Wesson's grandmother.

steading for his and Elizabeth's growing family, which eventually numbered seven. John's brothers Samuel and Matthew—having heard that indeed the water was fine—had shown up in upper New York State about the same time John did, traveling down the Saint Lawrence River past Quebec and Montreal and into Lake Champlain. They stayed on in the East, but John, with three sons soon to need land, joined the growing throngs who were using the great new and inexpensive highway that opened up the West and all its riches to settlers. He gathered his goods and his family, traveled the canal to Lake Erie, traversed the Great Lakes, disembarked at Milwaukee, and moved west in Wisconsin to the Lake Winnebago-Beaver Dam area where Lowell is located. The geography of the region was the image of County Armaugh. And by 1848, Wisconsin had increased its population enough to become a state. It is here that Grampa, Wesson Joseph, was born to John's son Arthur, "Square" Dougan.

5 ⊰ DELCYETTA

It's a marvel that Grampa was born at all. His mother, Delcyetta, was forty-five when she bore him, in 1868, the last of six children, and five years after his closest sibling. From a previous marriage she had a son, Chauncey Lansing Marvin. A family album has two handsome pictures of him as a man, spelling his name Chancy. The only written records are in two letters. On a nearby farm lived Arthur's brother Sam, who had three daughters — Gertrude, Viola, and Leonora; these were all Grampa's first cousins. In 1954 Leonora Dougan writes to Jackie, "Delciette had one son, older than any of us, and we children called him 'Chancy, Lancy, Leander, Clinton, Walket, Talket, Peabody Marvin.' We used to like to say that when we were little. He died when he was still a young man." Later, she again writes Jackie, "Aunt Delcyetta had been married before and had a son Chauncy Marvin who didn't amount to much. He died young." The vague family rumor is that he was an alcoholic. The rest of Delcyetta's children, fathered by Arthur, were Ida May (1857), Agnes Augusta (1859; who died at three, before Grampa was born), Polly Adell (1863), Lillian Loretta (1864), and Grampa (1868) — Wesson Joseph.

Leonora's letter goes on to tell a story. It also encloses a photograph.

> This picture is of Delcyetta. I want you to have it as she was your great-grandmother and not a blood relation of mine, but I loved her. She was a shining light of my childhood. I think she loved children. Perhaps I've told you how she cut our hair. Viola and I both had long curls, but it was wash day so Mother just saved time by braiding it. Father had to go over to Uncle Arthur's and took us along. Aunt Delcyetta talked him into consenting to her cutting off our braids. She did just that. Didn't Mother and especially our sister Gertrude have spasms when they saw us! We had to stay upstairs all day. Gertrude's young man gave us a real cut later. The first oatmeal I ever ate was at Aunt Delcyetta's. Their farm was about two miles from ours.... Uncle Arthur was father's brother. He died of a cancer on his face. I remember as

Three generations: Delcyetta, Ronald, and Wesson.

a child his coming to our house and always having a hand mirror to look at the cancer.

When Jackie's father reads the letter he says he recalls his grandmother only as a stern old woman who swiped his toys. She lived in the Big House with them in her final years, and she'd often say, "If Ronald doesn't take care of his playthings he shouldn't have them." After her death, says Daddy, they found her bottom bureau drawer crammed with his and Trever's missing treasures.

Jackie's mother, too, has a story that is not to Delcyetta's credit. "Grampa always felt sorry because his mother never thought he was good enough, pious enough, to be a minister," she says. "He said to me, 'She tried to dissuade me.' He told me it hurt him."

One photo of Delcyetta shows a grim and aged face under a sunbonnet. But most photos from that time make their subjects look grim; it was hard to hold a smile for a time exposure. And people did look old beyond their years, from lack of dental care and from incessant hard work. Jackie guesses she is glad for Leonora's report. Delcyetta must have had some virtue to raise Grampa as she did, even if she had doubts about his piety, and to manage things with such spunk during her husband's decline and death. And to manage, finally, for her son to get an education.

6 ⊰ GRAMPA'S GROWING UP

The earliest story-bit about Grampa shows what a narrow squeak it was that, once born to his aging mother, he lived to have descendents. His older sister, Aunt Lillian, tells it to Jackie and Craig, Patsy and Joan. Wesson, under two years old, was trotting across the yard when one of the big sows got out. He ran straight towards the sow, his little arms stretched. The snarling beast caught him by the middle and rolled him in the dirt. "I was seven, and I saw it from the porch!" Aunt Lillian says. "I screamed, and I could scream good and loud! One of the men came and saved him. I'll never forget that sight! A sow can be one of the fiercest creatures in the world."

Aunt Lillian also tells how her father bred horses and that her brother loved to let the horses run. He'd race along the road with a neighbor to see who had the fastest team. "Wesson was in his glory! But once he was looking at the other fellow and ran into the culvert—the wagon wheel did. It tossed him in the air and he came down on his head in front of the wagon box. I think that fall had something to do with his going deaf later. That, or the awful attacks of grippe he used to have—two and three in one winter."

Stories of other accidents have survived. In Watertown, near Lowell, there's a large Catholic church at the top of a hill. The street runs down to the business district. Wesson had Ida, Della, and Lillian with him in the buckboard. He turned onto the street up by the church. The horses got it into their heads to bolt down the grade. A girl flew off here, another there, a third farther along. By the time he managed to control the horses, Grampa had sisters scattered behind him for two blocks.

Another time his mother was driving a single buggy with a little platform back. Wesson was standing on this platform holding onto the back of the seat. Near their farm a bridge was out, and a bypass cut in the steep banks. The horses made it down into the creek all right, but when they grappled with the farther bank they did it with a rush. The jolt broke Wesson's hold and flipped him into the water. His mother had to stop and fish him out.

Grampa himself supplies an occasional glimpse of his early life. In a talk he gives in 1924 about the problems of keeping records of a dairy herd: "I remember on my boyhood farm home in the grain section [i.e., a part of Wisconsin where grain raising was dominant] a few cows were kept as a necessity to provide for groceries, and I remember in that herd there was a white cow, a brindle cow, a black cow, and each one took her name from the color — Whitie, Brindle, Reddie — yes, and the Kicker, and each one usually had a calf marked exactly like the mother, the white one had a white calf, and I guess the kicker always had a kicker. So we had a splendid system of naming cows and

The earliest photo we have of Wesson. He is fourteen, in 1882.

following the generations right down from one to another, no trouble whatever. But when the cows produced different looking calves, unless one were to feed them every day looking them right in the faces and getting to know their countenance and expression, he would soon lose their identity."

There are a few miscellaneous remembrances: that Grampa had a big dog he'd trained to haul his sled; and that he could look at a woodpile and accurately estimate how many cords were in it.

Arthur Dougan's death must have been a lingering trauma for everybody. The story is that the cancer developed from a kick in the face by a horse, when Wesson was fourteen, though the kick may not have been the cause. At any rate, Arthur spent over three years dying. Wesson assumed most of the farm work. He says in a 1945 letter to a future grandson-in-law, "From my personal experience and observation I am persuaded that too much emphasis cannot be put upon early mental and cultural training of youth. My elementary schooling was very weak and sketchy; from eleven to nineteen I averaged less than three months of school per year, and that in a very poor district school."

When Arthur dies and the estate is settled, Delcyetta, herself almost illiterate, wisely decides her son must have more education. She sells the farm and buys a home in Beaver Dam, where she and Wesson live, and where Wesson enters a private school, Wayland Academy. This is because he's so much older than the high school boys, and Wayland promises to push him along as fast as he can go.

Wesson is a "chair boy" at the World's Columbian Exposition in Chicago in 1893. This crew moved folding chairs from place to place for various demonstrations.

Grampa is bright and industrious. He crowds three years of high school into less than two. When he's twenty-one, Wayland decides he's ready for the university even though he's not yet graduated. Wisconsin takes him as a special adult student, conditionally. Delcyetta moves with her son to Madison. Grampa brings along his team of carriage horses but sells them when he finds it too hard to keep horses in the city.

He does well as a freshman. It is one of the proudest days of his life when the dean calls him in to his office and says, "Dougan, we're going to take you off probation. You're going to make it."

Grampa indeed makes it, and with honors. A new building is erected while he's there, a red brick fortress right on Lake Mendota, "Library Hall." Grampa's Commencement is held there, a "novel event, nothing of the kind having been attempted by any previous class." It's a version of Midsummer Night's Dream, complete with Mendelssohn, fairies, and plays presented before the Duke—with these latter being the Commencement Orations. Grampa gives one of the orations, "The Present Spirit of Truth Seeking," its thesis being that we must use our growing scientific knowledge to test old hypotheses in order to reach the truth. He says the astronomer "interrogates the heavens, sails the seas of space, and steps from star to star." That devoted churchmen and scholars are becoming more and more accustomed "to accept truth from every source; to study the circumstances and conditions under which the

Bible has been given to man." These searchers for truth "read side by side the Bible account of the creation and the accepted conclusions of modern science." Grampa is a Darwinist, and twenty-five when he graduates. (The Class Prophecy, a parody of the witches scene in Macbeth, is held later at another venue, and Wesson Dougan's projected fate is not recorded.)

Grampa is raised Methodist. When he's a boy he signs the Pledge never to drink, and he never does. During his college years he's active in the YMCA and the church. He starts a Sunday School in South Madison, which evolves into a church, and he fills in here and there as a student pastor. He finds he's called to the ministry. He studies theology through the Methodist conference, taking an extra year at the university to study Greek and Hebrew, and is ordained. He has a little parsonage at McFarland, near Madison. His salary is $250 a year, often paid in pigs and potatoes. His mother lives with him there until he marries Grama in 1898; then she moves to Beloit to live with her daughter Lillian.

Grama's background is similar in many ways to Grampa's. She's raised on a farm, third to youngest of a large family, and knows farm work intimately enough to vow she'll never marry a farmer. She inherits from her parents a strict Methodism and a strict work ethic. She, too, is delayed in her education, not starting high school till she's seventeen, for farm children — if they wanted more schooling; the terminal degree in those days was eighth grade — had to board in a town in order to attend regularly. Her opportunity comes when her oldest brother George is called to be the minister of Beloit's Methodist Church, and she can live with him and his wife Mabel while she attends Beloit High. After that, she receives scholarships and goes on to college at Lawrence in Appleton. She meets Grampa while they are both working at a summer camp on Lake Geneva. He's not a farmer; he's going to be a minister. She is happy to be a minister's wife.

In those days Methodist ministers were moved around every few years. It is at Juda that Grampa and Grama's first baby is born, a beautiful little girl. The doctor cuts the umbilicus and wraps the baby in blankets. Grampa is filled with joy and wonder. He goes out to the barn behind the parsonage and tells his cow and horse and pig the good news about the wee lassie. But when they go to tend her, the baby is dead. They open her blankets and find her soaked with blood. The doctor had been drinking; he'd cut the cord too close to the body and the baby has bled to death. Many years later, in Dr. Bennett's glowing obituary, Jackie's father reads the statement that of the many hundreds of babies Dr. Bennett delivered, he never lost one.

Daddy, Arthur Ronald, is born at the next parsonage, Oregon, in 1902. Uncle Trever, Trever Cranston, is born there in 1904.

And all this while Grampa is losing his hearing. Back in college he'd started recording his worries, and seeking help: "Jan. 93: After grippe noticed hearing was failing. Gargle and heat inflation." "Feb. 94: To Dr. Brown after attack of grippe. Treatment: spraying post nasal space with a weak solution of silver nitrate and inflating of middle ear. Noticed no great change for better, seemed to be held in check was all." "Nov. 94: Went to another doctor, Abaly. Had left side cauterized. Two weeks later bone or cartilage cut out. Since, the nostril has seemed more open and freer but no improvement in hearing." Wesson wonders if any of his treatments have been detrimental—should he continue the probing, cutting, and cauterizing. He twice makes visits to a famous Boston doctor; his second letter, February 1896, states, "The right ear has failed very rapidly. I cannot hear a watch tick, even in close contact, and cannot distinguish the syllables in ordinary conversation, can simply hear that there is a sound. I think the left ear has nearly held its own. That is, as well as it was a year ago. It was somewhat improved till cold weather set in but has failed some lately. I think the eustachian tube is clear, for there is no sensation of the ears being stopped up. However, the catarrh seems a little worse.... I am not seriously impaired in my work as yet, but should the left ear ever become as bad as the right one is now I could do nothing requiring use of this sense." The Boston doctor replies that he can do nothing.

A pastoral journal that Grampa sporadically keeps during those McFarland years chronicles, in its final entry, his anguish and hurt. The next-to-final entry, dated April 14, 1897, reads:

> The Easter services were well attended. I spoke in the morning of the importance of Christ's resurrection both to our own salvation and for the salvation of the whole world.
>
> Our missionary collection more than doubled that ever before given by this appointment alone. It was $20. Work is moving well but with the usual discouragements regarding the spirituality of the members. My prayer is that God will draw me near to Him that I may be able to lead the weak ones to higher living.
>
> I am aware of the truth that a pastor cannot lead his people higher than he is himself—"The good shepherd goeth before his flock."

Then comes the final entry, September 22, 1897:

Wesson and Eunice in their newlywed parlor at McFarland, Wisconsin.

Since last writing many months have passed — The conference year closed quite favorably — The people seemed to wish my return — Finances were all nicely straightened up without over exertion.

I went to the conference hopeful of the future but my hopes were to be crushed by having my infirmities made conspicuous and having my grade in the conference shown me by the Eau Claire incident in Reverend Benson's words, "We do not want such men."

I have been in an extreme state of mind since then. My thought is continually on the future. What shall I do. Is it my duty to continue in the ministry or ought I turn to some more private line of work. Oh that God would make the way plain. I cannot bear to think of giving up the work and I dare not continue in it. It seems as though my life is to be a failure throughout. Here I am nearly 30 and must change my life work. Then comes the question to what shall I change. I am incapacitated for almost everything. God forgive me for getting so discouraged. I will try to cheer up and work for the present and trust the future to God. Who, let us believe, doeth all things well.

But it is not until 1905, with Grampa having served appointments at Mc-Farland, Juda, Oregon, and Poynette, that he sees his way clear to leave the ministry. He had been casting about for some time for an alternate vocation, favoring the security of one with a salary. In 1936, the height of the Great

Depression, he writes his reflections about his search to a former employee who is facing a similar change in vocation:

> I had the opportunity of going into a coal business in a partnership affair. That business went to the wall. I had an opportunity of getting into a chain lumber business and in that I could never have been independent nor held my position securely. I feel it is true of many of the positions that are offered now. As I have seen the inside working of some of the large companies there is constantly held over the head of every employee from the least to the greatest, the fear of the ax falling. I am very thankful now I struck out independently. I feel I have had much in opportunities, much better opportunity for service, and I am much more secure now than I would have been under any possible position with any large company.

Grampa turns his attention to the milk business. At that time the production of milk is haphazard. There are horror stories from before the turn of the century. There is little emphasis on cleanliness. In many places milk is delivered in cans and dipped out into customers' containers. Few cows are tested for disease, and tubercular cows pass on tuberculosis to people. Milk drinkers get sick from a variety of ailments. In a University of Wisconsin commencement speech in 1911 a senior orator representing the College of Agriculture gives the results of his research: of 29 samples taken from Madison milk wagons on their regular rounds, only nine comply with the standard of pure milk production which declares that a content of bacteria exceeding 500,000 per cubic centimeter makes milk unfit for human consumption. Twelve of the samples had between 5 million and 300 million bacteria per cubic centimeter. "The fearful consequences of feeding impure milk to children were shown by Mr. Baer who declared that one sixth of all the children born in the U.S. die before they are one year old, and one-half of these babies succumb to diseases directly attributed to the milk that is fed them. This means that every year 200,000 children die because of the lack of pure milk."

But in 1905 Grampa is already aware of the dangers of impure milk. He decides to continue to serve the Lord by going into scientific dairying. He will be independent, and he will produce clean, safe milk for babies. Though still tending his clerical duties, he commutes to the university from Poynette, and takes classes in the School of Agriculture. He becomes friends with the professors, one of whom happens to be his wife's first cousin, George Mortimer.

He looks around for a farm to buy. Beloit is a natural place to start for his sister and brother-in-law, Ida and James Croft, live there, as now also does his mother with his sister Lillian. He visits Beloit, takes a walk in the country, and sees a farm he likes. It is close enough to town to make milk deliveries possible. The farm looks quite different from the one Jackie will come to know: no round barn, no milkhouse, no Little House. Its barn is what will later be the side barn, and the Big House is not nearly so big. At the side of the Big House is a windmill that is dismantled long before Jackie's birth. The granary sits on the spot where the round barn will some day be. The horse barn, though, is there, a long shed behind the granary. The farm is being rented to tenants.

Wesson walks back to town and knocks on the door of the farm's owner. Mrs. Colley ushers him into the living room. Also in the room is her nephew, a young man from the Beloit Academy, who later becomes a chemistry professor at Beloit College. Paul Boutwell reports to Ronald when Ronald is in his college chemistry class, "Your father's Irish charm so captivated my aunt that she was ready to *give* him the farm!"

But first Grampa has people from the university come down. They study the drainage, they look at the water supply. They take numerous soil samples. They declare the Colley farm to be among the best farmland in the world: Waukesha silt loam over gravel, the same soil composition as in the fertile Caucasus of Russia.

Grampa buys the farm, 110 acres, in 1906. He pays ninety dollars an acre, with no money down. A 1945 *Milwaukee Journal* article describes the departure from Poynette: "Mr. Dougan, his fine and brave wife, with their two infant sons, climbed aboard a worn spring wagon pulled by a horse, and plodded the road to a farm east of Beloit. They had a hoe, a crate of chickens and, tagging along behind, the family cow."

On May 1, 1907, Grampa begins the retail delivery of milk in Beloit. He writes his name and slogan on his first milk wagon, "W.J. Dougan, The Babies' Milkman." Ronald and Trever are known throughout their high school years as "The Milkman's Babies." They glory in what their city classmates intend as insult. Ronald's children inherit the label in turn. They, too, wear it as a badge of honor.

7 ❧ THE PRESENT SPIRIT

Wesson J. Dougan excels at the University of Wisconsin, and is invited to give a commencement speech, which is later republished. In his speech, titled "The Present Spirit of Truth Searching," W.J. argues that reason and science are compatible with religious belief. It's an eloquent statement of principles that will guide his life.

"Half a century ago a shrewd observer of his contemporaries said, 'Few human beings in their moral and religious inquiries are possessed with the simple wish of attaining truth.' But during the last few decades we note among religious thinkers an ever increasing spirit of thoughtfulness; a subtle change in methods of investigation; a growing spirit of rectitude in the search for truth.

"The scientist diligently gathers facts from innumerable observations; classifies and weighs phenomena until the general laws of matter and of life are discovered and stated. The geologist studies the workings of the powerful natural forces by which the rocks are formed, folded, and plicated, and lifted from old ocean's bed to glitter above the clouds. The astronomer interrogates the heavens, sails seas of space, and steps from star to star. Since the time of Galileo 'the artillery of science has nightly assaulted the skies.' One by one the secrets are being yielded up and man is coming nearer and nearer to a complete knowledge of the universe. The future lies as an open book before him and he endeavors to lift the veil from all the misty past. These men seek only for the truth, gladly welcome new evidence, and willingly restate long established hypotheses.

"This desire for the truth and the whole truth wherever it may be found; this willingness to stand for the truth; to give up old theories and accepted opinions for new and better substantiated conclusions is the scientific spirit of the age.

"But this scientific spirit is not limited in its scope and operation. In the field of religious inquiry it affirms 'that no ground is too holy to be trodden by reason if only with a reverent spirit.' The earnest Bible student seeing the many possibilities for error through translation, through interpretation, are bending all their energies to a scientific and historical study of the book of books. Devoted churchmen and scholars are becoming more and more accustomed to accept truth from every source; to study the circumstances and conditions under which the Bible has been given to man. These searchers for truth read side by side the Bible account of the creation and the accepted conclusions of modern science. They ask the astronomer to interpret the lofty phrase of Genesis — that 'the earth was a desolation and a waste; and darkness was upon the faces of abyss.' They interrogate the geologist as to the age of the earth and the length of the world-building day. The whole field of history is their province; they decipher the hieroglyphics upon the monuments and tombs of Egypt, study the common daily life of the Nile valley under the Pharoahs, read the Egyptian romances about Joseph, the events of the Israelites' bondage, and the account of the Exodus. They unearth the libraries of bricks and tiles and cylinders of Assyria, decipher the legends of the old Chaldeans, read the records of the Assyrian and Babylonian monarchs. They compare the Hebrew stories with the legends and records of contemporary peoples, submit the Bible to the most scrutinizing historical criticism. They

Wesson's University of Wisconsin graduation picture.

search for old manuscripts; they exhaust the resources of chemistry and of the microscope in reviving the dimmed and defaced records of the early Hebrew people and their mighty neighbors.

"All of this research and investigation is to find the historical value of the Bible; to find the very meaning, the deepest, truest import of the wonderful book.

"It is not to prove or disprove the truth of the conception of God held by some church-father that these investigators are laboring; it is not to uphold any creed or any sect; nor is it to prove the truth of their own theories with regard to the Divine. But imbued with the thought that man's knowledge is yet poor and imperfect, that he has not after all the long years of journeying reached the absolute truth, these devoted scholars strain every nerve; exert every power human; and implore guidance Divine to reach a true conception of God, of his word, of his creation, and of all that pertains to the relationship of the Divine to man.

"So we see that just as the scientist studies the animate world about him; reads the lesson of creation written upon the pages of granite; stands in awe before the titan spirits that built the Universe; just so does the devout searcher for religious truth knock at all the doors of knowledge and in the name of humanity demand admission. He interrogates all modern science, all history, he calls dead and forgotten empires from their dusty tombs to bear testimony to the truth of these Hebrew scriptures. This scientific spirit in religion shall some day bring man face to face with the absolute truth, and that truth shall make him free."

8 ❧ S. O. B.

It's 1932. In the side barn off the round barn where the newborn calves are kept, there's a calf with a broken leg. Grampa thinks her mother lay on her. Daddy calls the vet.

Dr. Russell comes. He glances at the calf. "Shoot the son of a bitch," he says, and leaves.

Daddy gets some narrow boards. He measures them long enough so that they'll make a walking splint. He sets the break and splints it. He binds up the leg. He calls a vet in Janesville and asks how long he should leave the splint on. Dr. Knilans tells him he'll come check the leg at three weeks, if Daddy wants him to. Daddy describes the splint and asks if it's all right for the calf to walk on it. Dr. Knilans says there's no way to keep her from it unless Daddy plans to hog-tie her.

The splinted calf, with a view of the farm buildings from the horse barn to the Big House.

Sure enough, before long the calf has struggled to her feet, hobbled to her mother and started to nurse.

Twice a day Daddy goes down to the barn and checks the splint and bandages, and inquires into the welfare of his patient. She leaves her mother, is weaned to a pail, is in with the other calves. When all the calves go out into the field behind the calf barn, she goes too, and manages a stiff-legged gambol. Grampa laughs and laughs when he goes past the fence. Joan and Patsy, Jackie and Craig, like to watch her, too. She becomes quite tame. They let her suck their fingers.

Dr. Knilans examines the leg and advises keeping the splint on a few weeks longer. At the end of the allotted time, Daddy takes off the splint. The leg looks fine. The calf has no trouble walking on it, although she does have a bit of hitch in her gait that she never gets over. She grows into a healthy heifer and productive cow. She spends twelve years in the round barn.

Daddy and Grampa don't call Dr. Russell any more. When they need a vet they call Dr. Arthur Knilans in Janesville. He becomes the farm vet.

Somebody once asks whatever happened to Dr. Russell.

"I shot the son of a bitch," says Daddy.

9 ⚮ BUILDING THE BARN

It is 1911. Professor Franklin King, Professor of Agricultural Physics at the university and inventor of the cylindrical silo, is also an advocate of cylindrical barns. When W.J. Dougan visits him in 1910, seeking advice on the building of his dairy barn, King urges a round one. He has no precise blueprints but has printed a book that contains a general plan. Grampa and his rule-of-thumb carpenter, Mark Kellor, study the book. They drive a horse and buggy north of Madison and spend two days examining a King-inspired barn there. They then make plans and sketches, and adapt the general plan to Grampa's site, though Grampa figures out a feature or two that Professor King hasn't thought of.

Before building can begin, the granary must be moved to another spot, for it sits where the new barn will be. Grampa wants the round barn to join up with the existing barn; that way they can be operated as a unit.

The inner silo is built first, of reinforced concrete—concrete laced with metal rods. This is unusual; most of the silos in the county are wooden stave silos, or tile. The base of the silo is sunk twelve feet below what will be the level of the cow barn floor. Its walls are seven inches thick. It is fourteen feet across and 154 feet around. When it's finished it's sixty feet high, as high as a six story building.

A gap in the concrete of the silo, a narrow slit, runs from bottom to top. The horizontal reinforcing rods are not cut; they pass through the gap on their way around the silo. They're spaced sixteen inches apart, and supply the rungs for climbing. Fitting neatly into the inside of the slit, one on top of the next, will be wooden slats, or shutters; these will keep the silage from spilling out. In summer when the silo is being filled, the men will set the shutters in one by one, as the silage level rises. They will plaster them airtight with a clay mix that won't hurt a cow if she happens to get any of it in her feed. During the rest of the year, as the silo is slowly emptied, they'll gradually remove the shutters, and store them in the passageway space between the new barn and the old.

Snugged against the silo on either side are two three-foot-square wooden columns, that run from the lower barn to the loft roof, where each meets a ventilator fan. When operating, these fans suck air up from the lower barn. One of the wooden shafts doubles as the housing for the long narrow gap; it has doors on the cow barn and loft levels, and a farmhand can swing into the shaft, grab the metal rungs, and climb up to the silage level. There's enough space between rungs and the shutters behind to afford finger and toe holds. Once arrived, the barnhand can crawl between the rungs out onto the silage bed, or—if it is Ronald or Trever—go on climbing for the joy and danger. They learn, as later do their children, that it's not wise to jump down on silage from a height, for silage doesn't give, like hay in a haymow. Once inside, the barnhand pitches silage down the shaft with a silage fork, which is wider than a hayfork and has more tines, closer together. Also the handle is shorter and has a hand grip like a corn or coal shovel. Once there, it's left inside the silo—not an item to carry regularly up and down a narrow shaft.

The pitched-down silage won't clog the bottom of the shaft, and require additional pitching. Grampa is cleverer than that. Near the foot of the shaft, opposite its cow barn door, is a hinged plank. The barnhand lifts the bottom of this plank and lays it on the edge of the silage cart, which has been trundled up against the open door. The plank is the width of the shaft, so that no silage can fall past its edges, and it slopes steeply into the cart. When the silage drops it hits the slanting plank and slides into the cart, which, when filled, is rolled from manger to manger and each cow given her ration. When the plank isn't in use, it is secured out of the way against the back of the chute.

The ever-growing silo, thrusting up, is an awesome sight. Ronald and Trever are told not to climb it, but of course (after work hours) they do. From the top they are lords of all they survey. They are able to see farther and farther over field and stream—first Spring Brook in the gravel pit in the back pasture, then Turtle Crick, eventually even Janesville and Rockford. The cows knee-deep in clover are like ants.

After the silo, Grampa puts in the rest of the concrete work. First come the thick walls of the cow barn, studded with multiple windows, and in between the windows, ventilation tunnels that allow fresh air from the outside ground level to enter, rise through the walls, and flow out near the top of the cow barn, only to sink to the floor and replace the warm stale air that is there. Both Franklin King and Grampa know that sunlight and fresh air are natural disinfectants, and that cows will thrive in a light and airy environment; they will be more resistant to tuberculosis and other cow diseases.

In building the barn, the silo comes first.

Then comes the complicated concrete flooring with its various levels, walkways, depressed mangers in front of the built-in stalls, and, for behind the cows, a gutter that is shallow on one end and gradually deeper as it circles the barn, to let gravity help facilitate cleaning. The two-by-six ribs of the loft are footed in the walls, and the broad planks of the barn floor form the ceiling of the cow barn. They are stout enough to bear the weight of two teams of horses, loaded hay wagons, and a loft full of hay, and not endanger the animals beneath. The cow barn ceiling has several gaps where chutes built above will allow hay to be pitched down to the cow barn floor. It also sports a rail for the manure trolley that will swing around the barn for cleanup, and can be raised and lowered. There is woodwork installed at the heads of the stalls that will serve for electric hookups when the time arrives to electrify the farm. There are stanchions attached to this woodwork, one for each stall.

Grampa builds a ramp from the ground to the loft floor; it will serve the round barn and make an entrance, part way up and to the side, to the loft of the original barn. This barn is already being called the side barn.

Now Grampa is ready for the roof. Ronald trots behind as his father and Mark Kellor, each carrying a two-by-six, go to a field behind the barn. He watches as they lay the planks on the ground and swivel one until an angle is formed that suits Grampa. Grampa explains that he is building a hip roof, one that bends part way up, and that "hip" means the joint of the two sloping parts. [Actually, he is building a "gambrel" roof.] He wants the roof to be harmonious and pleasing to the eye, not too steep, not too flat. Mark Kellor hammers Grampa's angle, and uses it as the form for the roof measurements.

A problem arises. The roof Grampa wants will turn out to be higher than the core silo, yet the roof must be hung on that core. There's nothing to be done but get out the forms and the scaffolding again, and mix more concrete. The workmen add twelve or fourteen feet, and then a few more feet of wooden superstructure with windows to let light into the silo. Only then can they start nailing into place the two-by-sixes that form the spokes of the roof. Once that's done, the roof boards and siding can go on, the inside rail for the hay fork added, and finally the shingles. Giving a talk late in his own life, Ronald says, "My father and Mark Kellor laid out the angle of the hip roof of the round barn by adjusting a rafter on the adjacent field until they arrived

The completed barn, "the major event of my childhood," says Ron. He's here with Bob, the collie.

at exactly the angle that pleased them, and to this day I think it as beautiful a roof as any conceived in the Middle Ages for any cathedral." He also says to Jackie, "The building of that barn was the high point of my childhood."

The outside of the finished barn is given a coat of primer and then white paint. The interior of the cow barn is completely whitewashed, as it will be regularly, every six months or so through the life of the barn. Whitewash is a mixture of white lime powder and water (called "slaked lime"); it is inexpensive and easily applied, and its purpose is twofold: it adds to the brightness and regular cleanliness of the barn, and has a high disinfecting value. It also sweetens the air by the absorption of odors.

The final hardware is installed in the cow barn, the partitions built in the loft, the passage finished to the side barn, the staircase to the loft built in the passageway. The plumbing is hooked up to the well. (The "Aims of This Farm" are not yet painted on the silo — Grampa's inspiration to do this comes several years later.)

Started in the spring, building goes on into the fall. But finally the barn is done, surprisingly quickly for its size and lack of precedent. It's ready for occupancy. Grampa and Grama celebrate by having a big open house and inviting the town out to see. The Beloit newspaper has paid scant attention over the summer to the innovative barn going up on the Dougan dairy farm, even in the "Turtle Township" weekly column. It has given more footage and a picture to the new barn going up at the county poorhouse.

But no matter. The town is happy to come to the open house. They have needed no newspaper to be watching all along.

10 ❧ THE PECAN GROVE

How can a young minister, paid two hundred and fifty dollars a year and some of that in chickens and firewood, save enough money to buy a farm? Grampa couldn't. But in 1906 one could buy land on "land contract," with no money down if the seller didn't demand it, and Mrs. Colley didn't. Grampa paid for the farm by borrowing. He borrowed money hand over fist. In those days, there was no plan for paying it back; for 6 percent a year, the borrower could have the money indefinitely. These land-contract mortgages on good farmland were considered the best mortgages in the world.

Jackie hears, a number of times in her growing up, the story of Uncle George and the pecan grove.

When Grampa first buys the farm, he doesn't intend to build, but he soon realizes that the barn is too small and too antiquated for his purposes. He needs money to finance a modern new barn and other buildings. After he's borrowed all he can from banks and local people, he still doesn't have enough. He asks his brother-in-law, Dr. George Trever, for a loan. Uncle George is a Methodist minister, the minister who married Wesson to George's sister, Eunice. He has a string of impressive degrees after his name. He's currently the president of a Negro theological seminary in Atlanta. Uncle George assures Wesson, "Surely, I'll lend you four thousand dollars. Let me know when you need it." So Wesson starts on the round barn. Before long, the point comes when he needs cash. He writes to Uncle George. George writes back that he no longer has the money. He's used it to buy a pecan grove.

That's when Grampa turns to his second cousins in Watertown, Jennie and Nellie Needham. They send the money. It's their four thousand dollars that makes possible the completion of the round barn.

For years and years, Grampa pays the Needham sisters interest on the four thousand dollars. During the Great Depression they decide that 6 percent is too high; they lower it to 4 percent without being asked. When Jackie is thirteen or fourteen, the old ladies decide they need the money to live on.

Daddy has bought the milk business by then—Grampa sold it to him along with all its debts—and so for a while Daddy has been the one paying the interest every year. Now, when it comes due every six months, they request some of the capital, too: five hundred dollars. Daddy says fine, but not unless they write him a letter, reminding him. So twice a year a newsy letter comes from Jennie or Nellie, never mentioning money, and then Daddy sends their payment. When it nears the time for the last five hundred dollars, they send him the loan documents marked PAID IN FULL. They write they have cancelled the final installment, for of all the relatives to whom they have loaned money, Wesson and Ronald are the only ones who have paid them back. Daddy thanks them gratefully. He says he regrets the end of the transactions, though, for it also means the end of the twice-yearly letters he has so come to enjoy. Never mentioning this remark, the Needham sisters continue to write him newsy letters in their quavering handwriting till the end of their lives.

Uncle George, says Daddy, lost his four thousand dollars on the pecan grove.

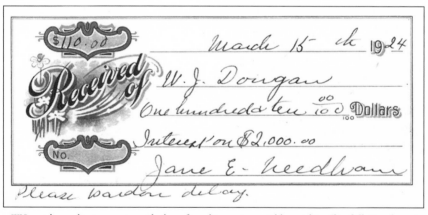

W.J. made regular payments on the loan from his cousins until he paid it off in full. For them, it turned out better to have invested in dairy cows; not, like Uncle George, in pecan trees.

11 ✼ WHY A ROUND BARN

Jackie is twelve. She's ridden her bike down to the dairy from Chez Nous, the farm a mile and a half up Colley Road where the family moved when she was starting fifth grade last year.

She goes into the lower barn. It's late morning, everything is clean and empty. She prefers when the cow barn is bustling with activity; the emptiness always makes her feel a little uneasy and desolate, just like Grama's kitchen in midafternoon when nothing is stirring there. But today is different. She has an errand. First, though, she stands looking at two handprints in the concrete floor. They are on the edge of a stall, near the gutter, near the doors out to the horse yard. Her father made the bigger print when he was nine. The smaller is her uncle's, made when he was seven. She sets her tablet and pencil on the walkway, kneels, and places her right hand in the larger print. Ever since she can remember, she has fit her hand into Daddy's handprint. He always seemed like such a big boy, until her hand caught up with his a few years ago. Now hers is larger.

She pictures Daddy as a little boy, kneeling in this same spot, pressing his hand into the wet concrete, while Trever crowds to be next. The sun and blue sky are above them, and no round barn on top yet, except maybe scaffolding. The bones of the barn. The inside silo is here, though; it was built first, and then the barn around it. The silo would have been a mammoth lonely column, like silos she's seen after a barn has burned down. But unlike them, not really lonely and abandoned, for there would have been a beehive of building going on around it. There's a picture in an old album of the silo, nearly constructed, and you can see all the activity.

She's never been interested in pressing her hand into Trever's handprint. Her own handprint, and bare footprint, too, are beside Craig's and Patsy's and Joan's, in a foundation in one of the many extensions of the milkhouse. Maybe her children will someday come and fit their hands and feet into her prints.

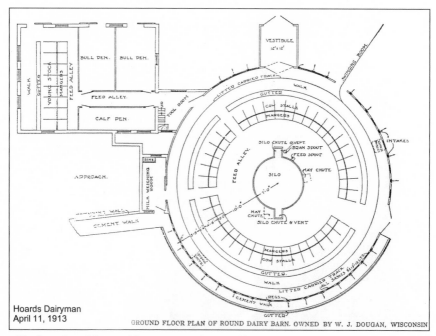

The following labels appear within the floor plan:

VESTIBULE 12' x 12'

SWINGING DOOR

BULL PEN. BULL PEN.

YOUNG STOCK

FEED ALLEY

WALK

GUTTER

MANGERS

WALK

LITTER CARRIER TRACK

GUTTER

COW STALL

MANGERS

FEED ALLEY.

CALF PEN.

TOOL ROOM

SILO CHUTE & VENT

DOWN SPOUT

FEED SPOUT

INTAKES

SILO CHUTE & VENT

SILO

HAY CHUTE

APPROACH.

MILK WEIGHING ROOM

SINK

HAY CHUTE

SILO CHUTE & VENT

CEMENT WALK

MANGERS

COW STALL

GUTTER.

WALK

LITTER CARRIER TRACK

CEMENT WALK

GUTTER

Hoards Dairyman
April 11, 1913

GROUND FLOOR PLAN OF ROUND DAIRY BARN. OWNED BY W. J. DOUGAN, WISCONSIN

The floor plan of the round barn, as printed in Hoard's Dairyman, *1913.*

Jackie picks up her tablet. She's been writing an essay for school. Her teacher is new to southern Wisconsin and drove past the round barn one Sunday. Now he wants to know, why did your grandfather build it *round?* He says he'll give her extra credit. Back at Chez Nous she's completed a composition that explains the advantages of roundness. Daddy gave her some help with names and facts and figures:

> When my grandfather bought the farm in 1906 there was just the side barn. It held nine or ten cows. That wasn't big enough for the kind of dairy that he wanted. He went up to the University of Wisconsin and talked to the agronomy professors at the Ag School, and other people interested in dairy farms. Professor Franklin King thought a round barn was ideal for a dairy barn.
>
> You can do all your work in a circle, your feeding, your milking, your cleaning, and end up where you started. That makes economy of motion.
>
> All the cows stand in a circle facing the silo in the center. The silo puts silage right in front of them. Grain and hay from the upper barn can come down chutes alongside the silo and end up in front of the cows, too.
>
> The design is economical. A barn braced on a concrete pillar for its core will not blow over in a tornado. The strong center means the rest of the barn

The lower barn ready for the cows. Grampa believed in lots of light. The openings just under the ceiling are part of the ventilation system.

can be of lighter materials. The side barn, which was built probably around 1850, had to have huge, square-hewn beams. The round barn needs only two-by-fours and two-by-sixes.

Then look at a cow's shape. From the top she looks something like a violin. She has a slender head (with ears, and sometimes horns, sticking out like the pegs). She has a moderate neck, rather skinny shoulders, and broad hips. She is rather wedge-shaped. Anyone who has cut an angel food cake knows that the pieces will be wedge-shaped. In the same way a round barn with the stalls in a ring will have each stall a little bit wedge-shaped. A cow fits comfortably into a such a stall. On account of her natural design she doesn't need much room by her shoulders, and she needs even extra room by her broad flanks, for milking and cleanup. It's an efficient use of space.

Even the feed depressions, the mangers, sunk into the concrete in front of each cow's stanchion, are slightly wedge-shaped. The larger end is closest to the cow, where she can best reach with her tongue. It is really surprising that more barns are not round barns.

That's really all her teacher has asked for. But Jackie decides to give over-flowing measure. She has written how the barn is white, not red like most barns. She has told that it's divided into the upper barn, the loft, and the low-er cow barn. She's described the green shingled roof, starting steep, then making a bend and sloping more gently to the top, which Daddy and Grampa call a "hip roof." She's described the two ventilators on opposite sides of the roof, like decorations on a giant's cap. And then—although she knows the barn as well as the inside of her own mouth, but if someone were to say, "How many teeth do you have?" she'd have to count them with her tongue to be sure—she takes her tablet and rides her bike from Chez Nous—the farm up the road they'd moved into last year—down to the dairy to take a close look.

She's recorded the upper barn details, the skylight windows and the windows directly under the eaves, in the hay section; the people-height windows in the other part. Two huge barn doors stretch from floor to eaves and are on a track. When opened, they hang against the outside barn walls. From the foot of the ramp you can look through the open doors and see "The Aims of This Farm" framed shadowy on the silo.

If you walk into the barn from the ramp, ahead of you is a huge open space, all the way to the silo, large enough for a team of horses and a hay wagon. On your right you'll see an incredible wall of hay, clear up to the roof if haying is just over. It stretches around behind the silo. The part of the loft that isn't hay and open barn floor has the feed grinder, usually with mounds of oats and unshelled corn beside it, the milking machine motor, and grain rooms with full and empty gunny sacks, and heavy paper sacks full of protein supplement for the pigs. Above the grain rooms are huge grain bins, stretching from silo to wall and almost to the roof; their broad wooden fronts are golden with age.

That is the upper barn. Now Jackie has come down the narrow inner staircase and, after the handprint ritual, is ready to record the cow barn.

The silo, of course, is the center, with the hay chutes coming down alongside but stopping at the ceiling, letting the hay fall free to the floor. The smaller grain chute, with its paddle to shove in or pull out, hangs over the grain cart. The silage cart stands close to the silage chute, which is also a ventilator shaft. This area close around the silo is where the barnhands work, feeding the cows, who stand in a wide circle facing them.

Jackie counts. Forty stalls, each separated by a curved metal bar. At the head end is the stanchion; it's like a wooden safety pin that opens at the top and can be snapped shut after the cow sticks in her head. She's happy to do this because her grain is waiting in front of her when she comes to be milked. The stanchion swivels at top and bottom, so the cow can turn her head comfortably when she tries to reach the silage and grain from her neighbors' mangers. A scaredy cow can swivel the whole stanchion around and with rolling eyes stare over her shoulder at Jackie, or a dog, or whatever is distracting her. Alternating between every stall hangs a water cup or a salt dish, at cow-mouth level.

At intervals, walkways interrupt the stalls, sloping up from the sidewalk behind the cows to the area in front of them. Behind the rear quarters of the cows is the gutter, where the pee splashes, and the cow pies mostly fall, and then the walkway from which the barnhands clean the gutter and do the milking. Finally come the thick whitewashed walls.

Jackie follows the walkway clockwise. Twenty-one windows set close together all the way around: they make the cow barn a light and airy place. There are also five doors. The people entrance, that goes through the washroom with its sinks and hoses to meet the sidewalk from the milkhouse. The Dutch door wide enough for a cow to go through into the passageway to the side barn. The double doors that reach from walkway to ceiling, which open into the vestibule to the barnyard and are flung wide to let the cows in for milking. The cows crowd through these, led by the head cow, and mill and stamp and find their stalls. The fourth is the manure trolley door. The trolley is pulled or pushed on its overhead track through this exit and its load dumped onto the manure pile at the edge of the barnyard. The final door, again cow-sized, opens onto the north barnyard, which is flanked by the horse barn and calf barn.

The main cow entrance is especially interesting. The vestibule is a porchway, a couple of cow lengths long, and has no windows. The light is dim. Near the middle a blanket the width of the entrance hangs down, low enough that a cow has to duck to pass under it. All the flies on her head and neck and back are swept off. They buzz around in the dimness, spot a bright slit overhead, fly up through it, and find themselves in a closed, empty room. It is full of windows. They haven't the wits to crawl back down through the gap they entered from, so after a while they die. A barnhand eventually sweeps them up by the bushel basketful.

The vestibule fly trap is Grampa's invention, to keep the fly population down inside the barn. Its only moving parts are flies and cows. Grampa says of his fly trap, "I succeeded by thinking like a fly!"

There's another interesting feature in the cow barn, the ventilation. In between almost every window, up against the ceiling, is a hole about a foot square with a sliding wooden shutter. On the outside of the cow barn, down between the windows, each square has its corresponding screened square. The two have a passage between them through the thick walls; they form a kind of periscope for air, and are part of the ventilation system for keeping the barn

The "back side" of the barn, showing the cow entrance from the barnyard. The two windows above the entrance illuminate W.J.'s "fly trap" room.

cool in summer and warm in winter, as well as getting the stale air out—all those cow burps and cow pie odors—and fresh air in. The other part of the system is the two tall wooden shafts that run alongside the silo, up through the upper barn to the fans on the roof. When the ventilator fans turn, they pull warm air up from the center of the cow barn to the roof. Then, to replace the warm air, cooler air enters through the little low outside windows and flows up the wall passages into the barn, entering at the ceiling-level square. The cool air sinks to the floor. The warm air, meanwhile, is flowing toward the center of the barn and up the big ventilator shafts to the outside. There's a continual current of warm leaving the top, and cool coming in the bottom.

It's one of Daddy's favorite tricks, when visitors come to the round barn, to demonstrate these ventilators. He takes his handkerchief and holds it under the shaft, and the wind going up nearly pulls it out of his hand. With this system it takes a terrible heat wave to make the barn anything but pleasant in the summer. In the winter, the shutters are closed and the cows' bodies heat the barn; the thick walls hold in the heat. The roof fans need change the air only once in a while.

Sometimes a sparrow manages to get into one of the ventilating passages in the outside wall and is trapped. Jackie or Craig discovers it beating its wings against the screening, and reports it. Then a barnhand loosens the screening and lifts the exhausted little body out.

Handprints of Trever and Ronald in the concrete of the lower barn.

Jackie goes through the washroom entrance to the outside and checks to see if there are any stray sparrows in a ventilating window. She follows the narrow concrete sidewalk around the barn to the horse yard. Because the barn is built on a slight slope, the sidewalk gets gradually lower while the windows remain the same height. By the time she gets beyond the horse yard, the windows are almost too high to look into. On the barnyard side, she knows, they'll be far too high.

There are no sparrows. And she has plenty of material for extra credit. She must remember to list "The Aims" when she describes the upper barn, but she knows these by heart. And at the end, to say how impressive the barn is, and that people often drive out on Sundays to see it and watch the milking. A good last line can be, "W.J. Dougan's round barn is a landmark in southern Wisconsin."

She goes into the Big House to get a sugar cookie from Grama, and to tell her about the essay, before riding her bike back up to Chez Nous.

12 ⊰ JIM HOWARD

Jim Howard grows up on a dairy farm near Tonica, Illinois. When his father sells the farm in 1925, Jim runs an employment-wanted ad in *Hoard's Dairyman*. W.J. Dougan answers it, saying he needs a herdsman. His letter states that there is no drinking or smoking on the farm, that he himself is deaf and a former minister.

Jim doesn't drink or smoke, and sees no problem in working under a minister-farmer. He thinks, privately, that it might be difficult to work for a deaf man, but he's willing to try. He writes that he will accept the job, provided the Reverend Mr. Dougan will take a man with a severe limp: osteomyelitis at age five has left him with one leg twisted and shorter than the other. But his handicap has never interfered with his ability to do a full day's work. W.J. writes back to come ahead.

When Jim arrives, Mother Dougan gives him the room in the Big House that has the little balcony. He meets the other hired men. Grampa shows him the farm. He reads the words on the silo and wonders to himself whether the last Aim, "Life as Well as a Living," is for the family only or includes the working man. He meets Ronald, who has just begun working full time on the farm that summer, in business with his father. Ronald is a few years older than he, and talks rapidly to his father by spelling out the words with his fingers. So does Mother Dougan. Jim pats his pocket. He's already purchased a little notebook and pencil to carry with him.

After dinner W.J. Dougan takes him into his office. "I never tell a man when to get up," he says. "I tell him when I want him on the job in the morning. You can get up an hour ahead, comb your hair, curl it, anything you want — or you can get up five minutes ahead. But I want you in the barn at four o'clock, ready to work."

He tells him about his day off: "You can sleep as late as you wish, and have breakfast here," he says, "but I want you to be gone part of the day. Get away from *here*! Even if you have to go downtown and stand on a street corner! If

you're away from here part of the time you'll be a better man for me when you're back. And also for yourself!"

He twinkles. "But you won't have to stand on a corner. There are church activities and Grange activities, and I have a membership at the YMCA for every man here, so you can swim and play basketball. There are rides to and from town, or if not, we have some bicycles."

Jim nods. A day off every seven or eight days, even without Y privileges, seems very liberal. He's been used to having only one a month at his former job. Nor does the work schedule seem unreasonable: milk from four to six-thirty, breakfast, then an hour's rest. Clean the barn and other chores till noon, then dinner and another hour off. Milking and cleanup from three till six, then supper and off for the evening, except for putting the cows to bed — though Jim doesn't know what "putting the cows to bed" entails.

W.J. says, "These are my criteria for cleanliness," and tells of the spotless white cap and apron he is to wear at every milking; of how the cows are brushed and shaved and washed; of what the steps are in clearing the manure, washing down the sidewalks and gutters, and spreading lime. He says that the walls are to be whitewashed regularly.

Jim's salary will be fifty dollars a month, including room and board. That, too, seems liberal. He knows that his employer has just returned from Chicago, where he gave a series of radio lectures over WLS, and received a Master Farmer award from *Prairie Farmer* magazine. He is a bit awed to be working for a Master Farmer, and is filled with respect. He determines to do his best.

The former herdsman stays on for a week to break in his successor, and then Jim is in charge. Not only does he respect W.J., "Daddy," as he is called by everyone, but finds that Daddy Dougan treats him with respect. He never tells him, "No, you're doing that wrong, do it this way." He never seems to be checking up on him. In the mornings when Jim pushes the two-wheeled cart with its four cans of milk on it from the barn to the milkhouse, and sees Daddy's head peeking from the small window of his bedroom in the Big House, he never feels he's looking out to spot loiterers, or count how many loads they are getting up. It's only Daddy surveying his world before emerging.

When the weather gets cold enough for the cows to stay inside, W.J. instructs Jim on putting the cows to bed. At 9:00 or 9:30 the two return to the barn. The cows are all lying down. They've eaten, they've knocked hay out of their mangers. W.J. and Jim get them all up. They sweep the hay back into the mangers, get more hay. A lot of the cows, once on their feet, make droppings. Not all the manure falls into the gutter. They scrape the walkway, tidy up around the cow, and shake up her bedding. All the while Grampa croons to his lassies. He also talks to Jim.

"You'll be surprised at how much cleaner the cows are in the morning, and how much more they'll eat, than if you just abandon them from 6 o'clock at night till 4 o'clock the next day."

He gives Jim other advice. "As Mr. Hoard says, 'The cow is a mother—treat her as such!'" And, "Every day, go around in front of each cow. Watch how she eats. Look her in the eye. See if it's got a bright sparkle or if it's losing luster. Then you know how that cow's feeling today. Go back around behind her, look at her droppings. From them you'll know how she's going to be feeling tomorrow."

Jim thinks everything Daddy tells him makes a lot of sense. He's also impressed with the routine of the Big House. The meals are served in the dining room, by Mother Dougan, Ronald's sister Esther, who is fifteen, and Hilda, the hired helper. The farmhands and Hilda eat with the family. Mother Dougan bakes all the bread, pies, and cakes, and spreads a lavish board. Breakfast is never merely bacon and eggs, but bacon, eggs, hotcakes, sausage, toast, jam, applesauce or another fruit sauce, fruit juice, milk, cream, and coffee. Dinners at noon make the table groan even more than breakfast. Suppers are simpler, but equally satisfying. At meals, W.J. doesn't sit at the head but at the middle of the table. He always says grace. After supper he reads aloud from the Bible, and from a commentary; the boarders stay for this lesson. Before bedtime Jim habitually polishes off a quart of milk: the day-old milk returned from the route is in a box inside the cooler door, and is free for the taking by the farm workers.

As a boarder, Jim has his bed made every morning, and his sheets and clothes laundered weekly. Mother Dougan and Hilda toil over the big washtubs in the men's washroom off the kitchen; in order to wash or to use the toilet in the closed room at the rear he must thread his way around tubs and women, and in the wintertime, clotheslines laden with overalls. More lines are stretched in the cellar near the furnace, and sometimes he helps hang the clothes or carry a basket. In fair weather, the clothes are hung outside to flap in the sunshine between the elms on the Big House lawn.

For his rest period, he can stretch out on his bed in his room or sit in the men's parlor off the dining room, where the radio is tuned in to WLS, and there are magazines, books, and papers to read. There is also a Victrola and records.

Out in the barn, when shorthanded, W.J. sometimes works along with him, taking the place of someone with a day off. Frequently, especially on Sunday afternoons, visitors from town come to see the milking. W.J. gives a mischievous glance at Jim, takes a cow leader, catches a cow through the nostrils, and exposes her gums. "This poor lass has no upper set of teeth," he says. "She was born this way." The visitors cluck with surprise and sympathy; they don't know that all cows are born like this. Daddy Dougan doesn't give away the ruminant joke, nor do Jim or the other barnhands.

Jim works a year on the farm. He and the other barn workers make a smooth team. Every week they scrape the barnyard. Every three months they whitewash the cow barn walls. Jim learns to swing all the way around the barn on the manure trolley track, hand over hand. Grampa sees him and says, "Hi! I didn't know this was the big top!"

Then Jim leaves for an operation that improves his hip. He returns to a roommate. Glen Gile acts a bit strange, and tells wild stories, but Jim reasons that every man is entitled to his peculiarities.

But Glen's strangeness increases. He gets it into his head that Mr. Griffiths, the oldest farmhand and trusted friend of Daddy Dougan, is losing his mind. Jim and the others laugh it off, but Jim feels uneasy. Then Glen decides that it's Daddy Dougan who is going crazy. He states that Daddy has a lot of worries with the farm, and with his flirtatious sweet-sixteen daughter, and with his harum-scarum college son, Trever. Jim and the others laugh this off, too, but Jim feels more uneasy.

On a summer night Jim and a milkhouse worker, Micky Baker, are sitting on a bench in the washroom off the kitchen, idly talking of this and that. Glen comes in. "I'm going to shoot Daddy Dougan," he says casually, and trots up the back stairs, slamming the stairwell door behind him.

Jim and Micky are speechless. They hear the floor creak and in a moment, Glen returning down the stairs, one slow step at a time. The door opens a crack; they turn mesmerized and see six inches of shotgun barrel ease out. Panic grips Jim's throat, but with the panic comes action. He reaches up and grabs the light cord. In the sudden darkness he and Micky sprint toward the front of the house, snapping off lights as they go. They find Mother Dougan in the dining room. "Get Daddy out, quick!" Jim orders. "Glen's loco, he's coming with a shotgun to shoot him!"

Eunice asks no questions. She rushes to Wesson, working at his desk in the front room, and spells that they must go over to Ron's place instantly. Wesson stumbles to his feet. "Is it a fire?" he cries, and follows her out the front door and down the sidewalk to the Little House. No one worries about Esther; she's staying the night with her chum Eloise down the road. Hilda is also away, visiting her sister.

Jim and Micky run to the cellar and hide behind the furnace. Overhead they hear Glen prowling back and forth in the empty house.

"I've never hurt anyone in my life," chatters Micky, clutching a coal shovel, "but if he comes down here, I'm gonna kill him!"

Over at the Little House Wesson is hustled upstairs and into Mother and Daddy's bedroom. He sits in the dark. Vera calls the police. Ronald goes outside and listens to Glen shooting up a cornfield. Then Glen comes to the garage, starts his car, and leaves. The police arrive a few minutes later. They are provoked that Glen has been allowed to get away.

"How do you argue with a shotgun?" asks Ron.

"He'll probably come back. Then call us again," say the police.

There's no sleep for anyone. Wesson, though he protests, remains in the dark in the uppermost corner of the Little House. Eunice stays with him. Ronald and Vera watch at the darkened downstairs windows.

Jim hasn't yet put the cows to bed. "Come with me, Micky," he begs. "What if he comes back while I'm out in the barn alone?"

Micky refuses to budge. Jim wavers, almost lets the cows be, but in the end he rushes down, practically kicks the bewildered beasts to their feet, and beds them more quickly than they've ever been bedded before. Then he and Micky watch from the front windows of the Big House.

About midnight Glen returns. Ron calls the police. Glen puts his car in the garage, goes upstairs, and gets into bed.

The police arrive quickly. "What's the best way to take him?" they ask.

"Every morning I call him about four o'clock," says Jim.

"Well—call him!"

From the top of the stairs Jim squeaks, "Glen, time to get up!"

Glen opens the door. Jim steps back, the police step forward, and it's all over.

That is the last any of them ever see of Glen. They hear he's been committed to the state mental hospital at Mendota. Everyone is sorry, but they're glad he didn't shoot Daddy Dougan, or anyone else. W.J. shakes his head. "Poor fellow," he says.

Jim stays on the farm for another year. Then he leaves and goes to ag school. He marries, and works as farm manager on a succession of farms in distant states. He eventually becomes a supervisor for Carnation Milk. He keeps in touch through Christmas cards and an occasional letter.

Some twenty years later Jim is in the area and drives out to the farm. He finds Grampa talking to Ronald in the barn. "Hello, Daddy," he writes on his pad. "I couldn't go by without saying hello to 'The Babies' Milkman.'"

Grampa and Ronald greet him warmly. They catch him up on some of the changes—the cows now almost entirely Holsteins; the improvements in the milkhouse; the growing hybrid seedcorn business with its buildings located at Ron's farm up the road; the Rock County Breeders' Co-op.

On the barn ramp, Jim says to Ronald, "Your father never preached to me, yet working and living with him was like a sermon every day." He motions toward the "Aims" on the silo. "My first day here I wondered if those words included me. I found out very soon they were meant for every person on the place. We were truly a family."

Ron reminds him of the Glen Gile episode, and spells the reminder to Grampa. His father shakes his head. "We had a touching letter from that lad's mother, about his mental troubles, and how they had not thought him dangerous when he was in one of his spells. My heart was sorrowful for that woman's trials, and for her handicapped son."

Jim grins wryly and writes, "Daddy, I have tended a number of herds since you taught me, and that night was the only time in my life that I almost didn't put the cows to bed!"

Grampa nods and nods over the message. His whole body shakes with silent laughter.

13 ✕ THE SIDE BARN AND THE CALF BARN

When Daddy is small, before 1911, the main barn on the farm is what later is called the side barn. It's in this barn, with its wooden floors and manure trough, that he learned to milk, and where twice daily, while he milked Daisy with her freckled udder, he gazed longingly at the carefree sparrows hopping among the horse apples on the drive.

The side barn was built around 1850, rectangular, framed with massive hand-hewn beams joined by wooden pegs. Its foundation, and the walls of the lower barn, are of local limestone blocks held together with a sand and lime mortar. Jackie asks once, when Mr. Griffiths is patching a spot on the side barn foundation, why they hadn't used cement in the first place. After all, the round barn is all cement, and so is the cowtank and paved cow yard. So is the milkhouse.

"Didn't know about cement back then," Mr. Griffiths responds.

Jackie has a long acquaintance with cement. It's one of the most interesting of sporadic activities on the farm. Cement is made in a large wooden rectangular box with low sides. Buckets of sand from the gravel pit are poured in it, and a sack of cement powder with its cloudy dust, and then water. Mr. Griffiths, who always seems to be the main cement-maker, mixes the sand and cement and water with a hoe, pushing and pulling it back and forth, and adding more water, until the ingredients are well blended, much the way Grama gradually adds liquid to the flour when she's making bread or cake. When the cement batter is a creamy, even, grainy gray, not too stiff, not too runny, it's ready to be transferred by the wheelbarrow-full to the spot where cement is needed. Then the spot is roped off so that no one will walk on it till the cement dries into concrete.

Concrete is funny. Most things wet will not harden; the clay at school is kept damp so that work can continue on the sculpture of a seal or pin dish the following art class. But there is a story about Grampa. Once, during the round barn's construction, he noticed a half-bucket of cement left over at the

end of the day. In order to save it, he covered it with several inches of water. The next morning it was totally solid, the cement useless, the bucket ruined. "Well, not quite useless," Daddy says when he tells the story. "One of the men took it as an anchor for his uncle's fishing boat."

When Jackie asks Daddy about cement, he suggests she look it up in their new *World Book Encyclopedia*. To her astonishment, the Romans had cement. They manufactured a masonry mortar, the sort the side barn has. But then they found a limestone that had the magic proportions of clay and lime, and learned that when they heated it, they had a product considerably better than anything they had before, one with strength, and which hardened under water. A natural cement. This was used (where the soil was right) up into the 1800s, when a bricklayer in England figured out the correct ingredients, proportions, and heating, which would produce a bond that was of consistent quality. That was Portland cement, named thus because it resembled the grey stone of the "Portland bill"—a well known projection of land into the sea, shaped like a bird's beak. It's made, she learns, of ground limestone mixed with clay and baked slowly in long ovens. It becomes hard through the chemical action of the limestone when water is added. It didn't come into much use in the United States till after the Civil War, and then mainly in the East, its general use filtering to Midwest farms by the last decade of the century. That is why no cement was used in the side barn, and why Grampa, building his concrete silo and barn in 1911, was somewhat of an innovator. At the time, his was one of the few concrete silos in Rock County; an inventory of 1917 gives only a smattering of the county's silos as concrete, the bulk being wooden, stave, or brick.

After the round barn is finished enough to house cattle, Grampa modernizes the side barn. He tears out the old floors and lays concrete. He cuts a doorway in the wall closest the round barn, and annexes the two buildings with a closed passageway. This allows cows, feed and machinery to be moved easily from one barn to the other. The original lower barn doors, through which the cows entered and exited, faced the north end of the Big House, and a narrow lane led the cows around the barn into the barnyard at its side. Grampa closes this entrance and cuts barn doors in the side of the barn, so that the doors now open onto the enlarged barnyard that serves both buildings. He paves the barnyard and builds a wide concrete tank for the cows to drink from.

Inside the remodeled lower barn, on one side, are box stalls. The newborn calves are kept in these stalls, with their mothers, before the mothers are returned to the round barn. When the mothers leave, the babies bawl and bawl. Jackie loves to hold her fingers out to a tiny calf. It grabs them, two at once, with frantic eagerness, its front legs splayed apart and its neck low with its head stretched up, as if under its mother. It rolls its huge wide eyes. Its tongue wraps around her fingers and it sucks with such force she almost loses her skin. When she finally jerks her fingers out they're tingling and sticky, and dripping with webs of saliva.

There is a walkway between the box stalls and the eight or nine cow stalls with their stanchions. Concrete mangers are in front, with the gutter and another walkway behind, as in the round barn. The box stall side has only one window at the very end, for the rest are now covered by the earth of the ramp going up to the round barn loft. But the stanchion side has windows the length of it, making this barn light. Grampa stresses lots of light inside a cow barn, and regularly preaches the value of sunlight's role in sanitation and cow health.

There is no chute into the lower barn from its hayloft above, only a trapdoor in the ceiling. Hay is forked down through the trapdoor.

Up above, the side barn loft is divided into three sections. Both ends are for hay, and in this hay is where you find the most eggs, probably because the loft is nearer the henhouse and less busy than the round barn's loft. It's also where you find the nests of newborn kittens. Between the two hay sections is a space open from floor to roof. From this middle space large loft doors face the ramp, and the back of the area is usually filled with a huge pile of sawdust for cow bedding. The massive beams span its sides and also cross over it. You can walk, high above the barn floor, from one hayloft to the other. There are always ropes to swing on, and if you jump down or fall, you land in sawdust.

This loft is an ideal place for a circus. The Dougan kids every now and then organize one, with any friends who happen to come out for the day. Connie Horn is always in on these; she's the daughter of the office girl, Ruby, and plays on the farm on Saturdays. The acts are mostly tight-rope walking on the beams and flying trapeze stunts with the ropes, punctuated by recitations and songs to swell out the program. For circus animals, unwilling dogs and a very unwilling goat are closed into the wooden slatted boxes that milk bottles are shipped in. Unhappy cats are dressed up. Sometimes there's a rabbit or a chicken or a crow that can be caged. From the Little House comes the big stuffed bear that is difficult to ride because one of its four wheels is half missing, and also the wooden horse which has a mechanism that makes its legs hitch along at a slow pace no matter how hard its rider spurs it forward. Jackie wears a candy-striped costume from one of Mother's dance recitals, and is a bareback rider on this unsatisfactory steed.

The audiences, Grama and Grampa and Mother and Ruby and anyone else the performers can round up, sit on milk cases and planks on the ramp, facing the open loft doors. The admission is usually safety pins. It doesn't occur to the four to charge anything else—in all their books, when children put on a show, the admission is safety pins, though the books never say what makes these legal tender. And there are refreshments, of course: chocolate milk and orange drink, and a tray of Grama's fat yellow sugar cookies.

One memorable Hallowe'en when Jackie is in second grade Mother puts on a party. It's held in the afternoon, in the doorway of the side barn loft. Friends of her sisters and brother come, as well as her own. Everyone wears a costume. Jackie is a Dutch girl with wooden shoes and an apron, also from one of Mother's dance recitals. They bob for apples, and play other Hallowe'en games, but the best part is when Mother sits them in a row on the straw, blindfolds them, and they pass around the parts of the witch. There is real liver for the witch's liver, a chicken foot with scaly skin and claws for the witch's hand, spaghetti cooked just enough to make it flexible for her guts, straw for

Cows in the side barn. Note the drinking cups on the left; the cup on the right is a salt cup.

hair, and a large peeled grape for her eyeball. To Jackie, that wet eyeball is the scariest of all, though the town kids scream most at the chicken claw.

There's one other place that holds calves; older calves who have graduated from the side barn box stalls but are not yet cows. This barn is more a long, low shed and it closes off the end of the horse yard behind the round barn. The calves can go out into a little pasture behind, where the strawstacks usually are. During the winter they mostly stay inside, and the hired men keep throwing fresh straw on top of the old straw and calf-pies. Grampa doesn't have the calf barn cleaned in winter, for the manure and straw make warmth for the calves. By spring the buildup can be a couple of feet high. Then on a fine spring day the calves are turned out to gambol in the sunshine, and there is a gigantic shoveling out. The magnificently terrible stench pervades the whole farm.

Once Joan bets her siblings that she can go in and stay the longest. They rise to the challenge. When they enter, holding their noses and gagging, two barnhands greet them cheerfully.

"How can you stand it?" Joan cries from the walkway, and the others echo her.

The four and the men chaff back and forth. Someone tells a story about something, then someone else does. After a while Joan suddenly remembers her bet. They've all been in there at least half an hour, and after the first few minutes, nobody has noticed the smell. It's a revelation to them that noses can get used to anything.

But the most interesting part of the calf barn is that part of its length, closed to calves, which is open to the horse yard and houses the bull walk. This is a slatted platform slightly wider than a bull. The reluctant bull is led up onto it, tethered to the front, and a lever thrown. The slats start to move backward, thus forcing the bull to walk forward, although he never gets anywhere. But he is exercising, which is the sole point of the bull walk. The bull is seldom on the bull walk, but Joan, Patsy, Jackie, Craig, and their friends often are, a line of them holding the rail and walking and walking on this treadmill. It's one of their favorite sports.

Earlier, before there was a bull walk, there was the bull sweep. This was an extremely long and stout pole, balanced in its middle on a post, by a swivel. The pole would go round and round, and not tighten up or loosen as it would were it screwed. A bull would be secured on one end of the pole by his nose ring, and then he could walk in a wide circle. A second bull could be at the other end of the pole, thus having both exercise at once. But there were two problems with the bull sweep — a bull could choose not to walk, to just stand there. If there were two bulls, it took a little cooperation, but they could both choose to just stand there. The second problem was more serious — the bulls were out in the open, behind the sheds beyond the Little House, and sometimes left to exercise unsupervised. After Jerry, Jackie's first cousin, at a young age somehow escaped supervision and was discovered toddling up to a bull with a handful of grass to feed the nice cow, the bull sweep was dismantled.

But there are dangers with the bull walk, too. Once, when Patsy is nine, she is walking on the bull walk with Jackie, Craig, and the herdsman's son, Warren Mathews, when she catches her foot between two slats and, screaming, she's dragged backwards. Warren has the presence of mind to leap off and pull the lever, just as Patsy is about to go under. She is lame for weeks.

"It's too dangerous," Grampa and everyone decide, and the children are instructed to stay off the treadmill. But the grownups forget, and when nobody is around to notice them, the four and their friends still walk, walk, walk, but oh so carefully, on the bull walk.

14 ⚔ CIRCUMCISION

There is a mysterious space in the round barn. It's a dim passageway between the cow barn and the lower part of the side barn. There's a window in this passageway, but it's so encrusted with dirt and lime and splashes of whitewash that only a murky light filters through. Under the window is a ledge, which is the lid to the slaked-lime bin. A narrow staircase winds up the wall of the passage past the bin and window to emerge in the loft of the round barn. On the other side of the passage is the inside opening to the outside silo. So all this is in the passageway, before you get to the lower barn: the window, the ledge, the stairs; and on the other side, the space before the silo opening, and the yawning black mouth of the outside silo. The passageway is whitewashed.

Jackie's earliest memory is of this passageway. It's an odd memory, like a dream. She's in this passageway, and so is the family doctor, old Doctor Thayer. He has her baby brother on the ledge under the window. The baby is naked. The doctor's back is to her; she can't see her brother. The doctor is doing something to her brother's bottom: she knows he's cutting the skin and stretching it over the buttocks. The baby is bawling. That's the extent of the memory: a setting, an activity, a sound. Jackie knows this is a genuine memory, for she never tells it to anyone until she's nearly grown, and realizes she's always been puzzled by it. Then she tells Mother.

Mother is startled. She has an explanation. Jackie was less than two years old, Patsy three, and Joan five when Dr. Thayer had come to the Little House to circumcise Craig. He did it on the dining-room table. Mother must have explained to her sisters, or perhaps the adults were talking. Little as Jackie was, she got the idea of skin, and cutting, and bottom. And when the doctor began, Craig started to scream. Mother hadn't realized this would happen; she'd rushed the sisters into their coats and taken them for a walk around the farm till it was over. It was January and the weather was cold; they'd stayed in the buildings. They'd gone to the cow barn to see the cows, and then into

Patsy, Joan, and Jackie on the day of Craig's birth, January 12, 1930. They are on the steps to the side door of the Big House, beside the cellar doors.

the lower barn to see the calves. In the passage, Jackie must have heard a calf bawling.

Jackie nods. Calves always bawl in the lower barn; it's where they stay right after they're separated from their mothers. It makes sense of the memory. She finds it satisfying to verify this as a memory, to see how it became garbled.

She tells her sisters, and gains further confirmation. "Sure," says Patsy. "We sat out the circumcision in that passageway, on the steps up to the loft. Mother made us keep going up and down those stairs, and we kept complaining we wanted to go back home."

"It was really COLD!" adds Joan.

Jackie's enormously pleased to know she has remembered something from before she was two. Craig, of course, is glad that he doesn't remember anything about it.

15 ✕ HEELS

Ronald is just twelve in May, 1914. When June comes, he graduates from the final grade, the eighth, at District School #12, across the field by the crick. Before being accepted at high school in town, all country school graduates must pass examinations. These are held at the county seat. Ronald goes to Janesville and spends two exhausting days taking tests. He fails in three subjects, a rude surprise, for he's a voracious reader, did well in the district school and also in Strong School, across from Aunt Ida's on Bushnell Street, where he attended for brief periods. He'd even skipped two grades.

But eighth is the terminal degree; students do not have to continue beyond that grade. Wisconsin, and Rock County, want to be sure their students are prepared for life as citizens in the adult world. They also want them to be ready for the rigors of high school if they continue their schooling; therefore the exams are stiff. The spelling exam, for instance, begins, "Write and define two words for each of the following roots: doct, fin, leg, rapt," and goes on to "Define syllable; accent; derivative word; disyllable." The arithmetic exam has story problems such as, "If a cow is tied with a rope thirty feet long to a peg in a pasture, how many square yards has she to graze over? How many feet around this part of the pasture?" as well as pure computation: "Extract the square root of 106,276."

Grampa and Grama confer. There isn't much point in sending their son back to country school. He'd feel disgraced, and the teaching, or his application, or a combination of the two, are obviously lacking. He should be tutored, and then give the exams another try. But there's no rush. He's two years younger than his classmates starting ninth grade. They decide to keep him home a year, have him study with his cousin Hazel Croft, now a teacher in Beloit, and work on the farm. He's small for his age. This plan will allow growing time for both mind and body.

Ronald is jubilant. He'll be a regular farmhand; he'll receive wages! A dollar a day! He'll have a title: Assistant Herdsman. Summer and riches spread gloriously before him. He doubts if he'll have much time for studying.

The evening before his starting day, his father calls him to his desk, has him sign his worker's contract, and gives him a solemn talk about responsibility. Ronald stands on the red rug, the spot where all new men stand to learn Daddy Dougan's expectations. Later, he knows, they are sometimes summoned there to be reprimanded or praised. He determines that he shall be one who is praised. He goes to bed before sundown.

He wakes early, filled with zeal. He hurries to the barn. It's clean and in readiness; it's been scraped and limed the evening before. The cows' grain is in their mangers. He would have liked to fetch the cows, but they don't need to be fetched. They're already in the barnyard, jostling at the vestibule, stamping and lowing. Their bags are heavy; some udders are so full that thin lines of milk are already streaming from a tit or two. They are nervous, for a storm's about to break. Ronald beats the herdsman to open the doors.

Bessie, the boss cow, leads in and heads along the sidewalk to the stall she always takes. The second most important cow is next, and then the third in rank. The old cows, the timid ones, and the new milkers bring up the rear and get whatever stalls are left to them. Bessie steps across the gutter, thrusts her head through her stanchion, and starts to eat. Ronald snaps the stanchion shut and goes around the circle, snapping the others.

All the hired men on the ramp of the round barn. Ronald, fourteen, is in the middle, his father to his right. Bob the dog is on the far left. Art Kassilke, the herdsman, is seated.

The men milk. Ronald does his share, his eight cows, but that isn't so very different; he's been milking cows regularly since he was six. What is different is the way he feels, grown up, joshing with the other men, being a real part of the group. Outside the thunder rumbles, the rain begins to pelt down. They finish the milking but leave the cows in their stanchions until the cloudburst ends.

Up in the kitchen Ronald eats a breakfast of sausages, eggs, and a huge stack of buckwheats. He finishes first and beats everyone back to the barn. He looks around for what to do next. The cows are restless, their mangers empty. He hurries to the upper barn and climbs the ladder into the haymow. The hay level is high from the June haying; it's near the top of the chutes. He grabs a pitchfork and vigorously attacks the hay. It's hard work getting it loosened and onto his pitchfork. He wrestles forkful after forkful into a chute. But the hay refuses to fall to the cow barn floor, some thirty feet below. It lies there, sagging slightly, caught against the chute's wooden sides.

Ronald has seen a hired man fill the chute, then hang on a slat and stamp the hay to dislodge it and send it down. He's even seen one occasionally ride the load down into the lower barn. He grasps the top slat, swings into the chute, and gives the hay a stamp. It's stamping on air, there's no resistance. In his surprise he loses hold of the slat and follows the hay down with a whoosh. He hits the concrete floor. The cows in their stanchions rear back in one wild, bulgy-eyed leap. The simultaneous clank of all the stanchions is sharp punctuation to the jar through his head and neck and teeth, to the pain that rips through his feet. There is hay under him, yes, but not enough to make a real cushion. He hadn't filled the chute full enough.

He sprawls there, contorted with agony. He gasps out words it's good his father can't hear, words he didn't even know he knew. He crawls around on his hands and knees before the startled cows, blinded with pain, weeping tears of humiliation, raging at himself for being a fool.

The herdsman comes in, finds him, carries him up to the house. Grampa examines his injuries, then hitches up the buggy, and he and Grama hurry him to the hospital. The doctor says he's broken both his heels.

Ronald is on crutches half the summer. He has plenty of time to work with Hazel on his fractions, to improve his spelling, and to memorize the major rivers of the world.

16 ⚬ YOU ARE A COW

You are a cow. Rather, you're about to become one. Half of what will be you is still an egg in one of your dam's ovaries. The other half is a sperm in one of your sire's testicles. Perhaps that half has been removed from your sire by stimulating him with an artificial cow or a nympho-cow, and now Amos, the artificial inseminator, has that part of you and a couple million of its siblings in a chilly test tube.

The moment arrives. Your mother is in heat. Either the bull's penis, or Amos's syringe, shoots the sperm part of you into your dam's vagina, close up to the cervix, the entrance to the uterus. That sperm swims vigorously, a little more vigorously than all the others, and meets the egg (called at this point an ovum) above the uterus in one of your dam's fallopian tubes. They join. You are now a fertilized egg.

Your cells immediately begin to divide. They divide all the time you travel down the tube and into the two-horned uterus. You implant yourself in one of the horns. The side of it is a thick, juicy wall, ready with nutrients for you. You grow in a sac called a placenta. You grow for about nine months. Then labor begins; your mother is calving. The contractions force you down the birth canal, preferably head first, and you are dropped — onto the ground, or barnyard, or stall floor.

Your mother turns around and licks and licks you. She licks you dry for you have come out wet from the fluid in the birth sac. The rough tongue invigorates you and teaches you 'mama.' Your mother licks you to your feet and nudges you, tottering, to her udder. You nose around, find a tit, and start to suck. You are born knowing how. You stay with your mother several days, then you're taken from her. She bellows her grief, you bawl like a banshee. You're put in a box stall in the barn that opens off the round barn, along with other newborn calves. You all smell like milk. You all bawl and bawl.

A barnhand brings a pail with a rubber tit sticking off the bottom rim. He holds it up so that you still suck as from an udder. The milk is warm and foamy, fresh from your mother in the cow barn. Her milk is rich with the antibodies you need as a newborn. If Craig or Jackie wanders by and offers you a finger, you'll suck the skin right off.

Before long your mother's milk goes into the regular milk pool. But you are brought milk from a nurse cow. This is a cow who's lost a quarter of her udder to mastitis but is too good a cow to ship to market. Cows with off-udders can't be used in the farm's milk supply, but they make good calf-cows. You like her milk as well as you like your mother's.

One day the barnhand brings you a pail without a tit. He gives you his fingers. You suck vigorously for you are ravenous. He gently guides your head down to the pail and, along with his fingers, you find you are sucking milk. He removes his fingers — you are drinking from a pail!

But perhaps you don't catch on that quickly. You won't follow his fingers down; to you, drinking is done with your neck arched upward. Finally he straddles you and holds you firmly between his legs. He grasps your wet, wide nostrils like a bowling ball and plunges your nose into the pail. You try to buck, to jerk your head out. You can't. You get a noseful. You also get a mouthful. MILK! You recognize it; you start to suck. You suck up the milk with your tongue curved like a straw. The fingers let go of your nostrils and you can breathe. Your breath is mixed with milk till you get the hang of it. You drain the bucket and bunt it around the stall with your head. You want more.

You are lucky to be a girl calf, a heifer calf. You will grow up. Had you been a bull calf (or a heifer twinned with a bull, a 'freemartin,' which heifers are almost always infertile) you'd have been shipped to market to make veal.

Up in the office, shortly after you are born, Daddy gives you a number and assigns you a page in his Herd Register. You are S-14, the fourteenth animal added to the herd in the year represented by S. He also gives you an elegant French name, *S. Quatorze de Chez Nous*, so that you can be registered in the American Dairy Cattle Club. He records your parentage. He draws a picture of you. When you're older, your pigment patterns will be mapped onto a printed picture of a cow, both sides, head and rear. Perhaps your photo will also be in the book. The amount of your milk production and your butterfat percentages will go in, along with any information about inoculations, illnesses, and other important matters, such as your breeding record.

The vet comes and gives you your shots. A metal tab is stapled to your ear which is your identification as well as your inoculation information.

You grow. You are moved to the older calf barn, the back shed that forms one side of the horse yard. The round barn, the horse barn, and a fence and

Here is a cow with a crumpled horn, surveying a pasture with others of the herd, living the way a cow might wish to live, if she could express her preference.

gate form the other three sides. You grow some more until you are no longer a calf but a heifer, a young lass. You are put out to pasture with the other heifers. You frisk like a lamb and do a lot of running. In between you graze on sweet grass and chew your cud.

Your body matures. At about fifteen months you come into heat. You've become a young lady. If you are bred, you can have a calf. Grampa sometimes lets a young bull run with the heifers when they're old enough: eighteen months is a good age for a first pregnancy. The bull is attracted to you by your special odor. Because you are in heat, you accept him. He mounts your back and impregnates you. The mating is successful. You are going to have a calf.

The calf grows inside you. You are out in the pasture when your labor begins. The other cows cluster around you in a circle, watching you give birth. Your calf drops onto the grass. You have 'freshened.' You lick and lick your calf. The other cows crowd around and try to lick your calf, too. One tries try to take over your calf, but you don't let her. The afterbirth comes out and you eat it. This will keep the wolves from knowing you've given birth. Perhaps the afterbirth has not all come out, for the placenta is buttoned to the uterus lining, and sometimes the labor action isn't enough to loosen it completely. Then in a day or two, Daddy or Grampa or the herdsman will reach down your vagina to your uterus, unbutton the placenta, and draw it carefully out. In a hard case, the vet will come. But usually the placenta comes out naturally.

Your calf is on its feet now, and sucking. You lead it to a far corner of the pasture and hide it in a clump of bushes. But a barnhand finds it, and takes you both to the barn. You nurse your calf for a few days. Then it is taken from you. You bellow and cry in loneliness. Off in the side barn, your calf echoes your grief.

You join the herd of milking cows and learn the rhythms of the round barn. You have a pleasant life there. You are fed hay and silage and a balanced grain ration. You drink from the drinking cup beside your stanchion, or from the cow tank in the barnyard, or from the crick in the pasture. You lick a salt block. You are protected from the cow diseases that have vaccines. No wild animals threaten you, only a little feisty dog who runs into the barnyard and yaps at your heels and makes you kick. Twice a day your udder gets to feeling uncomfortably full, and you make your way up from the pasture to the barnyard and into the round barn. You thrust your head into a stanchion, and a barnhand snaps it shut. There is grain in your manger. Behind you, in your stall, you are cleaned and curried. Your udder and tits are washed. A strap is slung across your back and a milking machine hung from the surcingle under you. The tit cups are snapped on, and you are milked. You listen to music on the radio. When your bag is empty, the milking machine is taken away. Your stanchion is unsnapped and you go back into the barnyard and pasture, if it is summer. Inside the barn, your manure is scooped up, the gutter rinsed, and the walkway limed. If it is winter, you come back into the barn after a brief stay in the barnyard. Grampa or the herdsman checks you in the evening, "puts you to bed." When you lie down, it's in straw or sawdust. In the summer, you sleep out under the stars.

Two or three months after you calve you come back into heat. Now is the time to inseminate you again, so that you will have a calf about once a year. But this is ideal spacing; no cow achieves it regularly. This keeps your milk flowing—305 days of lactation, the rest of the year a dry period before the birth of your next calf. Amos comes this time and inseminates you artificially. The sire of your calf is a famous bull at the American Breeders Service bull stud north of Madison.

You grow old in service. You may live and milk for as long as twelve or thirteen years. At the end of a noble life, when your milk is waning for the final time, and you've had seven or eight calves, you will be patted on the flank, put in a truck, and driven to the slaughterhouse. You will be killed painlessly. You'll not make USDA Prime, for you weren't bred to be a beef cow. You are also too old. You are an old and faithful dairy cow. You will end up as hamburger.

17 ❧ ESSENTIALS FOR THE PRODUCTION OF CLEAN MILK

It's a decade since W.J. Dougan left the ministry and turned to dairying. He's achieved enough success and notice that *Hoard's Dairyman*, the industry's bible, has published articles about him. These appear in the magazine in 1913 and 1914, and one written by him in 1914, too. Now in 1916 they solicit another article from him, "Essentials for the Production of Clean Milk."

This is a time of intense busyness for Grampa. The milkhouse is being designed and built, and there are other activities beyond the usual full engagements of field, barn, milk processing, and marketing. Nonetheless Grampa sits at his desk and composes a long and thoughtful piece. It appears in the December 22 issue, illustrated with seven photographs. Grampa begins:

> There are two fundamental economic principles underlying the clean milk industry. The first is that the selling price must be within the reach of the family with a moderate income and low enough so that clean milk may be classed as an economical food. The second is that the selling price must be high enough to compensate the dairy farmer and the distributor for their labor. It seems at first thought that here are two directly opposing tendencies — cheap to the consumer and high price for the producer. A comprehension of the essentials in clean milk production on the one hand and appreciation of the relative value of clean milk as a food on the other, brings these two apparently opposing tendencies into a harmonious relation where both consumer and producer may have their just due.
>
> Dirty milk is dear at any price, and clean, wholesome milk is a relatively cheap food at eight to ten cents per quart. The purpose of this article is to show how a satisfactory high class milk may be supplied at these prices.

By "clean" both *Hoard's* and W.J. mean milk with a low bacterial count. W.J. goes on to say that it is universally accepted that there are just two essentials in producing clean milk: it must be kept clean, and it must be kept cool.

Some would sterilize the cow, the stable, the feed, the milker, and the whole world about. Then they would immediately freeze the whole into a solid mass. Speaking seriously, some do contend for a surgically clean stable...and a cooling temperature close to freezing.... No one who knows the condition of bacterial growth but appreciates that these methods will get results. But these methods so increase the cost of production that the possible consumers are limited and the chance of profit to the producer is scant.

W.J. contends a dairy needn't go to these extremes. Only three things must absolutely be clean: the cow, the utensils, and the dairyman. A clean cow, he lists, is healthy, thrifty, uplooking, well fed, and well groomed. She must be tested for tuberculosis regularly. A careful physical examination should also be made frequently by a good veterinarian. The dairyman must be alert to detect any off condition in the herd, and especially be on guard against udder troubles. This care doesn't add to the cost of production but lessens it, for "the sick cow, the gargetty cow, and the three- and two-teaters are seldom profitable producers. Weeding them out in the interest of clean milk lessens the cost of producing milk."

A well-groomed cow isn't necessarily one who's been washed and swashed in an elegant stable. "We follow the principle of keeping the dirt off the cows... rather than getting it off after it has been allowed to get on." The necessary

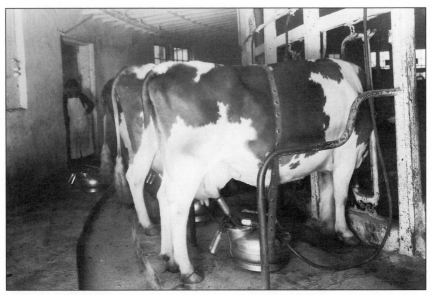

The three essentials for clean milk are clean cows, clean utensils, and clean dairymen.

ESSENTIALS FOR THE PRODUCTION OF CLEAN MILK   65

grooming of a cow well bedded and kept normally clean in an ordinary barn is a simple and inexpensive process—with card and a good brush the dairyman loosens and brushes off coarse dirt and hairs from shoulders, back, flanks, hips, legs, and tail. Careful attention is given to the udder, "especially that soil and bacteria fertile little pocket between the four teats. Then with a pail of clean water and a sponge to fit the hand, wet the udder and wash carefully each teat, then rinse and squeeze out the sponge and wipe each teat, the udder, flank, and the escutcheon. That cow is clean unless she has been allowed to wallow in filth. In that case no amount of grooming can put her in proper shape to milk that day." One man can groom twenty properly kept cows in an hour, and the cows largely pay for this grooming in a better flow of milk.

As to utensils, "our methods are to brush each piece clean in an abundance of cold water; wash in hot water containing a cleansing solution; rinse in hot water; and sterilize with live steam. We use the covered pail with the small opening covered with sterilized gauze and absorbent cotton. The purpose of these strainer clothes is not to take the dirt out of the milk but to detect if any has gotten into it."

But overshadowing all else is the clean dairyman. W.J. says that a pair of blue overalls can be as clean as the proverbially white suit. "We urge reasonably clean clothing and provide milking aprons that are washed twice each week. We insist on clean hands. We keep soap, water, and towels in the weighing room and each man is expected to keep his hands clean and dry. He may wash after milking each cow or he may milk three or four before washing, but whenever his hands become damp or soiled he must wash and dry them."

The dairyman, says Grampa, must be clean not only in appearance but have a clean, conscientious mind. "His every act should be governed by the thought that the consumer of his product expects him to do his best. If he willfully or carelessly neglects, he is morally responsible for the health, aye! even the lives of his patrons."

When Grampa turns to the other word in producing bacterially clean milk, "cool," he agrees that cooling the milk to near freezing is efficacious but expensive, and he doubts that it's essential. "In our section, deep well water is about 51 degrees F. Water pumped direct from the well through an efficient cooler and thence to the stock tank will cool the milk quickly to 52 degrees. This process costs nothing to speak of. The question is, will this do?" It won't, in the judgment of most boards of health and inspectors, yet the Dougan farm has followed this practice for ten years, and produced a milk of low bacterial count "and of perfect satisfaction to our trade."

W.J. points out that he has said nothing regarding stables, floors, dust at milking time, and all the environment of the dairy. "Good milk can be produced in ordinary, even shabby surroundings, while poor milk is often produced with the most expensive equipment. It is the things that come into direct contact with the milk: the cow, the utensils, and the man, that determine the quality of its cleanliness." He backs up his argument with a 1915 New York Experimental Station report, where barn conditions were compared with bacteria count in milk: the barn with a score so poor "that its products would have been refused admittance to the New York City Market" had the lowest bacterial count. "On the other hand, the dairy that received the highest score on all the cards, a dairy which in appearance and equipment would be placed among the best in the state, was bringing in milk that invariably had a bacterial count in the millions." In the words of one of the New York researchers, "The whole colossal blunder lies in making a fetish of the barn instead of requiring clean and sanitary methods."

Grampa gives his own history:

> We found that we could produce a high class milk under most unfavorable conditions. We started in the dairy business handicapped for capital. Therefore we must use the buildings and equipment we had. Our barn was an old style basement. It had small windows and no ventilating system. There was

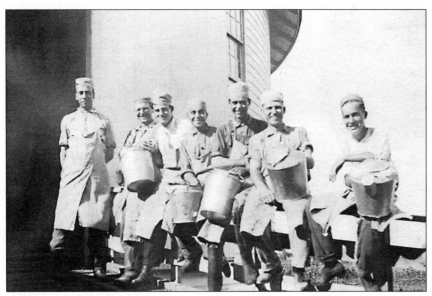

Clean dairymen, clean utensils!

a board floor, under which water often stood. The floor above was not tight so more or less dust worked through. Our milkhouse was a back room of the dwelling fitted and pressed into service as a milk room. In this barn and under these conditions we endeavored to produce a high grade of market milk by following the essentials of clean and cool as outlined above.

W.J. tells how he sent his milk regularly to Madison to be tested for bacteria, the samples being taken from the regular cases as the wagon was ready to start on the route. He gives impressive figures of low bacterial counts from these early years, and includes a table that compares his guaranteed market milk with two farms producing certified milk. Dougan's Dairy is substantially superior. "We give this comparison to enforce the truth that the essentials of clean milk production are simple and attainable by those who are willing to do the work. Since these tests we have built barns and improved equipment. However, we do not put our trust in these to the lessening of vigilance regarding the essentials."

Grampa finishes his article by broadening it. One thinks of clean milk for direct consumption, but it is just as important for creamery or factory:

> The cry is that we cannot go to all this expense for the ordinary market. We answer this by a resume of the foregoing. It pays, from the increase in production, to keep healthy cows, to keep them reasonably clean, and to groom them. The better equipment necessary to keep the utensils clean pays in time saved in caring for the utensils; cooling is inexpensive. A dairyman that has pride in the cleanliness of his dairy will look after all details so much better that the system and spirit put into the dairy work will make the whole place more efficient. Then, let any factory or creamery get a uniformly clean milk and it can manufacture a product that will be far famed and sell at the top price.
>
> Back of these material rewards is the consciousness, to the dairyman, of performing a high service to humanity.

The response of *Hoard's Dairyman*'s readership to "Essentials for the Production of Clean Milk" is excellent, the editor writes to Grampa. They will be pleased if W.J. Dougan will write for them again.

18 ⚔ SICILIAN

It's a scorching summer day in 1917. Grampa and everybody are busy haying. The job takes more men than Grampa has; he signs on an itinerant laborer, a huge Sicilian with a black bushy moustache. Grampa often hires immigrants and men of various ethnic stripe, for day or for regular labor. (Jackie, when she's small in the 1930s, for several days trails behind an employee who, Joan tells her, is an Indian: but she abandons her observations when she finds nothing extraordinary about him.)

The Sicilian works in the loft of the side barn, pitching the hay into the corners after the hayfork has dropped it. Late in the afternoon Grampa climbs a ladder against the wall of hay that now fills the barn, and peers over the top of it. Heat sears his face. The loft is an oven. The Sicilian is there, stripped to the waist, covered with dust. His body is channeled with gleaming rivulets of sweat. He sees Grampa, makes a menacing face, pulls out a pocket knife and slashes it in the air across his throat. Grampa ducks his head like a gopher back into its hole and beats a hasty retreat down the ladder. At the end of the day he pays the Sicilian and tells him he won't be needing him on the morrow.

"I don't know if he means to slit his own throat or mine," says Grampa ruefully. "If he does it to himself, it'll be sort of messy, and if he does it to me, why, that will be a tragedy!"

19 ✕ GOOD COPY

When W.J. Dougan comes to Beloit in 1906 to start farming, he's noticed for many reasons. He's left the ministry from deafness. He's well educated. He and his college-bred wife have promptly become active in the community: the town and county as well as Turtle Township. He starts a milk route and advertises his products in an unusual way. His "help wanted" ads are unorthodox. He enlists the university in testing his soils, cows, and milk, and in advising him on crops. He follows Professor King's recommendation in building a round barn. He paints his philosophy on his silo, in letters a foot high.

As a result W.J. is often invited to guest preach and to guest speak, which he does with eloquence and earnestness, grace and humor. It's not long before newspapers and magazines realize that W.J. Dougan, his milk, his methods, and himself, are good copy.

In April, 1909, less than two years after W.J. makes his first retail delivery of six quarts of raw Guernsey milk, the *Beloit Daily News* runs a series of headlines:

PRAISE GIVEN BELOIT MILK

SUPERIOR ARTICLE IS FOUND HERE BY WISCONSIN EX-PERIMENT STATION.

BELOIT IS FORTUNATE

In W. J. Dougan's Dairy It Has Plant That Is Producing Practically Certified Milk At a Moderate Price, Say State Authorities.

There follows an informative article: a reprinting of the entire text of a *communiqué* from the Agricultural Experimental Station at Madison, about the production of milk in general, and W.J. Dougan's enterprise in particular. It includes a favorable comparison of the bacterial count of Dougan's milk with three dairies of national reputation, dairies selling milk at 14 cents a quart while Dougan is selling his for eight cents. It ends with the assurance that the experimental station is not in the advertising business, but "is interested in the general movement for clean and healthful milk and desires to help this movement by aiding, in every legitimate way, the dairyman who is attempting to improve the quality of his milk."

The article is soon reprinted verbatim in *The Milk News*, a magazine published out of Chicago. This early documented praise of "The Babies' Milkman" gives a boost to Dougan sales. It also indicates W.J.'s cooperation with the university, for the Dougan milk samples don't arrive in Madison by magic.

The following year, another bulletin from the experimental station is given complete coverage by *The Beloit Free Press*. The emphasis of its author, E.G. Hastings, is this time on the testing of cows for tuberculosis:

> Many towns and cities ... have passed ordinances requiring that milk shall be from animals known to be free from tuberculosis. ... The experience of most places is that it is very difficult or impossible to enforce such ordinances. ... Some of the farmers furnishing milk to Milwaukee are fighting to the last ditch the enforcement of the ordinance requiring cows to be tested for tuberculosis and the diseased animals removed from the herds. These farmers should know that it is to their financial advantage to do the things the cities are asking, but instead they are willing to spend thousands of dollars in the courts, and besides lose money from the low efficiency of diseased cows. Any town that numbers among its dairymen one who of his own volition is doing the things that other towns are attempting to obtain by ordinance is to be congratulated. One of the farms from which we have examined the milk is that of Mr. W.J. Dougan of Beloit.

Hastings goes on to praise Dougan for low bacterial count, giving comparison tables with other farms, then says, "In Madison it is so difficult to obtain good milk that many people are willing to go to the university to secure their supply. Eight cents per quart is charged; at the present time about $300 of milk and cream is sold monthly. It can easily be seen what would be the demand for such milk delivered to the consumer's door. It is also evident why the people of Beloit are to be congratulated on having such milk delivered to them, and they should realize it is worth the money they are paying."

The *Rockford Morning Star*, in January, 1911, devotes a full page to the Winnebago County Farmer's Institute. Winnebago County, in which Rockford is situated, is adjacent to Rock County, where the farm is located. At the farm's south fence one can (with the aid of a high north wind) spit almost into Illinois. So W.J. Dougan is a natural to call in when an expert from the Illinois state capital is unable to be present at the Institute to give his talk on the diseases of farm animals. The headlines run,

FARMERS TAKING GREAT INTEREST IN INSTITUTE

PRACTICAL WORK IS BEING GIVEN

UNUSUALLY FINE ADDRESSES OF-
FERED BY EXPERTS

TEST BY TUBERCULIN

Beloit Dairyman Makes Convincing
Talk On Value of This Procedure.

The article states attendance at this twentieth session of the Institute to be large. It reports briefly on the president's address, how farm life has changed in twenty years: students now going to centralized high schools; the increased comfort and convenience of country life; and there are "greater rewards of farming under the more scientific methods now possible for every farmer to use to advantage." It gives a nod to the response of the Institute's first president, and then gets down to real meat: "Dougan in Fine Talk." "The gem of the day was the address of W.J. Dougan of Beloit, a dairyman. Mr. Dougan has a herd of twenty five dairy cattle which he has tested with tuberculin each year and has weeded out those affected by tuberculosis until he has freed the herd of that disease. He sells the milk at an increased rate to those who desire a product free from possibility of taint." W.J. is called "an eloquent and logical" speaker:

> He says that tuberculosis in cattle doubtless can be cured by the same means employed to obtain that result in human beings: rest, food and fresh air. Then he showed how long a time the treatment takes and the futility of using that means. Destruction of the affected members of the herd...is the only safe procedure. Ten percent now may be ninety percent in a few years. In his own case, the test showed the finest milk cow in his herd to be affected and examination after slaughter proved the truth of the diagnosis. Subsequent

tests found here and there a case and he has none in the herd now.... He holds that the test should be administered by some competent person who is not interested in the herd, as possibility of loss and fondness for fine animals is likely to warp the judgment of the owner. The result of his own experience is that his cattle are sleek and contented, show no sign of harm from application of the tuberculin test and return him a profit that has enabled him to improve his farm and buildings and buy equipment for marketing a high grade milk.

The article, after quoting a story about a friend of W.J.'s who neglected testing and lost his herd, finishes, "This talk was of the greatest interest in view of the fact that the test is being opposed in this state. No more earnest, practical advocate of any procedure has been heard than Mr. Dougan and his talk was most convincing."

A much later article, 1928 or 1929, shows W.J. still preaching the gospel of tuberculin testing; the *Beloit Daily News* headline is, DOUGAN HERD PASSES ANNUAL TUBERCULIN TEST; NO REACTORS. It quotes him, "It is possible for entire communities, a county or state, to enjoy the same security of healthy herds that this farm enjoys, by systematic, conscientious, and intelligent application of the tuberculin test." W.J., called a pioneer in testing twenty-two years ago, "was also one of the first to advocate that milk for human consumption should be from only tuberculin tested cattle." W.J. himself says,

Dean Russell [of the university] was one of the first to say that bovine tuberculosis was communicable to mankind. At that time most scientists held there were two different kinds of bacteria, and that the bovine type should be tested, so when I started my dairy I tried to find tested cows but found it difficult because many farmers and dealers were opposed to the test, and there were enough buyers who asked no questions. I managed to buy ten head to be tested before I took them. I had little confidence in the veterinarian who did the testing, so I retested them as soon as allowable, and found two reactors. These I had the state veterinarian and our local veterinarian slaughter and give the post mortem examination on the farm for the information of myself and neighbors.

The article finishes with W.J.'s fundamental principles of the tuberculin test: that in the hands of intelligent and honest men it is as reliable as most of the diagnostic methods of medical science; that a diseased herd is an un-profitable herd; and that milk from tubercular cows is unfit for human food. "These principles are becoming better understood and more widely accepted every year, and we may now hope for the time when bovine tuberculosis will be entirely eliminated."

In April of 1913 E.G. Hastings writes another article on W.J. Dougan, this time for *Hoard's Dairyman*. When a dairyman reaches *Hoard's* he has arrived, for that international journal, since 1885 published out of Fort At-kinson, Wisconsin, is every dairyman's bible. There's a photo of W.J. which, while not quite stern, is certainly straightforward, but gives no indication of his Irish charm and wit. The title is "A Successful Farmer," and starts, "Seven years ago Mr. W.J. Dougan, who had been forced to give up his ministerial work through deafness, purchased a farm of 115 acres one mile from the city of Beloit, Wisconsin. His idea was to produce a high grade milk for sale in the city." There follows a lengthy and detailed account of W.J.'s way of rais-ing the price of his milk, finishing, "The usual way of increasing trade is to lower the price until the increased demand has been gained and then raise the price." W.J. has, through some complicated maneuvers, managed the op-posite. Hastings adds figures for the steadily increasing income of the farm.

His next section tells that Mr. Dougan at his start had to buy and breed up an efficient herd, establish a just price, create a taste and demand for his product, and develop a business. The herd is mostly Guernsey, now number-ing 35, with a growing stock of 25. In cash income the herd averages over $200 each per annum. The purchased cows produced more their second year than the first; Mr. Dougan attributes this to the care and feed the animals re-ceive. There are one or two men whose main duty is to care for the herd, and each cow is given a thorough grooming each day. The increased care results in increased production, and more than pays the wages of the herdsmen.

Hastings then launches into his favorite subject, the tuberculin test for cows that W.J. conducts with no ordinance ordering him to do so. He stresses cleanliness — the washing of the udders at each milking, the use of the Gurler and Sterilac milk pails, the hiring of men who appreciate the value of cleanli-ness, and over all, Mr. Dougan's constant supervision. He paraphrases W.J.: "One of the most important factors in the production of clean milk is the personal element, and where the work must be totally turned over to hired help it is extremely difficult to produce the highest grade. Dougan hires men of character and intelligence, which he deems essential to producing good milk and in the long run are the cheapest help. He employs five or six good men the year around and pays high wages." He adds, "Until two years ago his barn was an old one with low ceilings, about as unsatisfactory type of barn as one could imagine, and yet in this, summer and winter, he was able to produce, and produce cheaply, the highest grade of milk. The model round barn now adds efficiency and comeliness to the plant."

Beloit's medical men endorse his milk for children's use, though he sells a considerable quantity for family use to laboring people, as most of them realize that it is the cheapest milk they can buy for it is rich — nearly 5 percent fat — and there is no loss through soured or dirty milk.

The final part of the article tells that W.J. believes dairy farming can be systematized so that each person can get life as well as a living. "He is working out a plan whereby every one can have opportunity for rest and recreation and to obey the fourth commandment. He gives each man one-half day off each week, and with abundance of help, each man has some time to himself on Sunday. He has his Sundays to himself, turning the work over to the men on that day. He also tries to do his work during the day, neither getting up in the night to eat breakfast nor letting the work drag into the night. All chores are expected to be done and the men ready to go to supper at 6 o'clock."

Hastings says the farm must pay, but not at the cost of men, women, and children working as long as daylight lasts and strength endures. He devotes a few sentences to considering the cow herself as a factor in the cost of producing milk, and then finishes, "It seems to the writer that the methods which are being used by Mr. Dougan are the only ones that will make farming what it should be, and that his case is a good example of what intelligence will do in obtaining success on a farm."

On January 30, 1914, W.J. Dougan delivers "the address of the day" at a meeting of the Farmers' Course division of the Country Life Conference, sponsored by the university. In this speech he gives such attention to the moral and spiritual aspects of farming that a member of the audience says to him afterwards in all sincerity, "I enjoyed your sermon, Reverend Dougan!" The *Beloit Daily Free Press* prints the speech the next day, along with the *Hoard's* picture; its headline trumpets, BELOIT MAN GIVES STRONG ADDRESS ON FARM PROBLEMS AT CONFERENCE. A second newspaper reprints the speech six weeks later, headlining it in a flowing quarter-inch script, "The Farmer and His Help." It is reprinted again, July 3, 1914, in *Hoard's Dairyman*, as "Solving the Farm Labor Problem." This is a heady moment for W.J. It is his first published article, albeit via a speech, and in three different publications, the pinnacle being *Hoard's*. With pride he reads

University agriculture professors lecture from field to field on W.J.'s alfalfa field day.

it to his brother-in-law, the Reverend Dr. George Trever, visiting at the farm that summer. George, who has theological articles published all the time, is sparing in his praise, but later, a supposed family slight causes him to write a blistering letter to Eunice that W.J. is looking at the profession of farming through rose-colored glasses.

May 27, 1914, had seen a gala day at the Dougan farm when W.J. and Eunice hosted a gathering devoted to alfalfa, a relative newcomer to Wisconsin agriculture, or to any agriculture. Besides farmers from all over the southern part of the state and northern Illinois, many Beloit businessmen and their wives came out to the farm. The *Beloit Daily News* said, in anticipation of the event,

> Mr. Dougan has been working for many years to get a start with alfalfa. Under the direction of the university he has tried different methods. Some have succeeded and some have failed. At present he has several plots of varying quality and in different stages of development. The College of Agriculture believes it is a good time to call a meeting at this farm to observe these plots and to discuss the important subject of growing alfalfa in this section.

The day after the meeting the paper reports in full. From the auditorium of the round barn, with the audience both on the barn floor and ranged up the ramp, "Mr. Dougan spoke hearty words of welcome," and "expressed in a few well chosen sentences the unlimited possibilities of Beloit farms and the necessity of cooperation in sympathy, fellow feeling, and brotherly helpfulness in order to reach these ideals."

Mr. Everett, the editor of *The Wisconsin Agriculturalist*, speaks next, and the address of the day is by Professor W.W. Weir of the university, who gives a practical talk on "How to Meet the Difficulties of Growing Alfalfa in This Section." This becomes a peripatetic lecture, for Professor Weir leads everyone to the actual fields, pausing at each plot to discuss its particularities with the interested crowd. He explains that alfalfa needs an abundance of lime; that natural drainage is essential; that the nature of the plant is to send its roots deep into the soil to find the moisture necessary to its growth, and for this reason the water level in the soils should be relatively stationary. That nurse crops of wheat, oats, rye, or barley have proved injurious to the alfalfa to follow. And that a top dressing of phosphate is highly beneficial to permanent growth. He discusses the importance of cultivation and the eradication of weeds, and lists the merits of various types of harrows. He sums up, "We here at the university, in conjunction with farsighted agriculturalists like W.J. Dougan who is hosting this event, recognize in alfalfa one of the best forage crops for all classes of livestock. It is excellent for feeding in connection with silage or starchy grains, and is a fine weed destroyer. It gets its nitrogen supply from the air and its mineral food from far below where ordinary crops feed. It harbors bacteria which work twenty-four hours a day, board themselves, and pay the farmer handsomely for the privilege!"

Alfalfa instruction is followed by refreshments and music on the lawn. "As for the ladies," says the paper, "while the men have been tramping the fields they've been shown the conveniences in the house, intending to lighten the burden of the caring for the large family necessary to do the work on this farm. The house is equipped with power washing machine, water system, power vacuum cleaner, and electric lighting." The rest of the farm is also on display, and the paper reports, "This latter [i.e., electricity] extends to all the barns and other buildings. The place as a whole is fast rounding into a perfect plant for efficient farm work and milk production."

Mr. Hoard himself attends, and is quoted as saying that in his travels through the state "he had not seen alfalfa and clover that compared with that growing on this farm. The College of Agriculture made no mistake when they said that this farm had some things worth showing to the community and from which good lessons could be drawn." The article ends with a hope for a repetition of this social and educational event.

W.J. and Eunice have a talent for making special occasions do extra duty. With the farm already spruced up, they flank the seminar with two open-house days, one for customers and one for potential customers, and finish the week by throwing a party described thus in the newspaper:

> The Philathea class of the Methodist Church were most royally entertained at the Dougan farm, about two miles east of the city, last evening. The guests were conveyed to the farm in two rigs furnished by the proprietors of the dairy farm. The company numbered about thirty. Games were played on the beautiful lawn which was illuminated with electricity and later the "round" barn was made the scene of much merriment. The guests were then served with ice cream, cookies and delicious milk, such as only the Dougan Guernsey farm has learned the secret of producing. Following the refreshments, outdoor pastimes were again indulged in for a short while longer after which the merry party was conveyed back to their respective homes.

Another event that summer makes front page news. "STUDENTS VISIT AT DOUGAN FARM," reads the headline on July 17:

> Professor Otis with his University of Wisconsin field class in farm management spent yesterday with W.J. Dougan at the Dougan Guernsey Farm. This class is made up of mature students of agriculture from eight states and as many colleges. Most of them are graduates. They have been studying some of the best farms in the state for the past month. They came to the Dougan farm yesterday morning twenty-two strong. The forenoon was spent in studying the crops, soils, drainage, crop rotation and general plan of the farm. After a picnic dinner on the lawn the following program was carried out by Mr. Dougan and his farm help:
>
> Piano solo by Percy Werner.
> College songs, by the whole crowd.
> Address, "The Farm Manager's Job," by Mr. Dougan.
> Address, "The Accredited Student," by Alan Turnbull.
> Address, "Getting the Work Done," by Joe Nelson.
>
> Prof. G.A. Billings, of the United States Department of Agriculture, who was present, spoke words of inspiration and encouragement.
>
> Mr. Dougan emphasized the importance of the work of conscientiously and faithfully managing a farm and the far reaching import of the two pioneer movements in Wisconsin, that is, the accredited farms and the state farm contest.
>
> Mr. Turnbull showed the work being done by himself as an accredited student on this farm and the benefits derived by the accredited relationship.

Mr. Nelson, who has been here nearly two years, showed the importance of adequate horse power, man power, and machinery to accomplish the desired ends. He illustrated his thought with examples and incidents in the two seasons on this farm.

The balance of the afternoon was spent in inspecting the conveniences of the house and dairy plant. After partaking of refreshments the company was taken to the 5 o'clock car for Janesville. They spend Saturday at Monroe.

Mr. Dougan suspended all field work and gave his help the chance to enjoy the day with the class. It proved to be a very enjoyable and helpful day to all.

The state farm contest, which W.J. Dougan emphasizes in his remarks, is an enterprise of Professor Otis and the Ag School, to encourage farmers to keep accurate farm records. Professor Otis has developed a system of book keeping, and farmers using the Otis method may enter the contest through their county agents; all receive free record books, and the winners also receive attractive prizes. W.J. has been using the Otis system on the Dougan farm. In 1915, in the wintertime, and again in 1916 he travels by train over the entire state of Wisconsin with Professor Otis, gone sometimes two weeks at a stretch. They stay at local hotels, meet with the county agents, and judge the reports of the farmers. W.J.'s role, besides participating in the judging, is to demonstrate and endorse the Otis system whenever there are local farmers' meetings enroute. There is publicity by the university, and publicity in the various counties the two men visit, about the Otis method, the contest, and W.J. Dougan and his successful farm.

In 1917 the Federal Government, through the Food Administration, creates a Commission to investigate the cost of production and distribution of milk. Hearings for the Midwest District are held in Chicago in early December, and last the better part of a week. Ex-Illinois governor Charles S. Deneen represents the producers, and the December issue of *The Milk News* reports the proceedings. Various notable people give testimony. Professor F.A. Pearson of the State Agricultural College of Illinois (the University of Illinois' Ag School) "left the impression...that he knew what he was talking about. His evidence was received as coming from an expert, now considered the best authority on this subject in the country." Professor G.F. Warner of Cornell New York State Agricultural College "is considered one of the best, if not the very best, posted man in the United States in Agriculture and Cost of Milk Production. His evidence was very interesting and instructive...and he was not permitted to leave the stand until just in time for him to get the 5:30

New York Central train for New York." Henry Wallace of *The Wallace Farmer* of Des Moines testifies on his studies of hog-corn ratios, "upon whose report the Food Administration's meat division established the market value of 100 pounds of average hog in terms of corn...in order to stabilize prices and stimulate production," and is "very interesting." Mr. A.J. Gafke, county agent for McHenry County in central Illinois, makes "a splendid witness."

The Milk News has so far given, to the testimonies of the top professorial experts from two prestigious universities, to the future Secretary of Agriculture during the Roosevelt administration, and to a knowledgeable county agent, a total of seven and a half inches of type. Next a foot soldier in the ranks is called to the stand, a dairy farmer from Beloit, Wisconsin, and to him alone are devoted the next thirteen inches:

> Mr. Dougan of Beloit, Wisconsin is very deaf and his wife acted as interpreter. He was, however, asked very few questions, but was permitted to give his testimony in his own way, which he did, much to the interest of the Commission.
>
> Mr. Dougan has the most complete farm accounting that has yet been brought to the attention of the Commission. Mr. Dougan distributes his own milk in the city of Beloit, but his books show the cost of production, cost of preparing and bottling, as well as the cost of distribution. His accounts of labor seem to be very accurate. In one instance they show where the herdsman was called to dig the potatoes for dinner, and the time taken, fifteen minutes, was charged to the household account instead of to the dairy. Mr. Dougan now gets 15 cents per quart for his Guernsey milk, testing 4% in butter fat, and has more customers than he can supply.
>
> He gave the Commission accurate data on cost of production on both feed and labor cost. He also explained his system of bookkeeping. He explained fully to the Commission the routine necessary to follow night and morning, and gave some good instances of the hard, tiresome work found upon the farm. He described in detail the work of haying during a long, hot summer day and how tired and sleepy one could get by bedtime. He told a little, but very interesting story about himself. After explaining how the hay rigging of his barn was arranged, he stated that when the team had pulled up the fork full of hay and taken it back into the barn far enough to dump they, the team, were so far away from the load that it took a very loud "whoa" to stop them. After a very hot day of getting in hay one Saturday, he went to church on Sunday, and soon found himself going through the agony of a tired dairy

Forking loose hay into a neighbor's loft.

farmer trying to keep awake. He found it hard to watch his pencil following the paper. He pinched himself, he kicked himself, looked at the minister, and tried to keep an intellectual look upon his face, but the minister kept getting farther and farther away and there arose in the minister's place a fine big fork full of hay. Up it went and swung back into the barn, and he yelled right out at the top of his voice, "Whoa." The best of the joke is, Mr. Dougan is an ex-minister!

Mr. Dougan urged the Commission to fix a price that would help elevate the dairy industry to the standard of other business callings, shorten the hours, and take the dairy farmer away from the characterization given him by Walt Whitman when he called him "the low browed, stunted man; the brother of the ox." He pictured the long blessed evenings on the farm, as well as the rolling in cream and all those splendid things of the farm, which have been inducing city men to give up lucrative office jobs to get back to it, only to find all an awful delusion. Mr. Dougan made a most interesting witness, because he interspersed his instructive testimony with sarcasm and wit.

In 1923, as radio is developing as a medium of general communication, WLS in Chicago, "The Prairie Farmer Station," engages W.J. to give a series of radio talks. Because many interested Beloiters don't yet have radios, the paper lets people know that a downtown store will open its doors, set out folding chairs, tune in, turn up the volume, and allow interested parties to drop by to listen. The newspaper duly writes up the bulk of each of W.J.'s speeches. The talks are so well received by the radio audience that W.J. does another series the following year; this time Eunice adds a talk. W.J. does a radio series again in 1925.

In 1924, *Hoard's Dairyman*, to which magazine W. J has contributed since 1914, turns to him as an expert. A farmer has written that a neighbor wishes him to take charge of his dairy barn and milk route on shares and details the proposed arrangement. He wonders what share he should receive. *Hoard's* refers him to W.J., gives his dairying credentials, then quotes him as advising the writer that the two would be working at opposing purposes: "The tenant's only means of increasing his income is to feed rather extravagantly and to lessen the work to a point where it would degrade the quality of the milk. On the other hand, the owner would desire to lessen the feed costs and increase the labor in connection with the care of the herd and the milk." He discourages the practice and suggests the writer be given a direct fee.

Wesson and Eunice, at the University of Wisconsin for induction to the Agricultural Hall of Fame.

The *Prairie Farmer* magazine names W.J. Dougan to its first "Master Farmers" list in 1925, the only farmer selected from Wisconsin. In 1926 the University of Wisconsin elects W.J. Dougan and his wife Eunice to their Agricultural Hall of Fame; their pictures and accomplishments are in newspapers all over the state. It is the first time a couple has received this honor. *Hoard's Dairyman*, not to be outdone, solicits W.J. to write a series of seven articles for the magazine. These are published throughout 1927. They also request and receive from Eunice an article on operating a farm boarding house and making it a home. *The Farmer's Wife* magazine picks up on this and writes a long article about Eunice, "Turning Handicaps to Gold." (Eunice, with three-year-old granddaughter Joan hovering, is pictured at her electric sewing machine, and, in another photo, operating her electric dishwasher.)

Shortly after the *Prairie Farmer* honor, the magazine runs an article (March 20, 1926) about W.J. that recaps his entire life: "W.J. Dougan—Master Farmer: The Story of A Preacher Who Went Back to the Farm":

If W.J. Dougan of Rock County, Wisconsin, hadn't lost his hearing some 25 years ago, he might never have been a Master Farmer. It was this unfortunate handicap that turned Dougan, the clergyman, from his profession as a Methodist minister in a Southern Wisconsin parish to the farm.

Graduating in the general science course from the University of Wisconsin in 1894, Mr. Dougan determined to devote his life to the ministry. As a student, his activities about the college campus led him into religious work. His earnestness and sincerity, and his ability as a convincing speaker won for him early recognition. While he was still an undergraduate, Dougan helped in organizing and conducting the mission Sunday school that has grown into the flourishing Trousdel church of S. Madison, Wisconsin. It was natural, therefore, for him to turn to the ministry for his career.

He took the conference course in religious education during which he continued preaching in the rural churches about Madison. Five years later, after he was well established in a church of his own, Mrs. Dougan, formerly Eunice M. Trever, a successful school teacher and graduate of Lawrence College, Appleton, Wis., came into the life of the young preacher. She was eminently fitted for the work of a minister's wife and she filled that position faithfully and well.

Then in 1906, after twelve years of successful ministry, the Dougans turned resolutely away from their work in which they had found happiness and satisfaction. Well along toward middle age, they deliberately entered on a new career on the farm.

"During my twelve years of ministry, I was unconsciously fitting myself for the farm," said Dougan as he reviewed his experiences leading to his decision to be a farmer. "I questioned my farmer members about everything and occasionally lent a helping hand. It must have been a great disappointment to my wife to marry a preacher and ultimately find him a farmer. However, she was a true wife and was willing to fit into the plan that seemed best for me."

Following a short course in agriculture at the University of Wisconsin,

Dougan found a farm in the spring of 1906 near Beloit in Rock County, Wisconsin. Thus the Dougans started their new career, not amidst the splendor of a country estate, but on an ordinary farm with poor buildings and equipment, heavily burdened with debt, and no better than the average in the neighborhood. They faced the future with courage, determined to win success in the dairy business.

It was not Dougan's first farm experience. He was merely returning to his boyhood life, for he was born on a Dodge County, Wisconsin farm in the spring of 1868 and spent the first 19 years of his life there.

Starting humbly, Dougan and his wife spent the first year getting a crop and finding their way. "We had the idea from the first to produce and market a high quality milk," he said. "We did not start our milk business until one year after coming to the farm. We began with very small capital and have had to carry a heavy debt."

Their first dairy herd was composed of a few grade Guernsey cows. These they gave good feed and care and added to the herd as their means afforded. Dougan's idealism asserted itself early in his life on the farm. As a boy he noticed that his uncle for whom he worked at different times, allowed too much of the crop, the straw, hay, and grain to be wasted, due to poor storage. "I made up my mind that if I ever farmed, proper storage for my crops would be one of the things I attended to," he said.

Dougan knew that to be successful the farm had to measure up to certain standards. So he established a goal that he might keep ever before him the things he wanted. He even wrote out his ideals, as follows: "The aims of this farm. 1. Good crops. 2. Proper storage. 3. Profitable livestock. 4. A stable market. 5. Life as well as a living."

Little by little the retail milk business grew and the Dougans moved along toward their goal. "Every year saw us a little further ahead. We never went backward," said Dougan as we sat in his comfortable study answering the questions I jotted down for him.

The Guernsey herd increased in size and quality as a result of the accurate records of production and ancestry kept on each cow. Only the heifers from the best cows were raised. From the beginning the herd was tested for tuberculosis and placed under federal supervision.

Today Dougan has an accredited herd of more than 70 Guernseys. Nearly half of them are purebreds and all are numbered and registered in the herd book with a unique system in which each animal's number discloses her breeding and ancestry. The 40 cows have been averaging around 8,000 pounds of milk with a test of 4.5%, year after year. The lower producers are culled out and the surplus stock is sold at their value based on breeding and records of production. All the milk is bottled on the farm and retailed at 20 cents a quart in Beloit. There is usually a waiting list of new customers because they know Dougan's milk is of high quality.

The 230-acre farm needed much improvement. It was broken and divided by railroads, highways and creeks, but all of it was tillable. The first objective was to make the farm feed the cows. A plot of the farm was made and the different fields studied as to location and fertility in working out a system of crop rotation. Limestone was applied for growing alfalfa, and today this is one of the most important and necessary crops grown. In 1923, 50 acres of the farm were in alfalfa, enough for the cattle, hogs, horses, and a surplus for sale.

Corn yields up to 80 bushels an acre, barley 50 bushels, oats 60 bushels, and alfalfa three to four tons an acre. The crops are rotated regularly, alternating with corn, small grain, clover and alfalfa.

A giant round barn 64 feet in diameter not only provides ample storage for hay and straw, but a large 14-foot silo, 56 feet high in the center, together with a similar one just outside the barn, holds plenty of silage for the cows and young stock. Dougan has arrived at his own goal of proper storage. Nothing goes to waste. The fields and fencerows on the farm are clean and tidy and the road in front of the house is mowed.

Dougan's aim is to make the farm return a gross income of $50 per acre. The income must be large to pay the heavy overhead expenses. Between six and eight men are employed to care for the herd, milk, bottle, deliver, and do the farm work. For the past few years the farm has returned approximately 8% each year on an investment of $56,000. The single hired men are brought into the home and given a share in the family life. Many of them have been college students out for a year or two of experience in dairying before starting out for themselves.

The house has all the modern conveniences, including electric lights, gas for cooking, running water, bathroom, electric stove, electric dishwasher, vacuum cleaner, pump, a shower bath for the men, and furnace heat.

Dougan's interests have led him far beyond the limits of his farm. He takes a keen interest in public affairs. He discusses politics and the election with his men, tells them his opinion, takes them with him to the polls, and encourages them to use their best judgment in voting. Naturally he has taken active part in church work. When there is a vacant pulpit to fill in the nearby city of Beloit, Dougan is asked to preach. He is active in the county YMCA and has led several county drives for membership and funds to support the organization.

His knowledge of the dairy business and his ability as a convincing speaker on the cow-testing association and management of the herd have made him much sought after at farmers' institutes, farm bureau meetings, and dairymen's gatherings throughout the Middle West. His farm is a mecca for tourists and visitors from far away. A banker from Beloit said that Dougan is perhaps the most outstanding farmer and public-spirited man in that community. "I'll tell you what kind of a neighbor he is," said Mrs. Albert Marston. "Last summer when my daughter was very ill and wasn't expected to live, Mr. Dougan brought his own milk for her free of charge and had one of his men bring ice every day for an ice-pack to relieve her fever."

Dougan's three children have all been given educational advantages. The older son, Ronald A., is a college graduate and is now home on the farm with his wife and baby daughter, taking an active part in managing the farm. A younger son is a student in the University of Wisconsin, and the daughter is now attending high school in Beloit.

"I'm not getting rich," said Dougan, "nor am I anywhere near as well off financially as many men I know who started out when I did in other lines of work. We have made many mistakes and sometimes I would like to write about them for the benefit of others. Nevertheless, I'm pointing young fellows to the farm, for after all the farm offers many advantages and a chance to serve and live a happy, satisfying life."

In the twenties and thirties, all over the local area W.J. is a speaker: to a U.W. Alumni group in Beloit; at Lima, Shopiere, Avalon, Emerald Grove, and elsewhere in Rock County on county YMCA work and other topics; farther north in Wisconsin at Fort Atkinson, farther south in Illinois at Harvard and Woodstock and DeKalb on various farm matters. He and Eunice together give talks around Wisconsin and Illinois, and sometimes farther afield, on aspects of dairy farming and homemaking; W.J.'s letters to Trever at college, between 1923 and 1928, mention these frequently, along with an occasional hint of weariness. One letter says,

Mother and myself go to Manchester, Iowa, to speak Wednesday. For the life of me I do not see what I have to say to pay them for that long trip with double expenses. I am working hard and hope to give a good talk (cow talk). You know I am to speak at a big state meeting in Illinois Feb. 20. I am cutting out this outside work on account of the difficulty of communication. I think after this Illinois meeting I shall absolutely refuse such calls. I would like to write more, but I am too lazy to properly edit my ideas. Mother or myself will probably be in Madison to the farmers' course beginning Feb. 4. I rather dread to go for the mingling, then both of us should not be away.

And again, to Trever, a wry comment: "My time is pretty full for a few weeks now. County work—lectures—my books and records—and incidentally my business."

Articles continue. In 1930 *The New York Sun*, in "An Understanding Milkman," quotes W.J. on modern science in dairying, saying that his opinion, originally recorded in *The Municipality*, has been condensed for *Health News* by the New York State Department of Health.

The University of Wisconsin's College of Agriculture, making plans to broach a publication highlighting matters pertaining to Wisconsin from all points of view, *The Wisconsin Magazine*, asks W.J. to become a member of the Advisory Editorial Staff, representing agricultural interests, and he accepts. The first issue contains a profile on him.

W.J. Dougan continues to be written up in newspapers and magazines all the rest of his life: *Better Farming* ("Daddy Dougan's Happy Hired Men," by an anonymous former employee, but most likely Elmer Carncross), *Successful Farming* ("Guernseys Pay Dougan—Here's How"), *Prairie Farmer, American Dairyman* ("Dougan's Thinking Does It"), *Farm and Fireside* ("Farming as a Mode of Living"), *Banker-Farmer* ("A Dairy Farm That Feeds Fifty"), *The Milwaukee Journal*, as well as a number of church magazines.

The deaf preacher-turned-farmer, with his wife beside him, is indeed good copy. W.J.'s own words might give a kind of sum-up. In a mid-1930s letter to a DeKalb professor who owns and manages a dairy on the side he writes: "I feel you are doing more with your side-line than most dairymen are doing who make it their regular business. I do not know how wonderful a teacher you are, but I'm wondering if this statement that was made to me a time after I went into the dairy business might not be applicable to you. A friend that had been under my ministry met me and complimented me on my dairy work, and casually dropped the remark, 'They came very near spoiling a good dairyman to make a poor preacher.'"

He friend was voicing then what everyone comes to know. W.J.'s dairying is his preaching.

20 ⊰ GOOD FOR SOMETHING

Ronald is fourteen. He's finishing his freshman year at Beloit High. Trever is going to Strong School, across from Aunt Ida's. Every day Ronald drives himself and Trever to school and back in the new Dodge. One afternoon in mid-June he pulls into the farm and parks the car by the back entrance to the Big House. Trever gets out with his books. Ronald stays in the car, in his good school clothes, his collar still on, reading.

It's hot. Beyond, at the side barn, Grampa is directing the first haying. A loaded hay wagon stands alongside the lower part of the barn, its mounded hay reaching almost up to the wide open end of the haymow. Men are busy on the load and in the mow. Chuck Hoag is in the roadway, driving the team that provides the power to lift the hayfork.

Ronald has admired Chuck ever since he arrived. He's a husky young man, curly headed, broad of chest, a student at the university, getting his M.A. in agricultural economics. He's down from Madison for a year-long internship on the farm. He's writing his thesis on the farm's economics. He's keeping data on all the processes. Chuck Hoag is everything that Ronald would like to be.

Today he's stripped to his waist, his body glistening with sweat and streaked with grime, his hair dusty. As soon as the huge tines of the fork are embedded in the hay on the wagon, Grampa yells, and Chuck drives the team toward the road. The ropes the horses pull tauten and strain, the pulleys roll, the hayfork grips and with its great burden slowly rises up to the track. It switches onto it in a right-angle turn, with a swish swings into the barn. Chuck drives the plodding horses past Ronald and the Dodge. When the next yell comes, signaling that the hay is now over the spot where it's to be dropped, Chuck calls "Whoa!" to the horses. He himself stops right beside the car's open window. He glances at the reading Ronald, turns the team, and returns to his starting place. A second time he drives as far as Ronald, glances in, and returns. The third time, as he turns, he speaks.

"Do you think you'll ever amount to anything?" he says.

Three springs later Ronald is seventeen and a senior. He receives his yearbook. His picture is in it, along with pictures of all the other graduates. Under every face is the name of the student, the grammar school, a nickname, and other data. At the last comes a brief comment about the person, written by somebody on the yearbook committee: "A lad with quiet ways," or "Dignity and reserve are two of the graces she possesses." Ronald turns the pages and finds himself.

In his picture he is solemn, small of face and fine of feature. He wears round, metal-rimmed glasses which make him look owlish. His high white

Ronald's high school graduation picture.

collar is up to his chin. Under his picture it reads, "Arthur Ronald Dougan, District School," and then "Doogy," a name he's never heard anyone call him. His place and date of birth follow: "Oregon, Wisconsin, May 20, 1902." Next are listed his high school activities: Literary Society, Thespian Club, Debate. Last comes the little squib: "Not only good, but good for something."

Ronald remembers Chuck Hoag, and wonders, good for what?

21 ❧ MISS EGAN

I t's 1928. In the same mail Grampa gets two letters. He reads them several times, then goes to the kitchen, holding them in his hand. Grama is punching down bread.

"Dearie," says Grampa, "I'm thinking of taking on a new barnhand, but first I need your approval."

"Whatever for?" exclaims Grama, and spells on her floury hand, "If there's a problem, don't take him!"

Grampa twinkles. "It isn't a him, it's a her!"

"Land sakes!" Grama snatches one of the letters and reads it with little exclamations of surprise while Grampa explains.

Miss Mary Josephine Egan is a maiden lady who has been teaching school for more than twenty years. She's recently inherited her parents' farm at Amboy, Illinois. She wants to make it into a stock farm, perhaps dairy. She wants to run it herself, but she knows little about modern scientific dairying. She inquired at the University of Wisconsin, and subsequently enrolled in their short course in agriculture. However, Professor George C. Humphrey, animal husbandry, has recommended that the best all-round education in practical dairy farming would be gained by spending a six-month apprenticeship under W.J. Dougan on his farm near Beloit. Therefore, she has written to see whether there might be an opening.

Grama reads aloud,

> This may seem rather foolish to you but I am willing to do any kind of work that you think I could do in connection with the dairy. And as I am fond of housework and cooking I would be glad to do that in any free time. Though I am middle aged I am very strong and well and, I think, used to hard work. Of course I understand how the introduction of an additional worker might be more of an inconvenience than a help but I am so anxious to try it that I am risking asking you.

"Very truly yours, Miss Mary Josephine Egan. Well, I never heard tell of such a thing!" Grama says, wonderingly. She reads the other letter:

I take this opportunity to say that Miss M.J. Egan, Amboy, Illinois, would like to have an opportunity to visit and work on a farm where she could observe and learn many things pertaining to the dairy business. Miss Egan was formerly a member of our short course in agriculture. She is concerned with a 350-acre farm, a part of which she feels might be utilized to good advantage for dairy purposes. She hesitates, however, to make the necessary investment in a herd and the equipment with her limited knowledge of dairy herd management. Miss Egan is a lady of mature judgment and apparently very nice in all her actions and attitude of mind. If you are in a position to have her come and learn something of the management of your farm and herd I would appreciate hearing from you or having you write her directly. I have taken the liberty of giving her your address, and trust you may be hearing from her soon.

Very truly yours,
George C. Humphrey
Animal Husbandman

"Well, I never!" Grama repeats. She pummels the mound of bread vigorously for a moment or two. "Well, we can't have her upstairs back there with all the men — she'll have to have the front bedroom!"

Grampa and Grama meet Miss Egan at the train. She's a stately, handsome woman with very pink cheeks. She's wearing a plain blue coat and a silk dress with tiny flowers. Her hair, visible under her flat blue hat, is pinned in a coil around her head. It's just beginning to gray. She's courteous, friendly, and reserved. She's definitely a lady of breeding. She and Grama take to each other immediately.

At the farm Grama shows her her bedroom, and Miss Egan makes short work of settling. She comes down to the noon meal dressed for the job, in overalls, blue work shirt, and men's over-the-ankle work boots. Grampa seats her to his left, and introduces her to all the help. They are speechless. The conversation, that first meal, is all between Grampa, Grama, and Miss Egan.

For a few days the talk of the neighborhood is the new hand in the round barn. Then everyone, including the men she works with, forgets that this is anything unusual. Miss Egan, in black rubber boots and white apron, learns rapidly how to curry the cows, wash udders, run the milking machines. She learns to milk by hand. She shovels manure, swills out the gutters, pitches down hay and silage. There's nothing the barn men do that she does not.

Grampa takes special pains with her, and she's curious and eager to learn. He has her assist at breeding, calving, and dehorning. He sees that she's at hand when the vet comes, and she asks Dr. Russell about heel flies and milk fever, mastitis and Bang's disease, conjunctivitis and swallowing foreign objects, and all other maladies large and small that cattle are subject to. When the schedule permits she's assigned farm chores—haying, silo filling. She learns to service and drive a tractor. She learns to manage the side delivery that rolls the dried hay into a windrow to be collected by the hay loader. She learns to pull the hay loader, and to balance a load. Grampa gives her time in the milkhouse, to learn the processing end of the business.

On the job, she mainly learns the hows. At night, in the family parlor where Miss Egan always sits, rather than in the hired men's sitting room, Grampa explains the whys. They talk about the merits of the various breeds of cattle and what makes a good cow. They talk crops and soils and machinery. They go over records and ledgers, and Grampa shows her how he enters every detail of farm care. They discuss government regulations and taxes.

Miss Egan doesn't neglect Grama. While they both knit, they discuss church missions, or the latest books, or, if it's Sunday, the morning's sermon. Miss Egan lived in foreign lands in her girlhood, and she tells her adventures. Sometimes all three play a game of anagrams. Grama is delighted that Miss Egan can play the piano. Miss Egan sings in a powerful soprano, and Grama joins in, in her strong alto. The room fairly quivers.

During Miss Egan's tenure as a hired man, there's at least one incident that everyone hears about. A salesman comes to demonstrate a new milking machine. He's on the walk behind the cows with the herdsman while Miss Egan is in the center section of the barn, shoveling silage from the cart into the mangers of the waiting cattle. He doesn't pay any attention to the tall barnhand as he goes about his demonstration. Midway, he interrupts his sales pitch.

"I know that Daddy Dougan can't hear this," he prefaces, "and so I'll just tell you this little joke I—"

The herdsman, aware by look and tone the direction the joke is going to take, protests and gestures toward the center of the barn, but the salesman is heedless. He charges headlong into a vulgar story as the herdsman becomes more frantic in his efforts to silence him. At that point Miss Egan takes matters into her own hands. "What—a friend we have in Jee-sus," she sings out in her rich voice, and between the cows glimpses the salesman's astonished face. He abruptly terminates his demonstration and has slunk away before Miss Egan rolls into the second verse. She and the herdsman, and soon everyone in the neighborhood, have a huge laugh.

After six months Miss Egan returns to her farm at Amboy. Grampa has researched cow breeds. He writes a general statement, which he sends to *Hoard's Daiyman*.

In the fall of 1929 I planned to build up a dairy herd of dual purpose Milking Shorthorns on a farm in Illinois. I consulted with several men and with various Breed associations. Of course many of the strictly dairy cattle breeders tried to discourage me. I corresponded with the Shorthorn Breeders Association, also visited their office in Chicago.

I put this question to this Association. Is there a milking strain of Shorthorns showing dairy type and inheriting dairy qualities, or is the so-called Milking Shorthorn a beef animal that occasionally is a good milker? To this question the office did not give me a satisfactory or definite answer, but from my contact I gathered the Association was inclined to regard the latter condition as true. They emphasized that we must hold to the beef form and capacity and not sacrifice it to the angular dairy type.

I will say I did not get as much encouragement in my dairy beef project from the Association as I expected. I was really advised to stick to dairy breeds if I intended to do dairying.

However, Grampa does advise milking shorthorns. Miss Egan buys them and sets up a combined beef and dairy industry. Over the years, it prospers. Grampa and Grama speak warmly and often of Miss Egan. They correspond. Miss Egan's letters are a combination of personal news, reports on how things are going, and questions. In February 1931, she writes:

I spoke to those new heifers about how much they cost, but they looked more depressed than ever. They are having a nice time eating and I occasionally see one that looks as if she had just swallowed a balloon.... There are a couple of things about which I need a little advice if you have any to spare. Two men came to the farm Saturday looking at bull calves and wanted a price on A-3's calf, intending to raise him and use him in their herd. We told them he was a grade but they did not seem to care. Do you think we should sell one for breeding and how much would he be worth?... Then about the Derwent heifer. Roy says she has been bred twice. Saturday the bull broke out and she was bred again. Roy wants to know if the breeding isn't successful this time, should we have Dr. Barth treat her?... The third question is one which I am afraid you will think I have a lot of nerve to ask. Is there any special account book you wish me to use this year? I suppose you think I am hopeless on accounts but I can at least make another effort to do them correctly.

Sometimes Grampa and Grama go to see Miss Egan; once, at the proposal of their coming, she responds with delight, then adds, "Tell Mrs. Dougan I have started house cleaning too. At present the attic and the cistern are as far as I have progressed, but I would be glad to entertain her in either one if she insists on a room that is really clean!"

At Amboy, Miss Egan and Grampa are able to confer about farm problems face-to-face. On one such visit, in reviewing the account books that Miss Egan has toiled over, Grampa discovers an item he didn't teach well enough during Miss Egan's apprenticeship. In the tax records he sees a tractor being regularly depreciated. He hasn't noticed this tractor among the farm machinery.

"Show me the Case tractor," he says.

Miss Egan leads him out behind the barn, where a tractor, overgrown with weeds, is rusting beside a fence post. It can't have been used in ten years.

"But Miss Egan," says Grampa. "You've depreciated this tractor several times over its value!"

"My, my!" exclaims Miss Egan. "Think of that!" She looks contemplatively at the wreck and runs a finger up and over a corroded lug. Then she turns to Grampa. "Who can put a value on an old friend?" she asks.

22 ⚹ DEAR MR. DOUGAN

In an August issue, 1925, *Hoard's Dairyman* publishes an article titled "The Future of Farming." It starts, "Young men, in particular, are interested in the future of farming. They desire to know whether they will have fair opportunity of success if they follow the occupation of farming; will they receive the remuneration necessary to maintain a good home, to educate their children, and to provide properly for themselves when they can no longer operate their farms." The editors say they are in receipt of two letters, one from John, a young farmer in Central Wisconsin trying to develop and pay for his farm, who formerly worked for "Daddy" Dougan, a practical, clear thinking, and God-fearing dairy farmer in Southern Wisconsin. The other is from Mr. Dougan, in response to John's letter. The article consists of the two letters reprinted in full.

John's letter to Daddy Dougan says, "So many speak of 'better times ahead' but do they mean higher prices? Surely not. Nor lower taxes. I remember your clear vision of the crash in 1920 when you told us boys of how you planned a radical cut in expenses and also how you warned the church people of the coming hard times. So thought you might be willing to voice an opinion as to what us younger farmers, deep in debt, can expect." W.J's reply to "My Dear Boy John" is warm. But he cautions, "My judgment regarding the future of agriculture is not infallible and may be somewhat tinged with my spirit of optimism. Here are some of the reasons for feeling there never was a better outlook for the young farmer than for the next twenty years."

He points out that the science of the past quarter century has given the farmer a mass of information on control of disease, improved stock and crops, and maintenance of soils. "He is in the best position in history to produce efficiently. And through the efforts of the agricultural agencies and co-operation of college and farm in extension work, this knowledge is accessible to all, even the unschooled."

Then, there are subtle and powerful forces working to influence and direct the economic conditions of the farmer in the immediate future. There is a change in the mind of the farmer from his former self-sufficiency and individualism to realizing his interdependence not only on fellow farmers, but also upon the assistance of the manufacturer, banker, and all other business. "His social mind has reached out beyond his family and school district to include all society." And this change is reciprocal—the urban population toward the rural is as marked.

W.J. elaborates on this. Both rural and urban dwellers are receiving ideas through the press, the convention, and in social affairs. Women's clubs of the county and city are mingling, farmers and city businessmen are sitting around the same conference table discussing problems of common interest and working out plans for mutual benefits. The young are mixing in social life and interchanging in marriage. "The line of demarcation between urban and rural is being obliterated. We are a common people and should have equal opportunity for the good things of life."

The reprinted letter to John goes on at length. It says the farmer's cry of hard times isn't only because of small income, but also that with these expanding conditions and opportunities there are expanded demands on that income. "Homespun" can no longer suffice—there must be a cash outgo, for the whole structure of society, from food, clothing, and education, to schools, churches, social centers, roads. Machinery must be purchased and maintained. The virgin soil, losing its fertility, must be restored, and there must be an income that will in reasonable time repay the capital invested. "Our present pinch is, when the necessary expenses of the farm are paid, there is no cash left to buy the education, food, clothing, and social life for the farm family; therefore the present discontent."

W.J. goes into a number of the economic problems of achieving equity. He preaches economy of production with the farmer's learning business methods, including keeping accurate records, improving soil, seeds, flocks, herds, and storage, and eliminating waste. Much of this is done in co-operation with other farmers, cow testing associations, agricultural colleges, farm bureaus.

He says the farmer's product must have a higher purchasing power. "There is something wrong in our present system of marketing. Either there is undue waste or too many handlers of the product between the producer and consumer, or someone is taking an undue toll as the product passes by." He suspects a combination of these. And, "There are many examples throughout the country where the individual farmer producing and distributing his own goods is controlling these factors [the ones he's listed] and is giving satisfactory service to the consumer and also receiving ample compensation himself. These isolated farms are producing a necessity and have established a standard brand. They have also used business methods and know the cost of production and can therefore fix a just price. What these individuals have done in their small way can and must be done by the great agricultural world cooperatively." The same factors hold for farmers collectively. "They are producing the necessities of life; without the farmer all other business would stagnate, the world would famish, and life become extinct."

W.J. ends his letter with a horrific image. "You give as your resolution to 'hang on' through the hard times, but you show in other parts

W.J. working at his desk.

how you are already 'hanging on' not as the aeronaut I once saw who started up with his hands holding onto the bar of the balloon trapeze. After a few unsuccessful struggles to gain a seat on the bar he hung back, without effort, just waiting for physical exhaustion and his drop to death. I advise you to 'hang on' not listlessly and hopelessly but by every effort improve your soil and herd, and above all improve your knowledge. Then co-operate for efficient production and better marketing. There is a vast field of opportunity for young farmers like you, not only in getting ample material rewards, but in the larger reward, consciousness of world service." "Daddy" Dougan.

A little over three years later, early in 1929, W.J. receives a bulky envelope from *Hoard's Dairyman*. They are forwarding a six-page letter. They indicate they do not intend to publish the exchange, but are hoping that W.J. Dougan, with his judgment and expertise, will answer it for them.

Mary Anna Pickett, with her husband, raises cattle on Long View Farm, in Bloomingdale, Indiana. She writes by hand. Without preface she tells W.D. Hoard and Sons how in 1917 she received a small legacy and used it to buy cattle. She then fills three closely written pages describing by dates, names, and numbers each Long View cow, bull, and progeny, often with added detail: "Betty of Long View Farm 109319 is a beautiful cow in full flow, I have milked 60 lb of milk a day and she tested 6.8 on the few times I have had her tested. In 1923 Betty produced Betty's Lady of L.V.F., 186665, in 1924 Betty's Peggy of L.V.F. 328093...."

It is not until page four that she comes to the reason for her letter. "I am writing all this first to show you what an uphill job I have had. Second to show you how far I have arrived.... Now these cows are not the most important part of this Long View Farm. We have raised Two Girls and Two Boys. They are better boys and girls than the average farm raises and I think these cows are responsible for it.... Now I want to tell you about just one of these boys and of course it is the youngest one."

This boy has milked cows since he was five, has made the highest grades in his classes, and graduated with the highest grades. "He is a good boy. He has no bad habits. He don't swear. He don't drink smoke or chew Tobacco. He is temperate in all things, He is a hard worker. He is a broad reader. He is good to his father and mother. But he is not a sissy either."

The other children are provided for. One girl is married well; one is a nurse; one boy has wanderlust and has been all over the West and East and South. "But this boy staid at home with us and after providing for the others there never seemed like there was much money left for this boy. His father lost one of his hands in a feed cutter years ago, and we were both smashed up in an automobile wreck. We're both past 52 years old."

The mother has wanted to send this son to college. A neighbor suggests he take a Herdsman Course. "But the boy wants to find some man who really knows cattle and work and learn for a while. He has asked his older brother to come home and fill his place and let him be free. He raised 70 acres of corn last summer and beat all the farmers around. Now this is the way of it. This boy has had everything we can give him except money. We have taught him all we can here. We will miss him, I can't begin to tell you how much. But we want him to have his chance before long."

The letter appeals to *Hoard's* for help and direction; gives references; confesses that the family is Quaker, has a mortgage on the farm, and it takes all they can rake and scrape to meet the Land Bank interest. And it finishes with the boy—that he is big, tolerably strong and good looking. He saves his money. He is honest. "The Bible says no man liveth unto himself. So do you think I am asking too much?"

It is a strange and wonderful letter, filled with pride, care, and anguish. It has surely taken Mary Anna Pickett a number of laborious evenings to write. W.J. pores over the pages, and then replies.

He begins by saying the letter has been referred to him, that he's a farmer, and is interested in the development of better agriculture and larger life on the farm. "I am convinced that even under present conditions the farm offers good opportunities to the youth of ability and vision." He congratulates the writer on her achievements in the breeding work, that no one but the breeder knows the disappointments and discouragements to be met, or of the satisfaction in a well bred and profitable herd. He devotes a paragraph to urging her to have her herd regularly tested under Herd Improvement Testing, that the cost will be less for the whole herd than testing a single animal officially. He then moves on to the heart of the letter.

> I am especially interested in your problem regarding your boy who is wanting a chance for an education. At the start I wish to make it plain that I have no sympathy to offer him. The boy who desires an education, but has not the funds to pay his way, needs no sympathy or pity. It is the poor "mutt" who has every chance to get an education but has not the desire, who needs our pity. You put the question, "Is there not a place for such a boy as this?" All a boy needs who has parts and an ambition is standing room, and he will make his place.

W.J. then says he will go into detail to help think through this problem. First, what should be the ultimate goal?

> In the field of agriculture there is a great variety of desirable activities: teaching, extension work, research, marketing, management, and actual tilling of the soil. At the start of one's schooling he need not decide definitely what he will specialize in, but he should make a careful study of his tastes and abilities, and the opportunities offered in the various fields of service.
>
> Second, he should consider how much time and effort he wishes to put into preparation. My view is: the field of agriculture is so great and the problems so intricate that he should plan to get the best possible mental, moral, and physical development. Your boy will need the broadening and quickening influence of a good strong college course, and he may be capable and desirous of going farther and using it to advantage.
>
> Third, how is he to get the preparation? The answer to this is short and easy. Let him go at it! As I read between the lines of your letter, I see that you

and your husband are anxious to assume the responsibility of the finances. If this boy has been giving faithful service and is filial as you indicate, surely you have a responsibility to the limit of your means to help, and that is all the lad will expect or need.

I emphasize again, you should let him go at it. Release him for his purpose to get an education, however difficult it may be for you. Hire a man to take his place on the farm, and let him go to better prepare for his life job.

The next logical question is, how and where can he do it? I think that he already has had first hand practical experience sufficient to enable him to make the best use of the schooling and of his preparation. I can picture him milking and caring for these cows, and tilling his fields, continually asking of nature the question, "Why?" Why does the cow grow thus and so? Why does one feed produce better results than another? Why, why, why? of the multitude of phenomena all about him. He should train his mind to think clearly and learn to get these answers in a scientific way. He can best do this in a good, thorough school. He also needs the broadening and enlarging influence of contact with thinking, active men. He can get this in a good school. Therefore I would advise him not to try for just dairy work on a good farm, but to aim toward getting into school by next fall.

There are many openings in our colleges and universities where a boy can earn a good share of his expenses. He can find and hold these positions if he is the kind of a boy I think he is. Where should he attend school? There are just two questions to determine this.

1. A thorough, well equipped school.
2. A school that can give a job to a worthy student.

I would advise him to investigate your own university first, and would caution against passing the nearby school to get to some famed far away institution. Keep as near home as possible, but get a good school that can offer a job. Take any job where he can show his purpose and ability; then the better jobs will seek him.

You are not asking too much to ask counsel and assistance of others in solving these life problems. And it is encouraging and exalts our faith in our fellows to know how willing, even anxious, our editors, educators, and other men of affairs are to give a helping hand to those who are endeavoring to get up.

I have no opening on my farm at present, and feel it is not just the opportunity your boy should look for. I may be mistaken but I feel his aim should be to get a start in school, then get this extra experience by working on different farms during vacations.

W.J. ends his letter by saying the boy should feel free to write him if he wishes further discussion.

It is long after this second exchange that Jackie comes across it in Grampa's files. She pictures Mr. and Mrs. Pickett and perhaps their splendid, deserving son—never named—poring over the letter (which hand did you lose, Mr. Arthur Pickett? No doubt your most useful one. And how badly were you and your wife smashed up in the car accident?). She suspects the mother is initially taken aback at Grampa's lack of sympathy, but then mollified and even strengthened by his further advice, including yes, she is right to seek counsel. Grampa's reading between the lines is an easy ascertainment: the parents really want to let the boy go, to live his own life, but oh how they will miss him. And they picture sacrifice—selling a precious cow or two—and college. Grampa is audacious enough to suggest they hire a man. With what? What?

Which brings Jackie to what Grampa doesn't say. He doesn't ask them to order home the wanderlust brother. He doesn't ask whence came the money for nurse's training; that's already indicated in the mother's letter. And Grampa's reply is entirely in keeping with what Jackie has always known of him. Her grandfather is that youngest child, the boy in the furrow, asking why, why, why; the boy who had so little schooling in the poor district school and was unable to start high school till he was nineteen, held on the farm by duty to an ill father. The boy, now man, who chose the local university and was faithful to it, to education—and to science—all his life.

She wonders if the Quaker boy started school at Indiana that fall, just before the stock market crash and onset of the Great Depression. She knows others on their own managed education at that time, through grit and sacrifice. She wonders if Long View Farm made it through, and what is the further story of this boy and his family.

The personal elements aside, she sees these letters from *Hoard's* represent what Grampa has become—a respected authority that a national magazine feels confident in calling upon. They know he will give a thorough, thoughtful, and—if called for—an appropriately personal answer to a farmer's or farm family's problem.

23 ❧ AN AMBITIOUS YOUNG MAN

In early April, 1923, W.J. Dougan, Proprietor Dougan's Dairy Farm, receives a letter from East Lansing, Michigan:

Dear Mr. Dougan:

You will probably be astonished at receiving a letter of this kind from a total stranger but I will explain how I learned of you. Up until about six years ago I lived in Beloit with my parents. While there we learned of your excellent reputation as a first class dairy farmer and I well remember several visits which I made to your place. We lived at the foot of Chapin Street in the house now occupied by Mr. McCumber of the 1st National Bank. My father was connected with Fairbanks-Morse Company and later with the Department of Engineering of the Michigan Agricultural College at East Lansing, where we now live.

Ever since I was a little boy I have had an ambition to be a dairy farmer and more recently, to stock my farm with high class Guernsey cattle. Last year in the Animal Husbandry course in the High School when we were studying this breed of cattle you were mentioned several times in different bulletins which we had as being one of the foremost breeders in the region. It is for these reasons that I write you.

I expect to graduate from the High School here next June and the following fall expect to enter the Dairy course at M.A.C. During the summer however I would like to get work on a high class dairy farm and learn a little of the practical side of dairying. If you have anything which you think I could do in this line you would do me a great favor by letting me know of it. I am 17 years old and large and strong for my age. I know a little about cattle as I have cared for a cow and 2 heifers which belong to my brother and me. Several years ago I showed such an interest in work of this sort that my parents encouraged me to buy a cow. My brother helped me finance the proposition but aside from that has no connection with it. We have two heifer calves from this cow, which is a grade Guernsey, which were sired by the purebred bull owned by the College. Of course this is not much but the reason that I am applying to you is that I want to know more and find out whether this is really to be my life work or whether it is just a fancy of mine.

I am enclosing a stamped, addressed envelope for your convenience and even if you have no job which you would be willing to try me on I would greatly appreciate an answer.

Hoping for an early reply,
I am yours entirely,
John A. Reuling

P.S. You will probably want some references. Those which I can give are, Professor Chace Newman, my Sunday School Teacher, Rev. N.A. McCune, my pastor, and W.C. Buchanan, Sup't of Schools.

W.J. is impressed with the letter, so much better composed and written than the usual replies he gets from job applicants when he runs a help wanted ad. He is cognizant of the lad's parentage and steady background. Nevertheless he mulls the proposition carefully, and on April 14 sends his answer:

Dear Sir:

I remember your people and Trever says you were in school with him.

You seem to be strongly inclined to dairying. It is possible that when you come to realize the many difficulties and disappointments in breeding and developing cows your ardor will diminish. You surely have done the right thing in trying out in a small way. Your plan to try out on a practical farm is excellent.

I have been trying to think how to make a place for you. The only way I can take you is as an extra man. I usually keep seven men during the summer. The herd work is a little lighter and I use the assistant herdsman in the field work to some extent. If I take you I would let you act as assistant herdsman and not expect you to do much of anything outside. This would entirely release the regular assistant herdsman for outside work.

This arrangement would give you just the experience that you desire. You would be one of the five men who have to do with the breeding, cleaning, feeding, in short the producing and distribution of high class milk. I keep complete production records so you could learn the practical side of dairying and become familiar with what a cow ought to do.

There are some reasons that I hesitate to decide to let you come.

1st. You are pretty young and will be rather soft to come right from school to the farm in the heat of June. Are you in school athletics?

2nd. Boys are apt to get too high an estimate of the value of their services.

From the tone of your letter I think you will appreciate what compensation you get will be in experience. The time that you must go back comes just at a rush period of silo filling and corn harvest. This will leave me short of help when needed most.

In spite of these objections to inexperienced vacation help I am inclined to give you the chance. Write to me relative to the wages you expect and also how this line of work suits you.

Sincerely,

W.J. Dougan

Young John Reuling may well have spent a summer on the farm, but he did not go into dairying. He became a missionary and executive with the overseas mission of the United Church of Christ. He spent many years in Africa. It's likely that he helped Africans improve their raising of cattle, and he surely milked African cows himself. He undoubtedly carried with him his own high ideals, and if he did work with W.J. Dougan, incorporated Grampa's ideals into his own.

24 ⊰ I REFUSE TO WORK
LIKE A HORSE

Not everyone who works at the Dougan Farm finds it a satisfying experience. A letter comes to Ron and to Russel Ullius, the current farm manager. Russel is the one in charge of moving men in and out of the barn, consulting with Harlan Whitmore, the herdsman, and Ron, if necessary. Even W.J., supposedly retired, might have a say. The letter is dated October, 1946, and reads:

Farm workers (and pet pig) in front of the milkhouse, none working like horses.

> Dear Ron and Russel,
> I am sorry I quit as sudden as I did but I stood Harlan's ordeal as long as I could. I didn't mind doing 2 mens work but when they start asking a man to do 3 mens work I simply refuse after when I came out here there were 3 men in the barn and one took care of the milk when the others feed silage then Harlan went to breakfast and the 2 of us put down hay and silage for the night. Then 2 weeks after I was there they pulled our third man out and I had to git silage and hay down and still feed them beside clean the barns the Monday night after we got done milking and cleaned the barns out and cows over then he wanted me to go clean out the box stall in the horse barn. I refused to work like a horse for anybody I don't care who it is. I liked it in the barn but when they kept shoving more work on me all the time there is a limit to what a man can do.
>   Please send me $30.00 now and when you figure the bonus later also last month I was only paid ¼ day for the Sunday morning I was called out on my

day off and I asked you about it and you said it was worth 1/2 day on your day off and also the two weeks I worked to from 4:30 to 11. I admit on 2 or 3 days I got done before 10:30 but I worked hard to git done so I could git a little work done at home. I would come back tomorrow if Harlan was out of the barn and I got a little more money because I have gone approx $100 in the hole the 2 months I have worked out there.

Yours truly,
LaVerne J. Austin
1632 Dewey Beloit Wis

Ron I can wright this better than I could come out and talk to you about it. Thank You.

Ron and Russel shake their heads over the letter, and show Harlan. He, too, shakes his head. "I didn't work him any harder than I did myself, or any of the others," he says. "He got mad about something and left us in the lurch."

"Probably just as well gone," says Ron, and Russell and Harlan agree.

25 ⚔ NO LIGHTS IN THE BARN!

Ron Dougan stops down to Roscoe with some corn for Red Richardson. "Red," he says, "what was it like when you were on the farm? You came on account of Lonnie, didn't you? I knew him when he was a kid, dating all the girls I was afraid to date." It doesn't take more than that for Red to launch into his story.

I came to the farm in 1940. Yes, my uncle, Lonnie Richardson, had been herdsman on the farm way back, I guess he was a favorite, and he wrote me a recommendation. Nobody called me Lester, they all called me Red, of course, on account of my hair. I worked in the barn most days. We had to be out there at 4:30 in the morning; we'd always hurry and turn the barn lights on first, then go to the milkhouse for the milk cans. That's because we could look up and see Daddy Dougan standing at his little bedroom window that gives a view of the barn, waiting to see whether the lights went on, that we were out of bed from our night out! He always knew when we got in—the headlights coming in would wake him up. We learned to turn off our headlights and coast in in the dark. Daddy couldn't hear the cars, just see the lights. So that's how we fooled him!

After I was married and living upstairs at Roy's, just down the road beyond Marstons', I had two days a week I wasn't supposed to milk, but be in the fields. There was a barn guy that wasn't reliable, and half the time on those days I'd get a phone call from Daddy—or someone calling for him—saying, "No lights in the barn!" So I'd roll out of bed and go start the milking. That became a saying in our family—"no lights in the barn" means we quick have to stop everything and go tend to something urgent. That, and Daddy's "Ouchy, ouchy, ouchy!" He always said that, waving his arms, when he got hurt. In our family, we all say "Ouchy, ouchy, ouchy," too.

With the field work. Daddy always knew if a field was worked properly, no rows missed. He wanted a field all turned. He'd come out and drag his toe

Lester and Rosemary Richardson on the day of their wedding.

clear across the field. He could tell if he found any missed ridges. We had to stay on *our* toes!

Ron, you told me Dr. Knilans suggested we vaccinate our calves, before the Department of Agriculture even authorized a vaccine. A trial deal. We got a couple years' jump on general authorization. If a cow reacted to the Bang's test, she had to be shipped. I heard one year the farm lost forty cows—a cow with Bang's could be sold for meat, though.

When Barney was testing cows every week, we had to test the cows at the Hill Farm. We'd get those heifers and run 'em into the barn, and there wasn't any holding pen or chute, we'd have to bulldog 'em up against the wall to get the nose lead in so Doc Knilans could get the sample—one heifer whapped Opelt up against the wall, lifted him right off his feet. He hardly knew what hit him. After a while, you figured out a series of gates. Till then the whole thing was a rodeo job.

Daddy Dougan dressed me down once. He was telling me what we had to do; I was the senior guy, and he was just talking about it. I already knew, so I wasn't paying much attention. I must have made a face, because afterward he called me into the office. "I didn't like that, your face," he said. "I want you to listen to me. I know you're doing it, but the impression I got was that the other men didn't think you were paying attention to what I was saying!" Well, he was right; I wasn't.

I got married during the War. After the wedding we came out to the farm to trade cars; you were letting me use your car for our honeymoon, mine was a real rambling wreck. I read my mail there in the office, and I had my draft notice! Hadn't even got off on my honeymoon yet! You took the notice and said, "I'll take care of that!" and you did, got me a farm deferment.

After our honeymoon, when we came to live upstairs at Roy and Fanny's, we expected a shivaree, had stuff in the house ready to feed everybody, but it didn't come and didn't come, and Fanny surmised what with the War and all, maybe everybody's too busy to give you a shivaree. So we got complacent. And then one night we were sound asleep when we heard all sorts of pans banging and horns blowing and there everybody in Turtle was, so our food didn't go to waste. But we didn't expect them to loose a gunny sack full of sparrows in our bedroom, or put our car up on the roof. Roy and Fanny were in on it, of course.

The day the War was over, we were thrashing. We had the tractors all running, the belts on, we were ready to go! I was spike pitcher. Daddy came out and told us we weren't working that day, the War was over and it had been declared a national holiday. I stuck my pitchfork in the stack and went downtown — there was dancing on every corner. You told me the same thing happened in World War I; everyone was in the streets, parading around, and then it turned out to be a false armistice — the real one came three days later, so they had the celebrating to do all over again. But there must have been some guys who were killed in those three days. I always felt sorry about them, and for their families.

Working for Daddy was good training. After I left you all I got my own farm. And as you know, I've been farming here ever since.

26 ⨯ BLOAT

There have probably been a number of incidents of bloat on the farm. Jackie knows the stories of two. The first happened well before she was born, the second well after she'd moved away, so she never sees a bloated animal dead or dying. But it takes little imagination to know it's a painful death.

She hears the first bloat story when she's thirteen. Dr. Knilans, the vet, leaving the farm office as she is coming in, mentions to Daddy in parting that a farmer in Lima township has just lost several cows to bloat.

"What's bloat?" Jackie asks, and Daddy tells her. His explanation goes like this.

It happens in cattle, and other cud chewing animals, when methane gas builds up in their first stomach, the rumen. The gas is produced by fermentation, through the bacterial action that breaks down the cellulose of the plants they eat. Ordinarily, gas escapes when the animal burps up its cud. But if the buildup is faster than the animal can belch, it bloats.

"Or if a cow, or goat, or yak—any ruminant—were to fall upside down in a ditch and not be able to get out again, it would bloat and die, for the food in the rumen would be blocking the natural outlet."

Jackie does not find this at all a pretty picture.

Bloat in cattle, Daddy goes on, is usually caused by a too-rich mix of protein which speeds up fermentation, and the regurgitation of the cud can't handle it fast enough. Rapidly growing spring grass has a strong growth protein which causes this faster fermentation. The cows bloat, and if they're not helped, they die from the pressure of the rumen on their lungs and heart.

"Some farmers keep their cattle off wet grass in the spring," Daddy says, "but it isn't the wetness that's the problem, it's that the wetness causes the grass to grow fast, producing lots of protein. What they should do is feed their cows on fresh growth sparingly, then move them to an older pasture, or augment the fresh growth with hay. At any time you should move cows to a fresh pasture with care, for their stomachs are used to the rate of fermentation of the pasture they're on. A new, richer pasture can give them too much protein and cause trouble."

"So what can cure them?" Jackie asks. "They just swell up and die and that's that?"

"You puncture them."

"What?" cries Jackie. "How?"

"Well, if there's time, there's a less drastic way. But a bloated cow has to have the pressure relieved. She can be tubed, that's when you work a length of hose down her throat into the rumen. The gas comes up the hose. But if a cow is too far gone for tubing, or a tube isn't handy, you puncture the rumen with anything sharp, and the gas rushes out like air from a pricked balloon. You can hear it whoosh."

Daddy rummages far into his desk drawer and brings out a small instrument. "This is standard equipment in most barns. A vet always carries a supply. It's a trocar."

He hands it to Jackie. She's fiddled with something like it before; there's one on a shelf beside the silo in the lower barn, where the daily records are kept, but she never wondered to ask what it was for.

"It has two parts," Daddy says. "That sharp triangular middle part is the stylet, it does the puncturing, and the tube that fits around it, the cannula, is left behind in the wound for a while to keep it open."

"How do you know where to puncture the cow? What if you hit her heart or something?"

Daddy laughs ruefully. "There's no question. The rumen is bulging so grotesquely, you just strike at the height of her distention. The left side, below her final rib."

"And then she's okay?"

"Once the pressure's relieved she usually recovers in short order. The wound never seems to present a problem — it may bleed or ooze a little, but it closes up and the cow gets on with her business."

Jackie pushes the stylet in and out a few times and then returns the instrument. "Why do you keep one here in the office?"

"I don't know. It's been in the drawer a long time. Maybe to remind myself of when I lost a bunch of Grampa's cows, myself, when I was seventeen."

Jackie waits expectantly, and Daddy tells her. He was working on the farm the year between high school and college. That spring his parents had to be away for three days, and they left him in charge. One night it frosted, and the next morning he turned the cows into a fresh pasture of Sudan grass.

The farm vet, Dr. Arthur Knilans, holding a serious syringe. His son Dick, a contemporary of Jackie, followed him as farm vet.

When he went to fetch them for milking he could hear them a long way off, groaning, trying to belch, but they couldn't. He ran and found most of them down, bloated.

"I was frantic. There wasn't time for tubing even if I'd had a tube. But I had a jackknife. I rushed from cow to cow, puncturing rumens. I saved a lot, but six didn't make it."

"How awful," breathes Jackie, hearing and picturing the scene of carnage.

"I was heartsick, of course, and dreaded Grampa's return. He felt terrible, too, for the suffering of the animals, and the economic hardship of their loss, but he didn't blame me. He blamed himself. I didn't know about Sudan grass, and he hadn't warned me. He said only an old, experienced cowman would have known. For it turned out that the cows that died really died of prussic acid poisoning; the poison made them bloat."

"Poison!" Jackie cries. "Where did they get prussic acid?"

"It was in the grass. It poisoned them, they went down, and bloated. I found out that young Sudan grass contains a high level of prussic acid, especially after a frost."

He goes to an office file cabinet and finds a booklet titled *Forage Crop Varieties and Seeding Mixtures*, published by the university's College of Agriculture. Jackie looks over his shoulder as he leafs through it. It deals with legumes, then grasses. Under "Sudans and Sorghum-Sudan Hybrids" Daddy points to a paragraph titled "For Pasture."

He reads aloud, "'Sudan grass and hybrid Sudan grass are suggested because of low prussic acid, few grazing management problems, and high yields. They should not be grazed before they are at least 18 to 20 inches tall since prussic acid content is always highest in the shorter growth and younger plant parts.'"

Daddy points further. Jackie reads for herself. "Piper" Sudan grass gets top billing under "Most Promising Varieties" for it is "low in glucoside which is converted to prussic acid and therefore much less poisonous to livestock." And under "Less Promising Varieties" is "Sweet Sudan," a Texas strain high in poisonous properties, only fair in yield when grown in Wisconsin, and moderately susceptible to diseases. It has, however, "sweet stalks and is palatable to cattle." "Common" Sudan grass is described as an old-type commercial Sudan grass, "moderately high in poisonous properties," and under "For Green Chopping," "The danger of prussic acid poisoning is generally greater with hybrids than with Sudan grass."

Jackie is highly dubious. Why should Sudan grass be grown at all, however palatable? If it kills what feeds on it, can it be profitable? She pokes through the booklet a bit more. She's impressed with all she doesn't know about pastures and forage crops, and the kind of land they thrive on. To her, a pasture has always been just a pasture—a place where grass comes up and cows eat it, whatever grass they don't ruin by making a cow pie on it.

She tosses the booklet down. "But why didn't they all die? Didn't they all eat the Sudan grass?"

Daddy shrugs. "Some maybe ate more than others. Maybe some were hardier cows. Not everybody in Europe died of the bubonic plague."

Jackie hears about the second bloat episode when she's more than twice thirteen. Dick Knilans, who's a little older than Jackie and has been in partnership with his father for a number of years, is treating a cow in the Chez Nous barn. Jackie, home for a visit, sees his van and goes down. He's clad in coveralls and boots and has his equipment in a large bucket, in contrast to his father's formal barn wear and Boston bag.

"What's up, Doc?" she asks.

Dick grins. "Mind you never call old Doc that," he says. "When my wife was first helping out at the Clinic she answered the phone one day, and repeated the message just as the farmer said it—'Tell Doc my cow has cast her withers and he should come right away.' My dad said to Marie, 'It is not "cast her withers," it's "the cow has an inverted uterus," and I am not a "doc," I am a Doctor of Veterinary Medicine. A "doc" is a horse trader.'"

"What did Marie say?" Jackie asks, grinning too. She's glad in all her years of knowing the senior vet she's never presumed to call him "Doc."

"He wasn't bawling her out," Dick assures. "He was teaching her, and she knew it. She smiled at him and said, oh so sweetly, 'Doctor Knilans, a farmer wants you to come see about a cow who has an inverted uterus.'"

They both laugh. Dick explains that once in a while in a difficult birth a cow will expel the calf with such force that the uterus comes out, too, and inside out. Then it has to be turned right side out and replaced. Jackie, who has birthed two daughters, grimaces.

Dick is treating a sore hoof. He goes on to entertain Jackie by giving her an account of the farm's recent mysterious bout with bloat. The cows at Chez Nous—as she knows—are the young ones, not milking yet, and the dry ones. And one day several of them are found dead or dying in the barnyard, bloated. The rest, wandering around, seem okay. Dick rushes down. By the time he gets there a few more are affected.

"Those that were dead, were dead," Dick says. "I didn't have any idea what was causing it, because they'd not been on pasture, and they'd all had the same feed, but I treated those that were down with dextrose, a detoxifier, and whatever it was, that saved 'em. Then we began an investigation, trying to find out what had happened. We asked questions of the help, and it took us a couple of hours to figure it out. You know the feed mill up in the round barn?"

Jackie knows it well. All her life oats and barley and corn have been ground in the feed mill, and the ground grain transferred to the bin with the double sloping bottom alongside the silo, ready to go down the chute to the feed cart below.

"Well," says Dick, "they've been using urea—a nitrate product—to add protein to the system. It helps with their rumination. You can get it in a lick, too, big cakes on a little wheel, and the cows lick it and get a small amount that way. But up in the round barn they have it in bags, powdered. At the feed mill they'll pour in a couple of bags of urea and so much corn, and oats, and anything else they're using as a supplement, and grind it all up and mix it thoroughly with a rake, and take it to the grain bin where it'll be ready to go down to the barn below. But first they fill three bags for the cows up here at Ron's, and set them by the barn door. Then the next morning somebody loads those three bags on a truck and brings them up here and pours them into that long wooden manger that's over there alongside the barn."

Jackie nods, following the story.

"Well, that morning they'd finished the milking and one of the Vanderkooi brothers went up to grind the grain. He threw the urea in the mill, and some corn, and then something happened and he was called away. Meanwhile Bob George—Ron's farm manager—decided that since more heifers had been brought up here they'd better give 'em more feed, so he told the one in charge of bringing the three bags to bring one more. The guy loaded the bags that were waiting, and then went to the mill and drew off a fourth, and this one had a terrific concentration of urea because

Dick Knilans notching a pig's ear for identification.

whichever Vanderkooi it was hadn't finished mixing. So the cows that got that bag were the ones poisoned. When you do have concentrations of feed that are toxic you have to be awfully careful—the Vanderkoois hadn't realized that somebody might come back and take feed. Often you never *do* discover what causes something."

Jackie tells Dick Daddy's story of the Sudan grass and prussic acid, which he hadn't heard before. Then he tells her that all bloat isn't simply gas that can be expelled by tubing or using a trocar.

"Sometimes it's a foam—we call it 'frothy bloat'—and that's a more complicated problem. We tube what we can, and give medication to slow the fermentation, and get a surface tension agent into the rumen so that the bubbles can't form, like you throw oil on water. Our standard treatment is detergent."

"Detergent!" Jackie exclaims.

"Yes, well, soap works, too, you could sprinkle soap over your cow's feed every day if you wanted to, and she'd never bloat, and some farmers used to do that as a preventative, but then after the War, when detergent had been developed, they started using that every day instead, and that was effective,

The barnyard at Chez Nous, showing the manger that held the poisoned grain.

too. Until they noticed that the fat content of their milk began to drop. The detergent circles the fat, or whatever it does, and the fat doesn't go into the milk. They found out they were getting about a 1 percent fat content. The deposition of fat in the udder changed. And on beef cattle they wouldn't get a good deposition of fat all over. It cut down the marbling. So they quit. But we still use it if a cow has frothy bloat."

Dick has long since finished treating the cow's hoof. He gives the animal a slap on the flank and picks up the bucket he carries his medicines in.

"Horses can bloat, too," he says. "A cow has all its gas up front, it belches all the time. But in a horse, the fermentation takes place in the cecum, the blind gut. Horses fart a lot. When a horse gets bloated he has to be relieved mechanically, by a vet. He's like a rodent.... Did you know horses and rats can't vomit? If they do, their stomachs rupture. That's why you can kill rats with products that cause them to vomit, like Warfarin.... Do you know I have a horse that can talk?"

"Sure," says Jackie. "You ask him if he wants some oats and he says, 'A feeeeeeeeew.'"

"I guess we grew up on the same raunchy jokes," says Dick.

Jackie walks with him to his van. "Where next, Doc?"

Dick grins. "Gotta go over on the Shopiere Road. There's a cow there that's cast her withers."

27 ⚔ NAMING COWS

At first the Dougan cows have cowy names. Jackie knows this because one of Daddy's most repeated stories is how, as a little boy milking in the side barn—then the only barn—he knew every freckle on Daisy's udder. How he looked out the barn door, envying the freedom of the sparrows as they pecked on the horse apples. The other cow it was his responsibility to milk was named Bess, who apparently had no freckles worth mentioning. Jackie studies udders, and finds not only freckles but spots and blotches and sometimes warts, though most are plain and creamy smooth.

But during the years that Jackie is in the round barn almost daily, each cow has her name over her appointed stanchion, on a metal plate. The names are J-16, L-3, P-7, or the notorious M-12, well known and avoided because she attacks little children.

Grampa makes this change in 1915, a few years after the round barn is built. He's enlarging his business and increasing his herd. The cows still bear cowy names: Marie, Beauty, Princess, Lassie, Easter, May, Fantine, Fern, Gladys, Elsie, Gretchen, Hester. But this is the year Grampa starts to name his herd

They named her Beauty because she wasn't.

more efficiently. He calls the year "A," and gives each cow a number. Marie is A-1, Beauty is A-2, Princess is A-3, till all cows, heifers and calves are numbered. When he buys a cow, or if a cow calves in the remainder of 1915, that animal receives the next A number. The year 1916 is year B, 1917, year C. Each cow also has her new designation on a metal tab clipped permanently to her ear. This system allows Grampa to know at a glance when a cow came into the herd and also to look up that cow quickly in his records. Some cowy names last at least into the early thirties, but new cows are seldom named, and old names are gradually forgotten.

When Daddy becomes involved with the cows, around 1926 or 1927, he decides it's to the farm's advantage to register all its purebred Guernseys with the American Guernsey Cattle Club. He sends a list of the cows' names: E-4, K-7, G-3, and all the others.

The cattle club writes back. They are sorry, but the Dougan Farm can't register their cows by number. It's required that each cow have a name.

Daddy studies the letter and shakes his head at the nuisance to the farm records of double-designating all the cows merely to have them registered. He expresses his irritation to Mother.

"Name them in French," Mother suggests.

"*Quelle* the hell *la difference?*" asks Daddy. "Bessie or Babette?"

"Name them their numbers," says Mother.

"A rose by any other name," shrugs Daddy.

Mother picks up Daddy's pencil, takes the list of cows, and translates each number: *E-Quatre, K-Sept, G-Trois...*

"It seems a little obvious," observes Daddy, "as well as spare."

"Then add something more," says Mother. "Add 'of our farm,' or 'of our home.'"

Daddy takes the pencil and adds "*de Chez Nous*," to each name: *E-Quatre de Chez Nous, K-Sept de Chez Nous...*

"Thank you," says Daddy. He kisses her. He says in French, "How smart I was to marry a woman smarter than I am."

He sends the altered list back to the cattle club. There's not a murmur at the other end. They register all the Dougan purebred Guernseys with their elegant French names. At the farm, these names go into the herd book. But each cow, on her metal plate and her ear clip, retains her simple numerical designation. All cows, grade and purebred, are equal in the round barn.

In 1940 Daddy and Grampa come to the end of the alphabet; the cows are finally Z-1, Z-2, Z-3. For the next year they switch, and the cows are 41-1, 41-2. They continue this in 1942. But the new system is cumbersome. Since all the A, B, and C cows from before 1920 are only sweet memories, Daddy starts through the alphabet again. He completes another cycle and has started around once more before he sells the herd in 1969 and retires from milking.

28 ⚬ BOSSY

When you want to round up a herd of cows you shout across the field, "Here, bossy, bossy! Come, boss! Boss, boss!" and the cows, ever curious, will start ambling and grazing toward you. To call pigs you screech at the top of your lungs, "SOO—ee, SOO—ee, SOO—ee" (which is why pig-calling contests at the county fairs are fun and popular), and the pigs, ever mindful of their bellies, come racing pell-mell so as to be first at the trough.

Jackie discovers something remarkable when she starts Latin in ninth grade. An early lesson is about a farmer, *agricola*. Well. It doesn't take much to realize that's where "agriculture" comes from. The *agricola* has a *bos*. Her vocabulary list says, *bos, bovis*: cow. So! A cow, in that ancient language, is a "*bos*," and present day cows are called bossies! From the genetive form of the word we must get "bovine."

Does the *agricola* have anything more? Aha, a *sus*! A pig! The plural is *sui*. Jackie has learned enough Latin to know that "*sui*" is pronounced "soo-ee." And that's the very word you screech to summon pigs!

It can't be coincidence. The common words to call cows and pigs on southern Wisconsin farms haven't come out of nowhere; they claim a history that stretches back well over two thousand years, and across oceans and continents. With *boves* and *sui* tended by *agricolae*, Latin doesn't seem a dead language at all!

She hurries to tell Mother and Daddy, Grampa and Grama. It turns out that they have all had Latin, too. They share her delight at discovery. "*Mirabile dictu!*" says Daddy.

29 ⋈ BUILDING A PROFITABLE DAIRY HERD

In 1926, *Hoard's Dairyman*, the international dairying magazine, in the wake of much publicity about Grampa, from *Prairie Farmer*, and the University of Wisconsin, and his popular radio talks, asks him to write a series of articles about his philosophy of farming. Grampa agrees. Seven articles appear in the magazine from January through April, 1927. *Hoard's*, on its January 10 editorial page, introduces Grampa and the articles:

A Farm and a Home

"What I Am Trying To Do On My Farm," is the title of a series of articles which will appear in *Hoard's Dairyman*, the first being published in this issue. These articles were prepared by W.J. Dougan, a successful dairy farmer in Southern Wisconsin, and they relate his farm practices and what he is striving to do to make an ideal farm home.

Before becoming a farmer Mr. Dougan was a Methodist minister but was forced to give up this profession because of impaired hearing. He had experience in farming in his early youth and it then became his ambition to be a successful dairy farmer and to produce and distribute the best quality milk, for he recognized its importance as a food for human beings. The time Mr. Dougan spent in the ministry did not unfit him for hard work and he has made an unusual success. He has worked hard but, fortunately, has had the help of an unusually good wife. This, with good health and a determination to succeed, has given him the distinction of being one of the best dairy farmers in Southern Wisconsin.

We desire to commend these articles because they present practical information on operating a first class dairy farm where the choicest food is produced. There is threaded through each article splendid ideals which are stimulating and lead to a better farm life. The person who is anxious to know how to operate a dairy farm successfully, to create an ideal farm home, and to participate intelligently in the activities of his community, should not neglect to read these articles written by Mr. Dougan.

The first article is on building soil fertility. The next, "What I Am Trying to Do On My Farm #2, is titled "In Building a Profitable Dairy Herd." Though high index bulls who can pass on desirable traits to their daughters are a thing of the near future, followed by artificial insemination that speeds the process of selection and makes excellent sires available to every farmer, this article shows that W.J. is already selecting for better production.

There are three outstanding essential features in building a profitable dairy herd. The first essential is cows capable of producing. This is so self evident that it seems almost unnecessary to state, yet any number of farmers are trying to secure profits from cows that cannot turn feed into milk. There is a wide difference in cows in this respect, even in cows that are well bred to type and appearance. The average Wisconsin cow gives only 190 lb. butterfat. The average of the 49,000 cow testing association cows in Wisconsin in 1923 was 273 lbs. Eighteen percent of the herds average over 300 lbs. butterfat. The highest producing cow gave 839 lbs. fat. Therefore the selection of producing cows is of prime importance.

Grampa in the barnyard behind a group of his cows.

The second necessity in building a profitable dairy herd is economical feeding. Not always the lowest priced feed is the cheapest. The feed that produces milk at the lowest cost is the economical feed to use.

The third necessity is proper management. Here is a good rule for housing and handling of cows: Keep the cows happy. The late Hon. W.D. Hoard expressed a fine sentiment and gave a good rule in this: 'The cow is a mother. Treat her as such.'

These three factors in building a profitable dairy herd, viz., good cows, good feed, and good management, are easily stated, but, oh, how difficult to work out in actual practice.

Knowledge is essential and to control these factors we must have complete and continuous records of production. These are absolutely required. What the cow does at the pail is the final criterion of the cow, her feed, and her manager.

There has grown up in the dairy world during the past decade, an institution of marvelous influence and almost unlimited possibilities. It is the foundation of intelligent and progressive dairying—the cow testing association. This is simply a co-operative movement. A group of farmers combine and hire a competent man to come to each of their farms once a month. He weighs and tests the milk from each cow, weighs the feed, and figures out for each cow just what she is doing and what profits she is making over the cost of feed. There are over 170 of these associations in Wisconsin, with over 78,000 cows under test. The continuous records gained in this way are determining to the dairyman his profitable cows and the unprofitable ones, the economical feed, and the right management.

I will give some facts from my own experience to illustrate these points. I had two cows of my own raising from the same dam but different sires. We will designate these cows by their stable names, F4 and G5. F4 with her first calf in 1920, gave over 7,000 lbs milk, then, increased to over 9,000 lbs. and is still a good producer in the herd. G5 gave only 5,000 lbs. with her first calf, and never got up to 7,000 lbs. She was an unprofitable producer and finally was sent to the block.

D5, a four-year-old cow purchased in 1918, started out as a fair producer, giving around 7,500 lbs. milk. By improving her feed, we found she had splendid capabilities. We brought her up to 9,000, 10,000, and 12,500 lbs. with 591 lbs. fat. F9 is another cow that could tell a similar story. A20, a fine looking grade cow bought in 1914, started in with only 4,000 lbs. milk per year. With the best of feed and care during several years, she never gave over

5,600 lbs. milk per year. The daughters of D5, the good cow, are proving good; the daughters of A20, the poor cow, were poor and there is none of her blood left in the herd.

The records of the C.T.A. help me to select sires for building up my herd. The sire is half the herd. The criterion of a valuable sire is whether or not his daughters are as good or better than their dams. With continuous and complete records of production of every cow that comes into my herd, I am able to select prepotent sires to continue in the breeding.

With complete records before me, I can judge the profitable feeds. At one time I was trying to make my cows produce on home-grown mixed clover and timothy hay — mostly timothy. I bought a carload of alfalfa. The increase in milk from feeding alfalfa more than paid the entire cost of the hay. Therefore I could afford to give away my timothy and buy alfalfa at $35.00 per ton and still be ahead.

For some time I thought I could not afford to put in drinking cups in the barn. I had a large tank of good water in the yard. I finally put in the cups. The records showed that this improvement in management paid for the cups in less than sixty days because of the increase in milk.

By keeping careful records and being guided by them in selecting cows, selecting feed, and directing management, I have built up a profitable herd. In 1922 the herd averaged 8,000 lbs. milk, 364 lbs. fat. For several years my herd of over 30 cows has averaged over 300 lbs. fat.

In conclusion, let me emphasize the importance of patience and perseverance. Don't be in too big a hurry to see results. Fix right principles and patiently wait and watch. Don't get discouraged with a few failures. To reach your goal, stick to your breed and your line of dairying. Eternal perseverance along intelligent, sane lines will surely bring results.

30 ❧ ODE TO A WISCONSIN FARMER

Grampa sometimes referred to himself as "an old sod." Here he looks every inch an Irish farmer.

I n seventh grade, Jackie writes a poem for the Roosevelt Junior High news-paper. It goes like this:

ODE TO A DOUGAN COW

The Guernsey cow, so calm and quiet,
Lives upon a yeasty diet,
And basking in the caking mud,
Calmly, quietly chews her cud.
Poor cow, no upper teeth has she,
Which is a great calamity.

Her world consists of pasture small,
She sticks her head into a stall.

But does she pine for sights anew
Of rippling brook and water blue,
Of grassy plain and mountain slope
Where carefree sheep and cattle lope?
Nay—happy and content is she
And does not long for life more free,
And doesn't seem to mind at all
Staring at a flyspecked wall.

Mother likes that Jackie has written the poem but objects to "flyspecked wall" and "caking mud." Jackie argues that she needs "mud" to rhyme with "cud," that you don't leave cuds out of poems about cows, and that all the other rhymes she thought of, such as "dud," were worse. As for "flyspecked," she needed an adjective to fill out the line with "wall."

"Why not use 'whitewashed'?" suggests Mother. "That fits the meter just as well." She points out that "flyspecked" makes the barn look bad. A dairy whose reputation is based on cleanliness should not look bad—especially when it isn't. The barn is clean, the cows are clean.

Jackie agrees, partly, and had she thought of "whitewashed" first, she probably would have used it. Still, both words are correct. The barn's walls gleam right after they're whitewashed, but they get more and more flyspecked till the time rolls around when they're whitewashed again. And the cows do lie in mud, sometimes—out in the pasture where there's a muddy place beside the crick, or in the well-trampled lane to the barnyard after a rain. The barnyard itself has no mud for it's paved with concrete. It does have cowpies. The barnhands scrape them up every day or so, but it would take all of someone's time to follow the cows around and shovel up after them. So sometimes the cows even lie in manure. They aren't very smart, like pigs. Lucky for the reputation of the farm that "cud" doesn't rhyme with "manure."

Since the poem has already been printed, Mother satisfies herself by saying, "You've used poetic license," and Jackie learns this means that in poems it's okay to make things not quite what they are (even if they sometimes are) in order to make the rhythm and the rhyme come out right.

Mother knows these things, for she has taught English, and also writes poems. She never wrote one specifically about cows, but she did write one once about Grampa, when Jackie was quite little. She rummages around in her desk and finds it. She says she didn't put in about Grampa being deaf, or going to the university with a team of horses, or studying to be a minister, because you can't complicate a poem with too much other stuff, and this one was about the farmer aspect of Grampa. It wasn't supposed to be his entire life history. Jackie reads it with interest:

WISCONSIN FARMER
A Portrait

This Wisconsin farmer is a man
Of weatherbeaten skin and sturdy frame;
His deep-set eyes hold valor, humor, too;
Determination sits his mouth and chin.
Bred of Irish and Scotch pioneers—
A rugged stock. His boyhood home a farm
Near Beaver Dam. His education first
The country schoolhouse, then Academy.
He said, "When I am grown, and if I farm,
I shall have life, as well as just a living."

So to that end he set his mind and went
To th' University at Madison.
With cultural and scientific bent
He studied; then beyond his Bachelor's
Degree, he learned about the soil, and cows;
Agronomy, Animal Husbandry.
A bride he took, farm reared yet college bred,
And brought her to his newly purchased home
Where Turtle Creek flows into River Rock
Lying a mile or two beyond Beloit.

The tilling of the soil he felt to be
An art. Painstakingly he labored, finding
Beauty in the turning of the furrow,
Satisfaction in the pull of the plow.
With care he fed the earth that which it lacked:
Minerals, manure, and legumes rich.

Wesson, Vera, and baby Joan in front of the Little House.

These things he wished: a spacious home,
Proud trees, wide lawns, and healthy pasture lands,
Broad fertile fields; and with a priestly urge
Labored until he saw his dreams fulfilled.

Within, his wife has made their home a place
Of comfort and of rest and inspiration.
White curtains at the windows, polished floors,
Bowls of flowers, books, a game of chess.
Yet in the kitchen one smells baking bread,
Sees the gleaming jars of summer fruit,
Watches the homely farm tasks going forward.
Their children are imbued with love of life,
Respect for toil, the feel of rich good earth,
A quest for knowledge and for all things good.

Maternity, however lowly, stirs
The farmer's deep compassion. Day and night
At farrowing time he goes among his sows

Heavy with unborn young and ill at ease,
And calms their restlessness. He understands
Pig talk; scratches their backs. Ugly with pain
They welcome him, their friend, and grunting, sprawl
In willing awkward postures to be rubbed,
And when the tiny squealing pigs arrive
He pats each mother proud and says, "Well done."

When barns are swept; the cattle clean and sleek;
Their warm milk cooled and set in sterile cans;
The sweating team unhitched and pastured out;
The hired men well fed at ample board;
The crops upspringing from the moist black soil
Of seed and science born, of brawn and brain,
Machines, electric power, rain and sun;
The farmer sees the evening come again,
Views the sunset fading in the west,
With uplift heart he walks the corridors of corn.

In civic life he plays an active part;
We hear his voice upon the radio.
He serves in church, in Grange, in County "Y",
Sponsors youth in 4-H club and camp.
His neighbors say, "His word is as his bond,"
And call him friend. His Alma Mater has
His portrait hanging in her Hall of Fame.
Upon his silo are these aims: "Good crops,
Proper storage, profitable livestock,
A stable market, Life was well as a Living."

—Vera Wardner Dougan

Jackie likes the poem, especially the stanza about the sprawling pigs. She
has watched Grampa with his pigs, heard him croon to them. And everything
Mother has put in about Grampa is true. She hasn't had to use any poetic
license.

31 ⚹ FIVE TIT NELLIES

In milking supply catalogues and farm magazine ads, "tit" is spelled "teat," as in "teat cup," or "teat balm," but it's always pronounced "tit," just as in Turtle Township, the creek is always "Turtle Crick."

One of Daddy's sayings is "as useless as a fifth tit."

For a cow has four tits; each tit services a quarter of the udder. Jackie has watched four tits per cow being milked all her life, except when one is deliberately omitted from the milking because of a sore or mastitis. But that tit is always milked by hand, later. Jackie assumes that Daddy's saying has no connection with cow reality, and she never even looks, until it occurs to her to ask him about it, once.

Some cows do have five, Daddy assures her. These are called supernumerary tits. "When a cow has an extra tit we just leave it, if it's only a nubbins,

A young man contemplates a well-formed tit. The cow's surcingle holds the milking machine above the floor.

for it usually doesn't develop. It won't be a nuisance," Daddy says. "But if it's large, or starts to grow, it has to be got rid of. We tie it off tightly, like a lamb's tail, till it drops off from lack of circulation. Or else the vet comes and removes it surgically."

Jackie is startled at Daddy's next statement. "People sometimes have extra tits, too," he says. "We had a hired man on the place for a while when I was a boy that the others called 'Three Tit Nellie.' For months I hung around on the fringes, and sneaking into the back washroom, hoping to see for myself, and I finally did, when Nellie took off his shirt during thrashing."

"Where was it?" Jackie asks. "In the middle?"

"No, it was off to one side, and slightly below—smaller than the other two. Not lined up neatly like a sow's or dog's. Just a genetic throwback to when we all were lying around with a litter working at our bosoms. The females, that is. Though a male pig has all the necessary equipment, too, just in case his chromosomes decided early on to turn the opposite direction."

After gleaning this bit of interesting information, Jackie prowls the barn studying tits. Regular tits are about the same size, and are usually pink, but an occasional Holstein has a pure black one. And she does find several Five Tit Nellies. In every case the supernumerary tit is very small; nothing has been done about it, or needs to be.

As for the current crop of hired men, there are no rumors about any of them. And since it isn't shirtless weather, Jackie can't spy out for herself whether the farm has any current Nellies or not. Probably not, or Daddy would have mentioned it.

32 ✎ ON TOP OF THE SILO

I t's 1934. Daddy is on top of the outside silo, between the round barn and side barn. The concrete silo is some fifty feet above the paved cow yard, and has an inverted saucer-shaped concrete cap with a skylight. The skylight is open. Metal rungs are spaced up the inside of the silo, by which means Daddy got to the top. Close inside hangs a plank platform; he and a helper are getting ready to plaster the inside of the empty silo before it's filled. It has deteriorated some and needs to be smooth so it won't spoil the silage. The platform is fastened at both ends and can be raised and lowered. A large coil of rope is alongside Daddy. One end is fastened to the plank; he's pulling up the rope and coiling it, getting rid of the slack. For the moment he's alone. His helper has left to fetch something from the toolshed.

Suddenly the inside platform gives way and crashes to the bottom of the

Gulbrand Gjestvang climbs to the top of the outside silo. The round barn roof is behind him.

silo. The coiled rope spins, whip-whip-whips beside Daddy's ankles and with a final fling upward of the end of the rope, is gone in a single stunning instant.

Daddy sinks down, crouching. Weakness sweeps over his body. He's in such shock he can hardly move. He feels waves of nausea; he feels dizzy. Had the rope lashed out and caught him, thrown him off balance, he would have plunged to the concrete cow yard below and been killed. Had he been holding it, as he just was, or straddling it, tangled up with it in any way, he'd have been flung down inside the silo an equal distance. In the silence the snapping of the rope reverberates in his head, the lightning-fast uncoiling replays. Emptiness quivers where the coil has just been.

He inches on his stomach to the skylight, afraid that his vertigo might yet send him catapulting. He reaches down, clutches iron, and slides onto the rungs. His body is like jelly. He clings there at least five minutes, his arms locked into the metal, waiting for the strength to climb down.

He tells Jackie, years later, "I still wake up once in a while with sweat pouring off me, reliving that moment. Just thinking about it makes me shudder. It was probably the closest shave of my life."

The outside silo, seen across a field of young corn. It would have been a long fall.

33 ⚹ DEHORNING

It's 1938. Russel Ullius is herdsman. They are dehorning calves in the side barn.

If left to nature, a calf will develop horns from the two little hornbuds on her forehead. But Grampa sees to it that the calves get a caustic salve when these buds are just little buttons, about half an inch high. The salve usually stunts the horns' growth. Some horns continue to grow, and these have to be removed when the calf is about a year old, to prevent harm to other cattle and to people.

Dehorning is not a happy procedure. The animal is held still with a halter, her head immobilized in a dehorning frame and with a nose leader. The horns are snubbed with a special miter saw, and then a cauterizing, healing powder is put on the cut surfaces. It's painful to the calf, as painful as having a tooth pulled without anesthetic, for there are nerves in the horn, and an artery which is sometimes large and squirts. If the artery continues to bleed, a calf can bleed to death. The vet has to be called.

Today, all the calves go through the agony, bawling with fright and pain, and are finally freed. But one is a bleeder. The herdsman can't stop it; Grampa can't stop it. They call the vet. Dr. Knilans reaches into the horn with tweezers, pulls out the artery, and ties it.

The animal is weak from loss of blood. "Give her a shot of gin," Dr. Knilans tells Grampa. "It will do her good. You can give her some more later on tonight."

Grampa drives to town and buys a bottle of gin. It's probably the first and last time he buys gin in his life. He returns to the barn, and he and Russel administer a good dose. It seems to do the calf good. They give her another dose that night. By morning the calf seems normal and is released from sick bay. Grampa takes the bottle and puts it on a shelf in the men's washroom behind the kitchen, back by the shower with the Petro-Carbo salve and other medicines. It sits there, gathering dust.

Russ Ullius drinking milk, not gin, from a cream-top bottle. Used for a short time by the dairy, it allowed cream, risen to the top, to be easily poured off, separate from the milk.

A year later Russel has a terrible cold. He can't shake it. Every night he goes to put the cows to bed, just dragging his feet. One night he returns from the barn, looks up, and sees the bottle. He thinks, "What's good for that cow is good for me!" He takes a hefty swig and goes to bed. He sleeps like a baby.

The next morning he feels more energy on the job. That night when he returns from putting the cows to bed he thinks again, "What's good for that cow is good for me!" He takes another shot, and enjoys another peaceful sleep. The third night he takes a final dose and considers himself cured. "It's good for calves, and it's done me good," he says to himself.

Only a day later Russel is in the back room washing up for supper when W.J. comes hurrying through. He glances up at the gin bottle and stops dead.

"Well!" he exclaims. "*That* thing's gone down!"

Russel doesn't confess, nor does Daddy Dougan probe. The bottle continues to sit on the shelf at its current level, gathering dust.

34 ✕ UNBUTTON

Jackie is fourteen. She changes into her jeans after school. Her horse doesn't want to go, but she rides him from Chez Nous down to the dairy. She sees the vet's old Buick near the cow barn door. She tethers Paint to the elm, goes down the step to the barn washroom, and into the barn. Whenever the vet is around it's interesting. She's known Dr. Knilans ever since she can remember.

The cow barn is empty except for Jackie-cow and Dr. Knilans. The vet is naked to the waist; his coat, tie, and white shirt are draped on a stall-divider. He's busy on the walk behind Jackie-cow, with his doctor's kit. A vet has a large doctor's kit.

Jackie-cow is a funny looking, who-knows-what-breed cow. She's one of the best milkers in the barn. Jackie likes it that she's called Jackie-cow. But now she's concerned about Jackie-cow's rear end.

Jackie has looked at cows' rear ends all her life. It's the major view in the round barn, forty cows' rear ends. But Jackie-cow has a lot of grayish tissue hanging out of hers, below her anus. It hangs in folds and loops halfway to the gutter. It's a little bloody. The cow seems unconcerned.

"What's the matter with her?" Jackie asks.

"It's the afterbirth," the vet says. "It didn't come out when she calved. I have to clean her. Unbutton her."

Jackie is astonished. "Unbutton?"

Dr. Knilans makes a fist. "See this fist? A cow has knobs sort of like that on the inside of her uterus."

Jackie nods.

Dr. Knilans cups his other hand over his fist. "This is the placenta, the sac the calf grows in. It grows around the knobs."

Jackie nods.

"Now, take your hand and peel the placenta off the knob. Gently."

Jackie carefully peels Dr. Knilans' hand off his fist.

"There," says the vet. "That's how you unbutton a cow. Nature usually does it, but when nature doesn't quite manage, we have to help."

Dr. Knilans gets out a long rubber glove, the sort Amos wears when he inseminates a cow. He dusts his arm with talcum powder.

"Is this cow a friend of yours?"

"Yes," says Jackie. "She lost the ends of her ears and tail from frostbite, before Grampa bought her. They call her Jackie-cow. For fun."

"Would you like to unbutton Jackie-cow? She's small enough — your arm might reach. And you have a gentle touch."

Jackie considers. "Yes," she says.

Dr. Knilans talcs her arm. He puts the rubber glove on her. It comes up and over her shoulder. He fits the fingers. He soaps all over the glove and arm. "Now," he says, "put your arm down and feel around for one of the buttons." He moves the hanging afterbirth and shows her where to insert her hand.

She makes her fingers into a point and pushes her hand gingerly into Jackie-cow's vulva. Her arm slides easily down the vagina. The passageway holds it snugly. She's surprised how warm it is inside the cow, it's like a warm bath. She's amazed how far the passageway goes. She reaches down, down. Dr. Knilans holds the tail aside. Her shoulder is right against the cow's anus.

"Are you there? Can you feel any buttons?"

Jackie gropes around. She feels a fleshy knob, like a mushroom. She nods.

"Now feel if there's anything to unbutton. Some of the knobs may be free already."

She feels something over the top of the mushroom. She works it gently with her

Dr. Arthur Knilans suited up for messy vet work.

fingers, feels it loosen.

"It's come off!" she says, grinning.

"See if there's another."

She feels around. It's working in the dark, by touch only. It's very warm. She unbuttons another knob. She feels further. She can't find any others. She pulls out her arm.

Dr. Knilans puts on the glove and reaches down. "One more, I think," he says.

He works around a bit. Then he pulls his arm out and all the afterbirth comes with it. "There," he says, dropping the gray mass in the gutter. He takes a tablet of medicine, big as a bar of soap, puts it deep in the vagina, and then peels the glove.

Jackie watches till he's done. Then she washes up in the barn washroom, and waits while Dr. Knilan washes up and puts his clothes back on. She walks out to his car with him and watches him stow his equipment.

"Do people have buttons?" she asks. "Women, in their uteruses?"

"No," Dr. Knilans says. "The placenta sticks without them."

He leaves to go to another farm.

Jackie goes to the milkhouse and gets a bottle of chocolate milk from the cooler. She drinks it, climbs on Paint, and rides back home. She tends the horse, practices her cello, takes her turn to set the table.

At supper she says, "I unbuttoned a cow this afternoon."

"Many's the cow I've cleaned," says Daddy.

"What's unbuttoning a cow?" Joan asks.

Jackie starts to tell her.

"Oh, not at the table!" Joan says. "Mother, make her stop! I can't stand to hear it!"

Mother asks Jackie to tell about it later.

Jackie explains after supper.

Joan is repulsed. "Honestly, Jackie, how can you stand to *do* those things?" she asks. "Why do you *want* to?"

"The cow needed it," Jackie says. "And I'd never felt a cow's buttons before. It was interesting."

35 ❧ AFTERBIRTH

Dr. Knilans has a son named Dick. He's Joan's age. He's going to be a veterinarian too. Sometimes he comes along with his father and helps with the sick animals.

Craig and Jackie are in the barn once when Dick is there. He tells them a joke about a farmer whose wife is going to have a baby. But when her labor pains begin there's a terrible blizzard raging. The farmer can't get out and the doctor can't get in. They talk on the telephone.

"Don't panic," says the doctor. "You've helped a cow deliver, haven't you? It's just like that, like a cow delivering a calf. Just follow that procedure exactly, and you shouldn't have any trouble. Call me back when it's over."

After a while the farmer calls back. He's jubilant. "Doctor!" he cries. "I have a little baby boy! He's perfect! Everybody's fine."

"You see?" says the doctor. "It was simple, wasn't it?"

"Well, yes," says the farmer, "up until the very last, and then I had a hell of a time getting her to eat the afterbirth."

36 ⚔ MARBLE GAME

Ronald is in the calf barn. He's eight. There's an older boy with him he doesn't know; the boy is twelve. The boy's parents are paying a visit to his father and mother. They are all inside talking. Trever is downtown at Aunt Ida's. There's nobody around the calf barn.

Ronald shows the boy the new calf. It has been recently separated from its mother. He shows how, when he gives his thumb to the calf, it grabs it and sucks frantically, showing the whites of its eyes. He pulls his thumb out, wet and tingling.

"He thinks it's the cow's tit," Ronald explains.

The boy tries it and laughs. He gives the calf his thumb again and then each of his fingers, one by one. He laughs. Ronald laughs.

The boy contemplates the calf, and then looks sidelong at Ronald. "You know what?" he says. "We have something that's even more like a cow's tit. Do you think he'd like that?"

"Like what?" asks Ronald.

The boy points to Ronald's crotch.

Ronald is puzzled for a moment, then realizes what the boy means. He finds the thought astounding. "No," he says, flushing.

"Oh, come on," the boy says. "Let's try it. It won't hurt, it'll just feel funny."

"No," Ronald repeats.

"I dare you," challenges the boy.

Ronald is silent. He gets dared at school. Dares are usually not pleasant.

"I dare you!" the boy says again. "There's no teeth. I bet it'll feel good. You're scared, aren't you!"

"You do it," Ronald says.

"I'll do it after you do it. I promise."

"You go first," Ronald says. "I won't do it unless you do it. I dare *you*."

"I dared you first, so you have to go first. Unless you're too scared. I'll only do it if you go first."

The calf is still at the bars. The boy gives it a finger to suck. "See? He's all ready and willing."

The idea seems a bad one to Ronald.

"Look," says the boy. He reaches in his pocket and pulls out a handful of marbles. "Real glass! You can choose whichever one you want, if you go first. You can choose the very best one. But not if I have to go first. So which one of us is going to go first?" He rolls the marbles around in his hand.

Ronald is confused. The situation has shifted. It's no longer 'if,' it's 'which.' But the idea still seems an uncomfortable one. "What if somebody comes in?"

"You're just taking a pee. Go ahead, I want my turn!"

Ronald shakes his head. He backs up.

"You don't want a marble?" the boy asks.

"No," says Ronald.

"What a baby you are!" the boy says scornfully. "Well, I'm going to. You can do it after me; I'll tell you what it's like. Just don't tell. I'll give you a marble provided you don't tell."

The boy pulls down his pants. Ronald sees his penis. It is larger and redder than any cow's tit, and sticking straight out without help of hands. Ronald gapes.

Laughing, the boy jostles him aside and thrusts his penis toward the calf. The calf grabs it with such a powerful tug that the boy's stomach is jerked right against the bars and the calf's nose. He lets out a whoop. Ronald sees the calf get in another incredible pull. Blood pounds in his ears; he turns and stumbles toward the barn door.

"He's ripping it right off!" the boy hollers. "C'mon back, it's your turn in a minute! It's crazy!"

The boy's voice is shrill, gasping, giggling hysterically. Ronald dodges around the calf barn, scrambles up the ladder to the icehouse and hides in the dark interior. He is shaking all over. He doesn't come down till he hears the visitors' buggy leaving the yard. He waits a while longer. It is dusk. He creeps down and goes into the kitchen.

"Lands sake!" cries his mother. "Where have you been? What sort of host are you? We send you out to play, and that boy says you ran off and left him! You've been brought up better than that, Ronald!"

Ronald doesn't reply.

"Well, you missed the angel food cake and raspberries," his mother says. "I guess that's punishment enough. Here, he said to give you this." She drops a red and yellow spiraled marble into his palm.

Ronald stares at it.

"He says he promised it to you. I think that's sweet of him, the way you behaved. He said you could have had another one, if you hadn't run off."

"I didn't want another one," Ronald mumbles.

"Well, he said he'll play marbles with you when he comes again, but I don't know when that'll be. It was a business visit."

The marble burns in Ronald's hand. He goes outside.

His mother's voice carries after him. "He did have such nice manners. I sat there wishing you had as nice manners as he has. You could take a lesson from him!"

Ronald flings the marble as hard as he can toward the ditch.

A year later someone finds it and gives it to Trever. It becomes the prized possession in Trever's marble bag. Ronald never tells him where it came from.

37 ⊰ THE MANURE TROLLEY

Craig is ten. His friends John Eldred and Ed Grutzner and Jim Hayes bike out to the farm one Saturday to play. They drink chocolate milk from the cooler, they slide down the strawstack, they drink more chocolate milk, they slip around on the corn ears in the corn crib, this time they drink orange. Then they go into the cow barn. It's empty, clean, and in readiness for the afternoon milking. They go into the center part by the mangers and fill all the cows' drinking cups by pressing down the perforated lips.

Craig spots the manure trolley hanging at its doorway ready to be hauled into the barn. He goes and hauls it in.

"You guys want a skyride?" Craig asks.

Jim and John and Ed look up. The trolley is high, close to its track.

"How can we get in it?" Jim asks.

"Follow me and I'll show you," says Craig. By its chain he hauls the trolley full circle around the barn. The boys trot along behind. The start of the track stops the trolley, just half a foot away from the turn at the other end that sends it out of the barn to the finish of the track over the manure pile. Craig pulls a chain and lowers the bucket till it is resting on the walkway.

"Get in," he instructs.

Ed is doubtful. "Is it safe?"

"Sure," says Craig. "I've done it lots of times. It's fun."

"It's dirty," says John.

Craig is scornful. "You call a little manure dirty? It's all dry. Do you want a skyride or not?"

The boys climb in. They sit in a row on the curving bottom of the manure bucket, Ed first, then John, then Jim. There's just room for three boys with their knees under their chins. Craig pulls on the chains. The pulley system makes it possible for him to lift the bucket. It starts going up.

"Hey!" says Ed, peering over the edge. The bucket rocks. John and Jim lean the other way. The bucket dips that way.

Harlan Whitmore and Bennie Harder admire the view over the manure spreader and trolley.

"Don't rock the boat!" Craig cries. "Just sit still and you'll be all right. Hang onto the sides. Pretend you're manure!" He goes on hoisting.

The boys sit still and hang onto the sides. They look dubious. Craig pulls them as high as they can go without hitting their heads on the track.

"This is sort of high," says Ed.

"Naw," scoffs Craig. "Only just don't wiggle. Ready?"

"Ready!" chorus John, Jim and Ed.

Craig begins to push the trolley. It creaks into motion. It begins to move slowly around the barn.

"Hey, this is fun," says Jim.

"Didn't I tell you?" says Craig. He pushes harder. The trolley picks up speed.

"Hey!" cries Ed in alarm. "Slow down!"

"It's all right," says Craig, pushing. "It's more fun, faster."

The boys hang on tight, scrunching their heads into their necks as the trolley careens around the barn. They don't rock the boat. Craig gives the trolley a final push. It rushes to the end of the barn-part of the track and makes a sudden right turn. It banks sideways, taking the turn like one of the airplanes-on-a-chain in the airplane ride at the county fair.

The three boys screech.

The trolley zips straight out of the barn and into the barnyard. The boys are terrified. They can't see where the track ends; they're afraid the trolley will speed right off the end of the track and crash them to the ground.

Ed grabs a lever at the end of the bucket. The bucket promptly turns over and spills them onto the manure pile. It hangs above them, empty and upside down and rocking gently.

Craig whoops with laughter.

John and Jim and Ed crawl off the manure pile like maggots off a fish head. They are dung from top to toe. They are not amused.

"You can wash in the cowtank," says Craig.

Another view of the manure trolley and the wagon, this one horse-drawn, that receives the trolley's valuable cargo.

"I'm going home," says John.

"Me too," say Jim and Ed.

"You can have some more chocolate milk," Craig offers hopefully.

His friends climb on their bikes and start back down Colley Road. Craig watches them as far as Marstons.

"Well, anyway," he says, "they can't deny it was a great ride till Ed pulled the lever."

38 ✻ BILLY BEADLE

Jackie is just thirteen. She's in love with Billy Beadle. She's never been in love before and she doesn't expect her love to be requited, for Billy is nine-teen and going to the Ag School at the University of Wisconsin. She is content to follow him around the barn, where he's working for the summer.

There is nothing about Billy that is not beautiful. She admires his jaunty whistling, his joshing back and forth with the other barnhands. She admires the way he slaps the cows around, not hurting them but making them step to. She admires the even rhythm he keeps up as he jabs the manure brush along the watery gutter, and the rhythmic ripple of his shoulder and back muscles under his white T-shirt. She admires the easy grace of his jeans clinging low on his hips, and the worn leather belt that holds them there. She admires his big rubber boots. She marvels at his strength when he pitches great waffles of hay into the chute, or, down by the crick, slings the milk cans of slops for the pigs up and over the fence as effortlessly as if he were pouring out a half-pint of chocolate milk. She loves to hear him sing the theme song of the band he stays up so late every night to listen to on the radio:

> Welcome all you listeners
> And here I am once more;
> It's quarter-past-eleven time
> And I'm knockin' on your door.

She knows every delineation of his profile. His hair cut is perfection.

Billy is kind to Jackie. Sometimes he says something directly to her and she glows all over. Sometimes he asks her to run an errand, for a pitchfork or a missing tit cup, and her feet are winged. Sometimes he teases her and she is filled with joy. He names the littlest and homeliest cow in the barn, the one with bob ears and bob tail from frostbite, "Jackie-cow," and Jackie is honored. She gives Jackie-cow an extra scoop of grain when she's allowed to go around with the grain trolley and feed the cows their ration.

Jackie follows Billy on his work around the farm like a devoted puppy dog. The other farmhands kid Billy about his shadow. Billy laughs and says, "She's learning! Some day she'll grow up and marry a hayseed like me, and then she'll be able to run the barn single-handed!"

Billy's father, Leonard, is Grampa's farm manager and the best Duroc man in the county, if not the state. When he came to the farm from teaching Ag at Beloit High he brought his Duroc expertise, and the farm went whole-hog into raising Durocs for breeding stock. Billy is a good Duroc man, too, and teaches Jackie a lot about pigs when she rides along with him in the farm truck as it clanks over the ruts in the lane down to the back pasture. She laughs when he flips a pig out of the trough where it's gobbling milk up to its ears, keeping other squealing pigs from getting their share. There is always at least one pig that scrambles right into the trough at feeding time.

But Billy is more interested in sheep than hogs. There weren't any sheep on the farm until Billy came along. Now there is one. He keeps his prize sheep, the one he's grooming for the state fair, in the orchard across the road. This way he can give her special care each day.

Jackie loves to go with Billy to tend his sheep. He plays with the little

Jackie, twelve, watering the Chez Nous garden.

animal, tussles a bit. The sheep trots along behind Billy when he goes to pick up windfall, just like Jackie does. Jackie loves the feel of the soft fleece, loves to bed her fingers in it, to test its depth. She loves the creamy whiteness under the grimy surface of the wool.

One day Billy has to go away for a week. "Will you take care of my sheep while I'm gone?" he asks Jackie. There is nothing she would rather do. Every day, after corn detasseling, she brings the sheep her rations and fresh water. She pulls grass and lets her nibble from her hand. She loves the soft breath on her fingers. Jackie has had goats, but there is a gentle nature to this sheep missing in her willful, sassy goats. She names the sheep Demi, after Demi in *Little Men*. She prints "DEMI" on the sheep's back in neat letters by every day embedding her fingers in the wool and then parting it, so that the separated wool gets used to staying separated and spells out the letters. She doesn't miss Billy as painfully as she thought she would; tending the sheep for him fills in the hollow.

Billy returns and thanks her. She prickles all over. He likes the name Demi better than the real one on the pedigree papers, and says he'll keep it for her nickname, but that he'll have to erase it from her back before the judging. That's okay with Jackie. He cleans Demi snowy white and takes her to the state fair. She wins a blue ribbon. Then he sells her. Jackie cannot see how he can do it.

Leonard William Beadle Jr.

"That's the way it is with livestock," says Billy. "You can't let yourself get too attached."

Inside, Jackie knows she will always let herself get too attached.

Fall comes; Jackie goes back to school, Billy goes back to college. On December 7 bombs fall on Pearl Harbor. Billy enlists in the Army Air Corps. When he wins his wings, his picture is in the *Beloit Daily News*. Jackie cuts it out and puts it in her wallet, where it's not visible to her friends. She is now in love with the boy who sits across from her in English class, the one who held her hand in the darkened bus on the church choir trip, but her first love will always be in an enshrined place in her heart, and now in her wallet.

At the back of the First Methodist Church is an honor roll. There's a long list of names on it. Each serviceman has a green star before his name. When Jackie reads the names she can picture many of the faces, from seeing them growing up in the church, always as big boys much older than herself. Billy's name is there, with its green star. Every Sunday she stops and reads it.

The war goes on. Billy goes to England and is co-pilot on a B-17 bomber plane flying over Germany. One day Grampa comes into the kitchen at Chez Nous. Jackie is modeling a puppet head out of glue and sawdust. Grampa's face is heavy. He sits down slowly, says to Mother, "The Beadles just got word. Billy's plane is missing. It was on its seventeenth mission. It never returned to its base." He shakes and shakes his head.

Jackie's heart stands still.

There is a chance that the plane's crew parachuted down over Occupied Europe. There is a chance that Billy is a POW. On the church honor roll, every so often a gold star replaces a green one, and from the pulpit the minister talks about the young hero. Billy is missing in action. His star stays green.

The war years go by. The tide turns toward the Allies. They push across Europe. The POW camps are opened, one by one. Billy does not come home. Finally the war is over. Billy and his crew members are not found; there is no record of the plane. The government notifies the Beadles that it went down in the North Sea. But, maybe, something else happened, and the crew will still turn up.

Time goes on, and something else does happen. Word comes that during the war Billy's body was washed up on a beach in Belgium, and a minister gave it burial in his churchyard. He writes the government. Billy's body is transferred to the Luxembourg American Cemetery, and the date of his death given as 12–16–44.

Jackie now knows Billy will never come home. Everyone must know it. She waits for somebody to change Billy's star to gold on the honor roll. Nobody does. The minister does not ever talk about Billy from the pulpit.

More time goes on. Jackie is grown up and has moved away. The war's been over many years. She's much older now than Billy was when she loved him, she's much older than he was when he died. The old First Methodist Church has been torn down and a modern one built in its place. On a visit home, Jackie stops in one day to look over the new church.

"What ever happened to the old World War II honor roll?" she asks a secretary she's never met. The secretary doesn't know. The new minister doesn't know. Finally, the new custodian remembers seeing it in a storeroom. He offers to find it for her.

"No," says Jackie, "just unlock the door." She goes and buys a box of small gold stars, the kind her piano teacher used to put on a piece when it was finished. She returns to the church and finds the storeroom. She pokes around. The honor roll is tilted in a corner. Its glass is dusty. She wipes it clean with her hand, and unhooks the lid. She licks a gold star and presses it over the faded green one in front of the name of Leonard William Beadle. She closes the case again and stands for a minute, remembering that thirteenth summer, and Demi-sheep in the orchard, and Jackie-cow in the round barn.

"There, Billy," she says, and leaves the storeroom.

39 ✕ ST. IVES

As I was going to St. Ives
I met a man with seven wives.
Every wife had seven sacks,
Every sack had seven cats,
Every cat had seven kits.
Kits, cats, sacks, wives—
How many were going to St. Ives?

There has been a distemper epidemic among the barn cats. There aren't any left. Mice are overrunning the round barn.

Daddy sees a farm auction advertised in the newspaper. Down in the kitchen he says to Mother, "I think I'll run over to that auction at Spring Green. There's a disk listed, and we need another."

Jackie overhears. She pricks up her ears in case Daddy adds, "I think I'll take Jackie." He doesn't. She jumps into her blue jeans anyway, instead of her school clothes, and goes down to breakfast.

"Oh, fine," says Daddy when he sees her. Daddy's always glad to have Jackie skip school; he enjoys her company. Jackie is always glad to skip school when there's something more interesting going on. "School is all right," is Daddy's philosophy, "but you have to keep it in its proper perspective." Daddy's perspective, when he taught school when he was seventeen in the District 12 schoolhouse that now stands beside the corncrib but then was down beyond the East Twenty, was to skate on the crick with the kids for hours, and then they'd all stay at school till five to get their work done. He also read them the continued story in *The Saturday Evening Post* every week. When Jackie brings home her report card and there's a minus after an A, Daddy squints and says, "What's that flyspeck doing there?"

The farm auction turns out to be not much. The auctioneer doesn't chant as well as Henry Wieland at Grampa's pig auctions. There's only a small cluster of people. Daddy looks over the disk before it comes up for bidding and decides not to bid on it. It's in poor shape. He wanders around to see if there's anything he wants.

Jackie sits on the wooden gate to the barnyard and watches the proceedings. She feels sorry for the farm wife—her husband was pinned under his tractor and killed, when it slid into a ditch a few months ago. The wife doesn't want to carry on the work alone. Jackie looks up the barn ramp and sees kittens playing in the sun. She climbs off the gate and wanders up. Even though they're barn cats, they aren't scaredy. They let her pet them. A large cat rubs against her leg and purrs. Two other cats sit on a beam, washing.

Daddy comes to fetch her. He sees all the cats. He goes back down to the auction. When the auctioneer pauses between sales and takes a gulp of water, Daddy stands at his elbow and says, "What'll you take for the barn cats?"

"Cats?" says the auctioneer in surprise. He wipes his mouth, turns to the crowd. "Folks, our next item is cats. Long, lean, sharp-eyed, sharp-clawed barn cats. Good mousers! Who'll start the bidding?"

"Fifty cents," says Daddy.

"Fifty, fifty, fifty, who'll make it a dollar?"

The farmers laugh, but nobody ups the bid.

"Seventy five, seventy five—what? Nobody wants any cats? Then sold, for fifty cents, to this gentleman. Fifty cents a cat."

"No, no," says Daddy. "Fifty cents the lot."

"The lot?" The auctioneer puts on a stern face. "You mean to tell me you're offering only fifty cents for all the fine cats and adorable kittens that you can catch?"

"The lot," repeats Daddy. "And a gunny sack."

"You drive a hard bargain, sir!" says the auctioneer, and the crowd guffaws.

Daddy gives the auctioneer a half dollar. He checks with the farm wife. She says he could have had them for nothing, she's been worried what to do with them when she goes to live with her daughter. Her daughter has a cat. She's just glad they're going to a good home. She says there were eleven cats the last time she counted, and not to miss the other kittens, behind the chute in the haymow.

Daddy and Jackie spend quite a while catching cats. Jackie climbs up and finds the kittens; they're old enough to travel. She guards the sack when it starts getting full, so that no cat will pop out when Daddy pops one in. They decide to use two gunny sacks.

The people see them carrying the sacks to the car, and laugh some more. The cats aren't happy in the sacks.

They drive toward home. The sacks in the back seat roil and complain.

They complain in grownup yowls and baby mews. Jackie talks soothingly to the sacks, that it won't be a very long trip, but the sacks aren't soothed.

At the dairy they each carry an active sack up the incline to the round barn. Jackie is careful to hold hers well away from her, on account of sudden claws through the burlap. It takes two hands.

Grampa is in the upper barn. He sees them coming and stops what he's doing. He makes his eyes wide with astonishment. He can't hear the cats. Daddy sets the heaving sacks down in front of him and undoes the twine. Eleven cats of all sizes streak out in every direction.

Grampa's eyes open even wider, and he laughs silently. Then he says, "Ronald, where have you been?"

Daddy spells it on his hand and says it out loud at the same time.

"To Saint Ives."

40 ⨯ RUSSEL ULLIUS

Russel Ullius has gone on to be manager of a large dairy up north. On a corn delivery trip, Ron stops by to see Russ's operation. Russ, a raconteur like Ron, takes the opportunity to talk about his years on the Dougan farm.

When I was in high school in Janesville, our Ag class visited the Dougan farm. That was the first time I'd ever seen you, Ron, you'd just returned from France, that'd be 1924, '25. Daddy Dougan talked to us about the aims of the farm. It was the first time I saw the writing on the silo, too. Those words have stayed in my life forever — they've meant so much to me!

I came to the farm in 1937; I stood on the red rug and Daddy wrote my name there in the ledger. I lived at the Big House. We'd play ball after supper, all the men, all the Dougan kids. I called Joan "Punky," she called me "Punkier." She was a good pitcher, and could she ever play the violin!

John Baker was herdsman. He was a conscientious man, but awfully rigid. He could argue any subject with anybody. I heard you say more than once that you wished you were as sure of one thing as John Baker was of everything, and that was my sentiment, too. For instance, we had four Surge milking machines in the barn and they were numbered 1, 2, 3, 4, and had matching numbers scratched on their lids, but all the parts were interchangeable. John had the theory that the machines had to match in order to work right, and also that the cows had to be milked in order, the first cow with machine number one, and so on, and that they should all be milked a set number of minutes, and then the machines moved to the next four cows. This meant some cows were being milked overlong, while others still had milk to give. Well, we'd start off his way but we'd take a machine off when a cow was finished, and put it on whatever cow was next in line, so that pretty quick the machines would be all mixed up. We didn't pay any attention to matching lids, either. Then John would come along and notice they were out of order, and stop everything and get them all matched and lined up again, bawling us out the whole time.

And if we ever spilled any manure, getting it to the manure spreader, he'd make us get a broom. He came into the barn one Saturday with guests of his—he was Seventh Day Adventist, so he always had Saturday off—and he was in a nice blue suit and white shirt. Henry Duerst was filling in. He had put a machine on a cow slightly tilted. John reached in to straighten the machine, and the cow kicked it into a hundred pieces, and knocked John into the gutter. He looked like a tractor had hit him! We told him his cow friends hadn't recognized him in his good clothes. He

Russel Ullius.

didn't think it was funny, but then he never thought anything was funny.

John and his family lived in the apartment over the milkhouse. Seventh Day Adventists don't eat meat—but those little kids of his, Carol and Clure, were always begging for it. Your kids told me they used to sneak bacon to them in the school cab, mornings they had bacon at the Little House.

John went down for the cows once; it was getting toward dawn, and the men—well, Red Richardson and me—had taken a great stuffed bear and put it on a post half way down the lane to the pasture. It looked realler than a teddy bear. John saw it there, its silhouette; he just knew it was some great dangerous animal and refused to go past it. He came back to the barn and made me go. I laughed all the way.

Another time when he refused to go, it had rained hard all night, a terrific lot of rain, and there was so much water in the crick that he couldn't get past it to get the cows. So I saddled up the horse. It was just getting light. I looked at that crick, it must have been sixty feet wide instead of six, and said, "I can make that." I waded the horse in and it got deeper and deeper, it was all he could do to keep his footing, and the water came in the saddle behind me. But we kept going. When we got across I looked back and realized we were lucky to have made it. I rounded the cows up—by now it was light—and when they got to the water they hesitated, then all of a sudden they surged in and started to swim. The force of the current threw some of them against the fence that runs down to the crick, but they all came through. They didn't know what they were getting into or they never would have started. But by then I knew! I left the horse in the pasture and walked all the way to Mackies and came over the bridge. When we tried to drive the cows back, after milking, they wouldn't go across. They refused until about the middle of the next day. So John and the cows were smarter than I was, that time. I could have drowned—I suppose I'd've washed up somewhere downtown in Rock River.

Cows have personality. I was herdsman when we left the cow down at the Catholic church for that bazaar for several days. When we closed up at night and turned the lights off, boy, would she talk to us. And when we got there in the morning, would she ever talk! She was so glad to see us. I think she missed us and the other cows and all the activity around the barn.

Henry Duerst had a funny accident in the upper barn. He was helping put hay silage in the silo—we did that for a few years, cut it green in the field, and it was so heavy we could only fill a wagon two thirds of what we usually would. It would go up the rick on the back—the hay loader—and the man on the wagon who distributed it had an awful job. Then it'd be chopped up in the silo-filler alongside the silo and blown up and in, but molasses had to go with it, for the fermenting—it wasn't naturally sweet enough to ferment by itself, you know. The steel molasses barrel was propped up high against the silo and there was a gravity feed, through a hose, that let in just the right amount. The next barrel to be used was waiting by the big barn doors in the sun, and it got so hot it blew its cap right off, and all the molasses shot out like Old Faithful. Henry got the full blast, over his head, down his neck—we had to peel his clothes off him. It's a good thing Daddy Dougan couldn't hear him swear! But most of the words were in German.

Another time, when we were putting in corn silage, Earl Brunke was driving a team. He'd bring the horses up onto the barn floor, and then want to back them down while he stayed driving. He thought he was a great driver. I was farm manager then; I told him to get off and hold their heads to back them down—those wagons are heavy and you need to talk to your team. He went ahead doing it his way and the wagon came out too fast and went over the edge of the ramp. It pulled one horse with it; she was upside down over the ledge, all twisted up. We talked to her—she didn't struggle too much—and when we got her harness unfastened she fell the rest of the way, not very far, down onto the walkway to the lower barn. She landed on her side upside down. Not really hurt. That was another time I was sure glad Daddy Dougan wasn't anywhere around! He'd have got awfully upset. That Brunke. He was a great fellow for someone else to get the job done.

Another accident. We were haying once up at your place, Ron—loose hay, we weren't baling yet—and Rodney Jennings was bringing a load down to the main farm. He had the new wagon Ed Pfaff made from an old truck chassis, with rubber tires, two horses pulling it, two of us riding on top. That wagon rolled so easy the horses must have thought they were in heaven till they got to that first grade, down to the curve. The whole weight of the load started pushing them; there wasn't enough friction, and they had to run faster and faster. They made that curve, and then it was level to the next one, but after that was the longer grade down to the drive into the dairy. They got galloping so fast, with that load forcing them, and made the turn so quick that the wagon tipped and dumped the hay into the ditch and buried the two of us. It was some wild ride! I think Ed had to figure out brakes for that wagon.

There's a technique to loading loose hay. You learned it as a kid, Ron, so did I—you loaded with me once when we were short handed—you cut the grass with the mower, all those scissor blades you don't want any cat to get caught in, and the grass keels over and lies flat a while to dry. Then you come with the side delivery—Mr. Griffiths always drove that—one horse and the little light side delivery that scoops up the hay and rolls it over and leaves it in a long neat windrow. Then when it's dry enough, you come with the horses and hay wagon and the hay rick behind, and you straddle a windrow and the hay loader rotates and picks it up and carries it up that broad ramp and it falls down onto the wagon in a continuous stream.

That's where the technique comes in. You don't just flop it in any old way, building up a load, or you'll rip your insides out trying to take it off again. You've got to overlap—lay out a section with your pitchfork, then take a new bunch, and overlap, like pancakes, like shingles, all the way around, and then start the next layer. I always liked to load with Jess Turman, he was Scotty Cook's brother, a magnificent black man, worked at Fairbanks—he came out in the summer time, and he knew how to do it. I didn't trust our regular men to put it in so we could get it out. Jess was 260, 270 pounds, and when we tramped it, it was tramped. You tramp it as you load.

Ron, you told me once about when you were fourteen, you were coming home from high school. They were getting in the first haying, alfalfa in that field west of the house, and you were still a little shrimp, maybe a 110 pounds—you didn't get his growth till later, when was it, college?—but you wanted to prove you were a man. You'd just got over the measles, too. You climbed out of the car and up on the wagon and said, "Let me take care of that hay!" So they handed you a pitchfork and had you stand at the back of the loader and grab the hay as it came down. You told me, "I wasn't going to give up, but I damn near killed myself! I think they speeded up the horses for me!" Though if it's a big windrow, and they let the loader run right along, it's all a full-grown man can do to really load that hay. It's a day's work with dry hay.

With bales, at first we pitched the bales up onto the wagon bed and loaded them like blocks, but later Erv made those balers that would kick a bale right out the end, and arc it up, and the wagon—a different sort of wagon with high sides and a catcher's net—would catch them. No jockeying them into order—they were just a big pile, like you'd knocked the blocks down. That was easy street. We still had to pile 'em at the barn, though.

I was in charge of haying at the Hill Farm once, after we were baling all our hay. We were loading on flatbed wagons. We knew a storm was brewing but the hay was just as dry as it could be, so we kept right on into the night, and then we could see it far off, all across the west, the lightning on the horizon, and hear the rumbles. I'd sent five loads down to the round barn, but all the men there had gone to bed so there wasn't any more unloading, so I'd ordered the milk trucks out of the garage and we were putting the loads in there. I finished the field ahead of the storm, about eleven-thirty, and I was racing it, driving the tractor as fast as I could go, bringing in the baler and the final load. Just as I was pulling into the yard the storm hit with such strength that it blew the shingles off the corncrib; they were spinning past me, and branches and everything. The sort of storm that should have scared us to death, should have set all the sirens blowing. We ran that load up onto the barn floor, so it got covered, too. I was awful glad I didn't meet anybody on the road!

Trever was living in Chicago; he sent a city kid to the farm. He knew the kid's parents. The kid passed out from heat in the haymow at your place, Ron. I had to get him to the chute and down the ladder. He was okay in a little while. But he telephoned his mother and she drove up and got him. You were disgusted. The kid shouldn't have called home. He was just getting broken in. He didn't give himself any chance to shape up.

Funny, how city people seem to think there's not much to farm work, how anybody can do it. I was with Daddy Dougan once, and we were bringing a heifer down from the Hill Farm, down to the round barn. We got her to the main farm and opened up the truck and she came out just a flyin'. We snubbed her up against a wheel, and we were both just about on the ground with her, struggling, and she had her tongue out and eyes rolling, and kicking—was she ever kicking!—and Grampa gasps, "I sure would like to have some of those city fellers out here right now!"

He couldn't hear me, of course, but he knew I was sure agreeing with him! I just shouted out, "Amen! Amen!" and we finally got her into the barn.

41 ⋇ HERD BOOKS

Grampa has always kept records. Among his papers can be found a small book of his frugal college spending, down to streetcar fares. And there are record books from the various pastorates he served during the ten years he was a minister. These latter are leatherbound, slim, and vest-pocket sized. They are not diaries, although one from McFarland, his first charge, has a poignant page near the end on his thoughts about losing his hearing. Four booklets, a set from his last charge, Poynette, are typical.

One is an alphabetized address book of parishioners' names. The initial list is not in Grampa's handwriting so he may have inherited it from his predecessor; more likely Grama carefully wrote in all the names and added her comments: "Mrs. Finury—*queer old soul*—indifferent" but names are added in Grampa's hand, with sometimes the person's state: "does not attend because of clothing," or state of grace: "good citizen," "consented to my private prayer." Two books are *The Systematic Church Record and Ritual for Pastors*, Volumes 1 and 2, and contain the titles, dates, and Biblical texts of the sermons Grampa preached both at Poynette and the other, smaller church nearby at Inch: "Three Unchanging Laws," "The Brother Who Stayed Home," "Learning to Look on the Bright Side," "The Bible in Our Daily Lives," also baptisms, marriages ($5.00 fee), funerals—quite a few infant ones, the numbers and dates of pastoral calls, and the weekly income from pledges and collection plate. The final book is a pocket diary almost empty; its inside cover calls it "Record and Notes of Anti-license Campaign and Civic Federation Work, Poynette, 1905" and merely lists contributors' names, and funds turned over to the Women's Christian Temperance Union. Apparently Poynette was trying to become, or stay, a dry town.

When Grampa leaves the ministry and comes to the farm, he keeps on keeping records. There is a shelf in the lower round barn, against the silo and in front of the cows, near the entrance door into the silo where it's handy, that contains a few things—a nose leader, a trocar for bloat, a small tin of Petro-

Carbo Salve for just about everything from an abrasion to a sore tit or worse, a pencil stub and small sharpener, and a nine-by-twelve cardboard-covered book, like a thick and sturdy tablet—the *Herd Record Book*. This book is provided by the Wisconsin Breeding Program. Inside, each page is printed on one side only, titled "Weekly Report of Breeding Data," and keeping that record is the principle purpose of this book. Across the top are these divisions:

YEAR	In Heat Not Served		SERVICE					PARTURITION				NOTES
Month	Ex-pect-ed	Ob-serv-ed	COW	BULL	Se-men No.	Hour of Day	Be-havior of Bull	COW		CALF		Cows sick; treatment given; Veterinarian calls; Retained afterbirth; Vaginal discharge. Deaths, Removals, Sales. Changes in Feed or pasture, Testers visits, etc.
									Sex	Birth Wt.	Herd No. Assigned	

Down the left side, under "Year," is "Month" and "Day of the Month." Each page covers a week. Each book, when filled, goes to the dairy office, where its pertinent data are recorded in a slightly smaller book, also called *Herd Record Book*. There is a whole library of these, from the start of records well before 1920, until Ron sells the herd in 1967.

The record book kept in the barn makes for interesting, if gloomy, reading. For what the book does not tell is that almost all the cows in the round barn are living happy, healthy lives, milking well, and calving regularly. What it does tell, in the "Parturition" column, is the birth of calves, the gender, sometimes the state: "sickly," sometimes the disposal: "Vealed," which is reserved for a male calf, or a heifer calf twinned with a bull. Sometimes it is "died." The final column, "Notes," with small printing underneath, "Cows sick; treatment given; Veterinarian calls; Retained afterbirth; Vaginal discharge. Deaths, Removals, Sales. Changes in Feed or Pasture. Testers visits, etc." is the richest though most uncomfortable reading. If the herdsman has been faithful, and gives details, it's here that we learn most about troubled cows.

The barn herd book is faithfully filled in every day by the current herdsman, and regularly and carefully checked, at first by W.J., later by Ronald. And while the "Notes" at the end of each entry often raise questions, there are seldom conclusions. Those—when they are to be found—are elsewhere in the farm records, or discovered by talking to the herdsmen, the vets, to W.J. or Ron. Take the barn herd book of 1952. It tells many tales.

—Jan 5: G1and D23 calf has scours. Give calf cordials.

—Jan. 6: I17 has sore eyes for unknown reason, Knilans sent meds

—Jan. 7: G4 got end of left hind quarter stepped on. [This, unfortunately, often happens—cows lie down, udders are big, and other cows are no respecters of where they put their hooves, on a bird's nest, in the pasture, or on another cow's udder or tit in the barnyard.]

—Jan. 9: D16 lame right hind leg due to heat period

—Jan. 11: C10 mastitis in front left quarter

—Jan. 22: Shipped E41—stepped on two quarters and couldn't milk

—Jan. 24: I29 acted like in heat. Too soon to breed so only observed. May be false.

—Feb. 12: D29 a heifer calf, F11 a bull. [Here Ron writes in the margin, "Both had what seem to be weak calves. F11 didn't clean." That is, her afterbirth did not come out. "Put three cleaning tablets in her."]

—Feb. 13: Vet opens teat on F11, cleans her, vaccinates five calves.

—Feb. 15: D3, a heifer calf, D29 mastitis in both hind quarters, is treated with Sulvetil.

—Feb. 20: F11's calf dies, was a weakling, didn't feed very good. [Here Ron writes to the herdsman, "I appreciate the way you worked on him."]

To summarize the rest of the year: In April, C33's left front quarter is stepped on. C46 has pneumonia, and the herdsman writes in detail the medicines administered to her. D25 has a bull calf, C34 twins—one bull, one heifer. In a few days both D25's and C34's calves are shipped. Bull calves are regularly shipped, except for an occasional one butchered on the farm, and mixed sex twins also, for the heifer twin, known as a freemartin, is almost always sterile.

Throughout the 1952 herd book there are a dismaying number of calf deaths, often scours or pneumonia, but a number of mysterious deaths "posted"—postmortemed—and the vet, or the university, can't detect what has caused the demise. Mastitis occurs regularly in one or more quarters of a cow, and is treated. Pneumonia is frequent for both cows and calves, and too many cows have tits, or a whole quarter, stepped on. There is a spate of foot rot, which takes several visits from the vet to eradicate in each afflicted cow. A cow dies of bloat, the vet arriving too late. A lame cow has a staple removed from her hoof. The vet clips the horns of 21 head.

A heifer calf is born with "lump jaw," a congenital deformity, and shipped, along with several bull calves. An occasional cow is down with milk fever but recovers quickly when treated in time. Another vomits frequently but the vet says there's nothing he can do, she'll gradually get over it. One cow, during birth, casts her withers—expels the uterus—and the vet is called. A calf is born twisted, backward, and upside down, but lives. Another, born the same way, dies. A cow is shipped because she has swallowed "hardware;" another has a blood transfusion. Several cows have bloody, or off-color milk, for various reasons, and are milked separately and treated. E-32 slung her calf, which probably means aborted. A bizarre entry, January 9, 1953, shows a busy time for the vet, who seems to come at least once a week, during some periods as often as once a day: "Had Knilans for F30 acted sick but appears fair when he got here he said may be slight case of acidominia. Also checked F11 for pregnancy, stays open and has large hard ovaries. Cut end of teat off C33 (right hind) took spider out of I15 left hind also checked G30 to stop her bulling says she should be bred in next appearing heat." Ten days later, the unfortunate F11, who has continued ailing, is shipped.

When we turn to the many office record books, they are different from the barn book. These are the ones issued by the United States Department of Agriculture, called, "Record of Dairy Herd," but subheaded, from about 1928 on, "Dairy Herd-Improvement Association." On the back of the later books—take 1938—is printed, "This herd record book is printed by the United States Department of Agriculture in furtherance of the Acts of Congress, May 8 and June 30, 1914. It is distributed free of charge by the Bureau of Dairy Industry, through State agricultural colleges, to cooperating dairymen, with the understanding that in return for the book the herd data collected during the year are to be reported to the Bureau of Dairy Industry, on Form

Jim Howard and I-9's daughter. He wrote on the back of the photo, "This picture taken for identification and records (the calf, not me)."

B.D.I.46, for study and analysis."

The earliest books give no directions to the cow tester, but once the "Dairy Herd-Improvement Association" joins forces with the USDA, each inside cover explains that the first records are made while this book is in the barn. On a day tested—once a month is the required spacing—the weight of each cow's night and morning milk must be recorded on her own page, their sum, and that multiplied by the number of days in that testing period. It says that the other columns on the page are self-explanatory

A registration page for The American Dairy Cattle Club. When lacking a photo, Ron would draw the cow's markings. (The registrations, of course, show only one side of the animal—perhaps enough.)

(Yield During Testing Period, Feed Consumed During Testing Period, which includes succulent [silage] and dry roughage [hay, stover, etc.], concentrates, Days on Pasture and Cost of Pasture, and then the various items with the costs and totals more specified, until finally, "Remarks"). This "Remarks" column is for giving dates as to when the cow was dry, freshened, bred, sold, died, sickness, and anything else.

There are directions for continuing to record the cow's milk weights, until at year's end there is a total for each cow, which is copied onto her individual record blank.

Also there are directions for the "Monthly Association Summary;" this for the USDA's Herd-Improvement Association. It gives the record of each herd in the Association for one month. It's recommended that the totals and averages for each herd be given, totals in black ink, averages in red. In most of the books up in the office the rows of figures are tidily kept this way.

Each page of the book, for an individual cow, also has a handsome line drawing of a cow, left and right side, presumably for identification. These are not colored in, for the farm has other ways of recording the looks of particular cows, and their pictures, drawn or photographed, are kept in other record books.

At the end of the book are several interesting pages: pedigree charts to be filled in for four different bulls, service record of herd sire (in the 1920 book), a gestation table for cows, yearly herd summary, yearly cost of feed, and finally, "Yearly Individual Cow Report Blank," three pages long, where all the data are gathered together. For these records to be serviceable, the tester is warned to fill in all pages very carefully, make the figures legible, and great care taken to avoid blots.

Later editions of the book have a section also for the herd owner, stressing the importance of cow testing and keeping accurate records. The first purpose of the testing, he is told, is to determine low producing cows and cull them out of the herd. The cows remaining should be fed according to their individual production so as to obtain the greatest return for the feed consumed. The ultimate purpose of the records is to enable the dairyman to improve his herd by intelligent breeding. Before 1938 the USDA was already advocating the use of proved sires along with daughter-dam comparisons, and ends the advice, "The herd owner should insist that the tester send in the necessary records from the herd to prove the herd sire."

Each individual book is not particularly interesting unless one is really into studying the red and black accumulation of figures and totals, and yet, overall, they tell a bigger story. There is seldom a remark in the "Remarks" column. The books are largely placid. But every now and then there is a horrendous year. 1941 is dreadful for Bang's disease. Cow after cow is shipped; the count is 32. 1940 sees the beginning of the Bang's epidemic, and a number of cows have garget, sore feet, udder trouble, injured quarters, indigestion, sterility. In 1938 too many calves die, a lot of cows are sold for beef; one for soap. 1937 is a bad year for garget and other deaths — poor S11 dies of heat, and S48 of a nail in her stomach. Others, both calves and cows, of scours. There are several lump jaws.

The vet comes, and comes, and comes again. Throughout these books, Ron's terse comments run like a Greek refrain — lamenting, lamenting.

One could, with patience, follow a single cow through her conception, her life in the herd, her breeding, her calves, her ailments, and her final demise or disposal. This of course isn't necessary, though, for each cow has her own page in a big ledger, complete with picture. Her full history is all gathered together, with more information besides, including her milking record. It is these records that allow Ron to begin work with proven sires, and make possible the most continuing and rewarding work of his professional life.

There are many more kinds of record books kept on the farm, each type meriting a story — some fascinating, some routine, even dull, except as you understand the subject of the records well enough to become engaged. All the customer accounts, all the producer-farmer accounts, the financial accounts, the records with various firms the farm does business with. Some of the records are in huge ledgers almost too heavy to lift, and bound with steel pins that can be removed to lift the thick covers and insert more pages. Perhaps one more recording merits mention: the three labor record books, from the start of the farm till it ceased hiring. These list the month by month names, salaries, and sometimes special data about each person who is employed by the farm. The information is not as detailed as if that person were a cow or bull, but in much the same way one can trace the history of a single worker through the days, months, and even years of his or her employ, though the itinerant workers, the scores of detasselers, are sometimes mentioned only by numbers. The customer working off a milk bill is given careful consideration. The worker who doesn't work out may get a notation. And if, from some other source, you know a story about some worker, usually not favorable (for often those are the stories that last), it's possible to look up the final day of employment, and nod and know that it was a firing.

All these records, taken together, and with the cattle herd books at the center, suggest something to Jackie. The suggestion is in the title of the books: herds imply shepherds. Shepherds "look out for." "Tend my sheep." One can look at Grampa's ministry record books of people; the barn and myriad office record books of people and animals; down to the labor books — again of people, as herd books. And that makes Grampa first, with Daddy after his father, shepherds. In her thought, shepherding in both its narrowest sense, and widest, is an honorable calling. She's glad she comes from a shepherding tradition.

42 ⁂ FAT MATTERS

I n 1923 W.J. receives a letter from H.W. Griswold, Secretary of the Wisconsin-Illinois Guernsey Breeders' Association. Grampa's fame is spreading, as an author of authority for *Hoard's Dairyman*, as a respected and entertaining speaker at important dairy events. This letter is asking him to speak at the Guernsey Breeders' annual meeting, Wednesday Afternoon, March 21, at the Park Hotel in Madison.

"We are going to try to impress on the Guernsey Breeders at this meeting the absolute superiority of Guernsey Milk both for Public consumption and Baby Feeding," he writes. "I believe when all the facts are brought to light that a baby can digest and grow on Guernsey milk better than any other. I know that you have had a long experience along this line and I have been instructed to ask you to have something to say along this line from your experience. Mr. Marsh is very enthusiastic about Guernsey milk and has a message for us. We shall be pleased with whatever you can give us."

There is a hand-written postscript: "We want to decorate the tables at the Banquet with milk bottle caps from the different Guernsey Breeders selling milk. Could you send to me about 200 of your bottle caps?"

W.J. answers this letter promptly.

"Yours of the 12th received today.

"I will send the caps as requested. My caps come in bands. I will include a strip of these. I will also send 200 cut discs.

"Your idea of the program is a good one.

"I have an idea that may not take well with the breeders. I have found that a milk not to exceed 4.5 percent of fat and not less that 4 percent or 4.2 percent is most satisfactory to my trade and the most economical to produce. I have good grade cows that give 10,000 to 12,000 lbs. of 4.2 to 4.5 percent milk.

"Would it be all right to present this idea of fixing, by our selection and breeding, a standard of production for the Guernsey cow that would insure the right per cent of fat for direct consumption and especially baby feeding. I fear that our tendency now in breeding is leading to an excessive percentage of fat."

The response to this letter is hasty, and is to "Dear Sir" rather than "Dear Mr. Dougan."

"Your letter received and I am afraid anything you say in regard to a too high a percent of fat would be grabbed on by the Holstein people and used against us. My experience is that milk from a cow that is fresh or nearly so is much easier digested especially for a baby than the milk from a stripper cow. If only the milk from fresh milk cows is used for the trade and the stripper milk separated for cream the fat percentage would not be high and the returns from the herd more. I would rather you would leave the percent of fat matter out. My idea was to get you to tell of cases where other milk was used and the child did not do too well and the change in the child when your milk was used. Something along this line was what I had in mind."

There is no record of W.J.'s accepting this invitation to speak, when he is being instructed what to say. Chances are he turned them down, though he may have gone to the meeting, and admired the bottle caps from all the Guernsey dairies. This exchange illustrates, however, the rivalry between purebred groups and implies the general contempt for grade cattle.

There is another exchange of letters with Guernsey breeders in 1926. The American Guernsey Cattle Club, headquarters in Peterboro, New Hampshire, writes W.J. as "Mr. Dorigan," and "Dear Sir." The letter is from C.M. Cummings, who is the head of the "Advanced Register" division, and begins, "Why is there such a small advance in the number of cows under Advanced Register test?"

He writes the letter because his division is not keeping pace with other activities of the Guernsey breed, which he lists: "Increase in the number of registrations and transfers of Guernsey cattle has been most encouraging. Growth, too, in the number of cows tested in cow testing associations has been steady. Studies of the annual Guernsey sales show a marked increase in the sales prices of animals that have pedigrees well balanced by Advanced Register records."

The letter finishes, "This office has you listed as one of the breeders testing at one time, but who has no cows under test at present. Naturally, we wonder if you are no longer interested and, if not, why?"

"Advanced register" is the practice of milking cattle four times a day instead of two, and feeding them enriched rations to support the increased lactation that results. Cows on this regimen (especially pedigreed ones who are registered by the American Guernsey Cattle Club, and regularly tested by them at some expense) boast a value — if they test well — that is elevated above other cows, for breeding and sale purposes.

W.J. has had experience with advanced register cows. When Ronald was seventeen he persuaded his father to buy three purebred Guernseys, from a farmer above Janesville who was dispersing his herd. All three cows had excellent production records; all three cows had originally come from the famed Isle of Guernsey. W.J. paid a premium price for them. But once they joined the Dougan herd, with twice a day milking and feed completely sufficient for their needs but no more, they reverted to the level of mediocre cows. They were no longer on "advanced register."

In responding to this query, W.J. hits the breed industry head on:

> I hesitate somewhat to answer your questions relative to Advanced Register testing. I do not like to be classed as a knocker or a retrograde. For years I have been working in the dairy business and watching the "Purebred Game." I have seen men jump in with all their enthusiasm, pay fancy prices, adopt a plan of elaborate and extensive A.R. testing. Then when we would expect them to be securely established the great herd would be put up for dispersion. I have the suspicion in many of these cases that the parties had to sell out to clear up. And many of us "Suckers" have helped them loyally. Now you are sure I am "yellow." I hope that I am not. Personally, I once had a large program for developing a herd of high (class) quality A.R. Guernseys. I made a modest start, paying from $500.00 to $1,100.00 for a few foundation cows. I became familiar with A.R. records through these cows. They were fair cows, 12,000 pounds of milk and from 595 to 671 butterfat. I also came to realize the financial expense of A.R. work. What it costs to give a cow her record and what one can expect this record to do in selling the progeny.
>
> At a sale I saw a good promising calf sold for $25.00. From the catalogue I figured up the cost that had been put into this calf through A.R. records of his near ancestors. It was several thousand dollars. Then another thing that I have discovered is that one must not carry through an A.R. test unless it promises to be good, for a poor test is worse than none at all. When we ask the question of a pure bred dealer, "Has this cow been tested?" and he excuses that she was dropped for some trivial reason, we know the reason is

poor production so she is below good grade cow price. Another observation I have made is that the A.R. test is not so much the measure of the blood of the cow as it is of the ability of the herdsman. In order to set a high record, the herdsman resorts to every device to increase the yield. FIRST — She is fitted by months of idleness. SECOND — She is fed with no regard for economy. THIRD — She is pampered as no dairyman can pamper a herd of cows. FOURTH — In many cases she is done for [i.e. exhausted], the one idea is to get a world record.

In my experience we only partially did the above things but we got a false record of the cow's ability. My cows have been under regular records since 1911. I have complete data on every cow that has been in my herd since 1914. Part of this time data was secured by my private work. Since 1920 they have been secured through the Cow Testing Association. The continuous records of cows I have had under tests are only a little over five-eighths of the A.R. record. I feel the continuous record is the better index of the cow and therefore the better guide to building of a productive herd and the selecting of breeding stock.

Again the A.R. testing falls down woefully in determining the prepotent bulls, because we get so few daughters of any bull on test. It is only exceptional that a bull has enough daughters tested to determine his value before he is too old. The bulls that are thus fortunate are those in big breeding establishments. The multitude of P.B. bulls out on the average farm never have a chance to show through A.R. testing what their daughters are doing.

I am also under the impression that many of these fortunate bulls with a goodly number of A.R. daughters would not be so highly thought of if all their daughters had been tested and the final criterion applied — i.e., the percent of their daughters that make under good conditions a profit and their production relative to their dams.

The trouble with our A.R. work is, it is a game. The best prospects are chosen. Their best records made under pampering conditions. Their achievements sung for advertising purposes.

I might have given my opinion in a single sentence without all this talk. I believe the A.R. work is falling off because the ordinary breeders find it does not pay. However, I am as positive that to get anywhere in breeding we must have records of production. Also, every individual farmer must have records before him for economical feeding and profitable dairying. Our C.T.A. work is not entirely meeting the requirements, but it is better than the A.R. work in that it is applied to the whole herd — it is inexpensive and therefore can become more nearly universal. It gives a more dependable record from which to judge the production of a family and the prepotency of bulls.

The Milking Shorthorn Association is recognizing C.T.A. records. I think the dairy breed associations should also do this. The C.T.A. work can be modified somewhat to meet the requirements of the Breed Associations. From my experience and observations, when I see an A.R. record on a sale bull, I knock off three-eights of the record and then compare the cow with cows in my own barn with such records. I think I am not an exception in this. In other words, the A.R. records, to an experienced dairyman, do not mean so much as they claim. I believe the time is fast approaching when a buyer will prefer a continuous C.T.A. record of ancestors in choosing a herd sire to the A.R. Pedigree. You are the only person I have spoken thus freely to. I'm not preaching against the A.R. work and trying to discourage it, I have been some time coming to these conclusions.

This letter must have severely rattled—perhaps enraged—C.M. Cummings. This is his livelihood, his life, that is being lambasted as a game and worse. There is, understandably, no thank you from Cummings in W.J.'s files.

It is this letter, and the one before it to the Wisconsin Guernsey Breeders, and perhaps others, plus all the thorough records that W.J. and then Ronald have been keeping on all the Dougan cows, grade and purebred, plus all their observations of their own herd and others, that make Ronald feel a thunderbolt has struck when he discovers Parmalee Prentice's "Mount Hope Index" article in the *Jersey Journal* in 1927. All this sets his path, and the farm's, on the track of proven sires regardless of pedigree, and, before long, all the intense involvement with artificial insemination.

43 ❧ THE MOUNT HOPE INDEX

There are two theories in breeding better cows. One is based on who you are, the other on what you do.

The Who-You-Are theory is this: all your great-great-grandparents came from the same place—the island of Jersey, the island of Guernsey, a valley in Switzerland, a duchy in Germany. For several generations the names of your ancestors, and usually nothing else about them, have been written down. You have a pedigree. Therefore, when you and your pedigreed siblings come along with your pedigreed ancestry, you'll grow up to be first-rate cattle. You have papers; you are registered with the breed associations. Your blood is pure. And, you may very well turn out to be an excellent animal. This is the same way the aristocracy of Europe maintained themselves: they inherited name, title, money, and the claim to blue blood. It's not surprising that the pedigrees of animals evolved in the same way.

But—and this is the What-You-Do school—there's a chance that one or more of you, animals or aristocracy, may inherit a combination of genes that aren't all that desirable. When the chromosomes divide, not every excellent gene gets chosen for the new germ cell. Sometimes the gene is an inferior one. If you're a cow, this could be a low-milk-productivity gene. You could, unfortunately, have inherited two of these. Then no matter who your granddam and grandsire were, you'll give less milk than your mother, or (if you're a bull) you'll pass on a giving-less-milk gene to your sons and daughters. You won't be able to help it; they're all the genes you have. In spite of your pedigree and your good looks, in the milk producing arena you're a bust.

So the What-You-Do theory comes from the opposite direction. It doesn't matter what your pedigree is. You can be wrong side of the tracks, with no papers at all. What matters, in again, say, milk producing (and that's what dairy farmers are interested in), is what you do: how much milk do you give? Are you an improvement on your mother? If you're female, that's not too hard to determine. Keep records, and it soon becomes clear which cows are

Williamstown House of Local History

Ezra Parmalee Prentice, at Mt. Hope Farm.

improved producers. This might be because you're fed better and kept healthier. However, when environment is factored out, the improvement must come from your genes.

But what if you're the father and will never give a drop of milk? (The saying is, "As useless as a bucket under a bull.") How will you know whether you're blessing your progeny with the desirable trait of productivity? For a calf gets only half her genetic makeup from her mother. If her father's daughters, under conditions similar to their mothers, turn out to be consistently better milkers, the theory is that the improvement must be coming from him. This is where "proved sires" come into the picture. As a sire, you prove your worth after the fact. The What-You-Do school is the Proved Sire school. You're tested by your progeny.

Daddy first comes on the proved sire theory in 1927. He reads an article in the *Jersey Journal* that interests him considerably. It's by E. Parmalee Prentice, about his experiments in crossbreeding cattle. His work shows that hereditary characteristics are transmitted without regard to so-called purebred lines, and there can be improvement in crossbred offspring. The important factor is the transmitting ability of the bull, whose value is determined by comparing the production records of his daughters with their mothers.

Taking environmental conditions into account, if the unselected daughters are averaging more than their dams, they must be inheriting that trait from their fathers. If one father has many daughters who are substantially better than their mothers, that is proof that, for increased production purposes, he's a superior bull, be his name Joe Doaks or Gregory Alexander Pettijohn the Third. In fact a Joe Doaks may well surpass a Pettijohn, Prentice maintains. His experiments in crossbreeding, using sires that have shown their worth through their daughters' records, are proving to produce better stock than by sticking to blood lines.

This is an outrageous idea at the time, although Prentice is not alone in investigating all this. It's been talked about in agricultural schools for some time, and the United States Department of Agriculture is even advocating outcrossing widely for superior stock. For several years Grampa has been suggesting this in his talks. In one from 1923:

> We have a saying, that the sire is half of the herd, and he is half, or possibly more, in the interest of increasing production. We know through the figures that have been accumulated through the Department of Agriculture that there are all kinds and descriptions of pure bred sires, relative to their ability to get daughters that are of as high production, or higher production than their dams. We have the saying, that the only test of a cow is what she will do at the pail. No matter where she stands in the show ring, nor how long her pedigree, nor how brilliant her show records are, what she will do at the pail is the test of her value. Just so the test of the value of a sire is, what will he do in getting daughters that are better than their dams.

But Prentice is the first, to Daddy's knowledge, to come out with an index for determining the worth of a bull. He has made it by comparison with cow testing records, and he calls it "The Mount Hope Index." It's an assignment of value that takes the form of a production figure. Since it's devised from the theory that daughters of a bull receive equal value from each parent, the bull's index can be calculated by placing the daughter's average production values halfway between those of the bull and her dam's production average. "The Mount Hope Index" is published in the *Jersey Journal* in full.

Daddy is greatly excited. The first cow testing records that Grampa has are for 1915. Testing continued regularly after that, and now he and Grampa have careful records on all their cows for at least twelve years. Most of these cows have lived under the same conditions. He gets out all the herd books. The figures are there. He organizes the cows under their sires. Some of these sires are, of course, no longer living. He then compares daughters' records to their dams. He uses Prentice's index to determine each bull's standing in reference to his daughters' production. The figuring takes him weeks and weeks of winter evenings at the Little House.

Finally he's ready to tally his results. He takes a huge sheet of graph paper, and using as his referents, pounds of butterfat up the left side, and sires across the bottom, plots each cow in this way: he enters her mother at her average level of butterfat, say, 350 pounds. Then he sees where the daughter falls—five squares above at 355, or three squares below, at 347. He then draws a line from mother to daughter, ending with an arrow. When all the lines are clustered together he can see at a glance whether a certain bull's daughters are on the whole superior or inferior to their mothers.

The results are dramatic. At the low end is "Jehu of the Dougan Farm"; his daughters almost all do worse than their mothers—the arrows point down. This bull is named for Jehu in the Bible, who "drove furiously." Daddy sees that Jehu, in spite of his frantic efforts, is dragging down the herd. He will advise Grampa to get rid of him. "Local Pride" and "Cherub Eureka" have daughters who hover near their mothers' marks. These bulls apparently did no harm but also did no good. The daughters of a current bull, "Valentine Rubina's Lad," however, make a remarkable showing: they are all substantially better than their dams. Every arrow points up, and some continue up square after square. It's true! On the whole, one bull will consistently father excellent daughters, another, indifferent or poor ones.

Daddy can't contain his enthusiasm. He writes E. Parmelee Prentice at the Mount Hope Farm in western Massachusetts, telling him that his own figuring verifies Prentice's thesis. He asks many questions and also asks where he might obtain a high index Guernsey bull.

Prentice writes back and they strike up a correspondence. He sends Daddy two crossbred bulls. These bulls are young ones, without indices, but a young bull has to get a start in life somewhere, to begin establishing his record. Why not at the Dougan Farm? The bulls will mate randomly with the Dougan cows. Their daughters, when they mature, will help be the basis for the bulls' indices. These bulls are the result of several generations of improvement. Chances are strong that they will prove to be good sires and then Daddy will have lucked out: he will have many daughters by sought-after bulls, daughters born before their sires were proved. If the bulls turn out to be only so-so, Daddy will have lost little on the gamble. Only if they are duds will the herd go down in quality. Later, the service Daddy supplies by taking these bulls is formalized: the bull studs that develop have "Associate Farmers" who will take a promising improved bull for a while, to get some record on him.

As to a high index Guernsey bull for Daddy, Prentice recommends the United States Department of Agriculture. It's been gathering records all over the country (some from the Dougan Farm herd books) and has now established a bull index. Daddy writes them, asking for a list of Guernsey bulls. When he receives it, he contacts all the owners within a radius of three hundred miles. He finds by the time a bull has had enough daughters to prove his worth, with all the records in and processed by the slow-moving bookkeeping of the government, that many of the bulls listed are incapable of any sort of Jehu performance. A number of them are already dead. From the large number he wrote inquiring about, he finds only a half dozen alive, able, and available. He studies the data on these carefully, then writes to M.L. Witz, Breeder of Guernsey Cattle, Kenmoor Farm, New Lisbon, Wisconsin. Mr. Witz answers, December 6, 1929:

> I find your letter on my desk when I arrived home today inquiring about the bull Luxerin Attestor. I was down to Ed Moriarity's, where the bull is, a few weeks ago and they said they were ready to sell him now if he is to be sold at all. He will be either 8 or 9 next spring, his papers are at Moriarity's.
>
> Upon poking around my desk I just found a pedigree of the bull we got from Barney Sheridan when we bought him as a calf. I see he was 8 last June. I will enclose the pedigree and a picture of him I snapped myself when he was at my place once. He is not a large bull, a little better rump than the picture shows. He is not in nearly as good flesh now as in the picture but has been kept down in order to keep him active, for in years gone by we have found that fat old bulls soon lose their usefulness.
>
> His daughters have wonderful udders, are nice milkers, one untested daughter brought me $525 in the state sale this fall. Mr. Moriarity has been using him for some time now and he told me he was serving very nicely and sure. Elmer Niles lives right across the way from Moriarity's and he has a bunch of his daughters milking. The cow tester told me he took a test of his herd in November and seven cows averaged 63 lbs. of fat.
>
> I asked the rest what they wanted me to ask for him and they wanted to know if $500 was too much. I nearly lost my breath but told them that I didn't think it was. He certainly is a good buy at that figure and I would suggest you drive up at once and look him over and his daughters. If you have any number at all to breed to him you will get your money back in a hurry.
>
> Moriarity lives on State trunk highway 71 three miles out of Mauston, between Mauston and Elroy. He and Niles are good fellows and will treat you right and any deal you make with them will be O.K. with me. They will give you any reasonable guarantee on the bull you may wish.

Daddy writes back immediately, appreciating the pedigree and description, and says "You men have surely handled him properly to get the maximum benefit from his good blood." He asks about Dairy Herd Improvement Association records on the daughters, the kind of records the Dougan Farm keeps, and would like to see daughter-dam pairs, figured for lactation periods. He says he plans to come north to see the bull after the holidays. He finishes, "The age of the bull is a little against him of course. We have a fair size herd, but we would have to get a lot of calves from him in order to get our money out of him."

Mr. Witz's response is that the only testing has been done by Mr. Niles, who has the records at his farm, "but you will not care to see them. All you have to do is to look at his daughters. You will know that you are looking at real cows the minute you see them." As to age, "Mr. Wright sold Dairymaid's Standard of Iowa to the Wis. University for $1,000 when he was 9 years old. They in turn sold him for $2,000 and I know he was in service at 16 years of age. If they are kept right they will breed on, but plenty of feed and no exercise will fix any bull in a few years. We paid $1,000 for this fellow at 10 months, and that is why I nearly lost my breath when they suggested $500 but Moriarity and Niles have the selling of him, and any bargain you drive with them goes." Mr. Witz says he looks forward to seeing Daddy after the holidays. "The roads are still good and I hope they continue to be the same."

Daddy drives up to Mauston, some 130 miles, in January. He's impressed with Luxerin Attestor and makes a counter offer. The men say they'll confer. Unfortunately, the roads don't continue good—the trip back is in a blinding blizzard. Daddy creeps along, bucking the drifts, knowing that if he stops he'll never get, as the nursery rhyme says, over the stile and home that night. He's so fatigued that at midnight he drives off the road into a snow bank. It happens on the last lap, happily, right between Marstons' and the dairy.

Mr. Niles writes the next day, "We have decided to let you have the bull, Luxerin Attestor, at the terms you offered, that is, $200 down, $100 one year from now if the bull is still servicable, and another hundred two years from now if the bull is still serviceable at that time. We guarantee this bull to be serviceable at this time. We are having a blood test taken this afternoon, also testing him for T.B., so you can send a truck for him as soon as convenient after the test is completed. If he reacts to either test we will either phone or telegraph."

Daddy tells the story of his search in a 1929 letter to a friend:

A few months ago I set out to find a bull that would do something for us. I ran down all Guernsey bulls in Wisconsin who showed a better daughter average than the dam average in 1928 and found only three alive and two available. I wrote to all the cow testers in predominantly Guernsey Associations asking for names of breeders owning proven sires. In following this up I gained practically nothing, as records were not complete enough to form a very good idea of the animals in question. At length I purchased one of the two bulls above mentioned. He is of exceptionally fine breeding—Luxerin

W.J. labelled this photograph, "Herd Sire, Celosia's Golden Secret 72814." He did not name the well-dressed man holding the bull beside the round barn, but it seems to be E. Parmalee Prentice.

Attestor 73417—nine years old. We feel that we have an outstanding bull. He seems to be in good shape, is fairly active, and serves quickly.

And a little later, in February, 1930, Daddy (age 28, not much older than some of his listeners) gives a talk to an Ag class at DeKalb, Illinois, then Dekalb State Teacher's College. He begins,

For twenty years the breeding history of our farm has not varied much. We have purchased fairly good purebred Guernsey bulls and good grade cows, and culled just as fast as an animal ceased to make a profit. Our losses from culling have been high, and do not seem to lessen as the years go by.... Our production varies widely from cow to cow—low, medium, high. Our direct losses from contagious abortion are about constant. If anything, our herd was in better shape in regard to production and abortion ten years ago than it is today. Surely this is a gloomy picture. Coupled with the fact that our labor cost is increasingly high, is it small wonder that it is the retailing of our own milk and our neighbors' milk at 16 to 17 cents per quart that is making us money, and not the actual production of the product at the barn figured at current prices for dairy products.

He goes on to say that this condition is not unique to Dougan's; with increased competition it's imperative that overhead be cut down while production is increased, or many dairy farms will cease to operate. Of his own farm,

"In the distribution work we have been successful, but in milk production not so happy." But, "We are, however, enthusiastic about the future of production work. We feel we are now in control of the two factors that can make or break a dairyman. I am referring to contagious abortion and a program of breeding up a herd by tried sires."

Daddy deals with abortion first, briefly telling of the progress in that arena, including the percentages of Dougan calves lost to abortion, a figure that is bound to diminish. He then goes on to the second. "Pardon my continual reference to our own herd. It is the group of animals I know best, and about which I can speak with most authority. It is my belief that they will measure up to almost any grade Guernsey herd in our state—and yet when I go into their records, getting out percentages and building up graphs, they don't look very good." He then warms to his subject—the use of daughter-dam comparisons, the importance of a bull that is known—statistically—to raise the performance of his daughters over their mothers: in other words, proven sires. He ends by telling of his obtaining Luxerin Attestor, how many calves this proven bull has already produced, and the farm's hopes for them. He urges proven sires on his listeners. He has become a missionary.

Daddy's prediction about the farm's first proven sire turns out to be correct. Luxerin Attestor fathers many heifer calves that attain maturity and go into the herd. These daughters are the best cows the farm has had to date. When Daddy starts adding Luxerin's daughters' records to his graph, their lines are great sweeps of achievement; they go right off the top of the chart and ring the bell.

Luxerin's fame spreads. He gains a picture and writeup in a Fond du Lac area paper. While the daughter-dam records quoted must have been made at his previous home, the number of daughters already in the Dougan herd prove that he has been a very busy lad indeed—most splendidly serviceable:

> This 11-year-old Guernsey bull, herd sire on the W.J. Dougan farm, Beloit, has a record of which to be proud. Records on seven pairs of dams and daughters of this bull show that the dams produced only 6,860 pounds of milk but the daughters made 8,323 pounds and the butterfat test was retained in the daughters' production. The average age of the daughters when these records were taken was two and one-half years and the age of the dams was five years. Old Luxerin, bred by Barney Sheridan, owner of Luxerin farm, was purchased from a group of four Mauston farmers at the age of nine by the Dougan farm. There are some 20 daughters of this bull in the Dougan herd of some 100 head of stock.

Daddy later has less success with a bull from Nebraska, Grandvu Forward, which he nicknames "Lochinvar" from a line in a poem by Sir Walter Scott: "Young Lochinvar is come out of the West." Lochinvar's daughters do not do at all well. Daddy is puzzled. He checks back and finds that when Lochinvar was being proved, the daughters were tested under much better conditions than their dams. They had been put on "advanced registry"—milking four times a day, and special feed. Under these circumstances any daughter can surpass her mother and make her father look like a winner. But under normal conditions, Lochinvar is a dud. He's returned to the West.

For a long time the Who-You-Are school, championed by the breed associations, wars with the What-You-Do school. In 1942 Parmalee Prentice writes about the controversy to Leland Lamb, the first professional employee of the American Dairy Cattle Club and later bull buyer for American Breeders Service:

> Mount Hope began the whole index business. We were the first to use the word index as applied to a formula showing a bull's breeding value.... All the breeding associations have resented the course of action we have followed, and very naturally, for it attacked the whole "pure-bred" idea. The Guernsey Club proposed to expel me from membership but when they found that it involved a law suit they gave up the idea.... The Guernsey Club was not alone however in its feeling of opposition, and the opposition and resentment of the breed associations have increased as time passed for we are constantly making more and more impression. Indeed, we have reached a point now where the associations are obliged to follow our work and every one of them wants to do so in such a way as to avoid giving Mount Hope credit.... Mr. Tufts would like to lead all breeders to forget the part Mt. Hope has played in developing modern breeding methods and to use a name which gives Mount Hope no credit. The name "equal parent [index]" and the name "intermediate [index]" were developed long after the formation of the Mount Hope index, now called the American index. So we want you to help maintain the American (Mount Hope) reputation.

Daddy, of course, and Grampa with him, has long been firmly in the What-You-Do camp. It's more than a theory; he's verified it by the records of the Dougan herd, by his own investigations, and the farm's investments. Jackie hears "proven sire" as soon as she hears "cow jumped over the moon." Maybe even sooner.

44 ⊰ BULL STORIES

J ackie is barely three when she goes to visit a bull that has somehow got loose. MooMoo Stam tells her about it when she's older.

"I came downstairs, out the door from the flat above the milkhouse where Lester and I were living, Jackie, and I saw you, trotting along in your bright red coat, you were so tiny, you trotted to that fence behind your house and lo and behold, there was a young bull there, he began to bellow and paw and snort and roar and snarl!

"I was scared to death, because I was afraid there might be a weak board in the gate—I was scared to go yet I knew I had to get you—I ran down there, my heart in my mouth, grabbed you up, carried you back to the milkhouse. You looked at me, and you said, 'MooMoo, that old bull, he went hmm hmm at me!' As tiny as you were, you were trying to tell me how he snorted! It was one of the funniest things."

Nobody, of course, thinks the situation funny, that Jackie somehow escaped supervision and met up with a bull. There's a similar incident when little Jerry Dougan, Jackie's first cousin, is visiting. He trots out to pat a "nice cow" fastened to the bull sweep. The bull sweep is a long slender tree trunk, pivoted to a stump midway, so that it rotates when the bull on the end walks, making the bull travel in a circle. The result of Jerry's encounter is the farm's getting rid of the bull sweep—the bull never exercised anyway, he just stood there. Or they, if another bull was fastened to the other end. Daddy had tried once to mechanize the bull sweep to make the bulls walk, but hadn't succeeded. He and Grampa now manage to find a used treadmill to force the bull to walk and walk, for his job requires his keeping in shape. (There is a note from Grampa to Ronald that the bull "Pride" has to be sold for beef, he has not been exercising enough to perform his duties and has now gone lame—styfled. That's a cattle disease, involving bone problems. "He is giving zero percent return, and will cost $300 to $400 to replace.")

The dairy has a number of other bull stories—no deaths or maimings, but closer calls than Jackie's or Jerry's.

Clair Mathews is herdsman in 1920 when he hears Daddy Dougan crying out in alarm. He rushes outside the barn to find W.J. knee deep on top of a high manure pile, cornered, his only protection a hammer, and the bull tearing his horns into the pile, getting closer and closer to Daddy. "The bull had come up from behind," says Clair, "and Daddy couldn't hear him — the only place he could go was climb the manure pile! I grabbed a pitchfork, a good strong one, and held the bull off until Daddy got out of there. Then I opened the pen, urged the bull over toward it with the pitchfork, and clapped the door on him. He'd somehow got loose.

"But Griffiths was nearer death than that!" he goes on. "There was a rack in the bullpen that could be filled from outside. There was another door for the bull to be taken in and out. I was out in back of the barn, in a separate building. I heard Mr. Griffiths just yelling his head off. I heard boards breaking! I went over. He'd gotten in there and the bull was between him and the door. That bull was just about to get him, so he crawled under the hayrack manger. The bull was tearing this hayrack apart piece by piece. I came running with my pitchfork again! I held him at bay until Griffiths got out of the building. Then I shut the door."

Milton Koenecke, in the early 1940s, meets a bull, again somehow loose, at the back door of the Big House when he goes before dawn to start the milking. He's afraid. But Bob Opelt, fearless, fares forth and gets the bull back in his pen. The tables are turned when later this same bull traps Bob right in the pen and Milton is the savior.

There are other stories of these close calls. There are also ones concerning less danger. MooMoo Stam tells Ron, "You went over to Brodhead to get a bull, you needed new breeding stock, when was it, around 1927? And when you brought him back, you put him in the same pen with your other bull — oh, what an uproar to hear those creatures bellowing at each other! They didn't fight much, just made a few passes — but the way they roared!"

"Bulls establish who's boss, very soon," Ron replies. "I had a big bull, always boss, and a much younger bull I'd put in a paddock between the round barn and horse barn — with much fear and trembling I put them together, in the big heavy pen. The old bull began to snort and paw, the little younger bull looked him over, then BANG! hit him right in the side, smashed him against those heavy iron rails. The big bull straightened himself up and walked quietly off."

"Now there's a thought," says MooMoo. "What about you and your father? I never saw you and Daddy Dougan snorting and pawing at each other.

Art Kassilke, the herdsman, holds a prize bull, on which Ted Selmer, left, and Lonnie Richardson are seated comfortably.

Yet he was the big bull. You never smashed him on the side and took over."

Ron ponders this. "We never did," he says. "Maybe it was because I grew up as the little bull alongside the big bull, and he let me have my head, in the milk business and with the seed corn. We worked together. Conferred on everything. We gave each other advice, and sometimes we took it and sometimes we didn't. We weren't competing."

There is a time that Ron doesn't tell MooMoo about; he does tell Jackie. It happens in the late forties. He'd had an alarm call from the sorority house; his older daughter, at the university, had stayed out all night with a young man, against sorority mores. "So I drove up to Madison," says Daddy, "to see what was going on. I think I was contemplating being the big bull! But then I met Karl, we drove out to Picnic Point to talk, and within ten minutes we'd decided we liked each other very much. Within a year or so, I think it was, he became my son-in-law. Now he always beats me in chess. I guess that's where the young bull is smashing the old one."

Another bull story has its humor. About 1917, Charles Kellor, a town kid, and Ron's school buddy, is a teen-age summer employee. He's distracted from his job nailing shingles to the Big House roof by his view down into the barnyard. Barnhands are bringing cows, one by one, to the bull, who, to Charles's astonishment, seems indefatigable as well as somewhat bored. Charles's father, W.J.'s head carpenter Mark Kellor, is irritated at his son's slow shingling and can't understand why a boy usually so quick at his work is now a laggard. Charles doesn't tell him why.

Artificial insemination brings an end to most bulls on farms, including the dubious bulls-for-rent that travel from farm to farm inseminating the few family cows. At the start of the Rock County Breeders Co-op in 1938 Ron contributes some of his own bulls, and they go to live on the River Road. They soon come back again, because the neighbors organize to object to a bull stud with several more than the Dougan bulls next door; they see it as a menace. But in 1944, Craig, in school in Arizona for his health, gets a letter from his father: "This is our new Bull Association stationery. We have moved in with Dr. Knilans at Janesville. We are now shipping semen from Elgin for Guernseys and Madison for Holsteins and are keeping on the farm no bulls of our own at all. The bull yard is empty."

Even without bulls, livestock can be dangerous. Sows are known for their viciousness. An occasional cow can be vicious, too. M-12's name is seared in the memory of the Dougan kids and cousins; they all barely escaped her attacks in the barnyard when they went to swim in the tank. And Jackie's youngest daughter will never forget being hastily thrown over a fence in a Chez Nous back pasture, when she's about six, followed by her mother's mad scramble, when they meet a cow coming at them with murder in her eye. This, after Elspeth had been reassured all her life that cows are gentle creatures, merely curious when they approach you.

The only local death Jackie hears of, caused by a bull or cow, does not happen on the place, but at the 4-H Fair. Art Raschke, who is a cow tester and works part time in the dairy office, has a slight and twisted body. He's taking a blood sample from a cow when she moves abruptly and leans against him, pinning him to the side of the pen. As far as anyone knows, the cow had no malice. But there is no one near enough to help him in time. He cannot push the heavy animal away, his body is too frail and crippled. He is crushed.

The farm does turn out for his funeral, even though he too had an irascible, bullish temper. But it is forgivable; it's all in the family.

45 ⋇ MILTON KOENECKE

In the midsixties, Daddy is driving through Reedsburg, Wisconsin. He decides to drop in on an old employee, Milton Koenecke. Milton settles in for a chat.

———•—•———

So, you're asking me, Ron, what was it like to work for Daddy Dougan? Well, I was just a kid when I came from Reedsburg in 1941 — twenty or twenty-one, and I was never so scared in my life, because I'd never been so far away from home alone for that long a time. I got there in the middle of the day, in the middle of June, and Daddy called me into his office — a room off the living room of the house — I stood on that little red rug — and he said, "I want to impress on you one thing. We have one rule here, and only one rule." He scared the devil out of me! Then he said, "The one rule is this: We treat our men like we would like to be treated ourselves." That really impressed me. I had a half day off every week, and every third Sunday — that was unusual for farmers in those days to treat hired men that way. He didn't tolerate smoking, drinking, rough language — I could see his point, having as many men as he had. He was good to his men, and expected them to be that way to him.

In the Big House, we had a sink and shower in the back room — we were required to take a shower, once, twice a day — Lord help the guy that got the last shower, the rest of us got all the hot water! There was a little coal-burner stove that heated the water for the shower. Effie usually started the fire so that we had warm water. There were two shower heads. We ate with the family — most employers wouldn't tolerate that. We had to come to meals showered and dressed nicely, not in our barn clothes, except for breakfast in the kitchen. Especially at noon, for we never knew who was going to be there — a salesman, a professor from the university, company for the family — and we were required to act like gentlemen! Daddy said a blessing every morning and every noon, and after supper at night we had family devotions. I didn't appreciate it much then but I do now, looking back—we weren't allowed to go till the last "amen" was said.

One time I thought I'd bring something really nice from home, from Reedsburg. I'm German, so I brought down some German sausage made from ground beef and flavored with allspice and sugar and salt and pepper—I only brought one, so it couldn't have gone far, and Daddy Dougan tasted it and said, "Man! This is awful!" so he didn't think much of my special treat. On Sunday nights he always had johnnycake; he crumbled it into his glass and filled his glass with milk and ate it with a spoon.

Daddy was an excellent speaker—even with his deafness I remember three or four occasions that I went to banquets with him. Your mother, Ron, never sat next to him, but straight across the table from him, and she signed to him. When he gave his speeches he emphasized the right words at the right times, and he made the most beautiful speeches I've ever heard.

Sometimes Daddy made a bed check on us fellows, we slept in those back rooms upstairs, in bunks—if we decided we were going out, we'd try to fool him. We'd put our suitcases under the covers; he'd come in with a flashlight. I don't know if we fooled him or not, but we thought we did. We'd drive into the yard with our lights out, we knew he couldn't hear the cars. Yet he seemed to know when we came in—he looked on us as his boys—he was responsible. If we came in late, we'd see him looking out his bedroom window, to see if we were fit to come home. Sometimes we weren't in the best condition; we'd go down to Morks and buy our booze—or Waverly Beach, or Delavan to go dancing! No matter when we got home, at ten or twelve or two, we had to be out in the barn at 2:30, ready to milk at 3. We had to have the milk up to the cooler and run over the coils before 7. They really wanted it by 6 o'clock. Daddy sometimes saw things he shouldn't have—once when Cleo Reinfeldt—he was from Reedsburg too—once when he got in at 2:30, Daddy said to him later, "It didn't take you long to change your clothes!"

When I came we had six milking units. This caused a lot of problems with mastitis; too many cows were being milked at once and a unit was being left on a cow too long after she'd finished milking. It hurt a cow to be milked after she was milked out, so I cut us back to four units—I had three men in the barn to help me. It was required to wash each cow, use the strip cup test, to see whether the cow had any disease that would show up in the strip cup, and afterwards we dipped the tits in a chlorine solution to be sure no bacteria would go up the tit—we put the milk into cans from the milking machines; when four cans were full we'd push them up to the milkhouse on those two wheeled carts. Not like that underground hose I saw you were using when I was down for Farm Progress Days in '61!

In summer, we used to sneak chocolate milk and orange drink, and hide it in a special place under the stairs between the round barn and the side barn annex, those stairs that went to the upper barn. Daddy didn't care if we drank it out in the open, but being kids we hid it—we thought nobody knew where we kept our treasure. Daddy caught us at it and gave us a little stern lecture, but he never did anything about it.... The most delicious thing I've ever drunk is a half pint of chocolate milk mixed with a half pint of stolen whipping cream—oh, that was good!

The manure trolley went around the barn, hung from that track, and in order to save steps we'd give it a tremendous push, jump on the back end, and ride it part way. Cleo was riding it one time. As he went past the main entrance, Daddy came in the door. He never said a word but that night he shook his finger at me and said, "You're the worst one of the bunch!" and to Cleo, "By golly, I don't know if we can use you any more!" but we knew he wasn't meaning it. Me—what had I done?

That was the cleanest barn I ever worked in—it was scrubbed daily—the cows too—we had a clipper that we used to clip the cows, we tried to clip several cows a day and sometimes we made it and sometimes we didn't, depending on the work load. When we got to the end of the line we started right over again. Every cow was logged, too, every day—if anything was wrong, maybe she was sick, or if she was off production, or in heat, it was all logged. One requirement of the barn help at milking time was a long white milking apron; this would be over the coveralls we wore, and this was required to be changed whenever it was dirty. That meant sometimes twice a milking, and at least once a day. They were spotless when we got them—Effie did the washing in that back room. On Mondays we could scarcely get to the showers for all those wash tubs and the washing machine!

There was a bull—a cross between a high producing Holstein and high producing Guernsey—and one pitch black morning I was coming out of that back room and this tremendous bull met me at the door, scared the heck out of me—I was scared to go down to the barn in the dark, I didn't know where he was. Bob Opelt was assistant to me, and he wasn't afraid of anything, so he took the bull lead down to the barn and found the bull and got him back in his pen, and as soon as he said it was all right, I went to the barn and started the milking. Later this same bull—the bullpen was back of the horse barn, and the door swung from the fence—when you clean the pen it's

mandatory you lock this door so when you shoot the bull out into his yard he can't come back in — some way Bob forgot to lock the door. I was in the barn, I heard him yell, "Help, help!" I couldn't understand why he was hollering so I went out there and the bull had him trapped, he was up in that manger built across the corner. The bull couldn't get at him, but he was working at it! Bob always carried a four foot stick, about like a broom handle but bigger, to protect himself when going close to the bull — the bull had whittled that stick down to about a foot and a half! For some reason when I came into the yard the bull saw me and turned around and walked out. I bet Bob remembers that to this day, that I actually saved his life.

The dry cows were kept up at your place, Ron, and whenever we had a cow or two to go up there we'd have to haul them, but lots of times we walked them, it was only a mile and a half. Take a couple of men, have a pleasant morning. One of us had to keep ahead and guard any gaps in fences so they wouldn't wander off into anyone's cornfield. One time the telephone company was taking down an overhead line and they'd cut the line every fourth or fifth pole. We had a fresh cow that needed to come down to the round barn, Bob and myself and probably Billy Beadle went up to get her, and she got tangled up in the wires and cut her leg terrifically — it was near the Blodgett farm. By the time we got her back to the round barn Daddy was out there looking around, he saw this blood, and it was the first time I ever saw a tourniquet used — he put one on and stopped the blood and saved the cow. He and I adopted this cow; but she was never very good on account of this, I think. Yes, Daddy taught me a few things about doctoring cattle!

After high school, before I came to the dairy, I was testing cattle for my home county, Sauk, through the Dairy Herd Improvement Association program, and I'd have to stay overnight at a farmer's place, and take evening and morning samples for butterfat. Then I became a check tester for the state—I'd travel all over and come in the following day and do a check test to be sure the tester was doing a good job—see if my check agreed with his, that the first check wasn't fictitious—but it was a lot of traveling. So I went to Roy Harris who was Professor of Dairy Science at the university, and head of the D.H.I.A. In two weeks he called me, said there was an opening at the Dougan farm.

One time they filled the silo in the barn—you had a chopper, first I'd ever seen in my life—you chopped the corn out in the field. They'd backed the load up onto the barn floor, and this horse, Molly, she got scared, ran away with a load of corn bundles and spread them all over the yard, and Daddy never got excited but walked up to her and the other horse, petted her, said in a soothing voice, "Now that wasn't very nice, to do this," and that old horse understood him and calmed right down and didn't give us any more trouble. But another time Molly tipped over the straw pile—when we cleaned the barn we pulled the old straw out and put it on the manure pile, and we always had a load of fresh straw out by the back door, brought up from the straw-stack, and she tipped over the hayrack she was hauling it on, and we had to pick it all up. We had to watch her behind the barn; she was a tricky one. She ran away with the manure spreader once.

We fed the cows irradiated yeast with their grain—so many shovels of corn, so many of oats, determined how much yeast we'd put in the mix to make vitamin D milk. We had a caster-wheeled feed cart and each cow on Vitamin D production got so many pounds of this Vitamin D mix every day. The Vitamin D would come out in the milk. Periodically, you'd send samples to the university where they'd test it for Vitamin D level—later on, of course, you got a concentrate and then you'd just put so much in a vat of milk. All milk now is Vitamin D, but not when you were doing it.

Flavor was a problem sometimes. We used the Holsteins for the hospital milk, they didn't have as high a test as the Guernseys and the lower butter-fat was better for babies, and sometimes the head nurse would call me and say, "Mr. Koenecke, your cows' milk is off flavor, the babies won't drink our formula." I wondered if it was because visitors would come to the milking and disturb the cows; they'd get excited, and we couldn't control that—once in a while, when we were short, we'd sneak in a little Guernsey milk, and that might have thrown the flavor off, too—but that was about when we began homogenizing; later you discovered the milk could have been exposed to sunlight that oxidized the butterfat and gave it a rancid taste—affected the flavor—so that was probably it. The cows never got any wild garlic, no garlic ever dared poke up a shoot in your pasture! But whenever you change a pasture the flavor changes, of course—even the customers would say, "Well, I guess the Dougan cows have changed pasture!"—and in the spring, changing over from hay, you get a grassy taste. And there was that producer you bought milk from, you always had trouble with him in the fall; he had a lot of oak trees in his pasture, and the cows would eat the acorns and it'd make their milk bitter.

I remember that first homogenizer. It was probably three feet high and two feet wide, and a series of pounders built up pressure and forced the milk through tiny openings. It was one of the very first that was engineered—this university prof was demonstrating it to you and us—so the Dougan farm had the first homogenizer in town. You put the blended milk through that homogenizer.

We had something rare, I don't believe any other farm had, we had charge accounts at Firestone, Goodyear, a few other places in town, where hired hands could charge things to the dairy—I was there when World War II was declared, and Daddy said, "You young fellows better go down and get yourself a good supply of tires before they're rationed, and some of us did and some of us didn't. I didn't, because I thought it was foolishness—I found out later it wasn't!

About that red rug by his desk—you never knew whether Daddy was going to praise you or if he was going to chew you out, but I liked that—because if you were a foreman, he never chewed you out in front of all the men. He did it after hours.

One thing about you, Ron, you never gave me a bad time. You never came in the barn. You were busy with the sales and in the office and in the milkhouse. Daddy was the head of the barn and the cattle, and required us to answer to him. If we had any problems, go to him; if he had any, he came to us. I was really impressed with that man. Do you still have the old cow record books, Ron? I'd sure like to see my own handwriting.

46 ≈ MAYPOLE DANCE

A once well-known ballad begins, "The Northern lights have seen strange sights— "

The loft of the round barn could write such a verse, too—"The large round barn might spin a yarn," for there are strange sights there now and again, especially in the loft. Some Jackie knows about.

Not at all strange are the usual farm activities—filling the hay mow, filling the silo, grinding grain in the little grinding mill. Nor is the hide-and-seek that is a part of any barn life where kids are around. The inventive games Trever and Ronald create move up the scale of strangeness, as well as danger, and the circuses of Ron's kids and their friends introduce some unusual feats and animals, such as Ed Pfaff's pet skunks. Grampa puts a basketball hoop in the loft for Trever, when he's in high school—this gives a dry place to practice in the winter, but no games are held there. Mother gives a Hallowee'n party, passing a witch's peeled-grape eyeballs and leathery ears to the squealing, blindfolded guests; that event is rather spooky and strange, but entirely appropriate in its gloomed surroundings. Its opposite, back when the high line first comes to the farm, is when Grama and Grampa serve a meal for forty people in the loft, with folding chairs and tables, and food wheeled up from the Big House kitchen in a milkhouse trolley. That banquet is brilliantly lit by the brand new electric lights.

Larger crowds aren't strange, either—a Kansas Chamber of Commerce delegation of a hundred people stands on the ramp, to hear Grampa give a lecture from the loft door; Farm Progress Days crowds wander in and out. Late in the barn's history Ronald introduces scores of schoolkids to the loft, where some even climb down into the empty silo. There's an occasional out-of-place item: the old sleigh stored there, balanced high on a beam, out of sight behind the center silo. The Dougan four know where it is, though, and go for sleigh rides surrounded by hay until Daddy loans it to a neighbor who never brings it back. But the strangest sight the barn might write is about the afternoon when the maypole dance takes place.

It isn't meant to happen in the barn. It's spring, 1934, and Mother is preparing a maypole dance for a festivity in Horace White Park. The dance will be the grand climax of the affair, after the speeches and glee clubs and mayor presenting the key to the city to someone important.

A maypole dance is not often seen, in barns or anywhere, for it's a complicated affair, and takes absolute coordination. It must work out perfectly. It takes skill on the part of the dancers and director. It's breathtaking in completion, but a daring thing to attempt.

As for the maypole itself, it's a tall pole with many streamers cascading down from the very top. These broad ribbons are always sweet colored, often pastel, but for Mother's event they are pink. They hang limp until the dancers in their corresponding pink costumes trip onto the stage and each takes her own ribbon's end. They fan out, and poised now in a wide and evenly spaced circle with the ribbons forming the ribs of a lovely parasol, and with their left toes pointed expectantly, the dancers are ready for the music to begin.

Mother's older, experienced students make up the core of the group. Dorothy Bach, Alice Noble, Marion van Lone, Anna Marie Alcan, and others. They wear pink organdy gowns with puffed sleeves, and their white-paneled bodices are laced criss-cross with black ribbons. They wear white pantaloons and black ballet slippers. They wear small pink sunbonnets tied under the chin. They look like storybook English girls on the village green. But this is not a green. This is the loft floor of the round barn.

There is a reason. Because the dance is so intricate, and because it has not yet worked out to perfection, it's imperative that Mother have a dress rehearsal. This was to have been on the Big House lawn. But it's storming outside; although the thunder and lightning are over, the rain is now pouring down steadily from a gray sky, and it will continue to do so for the rest of the day. So, Mother's solution: set up the maypole in the barn's dry loft! The Victrola (under a tarp) has been carried up, wound up, and the dance's record placed on the turntable. All the dancers—giggling—have changed in the grain rooms

Patsy Dougan in her maypole costume.

amid the spider webs and gunny sacks. Assorted mothers sit around the edges, some on folding chairs or camp stools, some on full grain sacks. The atmosphere is merry.

But there is one small dancer who is not merry. She clutches the end of her ribbon and is filled with dread. For Mother did not have quite enough older girls for the maypole dance, and so has filled in with her own daughters. Not Jackie, she is far too little to manage at all. But Joan is there, and confident, as she always is, and Patsy. And Patsy has no confidence.

She has tried, in the earlier rehearsals. It always starts off well. The steps are easy for the first part of the web. Everyone crosses over one way, and then back the other. It is not hard to follow. But as the dance progresses, the crossings become more intricate. There is going under arms and around your partner, under another partner. (Who is my partner? Where is my partner?)

Patsy gets more and more panicky; sometimes she drops her streamer and has to snatch it back up again before it falls toward the middle, until at the grand finale, when the music stops and you look up, instead of the perfect web there should be, it is all tangled and awful. It looks like those webs you see pictures of, where some scientist has fed the spider liquor.

Today in the barn is no different. When Patsy gets to those last few steps she cannot remember where to go, what to do. She panics. The perfect web turns out a mess. Mother explains to Patsy, walks through the finale with her, sets the needle back at the start of the music, and they all try again. Again Patsy fails miserably. The rain is falling as heavily in her heart as it is outside the loft entrance. She fights back tears.

But at the third try she gets it. Somehow, her feet go right. The partners are where they are supposed to be. The web above finishes perfect in its weaving. Everyone cheers. Patsy feels more relief than jubilation. The dance is tried once more, to seal in the success. "Now you have it," Mother says, "remember it. I'll practice with you once more alone, tonight at the Little House."

The next day, the day of the performance, is clear and sunny. The maypole dance in the park goes off without a hitch. The large audience is enchanted. There is applause upon applause. Again, Patsy feels more relief than jubilation, though the jubilation does creep in when ice cream cups with their little wooden paddles are passed out to everyone.

In the *Beloit Daily News* report of the event, the maypole dance is singled out as "an extraordinary feat, performed by ones so young." Patsy clips the article carefully and pastes it in her scrapbook. She knows they must be writing about her. After all, she is the youngest.

47 ⊀ KORN KURLS

It is 1931; Jackie is three. The herdsman in the round barn, Clair Mathews, is experimenting with feed for the cows. Jackie likes to go up onto the floor of the upper barn. So do her older sisters and little brother. They troop up the incline to see what's under Clair Mathews' machine today. What's under it are chips, or flakes, or peels of toasted grain. They pick up the chips or flakes or peels and eat them. You never know what you'll find under the machine, but whatever it is will have an interesting shape, crunch, or taste—sometimes all three.

The Dougan cows have eaten ground grain since Daddy was a little boy; the machine that grinds the grain, when Jackie is very small, is called a burr mill. It consists of two metal plates that rub together. The corn between the plates is cracked into large chunks, and then into smaller, finer bits. But the bits remain jaggedy.

Clair has been trained in agronomy at the University of Wisconsin. He knows what goes into the feed troughs; he also notices what ends up in the gutter behind the cows. He sees that a goodly amount of grain manages to get through the cows' chewing, digesting, rechewing and redigesting mechanisms without being fully digested. Clair points out to Grampa that the cows are not getting the full benefit of their feed.

Grampa agrees. He knows there are roller mills on the market that flatten grain, but these are huge things and more than the farm can afford. Clair thinks he can make his own roller mill.

Years later, he tells Ron and Jackie how he did it.

Ron prompts, "As I recall, you and my father got concerned about the burr grinder. You thought you could make a better feed—that you could flatten the grain out so there wouldn't be so much to go through the cows to feed the pigs."

"I went over to Afton," Clair replies, "where they had a sort of milling plant for the roller mill, and I saw what that could do. Then downtown in

In natty attire, a young Clair Mathews poses with his ukelele.

Beloit I saw a drug store with a mortar and pestle on the front, and they had this grinding affair with pressure rotating in there—I thought, could I make this principle work? You remember the Walsh cabbage farm? With that tremendous junk pile with odd pieces of wagon and everything else? I brought home a wagon wheel, thinking, why couldn't I take the sawed off axle, the skein—that's the hub—and the tapering bit there, and groove that in a way."

"I don't think you grooved it at first," says Ron. "You took the axle and the hub and put them together, and turned the axle, but the grain wouldn't go down through the skein to be compressed, and when it did, a little, it'd burn and clog. It was then you cut the spiral."

Clair agrees. "For the hopper I used one of the strainer funnels that you poured milk into, and had a tray at the bottom. And to have power to operate, I first used a washing machine motor, but that wasn't strong enough, so I took the outfit to the round barn where you had a 1.5 Fairbanks. I still needed a belt, and so I found some narrow 2, 3 inches wide pieces, and that powered the machine. I started to do business—and after it had run a little bit, I put in some corn meal that you had there, and to my surprise, it came out PUFFED. And I said, 'Lo and behold, what goes on here?'"

Ron says, "And Korn Kurls were born."

But there is more to it than that. The groove now pulls the grain down between the skein and the turning hub, but Clair doesn't count on the heat produced by the friction of the contraption, which chars, partially cooks, or puffs the grain. He tries wheat and oats and barley; he tries combining the different grains, even alfalfa leaves. Whatever he makes comes out tasty. The cows lick it up. Farm workers come by and nibble on the flakes and chips. Patsy and Joan, Jackie and Craig, nibble on them, too. Daddy brings some over to the Little House. Mother tries salting them and adding a little butter. They taste better yet.

Clair gets a local machinist to make a professional model of his invention. He tries to interest Quaker Oats. He hears Henry Ford is going to have an exhibit at the Chicago World's Fair, an oil extracting machine. He visits, and sees an Allis Chalmers roller mill on display. He tells those officials, "I have a machine that can do the same thing and it's only the size of a card table." He and his machinist make up a large box of soybean flakes and send it to the Ford exhibit. A few days later a car comes tearing up to the barn, slamming on the brakes. Two men jump out. They want Clair to get on the next train to Detroit. He does; the machine follows in the back of Clair's Chevrolet.

Henry Ford is interested. He works with Clair for a week in his research laboratories, then instructs that the machine be put up in the Ford display at the World's Fair, even though his other executives warn him that the machine isn't proven. It does not do soy oil extracting as efficiently as Ford had hoped, but his interest nonetheless gives a boost to the invention.

Back in Beloit, Clair can't make a whole lot of feed with his little machine. He needs better tools and a machine shop. He gives one half of his idea to a friend with space and equipment. They build a somewhat bigger model, and make a small profit producing Alpha Flakes from alfalfa, for rabbit food. It's the Depression and many people are keeping rabbits, for these are easy to care for and rabbit is a relatively inexpensive food. Clair and his friend decide they need more help and money in order to expand. They go to Harry Adams, a local lawyer and former Beloit mayor, and interest him in their machine. An engineer at the Beloit Iron Works helps refine the process. They form the Flakall Corporation in 1933; the machine isn't patented till 1938. The local lawyer's son, Arthur Adams, has written this account:

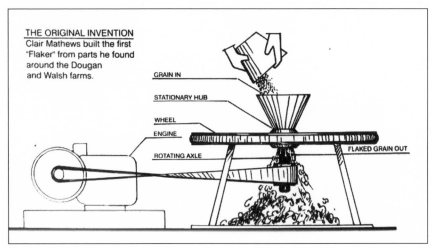

THE ORIGINAL INVENTION
Clair Mathews built the first "Flaker" from parts he found around the Dougan and Walsh farms.

GRAIN IN

STATIONARY HUB

WHEEL

ENGINE

ROTATING AXLE

FLAKED GRAIN OUT

A drawing of the original invention, in the Korn Kurls room of the Wheeler House Museum in South Beloit.

"Collettes" coming from an early improvement of the invention. These became the original Korn Kurls.

In the thirties, Clair Mathews, an agronomist at the Dougan Dairy farm, came to Father's office with a device fashioned from a wagon wheel, designed to grind grains together under pressure, to produce partially cooked flakes that when fed to the cows would increase the quantity and quality of milk. The rest is history. Father was intrigued. He, with Clarence Schwebke, a machinist friend of Clair Mathews, interested Earl Berry, an inventive genius of Beloit Iron Works, to perfect the device. After many nights of experiment he refined the machine we call the flaker to produce a good volume of this product; the first product of flaked grains was for rabbit food. My brother Allan was the first salesman.

One night of testing, the machine clogged; I remember it well. Corn meal had been introduced. The machine quivered and suddenly there appeared fingerlets of partially cooked corn meal. We called them "collettes." Mr. Wilson, a stockholder of the recently formed Flakall Corportion, took a bag of the product home. His wife dipped them in boiling oil, sprayed them with cheese and added a pinch of salt. Then and there, Korn Kurls was born.

Allan and I persuaded Father and Flakall stockholders to permit us to organize Adams Corporation, to manufacture and distribute Adams Korn Kurls throughout the country. Times were tough. We had little money. We were fortunate to induce a good friend to invest $5,000 to put us in business. There was a young naval officer stationed at Fairbanks Morse, Eugene McCleary, a good friend of Allan's. He was engrossed with the prospects of the venture and came with us to set up operations. We started in a small, one room building. I think it was a small rotary cement mixer that we used to prepare the finished product from partially cooked cornmeal collettes.

Soon, we needed a larger and more efficient plant. Elmer Luety, a Beloit contractor and good friend of mine, built us a plant to our specifications on land owned by him, which he leased to us with an option to buy. To Eugene McCleary, often assisted by Cy Heigl of Nielson Engineering Company, we owe the bulk of the credit for the successful operation that followed. Allan, Father, and I were in our glory. Father was Chairman of the Board, Allan, President, and I, Treasurer. Soon we had all the business we could handle. Allan and I arranged an advertising program in New York, featuring Dave Garroway and Hugh Downs munching Adams Korn Kurls. We went to Germany to establish a manufacturing arrangement. Branch operations were established in California and Lamberville, New Jersey, where Alvin Schickel, husband of our sister Elgeva, was manager of the plant.

Early on, Father and a specialist in cheese mixes, Carl DeWeese, organized Dell Foods, of which Adams Corporation held controlling interest.... In 1961, we sold Flakall, Adams, and Dell Food Companies to Beatrice Foods with offices in Chicago. Allan remained with Beatrice as President of Adams International, engaged in selling flaking machines and setting up independent snack food operations throughout Europe and South America.

This is the way Art Adams tells it. The tale varies a bit, depending on point of view.

Clair Mathews feels his invention was swept out from under him; he was the one who invented the machine that produced the corn curl and should have more of the credit and profits.

Later Daddy tells Jackie, "Well, a whole book could be written just about that machine, and the personalities involved, and what happened to the collette. A number of manufacturers got interested, besides Henry Ford, but there still wasn't much money in it for Clair. He quit cows to concentrate on his invention. While he was herdsman for us, part of his salary was free milk and the rent on his house. Gramp and I went on giving him rent and free milk. Once in a while I'd say, 'Clair, can't you give us a little something on our investment in you?' Then Clair would give us some stock in the company. We eventually had 3 percent."

At this point the stock isn't worth much. The corporation is just breaking even. But Daddy enjoys going to the stockholders' meetings to see people jockeying for control. Harry Adams several times tries to buy the Dougan stock but Daddy doesn't sell.

There's a copy of a note Daddy writes to Grampa, about the shares. "Isn't it strange," he writes, "that the only business you have ever put any money in save your own is panning out so well." Grampa doubts how well it's doing and Daddy replies, "It can do a lot worse and still be quite a business. After all the drain on the business of salaries, bonuses, expense accounts, etc., it still made 25% profit on gross sales. The milk business on $200,000 gross sales makes about 15 thousand, so I make about 7 1/2 % profit on gross sales, and I do not have a huge salary taken out before profits. Harry probably gets $35,000 out of it; he hires 35 men." Grampa asks about the pressure to sell the stock. Daddy answers, "He wants our stock so that he need not explain everything so fully. So that there will be no danger of the stock getting into enemy hands. They have the plant under lock and key—when I was down there they wouldn't let me in until I called Adams!"

The Adams family finally manages to buy up 51 percent. At that point a factory is built in South Beloit, many people are hired, and profits begin to grow. Daddy now enjoys going to stockholders' meetings in order to nominate Harry Adams for Chairman of the Board, Allan Adams for President and Arthur Adams for Treasurer.

For many years Daddy hangs on to his 3 percent. At Christmas, every stockholder gets a huge carton containing dozens of packets of different sorts of snacks. Sorting through them, Joan, Patsy, Jackie, and Craig are glad that the family owns a small piece of the Flakall/Adams Corporation.

Flakall, Dell, and Adams become international organizations. They sell snack food all over the world. Clair Mathews never makes the money he thinks he ought and writes pages of bitterness and detail of wrongdoing and double crossing to Grampa. Grampa answers with a placating letter. Daddy points out to the family that Clair's machine is providing the Mathewses with a comfortable living. When Beatrice takes over after Korn Kurls, Daddy finally sells his stock and makes a tidy profit.

The *Beloit Daily News*, in an editorial at the time of Clair Mathews' death in 1985, says,

> Wilson dubbed the discovery 'Korn Kurls.' And we all know Korn Kurls, don't we! They revolutionized the snack food industry, formerly dominated by potato chips. The story of how Clair Mathews attempted to make a better cattle feed led to the development of a flaking process that is widely used in the snack food industry today.... Inasmuch as Beloit now claims to be a snack food processing capital, the role of Mr. Mathews can hardly be overstated. Had he not paid attention to the gutter behind the Dougan Dairy

herd, we might never have had Korn Kurls and their array of cousin-products worldwide to enjoy.

So Clair gets strong credit in the *Daily News*. And a number of years later, in the Wheeler House, a renovated mansion with certain rooms dedicated to South Beloit industries, Korn Kurls claims the room of honor. A picture of the round barn covers one wall, and there is a facsimile of the original machine built by Hap Hornbostel, using the description of it that Clair Mathews gave to Ron, and that Jackie, listening, faithfully wrote down. That description is framed, along with a diagram of the machine, and a number of framed informational pages on the further history of Korn Kurls, along with pictures of the Adamses. There is even a photograph of Clair as a natty young man playing a mandolin. This is all even stronger credit.

True, the wormy little collette that issued puffed and toasted and tasty out of the skein—or perhaps the flaker—is the father of Adams' Korn Kurls, the first corn curl on the market, the first snack food marketed of any sort except, as the editorial indicates, potato chips—though it forgets to mention the one other, popcorn. It is the father (not the cousin) of all the products that evolve from or imitate corn curls all over the country, all over the world. It makes its owners and shareholders a mint of money.

The grandfather of the corn curl, though, goes back to Colley Road. "It's those chips and flakes and peels that us kids used to pick up and eat, under Clair Mathews' little grinding mill on the floor of the round barn," Jackie says, "when I was three."

48 ✕ SHINGLES

Grampa always carries a small tablet and pencil in the breast pocket of his bib overalls. This is so that the person he is talking to can respond easily.

The writing on the tablet is one sided, and seldom are these half-dialogues saved. Some do survive, and while a subject may be indicated: cows, crops, machinery, money, there is usually little understanding to be gained of the treatment of the topic, or the feelings of those involved. But in one that Jackie comes across, several years after Grampa has died, a small drama might be reconstructed.

She knows it's in the early Forties, during the War. The round barn is in need of reshingling, and Grampa has called in a professional roofer, Elmer H. Reimer, to see about doing the job. Mr. Reimer sets out to measure the roof. Grampa does not give him very long before asking what his measurements are.

Reimer (writing on the tablet), "I have not got it all yet—Just the round barn front—200—"

Grampa then writes some figures on the tablet:

"68.34 x 3.1416 = 214.6969"

Reimer: "We were on the top and have that. We have that."

There follows a rough circular drawing, apparently by Grampa, and on the next page, a rough right angle triangle, all lines labeled with figures, and a double hypotenuse—the upper line bent, obviously the roof line, which in a gambrel roof, the round barn's roof, has an angle in it.

Reimer: "Can you get wood shingles? I believe if you could get good wood shingles, they are not bad."

Next comes a drawing of the barn, and, in Reimer's hand: "It would take about 300 feet." He is referring to some sort of flashing, and W.J. questions the necessity of this.

Reimer: "If you do not put this on, in just a few years the wood shingles would rot away. You see it does not dry out—a 9 inch strip first—aluminum—"

Grampa questions the choice of metal.

The shingled roof of the round barn. Colley Road is in the back ground, and on the far eastern horizon, Chez Nous.

Reimer: "War time metal. Have you a few wood shingles? Bring just a couple."

Grampa does. Reimer demonstrates, apparently with shingle and flashing. "This sharp edge cuts the water off."

Grampa's next words must deal with holding the shingles down.

Reimer: "It is not necessary. The best staples we can buy. 168# or approximately 134#."

Grampa questions the color of the shingles; he wants a green roof. Reimer tells him this is possible. "Only color at present."

Now Grampa wants to know if Reimer's men smoke.

Reimer: "It's not usual. We do not allow any man to smoke on the roof. We ask them to sit down by the truck and smoke."

Satisfied, Grampa then inquires about the lap of the shingles.

Reimer: "We try to give at least a 2 inch lap on top and 3 inch lap on side. More often over because of spacing on roof boards."

From Grampa, another technical question.

Reimer: "Instead of going up with (undecipherable: — nt) we go down. I believe you will find it will run 9 inches rather than 10 inches. We do not use a rule."

Here, Grampa asks for a warranty on how long the roof will last, and mentions another company that has given a ten-year warranty on some work they have done for him.

Reimer: "That is only as good as the company. It means very little. We could be out of business tomorrow. We hope and try to make every job give good service. If we are here ten years from now we too will stand in back of our work. I always tell my men the best work we do is rotten. We have to do better every day."

Grampa inquires how many men he has who will be working on the roof.

Reimer: "I only have two and three men."

Grampa expresses doubt about so few men for such a big job.

Reimer: "I can get more and will have to get outside help on this job but I will be here myself and oversee and work personally on this job."

Now Grampa comes back to the question of lap, and Reimer is beginning to weary of the discussion. "It will I assure you be sufficient lap if we do it. We do not use a rule on each shingle, it would take too long. Besides your roof is round and would pull the shingle down. We would have to keep it down to make them cover."

Grampa is still holding out for a larger, specific lap.

Reimer: "Regardless of who you have do it. I would be willing to bet our lap would be as much as anyone's. I know just how that works."

Grampa now expresses such doubt that Reimer is testy. He tells Grampa, in essence, that he doesn't need to roof the round barn if Grampa has no faith in the way he will do it. "I have plenty of work and only yesterday I turned down a $1,400 job. I just said no because I could not take care of it at once."

Grampa shakes his head and says that in that case Reimer can't do the barn, because he wants the job done right away. Reimer sees the contract slipping away and quickly writes, "It just so happens that I can do it within a week or perhaps even sooner."

He now brings in the ammunition of his reputation, and names the men who suggested him to Grampa for the job, men he knows Grampa respects. "With men like Mr. Qualman and Mr. Klingberg recommending you, one must do good work."

Grampa is still bringing up quality problems, and Mr. Reimer is now angry. Would he do a shoddy job and jeopardize his reputation? He lets Grampa know his feelings; he throws away the job. "I would not sell my reputation for the barn. You are the *Boss*. If what we have considered is not worth your time giving it thought you better not do business with me. You need not."

Grampa realizes he has gone too far, and asks more conciliatorily about what Reimer means about lap.

Reimer: "The only reason I will not say 3 inches lap and 3 inches side is because in some instances it may be a trifle less, and then what."

Grampa then gives Reimer back his own reasoning, that because of the roundness of the barn, these measurements can't be strictly held to; there has to be a little give in the measurements.

Reimer: "I had fully made up my mind to give it a 3 inch lap but that is the point exactly. I do not believe we ever put on a job that was less than 3 inches in most cases."

Grampa now is ready to firm up the problem. He takes his pad and pencil and writes, "Relative to the top and side lap of shingles, the rule will be to have *approximately* a 3 inch lap at both top and side." It is a mini-contract.

Reimer: "That is O.K." In ink he signs his name, "Elmer H. Reimer."

Under his signature, apparently to remind Grampa of the flashing, he writes, "aluminum."

Now Grampa tells him to go ahead with the job, that he has confidence in him.

Reimer: "Thank you. I will write up a contract to that effect and you can sign it later. So the company will say when I purchased it."

Grampa then asks whether Mr. Reimer would like an advance on the job.

Reimer: "If you would it would be appreciated. When we start you can pay some."

Grampa says something more here, perhaps about supplying the flashing.

Reimer: "I will see about that later. You furnish roof boards and the wood shingles necessary."

At this point the writing in the little notebook comes to an end. The barn roof is reshingled. Jackie recalls watching a time or two, being impressed with the men crawling along the roof and the ladders all laid in place, but it was not an activity she spent hours observing. And she did not know, then, to study lap or flashing.

But the job is a good one. The green shingles last forty years, and more.

49 ⚡ THE SPLIT IN THE SILO

L ibby's has a large factory at Janesville, fifteen miles north of Beloit, where
they can peas, beans, tomatoes, and sweet corn. The summer that Jackie
has just finished high school, they offer all their sweet corn residue — chopped
green ears and husks, mixed with some ripe discard ears — to farmers for use
as silage. The factory will truck it; all the farmer has to pay is the cost of
transport.

Grampa and Daddy are delighted with this bonanza. They contract with
Libby's; they ready the central silo; they move the silo-filling machinery up
onto the barn floor of the round barn. At the scheduled time, everyone is
poised for action. They wait all day, but the trucks don't arrive. Finally, during suppertime, Daddy gets a call that they're on the way. He and Jackie and
Craig jump into the car and drive down to the dairy. They are in time to see
the first of the big trucks lumber in off Colley Road and wait in line on the
gravel area before the ramp up to the barn floor. Their open backs are piled
high with pale green foliage. Jackie notices that each truck is streaming water
onto the ground, as if there were a hose in the silage, washing it down. She
figures it must take a lot of water to process sweet corn at the factory.

Late into the evening, in intermittent convoys, the trucks keep coming.
Their headlights sweep the lawns and buildings as they turn in. Daddy and
many hired men are up half the night, silo filling. Jackie is intrigued with
this unusual nocturnal activity, but finally she and Craig walk the mile and
a half home to Chez Nous. Corn detasseling starts early, and they are both
employed.

At dawn Jackie hears the phone ring. She hears Daddy exclaim, "Well, I'll
be a son of a bitch! I'm on my way down!"

She leaps from bed and pulls on her jeans. She doesn't ask the emergency.
She knows from experience that if you wait for details, you might be left
behind. With Daddy talking that way, whatever it is will be important. Were
it merely the bottle washer again, or a problem with the well, he'd have said,

"I'll be down as soon as I have my coffee," and she'd have rolled over and gone back to sleep till six o'clock and detasseling time.

She hops into the passenger seat just as Daddy slides into the driver's. He shakes his head and explains as they roar down the lane and onto Colley Road.

"The silo's splitting. Libby's silage is wet, wetter than anything we've ever put in before. It must weigh tons more than the silo's designed to withstand in lateral thrust. Harlan just discovered a crack—down in the cow barn. He slipped on some ooze in the center by the grain bins and nearly broke his skull."

A chill grips Jackie. A herdsman's skull is bad enough, but what about the silo? What if it splits right in two? What will happen to the barn?

"Those trucks were leaking like an old man's nose," Daddy says, "even after coming all the way from Janesville. I should have thought about it." He careens into the drive, pulls right up to the cow barn door and slams on the brakes.

Jackie jumps out on her side. She can hear the milking motor in the up-stairs barn pulsing calmly, as if nothing were the matter. Inside the cow barn, she can hear it too, only more muffled. She follows Daddy around the side-walk and up a walk between the cows to the inner circle of the barn. The cows are rolling their eyes and snorting at the activity before them. Grampa and four or five hired men are standing between the cows and the silo, looking at the concrete.

"Ron's here," somebody says. They stand back as Daddy comes up.

Harlan, the herdsman, points. "There it is."

Jackie looks. There it is, all right—a narrow wavering vertical fissure, whitish against the grayer concrete, starting almost at the floor and disap-pearing into the ceiling.

"I'll be a son of a bitch," Daddy repeats. The men glance at Grampa, for when they were hired they had to promise not to smoke, drink, or use im-proper language on the place. But Ron is Ron, and Grampa can't hear him.

Juice is oozing from the bottom of the crack and making a pool on the con-crete. "That's how I discovered it," says Harlan. "I slipped on the puddle."

A gunny sack is lying in the juice, but it's caked with grain dust. Even if it weren't, it wouldn't be effective as a sponge. Wet trickles from under it into a cow's manger. The cow whose trough it is licks it up as fast as it runs in. Her neighbors on either side stretch their long necks and tongues in vain. Jackie understands their desire; she's sucked on many a corn stalk and knows how sweet the juice is.

Her attention returns to the crack. She's sick with foreboding. What can possibly be done? She listens to Daddy, Grampa, the men. They all talk about the problem. Daddy spells to Grampa; Grampa considers. They all consider. Will the reinforcing iron rods in the concrete hold, or will the pressure snap them? To take the silage out of the silo would be a difficult and dangerous job, more so because it would have to be done quickly. And there's no technique for emptying a silo quickly; silos are emptied fork by fork. But can they repair the silo with the silage left in? Might the water somehow be siphoned off, to relieve the pressure? How long do they have before the silo splits more?

"Yes," says Daddy to Harlan, "finish the milking, but get the cows out as quick as you can."

The dread in Jackie's heart increases.

Daddy remembers where there's an old dismantled stave silo west of town. Jackie knows stave silos. They are wooden, made up of many vertical slats belted at intervals by steel bands. Daddy spells to Grampa: might they belt up the splitting concrete silo with stave silo bands? Grampa nods thoughtfully and follows Daddy toward the office telephone. The barnhands get on with the milking. Everyone else waits, watching, conjecturing, running a finger along the crack, as if to feel it makes it more believable.

Jackie looks at the fissure where it disappears into the cow barn ceiling. She goes into the passageway between the round barn and side barn and climbs the narrow stairs to the upper barn. She wants to find where the crack ends. As she comes out onto the barn floor the milking motor throbs suddenly loud, and THE AIMS OF THIS FARM high on the silo's side seem to throb, too. She averts her eyes and scrambles up onto the hay. She springs around to the far side of the silo, for she calculates the crack must come up behind the grain storage bins. She climbs the chute and studies the concrete, but can find no sign of a break. That's a relief.

She returns to the loft floor and studies the silo. She pictures it splitting, taking the barn, fragile as an eggshell in comparison with that gigantic core, right with it. She sees the barn's curved, white-painted sides smashed like kindling, spilling out grain, spilling out hay, the silo pinning the barn down like a tree struck by lightning. She sees the AIMS cracked and exposed to the sky.

She addresses the silo out loud. "You've gotta hang on! Help is coming!"

Inaction is more than she can bear. She opens the narrow door into the dark silo shaft and swinging onto the rungs scales them fast as a monkey. She pictures herself part of the kindling, but she wants to see. She can hear voices coming up the shaft from the cow barn. She climbs toward the light to where

The Aims of This Farm:
1. Good Crops;
2. Proper Storage;
3. Profitable Live Stock;
4. A stable Market;
5. Life as well as a Living;
W. J. Dougan

Cunningham School first-graders visit the farm in 1955, and pose before the steel-banded silo.

the last shutter ends, and peers over its lip. The silo interior is dim, but she can make out the silage level three or four feet below her. The well of the great cylinder is more than half full. The chopped cornstalks lie there, looking and smelling green and fresh, unfermented. As soon as they smell like silage, the cow whose manger gets the trickle will be perpetually drunk. She gives a snort of laughter.

She looks for the crack, where it should be, but can't see it up here, either. Maybe it doesn't extend very far. She climbs back down and onto the loft floor. Through the open doors she sees Daddy and Grampa hurrying from the office. She swings into the shaft again and climbs to the lower level. No one sees her emerge; they are all attending the crack.

Daddy reports that the farmer will sell the silo. He and Grampa will take two men to go after the bands, and Erv will head into town for bolts as soon as the hardware store is open. Farm stores open early, Jackie knows, often before seven. Grampa squares his shoulders resolutely and cries in ringing tones, "We'll fetch it!" which is what he always says when things get rough. It seems particularly appropriate for this occasion: the situation is very rough, and there is actual fetching to be done. Grampa's phrase cheers Jackie.

A milkhouse hand, just arrived, wanders onto the scene and peers through the crowd. "Hey, that silo's got a crack in it!" he exclaims. "Shouldn't somebody be doing something about it?"

"You're the very man I need, Sparky," says Daddy. "Come here."

Sparky does.

"Put your thumb there where it widens out a little," Daddy instructs.

Sparky puts his thumb in the crack. "Now what?"

"Now," says Daddy, "stay right there until we get back, and holler like anything if the dike breaks!"

Everybody laughs except Sparky, who turns a little red and pulls back his hand.

Jackie decides she'll show up late for detasseling and follow the action. She climbs into the back of the truck with the men. As they bump up the lane to the farm west of town, she spots the remains of the stave silo near the barnyard. The staves are in neat fat rolls, like giant snow fencing. The steel bands are in much smaller, narrower rolls. The men jump down and hoist the bands onto the truck while Grampa and Daddy talk to the farmer. Jackie listens again to the details of the possible catastrophe. A collie appears and rubs against her, and three gray kittens come running, their little tails straight up like spikes, and their fur, when she pats them, soft as thistledown.

When the price is agreed on and the bands loaded—Daddy says they'll return for the staves another time—she climbs back in the truck and settles herself amid the coils. The sun caresses her face, the wind tousles her hair. The men laugh and joke as they speed back toward the dairy. Jackie sends a mental message to the silo. "Keep hanging on! We're fetching it!"

In the now empty cow barn, Erv is ready with his arc welder. The barnhands leave off the cleanup to help. The men thread a steel band around the silo, just under the ceiling. It goes behind the chute and the ventilator, over the crack, and behind the grain bin. As it comes around to the start, Jackie's heart gives a lurch. There's a two foot gap between the ends! But Erv bends the ends out, burns a hole in each with his acetylene torch, and inserts a long double-threaded steel rod. He screws nuts on the ends and twists. The more he twists, the more the two ends of the belt are pulled together.

She watches as they put another band below the first one and tighten it. The crack isn't closing, but it can't widen anymore, either, unless it breaks the steel. And with enough steel bands, it won't be able to. Grampa tells them that when the silo is empty and the crack has dried out, they'll caulk it. Till that can happen, some time in the winter, corn juices will leak out. They'll have to keep cloths down, on account of the slipperiness of the concrete floor. On account of the tipsy cow, too, thinks Jackie.

Erv and his team decide they can fit three more bands in the cow barn, then eight in the upper barn, stopping just under the AIMS. It's going to work! Daddy is cheerful. Grampa is cheerful. Jackie is cheerful, too, and gives the concrete a pat. "We fetched it," she tells the silo.

She's suddenly hungry. She goes to the milkhouse. Chocolate milk is rippling down the cooling coils above the bottling machine. She darts her hand in and plucks a just-filled half-pint off the assembly line, leaving the capping machine to stamp down on emptiness. She goes out in the sunshine to drink.

She looks up the ramp, through the open barn doors, to the AIMS. She thinks about the second one, "Proper Storage." The silo has stored faithfully and properly, ever since it was built. It just never had to cope with Libby's soaking wet silage before. Soon, with thirteen belts, it will store properly again.

She finishes her milk and strolls toward the office, to find out what field the detasslers are in. The excitement is over. She guesses it's time to get to work. She looks forward to telling Craig all about it.

50 ✥ MATCHES

It's September, 1944. Two kids who live on the edge of town are out, messing about on the farm. Tom Nesbit and Teddy McLeod. Tom is thirteen, Teddy eleven. They aren't the guests of anyone, or particular friends, they've just come on their own, as town kids sometimes do, hoping to find something of interest going on, hoping for some chocolate milk. This isn't their first visit. They wander in the cow barn, they wander in the horse barn, they go up into the loft of the round barn. After a while they leave.

Don Hunter, the herdsman, goes upstairs in the round barn for feed. He finds the feed room full of smoke. He rushes in and stamps out a small fire smoldering in the gunny sacks. He drags the scorched sacks out to the ramp. He gets water and douses them, making sure the fire is entirely out. He checks the feed room for other feed bags, and the whole loft for danger. Then he reports to Ron. Ron calls the police, tells who the culprits are.

The police catch Tom and Teddy trotting home along the railroad tracks. A squad car escorts them back to the farm. The officers stand with the boys between them when they face the Dougan Farm proprietors.

Yes, they admit to Daddy and Grampa, they had been lighting matches in the loft. They thought all of them had gone out. They hadn't meant to start a fire.

"Yet if it weren't for our herdsman, you'd have burned down the barn and the side barn, ruined two silos, probably killed cows, and certainly put us out of business," says Daddy severely. "And with today's wind, you could have taken the horse barn and the calf barn, too."

Grampa is grave. "You had no reason to be in the barn in the first place, and no business lighting matches anywhere near here. This is carelessness, but it is criminal carelessness. You are old enough lads to be responsible."

The boys alternately squirm and look defiant as Daddy and Grampa confer. They know the parents of both boys. They know Tom has been in trouble before, and perhaps led on the younger boy. They decide not to press charges, but ask the officers to escort the pair to their homes, and to speak to each set of parents about the seriousness of the averted disaster. They tell Tom and Teddy they are no longer welcome at the farm, ever again.

Jackie writes the details to Craig, who is away at school in Arizona. She knows he'll be especially interested, because Tom has been in his class all through grade school, has come to birthday parties. "I'll bet there was much weeping and wailing in the Nesbit and McLeod houses last night," she finishes her letter.

Daddy knows there was. For both fathers pay visits to the farm the next day, their sons in tow, to apologize, and to report what punishments are being exacted. Neither Jackie nor Craig hear about these, but they do know that neither Tom nor Teddy ever comes out to the farm again.

51 ⨯ DAN GOLDSMITH

Almost always when Jackie goes into the round barn and anyone is there, music is playing. The men listen to the radio while they milk or clean. The radio is on a little shelf up against the central silo, the shelf that holds the day-to-day barn records and the cows' nose-lead. And always the radio station they have tuned in to is WLS, the Prairie Farmer Station.

Jackie is familiar with this station. It's the same one the men listen to in their sitting room over at the Big House when they're waiting for dinner. In the early mornings, on nights when she's slept over at the Big House, she herself listens to Jolly Joe advertising CoCo Wheats and conducting dressing races that sometimes the boys win and sometimes the girls. Jackie and Craig are scornful—he must make it up, for how can he *see*? WLS has Lulubelle and Scotty, with their guitars, and the Hoosier Hot Shots, Craig's favorites; and people sing twangy songs like "Yippee Ti-Yi-Yo, Git Along, Little Dogies," or "Don't Fence Me In!" There are also whiney ones, "I'm Gonna Buy a Paper Doll," and a singer called the Betsy Ross Girl who belts out "Yankee Doodle Dandy."

Down in the barn the cows listen to "Yippee Ti-Yi-Yo" while they munch their hay and while the milking machines tug rhythmically at their tits.

"Do the cows really *like* music?" Jackie asks Billy Beadle once.

"They love it," Billy responds. "It soothes 'em and calms 'em and they let down their milk and give lots of it." He whistles along with "Yippee Ti-Yi-Yo" while he changes a milking machine. Jackie thinks privately that if she were a cow, her milk would come out all curdled if she were listening to one rhythm while her milking machine was pumping away on a different beat.

One year Daddy puts an ad in *Hoard's Dairyman* for a herdsman. He gets an answer from a man named Dan Goldsmith in White River Junction, Vermont. Daddy likes the sound of Dan's letter, writes him, and offers him the job. Six months later Dan shows up on the farm. He's been slow coming, he explains, because the letter went to White River Junction, New Hampshire. It only just reached him.

Dan Goldsmith, the herds-man in the round barn, plays the bass in Lewie Dalvit's danceband. Craig Dougan, also in the band, took this picture.

Dan is a tall man, thin, loose jointed, and bald. He has a prominent nose, and the tragedy of all Jewish history is in the depths of his deep brown eyes. Daddy makes room for him in the barn and the Big House.

Jackie is now busy at Beloit College. She's not around the barn much these days, and with Grama and Grampa retired and living on the edge of town, she doesn't go often into the Big House, either. She doesn't know anything about Dan Goldsmith until Daddy remarks one night at supper, "We have an unusual man in the barn."

"Oh?" says Mother. "What's unusual about him?"

"Have you noticed any difference in the milk? He's got the cows listening to Mozart symphonies," Daddy says.

Jackie and Pat—who is also going to Beloit College and living at home—prick up their ears.

"He tunes in WHA instead of WLS," Daddy goes on. "He listens to 'Chapter A Day' and is following Professor Easum's history lectures on the Middle Ages. We had quite a chat about Alcuin."

WHA is "the Oldest Station in the Nation," broadcast out of the University of Wisconsin at Madison. It's totally educational. The family is even more intrigued.

Daddy says, "I heard him whistling a Bach cantata today and I said, 'You must have a love of good music, Dan.' He told me he has a degree in string bass from Julliard."

Julliard! At this point Jackie and Pat are electrified; the account has become distinctly practical. Julliard is one of the finest music conservatories in the country. A Julliard graduate milking cows in the round barn! It's unbelievable. They leave the table, leap in the car, and speed down to the Big House.

They meet Dan. Yes, he's a Julliard graduate. No, he doesn't have his bass with him, though he owns a fine one of native birds-eye maple, made early last century by the New Hampshire contrabass maker, Abraham Prescott. Yes, he misses playing. If they can find him a decent instrument he'd be delighted to join the Madison String Sinfonia that Pat and Jackie play in on Saturday afternoons.

Thereafter, at noon every Saturday, Jackie sprints out of her class at Morse-Ingersoll Hall. Pat doesn't have a Saturday class. She and Dan are waiting with a farm truck. Jackie's cello, Pat's violin, and Dan's borrowed bass are in the back. They gun the fifteen miles up to Janesville where Betty, Corky, and Suzie, carrying two more cellos and a string bass, vault into the back of the truck. They then all speed to Madison, thirty-five miles farther. At one-thirty, Marie Endres starts rehearsal, and the Beloit-Janesville contingent, still breathless, have their strings tuned and bows tightened in time for the first downbeat. Dan folds his long frame over his string bass, and watching the conductor with his deep, sad eyes, he draws deep, sad tones from the guts of his instrument. He's a first-rate player. Everyone is enthusiastic about the Dougan herdsman.

Sinfonia isn't the only orchestra Dan joins. Pat's fiance, Lewie Dalvit, has a dance band in which Pat plays jazz fiddle and Craig plays saxophone. Now Dan goes along, too, on Friday and Saturday nights, and plunks out the rhythms. Sometimes he arrives home barely in time to fetch the cows from the pasture for early milking.

One night the band plays for a dance at the Turtle Grange. A husky farmer who has recently inherited a ramshackle farm and woodlot over on the State Line Road watches the players. At a break he speaks to Dan. His name is Marshall Miller, he says, and diffidently adds that he himself plays the string bass. Dan presses him to take a turn on the next set. Marshall plays a mean bass. It turns out that he's a graduate of Curtiss, another stellar music school. From then on there's another passenger and another bass fiddle in the truck on Saturdays.

Daddy tells the story to a group of Mother's Federation of Music Clubs friends who visit the round barn and are surprised that the cows are milking to Mendelssohn.

"Lift up a burdock leaf anywhere in Turtle Township," he brags, "and chances are you'll find a conservatory-trained, string-bass-playing farmer!"

52 ⚔ HARI-KARI

Ed Pfaff is a long-time worker on the farm. One of his sons, Jerry, is eight. Jerry likes to ride his bike out to the farm and fool around. He's particularly fascinated with the electric screens on the windows of the round barn. He likes to watch flies get zapped. If there aren't any flies committing hari-kari, he'll take a grass stem and hold it to the screen, and watch it sizzle with a bright blue flame.

One day a screen has fallen. It's lying under the window, partly on the sidewalk that circles the round barn, partly on the grass. It's still getting power, though; Jerry drops a beetle on it and the beetle takes a long brilliant time incinerating.

Jerry looks around. Nobody is in sight. He fumbles with his trousers, pulls out his thingie, and pees on the screen. The jolt throws him to the ground. He has nearly committed hari-kari, himself.

53 ❧ THE GREAT HAYLOFT IN THE SKY

Ron Dougan, in the Chez Nous corn storage warehouse, holds a bag of Dougan Hybrid Seed Corn.

Daddy has a health scare when he's 57 or so. He goes breakfastless to the dentist; emerging from the office he lights a cigarette. He gets dizzy, blacks out, and collapses in the hall. At the hospital he undergoes tests. His doctor tells him he's had a very small stroke, his arteries are vulnerable, and he must never smoke another cigarette. Daddy quits smoking.

A new American Breeders Service vet, Les Larson, an assistant to the head vet, Dr. Bartlett, has been coming down to the farm about once a month to work with Daddy on infertility problems in the Dougan herd. Les, as well as Dave Bartlett, is a "theriogenologist," that is, a specialist in animal reproduction. Les has devised a little plywood shelf that he can move from windowsill to windowsill in the round barn as he works along behind the cows. It holds the paperwork on each animal.

Daddy leans on the little shelf, telling Les a story. A prop gives way and the shelf tips. Daddy crashes to the floor. He's greatly relieved when he learns it isn't dizziness that caused his tumble.

"I thought this was it," he confides to Les. "I thought I was looking over Jordan—but it was only the manure trough."

Later he expands to Mother on the Great-Hayloft-in-the-Sky. "I rather hope it's like that," he says. "I'd feel at home. The pearly gates will be stanchions—a little easier to squeeze through than a needle's eye, though I don't have to worry about being a rich man. . . . Now, angels. They're obvious, with their big eyes and long lashes and soft breath and sweet voices continually mooing and hymning before the throne. But where is the throne? It'd have to be at the top of the silo, up there with the pigeons. The only thing I'd not care about would be swimming that river. Do you suppose it's narrow enough to step across?"

"Maybe you're not destined for heaven," Mother says. "What do you see as the other place? A pig sty?"

Daddy is shocked. "Oh, no! There's a place for them there, too. One of the many mansions. Why, heaven might be all one big wallow. Maybe there's no space for us there, at all. I can't for the life of me see why the Almighty would want humans. Except Gramp, of course. What is God, anyway? The Great I-Am."

Mother quotes Popeye: "I yam what I yam."

"God as sweet potato," Daddy muses. "That opens a whole new realm. I wonder where among the dominions and powers the rutabagies rank?"

Many years later, Daddy comes back from being a pallbearer at a funeral. He's depressed by the whole event. At the table he announces gloomily, "When I die, just dig a posthole and drop me in."

"Head first or feet first?" a granddaughter asks.

"It depends what direction you think I'm going," Ron Dougan replies.

BOOK TWO
THE
MILKHOUSE

The milkhouse, viewed from the top of the outside silo. The tool house is on the left, the Little House behind. Beyond is Colley Road. And in front, horse-drawn milk wagons and milk trucks.

1 ⋈ THE MILK ROOM

There is no milkhouse at the start of the milk business. There is a milk room. It's off the kitchen of the Big House, the end closest the barn. It's to this room that Grampa carries the milk cans from the morning and evening milkings and cools the milk. It's here, in the long sink, before Grampa has a hired man, that Grama rinses the milking and bottling utensils in cold water so that the residue of milk will not cook and set, then washes and scalds them and puts them upside down on a rack to dry. She also washes and scalds the bottles back from the route. It's here that Grampa fills the bottles and caps them.

The waste water from the milk room is funneled into a drain that goes out through the base of the north wall and flows into a foot-wide wooden trough that Grampa builds. The trough, sloping slightly, runs along the foundation of the house. It continues a few feet beyond the foundation's west end; from there the rivulet is eased onto the ground and in a shallow ditch runs down toward the barnyard where it joins with the sporadic overflow from the flushing out of the barn's gutters.

Till the round barn is built there is only the original barn, with its board floors raised above the wooden manure trenches. At first the run-off from both barn and milk room goes directly into the field west of the house and is absorbed into the soil. When Grampa builds the round barn, with all its concrete work, he makes improvements. The wood trough along the house foundation is replaced with a concrete one. The floor and gutters of the original barn—now the side barn—are torn up and replaced with concrete. A large concrete cow tank is built in the enlarged barnyard; the clean water used for cooling milk in the milk room is piped into it. Down below the barnyard Grampa has a stand-pit dug and covered. The waste water from the milk room, the overflow of the cow tank, and the liquids of cows and cleaning from the barn drain into the pit; it is only the pit's overflow that now is funneled into the west field, where it spreads out and percolates down through the soil as moisture and fertilizer. At this point in the dairy's operation, there isn't enough waste water to cause any concern.

From the start, the trough along the base of the house is a play-spot for Ronald and Trever. It's an intermittent stream. When water is running out from the milk room they squat by the river and let their little boats of chips or sticks or leaves sail the length of it. Then they run back and float more boats. When the water begins to wane they quickly construct dams, so that their boats will have a place to float a little longer.

On the west side of the milk room, behind a partial partition with a swinging door, is a privy. The user sits inside the house, but the product falls outside, down through a hole into a wagon placed directly below. The slope of the ground leaves the north wing of the house elevated enough that there is space for this wagon; Grampa has had a large indentation built into the foundation for it. Periodically the wagon is hitched to a team, pulled out to a field, and the human refuse dumped with the manure from the barn. There is also an outdoor privy, down beyond the wood pile, so that it isn't necessary for everyone on the farm to come tramping into the house.

When Ronald is ten, his father and Mr. Osborn, the plumber, add two showers to one end of the narrow privy room. This is a luxury, for up till now bathing has been in a tub rolled into the milk room, where there is hot water from the boiler. Morning washing has been with basins and pitchers in the various bedrooms. When the work is complete the two men strip down and initiate the showers. They emerge rubbing with towels, and Ronald, swinging his heels on a high stool in the milk room, observes with some surprise what a round little pot-belly the plumber has. It is more than five years before Mr. Osborn fits the entire house with indoor plumbing.

At the start of the business Grampa and Grama do all the milk room work, as well as all the work of the farm, but within a year Grampa is able to hire help. By 1914 there are seven full time men; eight in 1916. In the early years the work is not specialized. A man at different times will work in the fields, in the barn, in the milk room. A deliveryman in the morning will be a farmhand in the afternoon. And at three-thirty, everyone stops other chores and cleans up to assist with the milking.

Alan Turnbull, in his University of Wisconsin Master's thesis, gives a brief picture of the milk room as it was in 1914 by describing its equipment: "For the dairy work there are the following implements: milking pails, a milk cooler, a power capper, separator, a steam boiler for heating water and running turbine bottle washer, bottles, and cases for holding bottles.... The engine power consists of a kerosene engine used for pumping water, washing bottles, capping milk bottles, and furnishing light." He does not describe the cooler; it is a grid of metal coils through which well water is run, so that the warm milk from the barn, rippling down over these coils, is cold in a matter of minutes.

Chuck Hoag, in his 1916 Master's thesis in Agricultural Accounting, adds to the description, though he describes the engine as gasoline, which is the more likely: "The milk or dairy room is 18 x 12, being a part of the one story wing of the dwelling.... A small engine room adjoins the [east] side of the house and contains a 2 H.P. gasoline engine, pump, and electric light plant. The engine runs both of these and furnishes power for the milk room machinery and washing machine for the house."

He continues, in a later section:

> We have thus far omitted any reference to the handling of the milk. At the barn, the cows are thoroughly curried and brushed, and the udder, flank, and belly wiped with a wet sponge, prior to each milking. The milkers wear clean aprons and the milk is drawn into a covered pail. The milk passes through a protecting layer of gauze and absorbent cotton in the head of this pail. The milk of each cow is weighed separately and emptied into a can. The can is set on a shelf which prevents the milker from leaning over the opening while pouring. No strainer is used on the can and the cover is replaced after pouring the milk.
>
> Each can, as filled, is taken directly to the milk room and the milk cooled at once, or separated, as the case may be. Cooling is done by water pumped directly from the well by which method the milk is cooled to about 52 degrees. All the morning milk is bottled and sold as whole milk at ten cents per quart. Enough of the night's milk is retained to make up the necessary amount of whole milk for the trade and the rest is separated for cream. This night's milk is kept overnight in cans placed in cold water and bottled in the morning with the morning milk. A special bottle with "Standard" cap and ring is used. In supplying the trade, care is taken to give only the morning milk to those customers who use the milk for babies and invalids.
>
> The demand for this grade of milk in the city of Beloit was so great at times, that it was necessary to discontinue the sale of cream and sell the entire output as whole milk. Towards the end of the year, arrangements were made to secure a small amount of milk from one of the neighbors. This was produced under Mr. Dougan's direction, delivered to the farm twice a day, and separated for cream.

In calculating the milk room costs only the bottles actually broken in the milk room have been charged to the bottling operation. Those broken on the wagons and by customers are charged against the delivery department.

Hoag finds a difference in the barn weights of the milk and the actual volume of "the finished product that is disposed of." He cannot easily account for this. He suggests the loss may be due to errors in weighing in the barn, to spilling, to residue left in the utensils and separator or on the cooling coils, and to the breakage of bottles in the wagons. Since it is justly a cost of operating the business and since the greater chance of loss is in the milk room, he charges the entire shrinkage to this department.

He then goes on to calculate the full cost of producing a quart of milk, against the entire profits of the milk business, sprinkling in more facts about the business along the way. Milk is sold in quarts only, thereby simplifying the handling and reducing the expense of using pint bottles. During warm weather, the milk cases are iced before being loaded. The two delivery wagons leave the farm about 6:30 a.m. and return at noon; the customers receive their milk within five hours of the time it leaves the cow, except for that which is from the milking of the previous afternoon. Milk which is not sold is separated for cream and never put out again as whole milk.

The daily demand for milk is quite uniform, which avoids the necessity of bottling a large surplus of milk that may not be sold. There were 5,121 quarts brought back during the entire year, an average of 14 per day. No milk is replaced, since complaints by customers are so infrequent. No reduced rates are offered to anyone. A ticket system is used, which makes the business at least 85 percent cash. A gross business of $13,063.84 was done for the year, of which only $38.67, less than 0.3 percent was uncollected. Cream was sold at 12½ cents per half pint until October, when it was raised to 15 cents. Skim milk was sold at five cents per quart, though only a relatively small amount was disposed of.

The summary of value: 122,386 quarts of milk were sold in 1916 for $12,238.60; 5,451 half pints of cream for $743.44; 1,636 quarts of skim for $81.80, making a total value of $13,063.84.

The costs: 55 tons of ice cost $1.65 per ton, which included the labor of 128 man hours and 97 horse hours, as well as cost of sawdust and machinery use. Producing a quart of milk (feed, barn labor, etc.) averaged 4.52 cents; bottling, 1.20 cents; delivery, 1.63 cents; for a total cost of 7.35 cents. With milk selling at ten cents a quart, this resulted in a profit of 2.65 cents a quart.

Hoag adds a note, though: "Reference to Table XL, 'Profit and Loss Statement,' will show two quite large losses, in the breeding herd account and the feed account, totaling $911.61. Since both of these losses belong largely to the milk production account, it is necessary to add .64 cents to the cost of production of each quart. This makes an average cost of production per quart of 5.16 cents; a total cost per quart of 7.99 cents; and an average profit per quart of 2.01 cents."

The year's profit for whole milk is $3,126.28; for secondary or by-products, $252.32. The total profit, for the dairy account: $3,378.60.

For nine years the milk room stays next door to Grama's breads and pies, with its equipment increasingly crowding the space. As the business gains customers, more cows are necessary, and there is more milk to process and store, more bottles and pails to wash. From almost the start, a separate milkhouse has been needed. An adequate barn, of course, had to be built first; the round barn is constructed in 1911. By 1916 Grampa has gathered enough capital to build the milkhouse, part being a loan of $1,500 from his sister, Ida Croft. He locates the structure directly east of the Big House and diagonally south-east of the round barn. He runs a sidewalk from the Big House's back door to the milkhouse, and from the milkhouse down to the round barn. The considerable amount of building in 1916 — and not just of the milkhouse — strains the other farm operations, but as Hoag says, "Practically all the improvements were quite necessary, since the increased size of the milk business made the old milk room inadequate."

The new milkhouse is ready for use early in 1917, and the old milk room is retired. Within a few years after 1917 there is major construction work done on the Big House. The roof is raised over the one-story north wing that contains the dining room, the kitchen, and former milk room, in order to provide a series of upstairs dormitory rooms for the hired men; one room even boasts a little balcony. The milk room then becomes the hired men's washroom, except for every Monday when the men must share it with Grama's washing machine and rinse tubs, and in rainy weather thread the maze of wet overalls and work shirts hung to dry on a latticework of indoor clotheslines.

Jackie never knows this room as the old milk room. No water gushes outside into the cement trough for her and her sibs to float boats down; they use the cowtank for their armadas. She never even notices the trough, or the cubicle for the manure wagon, either, till these are pointed out to her by Uncle Trever.

The room is familiar to her nonetheless. She avoids it when Grama and

Effie are doing the wash. She occasionally uses the toilet in the back, when she's in a hurry, and she regularly uses the room as a thoroughfare to go from the Big House back door into Grama's kitchen. Grampa sometimes doctors a cut or scrape of hers there, using the supplies lined up on a shelf over the long sink. And she and her sisters and brother know that long sink intimately, for every now and then Daddy marches them over from the Little House, lines them up—the smaller on chairs or stools—bends them over the lip and with their upside-down noses practically pressing the enamel and their eyes scrunched tight, washes their hair assembly-line fashion. The reason for this change of bathing venue is that Grama's big wood stove has soft rain water in a compartment on its side, which can rinse out the soap scum much better than the hard water from every tap in the Little House, from every other tap on the farm. Daddy scrubs so fast and so hard that the job on all four is done in two shakes of a lamb's tail, and the vigorous toweling that follows is almost as rapid as the shaking of that or any other tail. The resulting soreness and tingling of Jackie's scalp, however, lasts at least half a day.

So it is the busy milkhouse, not the milk room, that Jackie grows up running in and out of to get her chocolate milk or orange. It's in the milkhouse that she watches the bottle washer gulping dirty bottles and disgorging clean ones, where she watches the milk rippling down the coils and filling the clean bottles, where she watches the milk swirling in the separator and coming out of various spouts as cream. All that sort of activity is no longer in Grama's back room off the kitchen. Jackie never knows, for a long time, that it ever was.

2 ⚹ SPIRITUAL MILK

The round barn is the hub of the farm. Hubs have spokes. The main spoke from the barn is a visible one: the sidewalk that runs from the barn entry on a diagonal up to the milkhouse door.

The geography of the round barn is easy to describe, to draw maps of, for after it was built it stayed basically the same forever: the silo in the middle, the loft above, the circle for the cows below.

But the milkhouse is always changing and shifting. New additions are added, a wing here, a shed closed in and incorporated there. The inside keeps shifting, too, like a delta in flood. The old cooler there, the new cooler here, the old bottle washing machine in one room, the new in a different one. The tanks for pasteurizing are moved several times during Jackie's growing up. An outside staircase leads up to a blank wall; once a door opened there, she discovers from an old photograph, and the cans of raw milk from the barn were poured directly into a tank over the cooling coils and bottler — the answer to Grampa's advertising assurance that the milk was cooled to 51 degrees within minutes after milking. A mysterious pool sunk into the floor where milk cans sometimes sat submerged disappears altogether, while the rickety raised track of rollers that shunt the clean milk cans out of the building for pickup by the neighbor milk-suppliers grows like a lizard's tail.

Jackie can't begin to describe the milkhouse at any one time, or chronicle the when of the changes. It is always in flux. Like a medieval cathedral it is begun in one style, added onto in another, remodeled and re-remodeled in bits and pieces so that Romanesque and Gothic and Perpendicular and Modern are all jumbled together.

But as in a cathedral, there are certain activities that go on inside, no matter what the spot or year. The daily service, the mass of the milkhouse, is the receiving of the milk, pasteurizing and homogenizing it, cooling it, bottling it, storing it briefly in the walk-in refrigerator, sending it out on the routes, and washing everything up. These are the essentials of the short ceremony.

The long one expands on these, and includes things added as the business grows or as dairy science progresses. Here are the things that happen in the milkhouse:

Weighing milk from the round barn; receiving milk from other farmers and weighing it in; placing all milk in holding tanks or directly into pasteurizing vats. Clarifying milk. Pasteurizing milk. Homogenizing milk. Bottling milk of different grades and in different size bottles. Separating cream into various grades and bottling it. Putting some of the skim milk from the separator into cans for the pigs.

Washing bottles by hand on swirling brushes, before the dairy acquired a mechanical bottle washer.

Preparing the mixes for chocolate milk and orange drink and bottling these beverages. Churning the butter, making it up and packaging it. Bottling buttermilk. Making and packaging cottage cheese. Refrigerating the dairy products in the cooler. Stoking the boiler. Washing the bottles returned from the routes. Tending to the unsold products returned from the routes, which includes putting milk aside for Big House use and for farm workers to take home, and pouring what's left into cans to take to the pigs. Washing milk cans. Washing the milking paraphernalia from the barn, washing the milkhouse pipes, and washing everything else, including washing down the walls. Fly, bug, and vermin control.

And the furniture in the milkhouse includes these:

The big Fairbanks scales; the clarifier; the holding tanks; the compact homogenizing unit; the many-dimensioned bottling machine with its giant icy reredos stretching to the ceiling, where the hot milk ripples down and by the bottom has become a cold river which is channeled into a tank above the bottles; cheese boxes and glasses; the separator; the churn; butter paddles; the cottage cheese vat; the cheese cutter; the bottle washing machine; milk pails; the big milk cans; the can washer; the large tubs for all the other washing; hoses; the walk-in cooler or refrigerator; the snow machine for icing the milk on the trucks; the metal milk cases each holding sixteen clean bottles; the metal dollies that can carry four or five of these piled cases; the boiler; the barrel of chocolate powder; the orange concentrate; sugar; the long cardboard tubes filled with bottle caps; small scales and other measures; the record books; the Vitamin D that goes into the pasteurizer to make Vitamin D milk; the testing equipment for incubating and counting the bacteria in milk samples; the barrels of caustic cleanser for the hoses and bottle washer.

The milkhouse workers (as well as the barnhands) have their vestments. They wear white caps covering their hair, white aprons from chest to knee, or when the job is wet, heavy rubber aprons, and tall black rubber boots.

The cathedral analogy might carry further. When Jackie is old enough to consider it, she finds Grampa's move from the ministry to milk an appropriate choice. It's a move from the giving of spiritual sustenance to the giving of physical sustenance, and the physical is of that most spiritual of foods, milk. Milk is used in this sense in the phrase, "milk of human kindness," and in the Bible, the Promised Land flows with milk and honey. She researches, in a History of Children's Literature class, a book written well over two hundred years ago, called *Spiritual Milk for Boston Babes, Drawn from the Breasts of Both Testaments, for the Nourishment of Their Souls.*

It fits, that milk is described as spiritual, that spiritual is described as milk. Grampa knows it. And doesn't that make the milkhouse, and the round barn, too, holy places?

Carol Hanson, a young farm visitor,
enjoying a bottle of chocolate kindness.

3 ⤜ MAD AT NOBODY

Every morning, like a doctor on the wards, Daddy Dougan makes the rounds of his business. He looks into the horse barn and converses with his horses. He stands at the heavy iron fence and communes respectfully with his bulls. He goes into the lower barn where milking is still going on and shouts cheerfully to his cows.

"Good morning, ladies! Good morning!" he cries. "Are you all happy? Are you all letting down your milk? What a generous gift you give us! We appreciate your efforts! Keep up the good work! Let us know if there's anything more you'd like from us!"

He goes into the side barn and examines the new little calves, and then to the older calves' barn. He checks the pig houses and croons over his mothers and babies. He does generally omit the hen house, for Grama keeps a sharp eye on the residents there.

Ralph Anderson with the milkhouse's modern bottle washer.

Nor are people neglected. He goes to the milkhouse where the bottle filling and capping is in full swing and greets everyone by name. Some days he just says, "Good morning, George!" or, "It's a bonnie day, Ralph!" but most mornings he comes in waving his arms like a windmill and crying out, "I ain't mad at nobody!"

On one such day Ron is inside the bottle washer, attempting one of his frequent and frustrating baling-wire repairs, when his father comes shouting his morning greetings. After he leaves George Schreiber bends down and peers into the maw of the monster. "You know what, Ron?" he says. "After Daddy comes through, I ain't mad at nobody, neither! What about you?"

In a muffled voice, though perhaps with not quite so much enthusiasm, Ron agrees.

4 ⊁ PA STAM

Jackie is almost four. She's sitting on the back step of the Big House beside the boot-scraper, where she always sits when she's eating a sugar cookie of Grama's. She's cuddling a kitten in her lap. Two more kittens wreathe her ankles. It's a serene, sunny April day.

Suddenly the milkhouse screen door slams open and Pa Stam springs out onto the stoop. He's called Pa Stam because he's the father of the milkman Lester Stam, and came to work on the farm after his son did. He has on a white apron down to his knees and black rubber boots. His face is scarlet. He holds a galvanized pail in his hand. He winds up and slings the bucket down the sidewalk toward the barn. It spins, bottom over handle, and lands two thirds of the way to the cow barn entry. It clangs and bangs and bounces the rest of the way and smacks up against the door. A startled head pokes out.

Pa Stam shakes his fist at the head and bellows, "Whadd'ya mean, you calfbrained, lazy, good-for-nothing sons o' Satan, sending up a pail all covered with shit? You do it agin, I'll come down and rub your tongues in it, you lousy lunkheads!" He disappears back into the milkhouse. The screen door slams behind him.

Jackie blinks. "Whadd'ya mean, you good-for-nothing sons o' Satan!" she echoes to the purring kitten in her lap. She takes a meditative bite of her cookie, pats the kittens at her ankles, and waits for something else interesting to happen. That's why she likes to sit on this back step, with its wide view of much of the farm. Something always does.

5 ✸ RHYTHMS

I n a high school English class, Mr. Wolfe is talking about rhythm in words
and phrases, both poetry and prose, and while he doesn't assign a composition, Jackie decides to try one, on a subject she's familiar with. She muses on
the round barn.

The cow barn has a rhythm, like a poem, like a song. It's a rhythm repeated daily, year in, year out, with only slight seasonal variations. I know this
rhythm, not from living it all day long, or even just for several days, for I've
never done that. But I have come into the barn a thousand times, a thousand
thousand times, when the work was going on, watching for a while, talking
to the barnhands, helping when someone gives me something to do.

I have come in when the barn is empty, except for a fleeting barn cat, and
wandered about, sometimes circling the stanchions and pushing down the
hinged lips in the cows' drinking cups till they brim with water. Or with my
brother and sisters I've raced our bikes and trikes and scooters and the Irish
Mail rowcycle round and round the walkway, as my father and uncle did
when they played in the barn long ago. I have gone with my grandfather to
put the cows to bed, late on a snowy night, and seen the sleepy cows, all lying down, blink when the lights are turned on. I've stood in the straw, deep-
breathing their warm cow breath.

So there has been lapping and overlapping, and all the laps fit together, lay-
ered over a thousand times; that's the way I know every beat of the rhythm.
This is true for my brother, too, and my sisters. If anyone were to ask us,
when we're off in some far section of the farm, what was going on in the barn
right now, we could respond with fair accuracy. Not by clock time but by
cow time. And if we were to feel the low throb of the milking machine motor, we could pinpoint the activity exactly.

We may not recognize that we are aware of the barn rhythm, the daily song
of the round barn. But for each of us, it is deeply embedded in our bones.

Bottles on their carousel in stately minuet, filled, capped, and tops wrapped in cellophane.

Now Jackie is at Beloit College. She is taking a poetry writing class. An assignment, "onomatopoeia," is to use words that imitate the sounds they're describing, such as buzz, or swish, or bob white, a bird easily identified by the words of its call. She finds that her frame of reference for rhythm is still the farm. She decides to concentrate on the onomatopoeia of the milkhouse. After working a bit, she realizes that she needs to not only mimic the sounds, but also to indicate the timing, the tempo. It might be good to contrast the sounds of the barn and milkhouse; she digs out her earlier essay.

A discovery is that the barn is basically leisurely, and has many words that take more time to pronounce than single syllable words normally do: "barn" itself, and "slow," and "cow," and "chew." The milkhouse has both slow and fast rhythms, and there are descriptive words for these, too. She has fun with this assignment. She titles it "farm rhythms" and cuts out all capitals, imitating e.e.cummings, whom her professor used as an onomatopoeic example.

> the round barn is
> on slow cow time,
> chew cud rhythm,
> swing udder soft.
> its tunes are
> single and simple:
> loudest the scra-a-ape...
> scra-a-ape...
> of the manure shovel,
> fastest the brush—brush—brush
> of the cleanup broom

in the water-filled gutter,
the lip of liquid flowing ahead
in leisurely flood-crest.

the milkhouse tunes
play all at once,
fight each other—
machine time quick-quick-quick-quick
and sorta-fast, sorta-fast
and slow—oh—oh—oh—ohly
as the andante vat paddles
swing gently back, forth,
moving milk.
hot, it travels to the ceiling,
ripples poco a poco
down the ramp of cooling coils
cantabile into the wide tank.
bottles on their carousel
rise, fill, lower, in stately minuet
meet the bottle capper then
clickup-stampdown-
spiiinn
clickup-stampdown-
spiiinn, a
driving whirling allegro.
milk cans swing
from the washing vat
in a cymbal clannnnnng,
bottles in their cases shhhiver and
chattttter slung from returning trucks.
the behemoth bottle washer
gives a lento trip through
scalding caustic
in its roiling stomach,
through cooler rinses
in its growling gut,
the action on either end is presto
when the wide maw's concave teeth

snatch six dirty bottles, gulp them in,
as six more teeth swing up to grab
six more at the other end where
gleaming bottles are disgorged
row by row onto a moving belt
taking them to the bottler.
homogenizer innards pound
fugue-fast relentless,
rhythmic fortissimo,
the butter churn splashes forte,
the cream separator's centrifugal race
hums piano.

the milkhouse rhythms, like
the barn's, are deep in the bones—
two separate songs fit together,
sometimes contrapuntally,
sometimes antiphonally,
all one composition.

Jackie's professor likes the poem. He likes her addition of musical terms. He points out, though, that the word "clang" rings sufficiently without any spelling change, nor do "scrape" and "shiver" and a number of the other words need any adjustment. Jackie sees that this is so.

All in all, it has been a satisfying exercise. She is especially pleased when she shows it to Grampa. He says, "Cubby, you are my ears."

6 ⊰ DAN KELLEY

I t's 1916; the milkhouse has just been built. There is a second floor to it, reached by a steep staircase, almost a ladder, that can be raised and lowered. Not all the farmhands live in the crowded Big House anymore; Mother and Daddy Dougan—as everyone on the place calls them—have moved several men to the bunkhouse above the milkhouse.

Dan Kelley is one of these. He's eighteen, a Roman Catholic. One Sunday he returns from delivering his route. It's about two o'clock and he's bought a paper. He is sitting in the bunkhouse, reading the news, and doesn't hear someone come up the staircase. Suddenly there's a crash and his paper is kicked out of his hands; he is narrowly missed by Daddy Dougan's boot. Grampa's face is severe. He bunts the newspaper down the stairwell and climbs down after it.

Dan Kelley driving a bobsled in front of the milkhouse and tool shed.

Dan is in shock. Then he's furious. He seethes to Ronald, who happens by, "I guess I'm not supposed to read a paper on Sunday! I guess I'm only supposed to be reading the Bible! But Daddy never told me I couldn't read a paper on Sunday!"

Ron says, "When we were younger we couldn't even throw a ball on Sunday."

A few days later a milkhouse worker says, "Daddy's looking for you."

Dan is apprehensive. "Why?"

"You went out of here with so many bottles of cream and you've come back with one not accounted for."

At that moment, W.J. puts his hand on Dan's shoulder. "What happened to the other bottle of cream, Dan?"

"I drank it," Dan says.

"What did you do that for?"

"Because I was hungry."

"All right!" says Grampa. "If you're hungry, take more. Take all you want."

Nothing else is said. Dan figures that sort of evens things up. That, and when a few months later, something terrible happens. It's a winter day; he is back from the route, eating a late dinner at the kitchen table in the Big House. Daddy comes to him, his face concerned.

"I can see a big fire to the north of us, Dan," he says. "It looks like your place. You go get something warm on; I'll saddle one of the horses, and you go home. And if there's an extra stall and you don't want to come back, that's all right—we'll double up on the work tomorrow."

Dan can tell, as he gallops across the fields toward the smoke and flames, that the fire is indeed at his home. When he gets there, everything is gone, but his family is safe. He helps out there for several days before returning to his job. Daddy Dougan is almost totally forgiven.

7 ❧ A BETTER BOTTLE

There are fashions in milk bottles. Jackie doesn't know what Grampa's very first bottles looked like in 1907 for it didn't occur to anybody to date and save one. Nor did anyone take a photograph or make a sketch. No early Dougan ad pictures a milk bottle, no office file on the companies the dairy dealt with over the years contains brochures that ancient. Daddy thinks the first bottles were rather like the ones Jackie remembers from when she was small: round sided, clear glass, tapered neck, curved lip, but perhaps wider-rimmed. A dairy supplies catalogue from 1905 or '06 would surely show the choices.

Jackie actually has a few old bottles, perhaps from the thirties, found in unlikely places around the farm—a quart bottle and three half pints—all with "Dougan" glass-scripted on them, one also with an additional capital "D." Each has its identifying code from the factory, circling its bottom, slightly different on the half pints; the quart also further identifies itself in small glass letters around the bottom, "one quart liquid." One half pint has almost unnoticeable printing under the broad upper lip—A BETTER BOTTLE OF MILK—nothing your own lips would notice, though, while downing a bottle of chocolate.

At the start Grampa bottled only milk, and only in quart bottles, but before long he added cream in half pints, for a 1916 farm document lists a substantial number of half pints of cream sold that year. The document also refers to a "special bottle with the 'Standard' cap and ring." This special bottle has a decidedly different lip from any Jackie remembers and must be an innovation.

Jackie is fortunate in having a father who is all his life curious, and has a habit of documenting, begun in boyhood. When he's fourteen, in 1916, he receives a camera as a birthday gift and for months prowls the farm taking pictures of all the building innovations going on. When he reaches the new milkhouse, he snaps milk cans and buckets—some rather battered—clean and drying on their racks; the bottle washing apparatus with bottles upside

Ron's photo of the cylinder of milkbottle caps to be punched out, the chimneys of copper wire to secure the caps to the bottle lips, empty and full bottles, and propped in front, the single caps, one uncrimped, one crimped.

down in large trays; five tiers of clean bottles, also upside down with necks and lips hidden; the bottler; the tub for hand washing implements and hard-to-clean bottles, with above it a Rube Goldberg maze of pipes, faucet knobs, belts, and pulleys, and an array of stout bottle brushes. It was on these pipes and faucets that the young Ronald propped his Shakespeare to memorize when he was doing duty in the milkhouse, bottle washing. (A dirty bottle is thrust onto whirling bristles and held there until clean — or overclean, if the student is concentrating on his Hamlet.)

And then Ronald arranges and photographs a still life worthy of a painting. He places for background, slightly diagonally, a large wheel of tape which is visibly printed with a succession of bottle caps: these will be punched out one by one at the bottler, and stamped onto the filled milk bottle. Alongside this stand two tall cylinders wound tightly with copper wire. In front of these items are two bottles — one empty and uncapped but with "DOUGAN" visible on the glass, the other full and capped. Propped against these bottles are two caps — one flat with uncrimped edges, as it is before it goes on the bottle, the other with edges crimped. It's all there, the "Standard cap and ring." One can see the specialness on both bottles — they have double lips. These make it possible for the cap to crimp down and be secured by a ring of copper wire between the two lips.

There is a later picture from the early thirties. One double-lipped bottle is visible in a brochure showing the inside of Dougan's "modern bottling plant." The large caps can be seen on the hanging tape above the capping machine, ready to be punched out. Pa Stam is managing the operation. There is also a motion picture of this same scene. The movie is only a few minutes long, an advertising film made to run in a local theater, with glimpses of grooming the cows, milking, bottling the milk, and putting cases into a milk truck with "The Babies' Milkman" prominent on its side. The bottle visible throughout the movie is double lipped. But this type bottle, as well as the crimped lid, is gone by the time Jackie is old enough to be a daily visitor in the milkhouse. So also is a handsome striated bottle that the dairy used for a short period—when? Long after Jackie is grown and leaves the farm, she sees one of these for the first time at a Dougan cousin's, and is astonished and envious.

Bottles, whatever their style, are ubiquitous in photos taken around the farm and on milk deliveries. There's an early snapshot of farmhand Ed Steinbaugh sitting on a woodpile in a snowy pasture, eating his lunch. An unopened quart of milk is beside him. A group of farmhands stand before a truck, downing milk. Howard Milner sits on the hood of his truck downtown, polishing off a quart of milk. The little Dougan kids have a tea party on the lawn of the Little House, and the featured drink is chocolate milk in half-pint bottles.

Quarts and half pints are not the only size bottles. There are pints, and for a brief time, a maverick, short-lived one-third quart bottle. The half-pints are the favorites of Jackie and her sibs, the ones that contain chocolate milk and orange drink. The Dougan name is featured from the earliest bottles, a raised-glass "Dougan" on the side, in the same flowing script as on the trucks. This has a practical as well as aesthetic purpose: a consumer knows where the bottle comes from, and has no excuse for not returning it. (Wright & Wagner's bottles also bear their name; when the farm ends up with enough W&W bottles, they return the case or two, and retrieve in turn whatever Dougan bottles have found their way to the wrong dairy.)

When the quart bottles with tapered necks are full they show white milk up to the base of the neck, then the rich yellow of Guernsey cream. Jackie always thought the tapered necks were only to make the bottles easy to grasp; your hand fitted nicely around the smaller circumference and was kept from sliding off the top by the wider lip. Then to shake up the cream you'd put one finger on top of the cap, to be sure it didn't pop off, and give the bottle several sharp turns back and forth with your wrist. You could see the yellow cream streaming out and mixing with the bluish white skim milk.

But Daddy says the taper was mostly a visual trick, to impress the customer with how much cream was in the bottle. The longer and more tapered the neck, the higher proportion of cream there appeared to be.

Many customers didn't buy half pints or pints of cream separately, but poured off the cream from the top of the quart of milk. This was tricky. The first part of the pour was pure cream, sometimes thick enough at the start to have to be nudged with a spoon, but the rest quickly became mixed with the milk below. This problem was addressed by a device Grampa bought in 1923, 500 for $80, on each of which was printed, "Presented by 'The Babies' Milkman'" The ad that beguiled Grampa reads, "A PERFECT CREAM LIFTER. Lifts the cream off the milk undisturbed by Simple Vacuum Process. Lifts one cup or one spoonful without disturbing the rest. CLEAN — QUICK — EFFICIENT."

The copy continues in smaller print, "It is practically impossible to pour more than two-thirds of the cream off the top of a bottle of milk without mixing some of the skim milk with the thick cream thus diluting it; while by using LANGE'S CREAM SAVER, all the thick cream from a quart of milk may be used for cereal or coffee, and the skim milk is just as good for cooking purposes, or, if desired, only enough thick cream need be removed for one cup of coffee and the rest is left undisturbed for future removing." There is considerably more rhetoric, but the pictures are what intrigue: a metal cylinder with a tall push-button in the middle of the top holds pride of place; then a male hand over a milk bottle demonstrates in three pictures (with text) how to use it — inserting it into the bottle, pushing the button which then sucks into the cylinder the desired amount of cream, gently lifting it out, and releasing the cream into a cup by raising the thumb. There is a caution: "Do not lower the cylinder below the cream line, for then skim milk will be sucked up along with the cream." Grampa's order blank carbon has added, "Satisfaction guaranteed or lifters may be returned." Apparently the lifters were not a smash success, for Jackie never hears about them, or notices such a device lurking in the back of some catch-all kitchen drawer. Grampa must not have ordered 500 more.

This same problem was solved in the early forties by changing the entire bottle. It was called a "cream-top" bottle. Its neck was a bulge somewhat smaller than a tennis ball, with a constriction at the base of the bulge; all the cream was contained in the bulge. To go with these bottles every customer received a little metal dish-shaped disk with a rod straight up the middle. The disk was

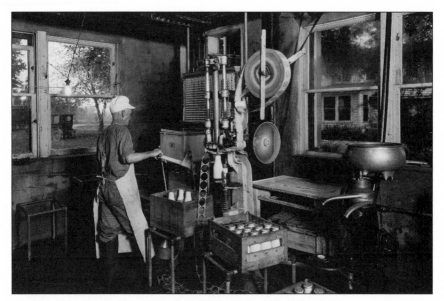

Pa Stam is bottling and capping in the milkhouse. The window behind the cream separator shows the proximity of the Big House.

gently pushed down through the cream till it rested on the constriction in the neck; then, with the disk firmly in place, the cream could be poured off with no intrusion from the skim milk below. It took two hands and a bit of practice to master the technique, but with the proper bottle, and the disk, extracting the cream was less complicated than with the Lange cream lifter.

The Dougan cream-top bottle's bulge was a simple unadorned sphere, with no more character than a tennis ball. But many years later Jackie sees a cream-top bottle from a dairy in Illinois where the shape had inspired a manufacturer to mold a baby's head. It's such a delightful bottle she wonders how the dairies that used it ever managed to get their empties returned.

There turned out to be a problem, though, with this cream-top bottle in the bottle filler. Heretofore, the bottles had been round with tapered necks; now the bottom of the bottle, below the bulge, was square. At the end of December, 1944, Daddy writes the Cherry-Burrell Corporation in Chicago ("Complete Equipment for Handling Milk and its Products") which has for a long time been the supplier for almost all the dairy's needs. "We are sending you under separate cover a square cream-top bottle. You will recall our phone conversation wherein I told you that this bottle would not work in our 6-20 filler. The bottle jams cornerwise between the metal star wheel and the bottle guard. I hope that you can give us some help in making this bottle work." A company official answers promptly that the factory recommendations are that he use a #6698 Iron Star Wheel in place of the fabricated type furnished with his filler; that he order this item and see if it does not overcome his difficulty. But two weeks later Daddy gets another letter from the official:

On January 16 we wrote you regarding the operation of your Bottle Filler with square bottles. Since that time our Milwaukee factory has been doing some further experimenting and they have learned that the last bottle invariably kicks back, which is apparently what your complaint is about. They have found that when installing an auxiliary bottle rail the trouble is definitely overcome. This auxiliary rail fastens to the infeed rail and originally was intended to overcome the trouble being experienced with half-pint bottles, but they find it works satisfactorily on the quart bottles. The required part is not in production at the present time but should be available on or about March 1.

We are very glad our factory has done this experimenting, as it seems they have discovered what is wrong and they particularly mentioned that they put your sample bottles through and they worked satisfactorily when this auxiliary rail was used.

Once milk begins to be homogenized, into the forties, the need for a cream-top bottle, or the earlier tapered-neck bottle, diminishes. For a while

Jackie's daughters Gillian, Megan, and Damaris, drink from Dougan bottles when they visit the farm.

bottles for homogenized milk, and for cream-top milk, run concurrently. By the time Craig is a freshman at Beloit College in 1948, the cream-top bottle's day is almost over. He makes use of its well-known image, however, on a medieval history exam by comparing "the church militant" to the skim bottom and "the church triumphant" to the creamy top. (Professor Irrman writes, "Splendid, Craig," in the margin.)

What homogenization does is to distribute the cream evenly throughout the milk. Homogenized milk proves popular; people prefer it to the milk that requires shaking. The new bottles are more compact, square sided, slightly concave, with gently rounded edges. The mouths are smaller and they have only the slightest neck.

But there's a problem with homogenization. Often the milk has a peculiar cardboardy taste. Jackie, Craig, Pat, and Jo refuse to drink the new homogenized milk. Enough customers complain of the taste to Dougan's Dairy and to other dairies throughout the country that various universities make studies. The problem is traced to sunlight. Its rays oxidize butterfat. Before homogenization, the individual globules of butterfat were large. The sun, working on a small surface area, didn't oxidize enough fat to change the taste of the milk to any degree. But homogenization, which forces milk through a tiny aperture at great pressure, breaks each globule into thousands of minute beads, making much more surface for the sun to affect. It takes only twenty minutes of sunlight to change significantly the flavor of a quart of homogenized milk. Once this is determined, milkmen are careful to keep the milk covered, and not leave it in the sun on a doorstep, even if the weather is cold. But occasionally sunlight will hit the milk anyway.

The problems with oxidation spur the development of opaque paper cartons. These cartons, in the stores from large suppliers, begin to cut into local sales. It's paradoxical, for to a discerning tongue paper cartons also flavor the milk with a cardboard taste.

At this time, in the early fifties, Wright & Wagner is selling about half of all the retail milk in town. Daddy is selling one-fourth to one-third, and the remainder is split up between some twelve small dairies. Before long, Wright & Wagner invests in paper. Daddy, however, feels he doesn't have the capital to risk jumping into paper bottles. It would mean a big investment in new machinery for bottling the gallons and half gallons, new cases for the handling, and then competing with store prices, for more and more people are finding it convenient to buy their milk at the store.

Furthermore, even without all the necessary new equipment, paper is more expensive than glass. Daddy figures a quart glass bottle, which costs about ten cents, averages some twenty trips. A half-pint bottle averages forty to fifty trips. This makes glass cost a half cent, or considerably less, a run. A paper carton which can be used only once costs one-and-one-half cents. Even figuring in the cost of labor, caustic, and hot water in the washing of the bottles, even figuring in the repairs to the bottle washer, glass comes out to be twice as cheap as paper.

One reason Daddy gets such a good return on his glass bottles is that he and Grampa have always avoided paying a deposit. Wright & Wagner and the other dairies give a nickel apiece for returned bottles. But this involves a tremendous amount of bookkeeping—charging bottles out to customers and figuring their refunds. It's more headache than it's worth. In door-to-door delivery it's easy for householders to rinse out the bottles and put them on the step. They have no wish to accumulate them. The same is true in the factories; cases for empties are left behind which the milkman collects the next day. Daddy now supplies milk to only a few stores and these are family groceries, like Wongs' on Maple Street. Even at the stores the customers routinely return their bottles.

So Daddy sticks with glass. He does promotional work. He points out that glass doesn't affect the taste of milk the way paper does. He goes around to schools and convinces the principals that a half-pint glass milk bottle is as safe as a paper container. He does this by dropping a bottle from waist level onto a corridor floor. It bounces.

"I'm always careful to drop it on a corner, where the glass is strongest," he tells Jackie.

Competitive pressure forces Daddy to go against one of Grampa's adages. His solution to the cheaper price of milk in gallon cartons is to now offer discounts on gallons, himself. If a customer buys four quarts, the discount will bring the price down to the store price. The quarts can be in any combination, a mixed gallon—a quart of Guernsey, one of blend, one of chocolate, one of buttermilk. And they don't have to be all purchased on the same day. At the end of the billing period, the number of quarts a customer has used is divided by four to determine the number of mixed, discounted gallons. It's a beautiful, well-thought-out service.

Longer in coming is Daddy's response to the off-taste in homogenized milk exposed to sunlight. It isn't till 1957 that he introduces the amber bottle. He starts by inserting a small but arresting box in the *Beloit Daily News*, stating in heavy black print:

> **IT WILL**
> **STARTLE YOU**
> **IT'S THE**
> **LATEST...**
> **from the**
> **DOUGAN FARM DAIRY**

The next day's ad is a larger box with larger print:

> # THE
> # AMBER BOTTLE
> # IS HERE!
> ## Watch This Paper Tomorrow
> ## Night For An Important
> ## Announcement
> ## from the
> # DOUGAN FARM DAIRY

The next issue brings a full-page ad headed "A Salute to the Past . . . A Challenge to the Future." Under this, in huge print, "50TH ANNIVERSARY" arches over a large cellophane-hooded amber-colored bottle (or as close to that color as the newspaper can manage) which fills the center of the page. "Dougan's" and "Beloit" are readable on the glass. Beneath the bottle the text reads,

> To Celebrate Our Fiftieth Anniversary We Present The
> AMBER BOTTLE
>
> Now our fine milk is further protected by light-filtering amber glass. Amber accomplishes two things. It preserves the high vitamin content of our milk, and it brings to your table the flavor of fine fresh milk until the last drop is used. We know that light damages flavor and vitamins, and that amber glass is the perfect container for preserving these essential qualities. All Dougan products are now packaged in impervious amber glass quarts. Of course, there is no additional cost to you, our customers.

This is signed by R.A. Dougan, and the bottom of the ad has DOUGAN FARM DAIRY in large block letters, with "The Babies' Milkman" in smaller print beneath. In a column to the left of the bottle is the salute to the past:

> In the summer of 1907 W.J. Dougan hitched up his horse to a single buggy and made his first milk delivery, to his sister, Mrs. James Croft, 917 Bushnell Street, to Dr. F.A. Thayer, 328 Euclid Avenue, and to Attorney Harry Adams, 836 Church Street.

Since that day, now fifty years ago, the business he founded and conducted until his death in 1949 has not missed a day's delivery on Beloit streets.

W.J. Dougan was a product of Wisconsin schools and the University of Wisconsin. Trained for the Methodist ministry, he preached for twelve years in Southern Wisconsin communities such as Juda, Oregon, and Poynette. When he lost his hearing at the age of forty, he bought a farm from Mrs. Colley, just east of Beloit. He brought to his new profession all the idealism which had marked his ministry. Soon known as "The Babies' Milkman," he eagerly adopted each advance in the better production and handling of milk.

This is followed by a list:

<u>1907</u>
120 acre farm
20 milking cows
One employee
A small "milkroom" and one milk route
Producing scrupulously clean raw milk of fabulous keeping qualities for a Beloit trading area of about 10,000

The space to the right of the pictured bottle is balanced with a parallel column, this one with a headline: "And Now The Next Fifty Years."

To family, friends and employees, W.J. Dougan was affectionately called "Daddy Dougan." Men associated with him over the years continue to return with stories of his influence on their lives. In looking ahead, we of the second generation can only hope to emulate his goal. Principally he was concerned with giving all involved with the business the opportunity for "Life as Well as a Living."

Of equal importance was his second goal and our continued aim. "To Produce the Best Milk to be Had in Any City at Any Price."

This, too, is followed by statistics:

<u>1957</u>
485 acre farm
25 employees
120 milking cows plus the production of a dozen neighboring farms

A Grade A milk plant and eleven big milk routes.

Producing the same fine milk but now adding Pasteurization and Homogenization plus vitamins—all for a Beloit trading area of about 70,000.

The ad is finished off with pictures of various Dougan babies from the customer baby ads.

In the months following, Daddy touts the amber bottle. He runs a promotional: free milk for returning the clippings of the slogans published in the newspaper. This means family and friends must come up with slogans in the first place. One of Mother's is, "For Dougan's Milk the folks all clamber, 'cause it is in the bottle Amber," and another, "Heigh-ho the Dairy-o, It's Amber Every Time." There are various puns on the recent risque book, *Forever Amber*. The family's brown boxer dog contributes, "I Ain't No Yaller Dog, I'm Amber." The milk itself takes voice and says, "I'm Proud to be Associated with the Amber Bottle." Because the four sides of the square bottle are slightly concave for easy gripping, one of Daddy's slogans reads, "Pinch Me—I LIKE IT! I am the pinch-type Amber Bottle." And, "FRESHER MILK? If Dougan's milk in the Amber Bottle was any fresher it should have its face slapped." Daddy also contributes, "I've Seen London, I've Seen France, Amber has Dougan in a Trance," and "Ronald A.* Dougan (*A for Amber)." As in the case of Burma Shave signs, there are some verses that can't be printed. Pat Dougan Dalvit mails in her entry, complete with a drawing of a very cross looking cow, but the *Daily News* doesn't run it:

> The cow is so angry she can't chew her cud.
> Her udder's so full that it drags in the mud.
> The obstinate calf, mama cow'd like to throttle,
> It will only drink milk from an amber glass bottle!

Craig, interning in Salt Lake City, contributes, "Doctors prefer the amber bottle because the specimen never fades," and, "Is it porpheria? No, just Dougan's amber bottle."

And Daddy himself thinks it prudent not to try to publish his own favorite slogan; had he done so (and had the paper printed it) he would have anticipated the Civil Rights Movement of the sixties:

> Integration is here to stay—
> The amber bottle has shown the way!

Daddy concludes his return-a-slogan promotion with two ads: The first features a picture of Ronald Cook, nine years old:

> Ronnie is as clever as he is good looking. When he read that Dougan's Dairy was giving free milk for returning the Amber Bottle slogans printed in the *Daily News* he got busy. His entry was completely original as one would expect from a boy doing so well in art classes at school. We will reproduce his entry in this space next Monday.
>
> Like thousands of other Beloiters the Cooks are learning that Dougan Milk is even better since its fine flavor and vitamin content are protected from destructive light by the Amber bottle.
>
> Ronnie and his sister Barbara are the children of the John Cooks of 214 Park Avenue. They attend Strong School as did their mother, not so many years ago when she was Clara Turman. Right now Mrs. Cook is a very busy woman, serving her second term as Worthy Matron of the Rebecca Chapter of Eastern Star. Congratulations from Dougan's Dairy to the outstanding Cook family. We are proud of you.

The second ad, Ronnie Cook's reproduced entry, gets a full half-page of the *Daily News*. In the middle Ronnie has painted a regal cow and pasted on her side the cut-out slogan, "With my coloring and my shape I'm a real hit!—Amber Bottle." Surrounding the cow are arranged some twenty other slogans. It's a splendid poster. The farm knows Ronnie. For many years his mother Clara—better known as Scottie—has been a cherished employee.

A later ad has a framed photo of an amber bottle, titled "Queen Amber the First in Full Royal Regalia." She is apparently reviewing her troops: "Since September 13 when the first wave of AMBER rolled through town, twenty thousand of these trim AMBER units have entered the fray. Thousands of Beloiters have found them on their doorsteps, in their milk boxes, and in their refrigerators. These AMBER soldiers from DOUGAN DAIRY are here to stay."

Another ad featuring the bottle says, "It's taken us fifty years of experience to bring you Dougan Milk at its ultimate goodness—not to mention the centuries it has taken the cow to learn her job." And yet another ad's headline reads, "DOUGAN AIN'T GOT NO SECRETS FROM NOBODY!" with the text,

> What's wrong with that sentence? Absolutely nothing except it ain't ain't, it's hain't, ain't it?—It ain't no secret that amber glass protects Dougan milk from harmful light flavor.—It ain't no secret that amber glass protects the vitamin

A and vitamin D in Dougan milk. — It ain't no secret that since last October we can't remember a customer complaint on flavor. — It ain't no secret that we are delighted with the amber bottle and that our customers continue to congratulate us on this forward step in protecting our fine milk.

The amber bottle is Daddy's holdout against the paper carton. People like the bottles, and Dougan's milk is delivered in them from 1957 until Daddy retires from retail home delivery ten years later. The farm is left with a number of cases. The family uses them for special gifts, or to be auctioned off at the Beloit-Janesville Symphony fundraisers.

Daddy writes a friend, "We hope you received our amber bottle which is becoming quite a collector's item. We were the last dairy to purchase amber from the last manufacturer before the colored bottle was discontinued entirely years ago. If you do not collect such items feel free to present it to a collector friend and accept the delighted reaction. The owner's embossed identification makes them rare, even in Wisconsin."

Queen Amber the First is dethroned by Daddy's retirement from the milk business. But before long the whole glass bottle portion of the dairy supply industry is vanquished. At the time of the fifty-year celebration of the Dougan business and the introduction of the amber bottle, Trever Dougan writes a congratulatory letter to his brother. He says he's got quite a kick out of the ads, but gives a postscript: "As far as the amber bottle is concerned I feel it is a gimmick, but as long as it is a first in the area it gives you a better sales pitch over competition. I may be wrong but I think the same end could be accomplished by containing in cardboard. By that I mean as long as the direct sun rays do not get to the milk, flavor is kept."

Trever seems unaware of the cost of moving to cardboard. But his is the voice of the future. In the end the paper carton reigns — but as a relatively minor ruler whose kingdom is measured in half pints, pints, quarts, and half gallons. The emperor, of course, is the familiar plastic gallon jug at the supermarket which, while showing the white milk, has a built-in sunblock.

But the old cliche, "What goes around, comes around," may be working with milk bottles. Glass and home delivery was never abandoned in England. And by the year 2000, in the United States, milk in glass bottles has been reintroduced both in stores and on elite home delivery routes, which are also making a comeback, as a prized and expensive item.

Fashions in milk bottles, after a many-year hiatus, may continue to evolve.

8 ⋊ JOHN'S MORNING RUN

There's no toilet in the round barn. At about the same time every morning John Baker, the herdsman, comes hurrying up the diagonal sidewalk to use the milkhouse toilet. It's located back in the boiler room, in a narrow cubicle. The door is a swinging wooden one. It doesn't reach the floor; if you bend over you can see whether anyone is in there.

John always bends to check and then rushes inside. One day George Schreiber takes a pair of the tall black rubber boots that are used in the milkhouse and positions them before the stool. Then everybody in the building waits for John's morning run.

He appears right on schedule, sees that the booth is occupied, and goes out by the loading platform. He paces up and down, snapping his knuckles, then hurries in again. The boots haven't moved. John makes an exclamation of dismay. He goes outside once more. George and the rest of the men have a hard time squelching their mirth.

A third time John hurries in. "Please!" he entreats, dancing around. "Could you hurry up, please? Won't you be out soon?"

There is no response from the cubicle, but beyond the boiler room someone stifles a titter. John is suddenly suspicious.

"Who's in there?" he demands, bending double to look again.

The boots have not moved.

John shoves the door. It swings open and reveals the empty boots before the empty stool.

He gives a roar of rage, flings the boots out of the booth one after the other, pulls shut the door and slams in the bolt, while the milkhouse crew whoops with raucous laughter.

9 ⨯ THE BABIES' MILKMAN

Graham McClay with an early milk wagon, carrier, and bottles.

O n April 30, 1907, three items having to do with milk appear in the
Beloit Daily News. One is a small news item tucked on the last page,
just above the "fair and warmer" weather forecast: "W.J. Dougan last week
shipped in eight head of fine Guernsey cows and heifers from Fort Atkinson
for his dairy farm east of the city."

The other two are articles. The first is headlined, "VALUE OF GOOD
MILK," and subheaded, "Many Things Go into Producing and Marketing
the Supply in Sanitary Condition." It is signed by W.J. Dougan, and is his
first message to the Beloit consumer. Its purpose is clearly to educate:

> There is no better food than pure, rich milk. It is the natural food for chil-
> dren. All through the history of man it has been one of the daily necessities

of life. To rightly produce and distribute this necessity for a city's consumption is a great and important work. It requires patience and perseverance. No food is purer when rightly produced and handled, nor is any more capable of infection without detection by the consumer. There are two factors in producing and distributing wholesome milk. First, the cow. Science has proved that the milk in a healthy cow's udder is perfectly germ-free—is pure. The cow determines the quality of the milk. Some cows produce only 2 per cent of butter fat, others as high as 6.5 per cent fat. Therefore, the healthy cow of rich quality is of first importance. Second, the handling of the milk. This is the whole process of conveying the milk from the cow to the table. In this transition there is much danger of contamination. The utmost care should be taken in the process of milking, aerating, and cooling. To this end the cows must be well groomed, the stable sanitary, the milking utensils and room thoroughly clean, the milk immediately aerated, cooled, and sealed in clean bottles for delivery. The dairymen must be neat and painstaking. No small factor is the care of the milk by the consumer. The milk must be kept in a clean, cool place free from all odors.

We endeavor to produce milk in accordance with these principles. We sell only milk from our own herd. Our herd is tuberculin tested annually. Any purchased stock must go into quarantine until tested and in every way found healthy. We feed the most wholesome food in liberal quantity. We are painstaking in every detail of handling the milk, using Gurler's sanitary milk pail and the Champion aerator and cooler. We deliver the milk in bottles because it is the most cleanly and preserves the quality of the milk.

We give this guarantee with every bottle of milk or cream: That it is from healthy cows; produced under sanitary conditions, and contains at least 4 per cent butter fat. The law requires only 3 per cent. We aim to supply your table with the very choicest milk and cream that the best breeding and selection of Guernsey cows can produce.

However, do not expect too much from a pint of milk. The milk that "mother" gave you for your bread and milk was from the top of the big pan.

—W.J. DOUGAN New 'phone 663.

The touch of humor at the end refers to the large shallow pan of the old fashioned kitchen, which allowed the cream to rise from the day's milking of the family cow. Skimmed off the top for a child's bread and milk, the cream would be almost butter.

The other article is directly alongside the first. It is headlined, "PURE

MILK FOR BELOIT," and signed, "Yours truly, Sturtevant and Wright."
While its purpose includes education, its main thrust is a hard pitch:

> We wish to announce to the people of Beloit that we are now ready to begin
> the delivery of sanitary bottled milk, cream, and buttermilk. We have been at
> work since Nov. 1st remodeling the plant on St. Paul Avenue near Mill St. We
> have installed all new and modern machinery including a Barber ice machine
> and a large cold storage room. We want every man and woman in the city to
> call and see how we intend to produce the very best milk that modern science
> can give to our cities. We understand our business. We do not guess. We can
> tell you what percentage of butterfat is in every bottle you buy. We guarantee
> every bottle of our milk or cream to be far above any state standard.
>
> Mr. Sturtevant, the senior member of the firm, has just completed a course
> in the city milk supply at the University of Illinois where he has been under
> the instruction of the best posted men in the United States in our line. Mr.
> Wright, the junior member, is well versed in the production and care of milk
> and will supervise the buying and selling. You will always find us at our post
> trying to give you and your children the very best, purest and most whole-
> some milk that money and skill can produce. Mr. T.H. Straw, our factory
> manager and butter maker, has spent his life at his profession. He has been
> with the best firms in the country and is an expert. "Cleanliness" is his motto.
>
> We will not be able to cover the city at once as it takes time to perfect
> a business of this kind, but will start with two wagons and cover as many
> streets as possible with them until the other wagons are ready. Thanking the
> people of Beloit in advance for the patronage we trust they will bestow upon
> us, we are, yours truly, STURTEVANT & WRIGHT.

Thus do the firms that will become the major Beloit dairies for the next sixty
years enter the business lists on the same day. It can hardly be coincidence.

The following day, May 1, W.J. delivers six quarts of milk in the town
of Beloit. Each company also runs another ad. W.J.'s is an inconspicuous
statement among the want ads: "GUARANTEED MILK from the Dougan
Guernsey Farm, W.J. Dougan, New Phone 561." But Sturtevant and Wright's
is an eye catcher, two inches by four, bordered twice, with a screaming headline underlined three times in black: "SAVE THE BABIES LIVES!" The copy
reads, "Nathan Straus, the philanthropist, demonstrated the superiority of
Pasteurized Milk when he established the New York City free depots where
such milk could be had, and later expansion in the use of this milk by the city

authorities has resulted in lowering the death rate of children under five years of age from 96.3 per thousand to 55 to the thousand in a few years. Make arrangements with STURTEVANT & WRIGHT to call on you." This ad runs for four days, and is followed by another grabber in the same format. This time the underlined headline is "WOULD YOU DRINK WATER," and the copy goes on in smaller print, "that stood in a cow barn under a cow for ten minutes without its being purified? Then why will you drink milk that stood in the same barn? You don't have to any more as you can get Pure Pasteurized & Clarified Milk of STURTEVANT & WRIGHT."

During the rest of the month the rival company runs four more ads, three of which continue to hammer on the pasteurization theme: Denmark requires pasteurization by law; Iowa compels it of skim milk that is fed to hogs and calves; New York has two bills before the legislature: "When the Great Search Light of Publicity is Turned Upon the City Milk Supply as it surely will be, out of the 'jungle' will come with triumph the man with the pasteurizer." The last ad promises to replace every bottle of milk containing any sediment. W.J. Dougan's modest one-liner among the want ads continues without change the entire month, nor does W.J., in any articles, make countercharges about the safety of his quality raw milk.

In June both companies cease their daily ads and from then on advertise in the newspaper weekly or sporadically.

From the start of his business, W.J. sends monthly samples of milk from the herd to the university for bacterial testing. In April, 1909, a report giving Dougan's milk high marks makes the paper. The author of the report, E.G. Hastings, makes clear that the University Experimental Station is not interested in advertising any particular dairy but in aiding any dairyman who is attempting to improve the quality of his milk. W.J. summarizes the findings in a brief half-sheet delivered to his customers, and adds that Dougan's milk also scored well at the recent National Dairy Show: "Our product was marked perfect in flavor, composition, i.e. fats and solids, and perfect in cleanliness and keeping quality." He thanks his customers for their patronage and finishes, "We are improving our milk room and equipment, and continually selecting cows with an aim of still improving our product."

The Experimental Station issues another favorable report the following year, headlined, "BELOIT BABIES ARE FORTUNATE." Mr. Hastings writes that many claim clean milk costs more to produce and must sell at a higher price. That some supplying the Milwaukee market are fighting the tuberculin testing ordinance. That "any town that numbers among its dairymen one who of his own volition is doing the things that other towns are attempting to obtain by ordinance is to be congratulated. One of the farms is Mr. W.J. Dougan's of Beloit. People at times fail to realize the advantages that are before them and need to have them pointed out."

This time, W.J. capitalizes on the report in a more thorough way. He prints up a neat pamphlet, "THE PRODUCTION OF PURE, CLEAN MILK ON THE DOUGAN GUERNSEY FARM." Inside, he reprints the entire report, prefaced with a page of direct advertising, of which Point #3 seems truly remarkable, and makes a reader wish to be standing between the barn and the milk room with a stopwatch:

THE DOUGAN GUERNSEY FARM

July 20, 1910

GREETING AND GOOD WILL

It is with satisfaction that I submit to you the inclosed indorsement of our products from the State University. Our aim has been unwavering from the first to produce the highest quality of milk at the lowest possible cost. That we are accomplishing this is proved by this scientific statement and by the testimony from multitudes of homes

In getting our milk you are sure of these factors:

1. Milk only from our herd of healthy Guernsey cows;

2. That, the cows are groomed, udders washed and stables in a sanitary condition before each milking;

3. That, the milk is always drawn into the Gurler pail, taken to the milk room and cooled to 50 degrees F., within one minute after milking;

4. That, the milk is handled and bottled in a sanitary milk room;

5. That, ice and cold water are used in the wagons to keep the milk cold until delivery to your door.

It is these features that puts our milk in a class by itself in Beloit and makes it a safe, clean milk for babies and family use.

Upon the merits of our product we solicit the patronage of those who desire the best.

Yours for Good Milk.

W. J. DOUGAN.

"The Babies' Milk Man."

In 1911 W.J. builds the round barn. When he brings out another pamphlet in 1912 he includes among his expanded points, "Our stable is new, sanitary and up-to-date in every detail." This time #7 is the point to ponder:

"We employ men of only high moral character who have no bad habits and who have never had contagious or infectious diseases." Though customers are left to draw their own conclusions, W.J. means by the latter, tuberculosis. The round barn, with its room for many more cows, prompts the final statement:

"FUTURE EXPANSION. We are ready to expand our trade largely. To this end we shall keep right on producing the best milk obtainable in any city at any price; and we shall endeavor to let the consumers of Beloit know what we are doing and try to demonstrate to them the satisfaction, safety, and economy of using the best in this delicate and valuable food for both babies and adults. We solicit your interest and patronage. Yours for clean milk, W.J. Dougan, 'The Babies' Milkman.'"

This final slogan had been Grampa's from the start; Ronald can't recall a time that he hadn't been teased as "The Milkman's Baby," nor can Trever.

With the advent of the round barn and Beloit's interest in it, a new avenue of advertising opens. W.J. lets the public know the time of afternoon milking and invites anyone to attend unannounced, to inspect the procedure. It becomes a gala thing for families and small groups to visit the farm, especially on a Sunday afternoon outing from town. Grampa is always on hand to chat with them and refresh them with a drink of milk. In May of 1914 he inaugurates the "First Annual Reception at the Dougan Farm." W.J.'s Scotch-Irish descent makes him a canny Scotsman as well as a member of the old sod. It so happens that on May 27, a Wednesday, he is hosting a large meet for area farmers, business men, and their wives, at which the topic alfalfa, the newcomer to forage crops, will be discussed by agronomy professors from the university. There will be tours of the alfalfa fields, the farm home, and all the farm buildings. Of course the place is seeing lots of elbow grease—painting and polishing, lawns trimmed, weeds cut, every gate oiled, every fence post firmed, every piece of farm equipment in its place. The farm is always kept tidy, a strong point with Grampa. But with the farm now in special show condition, why not let one party be the cause for two, three, or even four? He flanks the alfalfa meet with two events. The First Annual Reception, to be held the day before, is announced to his customers by a note on their doorsteps: "You are cordially invited to meet at our farm Tuesday, May 26, at 3 p.m. Inspection of the farm and dairy and a demonstration of our methods of milk production. Come and bring your friends." It isn't signed by Grampa as a business man, but cordially by "Mr. and Mrs. W.J. Dougan" as hosts. There is a P.S.: "Conveyance will be furnished for those who have no other way of coming. All who wish our conveyance meet at corner Broad and Pleasant Sts., at 2 p.m." Then on the day after the alfalfa meet there's a repeat reception, this one for the general public, and announced by a notice in the newspaper, again with transportation provided. The fourth event is an evening one, the Philathea class of the Methodist Church, which comes for supper and merrymaking, and also is transported from downtown by farm conveyance. So for three successive afternoons and one evening the farm is crowded with visitors.

This is the year, 1914, that W.J. institutes electricity on the farm, via a home generator. Electric lights are installed in barn and house, and most labor processes electrified. Rural electricity is enough of a rarity that the newspaper articles writing up the several parties all mention it, some in detail. In 1917, when Grampa pays Beloit Water, Gas and Electric—later Wisconsin Power and Light—to run a high line out to the farm and retires the generator, he and Grama host another party to show what electricity can do to enhance farm life, complete with lectures and an actual sit-down meal up in the round barn. Food is bussed from the Big House kitchen. This party draws a large and enthusiastic crowd.

Such events bring the public to the farm. There are also ways of bringing the farm to the public.

Every year the city has a Fourth of July parade. The parade of 1916 is of such proportions and success that the *Beloit Daily News* trumpets, "CIVIC PARADE SETS RECORD OF SPLENDOR." The first subhead, "Industrial Procession Witnessed by Vast Throng is Riot of Color," reflects that businesses were expected to participate. The article, after two more glowing subheads ("Floats are Unique" and "New and Original Ideas Lend Touch of Freshness to Holiday Exhibits"), goes on to give a lengthy description of the parade: the bands; the drill teams; the mayor and aldermen decked out in bona fide or improvised top hats; the fifty veterans of the old volunteer fire department pulling and pumping on the Water Witch; the Sunday School groups; the "score of Lithuanians clad in their native costumes and carrying the flags of their native and adopted countries;" and the "more than fifty Greek members of the Pan-Hellenic Union in ancient Greek costumes." Pronounced as "one of the most brilliant features of the parade" was a Greek chariot in which "rode a warrior and on a litter dragged behind the chariot was the body of a fallen foe."

The bulk of the article, however, is the description of every one of the more than eighty "industrial" floats. Some merit only a mention: "The Smith Republic truck agency was represented by a bunting covered truck," and others, especially toward the end of the article, are summarily lumped together: "The Sanitary Dairy Company, the Pire Grocery, and the McGavock Coal

The first three in a four-vehicle Dougan caravan in a Fourth-of-July Beloit parade, telling the story of the milk business. The initial truck has the beginning: on either side of the driver's cab hangs a cage with a calf; the nursing mother is behind. The horse-drawn wagon shows a cow ready for milking. The third is capping, bottling, distribution, while the fourth, not shown, carries the consumers—a contingent of healthy children and mothers.

and Lumber Company all had attractive exhibits, as did the Charles R. Foster Lumber Company." But many floats get complete and vivid coverage:

> One of the most artistic was that of the Beloit Savings Bank. Mounted on a large truck was a great straw beehive. Children in gold representing bees were filling the hive with the fruits of their labor. A portion of the truck was a replica of a flower-filled field from which the bees poured in a steady stream to the hive. "Industry" was the motto of the exhibit.

Or, "The Brill and Stier jewelry establishment was represented by a white flower-covered automobile, in the tonneau of which had been built a jeweler's bench. Seated at the bench were two white-clad boys industriously pounding away at clocks and watches." And leaving much to the readers' happy imaginations or memories, "The Eureka Laundry had an automobile decorated with bunting and filled with Swiss yodelers."

The description of the Dougan float nearly closes the article, and receives its own subheadline: "Attractive Dairy Exhibit."

> W.J. Dougan's Guernsey dairy set a new standard for dairy exhibits. On a large truck he had one of his finest cows. Dairymen in white were grooming

it, cleaning pails and pans, and bottling milk. The truck was covered with gold and white bunting and flowers. Two of the Dougan delivery wagons followed the dairy float, and following these were two motor trucks loaded with "Dougan Babies" and their mothers.

W.J. follows up the parade with a handsome advertisement in the paper, in which he interprets the float and gives a promise of good times to come for "our little people" of Beloit:

The Dougan Guernsey Farm

Our Part In the Parade

I intentionally put all my horses and men in the parade with the intent of giving some idea of the work in producing and distributing our clean milk.

It takes ten horses to produce the feed for the herd and to deliver the milk.

The eight men in the parade are all my regular help. It takes lots of labor 365¼ days in the year to do the work. The herdsman gives his entire time to the herd. The cows have to be curried and washed before every milking and the stables kept in a sanitary condition. One man gives his time to the milkroom work, cleaning utensils and bottles and handling the milk. It takes two men to deliver. The rest of the bunch are kept busy producing the feed and assisting with the dairy work. These men are no ordinary lot of farm laborers. They are all clean in character and men who do their work on honor.

The cow was representative of about eighty in the herd including the heifers. The children in the float and the tiny babes in their mothers' arms in the auto are a few of the many we are feeding. We should like to have had in the parade all of our little people. We intend some time to have them out to the farm for a gala day.

W. J. DOUGAN

"The Babies' Milkman."

True to his word that he will let his customers know what Dougan's is doing, it is around this time that W.J. publishes a statement in the paper concerning an epidemic of hoof and mouth disease. This highly contagious disease has no cure; when a cow comes down with it there's no recourse but to destroy the entire herd, sterilize the whole area, and, if the farmer can, start over. The statement is a kind of ad, a pact with his customers.

During World War I, other dairies raise their prices. Dougan's does not. As a result they are swamped with business. Guided by his slogan, W.J. takes on as new customers only those with babies or small children. But after the war, other dairies' prices fall dramatically, and the demand for Dougan milk drops. Because W.J. has been running on too narrow a margin, he can't match the competition by dropping his price even lower. Through the newspaper he cautiously informs the public, "We have been compelled to refuse many applicants for milk during the past few months. We hope for the future to keep the supply up to the demand. We can now take new customers." This is shortly followed, November 7, 1919, by a public "Notice to Our Customers," perhaps a brave front. "Because of our shortage of milk for some time we have had to skimp our customers and refuse to take new ones. We are now increasing our supply of milk and will soon be able to take good care of our trade. Before taking up many new customers from our waiting list we want our old customers to be well cared for. Therefore please resume, as soon as possible, taking the normal quantity of milk you will want."

This does not bring the needed results. He now distributes, through his milk men, a personal leaflet to all his customers, explaining why it may be necessary to raise prices. He suggests a solution, that both the customer and the dairy cut loss and waste together; one among several ingenious ideas is that customers pay cash, to eliminate the cost of the dairy's bookkeeping.

These measures are not enough. W.J. knows he must either raise prices, reduce quality, or quit the business. His Beloit friends — doctors and businessmen — advise him to raise prices and he does so, to 20 cents a quart. But with a minor depression in 1920, his competitors lower prices still further. W.J. retains his price but in 1921 carefully explains the history of area milk pricing to his customers. He then courts them with a contest: "We will give a $2.00 sheet of milk tickets to every customer who will keep a quart of our

> ### A GUARANTEE OF A SAFE MILK TO MY CUSTOMERS.
>
> I feel it is due to my customers that I assure them of the conditions under which their milk supply is produced at this critical time. We have bought no stock since the forepart of August. These were secured in the northern part of this state, from farms on which they were raised. Our herd is in perfect health and is under the constant inspection of Dr. Pattison. We allow no strangers to visit our barns without first being assured that there is no chance of their bringing the foot and mouth disease.
>
> With our sanitary conditions, with cement floors, both in stables and yards and the abundant use of lime and disinfectants about barns and herd we feel there is little danger of our herd becoming infected. I assure my trade that should there be the first indications of the disease in my herd I will notify the public and stop my supply of milk. So long as you have no word from me you may rest assured that your milk supply is safe.
>
> W. J. DOUGAN.

A final float from a Beloit Fourth-of-July parade proves the healthy outcome of Dougan products.

milk sweet and fit for use one week." The response is enthusiastic. Eighty-seven contestants enter, and sixty-one are winners. Mr. Amend, owner of the Racine Feet Knitting Factory, triumphantly keeps a bottle sweet for over two weeks. W.J. awards him a double prize. At the close of the contest he runs an ad-article that is three columns wide and the length of a page. He first explains the contest: "The practical test of milk is the length of time it will keep sweet. Our milk has stood this test in the homes of Beloit for over fourteen years. To bring this fact to the attention of the public we staged a contest." He then gives the names and addresses of all the winners, including testimonials: "Permit me to thank you for the sheet of tickets you gave us as a reward for keeping a bottle of milk sweet for one week. We have been continuous users of your milk for about twelve years and know what Dougan's milk is. While gratified with the result of the test, yet we were certain it would result as it did, for our experience has taught us to rely implicitly in the high quality of your milk. Again, thanking you, I am very truly yours, Clinton Karsteadt."

This imaginative advertising brings in many more customers, so that by February of 1922 W.J. is able to return to an old theme: "TO OUR CUSTOMERS: We will be a little short of milk and cream for a few weeks. The demand for our product has been constantly increasing for some time and it is impossible for us to go out and buy ordinary cows to meet the demand. It takes time for us to test out new cows for health and quality, before placing them in our producing herd. For the present, therefore, we cannot take on any new customers except for urgent cases of sickness or for small babies."

In *Hoard's Dairyman* in 1927, W.J. states his views on advertising:

> I have used various means: newspaper ads, circular letters, store window displays, floats in business parades, demonstrations at fairs, etc. Through all my advertising is a fixed purpose. I never beg nor never ask for customers. I never hit the other dealers. I never advertise a cut price sale but I aim to give information of how my milk is produced, its great value as food, and its extreme value in saving the babies. I aim to keep my name and methods so completely before the people of our town that if a stranger should ask any man, woman, or child, "Who produces the best milk in Beloit," they would answer without hesitation, "Why, Dougan, of course."

W.J.'s advertising is characterized by carefully explained information to educate the consumer. If the public knows the facts about healthy cows, clean milk production, and proper distribution, and if the facts prove that the Dougan Farm fulfils all requirements for a quality product and is also selling milk at the lowest possible price consistent with a reasonable profit, then consumers, whom he credits with intelligence, will buy. They don't have to be

"The makings of Vitamin D Milk." A Dougan display at a home and industry show, 1935.

shocked with any "WOULD YOU DRINK WATER" type ads.

W.J.'s truth and sincerity can't be doubted. That the words are from the pen of a clergyman is in his favor. Though it would never occur to him to capitalize on this fact, such publicity about him in articles and farm magazines keeps reminding the public. Then, too, he's frequently called on to guest preach, to perform marriages, to deliver the invocations at business meetings. People know that his advertising reflects the sacred trust he brings to his second vocation.

W.J. never loses faith in his initial advertising beliefs. In 1948, in his father's late seventies, Ronald asks him to write down thoughts on his philosophy and ideas about various aspects of the business. W.J., in his careful and methodical way, produces the following thoughts on advertising, critiquing first the specifics of Ronald's current campaigns, with suggestions.

Ronald, regarding advertising —

(1) The ad in the buses

I think an ad there is a good thing; however, it is difficult to word one so as to carry an impression and not to stir up an argument. It wants to be so the reader will assent to its truth and its importance. For example, the one now in the cars brings up a mental argument. You enumerate the points of value in our milk: Vitamin D, Homogenized, Grade A, at no extra cost; but the reader can say "I am giving a higher price than my neighbors," or, "I am buying a splendid milk for 18 cents and you charge 20 cents."

True, the 18-cent milk is not Grade A, Homogenized, etc., but your milk is two cents higher—and you have no means of discussion. It seems to me that may discount your ad. I think the ad would be worth more without that statement.

(2) Relative to the *Daily News* ads:

The public is very well informed regarding our milk—yet it is necessary to keep facts relative to our milk before the consumers. Is not our milk the only Wisconsin Grade A in the County? If so, publish an ad telling of the State requirements of Grade A milk and that our milk has fulfilled these requirements. State it in a simple way; i.e., Dougan's milk has qualified for Grade A since (date of starting it).

(3) Another ad:

"Babies' Milk Man—my coming to the farm in 1906. With an avowed purpose of producing and distributing a high quality of this necessary food for Beloit Babies.

However, right now the big question with the housewife is, how can I reduce my living costs? (Your letter to some of the customers lately had a good sound, showing you are anxious to hold down the price rather than to get all you can.) With the price of milk now and the amount that the milk industry advises per person per day it is hard to convince the consumer that they should not scrimp at all on milk.

I think that a definite effort needs to be made on the part of the producer, processor, and distributor to reduce costs all along the line and a willingness for all of us to produce more and better milk at no increase in costs.

And for the consumer to use regular and adequate quantities of milk and pay as regularly as possible.

I would suggest having a meeting of all producers and form some sort of purpose to do our best in producing in quantity at a reasonable price. Same with our workers in plant and on routes. I would conduct these meetings in an open and frank way and have a reporter present.

Then I would suggest a customer's day on the farm to demonstrate our methods and our effort to keep inflation down. Could make this day a Saturday picnic furnishing milk, etc. free—

I do not favor the idea of writing and publishing a milk cookbook or ads. The dairy industry's advertising is getting enough of this before the public.

The essay finishes with W.J.'s lifelong belief, "Let our ads hold some definite principles that will impress the consumer with faith in milk as a food and confidence in the producers and distributors to produce it at the lowest possible cost and reasonable profit."

There is one facet of W.J.'s personality, however, that rarely shows up in his type of earnest, informational advertising: his sense of humor. There's a hint of it in the early "shallow pan." Another hint is in a 1921 ad that pokes gentle fun at British products marked, "By appointment to his Majesty, the King." Pictured is a coat of arms bearing blocks, ball, and baby shoes: a commercial print that Grampa must have come across with delight. For above the shield is a small crowned babe and the line, "By Appointment to His Majesty, the Baby."

W.J.'s ads start his milk business with a promising dawn and go on to illuminate its morning with clarity. When Ronald begins contributing his ideas and humor, after he joins his father in 1925, the sun of Dougan advertising climbs swiftly to its zenith and stays there throughout all the remaining years of the business. It's an extended noonday, with Their Majesties, the Babies, firmly holding the golden orb.

10 ❧ CHICKEN POX

Joan, Patsy, and Jackie have recovered from the chicken pox. But they've passed it on to baby Craig. They've also given it to Daddy, who somehow never got it when he was a child.

Both males are wretched. All day long Mother swabs Craig with calamine lotion. Daddy swabs himself, sitting naked in his chair, over which has been draped first an oilcloth and then a sheet. Mother swabs where he can't reach. Both sufferers are bright pink.

Now it's three in the morning. Mother is upstairs, tending the fretful baby. Daddy can't sleep, either. He sits in his chair, bored, trying to read, swabbing calamine. He hears the chatter of milk cases as a truck stops, out by the milkhouse, and he wanders over to the little window at the foot of the stairs.

The light is on by the gas pump. He stares morosely while Byron Moore starts to gas up his truck.

Suddenly Daddy spots a flicker behind Byron. Fire! Creeping up the side of the pump! In a minute the underground tank will explode, and blow Byron, his truck, and half the milkhouse to Kingdom Come!

"FIRE! FIRE!" Daddy bellows, and is out the door in a

An early gas pump behind the milkhouse.

flash. He races barefoot across the snow to the milkhouse and grabs up the fire extinguisher from its hook inside the boiler room door. Then he's over to the pump, spraying the flames, while Byron is still rooted in shock.

Daddy leaps about naked, screeching curses in French, and gibbering prayers in English. The extinguisher hisses out clouds of foam. Both Daddy and the billows are a brilliant pink-red in the light. Byron comes to, and roars his truck back out of danger. Daddy manages to douse the flames. The buildings haven't caught; the pump hasn't exploded.

Daddy remembers he's unclothed, and ankle-deep in snow. He heads toward the Little House where his wife is on the step.

Mother calls anxiously, "What's the matter, Ron? Is everybody all right? Was it a fire? What started it? Get in here, you'll catch your death!"

"I don't know what started it," Daddy says, coming in. "We'll have to have the pump gone over and repaired before we use any more gas. As to your other question, yes, everybody's all right." He chuckles. "Except I don't think Byron will ever be the same again."

"Why? What's happened to Byron?"

"I think he's on his way to Confession," says Daddy. "Or checking the snow for cloven hoofprints. I bet he thought his time had come—that I was Mephistopheles himself, dancing in those flames!"

11 ❧ COUNTING BUGS

When Jackie is small, a mysterious occupation of Daddy's is to go over to the milkhouse and count bugs. This is often on a Sunday afternoon, when Mother is lying on the couch with the newspaper over her eyes, listening to the symphony on the radio. Jackie sometimes wanders into the milkhouse to watch Daddy. The actuality of his activity always falls short of the promise of its title. He sits in the back room, near the boiler, on a stool before a long shelf, his back hunched, his eye to a microscope, a gooseneck light illuminating a little bright mirror that shines up onto the microscope bed. A pencil scratches busily in one of Daddy's hands; the other hand manipulates a glass slide.

Jackie can't see any bugs anywhere. Daddy lets her look through the microscope, and she sees a dazzling disk with spots, some bigger than others. Those, he says, are the bugs he's counting. But they don't look like bugs. Where are the legs and hair and pinchers? If she or Craig stick around too long, or ask too many questions, Daddy says, "Scram, kids," or more likely, "*veux-tu te taire*," which is French for the same thing. Or "vamoose!" which carries a similar message.

When she's older she understands what Daddy is doing, and knows what she's looking at. Daddy has taken samples of different varieties of Dougan's milk, and samples of milk from all the farms that sell to the dairy. He's put agar, a jelly derived from algae, on slides. He uses the Frost Little-Plate Method that employs a slide rather than an agar plate or round petri dish; this method cuts down the incubation time. He has then put drops of the different milks on the agar slides and cultured them in the big white box on the shelf beside him, the incubator. The bacteria thrive on the agar. After a certain amount of time he counts the bacterial colonies that have developed on each slide. This tells him how clean each kind of milk is. The lower the bacterial count, the better and safer the milk.

Daddy isn't the only one who counts bugs. The State does, too. Every month the farm sends samples up to Madison, and the bacterial count of the dairy and its producers is determined. At first this is voluntary. If counts are high, the state alerts the offender. Later, when this becomes mandatory, an offender whose counts continue high will lose his license to sell milk.

In order to produce milk that tests low, every step of the milking process must be kept clean. Grampa, in an early article published in *Hoard's Dairyman*, says there are three main factors: the condition of the cow, the condition of the equipment, and the cleanliness and conscientiousness of the milker. He stresses that the barn needn't be a palace — that he was able to produce quality milk despite the deficiencies of his first barn, while in much fancier barns, if there is carelessness about any one of the essential three, the milk could be unfit to drink.

At first Grampa, and then Daddy with him, have only to be concerned about the barns, milkhouse, and workers on the dairy. In 1928 they begin buying milk from a few selected farms, paying a premium for bacterial counts under 50,000. They use this milk for cream, chocolate milk, and distribution in Beloit factories. They voluntarily inspect these farms' milking conditions at regular intervals. Grampa includes inspection of his own operation as well, and judges himself as stringently as he does the others. He can always come up with a suggestion to whitewash something, or a warning that more care must be taken with the equipment.

In mid-1929 Grampa writes his customers, "For twenty-two years Dougan has been producing the best milk to be had, and selling it as such under his personal guarantee.... Less than a year ago the Wisconsin Bureau of Markets adopted a model milk ordinance guided by the ordinance of the United States Public Health Service. Realizing the advantage to the consumer of a standard product graded and controlled by the State (especially to the newer residents of the city who have not yet had the opportunity to know the Dougan ideals of quality and service), Dougan has brought his product under this control." He states that Dougan's milk now carries a fourfold seal of its quality: The new Wisconsin Bureau of Markets, the American Guernsey Cattle Club, the Rock County Medical Milk Commission, and W.J. Dougan's twenty-two years of faithful service in producing a quality milk.

For Grampa and Daddy the inspection is optional, while in the larger towns and cities it is official. In April of 1930 the State of Wisconsin's Department of Agriculture and Markets calls together a group of prominent dairymen, professors, and State Board of Health members to draw up a suggested milk ordinance for towns in Wisconsin too small to have a milk control officer of their own. W.J. is one of this group. The ordinance they develop is adopted by various small towns, and W.J. and Ronald become official inspectors for their producers. By now the number of these has increased, for the dairy has introduced blended milk at ten cents a quart, and has had to expand its milk supply. The Wisconsin Guernsey Breeders Association (Wisconsin's branch of the American Guernsey Cattle Club, which gives the Golden Guernsey Seal of Approval) also inspects, and the farm cooperates with their inspector, Gavin McKerrow, as they do with the Rock County Medical Milk Commission inspectors, who in one report about the Dougan farm say "Cow barn — sweep down cobwebs. Some cows need reclipping. Milkhouse — Sanitary milk piping should not be put into place until just before time to use."

Gavin McKerrow sends a score sheet to one of the Dougan producers checking off many things that need attention. He chides at the end, "I really think it would be well worth your while to pay some attention to these things as the market which Mr. Dougan offers you is certainly much better than the average milk market in Wisconsin today."

The producer, upset, appeals to W.J., for many of the problems are beyond his control as a tenant farmer. W.J. writes to the owner of the farm:

> I told your tenant Mr. Carl Synstegard I would write you regarding fixing up your cow barn so as to be sanitary for producing milk. Here are the conditions:
>
> Floors: The cement floors are in patches and undermined with rats. The gutter on north side is so rough and uneven, especially its sides, it can not be kept sanitary. The walk back of the cows on the north side is broken, uneven, and full of rat holes along the wall. The gutters have no outlet and cannot be flushed and properly cleaned. Also, they half fill with liquid and keep the cows dirty. Under the stanchions the floor is broken. The rats keep throwing up dirt and filth in the mangers. I have told Carl to keep mangers clean. He tells me the rats dig up this dirt and filth into the mangers. You can not keep clean healthy cows with the floors in this condition. I would advise tearing out the mangers and stanchions, breaking out the gutter and back wall on the north side, opening a drain for each gutter to outside of barn, putting in new gutter and walk on north side and new cement mangers and iron stanchions on both sides. I think the floor and gutter on the south side will do.
>
> Light and ventilation: Repair all windows and fix so they tip in to give ventilation. Add windows on south side. The ceiling is too low under the old barn floor to give sufficient air space per cow. It also interferes with light.

Ronald at fourteen took this photo of clean milk cans in the milkhouse.

You can easily remedy this by taking up this floor, turning the joists east and west and placing them the same height as those under the east mow, then relay the floor being careful to have all cracks battened. Also the floor under the mows should have attention to see that there are no cracks or holes for dirt and chaff to get through.

Finally, exterminate the rats. What it cost you last year would have completely rid your place of rats. They are an expensive luxury.

I forgot to mention about the milkhouse. It is good. There should be a sill under door, a cover for water tank, and screens over all openings. Everything should be kept out except milk utensils.

We are anxious to have your place produce a satisfactory milk, and feel these repairs are not expensive, and will repay you in better health and production of your herd and also add to the selling value of your farm. As things now are it is impossible for anyone to produce a consistently low count milk. Existing conditions are a constant menace to the quality of the milk, and a threat to our business which we are doing everything possible to strengthen and safeguard.

We feel it necessary to set a time limit in which these repairs should be completed, in order for us to continue to use your milk. It must be done before weather gets warm. If the work is not well underway by the May 15th pay, we will have to withhold the premium for sanitary milk, and if not completed by May 31, we will have to suspend your product.

I hope you can do this repair work at once before the menace of flies and heat.

Yours truly,

W.J. Dougan

Not all Gavin McKerrow's reports are negative. On the same day he writes to Mr. Synstegard, prompting W.J.'s letter, he also writes Albert Marston, W.J.'s first producer, the farmer directly west of the dairy: "We wish to congratulate you upon the nice conditions existing around your barn and undoubtedly before I get back to visit you again the red cow will have gone." There is no hint in the report, unfortunately, of why the red cow should go.

In October, 1931, a letter to Dougan customers gives a description of the new blended milk. It contains an explanation of producers and bacterial count:

This milk is bought from seven local dairymen, selected because of their natural aptitude for producing clean milk. Some men can never be trained to handle milk properly, while others do the right thing almost instinctively.

These men sell their milk to us on a bacterial count basis. That is, we set a rigid limit, and deduct 25 cents per hundred pounds of milk from their paycheck if this limit is exceeded. We have a regular check in our own laboratory, using the Frost Little-Plate Method for counting bacteria. Coupled with this precaution, we frequently inspect barns, cows, equipment, and control methods.

Due to this careful supervision we are able to distribute a milk with a lower bacterial count than any other in town except for our own Grade A milk. Following are the average counts for Beloit dairies taken by the Beloit Health Office from May 9 to September 10, 1931. In case a sample had too many colonies to count, I have figured it into the average at the conservative figure of 500,000:

Pasteurized milks:

Dairy 1	147,000 bact. per c.c.
Dairy 2	109,000 " " "
Dairy 3	86,500 " " "
Dairy 4	64,400 " " "

Raw milks:

Dairy 5	265,600 bact. per c.c.
Dairy 6	171,000 " " "
Dairy 7	63,000 " " "
Dairy 8	36,900 " " "

DOUGAN'S BLENDED RAW MILK: 26,900 bacteria per c.c.
DOUGAN'S WIS-Grade A Raw Milk: 5,860 bacteria per c.c.

Because our milk is bought exclusively for fluid consumption and because we market very closely, we are able to pay our dairymen about one-third more for their milk than they would get in the open market. This additional price is a great incentive to clean production.

A statement to customers in April of 1934 lists the average of all regular bacterial counts taken by the City of Beloit from the previous November through March. Dougan's Grade A Pasteurized leads the rest at 1,500, followed by Dougan's Grade A Raw Guernsey, 2,000. Dealer A and Farmer A come next, with 3,400 and 3,700 respectively. Then comes Dougan's Blended Raw, checking in at 5,600. The rest of the list, fourteen more dealers and farmers, range from 9,500 up to 142,500.

And in a letter to Vic Emilson, treasurer at Beloit College in August '35, courting the college trade, Ron averages bacterial count by the city health office for a year, and names names: Wright & Wagner Guernsey Pasteurized is lowest, at 1,780, then come all three Dougan varieties of milk in quick succession, with another Wright & Wagner several slots down the list. Bacterial count mounts until Maples Dairy, at the end of the line, averages 372,800. He gets the bid, and three weeks later writes to the woman in charge of purchasing, "As you know we are more than grateful for the business you are giving us. It's a grand stop and no mistake. However, we are hoping that the quality of our product merits the continuation of the Emerson Hall delivery. Enclosed is a report on our pasteurized milk of September 12, made by the state laboratory." It is, of course, an excellent one. The health department's count in late September has Dougan's three milks far and away lower than the rest, from 1,100 to 9,000 while Maples, at 780,000 has lost its last place status to Triangle Dairy which has a count of more than a million.

The hospital, too, uses Dougan's milk, and Beloit doctors prescribe Dougan's Grade A Raw for their patients. Grampa ensures that they have full knowledge of the quality of Dougan's milk by every spring hosting a doctors' party at the farm, where, along with statistical evidence, the doctors are given a tour of the barns and the milkhouse, and are plied with fresh strawberries and homemade ice cream on the well-tended Big House lawn.

Every producer is regularly apprised of his bacterial count. If it stays below 50,000 he is now rewarded with a premium above the standard price, rather than the earlier practice of docking from standard price if his count is too high. His butterfat content is also taken into account, and a higher butterfat brings a higher premium. Once in a while every producer has an abnormally high count. Then Ronald suggests where to look for the problem and the farmer must find and correct it. If the count is outrageously high, or persists beyond one testing, Ronald hightails it over to the offending farm and tries to root out the trouble himself. Very occasionally the high count is from the round barn. Then there is silence in heaven for the space of half an hour.

The producers, too, receive detailed reports on their milking operations. Ron and W.J. (who is known universally as Daddy) usually go as a team.

Dear Lee,

Daddy and I inspected your place yesterday and found everything in good order. The only suggestion that occurred to us was the possibility of clipping. We have a hand clipper with several sets of sharp blades. If you do not have access to a clipper you may use this one, which we have on hand for producers. The only charge is for sharpening a set of blades. If more than one producer uses them without resharpening, the cost is cut that much.

We appreciate your fine regular care in production, and the uniformly high quality of your milk.

Dear George,

Daddy and I stopped yesterday but missed you. The barn and herd are in good shape. The herd seemed to be physicking a little. [i.e., loose bowels] I wish you would take a pail of water and soap and wash out the tails. Some of them are pretty bad. The yard isn't very satisfactory.... You would be ahead to keep cattle away from the manure pile, and hogs away from cattle.... The utensils are in fair shape. The milk pail has an open seam which should be soldered flush immediately, before warm weather comes and you get a boost in bacteria from that source. The strainer is a little rusty but I wouldn't advise a new one yet. Maybe when you get the pail soldered that rusty strip on the strainer could be covered with a coat of solder, or better yet, painted with tin. I don't know how they tin a small spot like that, but I should think they could heat up a little and apply it directly without dipping the whole article.

Dear Mr. Davis,

We are very much pleased with your barn and milkhouse and methods of handling milk for us.... Let us congratulate you again on the good bacteria counts you have had, and on the high quality of milk you have furnished us since starting delivery here.... P.S. It would probably make you some money if you would get the average test up to 3.5%. I hate to deduct 40 cents per pound for butterfat under that figure.

Dear Carl,

Daddy talked to you about your herd. I wish some of them had more meat on them. Do you suppose your present low butterfat test reflects the condi-

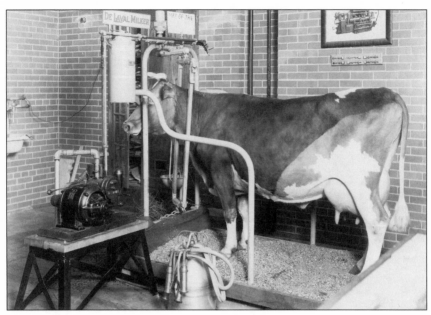

This Dougan cow, on display at a farm exhibition, clearly shows how she has been clipped to keep her hind quarters clean for milking.

tion of the herd.... The barn needs brightening up. Lime on the floor would help. If a little limite or slaked lime were mixed with a quantity of crushed limestone, the limite would brighten the floor and the limestone would help keep the manure from drying on, and would help grind down to the cement. The windows should be washed immediately.... Of course feeding silage before milking is all wrong, and I think you know it. That accounts for the strong odor and taste we have detected from time to time, no doubt.

Dear Floyd,
I don't see how we can stand guarantee for producers' cans. If we establish that precedent there would always be an argument.... On this particular can, I'll try to make it up to you some other way, although I can't establish responsibility for the damage done.

One of W.J.'s longer "Inspection and Recommendations" sheets runs as follows. It's for Dr. C.E. Smith's Dairy Farm, January 31, 1932:

Milkhouse: Secure better ventilation by use of fresh cheesecloth over windows, and make provision for opening windows except in very cold weather. Tank should be insulated and have insulated cover, or else water should be changed every few hours. Paint. Floors, walls, and tank should be thoroughly washed and disinfected. This also applies to the wooden rack.

Utensils: Wash thoroughly after each use and stack so that they may dry. Scald, or rinse with chlorine solution each time before use.

Barn: Thoroughly clean. Scrape floors throughout. Sweep all dust and cobwebs from ledges and walls and ceiling. Whitewash. Keep windows clean to let in light. Keep silage cleaned up from floors of silage room and alley ways. Feed silage after milking both morning and night. Keep several south windows open all of the time, and all of them open at least part way in mild weather. The silo flues act as outlet ventilators if the south windows are used as intakes. The floors and gutters are the hardest problem. The platform seems to slope forward so that the urine runs too far under the cow. Also the gutters are too shallow, and no outlet is furnished for flushing. I think by close attention and plenty of work, and lots of bedding, the cows can be kept clean.

Cows: Regularly tested for T.B. It is suggested that all be blood tested, especially in view of the fact that you expect to be buying in more cows. We do not require this however. Flanks, udders, and tails to be kept clipped. All dirt and manure kept off of cows. Udders to be washed and dried before each milking. A chlorine solution is quite helpful. We are now selling B.K. to producers for 30 cents per gal. No cows milk to be put in the supply if any defect in udder such as garget is present. Three teated cows are not to be used for supply.

I would suggest that each gutter have an outlet through the wall. I have not taken the levels, but I think by extending the gutter a few feet, the bottom would come to a level of yard surface. This may not be practical. The only alternative is constant care to keep gutter clean.

On the whole, both the tenant farmers and the owner-farmers respond gratefully to the detailed inspections. After all, it is to their benefit to have the kind of barn and milking that will produce the lowest bacterial counts, and give them the most return for their labors. A 1939 letter from Beloit lawyer Ted Woolsey, who owns a farm on the State Line Road in Turtle Township, says it well:

Dear Ron,

Referring to your letter of July 27 to Clawson Clair, I wish to advise that we have done our best to make all the corrections suggested by you.

We now clean the tank regularly. In fact, just as you suggested, we empty it every night and pump in fresh water. We have built a rack for the milk cans over the tank. We have removed the shelves entirely and substituted iron pipe. The rack for the milk cans is also built of iron pipe. We have put a cheese cloth over the window that was boarded shut. We have cleaned and disinfected the milkhouse and given the entire inside a coat of white paint. We have also carefully cleaned the pails and other utensils. In addition to this, we have whitewashed the barn, cleaned the floors carefully, and sprinkled them with lime.

If our count is still high it will not be because we haven't done our best to put our equipment in good order and in accordance with your suggestions.

Another letter is a shade more dubious, not of the inspection, but of the tenant farmers:

Dear Mr. Dougan,
Thank you for your letter of February 4 and copy of your letter to Cleo Beaver. I am confident that this young man and his wife have definite possibilities as a farmer and dairyman. They are ambitious and both like cows and take good care of the herd which is evidenced by their appearance and general health.

However I have noticed a lack of care with the milk and utensils but have hesitated to mention the subject as both seem to resent any criticism. I had a talk with them yesterday on the subject while they were doing a thorough job of cleaning the milker units and they were expecting you to call later in the day.

I am quite sure that after this there will be a definite improvement in the quality of the product you are purchasing from us. I hope you will work with them and the writer that we may continue as producer and customer.

Yours truly,
Ralph W. Young

It is, of course, to W.J. and Ronald's best interest to have all the producers' farms in excellent shape. They go out of their way to help. Ronald writes:

To: All Our Producers
Subject: Whitewashing & Barn and Milkhouse Inspection
I have not yet heard from the state inspector relative to individual recommendations for each producer to follow in order to bring his farm up to the standards of Wisconsin Grade A milk production. Some of you are now in

line, but many have corrections to make. When the two men were here, late in March, they set about May 1 as the time for a reinspection. I am disappointed not to have heard from them on individual reports, and wrote to Mr. Linde about a week ago asking if he had forgotten us.

All of you have had the inspection sheet so you know in a general way the things that need to be done. If you have not yet already done so, I would suggest that you bend every effort to correct any of the conditions mentioned, as the inspectors mean business. We do not wish to discontinue the purchase of milk from any of our present producers. On the other hand, our Wisconsin Grade A label is one of our most valuable trade assets. Not only is it valuable to us, but to every producer who benefits by the fact that partly because of it we are able to sell a large portion of his milk in a Class I price bracket.

We have arranged with Mr. Bailey from Belvidere to whitewash those barns that are not painted inside. He will also whitewash any other buildings, such as chicken houses, at the time he is on your place, I am sure. He is going to come up here the week starting Monday, April 30, and wishes to whitewash steadily until he has finished the work for all the farmers interested. His charges are 20 cents per stall, and he furnishes the lime and labor. The barn should be clean when he gets there. He will whitewash our round barn for $8.00 and the lower side barn for $4.00. We will be glad to take care of paying him and put the charges against your milk check for May. He figures box stalls on the basis of the number of stanchions they would hold if so arranged.

I appreciate how busy you are and how late the spring is. This business of meeting inspection and qualifying under Grade A in the future as we have in the past is vital, however. I will appreciate all that you do.

In all the inspecting Daddy and Grampa do, the very harshest criticism is reserved for Willard "Ike" Halderson. In March of 1933, Ronald, after saying the condition of the herd is very good and the milkhouse satisfactory (except for a door that should be adjusted to close completely), goes on:

Your utensils were a shock to me. Leaving them with dried milk and manure on them all day is bad enough, but it is evident from the amount of flaky milk stone on them that they are not getting satisfactory care. Pails and strainer are so jammed up and there are so many deep crevasses in the pails that I am surprised that even in this cold weather you have kept counts down.

You were wrong on the phone today when you said that the time to look for trouble is when counts go up. We did that once before with you, and for six weeks were in hot water with our trade every day. I'd pay a hundred dollars rather than have a few days of high counts, and if there is any way for us to avoid them we are going to do it.

You know how utensils should be cleaned, so it is a disappointment to find them in such shape. The only satisfactory method to us is to have all manure and milk washed off with cold water. This will prevent hot water fixing milk stone. Then the utensils must be washed with hot water and soap, and then rinsed. Just before milking, pails, strainer, and cans should be rinsed in B.K. solution of about one tablespoon to a gallon of water. Between washing and the use of B.K. the pails should be inverted and dry. After night milking, the same procedure should be followed as in the morning, including the use of cold water, hot soapy water, and rinse. B.K. should be used in morning just before milking.

I can't tell you how strongly I feel about sloppy methods of production, and care of utensils in producing milk for this market. Our success in handling a raw milk is built upon the intelligent cooperation of our producers, and one or two indifferent or careless producers can ruin the market for the rest of us.

But Halderson's bacterial count continues to run intolerably high, month after month. Ron drives over to inspect the farm again. He finds general improvement in the cleanliness of the utensils. Major sources of contamination are no longer in evidence. He examines pails and cans and metal strainers.

For his milking Ike is using the recommended Gurler pail, specially constructed to decrease contamination. The pail curves up and over the top, leaving an aperture of about one third the space of a regular pail. This aperture is fitted with a flannel cloth, cut to size and purchased in bulk from the pail manufacturers. The milker milks onto the cloth, which filters the milk for one milking session. A fresh one is put on the cleaned pail for the next session.

Ronald, in his poking around the Halderson milk room, suddenly notices some flannels hanging from hooks near the ceiling. A few are stiff and dried, one is still wet. He takes them down, shakes and sniffs. They are flaky and sour smelling. They are used cloths from the Gurler milk pail, not discarded but hung up, and hung up unrinsed. The bacteria are having a heyday.

He goes in search of Ike who faced with the evidence admits that he's been reusing the flannels. Ronald and W.J. conclude that Halderson is one of those men who, far from doing the right thing instinctively, can never be trained to handle milk properly. They terminate their contract with him. Within two years Halderson is running a dairy of his own. His bacterial counts, recorded by the city, are on a par with Triangle and Maples.

As one of his own producers, with the Corporation buying milk from the round barn (the Corporation being the incorporated production end of the dairy, done so during the Depression to stave off bankruptcy), W.J. is officially bound to inspect his own operations. In March of 1935 he writes this report:

Dougan Guernsey Farm Dairy, Inc.
Beloit, Wisconsin

Dear Sir:
I inspected the premises of your producer, W.J. Dougan, today.

I am especially interested in the handling of cans and the cleanliness and condition of barns and yards, the thrift [i.e. health] of the herd, and careful methods.

I realize the difficulties in poor bedding material. This condition requires extra effort to maintain the high quality of milk that our plant requires. In your case I would suggest two precautions. Clean the manure out of the gutter more thoroughly when putting the cows to bed, and adjust bedding and clean gutters frequently during the day when the cows spend so much time in the barn.

Your herd is in splendid thrift and clean. The use of more lime on the walk would add to the appearance of the barn. I note there are two cows in barn with defective udders. I understand these are not used in the market milk production and will be disposed of soon.

The yards look bad in spite of your cement yard floors. The lower yard should be scraped to the bone at once, and no manure can be dumped in this yard. Either load and haul away every day, or wheel to the manure yard. The same holds true regarding the horse yard. No manure will be allowed to accumulate about the barns or yards.

Keep doors in place and closed when not in use. Do not your methods of handling silage give a bad odor to the barn? Correct this so as to handle silage only after milking and sweep all leavings clear.

Sincerely,
W.J. Dougan, Insp.

Grampa and Daddy read the inspector's report. They decide that they will correct the deficiencies, and keep on doing business with themselves.

12 ⚔ RANGER MAC

Jackie is in fourth grade. In school, every Monday morning, the class listens to Ranger Mac. He broadcasts over WHA, the Wisconsin State Station, the School of the Air. Her entire class is enrolled as Ranger Mac's Trailhitters. He talks about all sorts of different things, mostly outdoor things you might not notice, and conservation, and life cycles. Most of the programs are interesting. All of them are educational. He holds contests. One Jackie thinks she'll enter. It's about cream and milk and butter, how they get from the cow to the back step. It's a topic she knows quite a bit about. At the Little House, at the table, she mentions that she's going to enter the contest.

"Cream, milk, or butter?" asks Daddy.

"Cream," Jackie says. "I think, the cream separator. Most kids will probably write about milk. And you and the milkhouse men have explained to me how centrifugal force works."

"Don't forget to mention skimmit," Daddy says.

"I've never even heard of skimmit," says Jackie.

Daddy explains. "The first separator we had in the milkhouse would build up a froth on the top, a kind of suds. The cream would go off in the higher funnel, and the skim milk in the lower, but then there'd be this froth riding on the top, getting thicker and thicker. We'd have to skim it off. We'd take bowls of it over to the Big House, put it right on the table, and everybody'd eat it on their oatmeal, or their potatoes, or bread, or just in a big heap with a spoonful of sugar on top. It was thick as sour cream, but it was sweet. It was delicious. And everybody called it 'skimmit.'"

"Why don't we have it now?" Craig asks. "It sounds good!"

Daddy shakes his head. "It was. But I suppose the people who design separators thought it was a defect."

"You could write how everybody on the place likes to drink half a bottle of chocolate milk," Patsy says, "and then hold the bottle under the cream funnel and fill it up with cream, and put a cap on it and shake it good and then drink it."

"That little caper costs me money," says Daddy, but he does it, too.

"I don't think we're supposed to write stories, just how something works," Jackie says.

She wanders over to the milkhouse to look at the separator. She spots a rotund separator-shaped machine on a pedestal near where Daddy counts bugs. She knows it's a Babcock tester, used to tell the butterfat content of milk; she's watched Daddy spin it and then take out the little bottles one by one and record the butterfat. She lifts off the metal lid and looks at the bottles. They nest in a circle, sixteen of them, each in its metal holder, tilted just slightly on their sides with their slender necks pointed toward the middle. The necks have gradation markings on them.

She changes her mind and decides to write on the Babcock tester. It's more interesting. Ranger Mac will probably get lots of papers on cream separators, anyway.

Stephen Babcock, inventor, in 1890, of the Babcock Tester.

She starts her essay. There are too many things she doesn't know. She gets busy with other matters and forgets about it.

A little while goes by. Mother asks, "When will you hear about the contest?"

Jackie says, "What contest?" and then remembers. "Oh, I never finished my essay."

"I'm surprised," says Mother. "You're a girl who usually finishes things."

Jackie rummages around and finds her paper. She sees that the postmark deadline is the next day. She goes to the office and asks Daddy about the Babcock tester. He explains how he puts a certain amount of milk in each little bottle and adds the proper amount of sulphuric acid, which will liberate the fat. He stoppers and shakes the bottles, sets them in their cradles in the centrifuge, and spins them. After about five minutes he adds hot water and spins the bottles again. Now the yellow fat rises in the neck of the bottle and the milk below is crystal clear, so that an exact butterfat reading can be made.

"It works rather like a thermometer," Daddy says. "The milk has to be the right temperature for the amount of acid, too, and it's a little more complicated procedure than I've made it, but that's mainly it. I keep records on every cow in our herd; that way we know the good producers from the poorer ones. And I regularly test the milk of the farmers who sell to us. We pay a bonus for higher butterfat."

Jackie chews over the information and finishes her essay. She goes out to the milkhouse and draws a picture of the Babcock tester, how it looks both from the outside and with the lid off. She also draws one graceful little bottle with the numbers on its neck. She thinks to look in the *World Book* and adds to her text that the tester was invented by Stephen Babcock, American agricultural chemist, in 1890. Then she recopies her composition and mails it and her drawings to Ranger Mac. She forgets all about it.

A month later she gets an envelope and a small package in the mail. The envelope contains two things: a certificate stating that she's won second prize on her essay on the Babcock tester, and a letter. She leaves the package till last, and skims the letter. It starts, "Dear Trailhitter, Congratulations!" and tells all about the contest, including a paragraph on Dr. Babcock's work. "Isn't it true that we so often take for granted the things about us, but when we investigate

TEN MINUTES

is all the time it requires to make a perfect test of milk if you use the

"OFFICIAL" BABCOCK TESTER

Used twice a month it gives you information that will save many dollars worth of feed every year. Anyone can use it. Full directions and all necessary glassware with each tester.

PRICES: 2 bottle size, $4.00
4 " " 6.00

For an "Official," testing both milk and cream add 50c. to above prices.

CORNISH, CURTIS & GREENE MANUFACTURING CO.,
AGENTS WANTED   FORT ATKINSON, WISCONSIN.

An early Babcock Tester, before addition of the enclosing metal drum that Jackie knew. It shows the thin-necked bottles in their hinged holders.

the cause of their existence we find behind them so much of patient work and persistent thought and maybe a whole life of hard endeavor?" Jackie agrees, but doesn't think a whole lot of people think about the Babcock tester enough to even know what it is, much less take it for granted. The point, though, is a good one. There are lots of things she takes for granted, probably most things. She notes the names of the couple who promoted the contest and secured the prizes for the rural schools; the Wisconsin Department of Agriculture and Markets furnished them for the village and city grades. She reads that if she wants to acknowledge the receipt of the prize and express her gratitude, that here are the addresses. She casts aside the letter to open the package.

The prize is a round pocket lens a little larger than a milk bottle cap. It's fastened to a leather case. It swings out of the case when you want to use it, and then swings back in when you're through. A horn rim borders the lens. It's a beautiful, well made little instrument. Jackie is enchanted. She rushes to show the family.

Playing with the lens, she finds, she can work magic. She can focus the sun's rays to a pinpoint on a piece of paper. The tiny yellow point turns brown, the brown spreads out like a stain, then the center blackens and spreads, begins to smoke, and the paper bursts into flame. She can make a little heap of dry leaves and shavings and start a bonfire with the lens. Or, she can focus sunlight to a point on somebody's neck or hand in school, if she's sitting in just the right place, and they'll suddenly say "Ouch!" and move and rub the spot and never know what caused it.

Jackie is glad Mother reminded her that she's a girl who usually finishes things. She's glad she finished her essay. She's particularly glad she won second prize. Whatever the first prize was, it couldn't be better than her little horn rimmed pocket lens. She saves the certificate and letter in a drawer, but never writes the suggested thank-you letter. Many years later, when she comes across the letter again, she hopes that someone did. For whoever put thought and effort into picking out a perfect prize would probably have been glad to know it was appreciated.

13 ⚔ RAW MILK

All during Ronald and Trever's growing up, their parents hold an annual luncheon on the Big House lawn, for all the area doctors and their wives. Creamed chicken on biscuits is served, and new peas. There is strawberry shortcake with ice cream cranked in the big wooden ice cream tub. There is coffee, too, with thick cream. Pitchers brim with milk. The doctors show up en masse for this popular event, sit around in lawn chairs, and have a relaxing time.

The purposes of the party, besides joviality, are not hidden: it's a thank-you to the medical community for recommending Dougan's as the best and safest milk to be had, well worth the extra expense, and to discuss and extol the health benefits and safety of Dougan's Grade A Guernsey raw milk. For regulated pasteurization has long been a threat—of course it makes milk safer from exterior pathogens that can contaminate the milk, and from sick or tubercular cows, but carefully produced raw milk from a monitored source causes no infection, and is healthier and tastier for babies and all consumers. W.J. wants the endorsement of the community to keep on producing his highest grade milk.

From the very start of his business W.J., in print, in speeches to farm gatherings, and over the radio, has been a crusader for cow testing. He advocates regular tests, and the elimination of any cow who tests positive for tuberculosis. He has suffered the loss of a number of cows over the years, but his herds have remained healthy—infected cows do not have time to infect healthy ones, nor to endanger milk. He has been written about and praised for his zeal in preventing the spread of tuberculosis.

He has stood fast, however, on raw milk. Pasteurization should not be necessary for untainted milk.

What is milk, anyway? One could give a complicated analysis, but simplified, and understanding that there is some variety with breed of cow and even with individual animals, whole milk is about 87 percent water, four percent milk fats, and the rest protein (casein and whey), milk sugar (lactose), immune factors, many minerals, acids, vitamins, enzymes, cholesterol. Pasteurization, by heating milk slowly over a period of time, kills most pathogens that may have contaminated the milk. But it also destroys much in raw milk that is vital to health, such as good bacteria. Vitamin content is also reduced and the calcium is less digestible. That is why W.J. makes clean raw milk his major and most expensive product, and advertises it for babies' health.

Around 1928, when mandatory pasteurization looms once again as an issue, he sends a letter to his customers titled, "Dougan, the Pioneer in Better Milk." Its purpose is to counter-attack pasteurization. He establishes that he's been in business more than twenty years, and why he chose Guernsey milk because of color, flavor, and the right proportion of fat and other nutrients. His third point reads, "Through persevering work and consistent advertising, I built up a demand for the highest quality raw Guernsey milk." Subsequent points are his high standards, the cleanliness of his tested cows, surgically clean utensils, and handled by healthy men. He finishes, "My whole business is grounded on the producing and handling of raw Guernsey milk. Upon this exclusive product I have established my twenty year reputation. I am confident of my quality of clean, raw Guernsey milk in Beloit, and I am here to give my best." He asks his customers to pass this word to their neighbors who may be looking for a better milk.

Ronald, now in partnership with his father, is in charge of the business end of the milk business. January, 1930, brings a letter from J.P. Riordan, director of the Agricultural Bureau of the Wisconsin Manufacturers Association, headquartered in Madison, whose slogan is, "Farm and Factory Must Prosper Together." W.J. and Ron have met Riordan. Here is the history:

Both father and son took notice of the motto, and since Beloit is an industrial town, have tried to implement it by selling milk in Beloit factories. In spring of 1927, W.J. writes E.B. Neese, Beloit's most prominent manufacturer, first acknowledging Neese's congratulatory letter earlier, on W.J.'s and Eunice's honor from the University of Wisconsin, and then using this opportunity to tell him of the new venture in the milk business throughout the country: to peddle milk in the factories, in order that workers might have a forenoon and afternoon milk break. He suggests how this would benefit the manufacturer in many ways (worker's health, increased productivity, efficiency, etc.) as well as the producer. "We have started with some of the smaller factories and shops," writes W.J., "and are working out our plans for producing and distributing to this special trade. We are now ready to enter some of the

Ronald's 1916 photo of clean milk bottles in the milkhouse.

larger plants." He encloses a page that has been submitted to Neese's superintendent, spelling out details. The first item is, " In the matter of quality and price, Mr. Dougan proposes to furnish a high quality of Grade A raw milk in pint and 1/2 pint bottles wholesale (i.e., delivered in cases to the refrigerator room at the plant) at seven cents per pint and four cents per 1/2 pint. The milk to be retailed at eight cents per pint and five cents per half pint." W.J. continues, in his letter to Neese, "Regarding our source of supply, of course I can not hope to produce on my own farm a sufficient volume of milk to supply my regular route together with this extra trade. Therefore I have been developing through the past months a special supply. I have selected a few Guernsey herds owned by intelligent farmers capable of producing just as good a milk as I can. I pay about one dollar per hundred pounds above Beloit dealers for cleanliness and care. These men are glad to follow my directions and are producing an excellent quality of raw milk which I handle in my plant and put out to the shops exceptionally fresh and cool. The milk that goes to my retail route is entirely of my own production, as it has always been." He finishes his letter on a separate note, soliciting a donation for the County YMCA.

There are also letters from Riordan during this period. In May of '27 he writes Ronald that he's had a good report from the owner of the Beloit Iron works about the success of milk in the factory; in August he responds to a letter where Ronald has related some of the difficulties of distributing milk in the shops: the collection of money when the milk is left in cases rather than sold to individuals, the return of bottles, other problems; and how the dairy is working to solve these. Riordan wants to come visit. He also wants to use

Ronald's letter for inspiration, "Do you have any objections to our taking excerpts from your good letter and sending them to some of the backward distributors?" And he says, in support of the factory sales, "These benefit the farmers, not only immediately around the factory city, but all the farmers in the state by withdrawing from the supply of milk from manufactured purposes the additional amount which is sent to the city. We have felt for some time that the large withdrawals of milk for the use of the city of Chicago have had a decided influence on the price of manufactured milk in the state of Wisconsin." He finishes this letter with a request for more of the Dougan story, and permission to reprint it as a circular. He also sends Ronald ten small pamphlets for factory distribution, each extolling in a different way the virtues of drinking milk, and of drinking it at the factory or in offices.

Now Ronald has before him Riordan's letter of 1930. Riordan is still a strong advocate of milk in the factories, but his job requires that he come up with other ideas, too. And this new one bothers Ronald.

Riordan writes, "Three years ago in the course of pushing the consumption of milk in the factories, I was impressed with the fact that while we might start distribution in the factory and while the efforts of the employer would go quite a way, there was quite a gap between the initial start and a proper education along lines showing milk values." He goes on to say that Milwaukee has had for years an effective "milk worker," a Miss Brady, supported in part by funds from the university, part by the distributors, and part by producer organizations.

Riordan feels it would be good to have such a worker in smaller cities, but that to support one would be too expensive for any one city. However, a group might manage. He reminds Ron of a meeting of the previous year that Ron had attended, which was investigating the formation of a state dairy council to supplement the work of the National Dairy Council in pushing the consumption of milk and milk products. To hire a man to assume charge of this state work seemed desirable, but no one could figure where the salary would come from. A later meeting discussed hiring a milk worker who would be sponsored by a number of towns: specifically Racine, Kenosha, Waukesha, Janesville, and Beloit, and paid by "check off" — the producers to contribute one, or one-half cent per hundred pounds of milk, and the distributors to meet that contribution. The worker would then spend time in each of the five cities. To get the producers and distributors to agree to this, Riordan suggests a "Milk Week" in which all the dairy forces in the state cooperate in pushing the value of milk, and that sometime during that week the two groups be brought together to agree to the check off, the amount from each city being turned over to the university, and the university in turn furnishing a milk worker to the cities.

With Miss Brady's success in mind, Riordan writes, "If this worker should get access, as she should coming from the university, to women's clubs, Red Cross circles, Parent and Teachers organizations, schools, and factories, she could preach not only milk but other dietary stuff as well. If she preaches dietetics and includes in her presentations every article of diet, the present value of milk and milk products will be extensively advertised and we will incur no hostility from other food producers." He points out that since Ronald is both producer and distributor it would be a little unfair, yet he thinks that one cent spent in advertising would be worth the money. He thinks the manufacturers from the cities involved might furnish the money for the initial "Milk Week," and that since he knows Ronald is a close thinking dairyman with quite a lot of experience, asks his judgment in the matter.

Ronald applauds Riordan's vision, but raises two objections. One, that this is a poor time, due to poor prices, to establish a check off. And two, he's afraid that a paid worker would be an enthusiast for pasteurized milk. He reminds Riordan that Dougan's Dairy has the endorsement of every doctor in town for its inspected and certified Grade A Raw Guernsey milk, and that is raw Guernsey milk that he is peddling in the factories..

Riordan responds, "Long experience with farmers and others convinces me that the time to get them to do anything is when there is an urgent need to do it. My own experience has been that that is the only time they are ready to contribute."

He concedes that Ron's second concern is much more serious and difficult.

> I think the point at issue has far more to do with health workers than with milk extension workers. Personally, if I know where the milk comes from, I should never want it pasteurized. I think physicians are agreed to that. There has come in this country, however, a wild and baseless, as I see it, agitation concerning undulant fever. It is a new thing and scientists who have long been unknown are trying in my judgment to work their way into renown by grabbing the story. Racine, by action of its health department, has forbidden the sale of any milk not pasteurized. There has been considerable agitation in Milwaukee to compel all milk to be pasteurized.

He continues that while pasteurization would eliminate any infection

What Does Dougan's New Seal Mean?

———◦◦◦———

1. "SUPERVISED WISCONSIN GUERNSEY FARMS" together with the cream container is the copyrighted seal of the American Guernsey Cattle Club, and its use allowed only on genuine Guernsey products.

2. "WISCONSIN GRADE-A-RAW," is the copyright held by the Bureau of Markets of the State of Wisconsin, and granted only to those producers who fulfill the rigid requirements established by the Bureau of Markets for Grade A quality.

3. "INSPECTED BY ROCK COUNTY MEDICAL MILK COMMISSION". The inspection and supervision of the milk is in the hands of this commission, which has been established by the Rock County Medical Society for this purpose.

4. "DOUGAN" stands for twenty-two years of service in the production of the best milk to be had in any city at any price.

Only

$16\frac{2}{3}$

Cents

per Quart

Every home in Beloit may be assured by the above outlined supervision and inspection that in Dougan's Milk they obtain the highest quality of Natural Guernsey Milk.

W.J. ran this ad in 1929, explaining his new bottle cap and the quality controls that guaranteed the delivery of clean, safe, raw milk.

from milk, veterinarians are divided as to whether undulant fever can be caused through infected milk, and that the university has a study underway to see whether it can originate in the use of milk. If they find that it can, "I am considerably worried about the future of certified and inspected raw milk. If I were selling this milk, I would arrange with my city health department to inspect my plant. How long that will stave off the action of the health department in the absence of any scientific discoveries I do not know."

(Undulant fever, also known as Brucellosis and Bang's disease, found with varying virulence in many animals, is caused by bacteria of one of the brucella species. In cattle it causes spontaneous abortion, and can indeed be transmitted to humans through diseased animals, which pasteurization prevents: milk mixed from many sources is safer pasteurized.)

Roirdan's final paragraph tries to reassure Ron. "I could not conceive, however, of a milk worker failing to support the use of clean, non-pasteurized milk. I would look for no trouble from that quarter. As a matter of fact, I would look for quite a bit of sane information concerning raw milk being given by this milk worker, she cannot do otherwise. I would like to point out, too, that the milk worker would be under control of the distributors and producers, with I assume each member having an equal choice in the form of policies."

But in the depth of the Depression, a Milk Week fails to materialize, nor is a milk worker hired, at least in Beloit. Ron and W.J. use their own advertising acumen to promote sales, and a major factor is the implementation of the idea—perhaps it was Riordan's—first promulgated by the Wisconsin Manufacturers Association, to sell milk in the factories. It is the factory workers' sales, and the spinoff to workers' homes, that enlarge the milk business and see the farm through the Depression. Ron does decide to produce a lower priced milk than its Grade A Guernsey Raw; in fact, in 1931, he produces two: Dougan's Blended Raw, which comes from the select number of producer farms W.J. mentions in his 1927 letter to E.B. Neese, and Dougan's Blended, from a larger pool of producers. This latter is pasteurized. Grade A Raw continues to be popular, though both cheaper Blends are best-sellers.

(Though not with all customers. The Monta Wing family, from the college, switch to Willowbrook after a month on Blended. Ron writes that he respects their decision, but would like to give them additional information. He compares Health Office figures on the milk of the two dairies, Dougan's coming out slightly ahead. "It seems to me that both from a control standpoint and the actual butterfat per dollar standpoint, our Blended milk is the best buy. I hope you will decide to come back to us when you can conveniently." He also encloses a copy of a sales letter to the college, telling how swiftly the milk comes from cow to delivery, the supervision of producer farms so that flavor is paramount—no silage fed before milking, for instance—and that Guernsey milk, of which Blend is 56 per cent with another 10 per cent Jersey, has exceptionally high food value. "It is particularly gratifying to us that the Municipal Hospital is using our Blended milk for patients and staff.... Aside from the hospital we have made no effort to interest wholesale users. However, we would appreciate trade from Beloit College, and have enough milk to supply your needs. The price is 30 cents per gallon.")

Grade A Raw remains the dairy's highest grade milk through the forties, although in 1945 small letters are added to its cap, saying, "from Dougan cows." This is to reassure the customer that only milk from the round barn, under W.J.'s direct supervision, is being sold as Grade A raw milk. This may be in response to a 1943 charge from a worker at the Warner Brake factory, who claims that his sickness is due to the use of Dougan's raw milk. Ron is hyper sensitive, writing to the worker's doctor, who has seen the patient once, "Even the unsubstantiated charge will cause us a great deal of harm. Naturally I wish to understand the situation as thoroughly as possible." He has checked with Warner Brake's employment office for the days Mr. Shakka was out, he writes, and with the driver as to his purchase of milk—no more than a half dozen in all. Shakka "held out on buying milk at eight cents a pint when he claimed he could get it so much cheaper at the milk station." He asks Dr. Brinkerhoff to get in touch after he has seen the worker again. In this instance, the charge against the Dougan raw milk is not disseminated nor upheld, and does no harm to the business or Warner Brake sales. But with the ubiquity of food sources increasingly spreading over the globe, Ron is right that unfounded allegations can ruin a business.

It is not until 1949 that the Wisconsin legislature passes a comprehensive milk pasteurization law, signed by Governor Rennebohm, himself a dairyman. It goes into effect the following year. This, they say, is to prevent disease "from any milk-borne diseases." Though there are various exceptions written into the law, the amount of work and money it would take to meet state requirements for these, makes the sale of raw milk beyond the means of the small dairyman. To the regret of the Dougan dairy, to the regret of Beloit area doctors, and to the regret of many customers, this is the end of Dougan's raw milk offerings.

And, as a final footnote, Daddy much later tells Jackie, "Ebby Neese was always a good friend, but he never put milk—raw or otherwise—into Beloit's largest factory."

14 ⊰ SCAFFOLD

It's autumn. Jackie is in fourth grade. She's not at home when Grampa falls off the scaffold.

They are building another addition onto the milkhouse, this time on the back. Mother is in the kitchen of the Little House. She can see the work going on through the kitchen window. Over the lilac bushes and beyond the apple tree she sees Grampa on a scaffold. Whenever activity is going on, Grampa's in the middle of it. She sees him take a step backward, as if to admire his work. But there's nothing behind him to step onto. Grampa falls. Mother can't see him land because of the lilac bushes.

She rushes from the house. Grampa is on the ground under the scaffold. The other workers are just recovering from their shock. Mother takes charge. She sends a man to call the ambulance. She sends another back to the Little House for blankets. She doesn't send anyone to the Big House to tell Grama or Daddy, for Grama is at church Circle, and Daddy's in Madison.

Mother covers Grampa with a blanket, to keep him warm in case of shock. She doesn't let anyone move him. Grampa struggles to get himself up, but Mother won't let him. She's had first aid training.

The ambulance races out to the dairy with its siren screaming. The attendants load Grampa into the back. Mother rides beside him to the hospital.

A few days ago Grampa had given Mother a *Christian Century* magazine, folded to an article. He had asked her to read the article so that he could discuss it with her. Now, in the ambulance, he asks her if she's read it. Mother says she has. He starts to tell her his views on the topic. In the middle of a sentence his voice falters and trails off. He's unconscious. Mother is sick with dread. She holds Grampa's unconscious hand.

At the hospital they take Grampa to the Emergency Room. He has a concussion. It's serious, but he'll recover. He stays several days in the hospital, with Mother or Grama sitting with him. Ron stops in regularly to check on his father, but doesn't confer on the work.

Grampa's face is discolored. Both eyes are black. He can talk but he can't see anyone's replies for the concussion has blurred his eyes. He can't read what anyone writes. He's able to write himself, though; after the first day, while he is still in doubt about his condition, he sends a pencilled note to Grama:

7 a.m., June 10.

My precious Dearie;

My love for you is pure, true, and abiding. You are a true companion and affectionate wife. If I live, and I expect to, I am sure of this—God careth for <u>me</u> and all my interests. If I do not pull through, this assurancy is just as firm, and he can care for my family and sisters as well as I can. My desires and my way is not essential to his grand plans. If I go, some larger blessing will come to my dear ones than should I stay. My text this morning is 1 Peter 5: 7 "Casting all your care on Him for He careth for thee." "God knows and cares." Must close now and rest. In about an hour the doctor will be here—I rested well last night and am perfectly content and peaceful this morning. Your loving husband

W.J. Dougan

When Mother sits with him, he confides in her. He says, "I'm wondering if I'm going to lose my eyesight. If the Lord has willed it, I'll accept it, as I accepted my deafness. But it will be hard, very hard. And it will be even harder on you, and Eunice, and everybody, if that happens."

Tears run down Mother's face. Grampa can't see them. She squeezes Grampa's hand to let him know that he will never be too hard on anybody.

But Grampa doesn't lose his sight. Gradually the black goes away from around his eyes. Gradually his vision clears. He comes home from the hospital. He's supposed to stay in bed.

Mother is ironing. She sees Grampa out the window, back in the thick of things. He's supervising the fitting of the large door to the back of the milkhouse. Mother goes out and writes to him, "<u>DO NOT OVERDO</u>!" She underscores the words heavily.

Grampa leaves the work. He comes in and sits at the dining room table while Mother goes on ironing. His eye catches sight of the *Christian Century* magazine. He picks it up and leafs through it. He stops at a page and studies it.

"Vera," he says, "This article looks interesting. I think I'll read it. Maybe you'd read it, too, and then we could discuss it together."

Mother, grateful, assures him that she will.

15 ⨯ NORM PEEBLES

Former employees frequently stop by to see Ron or Grampa, to relate their own travels and travails since leaving, and to talk about their time on the farm. Norman Peebles visits in 1958.

———

I came in October of '27, Ron, you remember, a couple years after you'd come back from France and moved into the Little House. I guess your dad didn't like my looks because it took four trips out to the farm before he hired me! I got $50 a month, lived at home. That first day Daddy set me to splitting wood for the kitchen stove; that only lasted half a day. Then I spent two or three days out in the field, picking corn—I didn't know a seed ear from a sweet corn ear, but DeWitt Griffiths helped me. Then Daddy came and got me and put me into the milkhouse. George Hotton was in charge, a boy out of the middle of Chicago going to ag school; I wondered how a boy from Chicago even *knew* he was interested in agriculture!

The milkhouse boiler room was nice to eat your lunch in, in cold weather. It was always warm and there were chairs in there—I took my lunch except when I was on the route; then I'd stop at home and Mother'd give me lunch. The injector that injected water into the boiler was a cranky thing, hard to get it going. One day I got that darn injector going and went back into the washroom where we washed cans and bottles, and I forgot the darn injector until all of a sudden—the boiler must have filled up completely—there was a huge POP! the top blew off, and I tell you it sprayed water all over that boiler room!

For a little while Daddy, or maybe it was you, Ron, tried to burn soft coal in the boiler, since it was much faster to get going than coke, but you gave up on it because it was too dirty.

Remember that route man who sometimes worked in the milkhouse afternoons, sometimes in the barn, Byron Moore? He was big and burly and jovial, but he took to picking on a little guy half his size in the milkhouse, a quiet easygoing chap, he was about my age, twenty. Whenever Byron teased him or made him the butt of a joke, he just gave a big grin and didn't say anything. One day Byron got to riding him pretty hard. It happened so fast that none of us knew how it happened, but suddenly Byron was flopped right over on the floor. I was never so surprised in my life. Byron got up and was awfully quiet for a while, and he never bothered the little guy again.

Then I got put on a milk route with Lester Stam; I drove the truck and had to learn to use a shift—took me about three days. Everyone was amazed I knew the town so well, but a kid that age, I'd been all over it. Chase Hess had been driving for Lester; he broke me in on the route, then went out and ran a tractor.

There was that big paratyphoid epidemic the spring of 1928. There was a carrier somewhere, and we all had to have typhoid shots, three each. Dr. Thayer started, he didn't hurt, then Dr. Delaney took over and delivered the third shot—it was all we could do to keep from screeching. Clair Mathews got deathly sick with the shots. The city started with the little dairies first, tested everybody. They tested Dougan's, too, and we came out clean, but everybody trusted Dougan's to begin with and business had already begun to boom even before we got tested. The trade grew so fast they had to split Lester's route and give me part of it; I used an old Buick touring car because that's all the farm had. We took the cushions out of it and I loaded the back end—I delivered milk in that old Buick for quite a while, it had the old Buick shift in it, which was backwards to the standard shift nowadays. Daddy Dougan had to pick up anything he could find—he got Byron Moore a tiny little black Ford truck. Byron hated that truck—the names he'd call it!—he threatened to smash it, you couldn't depend on it through one day's delivery. My Buick worked okay, but I was proud as punch when the farm bought me that new Erskine panel job, all nice and bright and shiny.

And then the farm ran short of milk bottles. You sent me and Ed Pfaff, a couple of small town boys, into Chicago. We took the Erskine truck; we ran the route in the morning with that truck, and then went to Chicago. I don't know how we found the place to get the bottles, but we did, only had to ask directions once—got a load, the truck was jammed full of crates. We made the round trip, a couple hundred miles, in one afternoon. In those days a trip like that was like going to the moon. We were pretty proud of ourselves.

They found the typhoid carrier finally, at the biggest dairy in town, Wright & Wagner. Everybody knew it, but they never admitted it publicly. There was

This picture of cows crossing the creek was used in Hoard's Dairyman. *The gravel pit is in the background, and the Mackie farm.*

somebody in the ice cream department there whose job was to lay that final circle of paper on the top of the tubs of ice cream, before the lid goes on. When he—or maybe she—picked up the papers and smoothed them over the ice cream, he was carrying bacteria into contact with the ice cream, and that's what caused the epidemic. As soon as they found him the epidemic died out. We all watched the *Daily News*, and every day there'd be a report on how many new cases there were, and how hard the city health officer was working on the case, and then state health officers were coming in to help, and in the Turtle column—all the townships had a column about once a week, Footville and Harmony and all, reports on what was going on, who was visiting who, and all—it said that all the children in Turtle and Clinton had now had their third toxin anti-toxin shots, so we dairy folk weren't the only ones who suffered those shots!

Anyway, about the middle of May there was a big article saying it was all unfounded rumors that the carrier was at Wright & Wagner dairy, or at any dairy, and then a few days later there was another big article, saying the source of the contamination had been found and the carrier was no longer in Beloit, and there wasn't any more danger of new infection, and that after about two weeks, which is how long it takes the bacteria to incubate, there wouldn't be any more new cases. I clipped the article. They never mentioned who it was or where they found him—everyone handled Wright & Wagner with kid gloves; they were the big outfit in town. You had to be careful what you said. Before they found the carrier, Daddy Dougan ran a statement in the paper that our milk was totally safe, but he didn't mention safe from what.

I'd got myself a Model T Ford, and in the spring thaw that year Turtle Crick overflowed Colley Road there by the bridges, and I couldn't get through, so I turned around and came out the State Line Road, the long way around. The frost had gone out of the ground and the road was just like a sponge, but it was all gravel, you couldn't get stuck. But it was just that I had to ride that doggone clutch the whole way because Model T's didn't have much power and in high gear just wouldn't pull it. So when I finally got to the farm I told you, Ron, that the road was out, and you were running a milk route too, you were using a Model A Tan truck. I told you the State Line Road was good. So you took the same route and had to ride that low clutch all the way into town; when you saw me that night you said, "Your idea of a good road isn't very good—it's like driving on Jell-O with a crust!"

Byron Moore and I were both helping out some in the afternoons in the barn. I was washing cows and he didn't notice I was there and I heard him sounding off about me to the other barn men about the way I was handling my truck. I didn't like that he was talking about me behind my back so I walked up to him and told him. He was bigger'n me, husky; I was just a skinny twerp. He grabbed me by the shirt front, backed me up against a cow, drew back like he was going to hit me, caught himself just in time and didn't deliver the punch. We never spoke after that, unless we had to. I might have been mistaken about what he was talking about, but it certainly sounded to me like he was giving me fits to the crew in the barn.

I quit near the end of 1928; I was making good money, $80. But my folks moved to Belvidere and I didn't think there was room for me in the Big House, and I didn't have any place in town to stay, so I just went with the family. My sister Frances worked on the farm, though, too, the summer of '28. She was sixteen and in high school and she came out to the Little House and did some housework and helped Vera with the children—your Joan was three or four, and then there was Patsy, and Jackie was just an infant in arms. And my brother Leo came out one day and got paid for picking pie cherries. I guess you could say the whole family worked at Dougan's, one way or another.

16 ⋇ CAPS

There are fashions in milk bottle caps, too. Nobody thinks, when Grampa presses those first caps on those first six bottles in May of 1907, to commemorate the occasion by pasting a cap in a scrapbook. Where did he get them? Who designed them? It seems probable that the first caps were like the standard disks of later years, with the pull tabs. It seems probable Grampa ordered them after studying the dairy equipment ads in *Hoard's Dairyman*.

There are photos, however, of a different sort of cap that Grampa is using by 1916, and continues to use until the early 1930s. There are pictures of the bottler and capper as well, and one can even view them in action, for a brief motion picture of the milk business was made, around 1932, for use as a short advertising feature at a local theater before the main film. One sees a huge roll of perhaps five-inch-wide tape at the top of the capper with cap after cap imprinted along the tape. The tape is threaded through the capper, and when the capper stamps down on a bottle, it cuts out the disk and clamps it over the bottle's lip, crimping the edges and at the same time winding a copper wire around the neck so that the cap holds firmly. The used tape, now with its series of holes, continues to the floor. The capper has space for two bottles. Its platform moves back and forth under the capper: a bottle is swinging to be capped while a capped one is being removed and placed in the milk case and a new uncapped one set in its stead.

That cap exists, or most of it (the crimp part has been cut off by hand), pinned to a carbon copy of a 1930 letter to the American Guernsey Cattle Club, Peterboro, New Hampshire. Grampa explains he has used their copyrighted "Golden Guernsey" seal for several years now, a privilege a firm may buy into, if their milk is of a certain quality. Grampa, and all Wisconsin members, have been paying for this privilege at the rate of one-fourth cent a quart. Grampa is anxious to make the label pay its way in increased sales. But the Club's advertising folder, "Golden Guernsey, America's Table Milk," doesn't fit his needs, nor does the Golden Guernsey cap, for his major competitor has caps

This bottle shows the crimped cap sealed with wire. Grampa abandoned the Golden Guernsey motto as well as the small attractive jug, for his competitors used the same advertising.

with "Golden Guernsey" writ large. If Grampa uses the folder for advertising, "Half of those receiving it would think it came from the other dairy." He asks for posters and advertising that will fit his needs, especially in the Beloit factories, where "possibly one-third of our total volume of milk handled goes." He says he is using an M-2 bottle with a hood seal of the same size. He continues:

> I am enclosing a sample of my new caps. I realize that the word Guernsey is not stressed on the cap. I feel that anyone buying a quart of milk will know that it is Guernsey—it is my hope that your copyrighted jug will become synonymous with Guernsey. At any rate I would prefer to tell the trade that the milk they are buying is Wisconsin Grade-A-Raw, produced under a standard ordinance and supervised by the County Medical Commission and the American Guernsey Cattle Club, than to talk up Golden Guernsey—a slogan which anyone can use, and which is used rather freely outside of the copyright.

The affixed cap (manufactured by the Crown Cap and Seal Company) is a yellow orange, with the Golden Guernsey jug on it, affidavits, and W.J. Dougan's signature. The material is a light but firm cardboard, waxed. There is no pull tab—the wire has to be loosened, the edges of the cap uncrimped and the cap peeled off. It can be pressed on again for storage.

This cap, and the relationship with Golden Guernsey, doesn't last much longer, for in the early thirties when Jackie and Craig and their older sisters are daily pulling up the tabs on milk bottle caps (more frequently if they are raiding the dairy cooler for chocolate milk or orange drink) the caps neither bear the Golden Guernsey jug nor cover the lip of the bottle. The change is almost certainly due to the Depression, and the cost of the elaborate crimp-top cap and wire compared to the simple cardboard disk.

These new pull-tab caps are varied and colorful. Daddy is now the one to tell the dairy supply company what caps he wants, and how he wants them to look, the one who approves their designs, and sometimes designs one himself.

The milkhouse gets almost all its supplies from the Cherry-Burrell Corporation in Chicago, "Geared to Serve the Dairy Industry," "Complete Equipment for Handling Milk and Its Products." Their representative to the Dougan Farm is Chet Hoesley, an affable man; he is well known to Jackie by his frequent appearances at the Chez Nous dinner table — she believes he times his visits to coincide with mealtimes.

On a Cherry-Burrell file folder from the dairy office, Daddy, sometime after the close of the milk business, has written, "This folder covers about 1946-47, possibly a little more. At any rate it demonstrates the details of maintaining milkroom equipment, the courtesy of the relationship, how I depended on Chet Hoesley, their salesman. The low prices are interesting, although they didn't seem low then, after all a penny post card cost 1 cent then! Hoesley had a sense of humor — also a nervous habit of brushing his sleeve or lapel for suspected lint." And then Daddy has punctuated that remark with a little smiling head on stick legs.

There are many Cherry-Burrell folders, stuffed with transactions. Some are as simple as:

Please send us the following bottle caps:
50M Guernsey Milk-Wisconsin Grade A-Raw
100M Dougan's-Blended
50M Dougan's-Homogenized-Vitamin D

Some are rush:

Gentlemen: Enclosed is an order for some viscolizer gaskets. We are completely out of the hat leathers and would appreciate immediate shipment or we will not be able to operate. The plant men failed to notify me that they were about out of the hat leathers until they were almost done with the last set."

Others are more complicated. A letter from 1944 indicates some specifics of what Daddy is talking about on his file folder notation, and gives details of how he has to spend his time, running a business:

Gentlemen: In 1940 we purchased a 6-20 Milwaukee Filler and Capper, Serial #136. We had a little trouble with it at first but you supplied us with some expert help and in spite of fairly rough treatment, the machine has been doing well for us until recently.

About six months ago you sent us a brass hook ring #55009 to replace one of lighter construction #6663. Once in a while a bottle would jam, and the lighter ring had been broken several times. The plant men tell me that since the brass ring was installed, we have had considerable trouble in breaking bottles, and that recently it has gotten much worse. We find that ring 55009 has teeth somewhat shorter than 6663 and that as the bottle is delivered from the filling table to the star wheel, the shorter teeth of 55009 have a tendency to deposit the bottle on the tip of the teeth of the starwheel. The bottle may then be jostled into place, or worse, become wedged between the star wheel and the opposite side of the bottle feed.

We have reinstalled the old battered 6663, and seem to be doing satisfactorily. We have rubber starwheels 6660 and 6661. Both of these are somewhat worn on the points, and I think should be replaced. Also we need a new set of filler rubbers. Probably we should have a new 6663 hook ring on hand, for the least strain will knock the one we are using to pieces.

Would it be possible for a factory representative to call and watch the machine working, and adjust it for us? Yours very truly —

The Cherry-Burrell products in the various folders range from gargantuan bottle washers and pasteurizing vats — which take special priority and even senatorial intervention to obtain during the World War II years — to the hundreds of mostly small individual parts, each of which can break or go wrong (and frequently do, as the letter above indicates) that make up an automatic bottler, or a bottle capper with heat sealing tape. From Cherry-Burrell the dairyman can buy, along with rubber starwheels and brass hook rings, myriad other items: rubber milkroom aprons, pasteurizer thermometers, cottage cheese strainers, butter boxes, metal sponges, milk-sample bottles with rubber stoppers, stainless steel seamless pails, bleached flannel napped on both sides, single seal hat leathers, those viscolizing valve seal gaskets, operating lever springs for the 6-20 Milwaukee filler, swedges for reforming pockets on a Model C Washer, to list but a few.

And, of course, milk bottle caps. These firm cardboard disks, each with a pull tab, are designed to fit snugly into the top of a bottle where the neck widens out into the lip, leaving an inner ledge. The ledge, less than an eighth of an inch down and no more than one-sixteenth of an inch wide, stops the cap from traveling right on down into the bottle. Bottles have different size apertures; when Daddy goes to the amber bottle, the cap size changes from 56 mm to 48 mm, which necessitates that all the designs be reduced. Fortunately none of them require any other changing in the translation, so the company makes this adjustment for no charge.

The Dougan caps are handsome. Their designs are on the whole simple and uncluttered, and there is some uniformity between them. The color often fits the product: chocolate milk's cap is printed on white in chocolate brown ink, orange drink in orange, grape drink in purple, buttermilk in butter yellow. Of the various milks and creams, Dougan's Guernsey Wisconsin Grade A raw milk is red, with "Vitamin D-Antirachitic" printed curved around the bottom: the latter word meaning rickets-preventing. Later, once the cows are no longer fed yeast to provide Vitamin D, fine print is added: "contains 400 USP units of Vitamin D per quart (Steenbock Process). Vitamin D Grade A Blended Raw, with a blue cap, bears the same message. Both raw milk caps assure "from DOUGAN cows," and for several years in the mid-1940s there is a special feature—raw milk caps in June and July are a jazzy red, white, and blue to celebrate Independence Day. Blended pasteurized has yellow-orange caps; homogenized, maroon. The caps are ordered in lots of twenty-five thousand, fifty thousand, and a hundred thousand, and these are applied on a one-million caps contract. They come, not on tapes to be stamped out, but in long cardboard tubes and are guaranteed sanitary. The chocolate, orange, and grape caps, and the caps on milk bottled in half pints sold to the schools, come with a hole under the tab for inserting a straw. Chocolate does not advertise its specific chocolate contents on the cap; indeed, it says, suspiciously, "chocolate drink." This is because chocolate milk is produced with a percentage of skim milk—although to all drinkers it tastes very rich, and is fully as nutritious though lacking some butterfat. The fruit drinks tell all: orange contains "15% or more orange juice, citric acid (made from lemons), sugar, and water." Grape drink contains "grape juice, sugar, and tartaric acid made from grapes—true fruit flavor." Around 1945, gradually as they are reordered, the bottle caps have added to them, again in small print, "Beloit, Wisconsin." Dougan's Dairy can now be located by its caps.

The clean bottles, in later years directly out of the bottle washer, go on a belt to the circular bottler and are filled a dozen at a time. At the end of the carousel ride they are shunted onto a moving metal jointed belt and carried under the capper. The capper stamps down on each bottle. The bottles move on under a small shower bath positioned just over the conveyer belt beyond the capper. At the end of the belt a milkhouse worker picks up the bottles two by two, gives them a flip with his wrist to get rid of the water in the cap area, and puts them in a milk case.

In sub-zero weather, if a bottle isn't protected or is left too long on a doorstep, the milk will freeze. Then a column of milk rises out of the neck, like a chimney, topped by the cap. Pictures of these "top hatted" bottles are favorites with newspaper photographers almost every winter.

In the late 1940s a customer, Mrs. Palmer, wife of a professor at the College, stirs up trouble about the Dougan cap. She tells Daddy that the unprotected lip of the bottle is an invitation to germs. Flies can sit on it in the milkhouse, in the milk trucks, on the doorstep. The milkhouse workers and delivery men who handle the bottles have hands of dubious cleanliness. She wants the entire top of the bottle protected.

Basically, Daddy agrees with her. A bottle would be more sanitary if it were completely covered. A fly can walk on it in a delivery truck. A dog can lick it on a doorstep. A milkman might not always wash his hands after he uses the lavatory. But covering a bottle means expense: new capping equipment, and the cost of the additional materials. He describes to Mrs. Palmer the safeguarding of cleanliness that goes into the production of every bottle of milk. But both of them know that this is not addressing the crux of the problem.

When Mrs. Palmer's urging does not move Daddy into swift action, she becomes a crusader. She circulates petitions. She gets customers not only to agitate but to threaten to quit. Her unrelenting efforts are so successful that there starts to be a loss of business near the college, and considerable ill will.

Ron shows off his cellophane hooded bottles to members of the Rock County Breeders Co-op.
From left: Amos Grundahl, Ron, Glen Knudson, Alfred Algrim, and David Gustafson.

Daddy capitulates. He and Mother take a trip through Michigan, visiting dairies and creameries. They find two main types of whole-lip covers. One is the heavy waxed cardboard circle that crimps down around the edges of the lip at capping, the kind the dairy quit using in the early thirties, but minus the copper ring that necessitated a ridged bottle. The other retains the inner cap but adds a square of cellophane chopped from a roll, placed over the bottle, crimped down, and as the bottle is given a spin, sealed with a heated tape at the narrowest point of the neck, just below the lip. The cellophane spreads out below the tape in an attractive manner. (There is a third type of cap just coming into use, the aluminum foil cap, which later becomes common in Chicago, Denver, and Milwaukee. In England, a clever little species of finch discovers it can peck through the foil cap and drink the cream; photographs of these small robbers in action become popular staples of the British press.)

Daddy decides to go with the cellophane hood. The transparent covering comes in a variety of colors. This calls for a decision about the caps underneath, for some colors of print are cancelled out by some colors of the cellophane. One can't read the words. Daddy will either have to redesign the caps to fit the cellophane, or have sufficient rolls of different colored cellophanes to fit the caps. And frequent changes of cellophane as well as caps, as different products come up to be bottled, is both a nuisance and time-consuming.

The decision is, in spite of the drawbacks, to keep all the familiar caps and use a complementary color of cellophane with each. Daddy orders red, clear, green, and "tango." And the tapes come in multicolors, too: black, blue, green, natural, purple, and red. He orders the special bottle capper assembly needed for this changeover.

The cellophane-hooded bottle, in use by the early fifties, is Mrs. Palmer's reward for her zeal. Daddy is no longer the Enemy. And the petitioning customers, or ex-customers, return to the fold. It is this combination on the amber bottles that Daddy uses until he retires from retail home delivery in 1967.

There is one other requirement for bottle caps over which Daddy has no control — he cannot entirely compose his own copy. In March of 1950 he receives a letter from the chief of the Dairy Division of the State of Wisconsin Department of Agriculture, who has been studying the Dougan caps — at Daddy's request — and finds them wanting. H.L. Weavers states,

> Wisconsin statutes do not define milk as being "fat free." That milk is defined as "skim milk" and must be so labeled. It is to appear on the cap in the same prominence as any other wording on the cap, together with the word "pasteurized," "Vit. D" and Vit. A if any of these are added.
>
> Your buttermilk is labeled as being "old fashioned buttermilk." The question is, is your buttermilk "old fashioned?" I am of the opinion that it may be "cultured buttermilk."
>
> Your Guernsey milk is not labeled as to whether it is pasteurized or not.
>
> Your Chocolate Drink in order to conform with the revised Wisconsin statutes of 1949 should be labeled "Chocolate Flavored Drink, Made with Skim Milk, Pasteurized."
>
> Since the city of Beloit has adopted the standard Grade A ordinance it will be necessary for you to comply with the Grade A requirements of this ordinance. The Wisconsin Grade A should, therefore, be deleted as soon as the grading provisions of the Beloit ordinance go into effect.

"*Mon Dieu*," mutters Daddy when he gets this letter, and is sorry he ever inquired of the Dairy Division. "How much can you print on a little cap, anyway?" Shaking his head, he sets about changing the wordings. He decides he will probably not get into trouble, though, if he uses up his now illegal supply on hand so long as he has put in an order for the changes.

17 ✕ RED AND LORETTA HOLMES

Hiring at the Dougan Farm is often a chain reaction. Hire one person, end up with the family. Lester Stam is followed by his father and mother. Herbert Hertzel's sister Josie comes to work in the Big House. Earl Bown travels down from Soldiers Grove in Kickapoo Valley; he tells Rod Jennings; Rod tells his first cousin Orland Potts who comes, followed by Orland's sister. Whole clans migrate. If a person doesn't get a job at Dougan's, he finds one in Beloit and stays on in the vicinity.

"The largest export of Kickapoo Valley is her young men," Ron Dougan has been heard to say.

Robert — "Red" — Holmes from Soldiers Grove is working for the WPA in Flora, Illinois, in 1941. His salary is $40 a month. His brother-in-law, Rod Jennings, writes from Beloit that he thinks Daddy Dougan will hire him for more than that. Red applies, and W.J. offers him a job at $65 a month, provided he doesn't smoke. Red and his wife of a year, Loretta, can hardly believe it. They pack up and drive their 1929 Model A to Beloit. They carry a dozen baby ducks in an iron kettle in the back seat.

Red assures Daddy Dougan that he doesn't smoke. It's a lie, the only lie he ever tells Daddy. He never smokes on the job, only at home. He figures what he does off the farm is his own business. "I'd have told him I didn't eat, if that was one of the requirements," he says. He tells W.J. he won't be able to do much right away, for he has the flu and is pretty weak.

"With all the Vitamin D milk you'll be drinking, we'll have you well and strong in no time," W.J. says. "I'll give you an easy job this morning."

The easy job is digging post holes.

Red and Loretta find a house near Waverly Beach. It's full of bedbugs and cockroaches. They fumigate for two days before they move in. The ducks go into a washtub.

At the end of the first month, Red gets raised to $100. He and Loretta drive down to Little Egypt to visit Loretta's folks. They debate all the way whether they should tell anyone how rich they are, and decide against it.

They move again, into the Larson place on a lane far back from Colley Road, alongside the Hill Farm. They have three little rooms and a windmill. The ducks go into a shed. When they return one night, the rats have eaten them all. They make another move, into one of the apartments at the Hill Farm. Pete Hoff lives downstairs and fires up the furnace so hot the upstairs dwellers, the Holmeses and Jennings, can hardly stand it.

At first Red does general farm work. W.J. watches him unload corn. "You're taking too many unnecessary steps," he says. "You're making work for yourself. Instead of shoving your scoop into the corn and stepping back to pitch it, just scoop it in and then pitch it." He demonstrates, leaving out the backward step.

Red tries. It throws him off balance, it hurts his back. But if he does it by stepping back to get into position before he throws, his balance is fine, his back is fine.

He does it W.J.'s way while the boss is watching. "Good," says W.J. "That's more efficient." When he leaves to supervise some other worker, Red returns to doing it his own way.

He's sent up to Chez Nous to

Red amd Loretta Holmes, when he was in the Service.

bring down a load of hay. He has a blind horse, old Molly, and a bay, May. Red has driven horses before, but never on a sharp curve with a load. At the turn above the dairy he chooses the higher side of the road. The slope pushes the load against the horses and the singletree hits their heels. They want to go faster and Red lets them. The horses and wagon get away from him. They are going so fast they don't even try to turn in at the farm. They hit the ditch below the drive. The blind horse falls; the wagon goes over her and lodges on top of her. Grampa comes rushing out, agitated, fearful for the horse. Red is agitated too, not only for the horse but for his job. It takes many men and a tractor to get the wagon clear and to free Molly, who miraculously is unhurt.

Red is next assigned to the milkhouse. Ronald is now his boss. Red is a self-confessed hothead; it must be in the hair, his wife says. He gets in fights with this and that fellow worker—"It never takes much," says Red—and every time figures he'll be canned. Ron always saves his hide. When Red is using an ice pick to remove caps from bottles returned from the route, and pouring the milk into a milk can, he gets into a heated arm-waving yelling match with John Baker. John reports to Ron that Red tried to stab him. Ron manages to calm Baker, and tells Red from now on to punctuate his arguments with his finger.

Not all confrontations are trivial. Red has the milkhouse job of dumping milk: of meeting the producer farmer coming in with his milk, taking the cans, weighing them on the scales and marking down the weights, then dumping the milk into the pasteurizing vat. One day he pulls the lid from a can and sees that the milk is off color: there's blood in it. Bloody milk can be caused by a number of reasons. When a cow first milks, the colostrum may be a little bloody. A tit can be worn down and bleed. There can be internal bleeding, too; an infection in the udder. Whatever the reason, the milk is unacceptable. Red refuses to take the producer's milk. Elliot gets angry; Red gets angrier. He goes to the office and tells Ron. Ron informs the producer that the dairy can't take bloody milk. The producer drives away in a rage, shouting at Red, "Blabbermouth!"—and worse.

Red also washes cans in the milkhouse, and sometimes puts the cream in the churn and makes butter and buttermilk. He sometimes adds the starter to the vat of milk for cottage cheese. A few times it doesn't set and has to be fed to the pigs. Ron is provoked that there's no cheese, but nobody can figure out what went wrong.

One winter night it snows so heavily that some of the drifts come up to Red's armpits. He and Rod Jennings drive to work from the Hill Farm in a '34 Ford, going around by Highway 15, then into town and out Colley Road. Halfway to the farm they get stuck. They walk. It's 16 below zero, the wind chill 30 below. The intense cold gets into Red's face and paralyzes one side. Ron takes him to the hospital where they diagnose the paralysis as Bell's palsy. The condition goes away very slowly.

Red asks for a milk route. When Ron can't give him one he quits and goes to work for the Beloit Corporation. A month later Ron offers him Sam Mackie's route; Sam is going into the service. The factory is unwilling to release Red. There is a wartime stipulation that they don't have to let a worker go, but Ron talks them into it.

Red works harder on the milk route than he's ever worked in his life. He comes home and falls on the couch, sleeps till three-thirty in the morning, then has to be up and back at work. By now he and Loretta and their children are living on Sixth Street. They have no car. Red has to ride his bicycle out to the farm in all weathers, six or seven miles from the west side. He neglects to fill out his route book regularly enough as he goes along, and then at the office has to grapple with whom to credit the two or four dollars left over, before he can check out and go home. He isn't fond of the shoe factory where the little strings on the floor get tangled with the small wheels of his milk trolley. He hates all the irksome coupons—the butter rationing, the gas rationing. He finds a milk route involves a lot of walking.

Red's draft notice comes after he's worked on the farm three and a half years. Ron can get him a deferment as a farm worker. But Red decides he'll take a chance on the service.

"Gung ho!" snorts his wife, telling about it years later. "Twenty-six years old, with a third child coming up! When was he ever going to get another chance like that? And then he goes and volunteers for the paratroopers!"

Ron, unable to find anyone to take over Red's milk route, has to take it himself.

In the infantry, Red reports, an old sergeant keeps hollering at him, "You're not a milkman anymore! You're not a milkman anymore!" He never figures out how the sergeant knows he's been a milkman.

At the end of the war, after serving in the Pacific and Philippines, Red returns to Beloit. Ron is ready to hire him back, but Red remembers how hard he worked on the route, and those icy three-thirty mornings.

"No thanks," says Red, "I'm not a milkman anymore," and he and Loretta buy a little farm west of town.

18 ⊀ REFUND

Craig is eight. He notices several older boys, boys he doesn't know, toiling along Colley Road from town, pulling a wagon over the gravel. When they get close he sees the wagon is full of empty milk bottles. They arrive at the farm, hot and sweaty, and expecting to be paid for all the bottles they've collected. The wagon holds a motley assortment—not only Dougan bottles, but Wright & Wagner, Merrick, Hillendale, and others.

"Daddy and Grampa don't give money for bottles," informs Craig. "Other dairies do, but not us."

The boys are incensed. They storm the office and demand to know why not. Daddy explains why not, that the bookkeeping involved costs more than the bottles are worth. Then he takes them to the milkhouse and they have all the chocolate and orange they can drink. Grampa comes on the scene and invites them to take a swim in the cowtank. After that they ride on an empty haywagon out to the fields and watch the haying. They even watch a little of the milking.

By the time they head back for town they've almost forgotten about money, but not quite. Craig, who has accompanied them on the entire outing, notes that they carefully separate out the Dougan bottles and set them in a row on the well lid, then trundle off with the other dairies' empties.

"They may cash 'em in," Craig tells Daddy, "but I bet those other places won't give them as good a refund!"

19 ⚛ MILK BOTTLE NECKLACE

Jackie is in junior high art class. They are making jewelry. The assignment is to design interesting beads out of clay, dry them, paint them, and then string them on braided raffia.

For all of sixth grade, and so far in seventh, Jackie has never handed in a paper without adding her trademark under her name. The trademark is a stylized, cartoony cow's head:

Jackie decides to make a trademark necklace.

She tries to model a cow's head, but her repeated efforts come out poorly. The emblem, for all its simplicity, is too complicated to model in clay. A related idea strikes her. How about a milk bottle? Milk bottles have no pointy horns or flaps of ears. They are a strong, simple shape.

She models a milk bottle. She makes it a little taller than her thumb-joint, but not so thick. She rounds it evenly, tapers the neck, flattens the top and the bottom. It comes out looking like a milk bottle. It is aesthetically pleasing.

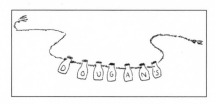

Jackie is hugely pleased.

She makes six more milk bottles, pierces their necks with an orange stick, and leaves them to dry. The next class period she paints them white with red caps. When the white is dry, on the lower part of each bottle she paints a black letter: D, O, U, G, A, N, 'S. After the letters are dry she shellacs the bottles. On the final day of the project she braids red raffia to make a chain. She strings the beads in order, spacing them with knots so they're not all bunched together, but will hang at even intervals. She leaves a length of raffia at either end to tie.

Her teacher looks dubious at the project throughout. Although she never criticizes, she never praises, either. She gives Jackie a "B" on the jewelry project.

Jackie doesn't care. She loves her milk bottle necklace. She wears it every time she wears her red pullover, which is frequently. And Grampa, every time he sees it, laughs and laughs until his eyes disappear. That is "A" enough for Jackie.

20 ❈ DADDY CHURNS

It is 1933, the Depression. The farm is barely surviving. If it weren't for the milk business, it would not have survived this long. Yet the profit margin is so slim that it's questionable whether either the milk business or the farm will be able to make it. W.J. is writing letters to Neil Bosworth in Elgin, a banker and his cousin-in-law, about procedures for declaring bankruptcy.

It is evening; the milkhouse has been a man short all day. Work is running behind. The butter is not yet made for tomorrow's delivery. Daddy goes out after supper to make it.

He's alone in the milkhouse. He fetches the cans of pasteurized sweet cream from the cooler, opens the churn, pours the liquid in, and seals the hatch. The churn is shaped like an oversize barrel on its side. He throws the switch; the churn rotates. Inside, the cream sloshes rhythmically.

All the butter-making equipment and containers have been previously cleaned, but Daddy now runs the steam hose into a vat of water till the water is boiling, and sterilizes the large stainless-steel pan, the wooden butter paddles, and the two-pound crockery tubs. He sterilizes the enamel-topped table with the boiling water, and arranges the tubs upside down along the back of it, pyramid fashion.

He listens for the change in sound that heralds the coming of the butter. He knows the sound from years of churning by hand, as a boy, in the kitchen of the Big House. It wasn't a job he enjoyed. Then, he could tell not only by the change in sound but by the change in feel.

After a while he hears that the butter's come. He stops the churn, opens it, and lifts out chunk after chunk of the golden butter floating in the buttermilk. He drops them in the pan. When he has all the lumps he slaps them together with the paddles into a huge ball. He rinses the ball in cold water, works it more, rinses it again, salts it lightly, and works the salt into the butter. He sets the mound of butter on the table. Then he fills the tubs one by one, pressing the butter down so there are no air pockets, and smoothing the

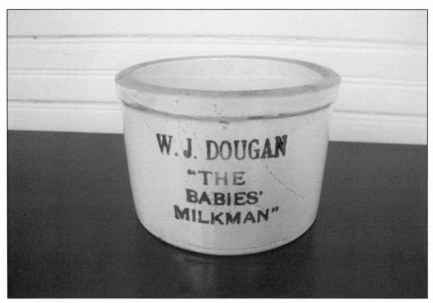

A two-pound butter crock, filled by hand, one by one.

top of the butter flush with the crockery rim. Over every tub he lays a circle of sterile parchment paper. He then wipes off the tubs, carries them to the cooler, and stacks them, again in a pyramid, on the shelf beside the cottage cheese. They are ready for the morning.

He returns to the churn with a clean milk can and starts emptying the buttermilk into it. Several quarts will be bottled before dawn for the few people on the route who swear by fresh buttermilk. The rest will go down the lane to the pigs.

As the buttermilk pours out he sees a dark lump flow by and hears it splosh into the can. He stops pouring, takes a dipper, and grapples in the can till he secures the lump. He pulls it out. There in the dipper, lying in in a pool of buttermilk, is a sodden drowned mouse.

Daddy stares at it. He feels sick. He can't believe it. He stares at it some more. He feels sicker. He nudges it with his finger. The mouse turns a bit in the pale liquid. It is intact; its little legs and tail are all there. Its eyes are half closed, its teeth show slightly. Daddy thinks he might vomit. He takes the mouse over to the boiler, opens the furnace door, and throws it in. He returns to the churn, finishes emptying the buttermilk, caps the can, and wheels it into the cooler. He stands looking at the neat row of butter tubs. He says a single French word. "*Merde.*"

He returns to the churn, muttering "*Merde, merde, merde,*" moving like a zombie. He rinses the churn and scrubs it with a stiff bristled brush. He rinses it again, puts in hot water and a caustic solution, then starts the machinery and the sloshing churn rotates for the prescribed number of minutes. He rinses out the solution, refills the churn with clean water, adds the steam hose until the water is scalding, rotates the churn some more, then empties the rinse water. He turns the churn upside down to drain, cool, and dry.

He walks back into the cooler and looks at the butter tubs. He bites the skin on the side of his thumb. He finds himself counting the tubs over and over. His mind is numb.

He knows what he must do. He thinks of the cost of the cream, the price the butter will bring. He feels sick. He knows what he must do.

He knows what he must do, but he doesn't do it. He walks past the lilac bushes to the Little House, speaks words to Mother that he himself doesn't hear, reads a story in the *The Saturday Evening Post* whose words he doesn't see, and goes to bed. He has nightmares.

He wakes up with the rattle and bang of the milk trucks loading; he hears the murmur of the milkmen's voices. Beside him, Mother's breath is quiet and even.

His stomach is knotted. He knows what he should do. It is still not too late. He knows what his father would do.

He lies staring at the dark ceiling.

21 ⨯ GEORGE SCHREIBER

George Schreiber is a mild, soft-spoken, stocky man, a bachelor, whose face seems perpetually frozen into a pleasant look. He works in the milkhouse. He makes the cottage cheese; he makes the butter. He works at the dairy thirty years, and lives there even longer.

Before coming to the farm he takes the short course in dairying at the university. He answers a Dougan ad for a butter maker. Daddy is going up to Antigo to see about a bull and says he'll meet George in front of the post office. George is there; they talk, and Daddy hires him. He comes in October, 1936.

During most of his employment he lives at the Big House, but when the work there gets too much for Grama, and she and Grampa move to the edge of town, LaBerta Ullius is in charge. She's upset about George. He's messy. He sometimes pees in his bed and pulls the bedclothes up over the wet, trying to hide it. George is upset about LaBerta, too. He complains about the Big House radio being on all the time; it interferes with his sleep.

So George quits and goes to work as the only clerk in a little grocery store in Milwaukee. But he's not happy there. Within a year he asks to come back. He buys an old silver trailer and Daddy gives him a spot for it, beyond the Little House at the edge of the lawn, just beside the East Twenty. George lives in his trailer and goes back to work in the milkhouse. He eats Sunday dinners in town with a family he knows. He buys their little boy a bicycle so that Whitey can ride out to the dairy and drink chocolate milk and see George at work. When Whitey gets older, Daddy gives him a job on the place during the summers, and George watches over him like a nervous mother hen. (It's lucky for Lowrey Greenburg that George is busy at the milkhouse when Lowrey throws Whitey in the stock tank: Lowrey, Whitey, and the herdsman Harlan Whitmore are cleaning the cow yard with long poles and metal scrapers, and Lowrey has gotten fed up with Whitey's lip.)

All George's life he talks about retiring, what he is going to do in those golden days. Then he retires. He leaves his trailer under the trees and goes off to Milwaukee again, this time into partnership with a friend who runs a saloon. The friend gives him a room over the saloon. Everyone jokes, this is the place for George, for he has the reputation of being a tippler, even though nobody ever sees him drink more than a few shots of blackberry brandy at the Tiffany tavern.

He leaves Daddy a letter on his desk:

Dear Ron—

I wish to thank you for putting up with me these many years. It will be 25 years on October 26th when I first set foot on Dougan soil. Our employer-employee relationship has been most gratifying to me. I feel I was fortunate to find such wonderful people to become associated with, as your parents and you. I'm sure a lot of their graciousness, and yours, has rubbed off on me.

I do not look forward to a life of self indulgence and ease, however I feel I could not go on indefinitely on my job. I am very happy to leave everything in such conscientious and competent hands.

These few lines may not be as eloquent as General Washington's Farewell Address to his Troops or become a masterpiece of oratory as Lincoln's Gettysburg Address but they are just as sincere. Once more I Thank You.

George returns in a week. There is too much street noise, too much racket downstairs in the tavern. He goes back to work in the milkhouse. After a while he considers retiring again. This time he goes down to Mississippi where he has another friend. He stays three weeks. It's too warm; there's no ice and snow. He doesn't think he can stand warm weather all year round.

He comes back to the dairy. "Can't I just keep on living here?" he asks.

"Of course," says Daddy. He never charges George any rent.

George lives on quietly in his trailer. He works for a number of years, and after that visits the milkhouse frequently to inspect how things are going, see how the new man is doing on the bottler. He helps out in emergencies. He leaves little notes on Daddy's desk from time to time; one (that could apply to himself as well as the recipient) reads, "Men may come and men may go, but Ron goes on forever." Sometimes he walks unsteadily out to the mailbox and someone usually remarks, "George is at the bottle again." He takes on as his special job the care of the farm cats, to the extent that the men dub him, "Vice President in Charge of Cats." He treats them tenderly. Now instead of just hanging around the barn they divide their time between the barn and George's trailer steps.

Only once does anyone see George do anything out of character. It's the Fourth of July. A milkman is gassing up his truck at the farm gas pump. Across the yard he watches George pour out milk in a broad shallow pan. The cats gather round; there are almost a dozen ringing the dish and lapping.

George lights a small firecracker and drops it in the center of the dish. It

George Schreiber's cats.

explodes. Milk flies, cats fly in every direction. George chuckles and goes back to his trailer while the milkman overflows his tank in astonishment.

George dies on the place. They approach his trailer with apprehension. They don't find many bottles inside. It's dirty, but not the filthy hole of a chronic alcoholic. His autopsy reveals diabetes and a mass of other ailments, quite enough to make him weave out to the mailbox without the help of spirits. George probably drank much less than everyone thought he did.

In his will he leaves milkman and co-milkhouse worker Roscoe Ocker and his wife $500. He leaves similar sums to his Milwaukee friend, his Mississippi friend, and a few other friends. To Ron, "In appreciation for the kindnesses which Mr. R.A. Dougan has shown to me throughout the years, I give and bequeath the sum of $200, my automobile, my house trailer, and the refrigerator, chairs, tables, hot plate, bed, mattresses, stove, lamps, television set and antennae located in my house trailer." He also leaves Daddy the new suitcase he'd bought for his trip to Biloxi.

The remainder of his life savings, some $6,000, he leaves to Whitey.

22 ❧ PARADISE

J oan, Patsy, Jackie, and Craig know what Paradise is. They have dwelt there. It's the room over the milkhouse.

When the milkhouse was first built, that space was a bunkhouse for the hired men. After the Big House had its roof raised and dormitory rooms put in, the bunkhouse became an apartment for a succession of married couples. One of these was Lester and MooMoo Stam, who moved out in the middle of the night after MooMoo and Grama had a fight over nobody ever knew what. It has been empty now for quite some time.

There are really several rooms, each commanding a view over a portion of the farm, so that a trip through the apartment lets you see from on high everything that is going on. The floors are broad golden planks, and the walls and ceilings painted white. It's a fresh and sunny place, with built-in cabinets and large drawers forming one whole wall of the largest room. It is this room that turns into Paradise.

It happens this way. The rich relatives that live in Elgin have bought new furniture. They offer to sell Daddy and Mother their old furniture at a very low price. Old Bosworth furniture is much finer than anything Mother and Daddy now have. Besides, they will soon need more furniture, for they are buying a farm up the road, and plan to remodel the large farmhouse.

Mother and Daddy drive a truck down to Elgin to look over the discards and pick out what they want. They return with a bird's-eye maple bedroom suite, a dining room table and eight chairs, several marble-topped bedroom tables, an ornate four-sided pivoting bookcase, and other assorted pieces. Aside from trying out the spin on the bookcase, the four children are not particularly interested in the spoils.

But then Daddy says, "They threw in something for you. Go look in the room over the milkhouse."

The four mount the stairs and enter through the many-paned door. Side by side in the empty front room stand a bear and a barrel. The bear is dark

brown, its four legs on wheels, and is big enough to ride. They all make a dash but Craig gets there first and straddles it. He promptly discovers a metal ring in the middle of the bear's shoulders. He pulls it and the bear says, in a low weary voice, "Uuunh." Craig scoots the bear forward. It turns out that one of the wheels is only half a wheel; the bear lists to the side and clunks when it rolls. But that hardly matters. It is a wonderful bear! They take turns riding it and making it go "Uuuunh."

They then turn their attention to the barrel. It is larger than the chocolate powder barrel in the old schoolhouse, larger than the copper sulphate barrel. It's open at the top but covered with tucked-in newspapers. They peel back the papers and make their flabbergasting find. *The barrel is filled with toys!*

After a stunned moment they reach in and start grabbing them out, loudly laying claim, until Joan declares that everything in the barrel has to belong to all of them, just like the bear has to, unless there's something nobody else wants. Patsy, Jackie, and Craig can see the justice of this. They also agree when Joan suggests they remove things one at a time, and examine them together.

Where did all the toys come from? That's easy to figure out. The rich relatives have four daughters, long grown up. The Dougan kids have never known these second cousins, except that Joan once met the youngest, Betsy. Betsy was visiting at the farm and riding a horse, and she told Joan, who was trotting along behind her, breathless with admiration, to go away and quit bothering her—she was too little and might get hurt. Joan was outraged to be ordered off her own fields by a virtual stranger. Forever after, she has resented Betsy Bosworth.

But now, all is forgiven. Somebody put the Bosworth girls' outgrown toys in a barrel and sent the barrel up to the farm, along with the marble-top tables and bird's-eye maple.

The barrel is a cornucopia. Wonder after wonder pours from it. There is a rag doll as tall as Patsy, with a smiling face and yellow yarn braids and a real child's dress and pinafore. Elastic bands are sewed to the bottoms of her feet, so that you can put your feet through the straps and dance with her. There is a metal platter painted with houses and trees and streams and bridges and a train station. When you wind a key on the underside, a little train runs round and round a groove in the edge of the platter. Most of the other windup toys no longer work, but one that still does is an amazement: a little tin woman, with long tin skirts and her hair in a mob cap. She holds a tin carpet sweeper with bristles that really go around, and wound up she darts here and there erratically, pushing the sweeper stiffly before her. She has a no-nonsense expression. Her name is printed on her apron: Bizzy Lizzy.

There are alphabet blocks and anchor blocks. There are books, among them several fat volumes of *Chatterbox*, which turn out to be bound collections of old children's magazines with games and puzzles and continued mystery stories. These come from England, and Jackie immediately adores them. There are toys with missing parts, and parts with missing toys. There are games with no directions jostling for space with games complete in their boxes. There are three ornate cut-glass perfume bottles, elegantly stoppered, fit for a queen's dressing table. The bottles are empty but each retains a trace of faraway fragrance.

These, and some of the toys, come wrapped in funny papers. The four spread the papers out and see comics they recognize, but most are from before their time, such as Little Nemo and Krazy Kat.

When the call for noon dinner comes, they hurry back to the Little House, each carrying a choice item to show Mother and Daddy. Joan brings the beautiful perfume bottles, Patsy clasps Bizzy Lizzy, Jackie and Craig between them lug the bear.

Their parents are happy to share their delight. Mother makes one rule. The barrel toys are to be kept over the milkhouse, for the Little House is cluttered enough, and the long window seat is already crammed to the top with toys. That is all right with the four.

Though usually worn and sometimes broken, the new toys are special for several reasons. Fundamentally, they have appeared out of nowhere, totally unsolicited, imagined, longed for, or deserved. It is not Christmas or Easter or anyone's birthday. They are pure manna from heaven. Then, because the Bosworth cousins are so much older, their toys are not the familiar ones in the stores and advertisements. Where could anyone possibly go to buy a Bizzy

Lizzy? Her day has come and gone. Add to that the wealth of the Bosworths. The toys they purchased are expensive ones, from unusual catalogues or Chicago department stores like Marshall Field's. They sit on a higher shelf in the economic toyshop than most of the Dougan kids' toys, however plentiful.

All this is not enough to make the room over the milkhouse Paradise. There is a final factor. At the Little House, play goes on on the living room rug. Extensive villages outlined with blocks and peopled with small ceramic dolls and dogs, elaborate Tinkertoy or Lincoln Log extravaganzas, can last only an afternoon. Sometimes Mother is persuaded to let a particularly absorbing creation stay up till the following day. Then everybody has to be careful to step over it or around it, including the family pets, who are particularly obtuse about such matters.

Over the milkhouse, the spacious room is totally theirs. No grownup presence taints it. Week after week, the four can play on the sunny floor and never have to pick up anything. *No one ever, ever, ever says: "Time to put your things away."* When they return, everything is as they left it.

But earthly paradises do not last. Patsy arrives at the room one day to find it bare. She is stricken, and so are Joan and Jackie and Craig. They rush to find out what has happened. Their parents don't know. But the answer is soon forthcoming. Grama has decided they've played with the toys long enough. It's time for Trever's children to have a turn. After all, they are Bosworth cousins, too. So, like MooMoo in the night, the barrel has vanished. It has been loaded up and shipped to Jerry and Karla.

Daddy says it's also history repeating itself in another way; that his Grandmother Delcyetta swiped his toys when he didn't pick them up and hid them in her bottom drawer. They weren't found till she died.

It doesn't make them feel any better. "You at least got them *back*," Patsy wails. She never does get over losing Bizzy Lizzy.

But two things are saved from Armageddon. Jackie happens to have a volume of *Chatterbox* under her pillow at the Little House. And Craig has only recently dragged the bear that says "Uuunh" over to the playhouse, as a guest at a stuffed animal tea party.

23 ⋈ THE TWEEDLE BROTHERS

R on Dougan writes often to his father. In 1948 he describes the milk-house help:

> Lowrey and Brunke don't get on. Brunke antagonizes all he works with. Russel doesn't want him on the fields, Harlan doesn't want him in the barn. Harlan thinks he's getting ready to push Lowrey out of the nest. I suspect he's dishonest to boot. On the surface he's a fine likable fellow. (Like someone said about Governor Dewey—you have to know him awfully well to dislike him thoroughly.) The rest of the milkhouse gang are pretty lightweight. Sparky Adams is weak in body and mind, can't read or write. He can do very little except wash cans. On the bottle washer, he's unreliable. They broke it this morning while he was running it. I don't know what he jammed up.

Jackie is witness to a Sparky incident. The family, in their Sunday best, is running late for church. A last minute call from a customer sends Daddy swerving into the dairy and slamming on the brakes in front of the milkhouse. He leaps from the car. The milkhouse door flies open and Sparky bursts out. He just misses colliding with his boss, but the bucket of water flung after him catches Daddy full in the face. Sparky, aghast, babbles apologies. Lowrey Greenburg, in the recesses of the milkhouse, doesn't dare step forward.

"Sparky," says Daddy, pulling out his handkerchief and wiping the water from his eyes and ears, "and Lowrey too: please continue this battle. Go drown each other in the cow tank. The gunny sacks are in the barn. But first fetch me a pint of whipping cream."

"Oh, Ron," says Mother as Daddy drips back to the car. "How can you go to church all drenched like this? There's no time to change!"

"You all go on; I'll take a truck and deliver the cream," Daddy says. "With luck, the Tweedle brothers will have settled their quarrel before I get back."

Jackie laughs. Knowing Dum and Dee, she gets the joke.

24 ⚹ FLAVOR

No product, other than medicine—or probably alcohol—will sell that tastes bad. Daddy and Grampa take pride that their milk tastes good.

But sometimes milk doesn't taste good. Sometimes it just tastes different, and customers, who are used to a certain taste, notice it and complain, or question, or, at least, comment. A regular shift in taste is seasonal. When cows go from winter hay to fresh grass, the change of diet is reflected in their milk. Grace Croneis, the wife of Beloit College's President Carey Croneis in the early fifties, is heard to remark, "Well, I can tell the Dougan cows are enjoying spring pasture!"

A really discerning tongue, like Daddy's, can tell when the cows have changed from one pasture to another. And even non-discerning tongues can recognize when the cows have relished a patch of wild garlic. "It's like mothers nursing their babies," Daddy says. "Some babies spit out the nipple when their mothers have eaten something they don't like. I pity any little Italian baby who doesn't like garlic. Or a Russian baby with an aversion to cabbage!"

A producer's milk, in the fall of 1943, starts coming up consistently bitter. Everyone can taste it. Howard Baldwin, whose cows are producing the bitter milk, insists he has done nothing different. Daddy visits the farm and looks over all the milking equipment, the stalls, the barns, and can spot no problem. He is mystified. He doesn't want to lose the Baldwin business, nor does Howard Baldwin want this to happen, but the milk continues bitter. Daddy tells Howard there has to be some reason. He comes back to investigate again. Finally, wandering over the farmer's fields, he discovers the truth. The cows have found a gap in a fence that separates their pasture from an oak grove and have wandered in among the trees. Daddy finds them munching acorns from a bountiful fall harvest. This is what is making the milk bitter. He tells Howard to repair the fence, and brings home a handful of the offending nuts. He passes them around at the dinner table. Everyone samples, and makes faces.

"Pigs like 'em, but I've not known cows to," Daddy says, "though cows will generally eat anything. Binder twine, you name it." He nibbles his acorn. "During famine times, you know, people ate these. There were recipe books that told how to fix grass, and bark, things like that. Acorn stew. You have to boil them and pour the water off, and then boil them up again, and again, and again, to get rid of the bitterness. You can even dry them, once they're sweet, and grind them into flour. Shall we try sweetening some?"

Daddy gets no takers, even when he mentions that the Indians knew all about acorns before the Europeans, but flavor gets him going. He tells how the farm milked by hand till he was seventeen or eighteen. At milking time everyone quit whatever else they were doing to help milk. "There were five or six of us, and forty cows. We all had Gurler pails, they had lids over two thirds of the top, and gauze over the last third, to catch any impurities. But then the great day came when we got our first milking machines—two Empires! They sat on the walkway behind the cows."

But shortly thereafter, the milk developed an unpleasant taste. "We had a bad flavor to the milk and we checked everything under the sun," Daddy says. "The university people came down. Finally they attributed it to the milking machines. They were made of German silver."

"What's wrong with German silver?" asks Craig. "What *is* German silver?"

Daddy ponders, but Mother knows. "It's a mixture of metals," she says. "I think a lot of copper. Some nickel. Maybe zinc. An alloy. Grampa told me about it."

"Anyway," Daddy goes on, "the action of the acid in milk with the German silver gave the milk a metallic taste. Gramp replaced the Empires with Surge milking machines, and everything was hunky-dory."

"Except for the Empire people," is Craig's comment. "Somebody should have told them."

"But now we have this problem with homogenization," Daddy says.

Jackie knows what that's about. Homogenized milk has recently been introduced, and there is sometimes an odd taste to the milk. Not bitter, not sour, not sweet—she describes it as "cardboardy." The problem has been traced to sunshine—the broken-down fat globules which are the product of homogenization present, collectively, a far greater surface area for the sun to strike, as it shines through glass bottles exposed on doorsteps. The taste of the milk is altered. Other dairies are converting to cardboard cartons which shield the milk from the sun, but cartons impart a cardboardy taste themselves. Daddy, who can't afford the changeover to paper, meets this problem by providing metal milkboxes for customers, but it isn't totally solved until he changes to amber bottles. The handsome colored glass effectively screens out the sunlight.

Taste is always a concern. But what Jackie and Craig enjoy most is when Daddy shows up at Chez Nous with a case of various Dougan milks, lines up a row of glasses on the kitchen counter, letters them from A to G on a paper beside each, fills each with a different grade of milk, and has the family taste — not to find off-flavor, but to see if they can identify each grade by the amount of butterfat, from the richest Guernsey through the various degrees of blend, to the pallid skim milk for the cats and pigs and people with special diets. They all score very well on these tests, to Daddy's satisfaction. They can also line up the creams, from whipping through coffee cream to half-and-half, recommended for cereal.

There is one final taste to milk, and this is Craig and Jackie's absolute favorite, and the favorite of every kid from town: the farm's chocolate milk. The dark unsweetened chocolate powder is kept in a barrel in the milkhouse, the sugar in another barrel, and George Schreiber or some milkhouse worker measures out the proper proportions into a large pasteurizing vat of milk where the slow paddles mix everything thoroughly. Then the chocolate milk is run in a pipe from the vat up to the ceiling over the bottler and courses down the cooling grid, into the tub above the bottle carousal, and the half pints are filled and capped with white caps with brown printing. Jackie often drinks several bottles of chocolate milk a day.

A school visitor enjoying the flavor of chocolate milk.

She knows there is only one thing more delicious. It's a well-known secret with everyone on the farm. That is to take a bottle of chocolate milk, half full, and sneak it under a spigot of the cream separator when that machine is whirling, so that the rest of the bottle is filled with cream.

"Trev and I did it ourselves," Daddy says, when she admits this to him when she's grown. "And of course Gramp knew right along — he even wrote a warning memo—but he never did anything to stop the practice."

Two flavored milks bomb. There is a period in the forties when the farm offers its customers half pints of strawberry milk and root beer milk. They are both on the market a few months, but never catch on. They are no competition for, nor addition to, the overwhelmingly popular chocolate milk. When they're discontinued, it's hardly noticed.

One flavored milk should have caught on, the kind Daddy drinks every morning for breakfast, and Mother, too, once powdered coffee is a product on the market. Daddy now stirs a heaping spoonful of instant into a cup of hot milk, adds sugar plentifully, and stirs. He sees this as a tremendous marketing opportunity and writes letters to dairy organizations. He demonstrates his drink in his kitchen or office, and all visitors, from cow testers to university professors, praise his milk-coffee. Many, including his grown children, begin drinking their coffee this way at home. They all like the flavor. But no organization will promote the idea.

Daddy shakes his head, especially in his later years, when *cafe au lait* becomes a household word. "They missed their opportunity," he says. "And ours. We farmers and producers could have had the jump on the market, and the credit. The profit. But nobody listened to me. *C'est la vie!*"

25 ❧ COCKROACHES

Daddy constantly battles cockroaches in the milkhouse. He often wins skirmishes, but never the war. Dairy plants are roach hotels—moist and warm, with places to hide, usually a bite to eat. When Daddy comes in at night and turns on a light, there's sometimes a flash of movement on floors, walls, ceilings as cockroaches scuttle for cover. He grabs the spray, but knows it won't penetrate the cracks where the eggs are, or kill the eggs if it does. He returns to the Little House swearing in French.

Even as stronger and more effective insecticides are developed, they can be used only sparingly and some not at all, for the milkhouse is producing a food product. But everything is washed daily, some things twice, many with steam. Everything that can be sterilized is sterilized. No cockroaches get in the clean bottles and milk cans, the bottling equipment, the pasteurizing vats, the separator, the pipes. No customers ever report cockroaches in their milk. An exterminator comes monthly and makes the roaches retreat for a bit. But soon they rally and retake the territory they've lost.

"They're survivors," says Daddy. "After all, they were here before Adam, and they'll be here after Armageddon."

They migrate in on the milk cases, traveling steerage in the cracks between the wooden slats. The cases have been sitting in a cafeteria, or a small cafe, or a corner grocery, or a factory. The cockroaches hitch a ride from town on a milk truck, look around the milkhouse, and know this for the Promised Land. They come from many colonies and social strata. There are, says Daddy, German roaches, Irish roaches, southern roaches, peg-leg roaches, cross eyed roaches. There are large varieties and small varieties, brown ones, black ones, and some with spots on their tra-la-la-la-loos.

Daddy is an advocate of crossbreeding. He uses cockroaches as an example. "Look at the hybrid vigor of our roaches," he says with glum pride. "The milkhouse is a melting pot. Give me your cold, your poor, your huddled masses."

When Daddy switches to all metal, wire-frame milk cases, the problem diminishes. These have no nooks for passengers, and are also lighter to handle and easier to keep clean. But the word is out on Dougan's Dairy. The immigration waves manage to continue.

In later years there's a drastic solution to vermin of any sort in one part of the milkhouse. The walk-in cooler, with its heavy insulated doors, is completely enclosed. The cold cannot get out. One would think cockroaches would find this clime inhospitable, but they adapt to all ecological niches. So periodically hydrogen cyanide is released inside the room, after the afternoon's milk is bottled, and left there till midnight or so. When this is done, both inside and outside doors are sealed, and warning signs of "POISON — KEEP OUT" are posted.

Lewis Dalvit has been married to Pat Dougan for several years. They've built a house on the edge of the dairy. They buy their dairy products from Daddy, at a family discount. Lewie comes in late one afternoon, on his way home from teaching wind instruments at Milton College, and stops for milk at the loading dock. He pulls on the handle of the cooler's massive outside door. The door doesn't budge. The heavy door always takes a bit of muscle, so he now applies more force and wrenches it open. He sees a slight mist. He instinctively knows something is different, something perhaps ominous. He takes a deep breath of outside air, goes in and grabs his milk. Then he comes out and slams the door.

He's just stowing the bottles in his car when Daddy, Miss Glenn, Helen Tapp, and a routeman come rushing down from the office upstairs, all of them gibbering with fright. They heard the door slam and know what that means. Their relief is vast when they see Lewie upright and breathing.

Daddy tells him it's a miracle he's alive. Why in God's name did he go in? Why didn't he obey the sign?

"What sign?" his son-in-law says. "But I did think something seemed a little funny, so I held my breath. I can hold it a long time, all wind instrument players can."

"You can be grateful your folks didn't start you on accordion!" Daddy says.

The exterminators, it turns out, had neglected to put a warning on the outside door, or else (as they insisted) someone had removed it, or it had blown away. As for the sealing, well, it hadn't been done quite as firmly as it ought to have been. From now on, the heaviest precautions will be taken. There must be no more unwitting openings.

Daddy says, "We tried to exterminate you, Lewie. But I guess we're stuck with you. You'll still be here in a million years!"

26 ⚔ BUTTER AND CHEESE

Daddy is familiar with making butter. Many are the tedious hours he spends as a boy, in the farm's kitchen, churning butter in the upright cylindrical wooden churn. His arms grow tired, pulling up, pushing down, pulling up, pushing down the wooden plunger.

There's a sound to it, a rhythmical slosh, which begins to change as the butter starts to come. Ronald screeches, "It's coming!" Then his mother hurries over, pulls out the plunger, examines it. If there are beads of butter on it, Ronald sighs, for he must churn a little longer. The butter needs to come out in one big chunk. When that time arrives, he willingly gives up the churn. Grama removes the chunk and puts it in saucer-pans she has ready on the kitchen table. She also has round wooden paddles, about grapefruit size, and with these she slaps the butter around till all the brine and buttermilk work out. Then she divides the butter into portions, and puts these, well covered, in the ice box. She pours the buttermilk from the churn into large pitchers, for pancakes, biscuits, and drinking. In the early years of the dairy, butter and buttermilk are only for home consumption.

In the mid-twenties, when Daddy has joined the business, there is sometimes the problem of surplus milk and cream. He encourages his father to add butter to the dairy's offerings. They buy a second-hand churn, positions it in the milkhouse, and produce a batch of sweet-cream butter. Everybody on the place pronounces it delicious. It goes out on the route, in handsome stoneware two-pound jars, as gifts to all the best customers.

The response is overwhelming. Compliments and orders pour in, for about three days. Then the tone of the calls changes. There is something wrong with the butter. Daddy tastes it; it's rancid. He hastens up to the university to see what he's doing wrong.

"Well, did you pasteurize the cream before churning?" asks the Dairy Sciences professor. "No? Well, try that."

From then on, the butter is excellent, and a best seller. The Dougan kids, growing up, embarrass Mother and Daddy, eating out with friends, by having a little bread with their butter.

The dairy also goes into the making of cottage cheese. A large vat in the milkhouse is filled with warm milk. A special culture is added, which clobbers the milk. When, after the proscribed time, it's all set, like junket, the farm's official cheesemaker, George Schreiber, who learned the technique at the university's Short Course, carefully lowers a close-fitting metal grill through the quivering mass. Each square of the grill is not as big as a square inch. The grill breaks the mass into curds and whey. The curds are lightly salted, and go into cottage cheese containers. The whey is drawn off and fed to the pigs.

Jackie loves to watch George make the cottage cheese. It gives meaning to Little Miss Muffett, though she's personally glad to let the pigs have the whey rather than drinking it herself.

Sometimes, in the spring, a special is advertised: chive cottage cheese. Then the office girl, Ruby Horn, goes out with scissors and cuts wild chives that grow here and there around the place. The long stems are further cut into little pieces and then added to the cheese, giving it a mild oniony taste and a handsome look. It is popular. Often the chive cottage cheese is packaged in thin pale yellow glasses, which much later become valuable as "Depression glass."

One spring, when Jackie is in third grade, there's a problem with the chive cottage cheese. Rather, the problem is with the chives. When Ruby goes with her scissors, searching for the tufts of wild chives, she can't find any. She looks and looks, for there were plenty of chives recently, and finally identifies places where the chives have been. They are nibbled right down to the ground. There can be only one culprit, Jackie's goat. Butter roams free in spite of efforts to pen her, and is always getting into trouble.

Jackie protests. "Butter can't like chives! They're onions!"

"Smell her breath," Ruby commands. "Your goat likes everything!"

Jackie straddles her struggling pet and manages to get a whiff. The breath is distinctly oniony.

The chive cottage cheese has already been announced--yesterday Craig and Jackie each earned a dime by standing beside the capper in the milkhouse and dropping a paper advertising cuff over the neck of each quart bottle of milk. So chives must be found. Ruby is up to the challenge. She walks down Colley Road to Marstons, and manages on their lawn, here and there, to find enough wild chives to go into the cottage cheese.

Not as often, Daddy has a special on pineapple cottage cheese--cans of chopped pineapple are added to the curds. Then Jackie and Craig each earn another dime, but the pineapple special is not as popular.

Cottage cheese lasts the life of the dairy, but not so butter. World War II comes, and with it rationing and price fixing. Rationed butter's price is so low that Daddy and Grampa lose on every pound. Before the mid-forties the churn is removed from the milkhouse so that the space can be used for something else. It's a sad day for everyone when the best butter ever is no longer to be had, and the Dougan family, along with the rest of the local populace, must use their ration stamps to buy butter from Wright & Wagner. They are a big enough dairy to swallow the price differential and keep on selling butter to the Beloit market.

Daddy and Homer Wright joke about it at the monthly Dinner Club both Wrights and Dougan's belong to.

"Here I am, adding to your deficit," Daddy says, slathering butter on his roll.

"Don't forget I bought the cream from you," says Homer, following suit, but with a large baked potato.

27 ⚔ ORLAND POTTS

O rland Potts works formally on the Dougan farm only a few years. He comes down from Soldiers Grove in the summer of 1941, at the urging of his first cousin Rodney Jennings—Daddy says half of Soldiers Grove young men worked on the farm at one time or another, the other half wished they did—and Orland stayed with Rodney's family. Daddy gets him a draft deferment, one of Daddy's feverish activities during the War, keeping enough men on the place to run it—and Grampa puts Orland to work in the milkhouse, washing bottles.

His first task every morning, though, is to pack up milking utensils and go up to Ron's place, where a dozen or so milking cows are in the barn, and milk them. They are an overflow from the round barn. When it gets to be winter, he grows to hate this job and to dislike cows. "That barn was frigid!" he says. "And the milking machine we kept there was balky in cold weather and had to be warmed up. Yep, that's what started my dislike of cows!" "What!" replies Daddy. "Even after you got milking and had your head against a warm belly?" "Nope," says Orland, "I never liked cows, even when I got farming for myself and had to have 'em, that was where the money was." Once, the snow is so deep that he can't get through with the truck. Grampa comes and fetches him, helps him harness the bobsled, and goes with him over the fields to do the milking. He has to do that chore by bobsled for several days.

Meanwhile, Orland has returned to Soldiers Grove, married Ruth, and come back to live in the apartment over the office in the Little House. It had been converted after Ron's family moved up the road to Chez Nous. He continues washing bottles, using the huge bottle washer that pulls in six at a time, and after a trip through its caustic guts, turns out six clean ones. "I reached in once," Orland says, "and cut my hand on a bottle that'd broke; I didn't go for stitches, though, just bound it up and went on."

"When I was a kid," says Daddy, "we had two tanks in the milkhouse, one hot and soapy for washing, one hot for rinsing. We'd dump a couple dozen bottles in the first tank, then put them on the swirling brushes two by two, and then into the clean water. A slow job, and a sweaty one in the summer. Now it's the big bottler, and it's always breaking down."

"Harley Bailey was working on the place," Orland says, "and he and Jim Gander were supposed to take a load of something up to the Hill Farm, in one of those huge lumbering flatbeds with the heavy tires we used during the war, and they didn't feel like doing it, so they set a nail so that a tire went flat and Pfaff and Lyle Bacon, the mechanics, spent half the morning pulling that big old tire off and fixing it, while Harley and Jim sat in the shade. I was there and saw it all; I got in on the blame."

"I was the one doing the blaming!" says Daddy. "I had to blame somebody, why not you? But I had my tongue in cheek about you."

"Harland Dull came from Soldiers Grove about the time I did, only worked three days. I was still staying with Jenningses at the Hill Farm—he got a bad throat, it swelled all up, strep, maybe, and Rodney's wife put hot compresses on it, and then thinking he needed more heat she fed him chili and put in darn near the whole box of chili powder. At that his throat got flaming so bad he could hardly breathe so we had to have the doctor out, he said cold compresses, we kept them on all night. Then he went to the hospital. That next day Harland's girl Charlene, or maybe she was his wife, came down from Soldiers Grove and drove him back again, and that's the last we ever seen of him."

Besides the milkhouse, Orland does general farm work. "We were filling silo up to Ron's place," he says, "and it was green hay silage, they did that for a while, and the hay would come up that old tall hay loader and down onto the flatbed, and we were loading, it was thick like rope, you couldn't hardly pull it apart. Daddy Dougan was driving the horses, and when we couldn't handle it fast enough to arrange it right, we'd yell 'whoa,' and the horses would start to stop, but Daddy couldn't hear and he'd slap and giddyap them, and they'd start up again, and we'd yell 'whoa' again, and the poor confused things would start to stop—it's a wonder we ever got that silo filled!

"I was there when the silo in the middle of the round barn split, all that wet silage, the silo was three fourths full and the juice oozing out into the gutters, the cows getting drunk, and then all those metal bands saved it. It could have burst at any time."

"We were all risking our lives, being in there," says Daddy.

Orland lives on the place about two years and then returns to Soldiers Grove, first to work his wife's folks' farm, then to work sixty acres of his own.

But he tires of farming—"I didn't like horses, either!"—gets a job at the Beloit Corp, then at the Chevy plant in Janesville, and stays on at Chevy till he retires. He and Ruth have a house in Shopiere that faces the park where the dam is, and Orland keeps busy with a huge garden, and with making charming airplanes from Budweiser cans, and low padded stools, green or brown, shaped like turtles.

He never returns to the farm to a salaried, everyday job, but Daddy is always saying, "I'll see if I can get Potts to do that," or, "I better call Potts, see whether he's free to help," so over the years he is a familiar figure to everyone.

"And I've always managed to find the time," says Orland.

Daddy says, "I imagine you know the running of this place as well as any of us!"

Jackie and her little daughters know Orland well. They usually pause there when they go to swim at the dam, along with stopping to coax a few words out of Howard Milner's talking crow nearby. Then when the Twin Cities—the villages of Shopiere and Tiffany—have their Fourth of July parade, with the Turtle Fife and Drum Corps marching, and Howard on a flatbed with a piano, pounding out patriotic songs, they have ringside seats on Ruth and Orland's front lawn. From a clothesline strung above them are a dozen bright Budweiser planes for sale, and they are seated on the padded turtles, also in a row for display. Ruth tells them about a huge snapping turtle that came up out of the crick, tore up a prize flower bed, and laid forty eggs in the pit she dug.

And on one of these visits Orland tells about when he was on the farm, and honey was running through the ceiling of the Big House, with bees so thick that everybody was getting stung. "Ed Pfaff tore nearly the whole front off that house, getting rid of those bees," he says, "and he pulled out a whole horse trough of honey."

"That much? Really?" marvels one of the daughters.

"Yep," says Orland. "The Big House had enough flapjack honey to last till the Second Coming!"

28 ⨯ THE BACTERIOLOGIST

It's 1942. Howard Greene of Brookhill Farm in Genesee Depot is a distinguished dairy farmer in southern Wisconsin, who sells his milk to the Chicago market. He's a good friend of Daddy's; they are the two farmers on the four-man board of the Wisconsin Scientific Breeders Institute. At a meeting, Daddy mentions to Howard that he needs a bacteriologist.

"I have one I can spare, if you want him," Howard says. "Arnold Akins."

Daddy rips at his hair. "I'm up at three every day running a milk route, and then putting in a full day at the office—with all the forms the government makes us fill out that's another job in itself, and then the Army keeps grabbing my help. Of course I want him!"

"He's accident prone," Howard warns. "You'll need to keep an eye on him."

Daddy hesitates, then says, "I'll take my chances. We're getting milk now from a dozen producers. I can't keep up with checking their bacterial counts, and as you know, in this business of ours, that's essential. I just lost a man in the milkhouse, too—so he can help there. Send him over, if he's a mind to."

Howard Greene's bacteriologist leaves Genesee Depot and settles in at the Dougan Farm. He lives at the Big House. He's a likable young man, and well educated, with a B.S. in Biology and an M.A. in Bacteriology from the University of Wisconsin. In the back room of the milkhouse he prepares the milk samples and reads the bacterial counts with an easy skill, but he does turn out to be accident prone. He has a succession of minor mishaps, all of which could have been avoided—injuries, broken equipment, neglect in ordering supplies. Then he has a biggish one, where he cuts his hand badly on a broken bottle. It requires stitches. It's the first time Daddy has had to secure benefits from Employment Compensation, which he has through Aetna for his employees.

After six months, though, Arnold decides to enter the military. He enlists in the Army Air Force. During training, the plane he is in crashes, and both he and his instructor are killed.

The young man is the son of a prominent Wisconsin family. At his funeral,

Howard Greene and Ron Dougan at a happier event.

Army airplanes fly over the memorial procession, and a number of high rank-ing military are in the cortege. There is a large gathering after the service. Daddy goes, and spots Howard Greene among the crowds of mourners. They retire to a corner and stand in silence a bit.

"He was a nice fellow," Daddy finally says.

Howard nods agreement. "Was he accident prone for you?"

"Yes," says Daddy. "In spite of needing him, I wasn't sorry to see him go. He was bright, but careless."

"The worst he did for us was the hundred petri dishes," says Howard. "All that expense of collecting the samples, and infusing them onto the agar, and incubating them, and they came out beautifully — but he'd mixed them up, so they were worthless. You couldn't tell whose was whose. All that necessary information down the drain." The two men stand silent again.

Daddy clears his throat. "I can't help wondering — well, maybe — maybe if up in that plane he was the one at the controls, and he messed up. And the instructor didn't have time to, well, do whatever had to be done in a hurry."

Howard nods. "That's crossed my mind, too."

"It's a terrible thing to consider," Daddy goes on, "but I can't help thinking it, what if once he got over to Europe, he might have caused more harm to our own side than he ever would have to the Germans."

Howard nods again. "No way we'll ever know," he says.

29 ⊰ CAFÉ AU LAIT

Ever since instant coffee has been available, Ron Dougan has switched from brewed coffee to adding instant to a cup of hot milk. Vera is a convert; this is the way they drank coffee in France, in their courting year back in the twenties—heavy on milk, and she loved it then. Others are often converts, too. The only drawback is that there are no more big tins of Hills Brothers coffee, with the sardine-can-type key that winds up the metal strip, allowing the lid to be opened and release that fragrance of fresh-ground coffee, the fragrance that makes one swoon. There's no more rich smell of brewing coffee penetrating the whole house.

However, it has long seemed to Ron that milk-coffee is a way to market milk. In 1957 he takes action. He writes his friend Lyman McKee of Madison, who is the Wisconsin president of the American Dairy Association, and also grows Dougan Hybrid Seed Corn. He explains how he makes *café au lait*, and its potential, especially with the surplus milk the dairy industry often has. He says he demonstrates his drink when anyone comes to his office, and most visitors praise his milk-coffee—enough for the ADA to give it serious consideration.

He suggests a tie-in with the coffee people on a Wisconsin "*Café au Lait*" campaign. The state ADA, for instance, would purchase milk from local Beloit dairies, and the Beloit Commercial Club would give away *café au lait* in their office to transients stopping for information. There could be road signs at the edge of this stateline town, boosting Wisconsin milk and urging tourists to stop at the Commercial Club for information and a drink of milk. The reason a particular dairy should not sponsor it is because it's almost institutional advertising, and of no direct benefit to the individual dairy, "as these folks are birds of passage."

Ron knows there is advertising money; he and his dairy's producers all make monthly contributions to the ADA for its national advertising efforts. Why not divert the local monies to this project? It would hardly make a dent in ADA's total budget. "Also, it might give local farmers a close tie-in to ADA activities which they don't get, I'm afraid, on the huge national promotions."

McKee passes Ron's idea on to the Chicago office.

Ron writes McKee, later in the month, "I don't blame Mr. Wilcox for giving me a rather polite brush off, as I can see how confusing and frustrating it must be to treat every crackpot idea that comes along so as to give the donor of the idea the sense that he has discovered something tremendous, as he usually thinks he has. However, he didn't answer my question as to the Chamber of Commerce arrangement—or he didn't understand what I was trying to get at."

There is sporadic communication back and forth with McKee, partly on hybrid corn orders, partly on the stalled *café au lait* proposal. Six months later, Ron sends McKee an exasperated letter. "After my total rebuff by ADA I have just simmered along." He repeats that he serves coffee milk to those who visit his office and they like it. He says a local hotel has offered to serve a cup with a new product, "Expresso," he thinks the name is, to every morning customer for a month or so, Expresso to furnish the coffee and he the milk.

"This is still in the maybe stage—personally, I think it would be better to make the coffee with one of the instant brands since if it takes hold, anybody in the country can make up the stuff as long as they have some instant coffee, a sauce pan, and a quart of milk. I must say that in my own office where everyone has a choice of milk coffee or water coffee, I haven't scored the 100% victory for the former. Still, if we could change the coffee drinking habits of a small percent of Americans, we would have no surplus problem."

He gives his opinion of professional advertisers. "They are a conservative lot—they don't fire easily. It is too easy to go along with the accepted way of doing things. If your folks, for instance, weren't inclined to be pretty smug about how well they were doing, somebody would have come down here into the woods to see what sort of screwball idea this farmer was kicking around."

Next Ron tries a grassroot approach; he goes to the local paper to try to stir up interest. He's rejected there, too, and writes McKee again.

> I talked to my own copy man on the *Daily News*—Yeah, it was a good idea. "Well, will you push it on a national level?" Well, I will talk to the national advertising man about it. Then I caught the advertising manager. Yes, Stockwell had talked about it, but he just wondered? I said, get the right man out to see me—how apathetic can you be? So out came their national man. In

spite of the fact that I thought I had explained everything very clearly to the others and they told him about it, he had no idea how the stuff was made up and why it is such a natural for the advertisers, the farmers, the coffee people and believe it or not, the restaurant equipment people. If this coffee is to be made up with a coffee extract like Expresso, it will mean all new coffee making equipment.

Think of the amount of advertising dairymen, large and small, would do if the coffee people helped defray the space, and think how happy the coffee people would be to get in on local advertising rates instead of being held up by National rates! And still ADA's policy is to avoid tie-ins of this sort—I think that is what their letter to me said.

I had no intention of getting off on this hobby horse—forgive me. But I've reached a point of tension where I just must stop and have my cup of ???? It needs a catchy natural name. I'll be back in a minute or two.... And now, about your corn order....

On April 11, A.C. Erickson, merchandising director of the Chicago office of ADA sends Ron a letter no doubt spurred by McKee. "Frankly I am not as fully apprised of exactly what you should do as I should be, but I intend to find out right now the complete story of your *café au lait* promotion." He then describes Ronald's process: "As I understand it you merchandise a coffee which consists of half coffee and half milk." Ron writes an emphatic "NO" in the margin. The rest of the letter is patronizing and condescending, telling of a television homemaker-type clip in which they have incorporated the *café au lait* idea. He's sure Ronald Dougan will be delighted, and wants to come to Beloit and show it to him: "Would you have access to equipment for running a television film?" Ron's dubious marginal comment is, "Maybe in Rockford."

Erickson's next paragraph says, "In addition we are going to take a closer look at other editorial approaches, publicity approaches, to this *café au lait*. If our publicity approaches play back to us in such a manner as to show sharp consumer acceptance nationally of such an idea, then it is a possibility that we might incorporate it into our advertising and merchandising plans. This is not a promise but a statement of fact as concerns consumer interest in basic food serving ideas. If they are there, it is incumbent on us to capitalize on them." Ron underlines these two sentences.

Erickson warms to his close by promising to look into national newspaper ads, even ones that "dairies could pick up to capitalize on this idea so well thought of by us." He finishes with an almost-apology for ADA's neglect of

Ronald's idea, and that he should rest assured of their continued interest in the dairy industry generally and Dougan Farms in particular.

But it isn't long after this that Lyman McKee confides to Ron, in a corn letter, that he's sorry the ADA hasn't been able to activate the *café au lait* deal into a real promotion, but "while in our Chicago office on another matter, Mr. Al Erickson told me that he had the Home Service Dept. prepare some for a mixed group of people who were in the office. The results, based on their tastes, were not good. As a result he was in a quandary as to his next move in your direction."

Ron is disgusted. Erickson must have made the drink by his own misunderstanding of the simple recipe, and of course it would not be as good. And how accurate is such a small, and no doubt biased, sampling? He gives up the idea of going through the dairy association, and in August writes the state ADA office that he's withdrawing his percentage of the advertising assessment, though not his producers', saying, "I am segregating these monies for special dairy promotion rather than our own brand promotion. If I find I have no flair for industrial promotion, I'll come back into the fold."

McKee's distressed response comes as soon as he returns from vacation and finds the carbon "regarding your position on the set-aside from your own farm."

> Although I presume your monthly investment was a fair amount, its real loss to the program is in prestige wherein one of the real gainers of the program, a producer-distributor, fails to participate. In 1958 we have already over 40 new plants who have joined the program, and as of this date there are practically no plants in the state not participating who have any volume. Our efforts to date are with the many small cheese factories. Some 126 plants in Wisconsin closed last year and we find that by and large many are non-member plants. This of course has no connection with their closing but it is interesting to note that the plants with the more dismal outlook and reluctance to build sales are the first ones to fall by the wayside. I realize that we were unable to activate your *café-au-lait* deal into a real promotion. I've asked our area representative, Dwain Dickenson, to call on you, Ron. Hoping that this finds you well, and I know, busy.

Ron gives up on the ADA, but he still has faith in his idea. He offers it to the area producers' cooperative, the Pure Milk Association, of which the farm is a member. He again arranges with the Hilton Hotel to furnish coffee to their guests, and he will donate the milk. The PMA doesn't warm to the idea. They too try it on a few office workers, who are not enthusiastic. The officers tell Ron that they don't want to advertise coffee along with milk. He retorts that if they can get one out of ten folks to become fond of it, there would be all those people drinking a pint a day who wouldn't ordinarily drink any milk at all. He reminds them of peaches and cream, and other combinations. But the PMA doesn't give it the go ahead.

As with the ADA, Ron decides he can spend his dues, some $70 a month, more effectively at home. The *Daily News* wins an award for the series of ads they do for him on Dougan babies. He takes pride that the ads he writes are much better than the ads being written by the PMA.

He finally gives up on pushing the idea. He lives almost forty more years, thirty of these retired from the milk business, long enough to witness Starbucks, local coffee cafes, every variety of latte and cappuccino. *Café au lait* is familiar to everyone, which it wasn't when he was advocating it to the big milk associations. His was an idea before its time.

30 ❧ TANKS

There is a concrete cowtank in the middle of the paved barnyard west of the round barn so large that a couple dozen cows can drink from it at once. It's a rectangle twenty-two feet long and twelve feet wide; the concrete ledge over which the cows stretch their necks is seven inches broad. The water, two feet deep, is constantly replenished from a low standpipe on the bottom of the tank. The overflow makes a streamlet that runs over the lip of the end closest the barn; the shallow depression provided for this outlet looks like a thumb scrape in the concrete, an afterthought. The streamlet spills down the side of the tank and runs along a somewhat broader depression to the main drainage gutter of the gently sloping concrete barnyard. There it joins any seepage from the manure pile, and the periodic river made by the water used to flush the gutters inside the round barn. All the drainage runs off into an underground catch-basin at the foot of the barnyard, and thence into the lower pasture where it evaporates. Any excess flows into the creek.

Joan, Patsy, Jackie, and Craig often go into the barnyard when the cows are absent. They float curled elm leaves on the surface of the tank, or wood-chips found beside the chopping block alongside the woodpile. These they rig out with lilac-leaf sails and blow them from shore to shore, if regular wind doesn't suffice. They make great tidal waves which founder their vessels and splash over the rim, sweeping the fleets to destruction, with perhaps one lucky survivor navigating the rough trip to the main drainage channel. Sometimes they bring their bathtub paddle wheelers, propelled by wound-up rubber bands, and let these see what it's like to leave their inland pond and embark on an ocean voyage.

The tank's broad lip is smooth, and a light gray stone color. The four dip their fingers in the water and draw pictures on this surface; water turns the concrete almost black. They watch as the sun shrivels the pictures away until nothing is left. Cowtank art requires speed: on a hot day the start of a picture can vanish before the end is drawn. Yet if they draw too quickly, darting their hands back and forth, their fingers drip and the picture is spoiled.

There are three episodes connected with the cowtank in Jackie's memory. In the first, she and her sisters are swimming in the tank, but Jackie can't yet swim. There is surely an adult supervising, though she doesn't remember one. She's pressing a foot on top of the stand pipe, enjoying the relentless force of the incoming water. She slips, and slides quietly under the surface. She remembers the slow slide that transports her into a still green world, and she remembers the feeling that accompanies it, a feeling which seems odd to her in later years. For she experiences no panic, only a kind of peaceful resignation. All is over. She knows without thinking that nothing she can do will save herself; she doesn't struggle or try to swim. And then the straps of her bathing suit are seized, she's hauled to the surface and set on her feet, and Joan goes on about her play while Jackie stands blinking in the sun. She realizes she's been rescued, and that to her sister the act has been purely routine. She is probably three.

The next isn't a true memory, though it's been told her so many times that it could be. Algae grow in the tank, feeding off the rich slobber from the cows' mouths. If the algae is let go, the sides and bottom of the tank become thick and slippery with green, and the water murky. It's not nice for swimming. Daddy buys a barrel of copper sulphate, which he keeps in the old schoolhouse. A little added to the water kills the algae. It also turns the water a brilliant blue. He and Mother move the slide from the backyard of the Little House and place it so that it straddles one side of the tank. The farm now boasts a pool as fancy as any in town.

One day Mother—who must be that supervising adult—observes her daughters playing around the slide with more than usual ceremony. Joan is standing in the sky blue water at its foot. Jackie climbs the steps and Patsy, at the top, receives her and sends her down the incline. Joan catches her, Patsy slides to join them, and the three take hands and do a splashy circle dance, accompanied by glad cries.

Mother watches this ritual twice and then asks, "Whatever are you girls doing?"

"Oh, I'm God," Joan explains, "and Patsy is Jesus, and Jackie is the good woman coming to heaven."

The third is a valid memory. All four have been playing at the tank edge. The cows come up from the pasture and stand at a short distance, looking and jostling, pushed from behind by more cows in the lane. They all want a drink before milking. The four know that in their own domain cows come before

A Holstein drinks from the cowtank in the barnyard of the round barn.

children, and so they turn and start picking their way among the dried cow-pies toward the gate. Suddenly a cow breaks from the ranks and charges them.

"M-12! M-12!" they all shriek, for they well know this aggressive cow and have been wary of her. Heedless now of dung they pelt for safety. Jackie feels terror, not for herself for she's almost to the edge of the barnyard, but for Craig, who had to reel in his sailboat and is still near the middle. Her memory shows figures scrambling over and through the gate's boards, herself skinning under the bottom one, and then whirling to watch Craig, pale and desperate of face, legs churning, with the great cow after him. It's in slow motion. All around her are screams; arms reach through the boards. Then Craig dives for the gate, he's dragged under, and M-12 skids to a stop, swinging her lowered head and snorting through wide wet nostrils. Even though the four are safe, they run crying to the Little House, with Craig still clutching his boat.

The horse trough has no stories connected with it, only pleasurable pictures. It's small, made of galvanized metal, and fastened to the north side of the round barn. It's fed by a pipe with a faucet, and the horses drink there when they leave and return to the horse yard. Jackie likes to watch them drink, sucking with their lips extended, chuffing with their nostrils, and finishing with a silver sheen of wet on their velvet muzzles. She leads her own horse there and lets him drink, when she's been out riding.

The tank at Chez Nous serves any stock kept there. It's freestanding, an old pasteurizing vat of stainless steel, and one eighth the size of the dairy's concrete tank, though deeper. It's fed automatically from the Chez Nous water system, with a float and valve as in a toilet tank.

There's a mystery associated with this tank. It receives only an occasional deep cleaning, every few years. When Jackie is in her midteens the tank is drained and a sunfish is found in it. No one will claim responsibility for putting it there. Everyone accuses Craig, but he denies it. And Jackie has several nightmares about that fish. She sees it circling year after year in its prison, none other of its kind to keep it company, eking out a marginal existence from algae and the bits dropped from the mouths of cattle.

On the Hill Farm, the third of the Dougan farms, there must be some sort of tank. Jackie has never noticed it. But there is one more tank to be described, one not for stock but for milk cans.

This tank is sunk in the milkhouse floor, around the corner from the main door. In its icy waters it will cool four large milk cans submerged up to their necks, or perhaps more than four, since the end of the pool can't be seen. It extends under the floor, under the machinery alongside it. More cans could possibly be shoved beneath that overhang.

And while there's no real mystery about this small tank, to Jackie it is always mysterious. For it's set apart from the hustle and bustle of the milkhouse. While milk cans are clanking, milk bottles chattering, the bottler spinning and circling and stamping, the bottlewasher spraying and groaning, the milkhouse workers calling back and forth, this little pool in its corner sits serene and still, its waters black and inscrutable, like a pool in a forest grotto whose bottom is lined with dark leaves. And even if milk cans are submerged in the pool they too are serene and still, their lids silver lily pads lying above the calm surface.

The best time to visit this pool is early evening, after the milkhouse has been put to bed. Sunset is slanting though the milkhouse windows, making rosy the white walls, the bottler's silver tank and grid, the silver pipes that crisscross overhead. At this time all the milkhouse is as still as the shadowed pool. And Jackie likes to sit on the concrete ledge, dipping a finger into the opaque waters. She imagines that the pool goes on and on, extending from that hidden, unknown side, until it merges with all the other still pools in the still evening forests; she imagines it is the Well at the World's End.

BOOK THREE
MILK
ROUTES

The Dougan Guernsey Farm delivery staff and one of the early trucks.

1 ✷ THE FIRST MILK ROUTE

It's May 1907, and Ronald's fifth birthday. He wakes before dawn. He looks out his window and sees a lantern bobbing toward the barn. His father is going down to milk Daisy and Bess and the eight new Guernsey cows that were shipped in from Fort Atkinson only last week. Ronald pulls on his clothes and follows. It's just starting to get light. It's fresh and clear outside; the air is balmy. A light breeze makes the windmill's wooden vanes whirr and rattle.

In the barn the cows are licking up their grain and munching hay. Grampa is sudsing Daisy's udder with a sponge. He sees Ronald enter the lantern light. "Happy birthday, cubby," he calls cheerfully.

Ronald watches while his father rinses the udder. He runs the sponge gently all over the four quarters and in the little upside-down pocket-cup the four tits surround, and then between and down the tits. Daisy's udder, Ronald has noticed before, is peppered with freckles. Bess's is creamy and unmarked. The udders on the new cows vary. All the time his father washes the cows he talks to them. "Coo, boss, coo, coo," he says soothingly. "Good bossy. Good cow. Let down your milk. Coo."

Then Grampa takes the milking pail. He lays a circle of gauze over its rim and fits a domed lid over the gauze. The lid has an opening in it, about a third of the surface. He puts the pail under Bess's udder and sets the little three-legged stool beside her. He sits on the stool and presses his head against the cow's side. Grasping the two tits farthest from him, one in each hand, he pulls down first one and then the other, in rhythm. The milk spurts into the opening of the sanitary bucket lid. Even through the gauze, Grampa makes the milk spurt with such force that it smacks into the pail and the metal sings. In a moment, as the bottom is covered, the song changes to a quieter one, milk splashing into milk. A little foam forms on the gauze around where the milk goes through. Grampa milks so well that the flow never pauses. While one tit is filling up, the other is shooting milk through the gauze.

Ronald squats on his haunches and waits. In just a moment now his father will say, "Open your mouth."

"Open your mouth," says his father.

Ronald opens his mouth as wide as he can and shuts his eyes, just in case. But Grampa doesn't miss — the stream of warm milk hits the back of his throat. Ronald chokes and swallows, and opens his eyes, laughing. Grampa laughs, too. Blackie the cat appears out of nowhere and opens her mouth. Grampa aims a tit at her, and even though her mouth is much smaller than Ronald's, he hits the center of the pink gap. She sits down suddenly, licking her chops.

Ronald with a cat, Trever with a rabbit. They are probably seven and five.

When the bucket is full Grampa empties it into a milk can. He finishes with Bess and then moves over to Daisy. Daisy keeps looking over her shoulder at Ronald.

"Come along," says his father. "She knows it's your birthday and says you're big enough to milk her now. Wash your hands."

Ronald washes first in the soapy bucket, then the rinse bucket. He dries with the clean towel on the hook on the wall. He sits down carefully on the milking stool. Daisy looms above. When he leans his head against her side, his hair butts against the lower curve of her firm belly. He can see every freckle on her udder.

"Some farmers milk wet and some milk dry," his father says. "That means some think a wet tit helps their grip. Some grip better with dry hands. In other barns, you'll see farmers spit on their hands in order to milk wet. But never, never will you see that happen *here!*" Grampa shakes his head and Ronald, pressed against Daisy, shakes his head too, but carefully. A cow's side is a strange, springy place to lean.

"Now hold the tits," Grampa instructs.

Ronald takes the two back ones. They feel firm and a little spongy, like a warm carrot with give. He squeezes. Nothing happens.

"You're squeezing the end so the milk can't get out," his father says. He holds a hand close to demonstrate. "You squeeze your fingers in order, starting with the top one, and at the same time you pull down. That moves the milk down and out the end. Then you let up, relax your grip, and the tit fills with milk for the next squeeze. And while you've eased up on that tit, you're pulling down the other. No, it isn't easy till you get onto it."

Ronald tries and tries. It's hard to squeeze his fingers in order. He feels very awkward. His father shows him again. At last Ronald produces a spurt from each tit, and then again. They miss the open part of the bucket lid, but Ronald feels victorious. So does Grampa. "You'll make a milker in no time, laddie!" he says. He sits down, finishes milking Daisy, then moves on to the new cows.

It's full daylight when they finish. Grampa looses the cows from their stanchions and turns them into the barnyard. They amble toward the pasture. Ronald carries the empty wash buckets and the empty milk pail up to the house. His father carries the heavy milk can.

In the back room, the milk room, there is new equipment. The milk cooler is a shiny metal grille that looks rather like a large scrub board but with the tub balanced on top. The coils of the grille are hollow and open above a tank at the bottom. His father starts cold well water running through the coils. When the water starts to spill out into the tank, he climbs a broad stepstool and pours the milk into the reservoir on top. The reservoir has holes all along its bottom length. The milk drains out in a row of small streams above the top coil and ripples down the cold grille. Ronald watches till the first of the milk reaches the tray at the bottom and is funneled off into a can. Then he goes to the kitchen. A kettle of hot water is steaming on the stove. A frying pan of bacon is sizzling.

"Happy birthday, Ronald," says his mother. "You're up early. Trever's still abed."

Grampa comes in. Together he and Ronald eat eggs and bacon and flapjacks. His father tells how Ronald has marked the day by milking his first cow, and Grama clucks with praise.

After breakfast, Ronald follows his father back to the milk room. Now Grampa washes up the pails and milk cans and scalds everything. He turns the pails and cans upside-down on a rack. He takes six of the new glass bottles and sets them on the enamel-top table. He takes the can of cold milk and pours some into a pitcher. He then carefully fills each bottle.

Now comes what Ronald has been waiting for. Since the bottles arrived, his father has filled a few of them daily, pressing on the caps with his thumb. "For practice," he has said, twinkling, about the whole unnecessary process, for after the family has admired the new gleaming capped bottles, they uncap

Delivering milk in Beloit. Ronald, the smaller of the two boys, is about eleven.

them and drink the milk. But now Grampa takes another piece of equipment, delivered just yesterday. It's a heavy metal hand-capper. It's already filled with cardboard disks from a long cardboard tube off the shelf. He positions the base of the capper over the rim of a bottle and presses down with the handle grip. With a ca-chunk, the bottle is capped. Ronald knows what the cap says, in deep golden yellow on white: "W.J. Dougan, The Babies' Milkman."

"There," says Grampa. "One day soon we'll have a bottler, too." He sets the bottles into a shallow tub of cold water.

Ronald trots behind his father out to the horse barn. Grampa harnesses Molly to the buggy. He leads her to the hitching post by the back door of the house. He goes inside, and when he returns he's taken off his overalls and is wearing town clothes. His ear trumpet hangs around his neck. He's carrying the milk bottles in a wooden case covered with a wet flour sack. "That will keep them cool," he explains to Ronald as he sets the case on the buggy floor. "Do you want to come? Hop up, then."

Ronald hops up and sits with his feet resting on the edge of the case. Grampa hops up, too, says, "Gee up, Molly," and the horse starts out the drive. Looking back, Ronald glimpses his little brother's face in the window.

Grampa turns west on Colley Road. Molly is full of energy; she trots briskly. Ronald looks at the plowed fields. He looks up and down the railroad tracks where they cross the road. He listens to his father sing at the top of his voice:

Rock of ages, cleft for me,
Let me hi-i-ide myself in thee!

Ronald can't see how you can hide yourself in a rock.

They cross the tall red iron bridge over Spring Brook, and Ronald looks at the little stream; they cross the low black bridge over Turtle Creek and Ronald looks at the larger stream. A hill marks the end of the Turtle Creek valley. They go up it and are in town. Grampa drives to a house on the west side. He takes two quarts of milk, goes to the door, and knocks. Ronald stays close beside him.

"This is Doctor Thayer's. Look there in the shed. Do you see that round platform? He drives his new automobile onto that platform, and then he turns it so that the automobile is facing out again, ready to go when a patient calls."

The dais is empty. Ronald wishes that Dr. Thayer would drive up, both so that he might see an automobile and witness the magical performance.

Mrs. Thayer answers the door. "This is a red-letter day!" she exclaims, and smiles at Ronald. Ronald agrees.

His father gives the milk to Mrs. Thayer. She gives him two nickels. Grampa writes something in a book. He and Mrs. Thayer chat, Grampa holding his ear trumpet while she shouts into it. Then she gives Ronald a cookie.

Grampa drives Molly back to the east side and stops before another house. "This is where Harry Adams lives," he tells his son. Ronald looks at the shed to see if it, too, has a rotating platform, but it doesn't.

Mrs. Adams comes to the door. "Here is a day to celebrate!" she shouts into Grampa's ear trumpet. Again Ronald agrees. Grampa gives two quarts to Mrs. Adams, and she gives Grampa a dime. He writes in his book. Mrs. Adams gives Ronald a cookie, too.

They drive a few more blocks, and Ronald doesn't need to be told whose house this is. It's Aunt Ida Croft's, across from Strong School. They've brought Aunt Ida milk before, when they've come for Sunday dinner, carrying it in a covered pitcher or two Mason jars, but never in a milk bottle with a "W.J. Dougan, the Babies' Milkman" cap. He jumps from the buggy and carefully carries one of the two remaining bottles to the door. His father carries the other.

"Happy birthday, Ronald!" says Aunt Ida. She takes the bottles and puts them in the icebox. She and Grampa talk a bit. Ronald stands on a chair and looks into the beady black eye of the yellow canary. The canary teeters on a little perch in its cage and looks right back at Ronald.

"Here's a present for a big boy," says Aunt Ida. She's holding two packages, one large and flat, one small and square. To Ronald, it looks like two presents. He climbs off the chair and undoes the tissue paper. The large package is a checkerboard, the smaller one the box of checkers to go with it. She also gives Ronald a cookie.

Then Ronald and Grampa climb in the buggy and drive back through the streets to Colley Road. When they get to the edge of town Ronald sits between his father's knees and holds the reins. He feels important. He's old enough to milk Daisy; he's old enough to take milk to town; he's old enough to drive Molly.

"Ronald," says his father as they are crossing Turtle Creek, "do you know that this is a very special day?"

Ronald nods vigorously. It certainly is! And Mrs. Thayer and Mrs. Adams and Aunt Ida have all known it, too. He indicates his box of checkers on the buggy seat.

"Yes," says Grampa, "it's your birthday and you're growing sturdy in body and spirit. That's quite enough to make this a special day. But we've also just gone on our first milk route, and delivered our own product to our first three customers. From this day on we're not only farmers, we're businessmen. You are riding with 'W.J. Dougan, the Babies' Milkman'!"

Grampa laughs till his eyes disappear.

Ronald laughs and laughs, too.

2 ⋇ WHIPPING CREAM

It's Thanksgiving dinner. The family is all there. Grampa has said the blessing. Daddy is carving the turkey. Everyone is waiting with watering mouths when the phone rings. It's an irate customer. Daddy slings on his coat.

"Where are you going, Ron?" Mother asks.

"Mr. Dowd says his cream won't whip," says Daddy. "The old curmudgeon."

Mother sighs. Everybody sighs. Customers call on Christmas and New Years and Sundays and late at night and early in the morning. Last month, the family remembers, Daddy drove ten miles at almost midnight to deliver a pint of milk to a young mother with a squalling baby. She'd forgotten to order enough milk to make up the formula for the night.

Daddy takes a big bowl and fills it with ice cubes. He takes the egg beater and buries the end in the ice cubes. He leaves the house. Jackie grabs her coat and follows. She's interested in seeing an old curmudgeon.

She holds the bowl of ice cubes between her knees in the car. Daddy picks up two half pints of whipping cream from the dairy cooler. They drive very fast down Colley Road to town.

Daddy explains that Mr. Dowd is a widower and has prepared Thanksgiving dinner for his children and grandchildren. He takes great pride in his cooking. They pull up at Mr. Dowd's house. Jackie follows Daddy in the front door, past all the guests seated at the table in the dining room, and into the kitchen. Mr. Dowd is waiting for them.

"L-l-look!" he says, thrusting the bowl at Daddy. Mr. Dowd has a speech impediment when he's upset. There's a little mound of butter floating in his bowl, caused by trying to whip the cream with a warm bowl and beater. It hasn't whipped, it's turned to butter and buttermilk.

Daddy goes right to work. He dumps the ice cubes in the sink and dries the bowl. He pours a half pint of whipping cream into it. He takes the cold egg beater from Jackie and beats briskly. Mr. Dowd stands and watches, scowling. The egg beater whirs. It takes only a few moments for the cream to whip. In a flourish of triumph, Daddy gives the cream a vigorous whirl, so vigorous that the bowl spins off the counter and turns upside down on the floor.

Jackie gasps. Mr. Dowd makes a gargling sound and turns red. He can only stutter, "D—d—d—d—"

Daddy picks up the bowl, steps over the mess, and empties the second bottle of whipping cream into the bowl. While he's whipping again, the dog comes into the kitchen and is pleasantly surprised by the cream on the floor. He licks it all up so there isn't a smidgen left. Jackie takes a dishrag and wipes over the spot anyway, for good measure.

In a few moments Daddy has another mound of perfect whipped cream. This time he omits the final flourish. He takes a spatula and transfers the whipped cream to one of Mr. Dowd's bowls.

Mr. Dowd sputters something that might be "thank you" and disappears with the bowl into the dining room. Jackie and Daddy leave through the kitchen door. Jackie licks the bowl and the beater all the way home.

They come in. They've been gone a little over half an hour; Thanksgiving dinner is well begun.

"Did the cream whip?" Mother asks.

"Of course," says Daddy, serving up Jackie's plate. "Our cream always whips."

3 ⊀ THE ONE-ARMED MILKMAN

I t's a sunny morning in late spring. Jackie and Craig are playing Find-the-Milkman. It's a game they've played all their lives. It goes like this: A milkman is out on his route and Daddy has to get ahold of him for some reason, such as to give him additional milk for a customer or to tell him there's one he's missed. Daddy drives to the area where the milkman is delivering. Any children in the car take opposite windows. "Keep your eyes peeled," says Daddy, and he cruises the streets, going slowly through the intersections while everybody peers up and down, looking for the familiar cream-colored vehicle. Finally someone spots it, yells out, and the game is over. Sometimes the game takes quite a while, for a truck has so many streets it can be on, and houses it can dodge behind, that it can stay hidden for a surprising stretch. And all this without the milkman doing it deliberately—he doesn't realize that he's the object of hide-and-seek. He reacts as though Daddy's running into him on his rounds is a pleasant coincidence.

Today, however, Daddy is perplexed. "Vanished!" he keeps saying. "He's evaporated off the face of the earth!"

"He" is Charlie Heisz, the one-armed milkman. Around eight o'clock calls began coming in from customers on his route that the milkman had missed them. After four or five such calls Daddy'd slung a case of milk in the trunk, taken Craig and Jackie, and headed for town to play Find-the-Milkman.

Following last month's route book, Daddy traces Charlie's route. Charlie, he finds, has delivered the start of it. Then, at a corner, and between one page and the next of the route book, he's disappeared. Everyone before has had milk, those after are the ones telephoning.

Daddy is more and more mystified. At first he'd figured Charlie's truck had broken down, but why then hadn't he called for Erv or Ed, the farm mechanics, to come fix it? And more to the point, where is the broken-down truck? It should be on this very corner.

Daddy goes into a customer's house and calls the police. He returns to the car shaking his head. There have been no accident reports involving a milk truck, but they'll alert all their patrolmen to be on the lookout for a one-armed milkman. The hospital, too, says they haven't recently admitted anyone with only one arm but will call the farm if they do. "Keep your eyes peeled," Daddy repeats to Craig and Jackie, and they all go back to playing Find-the-Milkman around the blocks of Charlie's route.

After ten more minutes Daddy gives up. He speeds back to the dairy, collars Roscoe Ocker, the relief driver who's working in the milkhouse today, and together they load up the farm truck with milk for Charlie's customers. Craig and Jackie perch on the loading platform and drink chocolate milk.

"You kids might as well stay home this time," says Daddy, but the two have no intention of abandoning the search now. They're eager to return to the scene. They climb into the back of the truck with the milk, and bounce and rattle to town.

At the disappearance corner everyone becomes a team. Roscoe drives and calls out orders from the route book. Up behind, Daddy loads carriers and hands them down to Jackie or Craig, who lug the milk and cream up to people's doors as hastily as the weight of the load will permit. Daddy laughs and says, "Never has a route been delivered so fast!" At every corner Jackie still peels her eyes for Charlie's missing truck.

For forty-five minutes they deliver. Then Roscoe rounds another corner, and they are radiator-to-radiator with a Dougan milk truck. The one-armed milkman is just returning to it, his wire carrier swinging jauntily from his single hand.

"Charlie!" shouts Daddy with relief and exasperation.

"Oh, hello," says Charlie, as if he hasn't been the concern of customers, management, police, and hospitals for the past several hours and as if meeting Daddy and Roscoe, Jackie and Craig running his route is an ordinary occurrence.

"What ever happened to you? Where've you been? We've searched everywhere!" Daddy expostulates. "Your customers have been calling since eight o'clock!"

Charlie looks surprised. He sets down his carrier, scratches his chin, gazes at the sky. Then he grins sheepishly. "Well, today, part way along, I suddenly realized how bored I was, delivering my route the same old way every day. So I just drove to the last house and started going backward. That's all."

Daddy shakes his head wearily. "*Mon Dieu*," he exclaims. "Tell *me* the next time you get bored, and I'll give you variety!"

But Jackie understands perfectly how Charlie feels. So does Craig.

"Just think," he says as they ride among the milk cases out Colley Road, with Charlie following them in his truck. "Just think how he saved you and me from a boring morning, too."

"And not just us," Jackie replies, considering how very many people were spared a boring morning by their one-armed milkman.

The milkhouse where the drivers loaded up, at about the time Charlie Heisz went missing.

4 ⨯ HOWARD MILNER

S ome of the milkmen, Jackie observes, go their appointed rounds year after year with no untoward events occurring. Others attract adventure as cats to a cream pan. The dairy's cream pan is Howard Milner. Daddy supposes that this is only partly due to the location of his route.

"Even the most placid of our men have had at least one adventure," he says. "Take Lester Stam. Stam is talking yet about that Sunday morning down on Athletic Avenue, along around two o' clock, when he came back and found an old woman had climbed right into his truck, singing, and drunker than a cow in an apple orchard—she turned out to be a customer, so he delivered her with her milk. But Howard! Howard has an adventure a week. It's got to be something about him."

Jackie agrees. When she was in Todd School she always liked it when Howard was the one to pick them up in his truck at noon, to take them the mile out to the farm for dinner. He often lets one of them sit in his lap and manage the steering wheel, and he tells such good milk route stories! They are always interesting, and always suited for young ears, such as the one about the old Greek woman living on a pension, who had run up a big bill, and when Howard told her he was worried about it, she said to him, "I already do plenty worryin'—no need for you to worry, too!" And she likes him to repeat the story about Mr. Durst, a wealthy man who owns Durst Manufacturing in the nearby village of Shopiere, and who used to drive around in a Stanley Steamer, and is a big game hunter. "He's got a gigantic room with all his stuffed trophies hanging in it," Howard tells them. "A lion's head, a rhinoceros, elephant, zebra, and every North American horned or antlered critter you can imagine. Well, I took a small grey mouse and carefully stuffed it, and mounted it on a square of polished wood, and presented it to this rich guy—we're friends, my little farm in Shopiere is just down the road from him. He's got it displayed now, 2½ inches high, on a special stand, surrounded by his other trophies!" They have a small thrill of horror when he tells them how he wired up a milk truck, but that Grampa climbed in first and got the hot seat intended — as a joke — for Roscoe. "I don't think he guessed it was done on purpose," says Howard, "and if he did, he didn't know who."

Their favorite story of all is about Howard's talking crow, which they often visit in Shopiere to hear it whinny like a horse, while they wrinkle their noses at the road kill Howard throws in the bottom of its big cage. Somehow it got loose one night. "I thought I'd lost him for good, it was pitch dark out," Howard says, "and I walked along the edge of the cornfield, calling to him, not feeling any hope, when out in the field I heard, 'Hello, Howard!' So I walked down a corn row, and found him, and put him back in his cage."

Howard's bawdier stories they sometimes hear later, from Daddy at the supper table. An early one is how Howard saved everybody's job. "I was working in the milkhouse, about spring of '35, and somebody — we never

Howard Milner by his truck.

knew who but we had our suspicions — had written some dirty words on the inside of the door of the toilet in the boiler room. When Grampa discovered it, he said to us, 'You're all fired! You may go. I don't want you anymore!' I got down on my knees, I begged him to change his mind. Then I planed the door, and painted it. Nobody ever tried that again!"

And there's the time, for instance, about three in the morning, that Howard is tippytoeing down the long ramshackle corridors of the Edgewater Flats, one dim light bulb burning at the far end of the hall, when he's tackled from behind. His bottles fly every which way as his assailant bellows, "I gotcha now! I'll teach you to sneak around seeing my wife!"

"I'm just the milkman!" squeaks Howard.

"Oh," says the angry husband, rolling off him. "Well, you're not the guy I'm laying for," and he helps him put his bottles back in the carrier.

Another early morning in another apartment building the door is flung open as Howard sets down the bottles, and an inebriated man cries, "Come on in! Come on in! Have a drink!"

"No, no," says Howard. "I don't drink."

"Come on in anyway! I'll show you my wife's Christmas present!" And the man grabs him by the arm and drags him into a lighted bedroom. A woman is lying asleep. The man throws back the covers and exposes her there, clad in a flowered robe. "See?" he says. "A silk housecoat! And look—it's got one of them brand new fasteners—a zipper! Watch! It zips!" He seizes the tab and rips open the length of the housecoat. The woman's eyes fly open, she lets out a screech, and Howard flees.

He has another housecoat story too, the one about the bride from Georgia. She told him to collect on Saturdays. The first Saturday is a gusty day. He knocks and knocks and knocks. Finally the young woman comes to the door, holding her housecoat closed with one hand. She opens the screen to pay him, the gale catches the screen, she grabs for it, and the housecoat flies apart, its sides flapping. She has nothing on underneath. Howard stands there turning red, but the young wife is equal to the event. She grins broadly as she gathers her housecoat back around her. "Well, Ah guess you done seen all there is to see—there ain't no more!" Howard collects his money and goes on his way.

Daddy also relates Howard's policeman stories, for Howard moonlights as a South Beloit policeman. He carries his service revolver on the milk route. This is okay with the Beloit police, as long as he also wears his badge. It would not be all right with Grampa, if Grampa knew. Daddy doesn't feel too comfortable about it himself, but he doesn't try to stop him. A few of Howard's customers, mostly the South Beloit ones, know about his double job.

Sometimes the jobs overlap. One early morning he's driving his milk truck past Hobbs's tavern just as there's a terrible brawl raging in front of it. There are shouts and oaths and screams. Bodies are flying every which way. Howard stops his truck and leaps into the fray. Mr. Hobbs sticks his head out from the tavern and spots him. "Quick, quick, Milner, in here!" he hollers. "Come in here where the fight is!"

And then there's the time Howard nearly gets killed. He hears a shot, and a woman, barefoot in the rain, runs right in front of his headlights. A man with a gun is a second behind her. Howard jumps from his milk truck, he and the man grapple, Howard feels the gun in his guts and hears the click, but the gun has shot its last shell. Howard overpowers the man and gets the gun from him as the woman comes back. "He'll be all right! He'll be all right!" she cries. Howard can't arrest him without a warrant, but he gets the man's name and takes his gun to the police station. He warns the chief to keep on eye on him.

And it's one Hallowe'en, or rather, early in the morning of the next day, when four or five big teenagers, dressed as pirates and skeletons, come up to his truck. "Trick or treat!" they threaten.

Howard says, "I can't give you any milk."

"We don't want milk, we want money!" the biggest says, and draws a knife. Howard draws his revolver.

"Man, he'll kill us!" yells one of the others, and they all vanish into the dark.

It's Howard who sees someone hunkered down in the bushes beside Colley Road. It's dark. No car or bicycle is nearby. Howard thinks this is suspicious, and stops. He calls to the man and there is no answer. He steps out, revolver in hand, and challenges the man to speak, but there is still no answer. He makes a show of aiming the revolver, and threatens to shoot. At this the man starts babbling. He's really still a boy, a freshman at Beloit College, and his fraternity hazers have dumped him in the country with orders not to speak for twenty-four hours. They've also taken his trousers and undershorts. Howard gives him a lift to the safety of the Beloit police station.

He himself spends some time in that police station, behind bars. He's delivering milk to Mrs. Herman, who lives in the Kemp Apartments on Highland. To get to her door he has to follow a sidewalk between waist-high hedges. It is just getting light. There's a body behind one of the hedges, a young woman murdered. He doesn't notice her. But when the body is found a short while later, someone recalls noticing him and his truck. A squad car intercepts him on his route, the police issue a warrant, and put him in jail. He calls Ron, who, along with the South Beloit police chief, spends the better part of the morning getting him sprung. He then resumes his delivering where he left off, and some people are irritated at getting their milk so late. The murderer is never found.

Howard's eyesight is better when it comes to flying saucers. He's seen them on two separate occasions. One time he comes on a saucer hovering over a tractor that's been night-plowing. The farmer, having abandoned his job, is crouched under the tractor. Howard runs across the field; the soft glow from the saucer and glare of the tractor's headlights make it bright. He ducks under the tractor with the farmer. He pulls his service revolver and aims it upward but the farmer clutches his arm and gurgles, "Don't shoot! Don't shoot!" Howard re-holsters his weapon. It's probably wise not to fire at aliens whose technology is obviously superior to our own. He waits with the farmer till the saucer darts suddenly away, and then helps the quaking man back to his house.

"Did you report it, Howard?" Daddy asks. "Or the little green men on the road, that other time? Isn't it your duty as a policeman?"

Howard grins his easy smile. "Why should I report something nobody'd believe?"

To the family Daddy says, "We lost a lot of excitement when we quit delivering so early in the morning, but trust Howard to turn it up at any time of day. Do you suppose there's another pistol-packin' milkman in Rock County?"

"I sometimes wonder if milk is all he drinks," Mother says.

5 ⚭ GRAMPA'S COURTSHIP

It is 1938. Jackie is ten. She and Patsy and Craig are in the living room at Grama and Grampa's. Patsy says, "Grama, how did you meet Grampa?"

Grama tells them. Grampa can't hear, but he knows what story is being told, by the looks and the laughs and the huge enjoyment of everybody. He enjoys it hugely, himself.

Grampa's courtship is like this. He's at the University of Wisconsin. He's intent on his studies; he's late in becoming a student, so he must apply himself seriously. He must also earn money. He supply preaches at a little church in McFarland, near Madison. He works one summer on the shores of Lake Geneva, a place called College Camp, where people come to live in the tents and cabins, eat in the large wooden dining hall, and, under a gigantic tent, listen to lectures and concerts. It's called College Camp because it gives people education and culture while they enjoy the cool water and lake breezes. It's a little Chautauqua. College students wait on the tables and do all the work around the camp.

Another college student working there is Grama. Her name is Eunice Trever; she goes to Lawrence College in Appleton, her home town, where she lives near her brother, the Reverend George Trever. She and Grampa wait on tables together. Grama likes the serious young divinity student.

One night after dinner, Grampa is picking a plate up off the table to put on the large tray of dishes he's balancing in the other hand. A pat of butter on the edge of the plate spills off onto the wooden floor. Grampa looks down at the butter pat, then looks around. He sees no one but Grama watching him. He gives her the merriest, most mischievous look she's ever seen; his eyes fairly disappear. With his toe he nudges the pat over and into a knothole in the floor. It vanishes.

At that instant Eunice's heart is won. She's in love, definitely, deeply, desperately. She knows that Wesson Joseph Dougan is the only one for her.

Grampa finds Grama attractive. But another young woman working at the camp has also recognized what a prize Grampa is, and she's set her cap for him.

"What does 'set her cap' mean?" asks Craig.

"Oh, the foolish thing!" Grama exclaims. "It means she did everything she could to make Wess notice her; she just made a fool of herself, she was so determined to get him!"

The unhappy situation is Grampa likes that other one, too. When he's with Eunice, she's in heaven; but when he pays attention to that other one, she suffers the pains of Hades.

The end of summer comes. Grampa is serious about his studies; he doesn't want his work complicated by the two young women he's become fond of. He can't make up his mind between them. He's not yet ready to make up his mind. Summer is summer, but winter is a different matter. "Don't mail me any letters," he tells Eunice. He says the same thing to her rival. He needs time. He returns to the university, Grama returns to Lawrence, and that other one returns to wherever she's going to school.

By Thanksgiving, Grama can stand it no longer. She writes Grampa a love letter. She pours out her heart to him. She doesn't mail it but sends it hand delivered by a mutual acquaintance from the summer who is traveling down to Madison.

When Wesson gets that letter, he's undone. The scales are tipped; he can

Wesson Joseph Dougan at the time of his marriage.

Eunice Medley Trever, at her graduation from Lawrence College.

resist no longer. He writes back to Grama and suggests they exchange pictures. He signs the letter "Love and kisses." He hopes she can soon make a visit to Madison. Grama does, and they become engaged.

Jackie, Patsy, and Craig clap and cheer. Patsy goes and sits on the arm of Grampa's chair and kisses him on the top of his head where his hair is thin and then makes a Kewpie-doll curl out of the thin hair. Craig and Jackie scrunch on the rug over to him and each hug a leg. They want to show him how glad they are that he picked Grama and not that other one. Patsy spells on her hand, M-A-I-L A L-E-T-T-E-R, and they all laugh at Grama's cleverness. Grampa's eyes disappear.

Grama gets a little white book out of the bookcase. It's called *Our Wedding*. She turns the pages and reads out loud to them from the faded ink. She shows them the first page:

She shows them the newspaper clipping:

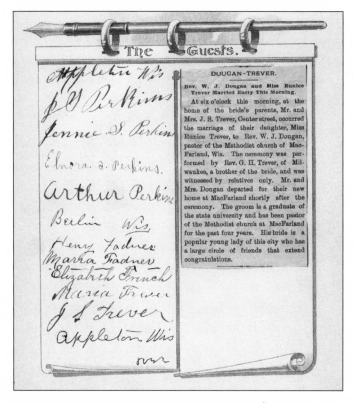

"Six o'clock in the morning!" cries Patsy in disbelief.

"The train left at seven," says Grama. She reads from the book her own account, on the page marked "The Guests."

> We had very few guests at our wedding. We were married at six in the morning by my minister brother George. We had a wedding breakfast, then took the seven o'clock train for McFarland. Mr. Dougan could not leave his flock for more than a day, even for his wedding. We spent some time in Madison buying some things, and arrived at McFarland at four o'clock in the afternoon. When the train stopped, it seemed like all the children of the village were at the train. Their mothers were in a nearby blacksmith shop peeking out to see the new bride after having the little parsonage well equipped with good things to eat and a table loaded with goodies, besides a fire in the wood stove with a teakettle of boiling water singing away a welcome. Since that day the guests have been coming.

On a different page, called "The Wedding Journey," Grama repeats herself: "We went right to our charge. Mr. Dougan was a very conscientious minister. We could not take time for a journey just then. We went right to McFarland where he was a student at the university, and a minister at McFarland."

There the account ends. "I was too busy to fill in the rest of the wedding book," Grama says. "And the journey didn't matter. Daddy and I have had a long, lovely journey through the years." She tells them about life as a minister's wife, how little they had to live on. She tells them about the two hundred and fifty dollars pay a year and the time a delegation of ladies of the church came to her and asked her about a Christmas present for Grampa.

"We are thinking of a nice buffalo robe, for his sleigh," they say. "It would keep him so warm when he has to drive all around the countryside, making pastoral calls. Do you think he'd like one? Do you think it would be a suitable gift?"

Grama assures them that he would, that it would.

"Do you suppose it will be all right if we take it out of his salary?" ask the ladies.

Jackie, Patsy, and Craig whoop and scrunch over to hug Grampa's legs again, this time in sympathy. B-U-F-F-A-L-O R-O-B-E, Jackie spells on her hand, and Grampa laughs silently.

Grama tells them about Grampa's going deaf and leaving the ministry. How sorry she was, when she thought she was set for life as a minister's wife, to be right back doing farm work, all that cooking and cleaning and canning, not only for the family but also for a whole lot of hired men.

It's a funny thing. Jackie is not really glad that Grampa went deaf, but yet she really is glad, for if he hadn't, he would have been a pastor in churches all his life, a new one every few years. That's the way Methodists do things. There would have been no round barn, no "Aims of This Farm," no cooler full of chocolate milk and orange drink for them to drink whenever they wanted it, no back-fence walks, no trucks with W.J. DOUGAN, THE BABIES' MILKMAN on them. And what would Daddy have done if he hadn't gone into business with Grampa? Because of Grampa's deafness, she can be both a minister's granddaughter *and* the milkman's baby. And everyone has had the farm.

"But you don't question the ways of the Lord," says Grama.

Patsy is thinking the same thoughts as Jackie. "The Lord *wanted* Grampa to be a farmer," she says positively.

Jackie nods agreement. Craig nods, too.

6 ⋅ JACKIE'S MILK ROUTE

At the start of the milk business, in 1907, Grampa thinks no one is capable of delivering milk but himself. Every day he takes the buggy and delivers the bottles to all the customers and to his sister Ida. The route grows and he purchases a milk wagon. It has brass trim and a glass front with a place for the reins to come through the glass. There's a well for him to stand in when he drives, and a space behind that big enough to hold many milk cases. The driver's side is open, so that a milkman can hop in and out easily. Grampa has his name and slogan painted in brown and gold on the cream-colored side, "W.J. Dougan, The Babies' Milkman."

Ronald sometimes rides with him on the route. As Grampa heads toward town, with the horses trotting at a brisk clip, he holds the reins and sings over the racket of the horses' hooves and iron wheels. It's the only time Ronald ever hears his father sing.

One day Grampa is on the route alone. He's returning home. Something startles the horses and they bolt. The wagon tips over. Grampa is caught between the wagon and the road, and dragged for a distance. The accident lacerates his legs and knees so badly that he's laid up for several weeks. He directs activities from a bed downstairs in the southwest room of the house. One of the hired men, Ross Martin, takes over the milk route. He thoroughly enjoys delivering the milk to the customers. When Daddy Dougan can finally be up and about again, there's no talk of his taking the route back. Ross Martin is, after Grampa, the first Dougan milkman.

No one can remember the name of a somewhat later milkman, only the story about him, which is that he never actually made it to a route. He was groomed for the job by accompanying an experienced driver, and before long was pronounced ready to solo. But when the morning arrived he was sick. He recovered, another morning rolled around, and again he was sick. It became apparent that the prospect of delivering milk was too much for him. Grampa left him at his job in the milkhouse and trained someone else for the route.

George Wermuth with the mules Foxy and Happy.

Daddy has a milk route at various times in his life. The summer he's fourteen he drives on the east side with a wagon and team of horses. The horses know the route so well that they'll stop in front of the proper house without bidding. This lets Ronald read a page or two of his current book in between stops. The streets in the Keeler and White Avenue area aren't paved, and when it rains the horses have rough going. It takes them longer, plodding through the ruts. Ronald has it so timed that in bad weather he can drink a quart of milk and eat the packet of cookies his mother sends with him for a morning snack, between the stop on White Avenue and the stop on Keeler.

Once, in fair weather on Keeler, Ronald gets left behind. He's a sociable sort and enjoys talking to the customers. He talks so long at one back step, with the mother of one of his schoolmates (the schoolmate much in evidence in the yard, hanging up wet curtains on stretchers), that when he returns to the street whistling and swinging his empty carrier, the horses have tired of waiting and gone around the block to the next stop. After that he always loads enough milk for both houses, gives the horses a giddyap, chats at the favored back porch, then jumps the fence, drops his order at the other door, and meets his team on the street as they arrive. That timing pleases him, too.

He's glad not to have been the driver when Foxy and Happy, the mules, run away with Tim Pedley on Wisconsin Avenue. The rampaging animals climb the curb, one on either side of a telegraph pole, meet themselves head on, and knock each other out. Milk is all over the street.

During the years when Jackie is growing up, Daddy fills in many times on different milk routes for two or three days, even a week or two, when someone is sick and there's no one to take his place. But during the war, in 1942, when so many men volunteer or are drafted, Daddy has to have his own route for six months. He leaves the house at two in the morning, takes the whole River Road route, then puts in a full day's work at the office. He's always tired. That's why he fails for so long to catch the new milkman who is embezzling route money. Besides having no expectation of being cheated, he isn't alert to discrepancies in the books. When Walter Abbot comes along willing to take the job of milkman, Daddy is grateful, even though Walter is a Seventh-Day Adventist and will under no circumstances deliver milk on Saturday. Daddy is glad to be a route man only one day a week.

Jackie's experience as a milkman is in two segments, the first in winter. She is fourteen. It's the start of Christmas vacation. Daddy is upset. One of the route men has slipped on the ice and developed housemaid's knee. He isn't allowed to walk for two weeks. There's no one to take Roscoe Ocker's place, least of all Daddy, who is still on a daily route.

"It's not as if he's really laid up," says Daddy at the supper table. "Even though he can barely get his pants on over the swelling, he says he can drive. He just can't do the running."

"I'll do the running," volunteers Jackie.

Daddy contemplates her. "*Grace a Dieu*," he says. "Better get to bed as soon as you can. I'll call Roscoe."

The next day Jackie leaves Chez Nous with Daddy at two in the morning. The stars are brilliant in the black velvet sky and it's bitter cold. She's bundled

Roscoe Ocker standing by Ockie Berg's truck.

up with coat, boots and snowpants, mittens and scarf and wool cap. At the dairy the yard lights are on and the trucks backed up to the loading dock. The milkmen are slinging cases into their trucks and arranging them. There is much chatter of milk bottles, and over it the banter of the men. Lester Stam, Howard Milner, Oscar Berg, Earl Bown — she knows them all. Roscoe Ocker is sitting on an upended milk case, directing the loading of his truck.

"There's my buddy," he calls cheerfully when he sees her. "I hear you're going to ride with me for two weeks."

Jackie nods and grins. She's always liked Roscoe.

The men cover Roscoe's load with a large gray quilted blanket to help keep the milk from freezing. They fix Jackie a niche up front to sit in. Roscoe swings into the driver's seat and warns her to be careful of the small kerosene stove that stands upright close to the dash, throwing off heat and a bright glow. Then they're off, out the farm driveway and down snow-covered Colley Road to town.

Roscoe explains that he's the swing man, the relief man, that every day he takes the route of one of the others who has the day off, and so Jackie will cover all of Beloit and South Beloit with him twice. That pleases her. Because of his leg they won't be going through the factories, though, when they take Howard's route. Ockie Berg will do those on Howard's day off, since Ockie's daily route is lighter right now on account of school vacations.

Today they are on the west side. They thread the dark streets, McKinley, St. Lawrence, Moore, lit only by street lamps at the intersections, and by an

The milk wagon has been transferred to runners for winter delivery. The new and as yet un-painted Little House is in the background.

occasional mid-block house whose Christmas tree lights, left on, cast a diffuse and many-colored glow out onto the snow. Roscoe explains the route book, how every month each customer has a page with the usual order of milk, and then what is actually taken on any given date. Even though Roscoe runs six routes, he knows most of the orders by heart and doesn't often need to refer to a page with his flashlight. He instructs Jackie what to put in the carrier and, with rueful warnings about ice, where to deliver the milk—into the front porch entryway, or on the back step in one of the insulated boxes that Dougan's provides, or into the kitchen—opening the back door and putting the bottles on the floor. When she gets to do that, Jackie sometimes slips inside and stands very still for a moment, breathing in the warm air, hearing the furnace rattle and the hum of the refrigerator. She feels strange as she listens to the sleeping house.

Jackie was fourteen when she drew this picture of herself delivering milk.

Roscoe gives information about the customers. This family has a new baby and her photograph has already been in a Dougan ad. This one's had a recent wedding; this family has a great-grandmother living with them whose hundredth birthday was in August. Her picture was in the paper.

"She didn't say she attributed her long life to drinking Dougan's milk, though," he adds.

Jackie calculates. Since the dairy began well after the great-grandmother was born, she'd have been able to drink Dougan's milk only during her last thirty-five years. But it could have contributed.

One family recently lost a son in the Pacific, and has two other sons in the service. "These are hard times," Roscoe says, and she is solemn as she crunches up the snowy driveway and leaves the milk on the back porch.

The hours go by. Jackie's arm aches from the heavy carrier. She's tired all over from getting up so early, and in spite of the heater in the truck her feet are frozen and her fingers numb.

Houses begin to light up as people awaken. Day will come late. It's close to the longest night of the year. Now kitchen windows make yellow patchworks on the driveways, and Roscoe instructs her to knock and give the milk directly to the housewife. This will ensure it won't freeze. He tells her whose house it is, so that she can greet the customer by name. The housewife, sometimes in a bathrobe and curlers, sometimes with a baby in a high chair or scooting on the floor, sometimes with a husband in work clothes, bent over his coffee, or an elderly father, bent over his, is surprised to see her, but always welcoming. Now Jackie gets to stand in a kitchen for a few minutes, invited, and warm her hands and feet over a hot air register and explain why they have a different milkman. They laugh, but sympathetically, about Roscoe's housemaid's knee, and they are always interested to learn she's Ron Dougan's daughter. Most of them know Daddy and Grampa at least a little. At one house she's given a slice of bacon, at another, a cup of hot chocolate and a doughnut, and she carries a mug of coffee and a doughnut out to Roscoe in the truck. Her energy revives with warmth and food.

"At this rate we won't have any room for breakfast," says Roscoe, finishing his doughnut. It's daylight in another hour, and he and Jackie stop at the Subway Cafe on Third Street. Geneva Bown, the owner of the Subway, is an old friend of Jackie's. She used to work on the farm and her husband, Earl, still does, delivering milk—he was at the loading dock this morning. Geneva serves them a full breakfast of sausage and eggs and flapjacks, and leans on the counter to exchange gossip and news. Earl comes in for his breakfast just as Jackie and Roscoe are leaving to return to the route. They finish it up and are back at the farm with a truck full of empties by late morning. Daddy, also back, runs her up to Chez Nous.

"Have a good time?" he asks.

"It was interesting," says Jackie, "but it's hard work." At home she's exhausted but fights taking a nap so that it will be easier to fall asleep right after supper.

The days go by, every one different, but with the same basic routine. The best day is Christmas, for she and Roscoe can scarcely get through their route, so many customers have cards and gifts for them—Christmas cookies on a colorful paper plate, or a jar of jelly, a box of candy. She keeps being invited in and dragged by the children to see what Santa brought, and then the adults have to get on their coats and come out to the truck to wish Roscoe a merry Christmas too.

"I'm not even their regular milkman," says Roscoe. "Look at all this stuff! And Stam's been bringing home presents from this route all week."

"They like you, too," says Jackie. She knows Roscoe is pleased.

The family saves opening its presents till afternoon, when Jackie and Daddy are home. The evening before, at the Big House party for all the help, Grampa tells her he's proud of the job she's doing. It's her turn then to be pleased. Grama says, "Think of our poor little Jackie doing all that running on a milk route!" Jackie doesn't think of herself as either poor or little.

The very worst day, and one of the worst days of Jackie's life, is the day after New Year's. It blizzards all night. In the car, she and Daddy slough down to the farm in a sea of drifts, unable to tell where the ditches are, the snow blinding them as it drives through the headlights into the windshield. When they finally make it, Jackie finds she has been holding her breath.

They find the farm alight and alive with activity. Grampa has a team out, breaking up the drifts so that the trucks can get through to town. Erv has the snowplow on the front of a farm truck, following up the team. Farmhands are helping with the plowing and shoveling and loading. Some of the milkmen came out the night before, when they realized it would be bad, and have slept in the Big House. Others have ridden out together, a lucky thing since they had to shovel and push more than once on the way. Ed Pfaff is getting chains on the trucks that don't already have them.

Everybody is late getting started. Today Roscoe's route is the River Road, stretching halfway to Janesville. The houses that fall between the highway and the river are often on little lanes, five or six to a lane, and the lanes are choked with snow. With all the drifting Roscoe doesn't dare take the truck down them, even with chains. In the dark Jackie mushes to the houses, often the ones at the very ends of the lanes, dragging her heavy carrier, and groans out loud when her stiff fingers unfurl a note stuck in a bottle and she finds the regular order has been augmented, making her take the trip twice. She has broken a path, but by the return the wind has already filled her tracks. The gale howls off the river and she can't feel her cheeks. The truck also can't get into Burrwood Park, a riverside shantytown of decrepit trailers, tarpaper shacks, and rickety summer cottages arranged haphazardly on a grid of un-paved streets. She makes trip after trip, leaning into the blizzard or, blissfully, being buffeted from behind as she returns to the truck for another load. It's worse delivering to Burrwood Park than to the snug bungalows on the lanes, for she's acutely aware of how cold the people must be who are crowded into those insufficient houses. She's never really noticed such things, till this win-ter on the milk route.

But worst of all is delivering to the big houses high on the hills on the other side of the River Road. Each of these has its own driveway—its own long, drifted driveway with the snow-laden wind whistling up and down and around it—and there's no way the truck can go up these, either. She has to battle her way uphill, step by laborious step, churning and flounder-ing through snow drifts. She's icy, yet sweat runs in rivulets down inside her clothes. Her eyelashes cake and her breath gasps until her throat is raw and aching from cold and exertion. Her carrier is lead, pulling her arm from its socket, for she brings along extra milk as insurance. But then if the order is the same or diminished, she has to carry it back again.

In the truck Roscoe keeps chocolate milk hot in a little pan on the kerosene stove. It's always ready for her when she staggers back. He's sympathetic and supportive, but doesn't apologize for his inability to help further, or smother her with praise. Jackie's glad of that. They are two people doing a job together. Their parts are defined. But midway along one of the long driveways she indulges in a tear or so of self-pity, before recalling Grama's words. Then she has a flush of shame, and rages at herself.

The snow lets up by mid-morning and the county has the River Road plowed to two of its three lanes, but drifting continues. Conditions are too bad to run back into town for a Subway breakfast. Before dawn Roscoe had produced two peanut butter sandwiches, and now they stop at a small grocery where they leave a case of milk and buy candy bars and apples. They warm up while discussing the weather with the elderly proprietors, who regale them with stories of much worse blizzards past. Jackie sits with her stockinged feet on the radiator and is gratified to find her toes gradually returning to her, red hot and itchy and full of needles and pins. She is reluctant to leave.

After the northernmost customer and longest driveway, Roscoe says, "Well, we've done it. It'll be easier from now on."

Jackie knows this from her previous River Road day, for now they'll turn inland and work their way back to town through more level and sheltered residential districts. She and Roscoe grin at each other in triumph. The harrowing day has firmly bonded their partnership.

Still, it's mid-afternoon before they finish the route and head back out Colley Road. Jackie has never been so worn out, but her fatigue is countered by a feeling of strength and accomplishment, of rising to a situation, battling through, getting done a job that had to be done. It's an exhilarating feeling, and turns the worst day into a best one. Nonetheless she falls asleep before suppertime.

The two weeks end. Roscoe's doctor permits him to use his leg, and Jackie returns to the routine of school. She has liked spending her vacation on the milk route.

Her second stint of delivering milk comes the summer she's sixteen. She and Craig both want summer jobs, other than the usual detasseling. They want to team up on a milk route—Jackie can quickly learn to drive and get her license.

Daddy says it's not a good idea. He has enough route men, and he'd have to carve a route for the two of them out of others' routes, then give the pieces back to the regular drivers in the fall. Besides, he needs them for detasseling—they're experienced and conscientious. However, Stam is slowing down and could use a boost this summer, and Roscoe, still the relief man, would probably enjoy his old partner back for a month or so. This wouldn't be make-work, for they'd both be learning the business. He could also use them after detasseling season for fieldwork. They'd receive detasseling wages throughout.

It's not what they'd hoped for, total responsibility and going together, but they see the problems. They accept Daddy's offer. Lester Stam agrees to teach Craig the ropes. And Roscoe is indeed pleased to have Jackie back as runner, though he will do his share of running, this time. She assumes her familiar spot at the front of the truck.

Delivering milk in summer turns out to be vastly different from delivering in winter. There are still the early hours. She and Craig bicycle the mile and a half from Chez Nous down to the dairy in the dark. But dawn comes soon, a faint graying of the black and gradually a lighter gray, followed by pinky fingers and gold-lined fleece, and finally the rim of the sun, piercing a sudden beam into Jackie's eyes and pinning her to the truck.

It's often rather chilly, predawn and dawn, and she starts out with a sweater, but soon after sunrise the day begins to warm. By noon, when they are returning to the farm, it's usually hot. The gray insulation blanket is now used to slow the melting of the ice that Roscoe shovels over the load. The running is easier with no snow or bulky clothes, though the carrier still strains her arm socket. People are out and about more, doing yard and garden work, hanging up the wash, painting their porch rails. Children are all over. Small ones in sandboxes. Middle-sized ones riding their tricycles and bicycles up and down the sidewalks. Bigger ones playing ball or kick-the-can in the streets or vacant lots.

Now, instead of putting the milk inside to prevent its freezing, Jackie often has instructions to come right into the kitchen and put it in the refrigerator to keep it from going sour. This happens in houses where everyone goes out to work, and they don't want the milk sitting all day even in an insulated box. Jackie loves to go into people's kitchens, see what they eat, how they live. She's always curious and takes a quick and searching look around, sometimes even darts into the next room or down the basement stairs to see what the cellar's like. At one house there's a genuine-looking treasure chest sitting on the basement landing. Jackie can't resist raising the lid. It's a disappointment, of course. It contains only old issues of *Popular Mechanics*.

People are just as friendly in the summer, probably more so. She gets cookies regularly, or a sample of whatever's baking. Once she has to stand and stir a pudding so it won't stick while a housewife answers the front doorbell. Once she watches a baby in a highchair while the mother rushes to respond to a minor emergency with an older child upstairs. She gives the baby a spoonful of something sloppy out of the dish the mother was feeding him from and is gratified when the baby, never taking his eyes from hers, eats it. And once, on Olympia Boulevard, she catches her jeans on a sharp edge of the truck and they tear, exposing a generous amount of underpants and thigh. Roscoe drives her to old Mrs. Carabini's house, where she sits with a towel around her middle while Mrs. Carabini's deft fingers sew up the rip.

Friendliest of all are the dogs, even the unfriendly ones who somehow stop their growling or snarling when she stands perfectly still and speaks to them in a conversational voice. They change their minds and come crawling up on their bellies, wagging their tails apologetically. The ones behind fences or on chains make little whiny noises, wheedling her to come pat them. Never once does she get bit. There is every size and shape and age and breed of dog that exists, and Jackie figures she knows them all, a lot of them by name. She also knows many cats.

She goes through the shoe factory again, as she did once when she request-ed the experience for her ninth birthday, and this time through the other fac-tories as well. They deliver to the service entrance of the hospital. They deliver to the Subway Cafe and have breakfast with Geneva. On Lester Stam's route they have a morning snack and gossip with Grama at 647 Milwaukee Road. The work at the Big House became too much for her, and she and Grampa and Effie are now living on the edge of town, close to the start of the road to the farm. Grampa is never there. He's still working all day in the fields and the barns, even though he's retired. Aunt Lillian and Hazel are also on Stam's route, and Jackie decides that some of Lester's slowness isn't due to age.

She covers every street in town and in South Beloit. She has more leisure and comfort to ponder the differences in neighborhoods, the grand houses on Sherwood Drive and Turtle Ridge, the old streets of substantial houses near the college, the streets of smaller houses to the north and west, the Athletic Avenue and Race Street area where almost all the Negroes in town are crowd-ed because they aren't allowed to live anywhere else. The street name, "Race," is ironic. The street wasn't named to point up the segregation, but because it ran along the now dry and shrub-filled mill race off Turtle Creek.

And she delivers to Burrwood Park, on the river, its littered streets unpaved and without sidewalks, swarming with scantily dressed little white children. Some of the shanties have flowers and paint and flat stones leading up to the doors. Others resemble derelict chicken coops. Old people sit on sagging porches, weary-looking mothers balance naked babies on one hip while they fill a bucket from an outside tap and their other children plash in the muddy water under the spigot. The farm has now gone to every-other-day delivery, on account of the war. It saves fuel and rubber to deliver twice as much milk to half a route one day and the other half the next, rather than to cover the total route every day. Burrwood Park, however, still gets every-day delivery because so few of the houses have refrigeration.

There is also little plumbing. At one house Jackie knocks and a small boy dressed in only an undershirt comes dancing out, holding a Dougan pint bottle half full of yellow liquid. "See this?" he shouts at her. "That's pee-pee! That's what it is, pee-pee! Pee-pee!" And he capers in again. Jackie delivers her bottle, collects two empties, and is glad that the caustic cleanser in the bottle washer is as strong as it is.

Near the end of the River Road route they deliver to an old farmhouse. There's a stake in the yard, and fastened to the stake is a long rope trailing over the grass. Beyond the end of the rope is a dirt path, circling all the way around the stake.

"See that?" says Roscoe. "The man who lives here had an accident and went blind last year, and that's the way he gets his exercise. He holds onto the end of the rope and walks."

The stake and rope and path haunt Jackie. In her mind she keeps seeing the man holding the rope and walking and walking, nowhere, like a bull on the bull sweep at the farm, or on the treadmill bull walk. In the several times they deliver to that house she never sees the blind man.

Detasseling time comes, and Jackie and Craig shift jobs. Jackie has enjoyed the milk route. She can see why most of the milkmen have been with the farm a long time. It's a worthwhile job, delivering clean milk to people. It has variety. It's as sociable as you want to make it. It's personal. You're directly in touch with your customer—a bottle of milk is not like a can of soup on a grocery shelf. You're up early, in the freshness of the morning, and usually through by noon. It's pleasant work with lots of exercise, but not as taxing as pitching bundles or haying or even detasseling, except when the weather is grueling. Then it can match anything. But terrible weather has its satisfactions, too, in the challenge of battling the elements and the sweet fatigue of victory.

All in all, milk delivering is a good occupation. She understands why Grampa was reluctant to give up his first milk route, and feels a bit sorry for that nameless near-milkman who never got up the courage to try.

7 ⋈ MOVIE, 1932

I t's early April of 1932; Patsy is five. She and her sisters and brother are on the screened-in porch of the Big House, keeping clean. They are waiting for the photographer. This isn't an ordinary photographer, the sort that takes their picture every Christmas for the Christmas card. That one sets up a camera on a tall three-legged stand. His camera has a black accordian pleated front which he stretches way out, and then he gets under a black cloth and fusses and fusses, and finally holds his arm up. There is a little heap of powder on a tray, and when he snaps the picture the powder flashes and smokes and smells, and you have spots in your eyes for a while. It takes a great deal of patience and staying still to have that sort of picture taken.

It takes patience for this sort, too. But this is different. They will get to move, for this is a movie. It's going to be shown in the movie theaters downtown, for advertising. Mother has rehearsed them on their part. They will come out of the porch and walk down the sidewalk, first herself, Patsy, pushing the toy wheelbarrow, then Joan, then Jackie with the wicker doll buggy, and last of all Craig, on his tricycle. Meanwhile she is infinitely bored. They are all infinitely bored.

Back in March, when Daddy and Mother and Grampa are planning the movie, sitting around the table in the Little House, Patsy listens in. So does Joan. Think of making a movie!

It cannot be a long one. People waiting for a film to begin don't want to sit through long advertisements. But it should show the whole story of producing milk.

"So we must start with the land," Grampa says. "The land is the foundation of everything, that fertile skin between bedrock and sky that makes our lives possible."

Grampa and Daddy plot the tractors, the plows, the harrow, the disk, the drag, and also the fields where these will be filmed. "I will manage the horses," says Grampa firmly.

Then the young stock will be shown, and the bulls, and next the cows and the milking in the round barn. Mother says cleanliness must be stressed, and Grampa and Daddy agree. From the milking the scene will shift to the milkhouse and the bottling and capping of the milk.

Then comes a master stroke. Daddy leads everyone outside while he demonstrates.

"We'll load full milk cases into this delivery truck," he says, slinging an empty case through the truck's open back doors. "And then the milk man will shut the doors—" Daddy shuts them, "—and the camera will fasten on the words on the door, our slogan, 'The Babies' Milk Man.' That will be a fitting end to the movie. Our milk on its way to the consumer." He points and writes and draws for Grampa.

Grampa studies the page and the truck, back and forth. He opens and shuts the doors, looking at the motto. He nods and nods. Patsy studies the doors, too. She nods.

"Except we have not yet finished the story," Grampa says. "We've left out the consumer, the only reason for our milk production. We must have the cubbies."

And that is why she and Joan and Craig and Jackie are waiting on the porch, in their sweaters and caps. They are to be the finale of the movie.

At long, long last the photographer gets to them. He sets up his camera in the driveway, and calls that he is ready. Mother lines them up and starts them off down the sidewalk. "Smile at the camera!" she instructs. Patsy does. Her part, as well as Joan's and Jackie's and Craig's, is swiftly over. She is glad. Now they can go play.

The cameraman walks back to the milkhouse. He confers with Daddy and Grampa. Then Daddy calls for them to come.

"There's a little film left; enough for one more shot of you kids," Daddy says. "Sit down here on the milkhouse step, and look natural. Smile."

Mother herds them to the step, and she and Daddy arrange them. Patsy is irritated. This isn't a step they ever,

A day well spent at the Dougan Guernsey Farm, the ultimate in cleanliness and modern dairy farming.

Frames from the film: manure to consumer in less than four minutes!

Joan, Craig, Jackie, and Patsy, sitting on the step at the movie's end.

ever sit on. How can they look natural? All they will look like is having their picture taken.

But the camera grinds, she squints into the sun, and the film is finished.

When it's shown in the Majestic Theater they are all allowed to go, even Craig, who is only two. Mother whispers the beginning print, but not for Patsy, for Patsy can read: "A day well spent at the Dougan Guernsey Farm, the ultimate in cleanliness and modern dairy farming." Then come horses pulling the manure spreader, huge on the huge screen, spewing manure out behind it, and then Larry on the big-lugged Case tractor, and Dave on the other tractor with a harrow, then the Case again, this time with a disk, and finally four horses with a drag, and behind the horses is Grampa, managing the many reins.

"Gompa!" shouts Craig, bouncing in Mother's lap, and everyone around them laughs.

The heifers stand in the barnyard; the bulls, fastened by their noses at either end of the bullsweep, make it turn. Print comes on again: "A Federal and State accredited herd—producers of Golden Guernsey products and Wisconsin Grade 'A' raw milk." In the barn washroom Maynard and Ralph wash and wash their hands. There is a view of cow sides and rears and switching tails, above an immaculate gutter and walk.

"Not one cowpie!" whispers Patsy and they all giggle at the thought of a cow letting loose in front of the camera.

The men then curry tails, wash udders, squirt milk from each tit into a covered cup.

"For garget," says Joan wisely.

A cow is milked by a milking machine. Milk from a full Surge is poured into a gauze-covered milk can. The milkhouse follows. The bottle caps on their long loops lead down to the capper, and a few bottles are capped before a milkman takes a full case and slings it into the back of a milk truck. He closes one door; it reads THE, and under it, MILK. He then closes the other door and the slogan is complete:

THE BABIES'
MILK MAN

And finally come the four of them walking along the sidewalk in front of Grama's porch! They too are huge on the huge screen. Patsy recognizes that the children are themselves, but those children hardly seem real.

They do to her brother. "Gockie!" shouts Craig, spotting his sister Jackie, and everyone around them laughs.

Now the four children are sitting on the step. Patsy surveys them critically. Really, they should all be drinking chocolate milk. But almost immediately the advertising short is over. Daddy stays for the feature, with Grama and Aunt Ida and Hazel. Mother drives Grampa and the four of them back to the farm.

"Vera, that is a splendid little movie, and only three and a half minutes long," Grampa says in the car. "My, how many weeks did it take us to plan it and film it!" He adds, "It will make up its cost in the business it brings in."

In the back seat Patsy agrees. Yes, it's a splendid movie. In spite of that long and boring wait on the porch. And in spite of that step they never sit on. It all went by too fast. She'd like to see it again.

8 ⨯ ACIDOPHILUS MILK

Jackie grows up loving the Oz books. But there's one literary technique L. Frank Baum uses in some of his books that she finds aggravating. It's this: he starts a story, with Ojo or the Nome King or the Patchwork Girl, and carries them along through all sorts of exciting adventures for about five chapters. You're reading avidly. Suddenly he begins Chapter Six with a whole new set of characters, in a different place, with a different adventure. You pause, dismayed. It's as if you're starting a new book, one you'd be happy to read later, but right now you want to get on with the first one. But you keep doggedly on, after a bit becoming absorbed in the new story, forgetting your interest in the old, and then it happens: at Chapter Ten or Eleven the two sets of characters come together, the roads have converged, the stories merge. After being tricked like this a number of times Jackie knows what's up when the original story abruptly stops and another begins. She merely sighs and begins the new tale. But she feels it's a shabby device no author should really stoop to.

However, to tell the tale of the acidophilus milk she realizes she must use this technique herself; that two unlikely roads must come together. The story happens when she's three, or maybe four, and all she remembers is being a bunny—and a terrified one at that.

It's the Depression. There are a number of rival milk companies in Beloit, all vying to keep afloat in a time of Unstable Market. Wright & Wagner, associated with a statewide advertising and certifying company, "Meadow Gold Milk," is a larger dairy than W.J. Dougan, the Babies' Milkman. Merrick's Dairy is one that's smaller.

Dougan's Dairy, along with its regular products, is selling something called "acidophilus" milk. Daddy gets it already bottled, from Brook Hill Farm in Genesee Depot. Brook Hill supplies all the certified milk to the Chicago area. It also sells other specialties, like acidophilus, to dairies here and there. The farm is owned by a man named Howard Greene.

Acidophilus milk tastes like very bland buttermilk. It's made by introducing the acidophilus culture into milk, acidophilus being a kind of bacteria. What it does, explains Daddy, is to replace some of the other types of bacteria in the intestines of the drinker. It crowds them out. It's supposed to be good for digestion. It also has the interesting property of making your farts smell good.

Jackie, hearing this at seventeen, is intrigued. She wishes acidophilus milk were still around so she could test it. She can't remember drinking it when she was three. She looks up "acidophilus" in the dictionary. The definition says that acidophilus milk "changes the intestinal flora." She's now doubly intrigued, contemplating her own intestines as flower beds, jungle loops.

But back now, to the other road. Forget acidophilus milk, and see Mother. She's a beautiful and talented dancer, and is teaching ballet. She has taught dance before, at Illinois Women's College, and in France, but now she has four small children close together in age. She is active in her new community. Her time is full. Yet the Depression is making itself felt, and this is a way she can help, receiving pay for doing what she loves. She sends out a letter, saying she's received many requests to teach, and has now decided to comply. She lists class times and duration (ten dollars per term), that private lessons

can be arranged, and that the work will consist entirely of Classical, Interpretive, Ballet, Character, and Folk Dancing. There will be special emphasis on technique, rhythm, grace, and correct posture. She gives her impressive credentials, her teachers (including Serova and Vestoff of the Russian Ballet), and the places where she has taught.

Her studio is downtown, upstairs over the Majestic Theater, in the big empty Knights of Columbus Hall. There are full length mirrors on the walls, and high and low barres. Jackie, age three, stands holding the low barre,

Mother: Vera Wardner Dougan.

her feet in their black ballet slippers carefully apart in second position. She watches Patsy ahead of her, and does exactly what Patsy does, plies and releves. Joan is in the class too, and twenty other little girls. Mother has a class of older girls that meets at a different time. Some of those girls are even into toe shoes.

The K of C Hall is all right for class. It's not all right for the kind of recital Mother wants to give this spring. She decides to stage the performance at the farm, on the lawn in front of the Big House. To the west of the lawn is a row of tall pine trees; before the pines is a line of shorter maples; and in front of the maples, a thick hedge of spirea, or bridal wreath bushes. The bushes will be in bloom, and snowy white. The audience will sit on folding chairs, facing the bushes, which with the double tier of trees will make a striking backdrop for the dancing. The dancers can stand behind the bushes, waiting for their cues, and enter and exit around the ends of, or even through, the bushes. The piano will be moved to the lawn; Grampa will get several hired men to do it with a farm truck. The grass will be mowed two days ahead, so that grass clippings won't stick to the dancers' legs. Mother has arranged for a small string ensemble, and even a male quartet.

One thing more is needed. Lights. The recital will start at twilight; most of the sunset will be blotted out by the backdrop, and the trees' shadows will cover the dancing area. Long before the program is over it will be dark. Mother has some regular flood lights on poles, but she especially fancies blue lights, to light up the little girls in their tutus, the older girls in their diaphanous white gowns, and the tumbling white waterfalls of bridal wreath blossoms during the Chopiniana. She wants it like fairyland.

But where to get blue lights? Christmas tree lights are the obvious answer, but it's June. No Christmas tree lights are available in the stores, and even if they were, to buy enough strings would be more than Mother and Daddy can afford. Daddy has an idea. The city has miles of Christmas tree lights! Every December, all over downtown, they are strung across the street, back and forth. They twinkle brightly all during the weeks of evening shopping hours, and even on Sundays. After New Years, city workmen on tall ladders take them down. They must be stored somewhere, until the next holiday season.

Daddy goes to see the city council and makes his request. Yes, they agree, he can borrow all the Christmas tree lights Mother needs. Daddy tracks down the lights. He discovers they're kept in a small storeroom off the Community Room, which is a meeting hall in the basement of the Beloit Savings Bank.

One hot June morning Daddy goes down to the Savings Bank. He walks through the Community Room and into the little storeroom. He turns on the light, closes the door. The Christmas lights are there, in great tangled masses. He settles down to untangle them. Once he has a string free he plugs it in to see if it works. He then switches all the red and white and green and yellow light bulbs—which are considerably larger than regular Christmas lights—to other strands, and replaces them with blue. He plugs in the strand again, to make sure all the blues light up properly. Finally he coils the finished strand on top of other finished strands, and goes on to the next. It's a long, laborious job. It takes hours. Daddy sweats a lot.

At last he has enough. He stands up, stretches, mops his brow, slings the great coil over his shoulder, turns off the light, opens the storeroom door, and goes out into the Community Room. A dozen heads swivel, a dozen pairs of eyes stare at him in astonishment.

When he went in, the Community Room was empty. Now there's a meeting going on. He recognizes the man conducting it. He's the head salesman from Brook Hill Farm. He recognizes the bottles on the table, and the word "Acidophilus" on the blackboard. He recognizes the people attending the meeting. They're the officials and milkmen of Merrick's Dairy. They all recognize Daddy, too. The salesman glares at him; the Merrick people glare at him. He gives a word of apology for interrupting their meeting, nods to the assemblage, and leaves. He stops at the Rosman-Uehling-Kinzer Funeral Home to pick up folding chairs before returning to the farm.

Once home, Daddy and some of the men festoon the lights from tree to tree. For footlights they arrange several strings along the grass in front of the first row of folding chairs. A piano tuner runs arpeggios up and down the piano and then returns to single plinks. Mother puts clips on the music stands, in case of wind. She lays out the costumes on card tables on the front porch of the Big House.

All the dancers and their families arrive; this is performance night. The dress rehearsal was the previous afternoon, without the lights. Scores of people drive out from town. Dicky Richardson, Daddy's history professor from Beloit College, is in the front row. So are Grampa and Grama. Grama holds little Craig in her lap. Aunt Lillian and Aunt Ida and Cousin Hazel are there. All the hired men are there, too, and neighbors from up and down Colley Road. Everyone sits facing the white spirea bushes.

Behind the bushes are Joan and Patsy and Jackie and all the other pupils, along with several mothers to help with entrances. There are no lights yet, it is a long June twilight. The program begins. Jackie, following Patsy so she

Jackie is a bunny. This is the dress rehearsal before the spirea bushes on the lawn of the Big House.

will know exactly what to do, marches out from behind the bushes with her toy musket over her shoulder. All the little girls dance the formations of "The March of the Wooden Soldiers" while the male quartet sings the words. With applause in their ears they rush to the porch to change.

Then Joan and five others do a Dutch dance in wooden shoes, on a low wooden platform so that the clop-clops are clearly heard. In the middle of the dance Mother signals and Daddy, at the edge of the bushes, opens a cage and shoos out a pair of geese. They come waddling and honking and hissing near the dancers. Everyone laughs and claps, and at the end of the dance Daddy and a hired man round them up again.

Next comes the bunny dance, the one Jackie never forgets. She remembers it not because she wears ears and a tail, but because at the end the bunnies hop behind the bushes and out again, faster and faster, circling several times while people clap. With a bunny hot on her heels and another behind that one, all in the gloom of the bushes, Jackie hops faster than she ever has before, trying to catch up to Patsy and safety, but she can't. She experiences terror, the very real panic of being chased.

But now the flood lights are on. Mother dances a solo, accompanied by the string ensemble. The quartet performs again. There are numbers by combinations of the older girls, with scarves and goings over and under. Then the flood lights dim, and the blue lights come on. A sigh like a ripple goes up from the audience. The older girls come stepping forth on their toe shoes like long legged birds, their white knee-length gowns shimmering in the blue lights. The strains of Chopin are mesmerizing. There is transformation to the lawn as the Chopiniana is performed, accompanied by the sweet strings. Fireflies add moving, blinking stars to the magical effect. The scene is indeed fairyland. Then the girls quietly vanish as the lights dim, and all is darkness. The trance holds.

Suddenly the floods light up, the mood changes, and there is a rollicking finale with all the dancers in it. It's a highly successful recital. Everyone enjoys it, and everyone remarks on the blue lights as they drink lemonade and eat cookies before driving back to town.

A few days later Daddy returns the lights to the storeroom in the Savings Bank. The same day he receives a letter from Howard Greene, the owner of Brook Hill Farm.

The letter is nasty. Howard Greene accuses Daddy of "unethical practices." He says what a low trick it was, to eavesdrop on the meeting with Merrick's people, that he would think such an activity beneath Ronald Dougan, son of the Reverend W.J. Dougan. Certainly W.J. would never stoop to such a base deed as spying on the competition.

Daddy now realizes what was going on at that meeting: Brook Hill was dissatisfied with how Dougan's Dairy had been selling the acidophilus milk, and so they were planning to give the franchise to another Beloit dairy that might do better. It was a secret meeting with Merrick's people to investigate this possibility. Nobody knows, Howard Greene says, how Daddy found out it was being held; everyone swears they didn't tell him, yet somehow Daddy got wind of it.

Daddy has always admired Howard Greene. He writes him a letter, explaining. The letter sounds hardly convincing, even to Daddy, with its talk of dance recitals and Christmas tree lights. It's absolutely too coincidental. Howard Greene doesn't believe that Daddy, sweating in the storeroom, never heard a thing. He takes the acidophilus milk away from Dougan's Dairy, and for several years treats Daddy like a bad smelling fart.

The situation isn't ameliorated until they both become members of the four-person board of the Wisconsin Scientific Breeding Institute. In working together they become fast friends. They eventually straighten out the acidophilus story and laugh over it. The intestinal flora come up roses.

9 ⚬ ROUTE BOOK

Every milkman has a monthly route book. Each customer has a page in it, in the order of the route. The milkmen are supposed to check off their routes in their route books as they go along, putting down how much milk and other dairy products each customer takes.

Howard Milner is a fast milkman, and prides himself on his memory. He doesn't like to be bothered with constant bookkeeping. He waits to fill in his route book till he's checking out in the office back at the farm. But Daddy is forever after him to fill in his route as he goes, like the other milkmen, for, good memory or not, he sometimes makes mistakes.

"I don't want to see you filling in your route book out here," says Daddy.

"All right, all right," agrees Howard. He changes his ways. But he still doesn't fill in his book after every delivery. At the end of his route, he pulls his truck up under a tree and, holding his route book in his lap, flips the pages and fills in every one.

One morning the phone rings in the office. Ruby answers it. A woman's voice states that she's not a customer, but she simply has to talk to Mr. Dougan. Daddy takes the receiver. The woman gives her address, and Daddy notes that it's near the end of Howard's route. She is clearly agitated.

"Mr. Dougan," she blurts, "I apologize for calling you this way, but I feel I must tell you! It's about your milkman. I'm sure you'd want to know and put a stop to it. Heaven knows *I'd* want to know, if I were running a business, and if I were having that going on, and me not knowing—and right out in public—on the street—he's over there right now, doing it again!"

"Doing what?" Daddy asks. "What is our milkman doing?" He knows that Howard, from time to time, does things that might baffle a customer, such as putting snakes on running boards, and waits to see what tricks Howard is up to now.

"We-ell"—Mrs. Milford takes a deep breath—"Your milkman—I really hate to say it—your milkman stops across from my house every day, there by the park entrance, at just about now — and I can see him through his truck window — looking down — and — and — "

"Yes?" encourages Daddy.

"Oh, Mr. Dougan," wails the woman, "I *can't* tell you what he's doing — but it's filthy, and he's been doing it every day at about eleven-fifteen or eleven-thirty — "

Daddy begins to get the picture but is doubtful. "You say you can see him?"

"Well, I can't exactly see him — I can't see his hands — but he's moving and moving them and, as I said, looking down, and it's perfectly *obvious* what he's doing!"

"I'll certainly see to it that he stops," Daddy vows. "We can't have *that* going on. I do appreciate your calling to tell me, Mrs. Milford."

"I just knew you'd want to know," the woman says in a relieved I've-done-my-duty tone, and hangs up.

When Daddy is able to stop laughing, he tells Ruby, and they both double over with mirth. They wait for Howard.

When he returns from his route and climbs up the stairs to the back room of the office over the milkhouse, Daddy accosts him. "Howard, haven't I been telling you to fill in your route book after every couple of deliveries or you'd get yourself in hot water? Well, you're in hot water!"

"I haven't made a mistake in two weeks!" Howard protests.

"Oh, yes, you have. You've made a big mistake to park across from the house of a Mrs. Milford while you leaf

Howard Milner enjoys a quart of milk while perched atop his truck.

through your route book. She's convinced you're a naughty boy." He tells him about the phone call, and all the milkmen in the office whoop. This time, Ruby laughs till the tears roll down her cheeks.

The episode doesn't cure Howard. He still doesn't fill in his route book after every delivery. He does, however, change his parking spot to an alley where no one can see him.

10 ⨯ THE GREAT DEPRESSION

M id-September, 1931, from W.J. Dougan to his employees:

STATEMENT OF THE NECESSITY FOR READJUSTMENT OF MY
WAGE SCALE AND THE WAGES OF EACH MAN BEGINNING
OCTOBER 1 1931

The necessity of my cutting expenses is imperative for these reasons: The farm is giving a small cash return this year, as you all realize. The volume of trade is difficult to maintain. The shops are being carried at little profit and collections are hard. The margin of profit after paying cost of raw material and labor is small, and the overhead expenses have not lessened greatly.

It is apparent to all of my help that in order to hold my place in these years of depression, I must manage so as to pay all current bills promptly, meet my interest and taxes, and pay some on my obligations regularly. My wage scale has grown with my ideals and it is a disappointment to me that I must lower the wages in conformity with these unusual financial conditions. However, I feel my men will still be better off than the average in city or country service.

It is a difficult problem for me to adjust the wage satisfactorily. There are so many factors to consider. Some of the factors are, (1) What are the needs of each man. (2) How does his service affect the income of the place. (3) What could I secure such help for on the open market. Then there are all the personal equations, i.e., his length of service on the place, his faithfulness and loyalty, and a score of other factors all of which must have a bearing on fixing this scale. Some may feel they are not getting a square deal as compared to others. I think if you could have all of the facts I have in mind, you would largely agree with me. I want to assure my help that if they can better their situation, I will give them every opportunity to do so, and will assist them in any way possible to find a better place and recommend them to any prospective employer. I can not tell how long this schedule will remain in force. I do not look for any sudden upstart in business, and when it does come it will take some time to recuperate. I may have to cut again, but hope not. I will not ask my men to contract for any definite period. Neither will I agree to keep them employed for a definite period. As in the past, if either party desires a change, give the other party reasonable notice and make the change so as to inconvenience the other as little as possible.

—W.J. Dougan

Employee	Salary	Bonus	In Kind
Lester Stam	60.00	5.00	House and milk
Harvey Hockerman	50.00	5.00	Board
Walter Grishaber	30.00	5.00	Board
Wilbur Metcalf	35.00	5.00	Board
Byron Moore	65.00	5.00	Milk
Roy Veihman	45.00	5.00	House and milk
DeWitt Griffiths	40.00	5.00	Board
Chas Taggart	45.00	5.00	House and milk
John Dummer	45.00	5.00	House and milk
Clair B. Mathews	80.00	5.00	Milk
Oscar Berg	35.00	5.00	Board

Thus do all on the farm have to tighten their belts, and not just the employees. Grampa and Grama, Mother and Daddy, tighten theirs as well. But Jackie, Craig, Patsy, and Joan are only dimly aware that the Great Depression is going on.

When it begins they are very little—in October of 1929 Jackie isn't yet two. They grow up through it, so that the word "depression" is a familiar one, and they know "money" is in short supply. But what does this mean to them? They have only word-knowledge of the Depression. They don't have heart-knowledge, belly-knowledge.

For there is always enough to eat, at the Big House, at the Little House, at Aunt Ida's. There is all the milk they can drink, and they drink gallons a day, plus all the half pints of chocolate milk and orange and grape drink that they freely take from the milkhouse. They spread butter on Grama's homemade bread with a trowel. Their oatmeal is a brown-sugary island in a sea of cream. There are fresh fruits and vegetables all summer; and from the pungent root cellar at the Big House, carrots and onions and parsnips and potatoes and

The milk-fed Dougan children at a picnic on the Little House lawn. There are two guests. Jackie and Craig are at the small table, Craig investigating a bug.

squashes and apples all winter. There are all the home-canned goods, tomatoes and string beans and applesauce and pickles and peas, lined up in dusty rows in Grama's canning cellar, or on the shelves at the top of the Big House back stairs. There are eggs. And there is plenty of meat: beef, pork, chicken. The four never know any hunger but that of healthy appetites.

Nor does the Depression occasion any discernable changes in their lives. They don't have to leave the farm, or move into a smaller house, or double up with relatives. Daddy doesn't lose his job; they aren't aware of how drastically his salary has been cut. They do not know that Grampa is investigating bankruptcy. Santa Claus always comes. A farm truck is more fun to ride in than a car. And doesn't every younger sibling wear hand-down clothes? Even the eldest inherit from a cousin?

Jackie has no realization of the hardships common to other families around the country, some even in Turtle Township. Her life is the way it is, complete with music lessons and birthday presents, and she doesn't question its bountifulness any more than she questions the sun rising over the Blodgett farm every morning, and sinking behind the Congregational Church steeple in far off Beloit every night.

However, Daddy and Mother, Grampa and Grama, and every grownup on the farm are well aware of the Depression. Everyone up and down Colley Road is. And of course, before it's over, even Craig, born in 1930, is old enough to have a grasp of the situation.

In the midsixties, Jackie hears Daddy tell about those early years. At any time, he says, not only the dairy but any farm along the road would have gone under if its creditors had all blown the whistle at the same time. But they didn't. Dougans were lucky that way, and Marstons and Blodgetts and the others. But there was more than luck. There was help from the government. The Federal Land Bank was ready to loan money to farmers who needed it, and Grampa and Daddy needed it. The farm was teetering on the brink. Grampa would probably have to declare bankruptcy unless he could get a farm loan. This money wasn't handed out willy-nilly, however. Requirements had to be met; there had to be a certain relationship between assets and liabilities. Daddy and Grampa figured out their situation and found that the farm had too many debts to qualify for a farm loan.

It was then that Daddy had a lifesaving idea. Why not incorporate the milk business as an entity separate from the farm? Let the corporation—which would legally be a "person," yet neither Daddy nor Grampa nor the farm—let that corporation assume the farm's debts. Then the farm would be eligible for a land bank loan, and they would all survive.

The corporation is a small one—Grampa as president; Hazel Croft, Daddy's first cousin, vice-president; and Daddy, secretary-treasurer. They draw up the articles of incorporation and "W.J. Dougan, the Babies' Milkman," becomes "Dougan Guernsey Farm Dairy, Inc." They change the lettering on the next order of stationery, but not on the trucks. Then Daddy takes all the local debts—money owed to the State Bank, the First National Bank, the debts on machinery, lumber, plumbing, seed, totaling some twenty thousand dollars, and asks everyone to take a private note on the milk business. And everyone does, even though the corporation has no collateral, only good will. This brings the farm debt down far enough to get a farm loan.

"And everyone on the road would have lost their farms if it weren't for the Rock County Federal Farm Loan Association," says Daddy. "We got our loan in 1933, and I'm still paying it off, as slow as I can. I'll probably have to finish it off pretty soon, though. Still, over thirty years, at that interest!"

But it takes more than luck, loans, and incorporation. Business is falling. As people are laid off, they cut their family milk consumption, or buy from the store, or carry a bucket out to the country to some farmer with a cow or two, or let their bills mount, or move out of the area entirely. Many leave milk bills behind. Can a business already running on such a slim margin survive such an unstable market? Daddy writes scores of letters to customers who aren't paying, asking if they might begin to reduce their debt little by little. These are courteous letters, and gentle, for he knows the straits of such families, and there but for the grace of God, the Federal Land Bank, and his own lenient creditors, goes he. Often he and Grampa let a man come out and work off his milk bill as a day laborer.

Daddy remembers taking a train up to Janesville. It is probably 1933, well after Grampa has had to cut everyone's wages so drastically. The distance is short but the train takes nearly two hours to get there. Daddy has the milk business on his mind. He has a scrap of paper and on it he is trying to figure out how to meet the payroll. There are many families supported by the farm: his and Grampa's, the milkmen and their families, the hired men, some of them with families. The helps' wages, factoring in board, milk, or other perks, is now averaging about sixty dollars a month.

"I decided the men simply had to have a hundred a month," Daddy says. "None of us could live on less than a hundred a month! But I didn't see how we could do it. I figured and figured. Then the train pulled into Janesville. I crumpled up the paper, I jammed it into my pocket, I stood up and said out loud, 'We'll pay a hundred a month!'"

It is after this that Daddy accomplishes another lifesaving action. Ever since joining his father in the business, he has been active in advertising. He came with experience—while at Northwestern University and Beloit College he paid much of his way by selling advertising for student desk blotters. Now he looks around for markets besides the door-to-door delivery one, places where people might buy a bottle of milk on a regular basis. Through his efforts, the hospital and a number of kindergartens are already buying Dougan's milk, though Todd School buys Wright & Wagner's so that Jackie has to bring her bottle from home. "We can't have you buying milk when we have plenty," Daddy says.

He now visits all the area grocery stores, scattered throughout town and far up the River Road, where Burrwood Park and the trailer courts are located. He gets many of the grocers to stock Dougan's milk in their coolers, and to add the dairy's name to their signs. This helps business some.

But an area the farm has under-utilized is the factories. Several years previous to the Depression Daddy had pondered a State motto, "Farm and Factory Must Prosper Together." The idea was just starting to develop that milk could be sold to men at their benches. Daddy knew of one factory that allowed this: Gisholts, in Madison. He and Grampa went up and talked to the management; they followed the delivery man up and down the aisles and into the foundry. They decided factories could be an outlet for The Babies' Milkman,

The fleet of Dougan delivery trucks, 1936.

and in 1927 approached a few of the smaller shops in Beloit, and one large one, The Beloit Iron Works. Grampa's letter was a solicitation for the county YMCA — one he would have sent anyway — but it added a query about the feasibility of milk delivery to the specific factory. Every day a routeman would peddle milk in its aisles. The response was largely favorable; a letter coming from the vice-president-treasurer of the Iron Works, Elbert Neese, said that he was personally in favor of it, but would take it up with "our Welfare Organization and the men will make their own decision." The men decided yes.

After several months of milk delivery, Grampa sent followup letters to the factory management, many of whom he and Ron knew personally, asking how the enterprise was working out. All the responses were positive; the longest and most detailed affidavit coming from M.W. Dundore at the Iron Works, who apparently gave the subject much thought:

> The reason we have for giving employees the privilege of securing milk during the daily work period are as follows:
>   1. Cold milk in summer will not induce dysentery as will iced water.
>   2. Milk seemingly is a better thirst-quenching medium than water.
>   3. Employees enjoy milk as a health food, i.e.: Molders suffering from stomach disorders drink it exclusively with result little time is lost in absence from work.

4. It is used as a wash during meal time by employees carrying their cold lunch in preference to coffee and other stimulants.

5. Less between meal lunches and sandwiches are eaten as milk fully satisfies.

6. Records indicate less lost time due to sickness and other ailments.

7. Employees performing heavy lifting and operating heavy machine tools are known to have added weight which is an asset on this kind of work.

8. Some employees claim the use of increased quantities of milk in the home since acquiring the habit in the shop.

9. Find that no time lost is occasioned by milk distribution.

The factory trade has helped, but the shops, Daddy realizes, could be bringing in much more. Armed with this and the other responses, he now decides to expand the factory trade aggressively. He first approaches Mr. John Amend, owner of the Racine Feet Knitting Factory in South Beloit. This factory makes only the feet of socks, which are then sent somewhere else for their tops.

"Yes," says Mr. Amend, "you can come in and sell to my knitters."

Daddy goes with Lester Stam the first day. They push a cart through the factory and explain to the women that they will be coming regularly. The knitters are delighted with a milk break in their morning, and many of them buy a half pint for a nickel. This is quite a profit, since the dairy is selling quarts for eight cents. That afternoon Daddy and Lester go into the office and empty nickels from their bulging pockets out onto the table. "Lester," says Daddy jubilantly as they count the money and roll it up in dusky-red

From a Dougan ad: the men are drinking pints of milk at their factory bench.

wrappers to go to the bank, "when we get our volume up to a hundred dollars a day, I'll take you out and get you drunk!" And since drinking is strictly forbidden to any employee of W.J. Dougan, he and Lester roar at the joke.

Daddy persuades Freeman's Shoe Factory and Mork's Foundry, both major manufacturers, to allow milk to be peddled. Other factories join in. In 1931 he runs an ad in the *Beloit Daily News*, "DOUGAN'S MILK IN BELOIT FACTORIES," with a photo of four overalled men with lunch buckets, eating near their machines, each with a pint bottle of milk — "Lunch Hour at the General Refrigeration Co." The copy reads, "Three years ago we made it possible for the employees in many Beloit factories to secure Dougan Guernsey products during working hours. Our drivers go through the factories every morning, selling milk to the men at their bench or in their office. At present the following factories are being supplied."

A full list follows: Beloit Iron Works is given pride of place, followed by General Refrigeration Company, Freeman Shoe Manufacturing Company, Gardner Machine Company, Warner Electric Brake Corporation, Beloit Box Board Company, Dowd Knife Works, Racine Feet Knitting Company, Gaston Scale Company, Beloit Daily News Publishing Company, Central Radio Corporation, Mork's Foundry, Wisconsin Power and Light Power Plant, Wisconsin Knife Works, Fish Rotary Oven Company.

The copy continues: "Milk is a man's food recommended by athletic coaches for their teams, and by doctors for men at heavy work. Because Dougan's Guernsey Milk is one-third higher in food value than the usual market milk it is an especially desirable food. Our factory sales have resulted in increased home retail stops. Men using the milk in the shops are anxious to furnish their families with this superior flavored Guernsey product."

That last is the lifesaving line. The milkmen are now meeting the men and women who have stable jobs, and the milkmen are friendly. They get to know their customers; after a while they suggest home delivery. Every time the business wins a new customer, or the monthly sales go up, everyone rejoices. And before long, Daddy has to add another home-delivery route, until from two routes at the start of the Depression, there are six by the end.

So it is during the terrible thirties that Daddy builds up the milk business. "We never did crack Fairbanks Morse," says Daddy. "But once we got into high gear in so many of the factories, I hardly realized the Depression was going on, either!"

11 ⋇ WHAT FARMERS NEED

On December 14, 1933, the *Beloit Daily News* prints a headline, on page 4, "DOUGAN SAYS LONG TERM CREDITS ARE BIGGEST FARM AID," and the subhead, "Says social and economic changes will bring more satisfactory future." The paper then reports in full the speech that W.J. has just given to the local Kiwanis Club:

> With adverse and favorable conditions as the items of his accounting, W.J. Dougan, Beloit farmer and dairyman, yesterday set up for the members of the Kiwanis Club a balance sheet of profits and losses accruing to the farmer in these days of difficulty.
>
> Then—spurning both the silly optimism and black despondency of the extremists—he predicted that sane and courageous thinking will at some not far distant date bring a better world for all of us than we have known in the past.
>
> Debits and Credits
>
> Among the unfavorable items in Mr. Dougan's balance sheet he listed produce surpluses, low prices, taxes, inadequate credits, and worse than all these, the spirit of rebellion which is developing in the farmer's mind—a rebellion which has made him mad at the farm, at business, at government, and at society in general.
>
> Whether from overproduction or underconsumption, the farm surpluses have brought prices so low that in many cases the entire produce of the farm is not enough to meet the fixed charges of taxes and mortgage interest, Mr. Dougan said, so that the farmer has nothing left with which to educate his children and to provide the decencies of satisfactory life. The lowering of the farmer's standard of living has hurt business and industry as a result.
>
> Especially does the farmer need adequate credit—long term credit on low rate of interest on a definite amortization plan—so that money borrowed in

flush times need not be repaid on short term demand in difficult times, when to pay is impossible and the loss of farms results, Mr. Dougan said.

The farmer needs a lifetime to develop his farm and to pay for it so he can pass it along to his children unencumbered and capable of making them a proper livelihood, the speaker said.

Especially serious, said Mr. Dougan, is the rebellious attitude which present difficulties have created — the spirit of hopelessness and indifference and antagonism.

Against these adverse items on the ledger sheet, Mr. Dougan placed such favorable items as the privilege of work, which he said is a "great safety valve," a good subsistence from the soil, safe investment (he said land is much more satisfactory than Insull stock), a public attitude that recognizes that the farmer must receive more for his produce and must be made self-sustaining, and the determined and conscientious effort of the government to be helpful to the farm industry.

Government Helps

Most helpful of all the government's efforts to aid the farmer is the attempt to create adequate long-term credits, Mr. Dougan said. The government alone can provide this, for under the present conditions no bank is able to make loans on long-term credits such as the farmer needs, said the speaker.

"The farmer doesn't need to call upon the public treasury for money that must come out of the public pocket, but he does need a credit structure planned for the long-term needs of farm life," Mr. Dougan said.

As for the future, Mr. Dougan said there will be tremendous changes in economic and social life. But if these changes are accompanied by sane thinking, courageous and cooperative effort, social conditions will not revert to an uncertain past but will bring about a vastly improved future, he declared.

"The farmer is the link between a hungry world and the inert soil. Let us make him contented and happy not by feeding him from the public treasury but by giving him an equal opportunity with every other group in our national life," urged Mr. Dougan.

That is Grampa's stance. No givaways, but solid government long-term credit to support the farmer through fair times and foul. This was forthcoming. Ron says, later, "Those farm loans saved us and all the farms on Colley Road! I'm still paying ours off, as slowly as I can."

12 ⚹ W. J. SCOLDS THE HELP

I t is 1936. The Depression is taking its toll. W.J. is investigating bankruptcy
procedures with his banker nephew, even as business is picking up in the
factories, and the Federal loan program is helping out. He practices econo-
mies, such as telling the Exact Weight Scale Company he prefers giving a
little extra butter to customers rather than purchase the expensive scale they
want to sell him so he can weigh it more precisely (though the scale company
protests, with figures, that this is a false economy). But it is in this climate
that he distributes the following letter, having to do with the milkhouse and
the business:

TO OUR EMPLOYEES:

January 27, 1936

I have been aware for some time that there is a tendency on the part of some
of our employees to take advantage of our leniency relative to the use of dairy
products and supplies. There are many incidents about the job that would
not be tolerated by any other employer.

I refer, among other things, to the help running to the milkhouse and
helping themselves to the best they can find, and all they want of it. The
practice of doping chocolate milk with cream, and slopping around the milkhouse in disregard to sanitary conditions and the convenience of the opera-
tors is illustrative.

In cooperation with the foreman of the milkroom, I have tried to correct
these abuses by notices, restrictions, personal talks, and even a lock on the ice
box. All these checks have been ignored. Not only is this spirit of help yourself to what you want incompatible with good management but also the way
in which it is done is objectionable. For example: Not long ago a man dipped
into the chocolate vat with the milk dipper, then immediately stuck the dipper into the whipping cream can without even rinsing it, in order to get his
swig of cream. This is sloppy work, and shows an ignorance and disregard of

sanitary methods, and disrespect for the whole job.

Another evidence of an entirely wrong attitude toward the job, is lamming of equipment and product in the milkhouse and ice box, and the rough handling of trucks. Men who have the interest of the business at heart handle company property with a consideration as great or even greater than they show toward their own.

I am not going to discharge anyone at present for these and similar examples of misconduct and attitude toward the job, nor am I going to endeavor to correct these practices by a

Earl Boun and Richard Husi, milkhouse workers and probable chocolate milk dopers.

lot of specific rules and regulations or by a lock and key or a bull dog to stand guard, but I am going to expect each man to conduct himself at all times as he would have me conduct myself if our positions were reversed. This same principle should govern in all of our relations between departments and workers.

I am writing this in all candor and am earnestly anxious that we may cooperate to make our job run smooth and strong and to maintain a high esteem of each other.

W.J. Dougan

Jackie, too young at the time, does not know of this letter, or whether it was effective. To her, running in and out daily, the milkhouse always seemed clean and on a predictable schedule. But seeing this missive later, she realizes that the problem of "doping" the chocolate milk with cream, at least, was never solved, though Grampa's words may have made the practice more sanitary. She and her sibs do it themselves, and every farm worker she talks to, including her own classmates who serve stints on the farm and in the milkhouse, mention it in glowing terms. Half-cream chocolate milk, all agree, is the ambrosia of the gods.

13 ⚔ MOM & POP GROCERS

I n the thirties, and before, and for quite a while after, before the ultimate takeover by the huge supermarkets, Beloit, like any other town in America, has small neighborhood groceries. A mother can send a child a block or two, a quarter clutched in hand, for a loaf of bread or bag of sugar. And for the local kids, the candy counter, often a sloping-fronted glass case in which all the tempting wares are displayed, is an endless fascination and frequent destination, especially if someone has a nickel. A husband, or a wife, or older children, tend the store. There are a few chain stores in the area — Krogers, the A&P, but these are not yet competition to drive local stores out of business. The local stores aren't all small — there are larger grocers downtown and here and there — the Crystal Food Store, the White Avenue Grocery. These are locally owned and run. Witte's. Kapitanoffs. A number of these will take your order over the phone, gather your groceries in a box, and deliver them — even into the country as far as the dairy. Witte's, the last grocer for home delivery, even comes as far out as Chez Nous, beyond the dairy.

The Dougan kids when small live too far from these stores, except when visiting town friends, or when they stop by with Daddy to drop off some milk. For during the Depression, and after, these small groceries become of vital importance to the dairy.

People are unable to pay their milk bills. They quit regular home delivery; when they need milk, they buy it from the downtown grocers, or from the neighborhood stores. Sometimes they go out into the country with a bucket, and buy unbottled milk from a farmer with a cow or two.

Daddy and Grampa quickly realize they need to stock the local grocers with Dougan's Milk. They have had a few store accounts in the 1920s, but now they go after all the stores, and with good success. One reason for this is their advertising — they run ads about the stores, giving their addresses, emphasizing their localness and convenience, and showing photos of the proprietors. This provides advertising for the stores as well as the dairy.

A Dougan ad combines some of the local grocers who are selling Dougan's milk.

Daddy usually writes the brief copy. The headline is usually, "Meet Dougan Dealer." There's no mention of hard times. Under a photo of a man behind a counter, "Pictured is John Spyreas, owner of Spyreas' Grocery Co, 1002 Pleasant Street, making a sale to a customer," is: "He doesn't have a milk wagon and a horse and he doesn't pack a milk bottle carrier, but just the same he's your Dougan Neighborhood Milk Man. John's store is open and selling lots of Dougan's milk when our trucks are off the street."

Jackie knows Mr. Spyreas. for his store is open on Sunday, only a few blocks from church, good for grabbing something essential that's been discovered missing for Sunday dinner. Mr. Spyreas is Greek, and he once pours some green leaves into Jackie's hand, which she mishears as "rigony," and carefully sniffs all the way home. It turns out to be oregano, a tasty herb she hasn't heretofore had in her spaghetti.

Almost all the ads point out that here is where you get your milk after the hours of regular truck delivery, and that the grocer is a milkman, too. Women aren't neglected—one even gets her own headline: "On The River Road It's Dougan Dealer Mrs. Irvin R. Buck," and she rates two photos. In one, Mrs. Buck stands beaming behind her counter. She is "proprietor of the busy little grocery store at Buck's Trailer Camp, 2120 Riverside Drive. Here she is pictured waiting on one of her camp customers." And we see, in the second photo, a welcoming figure holding open the "Camp Store" door to two small children.

Mrs. Doty doesn't get as thorough coverage, but her copy contains the essential information: "Doty's Grocery owned and operated by Mrs. Norman Doty at 2407 Riverside Drive serves the Beloit Trailer Camp and nearby area."

The other stores whose ads are pasted in the dairy scrapbook are Craddick's, of Craddick and Witte on West Grand, Witte's Market (farther toward the downtown than the other store), Frankland's at 3236 Riverside Drive, the Beloit Co-op Food Store with its manager, Chester Hammes, Joe Kapitanoff in front of one of his Crystal Food Stores, James Pipitone whose grocery is on State Street, Paul's Food Market on Euclid, owned and run by Paul Yeager, George Wolfe and his partner Arthur Gervais who operate the White Avenue Grocery, and Henry Wu. Salamone's, owned by Phil Salamone, on 412 East Grand, is the last local grocery to give up to the supermarkets, in 1970. There is much publicity and lamenting about its closing, but there's no way to save it. It's the way of small businesses, as the century moves on.

14 ⊰ SKIM MILK

I t's the Depression. Near the end of December, 1930, Grampa writes an article that is published in the *Beloit Daily News*. Its purport is that the farmer does not get proportionate value for the majority of his crops. He receives a letter from L.G. Burgess, of the South Beloit Fuel and Manufacturing Company, who agrees with him. Mr. Burgess goes on to say:

"We have realized for a long time there is entirely too great a difference between the retail price which the consumer pays for farm products, and the price the producer secures. There should be some readjustment so the consuming public could buy food products at considerable less while at the same time the producer should receive a larger proportion of the purchaser's money. Some day this will be undoubtedly worked out and our present method of inter-city distribution will be discarded."

He uses milk as an example. "The public today is paying more for the ordinary quality milk they are consuming than it is worth. In our personal opinion your milk is the only milk in this locality which is fit for human consumption but the cost per quart is entirely too much for the ordinary person to pay."

Mr. Burgess now confesses his family to be Dougan customers for a long time, "but we have never been able to afford the amount we would like to use and recently have seriously considered discontinuing it in favor of a poorer grade of milk on account of its price. We hesitate to do this because we feel milk plays an important part in growing children's diet." He says that the slackness of business and the necessary curtailment of expenses is driving them toward this decision, but since they do not care to give their children milk which they know is not clean, "we would purchase other milk for cooking purposes only. With these two views in mind, the thought came to us there might be some other way in which we could get together so we could still continue taking milk and you could continue to furnish it at a price you could afford. If this were worked out for our family, it might appeal to other families also."

The idea is, that "instead of getting one quart one day, two or three the next day, two or three times a week, couldn't we agree to purchase a gallon of milk each day say at 50 cents per gallon, and instead of having it delivered in quart bottles have you deliver it in a gallon container. It is immaterial to us whether the certified grade A label is on the milk or not so long as we get it from you and we are assured the milk is clean and of the same quality as Grade A milk and the same care and precautions taken in producing it. We do not drink the container, what we want is the milk."

Grampa takes this serious letter seriously, and with Ronald assisting they hew out a reply. It is in Grampa's voice:

Dear Mr. Burgess:

Your frank and interesting letter has been very carefully considered. When I think of the complex problems in our economic system, it sometimes bewilders me. In my own business, I have endeavored to produce and distribute economically and be just in giving fair compensation to my helpers and full value to my customers.

In reference to your statement that our milk is too high "for the ordinary person to pay," I could give you a long argument showing that this milk is an economical food as compared to other foods, even at present food prices. We are not yet aware what a large place the milk may take in a ration for the whole family. When a child, or adult either, is fed regularly on a wholesome milk, and it is used liberally in the cooking, he is not craving constantly the expensive luxuries and nicknacks.

I have considered very carefully your proposition to buy in larger quantities and in an open container at a reduced price. I must let you into my thinking and experience in this. First as a principle in my business I have held to one price to all. In business there is usually favor shown to the larger buyer and good payer. I have always felt that this message gives advantage to just the ones who need it least. We have well-to-do customers who are taking four to six quarts of milk a day besides cream in abundance. Now to make a cut on quantity and cash would give these, who can afford to pay, an advantage that would take the profits from the quart of milk a poor family has to have for the sick baby. I have been asked what I pay the doctors to prescribe my milk. As matter of fact, never has a doctor or an influential citizen received any favor in price or service over the humblest foreigner who takes my product for the well being of his children.

I know you suggest cutting the actual cost by using a cheaper container and seal. I have been asked before to do this, and in two or three cases have yielded in this way. You know we have developed a few of our neighbors to produce a high quality Guernsey milk for us which we use for separating for cream, and sell in the shops as whole milk in pint and half-pint bottles under the seal, "Dougan's Golden Guernsey Milk." We pay the farmers a premium for extra care in production, test the milk for bacteria every week, make regular inspections ourselves, and pay the American Guernsey Cattle Club a royalty on sales for furnishing us with their excellent inspection and for giving us the right to use their label. In two or three cases, I have delivered this milk in quantities of four to six quarts at a slight reduction where the parties were forced to go on a milk diet for a brief period and did not feel it possible to purchase so much milk at the regular price. These few cases were only temporary, and could not be continued as a policy, and did not prove very satisfactory.

There is also a real difficulty in trying to cheapen cost of container. There is a city regulation forbidding this practice, and we ourselves realize it is extremely difficult to handle milk in this way, and have it approach the quality of that bottled and sealed automatically, and only opened when needed for use.

I appreciate your confidence in me to produce and sell the Grade A quality without the seal and the guarantee of quality it carries from State, County, and the Guernsey Cattle Club. However, strangers in the town and many who do not know me need this assurance. Most dealers will make the claim their milk is the best to be had. I feel, with our enlarging community, this seal is essential to standard quality.

I feel I am extending this letter to an undue length without fully answering your questions. I appreciate the pinch in which all business men find themselves at this time, and feel we should each do all within our power to help the others to carry on. I know that in your letter you had no thought of soliciting trade or putting up a hard luck story. However, my sister, Mrs. Croft, and my herdsman, Mr. Mathews, have spoken to me regarding your excellent services and high quality of products. While I have been quite given to trade exclusively with one firm, I realize you merit a share of my purchases in the fuel line, and you may expect me to give you some orders.

We prize your opinion of our product and covet the privilege of continuing the supply to your family. However, I want you to know you will ever be held in high esteem whether or not you have to change your milk supply.

I wish to make a suggestion that may be of help to you in lessening your milk cost, and getting even a larger food value. We know that skim milk contains all of the solids of whole milk except fat. It is in these solids we find the protein which is the necessary and costly element in all animal food. The skim milk carries carbohydrates, minerals, and to a great extent the vitamins.

For cooking and adult drinking this is a valuable food. I have in the past regularly bottled skim milk, but to my surprise the housewives shy at it and some become really offended at the suggestion.

I am going to send you a bottle a day for a few days. If you like it, we will price it exceedingly low. This milk is "Dougan's Golden Guernsey Milk," separated. The driver will start leaving it Friday morning.

I am particularly anxious to hear your reaction to this use of skim milk, for if we deem it advisable, we shall advertise it to our customers. We have a number of them who use our milk for drinking, and the commercial milk for cooking. If we could supply them with a skim milk at a saving to them it would be to the advantage of both.

Sincerely,

W.J. Dougan

Jackie comes across these letters, and finds the exchange remarkable in a number of ways. Burgess, a businessman like Grampa, with both caught in the Depression, has taken the time to study Grampa's article, see how it involves himself, and has written a serious letter, taking W.J. into his confidence. He's offered a suggestion. W.J. in turn has studied Burgess's letter and replied with a serious one of his own, where in turn he takes Burgess into his confidence about the problems of his business, and Mr. Burgess's suggestion. There is courtesy and respect on both sides. How many letters of this sort, written in this way, would be exchanged today? They reveal a customer relationship that is close to extinct.

Furthermore, Grampa's letter is really more than to Burgess; it's a letter to the world, stating his philosophy on pricing: and it's exactly opposite the usual one of dropping the price to big buyers and payers. He takes the initiative in saying he's violated this principle on a few occasions, gives the reasons, but states he has not made this policy.

He also assures Mr. Burgess that he's given no favors to doctors who endorse his milk, nor have any ever asked him to. And he explains why Mr. Burgess's suggestion of the open and unmarked container is not feasible, both economically and politically.

Another point Jackie understands well. It may sound suspicious to the reader, that Grampa is offering to patronize Mr. Burgess's business, the implication being it will be good for the South Beloit Fuel and Manufacturing Company if it continues taking milk. But the farm policy has always been to give its business to its customers when it can. That's why Joan and Patsy have Dr. Idhe as their dentist, while Jackie and Craig go to Dr. McCaul. Both dentists take Dougan's milk.

Finally, at the end, Grampa comes up with a counter suggestion. Skim milk is underrated in food value. Grampa knows, but doesn't mention, that housewives shy from it because they think of skim as pig food. But Dougan skim is as good as Dougan Grade A, with all the valuable solids, and practically all the vitamins. It is simply minus the fat. If the Burgess family were to use inexpensive skim in their cooking and adult drinking, and Grade A exclusively for children's drinking, they could take more milk yet cut their milk bill considerably. He says he'll leave skim, gratis, for several days, and will appreciate Mr. Burgess's assessment. If this is something that will help the Burgess family in these difficult times, then W.J. might advertise to other customers in difficulty, and many families might be helped with their milk bills. This honest enlisting of Mr. Burgess's aid must certainly have taken the sting out of Grampa's rejecting the open gallon proposal.

All in all, it's a masterpiece of a letter. Later on, Jackie knows, one of the dairy's staples becomes skim, or "fat free" milk. The gain to human drinkers is of course a loss to the pigs, but that's a subject Grampa doesn't mention. The pigs will continue to be fed adequately in other ways, and no doubt there will still be plenty of skim left for them at the end of the day.

Pigs in the milk trough, milk in the pig trough.

It is somewhat later that Jackie, to her delight, comes across a third letter, one that rounds out the story, at least for 1931. It's Mr. Burgess's response to Grampa's skim milk offer. He says his family has been using the skim milk and has found it entirely satisfactory for cooking and adult drinking. That they've been taking one bottle of Grade A which their five-year-old drinks, with cream poured off for his wife's coffee. That he and his older boys thus don't see much difference in their habits, since the drink they had before was mostly skim — they are now just drinking much more of it. He thinks, since the milk is sanitary and the price right, there should be a ready market for it, and that Dougan's may continue to deliver four quarts of skim milk daily until further notice. He thanks W.J. for his cooperation in helping them cut down on their milk bill while still giving them the amount of milk they want to drink.

And then he comes up with another suggestion. He's mindful, from Grampa's letter and perhaps from other sources, that there is a prejudice against skim milk. He writes, "If you feel you might have difficulty with the public in general marketing your milk under the name of skim milk, why not create a new market name calling your milk 'Prepared Milk' and add a very small percentage of cream to the skim, charging a slightly higher price?" He finishes by saying his name may be used as a recommendation.

This suggestion pinpoints the problem of marketing skim milk. Grampa and Daddy do not prepare their milk, but continue with skim. Despite its low price, it doesn't catch on. The business grows during the Depression years mainly through factory, school, and hospital sales of regular and blended milk.

Fast forward, though, almost 20 years. Daddy sends all area doctors and dentists a letter:

> September, 1950. It has come to us as something of a surprise that there is a steady demand for milk with fat removed. We are finding more and more call for this product for infants — particularly premature infants and others with a low fat tolerance. Expectant mothers frequently have told us, "my doctor said I should drink skimmed milk." Similar comments often are heard from those many persons who suffer from digestive disturbances and fat allergies. A number of people past middle age also have quit milk, because they believe that shutting out the butterfat is one of the first steps they should take in keeping their weight down.
>
> For these and other medical reasons that have come to our attention, we recently introduced a new milk product. This is our Grade A Fat Free Milk with 400 Vitamin D units and 2000 Vitamin A U.S.P. units added per quart. We are also adding 2% milk solids not fat.
>
> Thus for those persons who find milk objectionable, we can provide Fat Free Milk with whole milk's high, summer, Vitamin A in each quart, but standardized on a year round basis. As you know, the 400 D units are essen-

tial to assure efficient retention and utilization of skim milk's high calcium and phosphorus content.

Daddy follows this up six months later: "Because of the nice reception our new Vitamin A and D fortified Fat Free Milk has received, and because we feel that Beloit doctors, dentists, and others interested in dietary problems are in a good way responsible for its growing acceptance, we'd like to thank you." He lists the sorts of folk who are using it, and "since most of our Fat Free Milk drinkers are nutrition conscious and seek the advice of their physicians before dieting, we like to regularly inform the doctors in our trading area of the progress of this new product." He includes a card that compares the nutritional values for Low Fat, High Protein Diets as compared to whole milk and skim.

But government regulations have stepped in at about this same time. Wisconsin's Department of Agriculture is demanding that fortified products be tested several times a year (at $30 an assay) to be sure that the fortification indicated on the label is in fact happening. "If you are fortifying milk, skim milk, or homogenized milk, buttermilk, etc., please list each type of product which is being fortified." Daddy is upset. He's been adding vitamins A and D to his Homogenized, Guernsey, Skim, and Chocolate. In a February 1951 letter to the Wisconsin Alumni Research Foundation, he says, "It appears the Department will require bio-assays on each fortified product. The whole regulation seems silly to me. If they are going to police each producer on every product, I should think it would be necessary to take a sample of every vat of milk on any particular day the check is made. For instance, we run three vats of Homogenized Milk. The fact that one vat is satisfactory doesn't mean that the other two have not been neglected."

He writes the supplier of his fortified chocolate powder; if the powder can't be cleared at the source, he will take a cheaper non-fortified powder. The company's response is that he will have to have assays on his finished product no matter what powder he uses.

In March, Daddy takes matters into his own hands. He goes to Madison, has lunch with legislators, explains the problems of labeling and assaying. He writes to the head of the Department of Markets, "Mr. Madler drafted an addition to the present definition of skim milk to allow a milk product containing a minimum of $8\frac{1}{2}$ percent solids not fat and under six one-hundredth percent butterfat to be labeled 'fat free.' I had lunch with Mr. Enlebretson and Dr. Rice and have their blessing. Englebretson is going to take it up with Mr. Pritchard, chairman of the agricultural committee, and then shove it

An ad designed to put a positive cast on skim milk.

right along." He also talks of the problems of the labeling and testing of his fortified products, which he has written to others about before.

Letters fly back and forth on the proposed bill, General Order 132. Daddy writes his friend, Howard Greene at Genesee Depot, owner of Brook Hill farm; Howard says he was the originator of selling fat-free milk in the Chicago market. "A physician asked us to prepare a case a day for a certain hospital and from this small beginning we developed quite a big business, particularly when homogenized milk came on the market and it was so difficult to get milk where the fat could be separated." He goes on, "At present many state laws require this product to be labeled skim or skimmed milk. This is unfortunate from a merchandising point of view as skim milk has popularly been thought of as food for hogs. Recent scientific work has shown that a great part of the value of milk is in non-fat solids, vitamins and enzymes carried by the fat-free milk." His letter contains more about laws and butterfat percentages, and finishes, "In these days when we're doing everything possible to stimulate the use of milk in all forms, it looks to me like our state, where milk is such a valuable farm product, should give every encouragement to the sale of dairy products." He advocates the law be changed to allow "non-fat solids," for the dry solids of skim milk, and "fat-free" for the actual milk, and commends Daddy for the effort he is putting into the bill.

In June of 1951 the bill comes before the Wisconsin legislature that would permit the use of "Fat Free" instead of skim. While this is a win, Daddy and the producers lose in their fight to cut down the numbers and costs of the bio-assays on all their fortified products. Daddy drops the fortification on his Guernsey and chocolate milks. He also has to change all his bottle caps to include exactly what is in the product he is selling.

In August a newsletter, *The Milk Dealer*, runs an article about a study by two UW professors, who conclude that it is feasible to process a fortified-modified skim milk—as Daddy has been doing—that is nutritious, economical, and delicious. It does not suggest naming or bring up testing.

Daddy does not forget his doctors. The following spring, in 1952, he writes to them individually:

> Under separate cover I am sending you the March issue of *Certified Milk Magazine*. The leading article discusses the wide acceptance of Fat Free milk by the medical profession. And in this letter I am enclosing a card giving the approximate nutritive value of our vitaminn A and D Fat Free milk as it is reinforced with 2% solids not fat.
>
> Since writing Beloit doctors some time ago we have been gratified by the growing popularity of our Fat Free milk. Recently we called many of our customers and found that in most cases the milk was being used by some member of the family by advice of the family doctor.
>
> This letter is to thank you for remembering us and to assure you that we plan to continue to supply a uniform quality, palatable Fat Free milk.

And so the skim milk battle is won, not to every dealer's complete satisfaction. But it allows the product to come down to this day with varying names, with the hog-food stigma fading into non-existence. Fortified "Fat Free" becomes a staple in the Dougan offerings, till Daddy retires from the milk business in 1967, when the Burgess children are grown and still buying a gallon of skim a day, for themselves and the Burgess grandchildren.

15 ⨯ RONALD AMOS

A salesman is in the dairy office. He's trying to get Daddy to buy some advertising in a book his company is getting out. It's a big book and comes in two colors: blue and pink.

"It's called *Our Baby*," he says, and flips the pages, pages blank except for titles and flowery decorated borders: "Baby's Birth," "Baby's Christening," "Baby's First Tooth," "Baby's First Words," "Baby's Likes and Dislikes," "Baby's Family Tree," "Baby's Inoculations."

Then he displays the pages of advertising, ads from another community where the book has been produced. There are ads for baby food, baby clothing, baby furniture, baby toys, soaps, soft water service, milk.

"You see," says the salesman enthusiastically, "we'll distribute this attractive and prized book free, to every mother who has a baby at the Beloit Hospital. Just think how your advertising will reach the precise market—the entire market—for which it's intended. 'The Babies' Milkman!'"

Daddy listens, doodling his name and little faces on a sheet of paper.

"And you'll notice," the salesman adds earnestly, "we allow only one ad for each commodity. One grocery store, one clothing store, one dairy, and so on. We choose the very best product of each sort in any given community, and advertise that one exclusively. No siree, you won't have any competition in our book. No Wright & Wagner's milk, no Hillendale. We're coming to you first. It'll be just Dougan's Dairy, the Babies' Milkman. Your page will go right here—across from 'Baby's First Foods.'"

Daddy doodles some more.

The salesman leans forward confidentially. "And Mr. Dougan, I want to tell you this book is exclusive in another way. We aren't permitting certain firms to advertise, much as they might want to. We're advertising only the... the clean products..." His voice lowers still further till it is almost a whisper, because Daddy doesn't seem to see the light. "You understand..."

"Clean?" asks Daddy.

"You know...no—" he whispers, "—Jews."

Daddy goes on doodling. With his pencil he finishes the last daisy in a string of daisy-faces surrounding his name. Then he pushes the paper toward the salesman. "Can you read that?" he asks.

"Why, yes, Mr. Dougan," says the salesman, surprised. "It's your name, 'R.A. Dougan'."

"Do you know what the 'R' stands for?" Daddy asks.

The salesman hesitates. "It's for—'Ronald'?"

"Yes. And do you know what the 'A' stands for?"

"Why no—can't say as I do."

"Amos," says Daddy. "And my father, W.J.—his middle name is Jacob." He stands up. "I'm afraid we wouldn't be permitted to advertise in your book."

The salesman grabs up his wares and scuttles out.

Later Daddy tells Mother the incident. "I think I was fibbing only about the names," he says. "You only have to look at Uncle Bert, and all those fine, sharp Trever noses, to figure that somewhere along the line a bull that wasn't Guernsey jumped the fence into the pasture."

For a moment he contemplates Uncle Bert—Dr. Albert Augustus Trever, head of the History Department at Lawrence College and author of the standard ancient history textbook in the field; he contemplates Uncle George, The Reverend Dr. George Trever, former president of a theological seminary in spite of his bad judgment about pecan groves. He contemplates his cousin Dr. George Mortimer, a respected agronomy professor up at Madison; George's mother was a Trever. He contemplates his cousin, Karl Trever, to whom he was always compared, growing up ("Why can't you be like Karl?") and who is now head of some department or other at the Library of Congress. He contemplates his own sharp-witted mother, Eunice Trever Dougan, and his favorite and even sharper-witted aunt, Ria Trever Fadner.

"And I think," he adds, "that having that bull—that outcrossing—was a very lucky break for all us Celtic Trevers!"

16 ⚔ DEAR BLAINE

One evening in 1932 Ronald is with Vera at an orchestra concert in the Fairbanks Morse auditorium. He's tired from having been up very early, battling the drifts of a March storm that dumped eight inches on the spring landscape in as many hours. He had to help the drivers get out on their routes, and help fetch the producers' milk from outlying farms to the dairy. His mind has wandered to the business, and to the talk he had recently with his friend Blaine Hanson. Blaine runs a ripsnorting newspaper, the *Beloit Daily Independent*, in competition with the more placid *Beloit Daily News*. Blaine, himself a ripsnorter, is fighting for survival. He thinks that Ron should help out the newspaper in these hard times, and Dougan's Dairy along with it, by running ads. Ron agrees, but he doesn't want to repeat his *Daily News* ads in the *Independent*. The *Independent* can take a more radical type ad.

He begins talking to Blaine in his mind, first about the newspaper business and then about the milk business, specifically the day he's just put in. He's so entertained by the monologue he's concocting that he gives a little laugh during a solemn part of the Brahms, and Vera looks at him askance. He lapses into silence but with a smile on his face. After a bit he takes out a pen and writes his first "Dear Blaine" ad on the program. At the intermission he reads it to Vera:

> March 24, 1932
> Dear Blaine:
>   A big storm like we had this week makes me feel great. I like to buck a tough day. Tuesday morning at three o'clock we started out with men and horses to get the milk through. Trucks wasn't worth nothin' in them drifts till we got the road broke.
>   A job like the milk business is what you might call a steadyin' interest in a man's life. Rain or shine, there is hundreds of babies waitin' for their milk,

and we is the guys to get it to 'em on time.

Your Dougan Driver.

P.S.—THERE IS MORE BABIES EVERY DAY WHAT DEPENDS ON DOUGAN DRIVERS. THE PRICE IS 10 CENTS FOR BLENDED MILK AND 14¼ CENTS FOR WISCONSIN GRADE-A RAW GUERN-SEY MILK.—D.D.

Vera laughs, but isn't convinced of its ad-worthiness. "*We is the guys!*" she exclaims. "Your drivers don't talk like that, they're all educated. You make them sound like illiterate hayseeds! What impression will you make on customers with 'Trucks wasn't worth nothin' in them drifts'?"

"They wasn't!" Ron protests. "Not until the teams broke out the track. Besides," he adds, "who's one of the sharpest and cleverest men around, whose every word is lapped up? Will Rogers, that's who, and if Will Rogers can do it, Ron Dougan can, too."

Vera shakes her head. "Let's hope Ron Dougan gets as rich and famous as Will Rogers! We wouldn't need any ads, then."

When W.J. sees the ad he shakes his head too, but also laughs. Blaine Hanson, however, has no reservations in his delight. He's even more enthusiastic over the next one, which rings in politics:

Dear Blaine:

I gets a laugh out of Pres. Hoover's "mobilization of the hoarded dollar." Maybe them big guys is right about folks hiding their shekels in a sock, but that ain't you and me, Blaine. Must be a coupla' other birds. Most of mine is doled out before I sees it. Here we have been married 8 yrs., and all we got is a bunch of kids to show for it. I suppose if it wasn't for them kids, we'd have money to hoard, but I'm tellin' you we wouldn't swap the naughtiest one for all the dough they say is hoarded west of Pittsburg.

Speakin' of kids, ain't it wonderful what good milk, fresh air, and sleep will do for 'em.

Your Dougan Driver.

P.S.—More folks is realizing every day that they makes their Depression dollar go farther by buying our good milk. Grade A costs 14-½ cents, and Blend is a great bargain at a dime.—D.D.

The *Independent*, of course, runs the ads. Blaine is happy with them, Ron is happy with them, and the public is entertained. Over the next two years Ron has fun with the homespun Dougan Driver, who is really himself:

Dear Blaine:

Does you know why us guys is called drivers? Years ago I chauffers Maud and Mollie. They was fine. They even pulls me through the bog what was Keeler Ave. when the mud is up to the hubs on my yellow wagon.

Then the boss thinks mules is the nuts, 'n he gives me Jack 'n Jill. My, My! The only trouble is you can't never tell what mules is thinkin', if anything. Mothers keeps their little kids off the streets, 'n the bigger ones climb trees to see me ra're by.

Runaways is all in the day's business. When they leaves me on Broad street, and I finds 'em straddlin' a post belongin' to the Utility Co. (you know who I mean, Blaine) up by Wright school, the boss gives up. Darned if he don't give me a Ford, and I has timer trouble.

Life is like that.

Your Dougan Driver.

P. S.—Times change, but the quality of our milk don't. You oughta hear folks rave about our Grade A Golden Guernsey at 14c. Then the way they takes to our Blend Milk at 10c is nobody's business.

D. D.

While Ronald's ads are heavy on humor, they follow W.J.'s in educating the public about various aspects of the business, and of the times:

DEAR BLAINE:

I GIVE THE BOSS A GOOD TIME THE OTHER DAY WHEN I TAKES HIM ALONG ON MY TRUCK AND SHOWS HIM JUST HOW FAST I RUNS TO SEE ALL MY FOLKS, BEFORE NOON.

YOUR FRIEND,
THE DOUGAN DRIVER.

P.S.—Tell your publix to phone the DOUGAN GUERNSEY FARM for

some of that good ten cent milk, or if the Depression ain't hit 'em too hard, they might treat themselves to the Grade A. Since the boss lowered the price more folks is taking advantage of it. See you tomorrow, D.D.

The Depression sinks the *Beloit Daily Independent* in 1934. The *Daily News* swallows it up and takes Blaine Hanson on as a proofreader. Ron misses the "Dear Blaine" ads, and Blaine's sympathetic ear. He finds himself writing personal notes to Blaine at the *Daily News*, in the "Dear Blaine" format, deploring the Depression practice of taking containers to "milk stations," or out into the country, to buy the cheapest possible milk from anybody's untested cow and anybody's unsupervised milking:

January 14, 1936
Dear Blaine,

When the boss started selling milk in this man's town, you was skippin' school over at Hackett. I was the only member of the first grade in old District #12, and felt pretty big when the first grade was told to stand up to recite.

Yes Sir, we has been sellin' milk for 26 years, and the boss says he ain't goin' to sacrifice his reputation for quality, earned by that quarter century, for any depression. If folks want to run around with a bucket after this here station milk, it's O.K. Some day they will be wantin' a supervised milk of established quality and that's where we come in.

Your Dougan Driver.

P.S.—You'd be surprised how much we are sellin' though. It's pretty hard to find a block where we ain't got one or more customers for either Grade A @ 14 1/2 cents or Blend @ 10 cents.

January 15, 1936
Dear Blaine:

I see you is still buyin' milk in bottles, but they tells me lots of folks is drivin' out in the country, when if the container ain't clean, it is their own fault. Course, it ain't nobody's business the shape the cows is in that gives the milk, nor the barns, 'cause it's cold weather now and milk is milk, they says.

Depression or no depression, the boss says he ain't sacrificing his reputation for quality for nothin'.

Sorta Steamed Up,
Your Dougan Driver.

Ron also continues commentary on local events dear to Blaine's heart, such as Blaine running yet again for city office, with only a snowball's chance of winning:

Dear Blaine:

I see you is steamin' up the old political calliope for the spring ruckus.

Maybe I ain't public spirited, but I just as soon mix up in the Shanghai mess as get put up for office. I been tellin' my wife what a good guy she married for so long, I'd hate to let you boys take pot shots at me. Offhand, I don't know what you could hang on me, but I gives you birds credit for ideas.

Ya' know, the City oughta give a Service Medal. It takes a brave man to lay himself open like that. A palm could be added for every time he runs, like the French do.

Election or no election, I got to sell milk, and boy am I doin' it. Folks appreciate a fine tastin' milk for 10 cents, and that's what I got.

Your Dougan Driver.

P.S. Say, this milk is FRESH! Last night's milk for breakfast, and this morning's milk on your table for lunch! Beat that, fella! D.D.

Blaine always enjoys Ron's letters, and remembers the ads with fondness. So does Ron. "Them ads sold milk," he says when he meets Blaine around town.

"Dern tootin' they did," agrees Blaine.

17 ❧ THE SHOE FACTORY

It's Jackie's ninth birthday. Her present is to go through the Freeman Shoe Factory with the milkman. This is something she's been longing to do ever since she discovered there was such a factory in Beloit.

It's a school day, but Daddy and Mother agree that anyone who requests such an educational present deserves to miss a morning of school. "Tell us what you've learned tonight," says Daddy, "and if there's any trouble, I'll go see your teacher personally."

Now Jackie follows Howard Milner from the loading platform into the factory. He has a wheeled cart that's low to the floor, piled high with milk cases. There are half pints of white milk, chocolate milk, and orange drink, as well as a few cases of white milk pints.

The first room is big as a barn. It's the cutting room, Howard explains. Jackie marvels. Here are the cowhides that are going to be made into shoes, all piled up like rugs in a furniture store. Howard introduces her to a foreman and he tells her that the hides have already been tanned and dyed, somewhere else.

When the workmen buy milk, they josh about Jackie. "We have a new milkman!" "Better watch out, Howard, she'll take your job away from you!" "That your best girl, Howard?"

Howard grins. "She is for today!" He seems to know all the men. "She wants to know what you do here."

The men show her how the preliminary cutting is done. They give her scraps so that she has pieces of all hues to take home with her—browns, blacks, tans, beiges, even reds.

Then she follows into an even larger room. Noise hits her ears like a blow: clacking, stamping, crunching, clunking. The room is filled with machines in long rows with aisles between them. There are men standing at the machines. Jackie trots behind Howard and the cart, and the workers pause, buy milk, and make remarks.

"What a pretty little milkmaid we have today!"

"What'll you take for her, Howard?"

Jackie doesn't mind the joking. She's fascinated with the machines. She lingers, watching a man stamp out sole after sole, like a giant cookie cutter. The next man is stamping out soles, too, of a different size and color. She wanders slowly down the aisles, staring at first one machine and then the next. Each machine does just one thing, often the next step of the machine before. She tries to follow the progress of a shoe.

At one machine she's startled to see a man from her church. Of course people at church must have jobs during the week, but this has never occurred to her before. Here is redheaded Mr. Harris, in work clothes, running a press! He recognizes her and grins, but there's no opportunity to speak, over the din.

Jackie watches. He puts a flat piece of black leather over a rounded form, clamps it, takes a brush from a pot and smears the leather with liquid, reaches overhead for a lever and hauls down the upper part of the machine. With a crunch it stamps into the leather. He holds it in place several seconds, while steam hisses from the juncture. Then he releases it. The leather beneath has become a permanently rounded shiny toe. He tosses it into a bin beside the machine with other identical toes, takes a fresh piece of leather the same shape as the first, fits it on the form, wets it, and stamps again. Jackie watches him steam the second toe, and a third and fourth, before she trots to catch up with the milkman.

She travels by fits and starts through the factory. They take a large service-type elevator, and as they ride up Howard tells her that the shoe factory milk-man before him, Don Stevens, had a temper. The men would tease him. He'd come back to where he'd left his cart and it would be hidden. Or they'd have smeared the handles with rubber cement, just to see him get mad. "But I josh around with them all," Howard says as the elevator door opens, "and they don't mess with me!"

They come into a room where it seems a thousand sewing machines are whirring. Jackie watches one woman sew a heel seam, and another heel seam, and another heel seam, over and over and over; the woman next to her takes the work and adds the next seam, over and over and over. The women glance up and smile but their flashing hands never miss a motion. She watches uppers stitched to soles, heels fastened and trimmed, lacing eyelets stamped in place. She sees the progress of a shoe, not always quite in order, but from beginning to end. She's absorbed and fascinated. The only problem is, she wants to stand and watch all day, while Howard keeps moving ahead too quickly

Jackie when she went through the shoe factory with Howard Milner.

with his cart and milk bottles.

When he's finished peddling he drops Jackie back at Todd School. She thinks about the shoe factory all afternoon. It was as interesting as she thought it would be. But something bothers her about the experience. She tries to figure out what it is.

At supper Mother says, "Well, tell all of us what you've learned."

"I learned how a shoe is made," says Jackie, and spends much of the meal describing with enthusiasm the huge rooms, the hides, the leather pieces moving along and becoming more and more shoelike as they go. Her voice is more tentative when she tells about Mr. Harris stamping out his toe, and the rows of women at their sewing machines, each stitching one seam over and over, over and over, all day long, every day all week, all month, all year.

"That's called mass production," says Joan. "That's the way factories run."

"The cobbler in the fairy tale, the one the elves helped, he'd make a shoe from beginning to end," says Jackie. "It was all his, like when I draw a picture I don't do one line and let somebody else do the next one."

"But he didn't make very many shoes, that way," says Patsy. "That was the trouble."

"We mass produce, too," Joan goes on. "The hired men, there's always the haying, and they milk the cows over and over, every day, and in the milkhouse the bottling is just like an assembly line, and the milkmen deliver the milk to the same old houses. It's just the same."

Jackie shakes her head vehemently. "It's not the same at all! The cows are fed, and then they're milked, and then they're stripped, and the barn is cleaned—the job's the *same*, but there's so much more *to* it, it keeps it in-

Howard Milner, at the time he took Jackie through the shoe factory.

teresting. And in the milkhouse they bottle the quarts, and then the pints, and then the half pints, and then the chocolate milk, and they wash the bottles and make butter and cheese—one man doesn't just stand there stamping caps on bottles all day, and that's all he does. And on the route, you're moving around town, and seeing people, and meeting dogs, and—and—well, going through shoe factories."

"And out in the field," adds Daddy, "the hay is only a little part of it. There's plowing and planting and cultivating, and worrying about the weather—"

Jackie nods. "The shoe factory was interesting because I wanted to see how shoes are made, and I went through with the milkman and saw the whole thing. But if I had to stay in one spot all day, indoors, sewing up one little thing, and not being able to talk to anyone on account of how noisy it is—I don't think I could stand it!"

"Unfortunately, a lot of jobs are tedious," says Daddy, "and a lot of people have to work at them whether they like them or not. But I must say I agree with Jackie. I often thank my lucky stars that I'm a farmer."

Jackie takes her last bite of birthday cake. "Me, too," she says.

18 ⊰ SNOW

After a spate of more-than-average snowstorms in January of 1936 there comes one of such proportions that after the worst is over, Grampa sits at his desk and writes an essay, which he sends off to the *Beloit Daily News*:

SOME HEROES OF PEACE TIME

When I was a boy I was thrilled by the stories of heroes of war time. Outstanding in my memory is the story of Washington crossing the Delaware. How men could face such hardships amazed me. In the course of my experience I have witnessed many heroic incidents not the least of these being in connection with the humble duty of getting the quart of milk to the consumer's door regardless of obstacles. There was a group of heroes about every milk plant serving the homes of the cities in the path of the recent blizzard.

The scenes about the Dougan plant were typical of the many. Our question was, "Can the milk get through to the plant and from the plant to the consumer?" Our answer was, "It must get through."—and this answer was a deep conviction in the mind and purpose of everyone connected with the business.

The farmers said, "We will get through," and immediately put their promise into action. Far into the night Saturday a group of farmers and employees of the plant struggled through the drifts with their teams and sleighs, and delivered the evening's milk to the plant, that the delivery trucks might be supplied early Sunday morning. At 3 A.M. the delivery men and helpers faced the cutting wind, met and mastered the mountainous drifts, and greeted their customers with a smile and a bottle of milk, almost on time. One delivery man took a case of milk on a hand sleigh a half mile through blocked streets in an outlying section, that his customers might be served.

The problem of the farmers getting their milk through Sunday was increasingly difficult. One group got together with bobsleigh and team. They fought the elements for hours, but finally were compelled to turn back. To quit? Never! Only to get reinforcements and to try another flank. And they got their milk through! See the picture. Seven men, two teams; slowly toiling over and through drifts along an impassable highway. They turn into fields and across lots; men with shovels preceding the teams, breaking the hard crust on the deepest banks, cutting wire fences, shoveling through drifts. The horses tugging, plodding, floundering, falling, only to arise and try again — the men muffled in all sorts of uniforms, their faces seared with the cold, but with their spirits high and determination to get through firm. As this group approached the milk plant another group with a four horse team tugging a full bobsleigh load, appeared from another direction, having gone through a like experience. A warm supper of hot soup, coffee, doughnuts, and sandwiches cheered the men after their long fight. The milk had gotten through to the plant.

All during the night the plant force with equal determination and high spirit attacked their belated job of properly handling and bottling the supply for morning delivery. Again the faithful delivery men and helpers battled the drifts, met the elements, and the finished product was placed at the consumer's door almost on time.

Heroes these as truly as any lauded knight of old or heroes in the glare of publicity and the favor of public acclaim.

Phil Holmes is one of those heroes trying to get the milk through. He's in high school, and when Clay Davis arrives to fetch the Holmes milk, his own milk already on a bobsled, Phil joins him. They load milk at Wellers and head for the Higgins farm. They can't see the road or even the horses in front of them; the snow is absolutely blinding. But when the bobsled comes to a standstill they get off to see the problem. They are up to their waists in snow, the horses up to their bellies. There is no going forward, or even turning around. They unload the milk cans into the snow, unhitch the horses and turn them separately, drag the sled around behind them and rehitch and reload. They then retrace their path home. Around noon they rally forces and try again, this time with two bobsleds. There is no way through to the town of Clinton, so they gather not only the milk for Dougan's, but the milk from Turtle that should be processed in Clinton. Men on foot break a trail with a team and empty bobsled, then the other team and the laden bobsled follow behind. They cut down to the State Line Road. Phil is one of the ones floundering ahead of the first team; he holds his scoop shovel up by the side of his

The farm often had to grapple with heavy snows. Here you see the Big House, side barn, round barn and milkhouse in a snowy season.

head to keep the wind off. When they are nearly opposite the dairy they cut across the fields. They arrive about four in the afternoon, in time to meet Ron Dougan and a group coming up from the southwest, and Fred Wallace and a crew from the north. The milkhouse workers pour out of the Big House to process and bottle the milk, while the bobsledders drag into the Big House for warmth and the hot meal that Grama has prepared, before battling the weather to get home.

There are other storm-based events which don't make it into Grampa's account. One of these concerns Tom Higgins. Tom sells his milk to Dougan's; he's a producer farmer. He and the other producers who live beyond the Hill Farm regularly bring their milk cans only that far, very early in the morning. Then Roy Veihman, a route man who lives on the lower floor of the Hill Farm house, carries them the three miles on to the main farm. He also makes a trip back home to collect the afternoon milk.

On the Monday after the storm, with the roads still impassable, Tom Higgins brings his milk by bobsled on a path that goes through a woods and over the fields to the drop point. It's an arduous and icy trek and takes him till midmorning. He's scarlet-nosed and covered with snow. As he turns his team to head home, he sees Fannie Veihman waving from the Hill Farm porch. "Tom! Coffee!"

Gratefully Tom brings his team into the drifted yard. Roy and Fannie are friends, active in the Grange; Tom's sons are in Roy's County Y group. The Veihmans are a popular and hospitable couple and their kitchen is always

Colley Road has been plowed. A milkman's baby, Craig Dougan, surveys the snow.

full of visitors. They know all the gossip.

Tom stamps the snow off his boots and leaves them just inside the door. He unwinds his caked muffler, pulls off his mittens and coat. Fannie drapes the garments on a rack and edges it as close to the stove as she dares. Tom settles with a sigh into a sag-bottomed easy chair and stretches his legs out to the warmth till his toes are nearly touching. He cups his hands around a mug of coffee. Its steam coils up to wreath and war with the steam from his barnyard woolens.

Fannie has kept the pot hot all the difficult weekend, and has been the recipient of stories from others who sought respite in the kitchen. She has heard Roy's tales of the dairy and the routes. Tom, coming from the other direction, knows the news from his place all the way to Clinton. The two keep each other entertained as the wind sings around the door and flings handfuls of snow against the windows. Tom's cup is refilled many times. Fannie notices that it is noon, and makes her guest a sandwich to fortify him for the hard trip home. He eats it, looking out a frosted pane and chewing slowly. At last he pulls on his dry clothing, stamps into his boots, and heads into the cold. On the porch he gazes, bewildered, at an empty white expanse. There is no team, no bobsled.

"Your horses must have got tired of waiting," says Fannie. "See the tracks heading toward home?"

Tom shakes his head and without a word crunches down the steps and follows them.

Back in the kitchen the phone rings. It's Tom's wife, frantic. The horses are in the yard, but where's Tom? He took the milk over, early morning. Didn't he get there? Has Fannie seen him?

Fannie explains about the coffee and warming up, and assures her that

Tom is on his way home. Tom's wife hangs up abruptly. It's forty years later that one of Tom's sons tells Fannie that his mother never forgave her for that morning. The revelation isn't news to Fannie.

Close on the heels of the gargantuan blizzard a second paralyzing storm socks the area. Ronald and Vera have parceled out their children and left for Florida, where Vera's sister has invited them to share a cottage on the ocean for two weeks. As the storm gathers strength, Grama chases them with a letter:

> The radio news was telling all day Wed. that there was another bad blizzard on the way. I tell you we hated to hear about it. Roy and Bill Purcell went for the milk last night and they had a hard enough time to get through. It had begun — so Roy, Bill, and John stayed here all night. This morning, Thur., the blizzard was on good — or bad. I was awakened by the grind and roar of trucks on our driveway. I got up and looked out and three trucks were stuck and the "brownies" were throwing snow in every direction. They got out and off about a quarter past six, but we don't know what this day and night will do to us. It is blowing quite hard and a lot of loose snow, as it snowed all day Weds. It is awful depressing so soon after the other. It may not be so bad and it may be worse. It is not so cold, and that is one consolation.

Grampa adds to Eunice's letter:

> About the work. Roy has managed getting the milk here and off this morning almost on time. The storm is not as bad as Sunday but had he not got the milk last night and also Freeman's we would be in a fix. Roy, Holmes and Bill stayed here last night. Roy put in pretty nearly all night.
> The pipe leading to barn at Hill Farm froze yesterday and I worked all day. Had plumber and finally Electric Co. They thawed it with 2300 volt current. I fear their job will be pretty expensive. I am going to have John and Gerue get the milk here tonight by team. And let Roy get sleep. Roy had yesterday off. Tuesday Henry was off. We will come on all right.

Had Grampa been talking instead of writing, he'd have said, with a ring of resolution in his voice, "We'll fetch it!"

Grama's consolation doesn't last long: the temperature drops to twenty below. The blizzard mounts. It turns out to be longer, deeper, and fiercer than the former. On the hill alongside the Hill Farm the horses mire and a bobsled of full milk cans overturns. It takes many hands to right it and get team and cargo to the dairy. By then the weather is so impossible that all the men have to stay the night, along with those from the night before. Grama writes Florida with some pride, that she was ready for the emergency with plenty of baked beans, soup, bread, doughnuts, and cookies.

The following night the hotel turns out to be at the Hill Farm; Fannie's kitchen is full of stranded men. The hilarity there includes phone calls to friends, so that one of the milkhouse workers, who lives in town, decides to try his luck and see whether he can make it to the party. Hank Florey's arrival proves that Highway 15 from Beloit to Milwaukee, a mile or so north, is being kept open, whereupon all the single men decide to mush out, retrieve Hank's car which he left near the highway, follow the plow into town, and attend the weekly dance at Waverly Beach dance hall. But they badly need baths.

The bathroom is off the kitchen. Johnny Holmes claims the first tubful. While he's splashing, Roy and the others fill a washtub with snow. They order Fannie into the bedroom, then burst in on Johnny and dump the snow on top of him. He roars into the kitchen, stark naked and beet red.

The storms taper off. When Ronald and Vera return from Florida, Colley Road is a tunnel with plowed drifts 15 feet high. They have been warned by more than letters: while still in St. Petersburg, Daddy opens a Florida newspaper that has a picture of mountains of northern snow, and the caption says the photo was taken "east of Beloit, Wisconsin." That's where the farm is; the photograph is of their road towards Marstons.

Joan, Patsy, Jackie, and Craig have never known such a winter. There is so much snow along the snow fences, and so easy to excavate under the crust, that they are able to dig cavernous rooms with almost cathedral ceilings. They connect these with a labyrinth of crawlways, and visit back and forth in each other's crystal palaces.

Grampa continues to take pride in the feats of the winter. He reports to his cousins in Watertown, Jane and Nellie Needham, in mid-February:

> I know you are wondering how we are making out during this severe winter. I will answer it with one word—good! We have not missed a day in getting our milk out and scarcely missed a customer. It has taken some pretty stiff pushing but I have a good bunch of loyal men and our producers have co-operated with us nicely in helping to get their milk here. We have had to go ahead of the county plows some because we could not hold up our delivery

until the wind stopped. Our trade is holding up good and the herd is producing well in spite of the cold weather.

March brings thaws and floods. In the back pasture, Spring Brook changes from a stream that a good spitter can spit across, to a racing torrent far too wide to span with an iceball. On the flood plain where Spring Brook meets Turtle Creek, just beyond the double bridges on Colley Road, there's a vast sea and both bridge surfaces are under water. For more than a week no vehicles can traverse the road. The milk trucks must first head away from town, then cut

Dobby (Everett Dobson) uses a sled to deliver to an impassable street.

over to the State Line Road and turn back, following higher land and bridges. It's a detour of many miles. The school cab has to follow the same route, and everyone must get up earlier to meet it. Jackie, her nose pressed to the cab window, looks across the valley at the inundated bridges and the gleaming expanse where water shouldn't be, and marvels at the great ice floes churning along with no regard for stream bed. As the water recedes the ice floes, some as big as barn floors, are left beached on the flood plain like a giant's abandoned checker game. Throughout the spring they slowly dwindle away.

The snows, the length of the sub-zero weather, and the floods of 1936 go down in the annals as the worst since 1881, and for decades they are the yardstick against which all winters and springs are measured. Grampa's essay doesn't exaggerate the heroism of the farm workers and milkmen. While the daily paper frequently did not get delivered, and the mail didn't make it, either, while schools and businesses closed, while Greyhound buses coughed to a stop in snowbanks and trains came through only sporadically, Dougan's Dairy battled drifts and floods and never for a day failed to deliver the milk to each customer's doorstep—although sometimes a few hours late.

19 ⋇ OSCAR BERG

Oscar Berg, known familiarly as Ockie, is one of several men who spend most of their working lives on the Dougan farm. He comes to Beloit in 1929 from Mondovi, a small farming village near Eau Claire, answering an ad Grampa placed in *Hoard's Dairyman*. He is 19. He writes asking that someone meet his train; he's never been in a big city before. And Beloit, about 20,000 population, must indeed seem huge. Ronald and Vera drive down to fetch him, in the Essex car.

Ockie lives seven years in the Big House. At meals he often sits by Grampa, who bonks him over the head yearly with the first green onion of the season. It's their private joke, and Ockie forgets the origin. He starts in the barn as assistant herdsman, then is made herdsman. When the Beloit Centennial is celebrated, in 1936, Ockie dons an old tunic and trousers, and rides the float in the parade, milking a cow in a wooden stanchion and sometimes squirting a titful of milk at little boys lining the street. Jackie Dougan, who is eight, and six-year-old Connie Horn, the daughter of the office girl, Ruby Horn, are on the float with him, in long gingham dresses and sunbonnets. The float is divided in two, the other half shows modern milking with a dairyman all in white with black rubber boots, stainless steel buckets, and milking machines.

It's not long after the parade that Ockie becomes a routeman. That is his chief farm identity, though he still helps out now and again in the barn or milkhouse when his route is finished.

"I never drank coffee till I went on the milk route," Ockie says, "but I felt sort of silly going into a restaurant for breakfast and drinking my own milk!"

Al Lasse is another single man who lives at the Big House. "I went to the State Fair once," says Ockie, "and brought back a prank car bomb that I installed in Al Lasse's motor. When Al started his car it went off with a noise like dynamite and a tremendous lot of smoke poured out. Al looked disgusted and said to all us whooping farmhands, 'I suppose you fellows are real proud!'"

After seven years, Ockie marries. His bride is a young woman he first meets at Waverly Beach. This is a Beloit dance hall on Rock River, just over the bridge on the west side, where many of the town young people, and some older, go for entertainment. There is always a band, playing country music or old time tunes; once in a while a band of some reputation makes a stop for a night or two. The dance floor is excellent polished wood. There is always a policeman at the door, and if anyone makes a disturbance, he is thrown out.

Ockie and Marian Berg in their wedding picture.

Ockie and Marian are nothing to each other but occasional pleasant dance partners, although Marian says to her friends, "Don't you touch him, he's mine!" But then Marian gets a job working for Mother on the farm, helping with the cooking and cleaning and children at the Little House. She has Wednesday afternoons off.

"What good does that do me?" she asks. "How can I get to town?" Mother considers. "Let's ask Ockie Berg. I think he'll run you into town."

This is how Marian learns that Ockie is also working on the farm.

Ockie is willing, so every Wednesday he gives Marian a ride to town. On the weekends, he takes her dancing at Waverly Beach. Their friendship ripens. They want to get married, have a place of their own. Good as the food is at Grama's table, comfortable as living is there, Ockie is ready to leave.

Ron tries to discourage him. "Don't do it, Ockie," he advises. "You're valuable living right here on the place, and you know she has a little girl her mother takes care of."

"I know," says Ockie, smiling. "I like her little girl, and she likes me."

The couple think that Ron and Vera don't want to lose either of them. It takes a while, but they marry, anyway, "on a shoestring," Marian remarks, and "I'd have got him out of there sooner if I could have! He thought the world of Grandpa Dougan, and they treated him so well. But then, he was never any trouble. He's the world's number one nice guy. Ask anybody on his route."

They move into town, on the west side. That winter there's a monstrous storm, with snow so deep that nothing is moving. Ockie puts on skis and starts out. Marian calls after him, "If you don't make it to deliver that milk, you know the whole farm will just have to close down! Nobody's going to get out!" But Ockie makes it, and delivers his load, along with all the other milkmen who also are either on the place, or get there some fashion or other. "The postmen didn't make it, but we did," Ockie says. "Letters can wait. Milk can't."

Marian gets a job at Fairbanks Morse, at 46 cents an hour to begin, and stays there 31 years. Ockie leaves Dougan's and works a bit at Wilford Lumber, but comes back shortly to continue being a milk man. The couple have a son, Dwayne, who grows up a very bright young man, excelling in everything he does, as does his older sister. Ockie and Marian have over fifty years of happy married life.

"I guess I was wrong," Ron Dougan confesses along the way. "I think I just didn't want Ockie to leave the place, he was such a nice and reliable fellow to have around."

Marian agrees. "Whenever anyone wanted to pick a fight, Ockie would just smile and walk away. Sometimes I try to get an argument going with him, just to see if I can, but he gives that great smile of his and walks away."

She smiles at Ockie, and Ockie smiles back.

20 ⋈ JUDGE LUEBKE

Arthur Luebke is Municipal Court Judge in Beloit. He's one of the town's splendid citizens. He's a tall, spare man who doesn't speak much, but when he does the words are eloquent and wise. He's a member of Daddy's chess club. If ever anyone manages to beat Judge Luebke at a game of chess, that person circles the date in red on his calendar. Judge Luebke is also an historian, and tracks down the diaries, journals, and letters of early settlers to the Beloit area. He's working on a book called *Pioneer Beloit*. His large family, out on Sherwood Drive, drinks a gallon of Dougan's milk every day.

After Art Luebke has been municipal judge for ten years, the circuit judge of Rock, Jefferson, and Green Counties dies. Governor Nelson appoints Judge Luebke to fill in the balance of Judge Harry Fox's term. The balance is very short, for Judge Fox had only a few months to go before standing for re-election. Judge Luebke decides he'd like to continue the job, and immediately is plunged into running for the six-year term. A number of his friends form a campaign committee. Daddy becomes treasurer.

To publicize Art's name the committee decides to use ads, telephone calls, cards in doors or mailboxes, and posters. One type of poster is a traveling one: a huge placard that will fit on top of a car and blazon, "ELECT ARTHUR LUEBKE CIRCUIT COURT JUDGE." Everywhere the vehicle goes, the sign will carry its message. The placards are stored out at the dairy, in two empty stalls in the horse barn.

When campaign blitz time arrives, all Judge Luebke's friends drive out to have signs affixed to the tops of their automobiles. Daddy puts one on his Buick. Although it's an unwritten business rule that companies don't express opinions on political subjects, Daddy pays no attention to this and also fastens a placard on the top of each Dougan milk truck. Thereafter every day during the campaign six trucks carry Arthur Luebke's name to all the streets and alleyways of the Beloit area. Judge Luebke and Dougan's Milk are advertised together, with the judge having top billing.

He won the election! Judge Arthur Luebke being sworn into office.

Election day comes. The retail milk business goes on as usual, with the trucks fanning out on their daily routes. At about nine in the morning Daddy gets a call from Oscar Berg.

"Hey, Ron," says Ockie. "Something's happened. You better get on down here. I think I'm being arrested."

Daddy is instantly alarmed. Ockie is the milkman who delivers to the schools at this time of morning. He pictures an unnoticed child darting behind a milk truck. "Have you had an accident?" he asks quickly. "Where are you?"

"No, no, nothing like that," says Ockie. "They're holding me at Strong School but I'm probably going to be taken to the station to be booked."

"Stay right where you are; tell them I'm on my way!"

"Wait! Ron!" cries Ockie. "What are you driving?"

"The Buick."

"Then park half a block down the street!"

Ockie hangs up before Daddy can ask why. Mystified, he leaps in the Buick and races for town. He parks half a block from Strong School, beside a thicket of campaign posters stuck on sticks in the ground. He sprints to the side of the building where he spots the milk truck. Ockie and a policeman are standing beside it.

"What's wrong? What's the charge?" asks Daddy.

"Is this your truck?" asks the policeman.

Daddy assents.

"Then it's campaigning too close to a polling place." The policeman jerks his thumb toward "ELECT ARTHUR LUEBKE CIRCUIT COURT JUDGE" atop the milk truck. "This school is the polling place for District 19."

"Half the schools I deliver to are polling places today," Ockie complains. "I'll keep getting arrested all morning long."

"You can park half a block away and lug the milk," suggests Daddy. "More than any of the other drivers you'll be doing your bit for the Cause!"

"Not if I'm in jail I won't," says Ockie.

Daddy turns to the policeman. "What's the penalty, Officer?"

"A fine, and you'll have to appear before the judge. But I guess as long as you take the sign off right here, and keep it off, we'll let it go this time."

Daddy shakes his head. "No, Officer, do your duty. Charge us. Will we be tried by the municipal or the circuit court?"

"Municipal," says the officer. "But you can appeal, and then it'll go to circuit. But I'm not going to charge you, since this is a first offence, and not deliberate—"

"No, no, please charge us! I'm determined to fight this all the way to the top," says Daddy. He adds, "I want to be prosecuted to the full extent of the law."

The officer looks perplexed. "No," he says finally. "Just take off that sign."

Daddy and Ockie take off the sign.

"There," says Daddy, "bare as a baby's tra-la-la. Get along, Ockie; only five trucks will carry the message to the masses this election day."

Ockie gets along. Daddy takes the offending sign as far as the grove of campaign posters and leaves it standing beside the sidewalk at the prescribed distance from the school. He laughs and shakes his head as he climbs into his decorated Buick. He thinks what fun he'll have, telling the story at chess club. Especially to a newly elected circuit judge.

"Too bad," he says aloud. "It would have been worth a couple of fines to make Art Luebke try this case!"

21 ⊰ PRICES

F ive cents a quart. This is the price when W.J. Dougan begins retail milk delivery in the spring of 1907. He holds to this until it's evident the business will not have a sufficient margin of profit, then raises the price to 6¼ cents. A Mrs. Smiley on Keeler Street quits in a pique. "I will never pay over five cents a quart for milk!" she declares.

Mrs. Smiley's name and statement echo down the years of the milk business. The price of milk is never again as low as five cents. However it fluctuates widely on its generally upward climb, due to market conditions.

In November of 1909 W.J. circulates a mimeographed flier to his customers, gently explaining the reasons for an increase in the price of cream:

> We started the production and delivery of milk two and one-half years ago. Our ideal from the start has been to produce the best possible milk. We are gratified in the results obtained thus far. From the testimony of scores of satisfied patrons we know our product is giving satisfaction. By the monthly test at the university our milk stands at the head. By the contest in market milk at the National Dairy Show our milk stood well among the select milk of Canada and the U.S. It scored 91, cream 91½; each received a diploma. Our product was marked perfect in flavor, composition, i.e. fats and solids, and perfect in cleanliness and keeping quality. These are the factors essential to good milk.
>
> We are improving our milk room and equipment and continually selecting cows with an aim of still improving our product.
>
> We are compelled to make a slight raise in the price of cream. We are selling our cream for less than most of the dealers. Our cream is always perfectly fresh and does not curdle in coffee and keeps sweet several days. We can furnish cream old enough to whip when ordered in advance. Hereafter we shall charge 10 cents for a half-pint bottle of cream. Milk remains at the old price.

Thanking you for past favors, and hoping to retain your patronage for both milk and cream, we remain

Yours for good milk,

W.J. Dougan

In April 1913 a detailed account of milk pricing is the start of a long article on W.J. by E.G. Hastings of the University of Wisconsin's Agricultural Experimental Station, and published in *Hoard's Dairyman*, the epitome of all dairying magazines. It's the first of many such articles through the years about W.J. Dougan and his farming. This one is titled "A Successful Farmer." After a brief introduction Hastings writes:

His idea was to produce a high grade milk for sale in the city.... Within a comparatively short time he succeeded in getting trade enough so that he was selling $120.00 worth of milk per month, and the trade constantly increasing. He raised the price to 6¼ cents shortly after he began selling. After a few months he realized that he could not produce the quality of milk which he was desirous of producing for this price; he figured a price of 8½ cents would enable him to produce the grade of milk he wished. He increased the price...losing but few of his old customers, in the following way: His milk was constantly recommended by the doctors for children's use. People were coming to him and asking if they could purchase milk. He would agree to take them as permanent customers with the understanding that they should pay 8½ cents a quart. His trade constantly increased and [soon] about one-half of his customers were paying 8½ cents; the other half paid the old price of 6¼ cents. Those paying the higher price knew what the others were paying and vice versa. Those paying the lower price realized that it was only a question of time when they too would have to pay the higher price.... He allowed this to continue for some time, then notified his customers that all would be expected to pay the higher price. The demand for the milk practically doubled and all new trade was gained at a price of over two cents per quart higher than was being paid by the older customers. The usual way of increasing trade is to lower the price until the increased demand has been gained and then raise the price. When the opposite process will work, it surely shows the demand for the goods and that the consumer is satisfied that he is getting good value for his money.

In 1916 W.J. is selling milk for ten cents a quart; its cost to produce is eight cents. When the United States enters World War I in 1917, costs escalate and the price of quality milk goes up to 20 cents all over the area. W.J. increases his price to 15 cents. He figures he's making a fair profit and doesn't match his competitors. Business prospers; there is a waiting list for customers. W.J. can afford to be choosy—only those families with small children are allowed to buy from The Babies' Milkman. And only rich Guernsey milk is sold.

But more customers don't solve the problem. The cost of everything continues to rise, and W.J. is hard pressed to hold down the price of milk. He realizes he's been running on too narrow a margin; nonetheless he tries not to raise prices. After the War, on October 24, 1919, he takes his customers into his confidence. In an enveloped leaflet, delivered to their doors, he enlists their aid.

He says he is unwilling to raise the price of milk but explains why it may be necessary to do so. He proposes a pact: "Let us cut loss and waste together." Customers will pay cash; he will eliminate bookkeeping. This will save also in not having the cost of running accounts. Customers will be careful of bottle breakage and return empties promptly, and the farm will not have to have as large an inventory of bottles on hand. And if customers send the bottles back clean, time consuming effort will be saved at the plant, for bottles returned with dried or sour milk dregs must have special treatment. Also, if bottles are placed in a convenient place the routeman's time will be saved. W.J. gives suggestions on the keeping of milk, so none will be wasted by spoilage. All these things together could work to keep the price of Dougan's milk from going up. W.J. finishes,

> I wish to advise my customers of how greatly I appreciate their patronage and the patience they have invariably shown during periods of milk shortage. I realize the people of Beloit have manifested a confidence in my ability and integrity in producing a milk of certified quality without the inspection and certificate of an official board for this purpose. I wish to assure you that I am earnestly trying not to betray that confidence. I am producing the best milk within my power and I am looking after those numerous details that insure a uniformly reliable quality.... While our milk has always been sold at a little higher price than the ordinary milk of this city, I am confident that it is the cheapest food in the end. Compared to other foods our clean wholesome milk is an economical food for your whole family.

However, enlisting aid, cutting costs, wooing former customers, isn't enough. With expenses of production increasing, yet prices in farm products falling all around him, W.J. realizes he must either raise prices, reduce quality, or quit the business altogether. He takes counsel with Beloit businessmen and doctors. They invariably urge him neither to quit nor reduce quality. The doctors say, "Beloit needs your product." Persuaded, W.J. raises his price to 20 cents a quart, the price of his competitors, and things stabilize for a bit.

But with the minor depression of 1920, the competition slash their prices. Since W.J.'s have been low all through World War I, he now has no reserves to tide him over, and has to keep his milk at 20 cents in order to meet spiraling costs and still have enough to live on. The result is he loses business to other local dairies, of which there are now quite a number. In early spring, 1921, he publishes a letter-ad in the *Beloit Daily News*, earnestly explaining the history of the area's, and his own, milk pricing.

DOUGAN'S MILK POLICY

A Statement to My Customers
and the Consuming Public

Fifteen years ago we came to our farm with a fixed purpose to produce and distribute to the babies of Beloit the best milk to be had in any city at any price.

During these years we have worked out the details of the business, ever keeping abreast with the advancement of ideas in clean milk production. We have built the plant, developed the herd, and put into effect the practical methods that secure to our patrons with unusual regularity a uniformly clean, cold, rich milk. To accomplish this we have worked out some principles of management:

— The right volume of business for the greatest efficiency and economy.
— Proper equipment.
— The problem of securing and managing help so as to have constant, intelligent, clean, and conscientious men to handle this most sensitive and important food.
— The right price.

That the people of Beloit have recognized our effort by placing full confidence in our ability and integrity is a matter of great gratification and encouragement to us. The following frank statement at this time, regarding our product, and the price we feel it necessary to maintain will doubtless be of value in strengthening this confidence.

The question may be raised, WHY DOES DOUGAN STILL CHARGE 20 CENTS PER QUART FOR MILK? The reasons are these: Our milk is now only 33⅓% higher than the price in October, 1917, at which time our price of 15 cents per quart was far below the price of milk of this grade in other cities. Many of the articles that are showing such marked declines at present were increased 200, 300, and 400%. Such articles can stand a big cut. On the other hand, most of the supplies that we use are still over 75% above pre-war prices. These supplies include bottles, caps, cleansing powder, fuel, utensils, and repairs.

The second reason is that during the war we held down the price of our milk to close to that of ordinary milk in Beloit, and far below that charged for milk of like quality in other cities by being conservative in the wages paid our help. Now I am not inclined to reduce their wages unjustly. Our labor expenses in 1921 will be 133% higher than it was in 1916, 40% above 1917 and 1918, and 20% above 1919. In view of these facts, it is necessary to maintain a higher price than before the war. We have been producing this milk on too small a margin of profit, and have been paying our labor too low a wage to insure the performance of the business. There is also a principle of permanent agriculture at stake. In order to hold sufficient and competent help on the farm, we must readjust the compensation so as to compare favorably with compensation for like service in the city. It is as much moment to the consumer as to the producer that farming, and especially milk production, should be established upon a profitable basis.

The third and greatest reason why I do not cut the price of milk is because the consumers do not want me to do so. I know that the people of Beloit can not afford to have me reduce the price at the expense of quality. Beloit needs a better milk for the sick and babies more than it needs a cheap milk. It is my purpose to produce the better milk. To this end I am going to large expense and investing my whole life in the work. In view of the shortage of ice this season I have installed a Lipman Refrigerating Plant at an expense of over two thousand dollars, so as to insure a cool wholesome milk for the babies and sick of Beloit. By the repeated tests of our milk in the University Laboratories and the Beloit Health Office, and by the still more critical test in saving babies' lives, our milk shows that we are actually producing year in and year out as good a milk as can be secured in any city, and at a price far below that charged in any other city for this quality of milk.

I am confident that I am putting full value into the milk, and I am trying to give a service to this city that can not be measured by monetary standards. I desire to thank my customers for their liberal patronage, and the professional and business men for their encouragement in building up this special milk business.

At present I have a surplus of about seventy-five quarts of milk per day. I feel that the people of Beloit can not afford to allow this quality of milk, which should be used in saving babies' lives and increasing the health and vigor of our children, to go into ordinary butter making, and I am aware that I can not produce this milk by the present expensive process, and sell any portion of it at butter prices.

I ask your continued patronage and encouragement in maintaining our present high standard for the milk supply of Beloit.

W.J. Dougan,

"The Babies' Milkman."

This letter is followed by a contest, how long can a bottle of Dougan's milk be kept sweet? With prizes of milk tickets, customers enthusiastically rise to the challenge.

Ronald is now in college, and his father's financial problems can be charted in his letters to his son. He lists, in May of 1921, the various groups visiting the farm, and regrets that he cannot afford this year to entertain all the Beloit doctors for lunch. "I have got to do something to advertise, however, the trade is very low, 250 to 260 qts. per day. This is over $10 a day short of necessary income. I will clear expenses but will have no salary with which to pay off indebtedness and for improvements."

But by February of 1922 the 20 cents a quart has remained steady, and the milk business is returning to an even keel. W.J. is again advising his customers that for the time being he cannot accept any new customers except for urgent cases of sickness, or those with small babies.

In 1923 Ronald works in France, he marries there in 1924, and by the spring of 1925 he's a father, has graduated from Beloit College, and has joined W.J. in the milk business. At Northwestern, where he spent three of his college years, he made money selling advertising for desk blotters, and found he was a good salesman. Now he flings himself into promoting the dairy business. He's a dung beetle in his determination to sell Guernsey milk at a premium. He attempts to persuade everyone that Guernsey is the best milk there is. He hires little boys to go up one street and down another, leaving leaflets in mailboxes. The leaflets tell why Guernsey milk's food value outweighs the several cents it costs over other milk. He enrolls the farm in the American Guernsey Cattle Club, which entitles Dougan's to use the handsome Golden Guernsey Products seal and the Cattle Club advertising, always with space to personalize the local advertiser. But again, business has become shaky. Costs continue to rise. There is not a waiting line to be a Dougan customer.

W.J., supporting his second son at the University of Wisconsin, sends Trever frequent letters, encouraging his studies and athletics and discouraging his spending. In March of '26 he writes Trever:

> It is nip and tuck to make ends meet. Any reverse would put us in bad shape. You see I am needing to apply the very principle to my business I preach to you in your races. I believe I can win but it is hard to keep myself in training on a 20 year stretch & then for another 20 years. There can be no let up in training in life's game. Should I relax for a single month my business would feel it & should I grow careless for a year I would be busted.

In April he reports that he is woefully short of money and has not paid the help for last month. In May he says he's had to borrow to pay Trever's college expenses, but can repay the loan if he has good luck and can sell hogs to advantage. "I am glad and willing to do this for you & all I want in return is the consciousness that you are developing into a strong, upright, noble Christian man." The following December, both sons are at Wisconsin; Ronald is attending the Ag School Short Course. W.J. tells them they must cut expenses to the bone. In January he urges Trever not to attend Prom, an expensive proposition: "My creditors are urging payment & I have to pay fast and stave off the rest. When I sell hogs it won't help much for I have had to borrow on them. We are dropping the price of milk to 16 2/3 cents. Hope the income will pick up." In February he writes Trever his appreciation:

> I do not want to talk hard luck but I want you to feel satisfied that you are doing the right thing by saving this expense. Be happy in it. You noticed I have not bought any clothes this year. I would feel uncomfortable in them knowing I cannot afford them.... Our past year has been a poor one. The milk sales fell 3,500 short of '25. The inventory $3,063 short & the expenses

were not cut. Whatever I have spent for the family this year has been taken from laid up capital. Therefore my net worth is $2,778 less than a year ago. But I could stand that and not flinch. It is the inability to meet my obligations. Notes come due and I have to stave them off. However there is no reason for a pessimistic view. We have the means to build a good business. Our change of price and our advertising are beginning to count.

The price change does help. But then comes the stock market crash, in October of 1929, followed by the Great Depression. People lose their jobs, wages drop, prices drop. Many families cancel home delivery. And even 16 2/3 cents is too high for most Depression customers.

In December, 1931, Ron writes a letter to the newspaper about the farmer's plight:

To the Editor: The desperate condition of the farmer is generally conceded. The recently released index figures compiled by the United States Department of Agriculture give a vivid picture of the situation.

Taking the prewar years, 1910 to 1914, as equal to 100, the farmer now receives 70 for all that he produces while he pays 125 for all that he has to purchase. He is paying 120 for labor, while his taxes have soared to 250.

Living costs for the urban dweller have fallen rapidly during the past year. The farmer's costs have also fallen, but his income has been nearly cut in two. Again quoting U.S. Department of Agriculture, the unit exchange value of farm products for other commodities is slightly over one-half what it was before the war.

What effect will the farmer's unprofitable operation have upon the quality of the product he sells? In cereals, fruits, and meats, the city buyers stand to gain by lower prices, because the buyer can judge by observation the quality of the product offered. With milk it is entirely different. The cleanliness of milk is affected by the attitude of a dairyman toward his job. The grade of an apple cannot be altered by market conditions. Just as good wheat comes to market this year as when wheat was two dollars a bushel. With milk, however, as the price goes down to the farmer, the quality goes down to the consumer. A disgruntled underpaid farm community will not furnish a high quality clean milk to the city depending upon it for its milk supply.

In bringing pressure for lower milk prices, the consumer should bear in mind that the biggest proportion of all price cuts come out of the farmer — that at present the farmer is marketing his milk as closely as it is possible to market a quality product—that any further cut to the farmer is bound to result in a lower quality of market milk.

RONALD DOUGAN

However, it occurs to Ron that Dougan's would do well to carry two grades of milk: their own barn's premium Guernsey, and a lower priced milk that could meet the competition. It would be a blend of Holstein, Brown Swiss, and Milking Shorthorn, all of which have a lower standard butterfat. W.J. agrees, and it is at this point that the farm begins buying milk from area farmers in earnest: they have already been buying from a few, whose standards they can supervise. Ron and W.J. decide they can price Dougan's Blended Milk at ten cents, and bring Wisconsin Grade A Raw Guernsey down to 14¼. Ron initiates a blitz of advertising. The day the first ad appears the phone never stops ringing. He figures they are finally in clover. Business steadies and starts to rise. True, the daily number of Guernsey quarts drops—it had been about 600 a day—but the Blend more than makes up for the loss.

But the Depression grinds on. W.J. considers bankruptcy, and papers are actually drawn up. The milk business is faltering, in spite of low prices and vigorous advertising. The price of blended quarts for door-to-door delivery sinks to 8 cents and the farm is losing money delivering them. On May 19, 1932, Ronald writes to Vera, who is away: "I've been figuring milk prices all day, and am beginning to come out. It looks as if our farmers will have to take a cut but even so they will be infinitely better off than the Pure Milk Association members."

At this low ebb, two important steps are taken. W.J. and Ronald incorporate the milk business, which splits off its debts from the farm and makes both farm and business eligible for loans. And W.J. offers something new from Dougan's Dairy. He writes his customers:

You will be interested to know that we have added a pasteurized milk to our line of dairy products. We are pasteurizing a portion of our supply of Blended Raw Milk, and marketing it under the supervision of the Wisconsin Department of Agriculture and Markets. The department has seen fit to give this milk the rating of Wisconsin Grade A Pasteurized.

For years we have been handling Wisconsin Grade A Raw milk. Now that we are entering the pasteurized field, it is particularly gratifying to us that the state should give us this high rating—the first Wisconsin Grade A Pasteurized milk produced in Rock County.

Prices are so low that liberal quantities of milk should be included in every food budget. Our raw blended milk and the new pasteurized milk sell for eight cents per quart, while our Wisconsin Grade A Raw Guernsey milk sells for ten cents.

From several years before the Depression the farm has been selling milk in pints and half pints to workers in a few of the small factories. Now Ron sets out to sell in all the factories and succeeds in getting his milkmen into Warner's, the Freeman Shoe Factory, the Iron Works, and quite a few others. Factory half pints are five cents, pints are eight cents. The increased factory sales now begin to help the deficit.

In 1933 the State steps in and bars below-cost selling: milk can't be sold for less than 10 cents a quart. For the last half of that year, the door-to-door milk business shows a profit, too.

With many factory customers agreeing to home delivery in addition to factory delivery—the personable and friendly milkmen press for this—business steadily picks up. The routes grow from one to six. Ronald introduces other products: a 2% butterfat milk which he calls "Low Fat," a skim milk called "Fat Free," butter, and cottage cheese. The cottage cheese is usually in a carton but sometimes, for promotional purposes, in a pale yellow glass that people like to collect for tableware. Sometimes, in the spring, chives are added, and the cheese has a different look, the green bits both attractive and flavorful in the white matrix. (When chive cottage cheese is to be made, anyone available around the place—often Ruby, the office girl—goes out to the garden and picks the green stems; they're washed and cut up with scissors.) Sometimes the dairy runs a special on pineapple cottage cheese. When promotions occur, Craig or Jackie or Patsy stand out in the milkhouse and drop paper cuffs over each quart bottle as it moves from the capper, the cuffs advertising the special product. The pay for this labor is never more than a dime.

In 1935 Ronald captures the Beloit College trade, and that, he writes the head purchaser, "is a grand stop and no mistake."

By 1940 the obligations of the milk business are pretty well paid off. There's no longer any need to maintain the corporation that got the farm and the business through the Depression. W.J., Hazel (Aunt Ida's daughter), and Ronald—president, vice president, and secretary-treasurer—dissolve it. The farm operations and the milk business are still kept separate, for it's at this change, consummated in 1942, that Ronald buys the business from his father. Now Ron, rather than the Corporation, purchases milk from W.J. and

W.J. looking for a six-day cow.

from the round barn, down the short sidewalk from the milkhouse, under the same arrangement as he buys milk from Albert Marston or Howard Johnson or Emil Punzel. He pays rent to the farm for his buildings. There is still the easy give-and-take between the two operations, however.

When the United States is drawn into World War II in December, 1941, there are many shortages that affect the milk business. Gas is rationed, new rubber tires are unavailable, worn tires must be retreaded. Running a truck every day over an extensive milk route is impractical. Wright & Wagner Dairy solves the gas and tire problem by returning to horse-drawn wagons. But there is another solution. What originally necessitated daily delivery—poor refrigeration—is scarcely a factor anymore. Iceboxes are relics of the past; almost all houses have refrigerators. Dairies have low-temperature coolers. Milk lasts better. Ronald recalls the 1920s contest: Two dollars worth of milk tickets to any household that could hold a quart of Dougan's raw milk sweet for a week. Many people collected a prize, and Mr. John Amend, of the Racine Feet Knitting Factory, boasted that he'd kept a quart sweet in his up-to-date refrigerator for nearly three weeks.

Now, with the War demanding conservation, dairies all over the country institute every-other-day delivery. "Your Dougan Deliveryman," on November 22, 1942, leaves a note on each customer's doorstep: "In rearranging our routes to conserve milage, we find it necessary to switch your delivery to another day, and to a later hour. Today I am leaving you your regular order. Tomorrow your delivery will be at about 11 o'clock and at the same hour every other day thereafter. We hope that this change in schedule will not inconvenience you." So a woman who used to take a pint of milk every day for herself and her cats now takes a quart every other day. Dougan's delivers the same total of milk to each house but drives only half as far. The exception is Burrwood Park, an area of trailers and shanties along the river, where the people have either iceboxes or nothing. Walter Abbot swings past Burrwood Park on both sections of his route, and delivers milk there every day.

With the War also comes price freezing. The ceilings on Dougan's milk are 13 cents a quart for either raw or pasteurized Blended, Low Fat, and Homogenized—homogenization is an innovation of the early forties—while Grade A Guernsey is 15 cents. Whipping cream is 23 cents a half pint. On the whole, these are what the prices were in September, 1941.

One Dougan product becomes unprofitable to continue: it costs almost as much to produce a pound of butter as the allowed price brings in. Butter to the consumer is also rationed, so sales are limited. Ron makes extensive calculations, comparing what Wright & Wagner and Merricks are paying for butterfat—five cents less than Dougan, as well as charging less, then writes to his father at the end of all the figures, "At the price we pay for cream for churning—37½ cents, it costs us 30 cents for raw material, allow 10 percent for manufacturing, and the regular drivers' commission, we come to 35-plus cents. With sale price at 39 cents, we have less than 4 cents to cover delivery overhead, office overhead, loss on testing, loss in accounting, and profit." Near the end of the war, Ronald regretfully chops up the large churn, and Dougan butter in its two-pound handsome gray stoneware tub is never sold again.

In a few years, every-other-day delivery is supplanted by a six-day delivery week. All customers are on a Monday-Wednesday-Friday, or Tuesday-Thursday-Saturday schedule. Sunday can now be a true day of rest for the delivery man, but not for the milkhouse workers or barnhands.

"We'll never all of us be able to go on a six-day week," W.J. says, "until we breed a six-day cow."

22 ⨯ HOWARD AND THE CREAM THIEF

Howard Milner delivers Dougan's milk to the Freeman Shoe Factory. He goes through the various areas, pushing a low cart with cases of milk piled on it, and the workers stop their machines for a moment, buy a pint and drink it on the spot, or put it aside for their lunch.

One day when he returns to his truck he finds a half pint of whipping cream missing. The next day another bottle is missing, and the next. The thief must be nipping out from the factory and taking the cream from the open truck while Howard is inside. It must be someone in the cutting room on the first floor, Howard figures, who waits till he sees the milkman take the elevator up to the higher floors.

Howard is annoyed. He doesn't like to lock his truck every time he leaves it. It would make his job last forever. Most people are honest. And as far as he knows, the truck doesn't lock, anyway. He goes to see the factory foreman.

"Catch him if you can," says the foreman. "Anybody that'll steal milk will steal shoes. Do whatever you want with him."

Howard mulls the problem. Then he goes into the milkhouse at the dairy. "George," he says to George Schreiber, "I want you to make me some very special whipping cream."

George does. He puts some of the caustic cleaning compound used for washing bottles in the bottom of a half pint. He adds some cream, fills the rest of the bottle with water, and presses on a whipping cream cap with his thumb. The bottle looks almost like whipping cream. He makes up eight or nine more special bottles and puts them in a case. Then Howard takes the case on his route.

At the shoe factory he hides the good whipping cream at the bottom of his load and leaves the bogus case right behind his seat. He loads up the milk for the factory workers, goes in, delivers the cutting room and the rest of the lower floor, and then goes up in the elevator. As soon as he reaches the top he leaves his milk and comes down again. He steps out the elevator door.

Right before him a factory worker is clutching the drinking fountain with one hand and holding a half pint in the other. He's retching and spitting and crying.

Howard rushes up to him and grips him by the shoulder. "Where'd you get that cream?"

"I bought it—" gasps the worker, "from a guy—over there—"

"I'm the only guy that sells cream around here," Howard says. "And you owe me a total of three bucks for the cream you've already stolen. Pay up right now, and keep out of my truck from now on, or it'll cost you your job!"

"I don't have three bucks," chokes the worker.

"Then get it," snaps Howard. He bounces his head against the wall a couple of times and releases him. The man borrows the money from a fellow worker going by and pays up.

Howard never has any trouble at the shoe factory again.

He runs into a similar situation, however, a few years later at Mork's Foundry. While his truck is standing unguarded a few workers are sneaking out and filching milk. This time he solves the problem differently. One afternoon he's passing Turtle Creek and spots a large water moccasin sunning on a rock. He shoots it with the revolver he's allowed to carry as a South Beloit policeman, and puts it in a box. The next day at the foundry he coils the snake into a lifelike position on his running board, just under the open door of his truck. Then he goes in to peddle milk.

It's not very many minutes before three workmen come pelting into the foundry crying to the others, "Man! Better keep outa his truck! He keeps *snakes* in there!"

After that, nobody bothers the milk truck at Mork's, either. Chances are the grapevine spreads to all the factories in town: better not mess with the Dougan milkman!

23 ⊰ THE MILKMAN'S BABIES

The genesis of the Dougan baby ads lies in W.J.'s slogan, "The Babies' Milkman." It's natural, when Ronald's children are born and he's taking over more and more of the work of the milk business, that he should think of using his own children in the advertising. There have been leaflets before, but

Patsy Dougan

Age: 15 Months
Weight: 25 Pounds
Daily Diet: One Quart Dougan's Milk
Fresh Vegetables
Fresh Fruits
Eggs, Cereals
Cod Liver Oil

**THE
DOUGAN
GUERNSEY
FARM**

A leaflet with Patsy Dougan on the cover is one of the precursors to the regular Dougan Baby ads that Ron Dougan starts in 1941.

without pictures. Now he gets one out showing cows in pasture, cows in an immaculate barn, pictures of the bottling, of the delivery trucks, and of a very healthy looking Joan and baby sister Patsy. On the back of the succeeding leaflet, underneath an invitation to visit afternoon milking from 3:30 to 4:30 any day, are added snaps of Joan, Patsy, Jackie, and a newborn Craig, with the line, "We drink a gallon of grandfather's milk every day."

It's but a short step from there to featuring customers' babies. Advertisers have always known that a baby will leap right off the page, carrying the product with it — how much more so local babies, the offspring of neighbors and friends?

After sporadically featuring customers' babies, in 1941 Ronald starts weekly baby ads in the *Beloit Daily News*. The milkmen pave the way by asking parents on their routes if they'd like their babies' pictures in the paper. Then Florence Johnson or Helen Tapp, who work in the office over the milkhouse, telephone and make arrangements. Once the ads become known, customers volunteer their little ones; often Ronald is stopped on the street or in the barber shop with "Hey Ron, how about running our kids in

your ads?" Sometimes this amounts to quite a few kids. The record is held by
the Van Kampen family, with eleven of their twelve children in one advertisement. Florence or Helen cuts out each ad as it appears and pastes it in a large
red scrapbook.

Ronald has an arrangement with a local photographer. The studio gives a
free sitting and enlarged portrait to the parents, plus a glossy to the newspaper. In return, the studio piggybacks on the Dougan ad, with "Photo by" in
a prominent place. No pressure is put on families, but a nice profit is made
by the photographer on the extra prints that the family almost always orders.
It's a symbiosis of dairy and studio. For several years the two businesses even
stage a joint "Most Photogenic Baby" contest, with contest ads sponsored by
the studio, but the several winners appearing in the ads of both. The prizes
are trophies, photographs, and milk tickets. Over two hundred children enter
every year. The paper always writes an article, with a group picture of winners, judges, and mothers. It's excellent free advertising, and no family is a
loser — the studio's entrance fee of four or five dollars includes two portraits
of each little contestant.

The texts of the baby ads are usually written by *Daily News* staff. They do their best but it's not easy to come up with sparkling copy about preschoolers week after week. The same headlines show up with monotonous frequency. "A TREASURE BEYOND MEASURE." "A PAIR OF BLONDE CUTIES." "MEN OF DISTINCTION." "A FAMILY TO BE PROUD OF." Tired puns are repeated: "TWO PEACHES MAKE A PAIR." The texts run to, "Andy likes to play with his blocks and trucks," and, "This very charming little girl with the big smile and pretty curls...." The writers aren't blessed with as large a measure of playfulness and originality as Ron Dougan, nor the advantage of a personal knowledge of and historical perspective on the families. Nor do they have his privilege of stepping in and writing an ad only when he's moved to do so. But it's when Ronald does this that the text leaps off the page along with the baby.

A child beside a toy piano, "SHADES OF RUBENSTEIN!" A beaming foursome, "QUARTETTE AS POPULAR AS VERDI'S RIGOLETTO!" A stairstep group, "REPRINTED BY POPULAR REQUEST," followed by:

Last week we featured the five children of Richard and Marian McCaul. Alack-a-day! Alack-a-day! Tiny Barbara almost missed getting into the picture. In fitting the glossy print to the available space, she had half her head cropped off. So here they all are again! In spite of her rough treatment, Barbie is still loyal to Dougan milk. I'll tell you what, Barbie. Have your daddy bring you out to the farm and you can name a cow! Maybe we'll let him name one, too. After all, he was a Dougan Baby, way back when!

Ronald is enthusiastic about the Quillen twins, whose older siblings have graced an earlier ad:

You'd think that the girls would be spoiled, unless you too have been a member of a large family. Then you know that everybody has responsibilities and lives up to them or else! We're sure there isn't a parent in Beloit who isn't envious of a family with twins. Must be absorbing to watch them develop. When even Dad can't tell them apart, what fun for the twins! But, let's not be carried away—how do we slide smoothly into selling milk? Well, the Quillens have used Dougan milk since they were married. Sandy tells her neighbors about it and Jim spreads the word at Fairbanks where he's a machinist, and at Yaglas where he's an expert camera and projector repairman.

The Quillens appear in ads over the years as their family grows. One is exclusively of their curly-headed twin daughters, not yet born at the time of this photo.

Ronald waxes lyrical when he writes about "FIVE LITTLE EYRES AND HOW THEY GREW." "No, these aren't 'grave Alice and laughing Allegra and Edith with the golden hair,' but think what a poem Longfellow could have composed if he'd had these five lasses to immortalize!" Later in the ad he tells us that in the year since their arrival in Beloit, the Eyre family has consumed 1,819 quarts of milk.

He kids the staffwriters' "men of distinction" headline with "Á DOS CA-BALLEROS DE DISTINCION!" This ad strays from young children; it shows two whiskered, serape-clad, guitar-playing young men:

> If you scraped away the luxuriant hirsute foliage you'd find that 'Pedro and Pancho' are really Wally and Ed Strong. Wally, just turned 20, has finished his Sophomore year at Swarthmore College and is now engaged in taking some underwater pictures somewhere off the coast of Carolina. If you lift that king-sized sombrero you'll find Ed, 17, just returned from Mexico with the Beloit College Anthropological Team. Tequila may be the national drink of Mexico, but these two popular lads cast their vote for Dougan's Milk. These talented young men are the sons of Mr. and Mrs. Walter A. Strong, Jr. Mr. Strong is a prominent civic leader and publisher of the *Beloit Daily News*.

Ronald's ad for the Amends' first child takes the form of a letter:

Dear Johnny,

Congratulations on your first birthday which falls on April 1. You sure fooled your folks, didn't you?

You are a lucky boy to be born into such a fine family and to live in such a friendly town. I know your daddy is employed by the Beloit Iron Works, and that is wonderful, too.

Johnny Amend. Ron goes all out on this family.

But it is your great-grandfather, John Amend, I knew best, for years ago he encouraged me to start a "milk break" service for his employees in the Racine Feet Knitting Company. That was the start of our growing up as a business.

Then when I was a little boy I remember your great-grandfather Dan Osborn and my father, who was the original "Babies' Milkman," planning the heating and plumbing out here at the dairy. Of course in those days I was called the "milkman's baby."

Your mother tells me you are learning to walk and are very proud of your Notre Dame sweater. I think the crew cut is pretty grown up for your age, too — and what is this bit about dropping clothes pins into amber Dougan milk bottles. It is a nice trick if you can do it.

Congratulations again on everything. Before you know it you will be in kindergarten and visiting Dougan's Dairy with your class. I'll be looking forward to seeing you.

Sincerely, Ron Dougan

Our customers say, "DOUGAN'S MILK tastes wonderful." That's good enough for us. We plan it that way, and protect the fine flavor with amber glass.

The Amends have more children, who inspire Ronald to additional epistles. The second one relates more history:

Dear Dougie,

I wrote your big brother a letter when he was your age, and told him how wonderful everything was going to be. Now he is four years old on April Fool's day but you missed that birthday by only two days, didn't you.

I envy you all the things that are going to happen during your lifetime. Why, long before you are as old as I am you will be living in the twenty-first century.

If things change as much in your lifetime as they have in mine — my, oh my. I was quite a boy before I rode in my first automobile. It was homemade, had hard rubber tires, and was driven by a chain. The telephone hung on the wall out of my reach and was cranked to make the bell ring. It was a big day when we put in our own little Fairbanks Morse light plant, and a bigger day when the high line came through. We had to pay to have that built ourselves. Then there are the newer fads of radio and television. My own children were older than you are before radio came along. As to television, I wonder if it is really here to stay. With all the wonderful things to do in this life I wonder if you will ever have time to bother with the silly thing.

Well, I can't talk to you forever. Just keep on doing what you're doing — drinking Dougan milk, pulling up your mother's yard plants, eating dirt, climbing all over the place, and every day running into new experiences. Pretty soon it will be the twenty-first century. See if I'm not right.

Sincerely, Ron Dougan

Danielle Jacqueline's letter starts with commentary on her brothers:

They will tease you a lot, but oh! how they will fight for you if any one else picks on you. What a lovely name you have. It reminds me of your great-grandfather, Dan Osborn, and your great-grandmother who passed away the morning you were born. Just as your brother John makes me think of your other great-grandfather, John Amend, Sr. When I was a boy I knew and admired them. No one will often call you Danielle, of course. It will be Dan or Danny for sure. We have three girls and they are called Jo, Pat, and Jack. Can you guess what Mrs. Dougan and I named them? It was Joan, Patricia, and Jacqueline. Drink your milk and eat your cereal and before long you will be following your brothers to Todd School.

Danielle Amend

Ronald's own children furnish him with ad material when they produce grandchildren. "LUCKY, LUCKY JOAN!" reads the headline over a glowing young woman with two small boys who couldn't look happier:

The Schmidts don't live here anymore. Their children can enjoy the luxury of Dougan's milk only when they return to Beloit to visit Grandma and Grandpa. Poor little Pete! Poor little Jerry! Unhappy little wretches!

Lucky, Lucky Joan

Portrait by Mathias-Houghton Studio

Joan Dougan Schmidt was fortunate in having Dougan's milk from the day of her birth . . . one way or another. Now it is a different story. The Schmidts don't live here anymore. Their children, Karl Peter, pushing two and Jeremy Craig, just one, can enjoy the luxury of Dougan's milk only when they return to Beloit to visit Grandma and Grandpa! Poor little Pete! Poor little Jerry! Unhappy little wretches!

Dougan's Vitamin D Homogenized Milk

AT YOUR DOOR **18ᶜ Qt.** OR AT YOUR STORE

See What You Buy — In Glass — Your Most Economical Package

Pat is shown with her daughter Jackie Jo, "UNTO THE THIRD AND FOURTH GENERATION."

> Jackie Jo's great-grandfather established the Dougan Farm and became known as "The Babies' Milkman" when Theodore Roosevelt was president. Her grandfather grew up in the business and brought his bride to the farm during the Coolidge administration. Her mother, Patty, a leggy little girl, grew up in the thirties. Now Jackie Jo and her little sister Stephanie are living close to the home farm. The ideal of their great-grandfather was to supply Beloit with the best milk it was possible to produce. Jackie Jo attests to the continuing attainment of this ideal as she develops strong and happy on Dougan's Milk—which, by the way, she calls "Gampa Juice."

When it's Jackie's turn, the headline is, "POOR GRANDPA DOUGAN!"

She is pictured with two small girls:

> Grandpa can see his granddaughters only once in a while when they come to visit. Jackie Dougan Jackson has Megan on her lap. Ol' Megan was born at Harvard. Damaris, the scamp, was born at Oxford and is a British subject as well as a United States citizen. Probably their sister will be born at Yale, where their father, Bob, is teaching this and that. POOR LITTLE NOMADS! If they'd come back to Beloit, Grampa would fill them up with Dougan milk out of amber bottles! No kid can resist that flavor. They'd drink till their eyes bulge.

Craig's four get the same treatment. "They can't get Grampa's milk and orange drink in Carson City, Nevada, where their daddy practices medicine, but how they lap it up when they're in Wisconsin!" Then Ronald tells of his Western grandchildren's visit: "Perhaps the high point was a canoe trip down Turtle Creek from the Shopiere dam to Colley Road. Turtles, carp, little green heron, great blue heron, kingfishers, cedar waxwings, and ducks galore—a Wilderness Area at our Door!"

Occasionally Ronald rings a change on his baby ads. Under the headline, "WE LOVE OUR HOME AT THE DOUGAN FARM DAIRY," a cow gazes mildly at the reader and says:

> They treat us like the ladies we are. Everything for our bovine pleasure and comfort is cheerily provided. Of course we appreciate all this, and in turn

Jackie with Damaris and Megan.

we give the finest milk we know how to produce. From the time we are milked until the bottle is set on your porch our milk has the finest care of any milk in the world.

A group of cows declare, "PAMPERED? OF COURSE WE ARE! The Dougan Farm Dairy not only pampers us, they pamper our milk until the moment it gets to your table." And again, "OURS IS A PROUD HISTORY!"

"We have to give Jacqueline Elspeth top billing even if she drinks Dougan milk only when she comes to visit her grandparents." This is baby Elspeth.

Some things have changed in the milk industry since great-great-grandmother's day. Scientific sterilization has replaced older methods of cleanliness, automation has replaced hand bottling, fast moving trucks have replaced slow horse drawn wagons, and better records are kept of our efforts. Better feeding methods have even improved the already high quality of our milk. The wonderful care and attention we get at the Dougan Farm Dairy inspires us all to give our very best, and we do! So when you taste the superb flavor of Dougan milk, and all Dougan's Dairy products, you'll know it didn't just happen. It was planned that way.

The boxer pups hit the paper twice. Under "THE FAME OF DOUGAN'S MILK MUST BE DESERVED!" all nine are nursing, cuddled up to their mother, while the text says, "The Boxer children know that if their present source of milk supply should fail them, they will always be able to switch to that delicious Dougan's Homogenized Vitamin D Milk.... Some of these splendid Boxer pups are for sale. Come and see them. You'll love 'em!" In the second ad the pups are older, making a pushing, shoving crowd around a basin of milk. "NINE EXPERTS SAMPLING DOUGAN'S MILK. VERDICT: POSITIVELY NONE BETTER!" And, "We've just switched and are finding out what we've been missing. Why did we wait so long?"

Ronald peddles kittens, too, and manages to advertise milk at the same time. "YOUNG WIDOW OFFERS FAMILY FOR ADOPTION" headlines a picture of a handsome feline gazing demurely into space:

Mrs. Felix Chat-Chat, formerly Miss Fleur Puss-Catt of this city, can no longer support her fatherless kittens. Felix, the debonair scoundrel, abandoned his family, leaving mother Fleur to do her best to raise them in decency and decorum. They walk modestly, albeit with head and tail held high. Mrs. Chat-Chat is an old fashioned mother, and has for months nourished her family as nature intended. When the time came to change, Dougan's was the inevitable choice.

Several weeks later, in small print at the bottom of a regular baby ad, appears this notice: "Her many friends will be happy to know that Fleur, the Dougan cat, has successfully placed her entire brood out for adoption except for a fluffy, slate grey male kitten. First come, first served."

Another cat ad is of a striking black and white tom, curled up but head raised and looking directly at the reader. "ME? RISK MY LIVES?"

I should say not! I'm choosy with my diet. That's why I have insisted on Dougan's Vitamin D Homogenized milk since kittenhood. Lately I have been thinking of watching my weight a little. Maybe I should switch to Dougan's marvelous Fat Free milk. I must ask my doctor about it. I share my home at 1244 LaSalle with Mr. and Mrs. Earl Rice. Earl is a crack salesman for the New York Life Insurance Company, but as a friend he tells me that with my nine lives I'd be silly to insure.

The Dougan baby ads, with their occasional variations, run with success to the end of the retail delivery business. They are surpassed only by the schoolchildren ads Ronald writes every spring and fall, when thousands of the area's kindergartners and first graders come out to visit the farm.

Stephanie, Patsy's second daughter, "A Proud 4th Generation."

Johnny, "the first American citizen in the Gjestvang family in hundreds of generations," is the son of Gulbrand, farm manager at Dougan's.

24 ⨯ JO-KING

It's the fall of 1942, wartime. With so many men enlisted or drafted, there's a help shortage on the farm. Daddy has been getting up at two o'clock to run a milk route, then returning to do his office work. This is more complicated and time consuming than ever, what with gas and tire rationing, Pure Milk Association regulations, Office of Price Administration regulations, and other exasperating extras.

Now he's become increasingly uneasy that all is not well somewhere on the routes: there seems to be a steady shortfall of money. He hasn't had time nor energy to do the sleuthing necessary to find out what's the matter, nor the heart to do it. He doesn't want to find one of his drivers a thief. He trusts them and they're his friends. Several of them have been employed by the farm for ten years, one for twenty.

In late September he forces time to do some careful checking, and the evidence indicts the newest routeman. Vernon Sperlin is a breezy eighteen-year-old who came to the farm a year ago from Endeavor, Wisconsin. He'd been used immediately to fill a vacancy on the routes. He'd learned quickly and was popular with his customers. At the Big House he was well liked by Grama and Grampa and the other boarders. At the start he'd been inclined to be both careless and lazy, and Daddy had had to call him up sharply. One day, when he found him loitering in the milkhouse after missing several customers on his route, he'd said to him, "You've heard of the three good kings, haven't you?"

"You mean the Three Wise Men?"

"Yes, Caspar, Melchior, and Balthazar. But have you ever heard of the three bad kings?"

"Can't say that I have," Vernon had replied jauntily.

"Oh, I think you have," said Daddy. "The first one is Smo-King. Can you name the second?"

"Drinking?" asked Vernon tentatively.

"You've got it. His Royal Highness Drink-King. What's the third?"

Vernon rolled his eyes heavenward. "I won't say that bad word!"

"It's Shirk-King," said Daddy grimly, "and you're doing a lot of it. Better shape up or I'll introduce you to the fourth king, Hike-King."

It had been an idle threat, for Daddy had no one for the route and Vernon knew it. But there was something in the exchange that sobered him, and he shaped up.

Now, he's just been drafted. On his last day on the job, Daddy finishes his computations and confronts him with the evidence. Vernon is distraught. He admits his guilt, says this is his first offense, and begs Mr. Dougan not to go to the police. In view of his youth and his forthcoming military service, Daddy decides not to prosecute, provided the money is paid back. Grampa agrees.

Vernon sits at the route check-in table in the back office and with a certain amount of technical help from Daddy, writes a confession. Daddy, and Gladys Moore, an office worker, sign as witnesses.

> During the summer or fall of 1941, I, Vernon Sperlin, began to take money from my employer, The Dougan Guernsey Farm Dairy, and continued the practice until I left their employment September 30, 1942.
>
> I manipulated my accounts to hide the theft as follows: When certain customers paid me I pocketed the money and gave them no credit for the payment on that day. Thus my daily report sheet balanced as neither a debit or a credit appeared on this transaction. After my daily report had been submitted, and usually a day or so later, I would enter a credit on the customer's account on the date the account had been paid. Thus my record with the customer was accurate and the customer received full credit for payments.
>
> I am extremely sorry for this misdeed and this violation of trust, and wish to do everything in my power to make restitution. As soon as the amount taken can be established, I will give a note covering it, and agree to make regular payments in reducing the obligation.
>
> Signed:
Vernon Sperlin
October 1, 1942

That same day Grampa, at his roll top desk in the bedroom, writes a letter:

> Dear troubled Vernon:
>
> I can not tell you how sorry I am that you should have been tempted to betray our trust in you and appropriated to yourself the money that did not

belong to you. You realize now how serious an offense it is. You should have thought of the sorrow it would cause you and your friends when tempted to take the money. Of course it will grieve your parents greatly, and it will be a difficult task for you to live this mistake down.

It is always sad to see one fall into the ditch, but it is infinitely sadder to see one stay in the ditch. You have fallen and fallen seriously, but there is no reason why you should go on in wrong doing and a life of crime. You have the ability to be a good bright business man. You know I told you this when you first came, and encouraged you to take business courses in the vocational school, and I was disappointed when you got a car and began running around.

Now your problem is how to get out of the ditch and make the man of yourself that you are capable of being.

You have done a wrong thing and that must first be righted. It may at first appear impossible to do this. Your first tendency will be to try to hush it up or regard it as a slight mistake. This attitude would only burn and sear your character and spoil your whole life. Have you read the novel, "The Scarlet Letter"? This story deals with this fundamental problem: Can sin be confessed and forgiven? In this story, Hester's sin was open, and her whole after life was devoted to purity, charity, and friendliness. The sin of Rev. Dimmesdale was hidden. He did not confess, though he was filled with remorse and his covered sin burned into his very soul and, as the story goes, burned the scarlet letter on his breast. It is the age old story of wrong doing and remorse, or wrong doing and sinners' repentance and the will to live it down.

Now, Vernon, applying this lesson to your case means this. You have wronged your employers. You have wronged your fellow delivery men. You have wronged your parents and friends who had confidence in you. You have broken a fundamental law of society and the State. You at present are deeply moved and full of remorse. So was Judas after his betrayal, but he took the wrong way out of it. You should now turn to sincere repentance for this wrong you have done. How can you do this? The steps are definite.

First: Study your own attitude. If you are deeply sorry (not that you were caught, but that you did the wrong) then there is hope for you and an honorable way out of it.

Second: Make a manful confession to all whom you have wronged. This confession will take a different form to different parties. Your letter and words of confession to your parents will be loaded with grief and deep emotion that you have fallen below their expectations of you. Your confession to your fellow drivers will be a business statement that your wrong will make it more difficult for all concerned in the business; possibly to the extent of requiring a bond securing each driver which is an unnecessary expense if there were no men doing such tricks as you have done. But you must confess and confess openly if you want to get out of the ditch and live a respectable and respected life.

Third: You must make restitution to your employers to the utmost of your ability. Your employers are in a position to make it very hard for you, even to a term in State prison or a reformatory. However, you know we do not desire to do this if you are truly repentant and want to live a right life which we believe you do.

Now, Vernon, what are you going to do about it? It is entirely in your hands. You can will to stay in the ditch; i.e., to continue wrong doing, cover up your past and try to make yourself and every one else believe you are straight whether you are or not. Or you can will to come right out and repent fully and start anew and become a strong straightforward man. We will do all in our power to help you follow the latter and heroic course.

Sincerely,
W.J. Dougan

Daddy and Gladys Moore spend the next several days figuring just how much Vernon has stolen. This means checking every day's reported total for over a year with the amount Vernon later recorded in his route book as collected. Some days, they find, he pocketed nothing at all, or as little as forty-three cents, others days it's ten or twelve dollars. The previous July he collected over nine hundred dollars, but reported less than eight. The year's total, as closely as they can figure, comes to almost $1,120. In barely post-Depression times, with wages at $200 a month, this is a substantial sum.

Daddy takes Vernon and his confession to his lawyer, and in those solemn offices the amount, and terms of payment: $20 per month at 4%, are added to the essence of the confession. The sheet is signed, witnessed, and notarized. Vernon then leaves town and enters the army.

In December, Daddy receives the first payment, sent by Vernon's father:

Kind Sir:

Enclosed you will find a check for $50.00 drawn on me for Vernon's payment to you, and please be so kind as to send a receipt for same in Vernon's name.

It is difficult for me to comprehend how such a state of affairs could come about without your knowledge; that you could check on him on his final month but find it impossible to do so six months previous.

I admit Vernon did wrong but I can not hold you blameless either.

I never transacted a "shady deal" in my life and thought I had trained my boys to be honest also; maybe he was too young for the responsibility, but who knows.

Any way he will make his retributions as he is paid, and his life is spared. He is sending all by way of me as he cannot get to a Post Office or Bank either one. I will send it on to you when I receive it.

If he has to give his life for his country his debt will be buried with him so far as I am concerned for as I previously stated I hold you responsible also.

Yours truly,
Kenneth Sperlin

In answer to this letter Daddy writes that his excuse for not bringing Vernon up short a good deal sooner was that he realized what a grave matter it would be to charge a young man with so serious a misdemeanor without absolute proof. That with limited office help, it took him some time to set up the necessary machinery to prove his suspicions. Also, with Vernon living in the house with the family, and other drivers equally well known and liked, it was a long time before he believed it possible that any one of them could be taking money. He finishes, "He is young and I have every hope that he will straighten out." He does not say that during this period he himself has been carrying a full route job along with his regular full-time job.

Throughout the war Vernon's payments come in regularly, usually more than the stipulated amount. The later money is sent by his mother, who in a near-final payment tells Ronald that Vernon has served in the Pacific theater for two years, the last six months in the northern Philippines.

In October of 1945 the last check is received. Ronald, sending the receipt, congratulates Mrs. Sperlin and her husband for standing by their son, and Vernon for making restitution. He writes,

My father and I feel that we have given Vernon a better opportunity than had we forced the matter more strenuously. He was a rather down-and-out boy until we trusted him to pay his account and not hold him further. We rejoice with you that the war is over and Vernon has been spared. We hope that he will call on us after his release. I have no idea what his plans are — maybe we can fit into them.

At supper that night Daddy relates the finish of the Vernon Sperlin saga. "I doubt if we'll ever see him again," he says, "but if he does show up, I'll be tempted to tell him about a few more kings. Such as that bad king, Ta-King Money, and that good king, Ma-King Amends."

Craig waggles his head wisely. "If you do, I think a certain Milk-King must be Ache-King for a Po-King in the kisser!"

Daddy gives him a fierce look. "You know, there's a king for smart-alecky kids, too—a good Lick-King!"

Craig hastily supplies a final king. "Hey, Jo-King! Just Jo-King!"

Records show that Vernon Sperlin performed honorably in the Service, married, had a child and grandchildren, apparently led a good and decent life as a mechanic, and died in 2004, just 13 miles from Endeavor, Wisconsin where he was born.

25 ⚔ LYALL BACON

R on Dougan is often out in the State, delivering corn. When he's near the home of a former employee, he sometimes stops by for a cup of coffee; this usually leads to reminiscences about that man's time on the farm. One day, south of Wonowoc, he remembers Lyall Bacon, a twerpy sort of chap, a bit weasely, who was pretty much a jack-of-all-trades and very useful around the place. Lyall is home and very ready to launch into his account.

———·———

I came in 1942, Ron, and then you hired my brother Nyall a year or so later. I was hired to work in the fields, Mr. Griffiths was field boss, but when Grampa saw I could fix trucks, he put me in the garage. It was right beside the milkhouse. None of those trucks would work right, they were in deplorable shape. In the winter only one would start; I'd use it to pull the other ones and get them started. I told you they all needed overhauling, so we bought a motor and I put it in one truck, and then rebuilt that truck's old motor and put it in the next truck, did that right down the line. Got 'em all running. Guess I earned my keep!

You sent me over to the Cherry-Burrell Company right on Lake Michigan; we needed alloy piping. You made a list, and gave me one of those canvas bank satchels. While they were filling the order I went for a walk along the lake, left the satchel on the seat of the truck. Then I took it inside to pay, and opened it up, and instead of a check here was all this cash, thirteen, fourteen hundred dollars! I was real mad that you'd given me all that money. When I got back I had Mrs. Moore in the office check it all out, item by item, to be sure it came out all right, and you said, "What? Didn't you use any for lunch?"

You put me on the route for a while. There were a lot of nice people. Any holiday, I'd go in people's houses, have coffee, cake, doughnuts.

They weren't all so nice, though. I had one of your friends on my route, I won't mention any names, you know who I mean. He was an attorney and in Rotary, probably still is, and month after month he let his bill get bigger and bigger, up to $140 on 14-cent milk. I was getting paid a salary and commission so of course I wanted him to pay up. I finally went right to his office and he said he'd mail a check out to the dairy. I said, "How'd you like your clients to know what sort of a guy you are?" So he wrote me a check. I jumped in my truck and rushed to the bank and cashed it, and just after I'd got the money the call came through not to honor the check, but I had the money. Next Rotary meeting you came back and said, "Lyall, did you do that?" I said, "Yes, I did that," and you chided me. You were running a milk route then, too, and I said, "If you want to deliver milk to him, you do it." And from then on, you did.

One place, they wanted me to deliver to the rear of the house. That always made more running, so I cut across the yard, I didn't know they had a dog there. I had my carrier in one hand and a quart of milk in the other. I came round the corner and that dog came leaping and snarling at me and I laid the bottle right across his head. He was flat on the ground; I thought I'd killed him. I delivered the milk quietly and slunk away. I wasn't stupid enough to go up to the house and say I hit your dog! The next time I went around there I had a quart of milk in my hand, and the dog was all right, but when he saw me he got as far away as he could and lay down and cringed.

Got a brand new customer, on Whipple Street on the west side. I was supposed to take it into a little entryway and set it down. I got a note to collect, so I knocked on the door and someone said come in, so I did, and here was a lady with an open house coat on and nothing else; she was young, pretty. I said I gotta get going, and just then her husband came out of the bedroom and said I had to bring them all the milk products they wanted or he'd say I tried to seduce his wife. They were blackmailing me, see, to get all their milk for nothing. I dodged out, and I talked to the Wright & Wagner delivery man, and he said they tried to pull the same stunt on him, and then switched milkmen. So I called them up and told them they had to buy coupon books and leave 'em outside with the bottle, with a note saying what they wanted, that was the only way I'd deliver to them. Funny thing is, they stuck with Dougan's. I guess they ran out of milkmen! Ron, I never told you about it at the time. But maybe someone tried to pull that on you, too, when you were delivering milk! Maybe it was tried on all of us, one time or another. Except probably old Lester Stam.

26 ❧ DUE CREDIT

Over the years, most people pay their milk bills. Ron Dougan makes no systematic effort to collect on overdue bills, except to have the milkmen keep reminding their customers. In case one disappears, he pursues him with a letter or two. Sometimes, after several reminders, he turns a batch of delinquents over to a collection agency. But the earlier reminders are variations on a theme: "Dear Mr. Hayes: In rechecking our books before turning old accounts over to an agency for collecting, we find that we are carrying a balance of $25.36 against you. We believe this has escaped your attention but we would appreciate either hearing from you or receiving your remittance as soon as possible." These letters usually bring results: the full sum paid, or an arrangement made to pay the bill in installments.

But unpaid bills become a more heavy problem during hard times. The Depression is one. In 1933 Ron sends out a barrage of notes to overdue accounts, addressing the customer personally, asking if he or she can pay a little on the bill. These letters are unusually gentle and courteous. He recognizes the common plight, he twists no arms. Some customers respond with small sums, more often they say they will pay when they can. And eventually most pay.

Some do this by coming out to the farm and working off their debt. A file card dated May, 1931:

> H.O. Downoway, 317 Springfield. Quit. Will never pay, worked out a bill of $12.30, and discontinued delivery. From now on cash only.

W.J. mentions this practice in a 1932 letter to Professor Duffy at the university, who, in the midst of the Depression, is sharply critical of what W.J. is spending for labor; profit is all that matters to Duffy. W.J. writes, in controlled exasperation: "My farm labor expense will not show economy for two reasons. First, as I have indicated, I have used a lot of extra help in order to work off milk bills of unemployed customers. And second, I presume I myself do not work hard enough, or push my men hard enough, and I pay too well."

It is at this time that Ron sets up a special account, a reserve for uncollectable bills. Into it he puts half of one percent of his total sales. Every year, when anyone pays on one of these bad bills that he's thought is gone forever, he deducts it from the accumulated total.

He also, over the succeeding years, sends out more dunning letters. These are also courteous and fair, and indicate how reluctant he is to lose a customer, no matter how small or large the debt. Some of these sums don't seem worth the time and postage to the modern mind, but postage then was three cents, and people's inability to pay even small amounts show how much money was worth, and how desperate the times.

The mailings indicate not only that a customer is in arrears, but also sometimes show the ambiguities of the business. Some are apologies for mistakes made. Some are painful to write, to a friend or business associate. There is an occasional letter of appreciation. And one, this from a customer, is a tart note about quality:

> Dear Mr. Stam,
>
> I am returning the cottage cheese that you exchanged last time. It simply doesn't taste fresh. I know that you did not pack the cheese and that therefore it is no fault of yours. Please tell the people at the dairy that it is better business to keep their customers satisfied than to get rid of stale merchandise.
>
> M. Feder

On September 8, 1942, Ron writes to a lapsed customer on Sixth Street:

> Dear Mr. Martin:
>
> I notice that you were taking milk and paying regularly until June 8. The driver's book states that you wished to discontinue until after the following payday. I am wondering if the driver failed to get in touch with you later in May, for we have not heard from you since then. Our customers are our greatest asset and we hate to lose touch with them.
>
> Your balance at the present time is $8.95. Let us know when it will be convenient to pay on this account and we will call back. Or better, let us start delivery again and at that time start paying up the balance.
>
> Yours very truly,
> R.A. Dougan

On February 11, 1942, to Mrs. Kenneth Caldwell on Tenth Street,

Thank you very much for your letter relative to your account. We have checked back and find that in the confusion of changing your account from one driver to another in March of 1938 we failed to give you the credit you indicate. We are doing this now by adjusting the old balance to $2.70, which we understand you are taking care of at the Associated Credit.

Late in the fall we asked them to help us with a number of accounts that were inactive or on which we had lost addresses. We appreciate your payment and beg your pardon for our failure in rendering the correct balance.

May 29, 1942, to a customer in South Beloit:

Dear Mrs. Fiore,

In re-checking our books we find a balance of $6.36 against you. Our driver has called at your home but has been unable to see you. We do not like to give our customers' accounts to a collector but we feel that after a certain number of trips, especially now in the present time of tire conservation, we have fulfilled our obligation, unless you would send your remittance in the mail or call to have the driver stop and see you.

The following letter presents a peculiar problem, and given the way people regularly leave money, or tickets worth money, in milk bottles, it's a testament to general honesty that theft doesn't occur more often:

Dear Mrs. Ainger,

I have just talked to the route man and the supervisor about your ticket book. The route man tells me that on Sunday he found neither note nor money in the bottles. Inasmuch as you always either have tickets out or money for a new book when out it struck him strange. The following delivery you talked to the supervisor, and he left you a book.

The only conclusion we can come to is that someone noticed the money in the bottle and picked it out between the time you put it out and when the driver called. At any rate, you put out the money, and we didn't get it.

Of course we can't accept responsibility for money put out and lost before the driver picks it up. However we hate to have you suffer the entire loss, and will be happy to divide the loss with you and charge you only $2.50 for the new book.

This letter, from August, 1942, shows Ron's reluctance to lose a customer:

Dear Mrs. Wright:

When you discontinued taking milk some months ago, I understood that you intended to start making payments against the balance as soon as convenient. I would appreciate hearing from you, and if things are working out, would like to have you start making payments.

In the mean time, I wonder what you are doing about milk. If you would care to take milk and pay for the current milk as you go, we would appreciate your trade. You could keep up the current account and pay off the old balance as you could.

At any rate let me hear from you.

Sincerely,

R.A. Dougan

Price list, 1963, delivered on the milk routes.

DOUGAN FARM DAIRY

Beloit, Wisconsin — Telephone EM 5-7786

PRICES IN EFFECT APRIL 1, 1963

GALLON PRICES ON LEADING PRODUCTS REDUCED TO **79¢**

79c will buy a gallon (four quarts bottled in amber glass), of any of our milk products in any combination —

This includes:

VITAMIN D HOMOGENIZED
CREAM LINE
FORTIFIED TWO PERCENT
FORTIFIED FAT FREE
CHOCOLATE MILK

Prices for other than 4 quart combinations (even gallons) are as follows:

Vitamin D Homogenized, Cream Line, and Chocolate Milk

One Half Gallon	44c
Quart	25c

Fortified Two Percent

One Half Gallon	42c
Quart	23c

Fortified Fat Free Vitamin A and D

One Half Gallon	40c
Quart	21c

By Products:

Buttermilk	Quart	22c
Orange Drink	Quart	18c
Cottage Cheese,	Creamed	25c

Cream:

Half and Half	Quart	70c
	Pint	37c
Coffee	Pint	52c
	½ Pint	27c
Whipping	½ Pint	39c

From October 14, 1942:

Dear Mr. Cliff:

We have discussed your account in the office. It is alarming that since April you have allowed it to get to nearly $60.00. We are probably somewhat to blame too in not urging payment more strongly.

The minimum arrangement to which we can agree relative to payment is that you give us $3.00 every week. This will pay for two quarts per day, and will pay $1.18 on the balance. If you can arrange to take care of this on this basis, we will go along with you and be happy to continue furnishing milk.

Of course you appreciate that in the eyes of any hardboiled credit manager, the account looks pretty bad. We do not wish to be unduly severe, but we must have a regular arrangement by which this big balance is worked down.

Ron often tries to take into account the possible plight of the customer: "Your balance of $196.27 represents the value of nearly twelve months delivery. It occurs to me that there may be some circumstance of which I am not fully aware—repercussions of the Iron Works strike, perhaps, which affects the situation, and which should be taken into consideration."

Stories of hardship come back to the farm in wake of the letters. A 1942 reply:

My husband has been in the army for four and one half months as yet I have not received any allotment money but as soon as I do I will pay it up in full.

Mrs. Earl Mitchell

In 1948 Ron writes to a former employee who has moved to another town:

I have not heard from you since your letter of April 13 promising monthly payments. I hesitate very much turning the account over to a collector. First I hate to subject one to their persistent methods of collection—especially one who has worked with me and whom I know. Furthermore, we get only part of the money a collector secures. The fact that we have carried you so long entitles us, I think, to be paid in full. However I am not equipped to continue following up accounts on which I can get no action, so I am forced to turn them over. I will appreciate it if you will get in touch with me at once, enclosing payment and setting up a plan whereby we can work this old balance of $58.80 off.

Mr. Shoemaker replies,

Dear Mr. Dougan — I am very sorry that I cannot send you payment at this time, also that out of circumstances which I have no control over I have been unable to take care of any of these bills. As you know I was forced out of work for the most of six months by the strike which cost me all the cash I had been able to save, then I lost my house and had to move up here to get my family in a place to live and at that time I got very sick and lost five and a half months again and haven't been able to work much since that time. However I am trying to make a farm loan so I can get these things taken care of. If I can't get a loan I will try to get down there in the spring and work for you.

Very Respectfully,
E. A. Shoemaker

From 1949:

I have received your notice about the past due account I have with you. I want very much to pay you as well as pay all my bills but I have been out of work one year and I can't seem to find anything as yet. Please give me a little more time. Yours truly, Andrew Steward

From 1950:

It has been with regret that we have been unable to meet our obligation to you. More especially since you have been so considerate and helpful to us.

It is not because we wish to burden you with our troubles, but more because we believe you have the right to know why we haven't met our obligation, that we offer the following information, our apologies, and beg your indulgence.

During last summer the writer sustained an injury which forced him into an extended layoff thus making our financial burden on the ensuing months more than double. Soon thereafter the stork made a very welcome, but untimely, visit at our home and blessed us with an heir.

We now have ourselves on a strict budget, and beg that you consider the following payments, which will, of course, increase as we are able to liquidate our smaller obligations.

Jackie never hears from her father that he lowered the boom on any of these hard-strapped people; subsequent letters show him working out graduated payment plans. Occasionally, though, it seems a customer may be trying to con the dairy, but there is no way of being certain. From a May 12, 1942 letter to a woman then located in California:

> I am extremely sorry but I can find no record of your payment of the $19.53 on our books against you. My mother, Mrs. W.J. Dougan, has no memory of such a transaction. If a payment had been made to her at church, the natural thing for her to do would be to put it through the office immediately. Both my bookkeeper and the routeman were well acquainted with the account, and would have been quite certain to run through the proper credit.
>
> I believe that in March you were still with the Bach Drug Store, or had recently discontinued the connection. I remember telling Mr. Bach about the account at that time, and later writing Janesville when you were located there. I think you must be mistaken relative to the payment.

A man from church, somewhat slow-witted, who lives with his mother and sister, writes a rambling letter asking Ron to look into his bill. "I want to do the square thing," he writes, "and I know everyone else does also. As I said I really do not think I owe this $6 and I hate like sin to pay it. I foolishly threw out all my old statements."

Ron goes over all the figures and in a full page letter gives various possibilities for error. He finishes, "At any rate talk to your mother and sister about it. Whatever you decide is O.K with me as I know you are only anxious to have the account correct."

In 1950, Ron receives a letter from a Mr. Heinz of South Beloit: "We appreciate so much the credit you have extended us that I feel I must acknowledge your letter without further delay. We will try to cooperate with your policy but could I ask that we do it in this manner." He then outlines a payment plan. This plan does not work, for eighteen months later Ron writes another letter in response to Mr. Heinz's latest proposal:

> Thank you for your recent check to apply on your account which amounted to $176.23 on that date. This left a balance of $11.23 which you requested

to be discounted.

Perhaps it has not occurred to you that this is a rather unusual request except in cases where the credit of an individual is uncertain and the creditor wishes to get out and stay out — that is to take his loss, forget about it, and not get involved again. From time to time we get into a position where the individual's ability to pay has gone to pieces and it gets to be a question of half loaf better than none.

As a matter of fact, in your case, we have carried you for a long time — on the basis of last month's delivery, the balance represents about twelve month's milk. We have carried this large balance without interest, although we have to pay for our milk and our labor monthly and like most businesses, are operating partly on borrowed capital and paying interest on this capital.

I appreciate the fact that the going has been rough for you this last year with changing jobs due to the strike and it has put you behind. In view of this, we would like to go along with you and will accept the $165.00 as paying in full what you owed up to that date. Since then you have had milk amounting to $3.44 to the last of August. May I suggest that we establish a collection schedule which will prevent you running behind again, and that we be quite hard-boiled in holding to it. By this I mean that if you decide to pay weekly, we will expect the money regularly and if for any reason payment lapses beyond two weeks, the driver will automatically cancel delivery.

I hope you understand the above arrangement is entirely impersonal on my part and my only interest is in developing a scheme whereby automatically the bill will be kept up and both you and I will be spared embarrassment in the future.

Mr. Heinz is not the only customer who has had extended credit. Charles Glover works for Wright & Wagner, Beloit's largest dairy, yet takes Dougan's milk. Ron sees him at Wright's and talks about his bill. He then writes, "I am sorry I did not have accurate information on your account when I saw you a few weeks ago. Following is your record." He then gives it, the sporadic $10 payments, and says the account now stands at $305.08. "During this long period of delinquent account we have never added interest as we would be justified in doing. Of course you realize the above record is far from satisfactory, and we would like to establish an account on some sort of automatic basis to get it paid. I talked to Homer Wright some time ago and he suggested they take an assignment against your check down there, so the money would come through on a monthly basis."

A customer occasionally comes up with a unique proposal for paying his bill. Ron answers such a one in 1952:

I'm afraid I am a poor collector. It was over a year ago that I last wrote you about your account, stating that I was going to turn it over to someone more capable than I in putting on the pressure. You countered with the idea on the boiler, and there the matter rested.

About the heat efficiency idea, I think that situation is the same as my farming set up. I know a whole lot better than I put into practice, and the most elaborate heat-loss study on the plant would only bring additional proof of facts I already am familiar with. No. I do not think such a study would do.

That brings us back to the fact that we have been carrying you for $144.98 for a long time with no interest. It seems to me that the responsibility is yours to take care of this, and my big mistake was to ever advance you the credit in the first place. If we had kept a tighter rein on the credit, you would still be using our milk and we wouldn't have this money tied up. It is a strange paradox, isn't it?

And here is a letter of contrition from the forties:

Dear Mrs. Gransee:

I owe you an apology for allowing as sharp a letter to get out as I did. As a matter of fact, we in the office assumed that the driver had regularly called, and as the account still showed on the book we sent the letter together with some others.

We have checked back to the original entries in January, and find this situation. Mr. Ullius, the driver at that time, started with your balance of $1.73 at the first of the month and added 14 qts. @ 13 cents, one whipping cream at 23 cents and a buttermilk at 8c, and arrived at a false total of $2.86 instead of the correct total of $3.86. When you discontinued on January 21, he figured rapidly, made the mistake, and I imagine receipted your bill in full to the amount of $2.86.

He of course knew you thought the account was fully settled, but by the time the office had refigured the book as we do on all books every month, Mr. Ullius was working for another employer, so we had no chance to talk over the various accounts with him. The new man was inexperienced on the route and did not know you. We made the mistake of assuming he had called back and you knew of the balance when he hadn't.

I can't blame you in the slightest for resenting our letter, and I would give a great deal if we hadn't offended you. The least I can do now is to have a credit run through to clear the account and hope you will forgive us our mistake.

Yours very truly,
R.A. Dougan

And then, there is the occasional complimentary letter, where Ron sometimes takes a customer into his confidence:

Dear Mr. Swanson,

First I want to tell you how much I appreciate your long term patronage and the fact that you use our products in such liberal quantities. Your account is like money in the bank. Furthermore I want to assure you that your arrangements for payment have been quite satisfactory, as evidenced by the fact that I cannot recall having written you on the subject.

I might mention in passing that I have been going over the books with Mr. Langklotz, sorting out accounts that need a prodding. We passed your page rapidly, and then I reconsidered. If I take time to write the troublesome accounts, why not tell a good customer he is appreciated?

You will be interested in my problem as to the price of milk. Our volume is down a little, and our costs, notably milk purchased from farmers, is working up. I have figured as closely as I know how, and in spite of the fact that most dairies in the middle west are raising their prices, I think we can continue at the present price, at least for awhile. Just to show you how complex it is, if nothing happens to force up the Plymouth cheese market on Friday, the chances are that the condensery price which is partially based on cheese will not advance. If condensery holds firm, our buying price which is based on condensery will not advance, and we can get by without a raise. At present we are three cents under Chicago, although our price to farmers is the same. We are two cents under Rockford, and from one to two cents under paper bottles in the Beloit stores and two cents under paper in Janesville stores. Our margin is closer now than it has been in a long time.

Thank you for bearing with me. I didn't start to write about my troubles in trying to maintain a margin in a business where I have very little to say about costs. It certainly is a merry-go-round and high time some of us stopped it. The trouble is no one is big enough to do it alone and stay in business.

Sincerely,
R.A. Dougan

A final letter about customer relationships, from the early sixties:

Dear Mr. Mitok:

At the time you stopped taking milk from us, I meant to write you, telling you we had appreciated your business and express the hope that sometime in the future you might want us to stop by again. Like many good intentions, I guess I never wrote the letter.

I was reminded of you today, when the driver who had your stop came in and said he had lost a customer to Mueller because Mueller was going to buy his gas from him. He then said that was the way we lost the Mitoks to John Holmes in the first place.

I only wish we were big enough to buy reciprocally with all our friends, but you can appreciate that with a commodity like gasoline, it is not practical to try to divide our business. The best I can do is stay as loyal as possible to suppliers who have treated me right and have given me no cause to change.

At any rate, I wanted to send you this belated letter. We are trying to put out the best milk we know how—as matter of fact, since we produce about 3/4 of the milk we bottle, and our herd is a mixed one, the average butterfat, and therefore the solids not fat run higher than the average milk of the country. We do think we have a superior flavor.

After many years Ron Dougan's special half-of-one percent account reaches a total of $7,000. He has never paid taxes on this money as it's a reserve for bad bills. It represents a credit of $7,000. He closes out the account and pays the tax.

"I suppose I forgot a lot of bad bills that never got into that account, that got written off, anyway," Ron says. "But even so, I don't think it would add up to more than a half cent on a dollar. When you think that less than half a cent on a dollar is what I was losing, while giving credit all over town, it says a lot for people's honesty."

27 ❧ LESTER STAM

On January 1, 1922, at age 32, Lester Stam leaves farming with his father in Sparta, Wisconsin, and follows a cousin to the Dougan Farm. He brings with him his wife, Mildred. For a while he works in the barn, the milkhouse, the fields. Then there's an opening for a route man. Lester takes the job, and never holds another.

He delivers milk well into old age. Over the decades he becomes a familiar, venerable figure as he daily totes his carrier of bottles up to the kitchen doors of Beloit and South Beloit homes. To his customers the word "milkman" is synonymous with "Mr. Stam." As he ages it takes him longer and longer to finish his route. Daddy shortens it, and sometimes in bad weather sends someone to give him a hand. When he falls asleep over his route book in the office, checking in, Daddy finishes it for him. Finally, at eighty, Lester retires. The *Beloit Daily News* interviews him.

Lester recalls that there were two routes in 1922; his was on the east side of the river. At first he had a partner who drove the truck while he did the running. Once his driver—Eddie Pfaff—took the corner at Central and White, an acute angle, at such speed that Lester sailed off the seat and lit on his bottom on the street. "A pretty hard landing," says Lester.

Later, when the routes multiplied, he had one alone. Sometimes Dougan's reverted to horses. After one March blizzard the roads and streets were so clogged that milk had to be delivered by team and bobsled for over a week. "Pretty slow going," Lester says.

In all his years he had only one accident. A front wheel rolled off his truck, and the vehicle tipped over. Says Lester, "That was a messy day."

He also once had his truck robbed. His cash box with his change and keys in it was removed from his truck, down on Broad Street one morning. He never got it back.

He was a hero once. He saw smoke curling out of the roof of St. Paul's Lutheran Church and called the fire department.

And then there was his adventure. A maid in a well-to-do household met him at the door in a state of agitation. Two little eyes were gleaming at her from under a bureau. She begged Mr. Stam to come in and get rid of whatever it was. He followed her to a bedroom, crouched down and peered beneath a broad chest of drawers. After a moment he reached under and pulled out a purse. "The eyes were those shiny knobs on top that cross over to hold the bag shut," chuckles Lester. "Catching the light."

Actually there was one other adventure, or sort-of adventure, which he doesn't tell the newspaper reporter. He tells Ron, who repeats it later with glee. He was down on Athletic Avenue, delivering, at about three in the morning. He returned to his truck to find one of his customers, an elderly woman, clambering into it. She was very drunk, he tells Ron, and kept repeating, "Dat debbil Dougan! Dat debbil Dougan!" Lester tried to get her out but she wouldn't budge. Finally he had her drink a pint of milk and gave her a ride home. She disappeared inside, still singing out, "Dat debbil Dougan!"

Lester Stam with 48 amber bottles representing his years as a Dougan milkman.

When Daddy gets to this part, he adds, "He delivered her along with the morning milk. We didn't charge for her, because we didn't know how full she was."

"Since we all know Daddy Dougan is a saint, she must have meant you were the debbil," Lester says to Ron.

Along with the *Daily News* article are pictures. One is of Lester holding a milk carrier, climbing out of his truck. One is a view through the truck, to Lester juggling milk cases. And one shows Dougan amber milk bottles, a pyramid of ascending rows, with Lester's grizzled face peeking over the top like a gopher out its hole, like a squirrel guarding its hoard. There are forty-eight bottles, one for each year of his service as a milkman, and he holds a pint bottle for the additional half year.

This final picture proves popular. It's reprinted in *The Rockford Morning Star* with the headline, "LESTER STAM 'MISTER MILK' TO BELOIT KIDS 48 YEARS." The accompanying article says he has jumped on and off his truck one million six hundred and fifty thousand times, and never spilled a drop. It says he once regularly started his route at 1 a.m. and is a dairy diplomat: "Asked what a milkman sees early in the morning, he replied, 'Beautiful sunrises.'" Though starting time is now closer to 6 a.m. than 1, Lester says he has had to start his route earlier and earlier, these days, because of slowing down, but that his wife Mildred always gets up when he does and packs his lunch of homemade bread and fresh garden produce.

The picture is also reprinted in Madison's *Wisconsin State Journal.* But someone has goofed: the caption under Lester and his forty-eight and one half bottles reads, "Harvey Elmer, Monroe City Engineer, With Supply of DDT," and the headline, "MONROE CONTINUES TO USE DDT TO CONTROL DUTCH ELM DISEASE." Two days later, with no DDT retraction, the *State Journal* prints the climbing-out-of-the-truck picture, captioned "He Gets His Energy From Milk," and a rehash of the Beloit and Rockford articles, but with a paragraph comparing postmen, who can refuse to cross an unshoveled sidewalk, and don't deliver on holidays and election days, with milkmen. The paper goes on: "The Dougan Farm calls itself 'The Babies' Milkman' and Stam takes it seriously. 'We have a great responsibility in seeing that babies get their milk,' he said. 'I have been very late, but never missed a day.'" He is also quoted, "I've delivered to the babies of the babies of the babies."

The 48-plus bottles picture has one further repercussion. A few months after its appearance, Lester receives a letter:

Dear Mr. Stam,

I read your article concerning your milk bottle collection in *The Rockford Morning Star.*

We own an Antique Shop on Highway 89, 6 miles north of Delavan, Wisconsin. While on a buying trip in Iowa we picked up an amber-colored bottle marked Dougan's, Beloit; near the bottom is "One Quart L.I.Q. X M679 Reg." On the bottom is impressed "Patent Design 174,591. 11. E 6 1."

As a rare colored milk bottle it sells for $2.00. If you are interested in adding this to your collection kindly advise and I will save it for you.

Bet you have had a lot of fun in getting your collection together.

Sincerely, Maude Totten
(Mrs. L. J. Totten)

"I think I'll pass on that bottle," says Lester.

28 ⚡ THE SCHOOL ADS

"**B**eloit children are fortunate in living so close to the country. It's a rare child who hasn't seen a cow milked, baby pigs nursing their mother, or a calf taking its first faltering steps."

So writes Ron Dougan, in a large ad that pictures a dozen Brownies, each wearing a white milkhouse paper cap, and ranged up the diagonal ramp of a corn elevator. He mentions himself only obliquely: "We at Dougan's enjoy our visitors and have fun showing them the complicated and fascinating steps in producing a high quality milk." It's up to the many visitors to point out that the farm tours are made unforgettable by the one who personally leads each outing, Ron Dougan himself. In his later years he continually meets adults—a bank teller, a hospital nurse, an insurance salesman—who say, "I sat on your lap when I was six," or, "You squirted milk right into my mouth," or, "I got to drive the tractor!"

Even at the time, the kids know what makes the trip so special: "Dear Mr. Dougan, We had fun at your farm. We liked crowding around you."

The letter, reproduced in a Dougan ad, continues:

> The things we liked most were, the ride on the hay, the hollering house, the witch's stairway, the ponies, all the farm animals, the tour of the dairy, jumping in the corn, milking the cow, tasting warm milk, Gertrude the talking hen. Chocolate milk never tasted so good. Thank you, Mr. Dougan. We hope you will get plenty of rain and sunshine for good crops this summer. Love, Cindy Divan, for Mrs. Burke's First Grade, Robinson School.

From its start in 1906 the farm extends a welcome to visitors. People are invited out to view the milking and bottling, and special events are planned for the public's pleasure, interest, and instruction, such as Sunday School picnics, alfalfa seminars, and corn yield trial days. School classes visit now and then. 1950, however, is the first year that Ronald Dougan formalizes these visits. He invites all the schools to bring out their kindergartens or first grades for educational playdays. The schools accept with alacrity, and Ron reserves several weeks in spring and fall for the outings. In an ad some ten years after their inception he writes, "What do they do?"

> There is Gertrude the talking chicken who thinks she is a rabbit. She likes freckled boys and girls and gives them souvenir feathers out of her neck. The children sing Princess Gertrude to sleep, and a Prince Charming wakens her with a kiss. Usually the song is Rock-a-Bye Baby, but the more sophisticated groups may surprise her with Brahms Lullaby.
>
> The children have a chance to help grind corn for the cows, to have a drink of milk squirted right into their mouths and try a hand at milking. Some lucky ones ride a cow or drive the tractor on the hay ride.
>
> Little animals abound. Every trip is different. One group played with rabbits, raccoons, chickens, and calves. They listened to bobolinks, red-winged blackbirds, meadowlarks, and dickcissels in the hay fields. They saw homing pigeons at close range, peeked into a wren's nest, and watched a field mouse who lives in a bird house.
>
> Oh, it's fun at Dougan's, especially when the party ends with chocolate milk, whistles, and everybody singing, "Old Man Ronald Has a Farm, Ee-i, Ee-i, O!"

In addition to the early grades there are sometimes older grades, Scout troops, Salvation Army Sunbeams, retarded children, handicapped children, even a smattering of birthday parties. Classes in neighboring towns pour out to the farm. Ron notes this in an ad. Beneath a photo of Rockton schoolchildren, "Poor little chill'uns. Living in Rockton they can't get Dougan's milk delivered to their homes like the lucky, lucky children in Beloit and vicinity."

It's of course superb advertising that every child in the area at some point has a wonderful time at the Dougan farm. Ron makes the most of it by having a pho-

A school child feeding hay to a heifer.

tographer on hand. During the spring and fall large pictures of school groups, with such headlines as, "53 WATERMAN 6 YEAR OLDS WORN DOWN TO NUB," supplant the Dougan baby ads in the *Beloit Daily News*.

Ron uses considerable ingenuity in finding a variety of places for the children to be photographed. They gaze out of the newspaper from in front of the round barn; from among the stanchions in the lower barn; on the ramp up to the hay mow; up in the hay mow; on a wagon ready for a hayride; perched on tractor, manure spreader, corn planter, or ranged on top of the mobile water tank. They are on a mountain of corn; inside a row of delivery trucks; watching the bottling; by the cow tank in the barnyard; up to their knees in the creek; in a corn field with shocks and pumpkins. They stand before the old schoolhouse, in front of the milkhouse, hang on a pasture gate. They're pictured with cows, calves, pigs, the pony. They're perched on the scaffolding of the mural-in-progress on the Chez Nous seed barn, seated on the grass singing a chicken to sleep, in a circle drinking chocolate milk. Often they are holding animals—kittens, dogs, rabbits, calves, piglets, a fox cub, a raccoon kitten, a descented skunk.

Ron always writes the copy. The headline under a group surveying small pigs at a trough is, "BURGE FIRST GRADERS VISIT SMART PIGS." The ad goes on:

> The three little pigs in the foreground are, from left to right, Petunia, Pansy, and Sausage. "The only trouble with Dougan's milk," says Sausage, "is that we don't get enough of it." "Look at those kids," chuckles Petunia. "They sure come in all shapes and sizes, but all nice. Isn't that Tom Pickett over there, and what is Dick Cheadle doing out here?" "I'm smart without going to school," claims Pansy. "Dougan's milk by the gallon is a wonderful bargain. I could use a gallon myself."

In an ad where kids are draped over a fence surveying nursing sows:

> These pigs found the children very amusing. How silly to walk on two feet when the smarter animals all walk on four. Why run and shout when one can lie on the cool ground and grunt? One little pig wondered why Suzie and Pauline Salmon looked so much alike. When told they were twins he said, "Oi, oi!"

We see Ron Dougan squirting milk into a row of open mouths, and the

A class hangs over a fence to watch barnyard activity. They wear milkhouse caps. The child on the right is Gillian Jackson, Jackie's daughter.

copy reads, "In the barn Mr. Dougan milked right into some of the girls' mouths—such a squealing time that was! And who were these brave girls? Nancy Whaley, Nancy Stadler, Linda Barkenhagen, and Sandra Jones. Not to be outdone by her daughter, Mrs. Jones took her turn!"

The ads combine this playful element with reporting some special event from each visit, often with information and education about farming. Beneath a cluster of small faces looking up from deep within a dark hole:

> This isn't the inside of a rain barrel or a bucket of live bait. It is Mrs. Gilbert Schultz's first/second grade from Converse School, standing at the bottom of a Dougan silo. They are learning first hand that these huge cement cylinders preserve summer feed for the cows to eat in winter. Grass made into hay loses much of its valuable Vitamin A. As silage, most of the Vitamin A carrying carotin is saved as the yellow character of the milk testifies. Later the children were fascinated as they watched the bottling equipment whirl attractive cellophane hoods onto shining glass bottles of milk. Only minutes before, in the Round Barn, they had lined up for the fastest milk delivery in history, from cow to consumer, and here it was again, pasteurized, cooled, and bottled, just like at home.

About kids ranged along a large piece of machinery,

> Perhaps none of Mrs. Henry Rowe's first graders will ever use a cultimulcher like this one at Dougan's Dairy. With modern techniques, a few of us produce abundant food for a growing population. Even Dougan cows are better. Each

one gives nearly twice as much milk and cream as her great-great-grandmother did in the twenties. That is why, even with rising costs, our milk is cheaper to your door than in the 1920-26 period. Less time is now needed to produce the necessities of life, so more of our nation's genius finds its expression in a flowering of the mind and spirit. Truly we are living in a Golden Age — the longest and most widely distributed the world has ever known.

Sometimes Ron gives a bit of personal history and reminiscence: "These Brownies had their picture taken beside a 75 year old schoolhouse that is now located on the farm. Mr. Dougan was once a pupil in this schoolhouse and later taught there." And since Ronald for various short periods attended Strong School in Beloit, which was right across the street from his Aunt Ida Croft's house, he writes, under a photo of Strong School students:

We attended Strong School before Bushnell Street was paved. When the schoolyard's famous Croft Elm, now a victim of Dutch Elm disease, was a puny thirty years old. In those days the neighbor kids played Duck on the Rock in the soft June twilight under the gas streetlight that swung over the Harrison Avenue and Bushnell Street intersection. In those days Dougan's Milk was delivered from horse drawn milk wagons as it had been since 1907. Oh well, Dougan's Milk is so good people will be buying it when these first graders are starting families of their own. Don't forget us, kids.

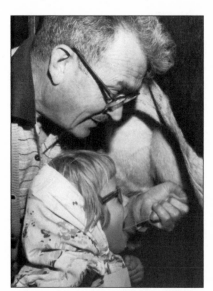

Ron Dougan delivers milk direct to the consumer. Kathy Martingilio is a first grader from Gaston School in Beloit.

As the activities and photo sites are varied, so too are the styles of the ads. The headline above a picnic lunch in front of the log cabin in the Hill Farm woods (transportation, a three-mile hayride from the dairy) reads, "TALK ABOUT BRIGHT EYED AND BUSHY TAILED ! ! !"

Hundreds of Beloit children visit Dougan's Dairy every spring and do you know why? Because they have more fun than anything. But oh, the questions they ask!

—Do some cows give chocolate milk?

—Why don't cows have upper teeth?

—DO THE CHICKENS STAY UP LATE WATCHING TELEVISION?

—Are they afraid of the dark? Is that why there are lights in the chicken house?

—ARE PIGS CLEANER AND SMARTER THAN COWS?

—When are we going on a hayride?

—KIN I HOLD A RABBIT? KIN I? KIN I? KIN I?

—Can we eat our lunch at the 'Lincoln Log Cabin' in the woods?

The ads are generous with children's names and individual activities, and Ron is quite often personal with his small visitors—and never condescending. Before the snowmaking machine:

WHAT? SNOWBALLS IN MAY?

Waterman First Graders Have a Snowball Fight at Dougan's Dairy.

Dear Mr. Dougan,

We had such a good visit to your farm. Thank you very much.

Waterman First Grade

Bobby Grundry, Secretary

We had fun with you, too, Bobby. Do you remember some of the things we did? In the girls' race in the Round Barn, Belva Frye outdistanced Melody Rast by a nose. In the boys' race, Jimmy Magnanenzi won over Danny Moyles by a neck. Sandra Brockner was the sharp-eyed little girl who found the robins' nest. Gail Gregus noticed that her rabbit exactly matched Miss Tuck's grey angora sweater. Did Mike Leisher tell you he found his Aunt Flossie in the office? Of all things, she was on a chair picking gas balloons off the ceiling for the class. Mrs. Florence Johnson is that nice voiced person who answers the phone at Dougan's.

The ad the following week passes on a message for a previous visitor: "The robin's nest that little Sandra Brockner found the day before was still hidden in the corner of the wagon box—(this time Bennie Devine found it)—and Bennie says to tell you, Sandra, that there weren't any eggs in it anymore, but four naked baby robins." It also sends get-well wishes to a non-attender, who had an appendix removed, and promises Carla she can come next year.

Ron Dougan holds a piglet.

As to the advertising of milk? Often it's nonexistent, but readers are usually reminded, in Ciceronian fashion, of this fact: "We started to write an ad about the milk business, and how the children learned where that good Dougan's milk comes from — then decided to share with you some of the thank you letters from the Brownies." And often it's by-the-bye: "Before they left they showed Mr. Dougan some magic. He set out some chocolate milk and they made it disappear in a flash. Good trick!" "As active a gang of six year olds as ever tore the red cellophane caps off bottles of Dougan's Homogenized, at school milk break."

If advertising is central to the ad, it's usually presented humorously. A Guernsey head, haloed by first grade heads, gazes benignly at the reader:

HAS DOUGAN'S DORA WATCHED YOU LATELY?
(Eyeball to Eyeball?)

> Thousands of Beloit children know Dora. They have climbed all over her and the more daring have milked her. Where does Dougan's milk come from? Well, Dora supplies over 5,000 quarts a year to Beloit homes. Dora and 165 sisters live and work at Dougan's — if you call it work. Ron Dougan thinks he does all the work. The same number of cousins just over the fence in neighbors' fields furnish an equal share. Call Dougan's Dairy for the best there is — Home produced, Home processed, Home delivered. A product unique to Beloit — truly a "*vin du pays.*"

In another ad, after talking to the children about the activities of their visit, Ronald says, "We hope you will drink more Dougan's MILK — now that you know the cows personally."

Occasionally an ad approaches poetry, but with any sentimentality deflected by a quick shift to humor:

A school group carefully crosses the crick and follows the cows to the round barn for milking.

PARKER BROWNIES VISIT DOUGANS

O what fun we have, mothers and daughters together...

Lovely little girls with charming lilting names. Listen to the song of their names:

> Cheri, Mary, Linda Sue;
>> Sharon, Maggie, Barbara Ann;
>>> Susan, Lynda Ray, Lu Ann;
>>>> Suzanne and Bonnie Sue.

Again we have forgotten the milk business, but who cares. We'll think about it come meal time, when each little nose will be buried in a brimming glass of the delicious stuff.

A school group, with Ron Dougan, watches pigs chow down. The small building behind, "Taliesin," is an eight-sided pig farrowing house.

But Ron doesn't put a humorous end on an ad that remembers his father, only a touch of wistfulness. The photo shows a crowd of heads peeping over the side of a wagon, which has been pulled up on the barn floor before the silo:

CHIN DEEP IN A GRAIN BOX

Above these heads, painted on the silo, are the famous "Aims of This Farm," first stated over forty years ago by W.J. Dougan, the original "Babies' Milkman." To these we might add another aim to which he dedicated his life. It was, "To Produce and Distribute to the Families of Beloit as Fine a Milk as Could be Secured in Any City at Any Price." "Daddy" Dougan is gone now, but he lives in our memory and his example and precepts guide us constantly. We enjoyed entertaining the Waterman Brownies and know that "Daddy" Dougan would have been delighted to have seen them having fun.

Surely having mobs of children swarming over the place for weeks on end would constitute a nuisance for most businesses and far exceeds the demands of advertising. But then, the school visits are more than advertising. This is evident in the affection with which Ronald writes his copy, and the occasional tender lines that creep in: "We've said it before and we'll say it again — of all the lovely small creatures of springtime, calves, kittens, fox cubs and downy ducks — six and seven year old children are our favorite species. Aren't they wonderful?" Or, "Either Carol Wilson or Sylvia Solem had Mr. Dougan by the hand most of the time. They didn't want to lose him." Or,

> This is our favorite thank-you here at the farm; we approve the simple direct style and reciprocate the sentiment:
> "Dear Mr. Dougan, I wish you would hire me for a helper at your farm and most of all thank you for lettin us see the gopher. I enjoyed the orange juice. Dear Mr. Dougan, I love you, do you love me?
> "Love, Shirley May Faust"

The school visits continue till Ron Dougan retires from dairying. He always hosts them personally, in spite of the seasonal demands of plowing and harvesting, the daily requirements of the milk business, and the unvarying variables—a sick animal, a burst boiler, a balky engine in the well, trouble in the bowels of the bottlewashing behemoth. He enjoys the kids, giving them new, enlightening and delightful experiences, sharing with them (and later, the readers of his advertisements) the fun and interest of the life he loves:

> Angus the calf knows Beloit children, all right! Maybe a thousand have pummeled him this spring, and hundreds have perched on his back, as Cathy Stanley is doing here. Morgan children can look across the road from school and see Dougan cows making milk for them. When we say fresh milk, we mean fresh milk. Ron Dougan and his men hustle all year long to keep the cows well fed and comfortable. Maybe there is an easier way to make a living, but none that is more fun.

Ronald, in his way, is as much a missionary as Grampa is in his. Not only that, he's happy to advertise it.

29 ⚹ WARNER BRAKE

I t's shortly after the start of World War II. Part of routeman Howard Milner's job is to deliver milk to the factories. Warner Brake, a large Beloit factory, has turned Daddy down on selling to their men. However, when Howard is driving by once, and stops at a stop sign, a man calls from a window. He wants to buy milk. Howard leaves his truck, goes to the window and hands the milk up, and the man hands down the money.

"I'll stop by for the empty bottle tomorrow," Howard says.

The next day the man is at the window again, but he's not alone. Two others are with him. Howard sells them all milk, and promises to come back for their empties.

The following day the men are again at the window, and there are also men at adjacent windows. It isn't long before Howard has built up a brisk trade at Warner Brake, handing milk up to the welcoming hands, and receiving money and empty bottles back down. There is good natured banter between the milkman and the factory workers, and a sense of sport, like doing something behind the teacher's back and not being caught.

About two weeks later Howard pulls up outside to discover someone on the ground below the windows. The windows are empty. Howard sizes the man up; he's dressed in a business suit. Oh-oh, thinks Howard.

"What's going on here, milkman?" asks the man. "I'm waiting to see you." He introduces himself.

Howard isn't sure, but thinks he recognizes the name as the president of Warner Brake. He also thinks this marks the end of a good thing, but they needn't have sent the head guy, a foreman would have done. He explains that the men want milk.

"Well, I don't like them hanging out the windows to get it," says the man. "Do you want to continue selling milk here?"

"Yes," Howard says. "I want all the business I can get."

"Then come in and go through the shop. First come with me to the office."

Howard can't believe his luck.

In the office the president says, "Here is my situation. Because of wage fixing, I can't give the men a raise. I can give them anything else except cash and a raise. So why don't I give them free milk? It would be eight hundred pints. Four hundred a shift. Can you handle it?"

Howard is dumbfounded. "I gotta ask my boss!"

"Bring him in. I'd like to start right away."

Howard hightails it out to the farm. He and Daddy go down to Warner Brake that afternoon, and Daddy sews up the deal. There are not enough pint bottles on the farm for eight hundred a day. The president—for it is he—says that the company will pay for the bottles if Daddy will get a hold of them. Daddy sends two men to the factory in Chicago, and they bring the bottles back the next morning. Daddy and Howard make the first delivery together, a whole truckload just for Warner Brake. They walk through the factory handing out milk.

After a few days, individual delivery proves too time consuming both for Howard and Warner Brake. The factory moves in a bulk cooler so that the men can fetch their milk at noon. Early in the morning Howard fills his truck, puts the milk in the Warner Brake cooler, and retrieves the empties. He then returns to the farm and loads his truck for his regular route.

This happy arrangement goes on for a few years. Then George Schreiber, in charge of the milkhouse, leaves for a different job. Without enough help, it's hard to get the bottling done. Daddy considers turning Warner Brake over to Wright & Wagner till the war is over. He is fighting just to hang on to the shoe factory and the Iron Works. And then, war pressure causes Warner Brake to add a third shift. They now want 1,200 pints a day. That cinches loaning the business to the larger dairy.

For Howard, losing Warner Brake means losing a hefty commission. Ron gives him the amount of the commission on three month's salary, to make up for the money he would have gotten. At the end of the war, though, Daddy makes a few very broad hints, but Wright & Wagner does not return Warner Brake.

"*C'est la guerre*," says Daddy, with a headshake and a shrug.

Howard figures that means, "That's life." He shrugs, too.

30 ⊰ WALTER ABBOTT

In the late sixties, Ron stops by to see Walter Abbott, living in town, retired now as a milkman.

———

You want to hear my milk route adventures, Ron? What makes you think I had any? But you know I was on the route for a lot of years, rain, shine, sleet, snow. Except on Saturdays. You liked to have a Seventh-Day Adventist milkman who would be glad to work on Sundays, and that was me.

I came during the War—I think it was '42—you were running a milk route yourself, you were glad to turn it over to me. But then later, when Red Holmes left, you had to take on his route. Those were the days!

In the first years, the work wasn't as compartmentalized. I was a route man, but I'd finish my route, and then put up hay, or pick corn, or detassel, or pick special corn—once I sawed up wood with a buzz saw, another time I went behind the potato digger in field west of the Big House and picked up potatoes. I'd help milk, or be in the plant—put in a day's work! So did the rest. None of us thought anything of it. When the electricity went off, we'd have quite a party at milking time!

On the route I had a pet peeve—well, it was worse than a peeve. It was when housewives who wouldn't put their bottles out till after you were down the street three or four houses, then they'd call, "Yoo hoo! Milkman! You forgot my bottles!" but they hadn't had them out when you were there. And once in a while I had a customer who never washed her bottles before she put them out, they'd be all slimy and smelly. When I helped out in the milkhouse, those bottles were the ones that always had to have a special wash.

Rosco—on the relief route, he went all over town and South Beloit—he said that in parts of town the bottles were put out dirty and other parts of town, they were put out clean—but that in the dirty part, there was always a house or two where the bottles were sparkling, and the same for the clean part—there'd be some houses where they never rinsed their bottles. My route was in a clean part, but I got some dirty bottles, too, as I said, so I know he was speaking the truth. The bottles from the shops never got rinsed out, of course.

Once I thought I'd rolled over a heavy stone or boulder. You told me later that day, "Did you know you ran over Mrs. Persinger's dog and killed it?" It was the sort that ran after wheels and grabbed them, he must have caught a spoke and got carried around. She thought I'd killed it because she hadn't paid her bill in a few months. I didn't ask if she then paid up! And I didn't get into trouble over it, with her or with you. Maybe you smoothed things out.

Then once I was rearranging the empties from the back of my truck and the wind slammed the door on me in the middle of my back, so I got out feeling sour, and a customer's little dog came running up and grabbed me on the ankle just as I stepped out. I said, "Get out of here, you!" and tossed an empty bottle at it. The bottle kept sliding across the grass and the dog running from it, and all of a sudden the bottle hit a little lump and bounced up under the dog, hit him in the belly, not enough to hurt him but to shock him, he went yip-yip-yip and the customer stepped out on her porch and said, "Is my dog bothering you?" and I said, "Not anymore he isn't!"

Walter's children helped promote the milk he delivered.

Fairbanks was having a strike, it lasted six months, and you said to trust people, as long as they were making a try at paying their bills. One fellow told me he couldn't pay, he didn't have the money, but he had all sorts of beer empties on his back porch. I felt like asking him to cash them in, but I don't think you get money back on beer bottles. At least I never saw any of it, and he wouldn't have got the sarcasm anyway.

But then there was that fellow on my route, name of Voss—you remember him?

He said you wouldn't, but he remembered you well. He said to me, "When I first came to town I didn't have a job, I had two children, taking your milk, and only a little money came in, the milkman got some of it, I got to running up a tremendous bill—Ron Dougan'd written me a couple of times about it—I finally came out to the farm and told him I recognized the debt and I'd pay what I could, but in the meantime I better quit taking milk. Ron said, 'Well, I'll tell you what I'll do. You keep taking the milk and I'll keep on trusting you, and you pay me when you can.' Shortly after that I got into insurance and real estate and I did all right. I paid my back bill, of course, and we continued to take milk. I'll never forget sitting in that office and Ron saying you take milk and I'll trust you and you pay me when you can."

Thinking back, Ron, over the years, and over some enlightened thinking about it, I realize there were instances when I should have accommodated better—I wish I hadn't been so unbending and helped you out once in a while on a Saturday when you were so desperate.

I know you thought so too, at the time, but you respected my need to have Saturday off; you said one needs to be firm, because you can always find a reason to work on Saturday, just like you can always find a reason to work on Sunday. But you never held it against me.

I didn't realize then that people were more important than dogma. I know that now.

31 ❧ THE THREE-LEGGED PIG

It's during World War II. There is rationing going on: gas rationing, tire rationing, meat rationing, sugar rationing. There are price ceilings on milk, on cheese, on cream and butter. It costs more to produce butter than Daddy and Grampa are allowed to charge for it, so they chop up the churn. At government urging, Grampa is raising a field of hemp for rope; he has to have a special license for a controlled substance. Daddy is shorthanded. He tries to get farm deferments for his men, and is often successful, but some of them enlist in spite of a deferment. He's on a milk route, along with all his other duties. Joan comes home from college to help out; she works in the office for a year. New trucks aren't available, machinery parts hard to get. It takes the inventive genius of two mechanics, plus plenty of binder twine, to keep things running, from tractors to pump to bottle washer. And everything has to be applied for and justified and written about and filled out in triplicate, and then, like as not, after long delays, there is some glitch and the papers come back and have to be done all over again. Sometimes twice.

Daddy is bone weary, but after all, it is the War. "Still," he complains, "if we only didn't have all that extra paperwork on our backs, if the government would just lay off us, we'd make out okay."

When Grampa starts the dairy in 1907, there are relatively few restrictions—and that is why he turned to dairying as his mission, to provide clean milk for babies, where the mortality rate was high, with deaths often due to unregulated, contaminated milk. He regulates himself, and that is where much of the good publicity comes to him—that without coercion he is testing every cow for tuberculosis, he's keeping a clean barn and milk room and a low bacterial count in his milk, and reporting regularly to the university.

But as the years go on, everything becomes licensed and regulated, from dairy plant licenses and the sale of raw and pasteurized milk and cream, to a "soda water beverage" license required for the non-carbonated orange and grape drink the dairy sells. And everything requires forms, statistics, and often letters back and forth. Beloit has to have its own set of ordinances on everything, and South Beloit, too, for the farm peddles milk in adjacent Illinois. One set from South Beloit is titled, "An ordinance providing for the licensing of milk and cream dealers, and the regulation of sale, disposal, exchange or delivery, possession, care, custody or control of milk or cream for human food," and runs to twenty-seven sections on five densely written, jargon-filled pages.

Regulations are not just for the milk business, but for the running of the whole farm. Detailed statistics are required on all inventory and finances, on what land is allowed for tillage and what withheld, and on much more.

In theory, and for the most part, Grampa and Daddy agree, regulations are good. Sanitary standards are now set. Inspection is now required. But bureaucracy has a way of feeding on itself, and much of Daddy's time is now spent on regulations. There are various fat files in his office filled with this paperwork. A lengthy 1945 questionnaire from the Wisconsin State Department of Agriculture gives a more than adequate example; its fine-print purpose at the top:

> In accordance with the provisions of Section 100.06 (5) of the Wisconsin statutes as enacted by the Wisconsin Legislature, we present for your consideration our sworn financial statement, in lieu of bond or other security. This statement is being presented for review by the Department as a consideration to the granting of our dairy plant license required under the provisions of Section 97.04 of the Wisconsin statutes.

The front page designates whether it is an individual, corporation, co-op, or another entity reporting, and the location. The second gets down to the nitty-gritty: "Assets," and "Liabilities and Net Worth." Assets is divided into Current Assets, Investments, Fixed Assets Invested in the Business, and Other Assets. Current Assets is subdivided into nine categories. Fixed Assets is divided into Land, Buildings, Machinery and Equipment, Cans, Trucks, Office Equipment, All Other Equipment Used in Business, and these are subdivided into Cost, Depreciation, and Book Value. When we get to Liabilities, these include Amount Owed to Producers, on Producers Assignments, to Haulers, Interest, Notes and Mortgages, and much more. So it goes, until we get Ron Dougan's total net worth at that time, $29,427.23.

There is a third page. This has nine Schedules, which the previous page has referred to for further detail. Schedule 3, Accounts Receivable wants to know, "Name and address from party from whom due; when due; and [enigmatically] for what is it due?" And finally, the amount. Schedule 8, Amounts Owed to All Others, again wants book, chapter, and verse.

The final page wants to know if there are "any judgments, suits, or claims pending against you?" Liens filed against you, etc. There is ample space for signature and surety that this is the whole truth and nothing but the truth. A long paragraph of small print at the end warns that incomplete reports cannot be considered. Ron Dougan has scrawled across the top of the file copy—for a clean copy is sent in—"This is the sort of stuff I have to do for the bureaucracy!"

There are many other items in the folders, including many South Beloit licenses to peddle milk and cream for one year, city of Beloit licenses to sell raw milk, to sell pasteurized milk, the Wisconsin State Department of Agriculture's hefty additions, plus numerous financial statements of both Ronald and W.J. Dougan. There is also a fat folder from the Federal government.

There is then all the wearisome correspondence in connection with the many rules and regulations. Letters back and forth, followed by letters about the letters. Most are nit-picking on the governmental side, but are important to the running of the business on Daddy and Grampa's side. They cannot be ignored.

At the supper table one night Daddy says, "I heard a joke today." He looks

Four-legged piglets.

around for everyone's attention, then continues. "It seems a traveling sales-man visited a farm, and in the barnyard he saw a pig limping around on three legs. He said to the farmer, 'What happened to your pig?' 'Let me tell you about that pig!' says the farmer with enthusiasm. 'Last February during the big thaw, the crick rose so fast and so high that it got right up to the barn-yard and was pouring into the barn and all the stock was in danger. That pig managed to get the barn door open, and the stalls unhooked, and he herded the stock up onto high ground, and saved them all.' 'My, my!' marveled the salesman. 'But that ain't all!' said the farmer."

Daddy pauses to take a bite of his salad. The family is listening. He goes on, "The farmer said, 'Remember the big tornado that struck around here last spring? Well, that pig seen it coming, and set up an awful squealing and grunting and alerted us all, so everybody managed to get down into the cellar hole. Lost the roof and the chicken house and all the chickens, but the rest of us come through okay.' 'My, my, my!' marveled the salesman. 'But that ain't all yet!' said the farmer. 'This summer the house got struck by lightning and caught on fire, and that pig got the screen door open and went up the stairs and managed to get the baby out of her crib and onto a blanket on the floor, and he took the end of the blanket in his mouth and hauled that baby down the stairs bump bump bump and outside, and saved our little baby's life.' 'My, my, my, *my!*' marveled the salesman. 'But you still haven't told me how your pig lost his leg.' 'Oh,' said the farmer. 'A valuable pig like that, you don't want to eat him all at once.'"

Daddy looks around, waiting for everybody to laugh. They finally do, explosively.

"Grampa appreciated that joke, too," Daddy says, attacking his baked potato.

32 ❧ LOYALTY

Jackie becomes aware, in the late thirties, of unions. Not just the sort big companies have, like Fairbanks Morse and the Iron Works, but unions for smaller businesses, such as dairies. It's mentioned at the supper table. Daddy doesn't know much more than rumors.

"They are here in town," he explains, "trying to unionize milk route drivers. That means that the drivers would negotiate their hours and their pay, through the union, and who knows what all else."

"Would all drivers have to join? Our drivers, too?" Joan asks.

"I don't know," says Daddy. "I'd think the drivers for any one firm would have to agree, and our men, or most of them, don't seem dissatisfied. They've stuck with us through the Depression, when we paid the best we could manage and we all tightened our belts, Grampa included—why should they demand more now, when everyone is gradually better off? If we're forced to up wages beyond what we can pay, we might have to cut the routes entirely, and sell our milk to creameries or to a bigger dairy, like Wright & Wagner. Then where would our drivers be?"

Jackie's stomach gives a lurch.

"Our drivers like it here," Craig states.

"Yes," Mother agrees. "Think of Stam joining a union—he's been here since before we were married, Ron. And Milner, and Roscoe Ocker. I don't think we have anything to worry about. You might chat with Homer Wright, though, see what he's heard, how Wright & Wagner feels."

"I'm not against unions in principle," says Daddy, "and I think they are pretty necessary when it's the little guys against the big steamroller companies. The companies that don't care. But when we're all little guys, in a small family business like ours, the owner included, when everybody does care about how the business fares, and about each other, then why set up an adversarial relationship?"

"What if they try to unionize farmhands, too?" asks Patsy. "They're up at three o'clock just like the milkmen."

"We couldn't do that till we unionize cows!" Daddy declares.

"It may not happen," says Mother. "Our milkmen are very loyal."

Jackie breathes out again. Yes, they are.

Talk of a possible union comes up sporadically over the next year or two, and then fades away entirely as the War absorbs everyone's effort, and there are not enough workers for the necessary jobs. On the farm, Daddy and Grampa's help leave for the factories or go into the service; Daddy works hard to get dispensations for young men to stay on the land. He himself holds down his regular office job of handling the milk business, and running a milk route besides. Both he and Grampa put in sixteen hour days, sometimes even more hours. And the corps of routemen they have stay on through the War, when Craig and herself help out on the routes during summers and vacations.

Years later Jackie comes across a written conversation between Daddy and Grampa, that spells out the problem. It also shows the extent to which Daddy and Grampa worked together and shared their thinking.

"Daddy," writes her father. "You know what our feeling about Rick has been for so long. His attitude is that the friends on his route and in town are his personal assets, and he holds his control over the milk buying of this group as a threat to us, his present employers. He championed this attitude very strongly yesterday when I brought up the question of John's leaving to work for Wallace, and wondered if many customers would follow him."

This is something that had never occurred to Jackie, in all her years growing up on the farm.

The document continues,

> As Rick put it, as many would follow him of their own accord as he would solicit. He maintained that it was entirely all right for him to use every effort to swing this group to follow him. As I told you, I grew quite indignant and said it was unethical. Said I did not have words strong enough to express my feeling for a man who would take an employer's money over the years and then in changing employers sell the first employer down the river. Said it was surely unChristian. When a man takes employment, he sells his physical and mental efforts and his loyalty.

Jackie pauses at this point. There is something here that bothers her. But she continues reading.

I also told him that I knew this had been his feeling about the routeman's attitude toward his customers right along. I couldn't forget the fact that something over a year ago he openly talked about the damage he could do us if he should pull out. He could cripple our barn, plant, and route force to the extent of four or five men, and could take away a big slice of the customers. I think in taking the opportunity to talk to him just as John is pulling out was a good thing. My excuse for jumping him was his reaction to John's possible action. It gave me a good chance to say what I thought, and let him know that his talk about what an important fellow he was a year back hadn't been forgotten and had never been taken well on our part.

I wonder if it wouldn't be just as well to urge him to find another job as soon as he conveniently can. I get tired of that attitude and don't trust it at all. I am sure he would have no compunction about jumping and in so doing, take as much as he possibly could. Of course he would swing a certain number of customers, but I am of the opinion that a man or a firm overestimates the amount a driver can drag away. Maybe we should urge him to quit, take our losses, and think no more about it.

This has nothing to do with the foregoing — I rather think we should let Rick go on the above. Besides this, however, he is the only fellow we have who is in sympathy with the union. I am convinced he will be the first one to fall in line, and I am sure he will be the most unreasonable man to deal with if and when the drivers of town are organized.

There is a note from Grampa in response. "If we do that we must first have a talk with Wallace, and warn him about hiring Rick. To this effect, show him just why we are letting Rick quit (because we know sooner or later he will find another opening and through it endeavor to break us if he can) or if he don't get an opening he will continue with us getting all he can and giving no more than absolutely necessary — a soured employee — and such a one in any group is a detriment."

Jackie thinks back, and realizes that Rick, an affable, likable milkman, did vanish from the place when she was ten or eleven. But she never asked why, nor ever really noticed. She returns to Daddy's line about loyalty. "He sells his physical and mental efforts, and his loyalty."

It seems Daddy's indignation about this unloyal employee is justified — when it's his and Grampa's own dairy, and he knows all the sweat and work and ideals that have gone into building it up, securing a solid customer base, and a better life for everybody — employees, employers, and the customers served, too, who have received a superior product. But what if it were Maple Dairy, say, or

Triangle, which both had been shoddy operations that regularly had bacterial counts in the millions? Firms that probably kept ailing or tubercular cows, whose milk was harming their customers? Should a milkman then be loyal? She thinks not.

There must be an ethic above loyalty, where a person should leave a bad employer, or a dishonest one, take what customers with him he can, for their good as well as his own—or stay, and blow the whistle. But what if he only suspects his employer is shoddy, or dishonest? Are there ways he can know? Further, how loyal should an employer be to an employee, if for any number of reasons that employee is not up to standard? And this can be extended to any relationship, to one's family, friends, to one's country, even.

It seems to be a case of situational ethics, which they'd discussed in her college Ethics class. Then she remembers a letter from Grampa that Uncle Trever had shown her, one written him when Trever, as a college kid, was working his way across the country. Many of Grampa's letters, to both his sons, contain advice. She had saved his words, she looks them up now. He writes, "If you take the grocery position fill the job more than full. Be more than an ordinary roustabout delivery boy. Learn the business, take a definite interest in your manager's welfare. Be loyal to your employer, if he deserves it, if he is a crank and unworthy of your loyalty, quit him. I have two or three men at present who are on the list to be fired—they are not loyal and do not appreciate what I am doing for them."

So there you have it, thinks Jackie. Loyalty goes both directions, and it is earned. It is not bought and sold. That is a satisfying conclusion.

33 ✼ MISFITS

Almost all the farm's milkmen are capable and reliable. Several spend their entire working lives on a Dougan route. There are a few, though, that cause Daddy enough concern that he keeps notes on them, in a hidden part of his desk. One such file, from the mid-1930s, is on John. There's no mention of his last name, but it can be found easily enough in the labor record book.

Verna Dobbs put out a note and we had a note on the office bulletin board not to leave any milk until Saturday, August 8, but John left every day. L. Plumb was to have milk by breakfast — He promised it when he picked up the shop load, but failed to deliver, and she called back.

Asked for his base pay to be raised, saying he was putting out a $50 a day average, but I looked over his figures and he isn't. His tickets were short $1.80. He did not stop to check. He never bothers to figure over his load, etc., as the other drivers do. He is rarely courteous in the office and impresses me as an unruly spoiled kid that hasn't been licked enough to have any consideration for others. I am certainly not inclined to placate a chap with higher pay when his every act indicates that the pay is all he is interested in. In a week or so Roscoe will be able to go alone. We will give Milner a rest, and then let John talk himself out of a job as soon as he likes.

Ruby asked John to fill in a sheet on a transfer. John answered rudely, completely squelching Ruby. He then proceeded to rush away a few minutes later, forgetting to do it.

Ungracious about a call-back to deliver acidophilus to his own customer, Ballard. Wanted somebody else to run it in. Disrupted office and upset Ruby. I took it.

Failed to deliver two customers. He didn't plan to take back. Ruby volunteered and took it. His truck was dirty. I told him so but because he was mad at Ruby and had to wait a few minutes for another driver to finish washing, he went home. I called him and he said he didn't understand it was to be washed right away etc and I should do as I pleased about having it washed.

There are several more pages of John not taking milk back to missed customers, not following up leads, or postponing doing it for days, not washing his truck even when Daddy writes "WASH" in the grime, and accounts of John's general cockiness. He does not date his route book, says he doesn't have time, nor fill in his shop book. He behaves boorishly at drivers' meetings. Then the entries end. John has talked himself out of a job. This milkman comes and goes when Jackie is very small.

The other large group of notes in the secret file is on Roy, who takes John's place, cleans up John's shop book, and is the relief driver for the other routes, a sort of "overseer" driver. Jackie does know him, for Roy is a flamboyant and personable fellow, and is around the farm for several stints of work: the last one continues until his death.

Daddy's initially favorable comments about Roy become cautious. "Tending to run a little late on whatever route he is on," and, "laid Swanson out for fare-thee-well because Swanson had changed a window in his truck — he holds Swanson personally responsible for most things that go wrong. His attitude makes it very difficult for him to take general leadership — he leads cliques and has sides. Swanson held himself better and showed up in better light than Roy by far."

Soon the comments turn all negative. Roy fails to leave customers their bills. "I took them back again. I find him no more valuable than a regular driver and a lot harder to handle. He will not conform to any office practice that he doesn't approve of or that will require more effort on his part." And, "He took back two misses on his route and one on another, under protest. As a rule he is hardest of the drivers to accept an additional service for the firm."

Daddy talks to Roy, and reads him the latest entry. Roy says his feeling was that he was asked to go back as a punishment. Daddy's, that he accepted the job in a grumbling frame of mind. "I told him his attitude at present isn't true of his attitude when he worked here formerly. He said that my feeling about him was a fine repayment for his years of service. He said that he would like another regular route — instead of his responsibilities becoming greater and work smoother, being the relief man meant his responsibilities were fewer and the work rougher."

Roy's sins mount. "He didn't have time to take care of a lead—said you better give it to Milner." Also, "Failed to use his head in criticizing me about cheese for Xmas—held me up before the drivers in a bad light—raised hob generally in the office and with Ruby—why can't he cooperate instead of antagonize?—His attitude is the answer why Roscoe should be advanced so fast etc as compared to the others. Roy is being overpaid on a competitive

Roy Veihman, one of the farm's best men.

basis, on rating of loyalty, and value to concern—he isn't much better off with a private route than as route jumper. I am tempted to suggest to him that he look around for another job."

Roy does leave, for a while pursues other occupations, then returns to the farm not as a milkman but as a seed salesman for Dougan Hybrids. There he finds a job he revels in; he's almost his own boss. Ron, in a letter to a corn dealer, says that John Sapp is leaving, but "I had a new man with me last week—Roy Veihman—who has been in our employ in other capacities for a long time. He will make an excellent representative for us in the corn business, I am sure."

True to Ron's prediction, Roy soon becomes head seed salesman, running all the Dougan Seeds booths at the area fairs where his expansive personality brings in friends and sales. He and Ron work well together, and Roy, with the help of his wife Fanny, who also enjoys the selling and the fairs, travels the Midwest, selling Dougan seed corn and oats. Ron even appoints him head of Farm Progress Days, when that statewide event is held on the Dougan farm in 1961. Roy grabs hold and makes it a smash hit. In selling and managing he has found his niche, and over the years he makes it big as a pig wallow.

Perhaps John goes on to a spot where he fits; Jackie never knows. But these two sets of notes, and the outcome of one, show her that not everyone is cut out to be a milkman.

34 ⚔ LAWRENCE LANGKLOTZ

The Langklotz family lives on a farm a few miles east of Chez Nous, over near Clinton. Lawrence Langklotz is a lanky, loose-jointed, sociable fellow, who is always popular as a milkman. When he gets a bad leg and retires from his route, his son takes over, but Ron likes to stop by and chat when he has to go to Clinton for nails or tools or something. One of their chats is about Lawrence's start at the farm.

I came in March, 1943, during the War. My first job wasn't as a milkman, though. It was with your dad, digging postholes for a fence east of the barn, so that the heifers could get outside. The ground was still pretty frozen, and I wrote to Daddy Dougan that the job was a waste of time. Daddy answered, "You don't know how important it is to get those heifers out!" so we went on digging postholes and I darn near broke my back.

Then you gave me your milk route, Ron—Red Holmes's route, I knew you'd been running it from October when he left, no days off, Sundays and Christmas and all. I was glad to get it, but I didn't like when I was loading up the truck that John Baker'd stand in the corner of the big ice box, checking everything I took, like I was stealing. He did that for everybody and nobody liked it. It was an unnecessary job.

You'd gone to every other day delivery by then, to save on gas and tires. I know Wright & Wagners went back to horses, but we didn't use the horses except for the bobsleds in the really deep snow. We did have an awful time getting those trucks going in the cold, well, actually any time, and keeping them going. Before the new garage, there was only room for two trucks, we had to start 'em all from each other. Old D15, from Halverson, we parked it on the barn ramp so we could roll it down and get it started in the morning.

There was that terrific snowstorm, Ron, remember? Colley Road was filling up fast. You drove me to the Turtle Town Hall, by way of the Milwaukee

Deep snow on Colley Road.

Road highway, and I hiked in to the Hill Farm, we were living there then. The next morning Colley Road had had a plow go through, so I started out walking. When I got to your place, there sat your Chevy at the foot of your lane—you hadn't been able to drive up the night before, so you'd just left it and walked in. I opened the door and the keys were in the ignition. So in I climbed, and drove the rest of the way to the dairy and went on my route. You were sure surprised when you mushed down a little while later and found nothing there; you had to walk to the dairy. You wondered how that car had managed to get there without you! I let you puzzle for a while before I told you about it!

I had an accident once, out in that hilly part of Turtle Ridge. The emergency brake failed, the truck rolled down and crossed the road and smashed into a tree. There was glass all over, broken bottles, the owner was mad, the police came. You had to square for the tree; it didn't make it. And I guess Erv and Ed had plenty of work fixing the truck.

When you had that route, Ron, you know that little old lady that was so crippled up with arthritis? Over on Moore Street? Yeah, how could you forget. Well, there she was, every morning, waiting for me. She couldn't bend over. So I'd deliver her her quart of milk, mebbe some cottage cheese, put it all in her refrigerator, and last thing, I'd kneel down and tie her shoes. Don't know what she did on the every-other-day that I didn't deliver to her. Mebbe went barefoot. Mebbe had the postman do it!

35 ✃ VOICE OF DOUGAN'S PRODUCERS

A little over two years into the Great Depression, the *Beloit Daily News* runs a series of unusual ads. They are Dougan ads, but not conceived by Ron or W.J., or paid for by the milk business's advertising budget. The idea comes from Albert Marston, next door neighbor to the farm. For over a year now the dairy has been buying milk from Turtle Township farmers and selling it as Dougan's Blended Milk, for 10 cents a quart. This is the farm's answer to the desperate times of the Depression, to help people buy a guaranteed milk they can afford. This milk is a boon not only to the consumer, but to the dairy and to the neighboring farmers. The farmers realize it, and appreciate the heavy advertising the dairy has done to promote the 10-cent milk.

At the start, W.J.'s and Ron's ads had introduced the new product with considerable fanfare. They'd assured the consumers that if they bought Blended, they would still be getting a quality milk. That the participating farms were clean, regularly inspected, and the cows tested for disease. That each individual farmer's milk must undergo frequent lab tests to insure its bacterial count stayed low. And there had been excellent response.

But the Depression is taking its toll even on 10-cent milk. Ron writes the newspaper, a letter to the editor, saying how little of the milk dollar is going to the farmer or to the distributor, how the price of producing is going up drastically, and how the quality of milk can be reduced, to save expense, in dangerous ways that the consumer will not recognize, as they would, say, a bruised or semi-rotten apple.

The farmers who are supplying the dairy realize that the Dougan budget for advertising is dipping low—W.J. has considered cutting back on ads, or eliminating them, important as they are, and has talked this over with Ron and Albert. Yet it's to the interest of everyone to keep on advertising.

It's then that Albert comes up with his idea. Enlist the farmers themselves to advertise the milk they are supplying! Both Daddy Dougan and Ron think this a unique approach, one sure to catch the eye of the reading public.

"This is not an advertising gimmick," W.J. says, studying Albert's idea written out for him. "It will be an honest statement from honest men, and its purpose will be to educate."

"I like the idea of not just contented cows, but contented producers," says Ron. He and his father urge Albert to pursue the idea. Albert goes to the other producers, and all are willing to participate. The farm agrees to accept their paying for the ads, and to supply some follow-up advertising of its own, at the end.

W.J. and Ron supervise the copy. They ask the men individually why they like to bring their milk to the Dougan farm, keep the answers as much as possible to the responses of the individual producer, add in suggestions, cut out repetition. The men agree not to reveal that they are the ones providing the ads until the end of the series, when a group ad will tell the secret, although each ad will give the name of the farmer who wrote it. The title of the series will be, "Voice of Dougan's Producers," and every ad will end with "Dougan's Blended Milk—Ten Cents Per Quart."

Albert's ad starts off early in January, 1932. His copy states, "I like my market in Dougan's Blended Milk because there is encouragement in working with a group of dairymen and a distributor who are producing and delivering a high grade of milk. The regular grading of my milk by Dougan's laboratory gives me a constant check on the quality of my milk and my care in production. —Published by Albert Marston."

A week later, Smith and Synstegard say they like Dougan's inspection because "1) Dougan goes at it as an educator and co-worker. He has come to our barns, scrubbed floors, curried cows, washed udders—showing us the essentials in producing clean milk. 2) Dougan knows where to locate and how to correct defects in methods and practices. 3) Dougan is practical in his recommendations. 4) By following his directions we get a milk that collects its premium."

Fred Eddy is brief. He says Dougan appreciates the efforts of clean dairymen, knows how to produce and handle clean milk, and looks to the interests of both producer and consumer.

The new information that J.M. Halderson adds is that "my premium last month was enough to pay good wages to one full time man." Howard Baldwin stresses Dougan's helpful criticisms and his high ideals in dealings with producer and consumer.

The final two ads, Lee Millington's and Floyd Brewer's, are variations on the earlier themes. And then comes the ad with the combined chorus, explaining:

THE VOICE OF DOUGAN'S PRODUCERS

We have combined our experience with that of Mr. Dougan in producing as fine a milk as we possibly can. Mr. Dougan's herd and farm inspection combined with his regular laboratory control is of great value in helping us maintain a uniformly high quality.

Two months ago we decided to contribute to the advertising budget of the Dougan Guernsey Farm, feeling that an increased knowledge of our product and methods by the consuming public would react to our mutual advantage and broaden the market for our good ten cent milk in Beloit.

Visitors are always welcome on our farms and in our barns.

Published by:

Howard Baldwin	J. M. Halderson
Floyd Brewer	Albert Marston
Fred Eddy	Lee Millington
Smith & Synstegard	

After the producers' confession come three contributions from the farm, the first informational:

W.J. Dougan, "The Babies' Milkman," gives the public five facts about Dougan's Blended Milk: It is produced by intelligent dairymen proud of their ability to supply us with clean milk; it is scientifically handled in our modern plant; it is regularly analyzed on the basis of bacterial count in our own laboratory; it is delivered fresh — last night's milk at your door before breakfast — this morning's milk on your table for lunch, and, it costs ten cents per quart.

The second ad is purely educational:

LABORATORY CONTROL

Our producers receive a substantial price for their milk. In addition to this they receive twenty-five cents per hundred as a premium providing their bacterial count is lower than our strict standard.

To determine counts, we employ the Frost Little Plate Method. This method consists of culturing samples of milk on agar, staining, and counting bacterial colonies under the microscope. It is particularly advantageous in controlling production, as an accurate check on a milk can be obtained in one-sixth the time required by the usual method. With Frost's method, a report can be secured between milkings, while with the big plate method two days are required.

Our close control, the quality of our farmer-producers, and the premium paid for quality, account for the splendid record of our milk at the City Health Offices the past year.

The series of ads then ends with a general thank-you to the consuming public, for their continuing support.

The producer ads run through April of 1932. Ron and W.J. are pleased with them, as are the farmers who made them possible. The ads show some results, but the success is qualified. For the story is not over, the Depression is worsening. At the end of August, Daddy is forced to write to the farm's producer friends the cruel realities of the situation.

When we decided to advertise starting last December and then in May decided to hold price, it was an open question whether or not we could hold volume enough to justify the course. As volume falls it automatically affects producer price. The question is, in which way can the best price be obtained for the producer, and the largest net for the distributor—by larger volume and lower base price, or by smaller volume and higher base price.

All you producers realize that while our wholesale milk and cream has been holding up, the amount of milk used in retail Blend has been shrinking.... We have reluctantly come to the conclusion that we must make a rather radical adjustment.

Most Beloit families have been hard hit by the Depression. The argument of higher food value at a higher price has little effect. Almost any fly-by-night dealer can put out a milk with a cream line that will surpass our Blend, and do it at a lower price. We must sell in competition to high fat milk, personally solicited by the owner-driver at prices ranging from 7 cents (Jensen) to 10 cents (Willowbrook). Below this milk is the commercial pasteurized. They automatically take a number of customers on basis of pasteurization propaganda. In addition, their 8 cent price is a tremendous incentive for customers to switch to them. And below them is the station milk—at 5 cents.

With the outlets to which we can look for volume restricted by the hard times, it seems we must fall in line or look to continued shrinkage.

Our change of policy must be drastic to be effective. Grade A. must come down to compete again with other Guernsey milk. We can not maintain our farm at the expense of the distribution business. Blend must be retailed at a price which will bring us a substantial volume increase. The retail price which we have in mind is 8 cents on Blend and 10 cents on Grade A. with a 1 cent discount on Blend if a customer takes 3 quarts per day or more.... This will, of course, affect what you producers will receive.

The producers recognize hard facts, and most of them hang in. The farm and the dairy hang in. And Turtle Township comes through battered but intact. Blended milk holds its own. This is aided by the government's edict, in 1933, which prohibits selling milk for under ten cents a quart, the determination being that at any less than that, milk is selling at a loss. Blend does not lose its popularity with the end of the Depression but continues on as one of the dairy's offerings until the end of the milk business in the late sixties.

Concerning the producer ads, there had been much earlier publicity that benefited the dairy in the pamphlets and articles of E.G. Hastings of the university, which praised the farm's cleanliness, low bacterial counts, and tuberculin testing, but this is the only time, Ron says, that direct advertising was sponsored and paid for by a group serving the farm. Otherwise, he and Grampa originated and paid for all their advertising.

"Those statements did as well for us as they possibly could," Ron says later. "The times were just too tough. But they got us a lot of attention. And Gramp was pleased and honored, and all our producers were. We all were."

36 ❧ KAZOOZLEHOSE

Howard Milner glances at his watch; it's almost eight o'clock. He turns his truck from his milk route and drives downtown. He parks before the *Beloit Daily News* building, pours coffee from his thermos and plucks a newspaper from behind his seat. It's last night's paper. He studies the classified page. There is an item hidden on the page, put there once a week to encourage people to read the classifieds. It's always different, and it offers $10 to the first person the next day who arrives at the *Daily News* office, fulfilling a certain requirement. "First person to arrive in a pink bathing suit." "First person to arrive with a home-baked pumpkin pie." "First person to arrive with half a beard." Howard has never competed in these contests, but the box this time reads, "$10 prize to the first person who arrives at the *Daily News* office and plays a musical instrument."

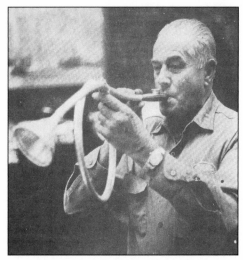

Howard Milner, master of the kazoozlehose.

Howard finishes his coffee. He then opens his glove compartment and takes out a battered kazoo, left there by one of his children. He takes the piece of hose and the funnel he keeps in his truck for any gas emergency. He jams the funnel into one end of the hose and the kazoo into the other. He loops the hose so that the contraption resembles a French horn with the funnel as the bell. He practices a few minutes, then hops out of his truck and enters the building. He stands by the information desk and plays "Happy Birthday." By the time he's finished, he's the center of a small crowd.

"There," Howard says. "I've played a musical instrument in your office and it's only 8:03. Am I the first?"

"I'm not sure that's a musical instrument," says the girl at the information desk. "What is it?"

"A kazoozlehose," Howard says promptly. "An instrument that plays music." He puts the kazoozlehose to his mouth again and plays "Yankee Doodle."

The group agrees the kazoozlehose is a musical instrument. They take him around to all the offices and he plays "Yankee Doodle" again, and "The Arkansas Traveler," and "Turkey in the Straw." When he comes back to the information desk there's a man with a saxophone, a woman with a clarinet, and a boy with a mouth organ. But Howard was the first. They give him $10 and a photographer takes his picture. He goes back to delivering his route.

That night Howard's picture is in the paper. It shows him playing his instrument. The headline reads, "Musical Milkman Konkocts Kazoozlehose."

37 ❧ PURE MILK ASSOCIATION

E arly in 1942 Ron Dougan receives an ultimatum from the milk business's producers, the farmers who sell their milk to the dairy, which puts
him in a squeeze. It's a letter bristling with bravado, for the writers know they
are confronting both Ron and W.J., who are old friends, longtime neighbors,
and who have always treated them fairly. But they are under pressure themselves, from the Pure Milk Association, a co-op founded shortly before the
Depression, to which they all now belong. A committee headed by a Chica-
goan, John Knox, who does not know the farm and has never visited Turtle
Township, has been urging them to stand up against evil management for
their monetary rights.

The PMA has a history of being an aggressive, slugging group in the interests of the dairy farm—or its interpretations of the interests. From a small
start in 1925 (the forming committee was the University of Illinois Agriculture
Extension Service, the Illinois Farm Bureau, and various dairy farmers) it grew
from less than 500 members at the start of 1929 to 15,000 by that year's end,
gaining most of these new members as a result of its successful 1929 Chicago
milk strike. The strike lasted eighteen days, farmers cooperated, tons of milk
were poured out into the streets, and milk was prevented from coming into the
Chicago market from Indiana and elsewhere. The PMA proved it had muscle,
and Chicago milk dealers were forced to capitulate and bargain. The PMA supported the breaking of a dairy workers' union in Joliet, and was perhaps impli-
cated in other dubious activities. An article in a 1936 issue of *Milwaukee Milk
Producer*, published by "Milwaukee Co-Operative Milk Producers," laments
the resignation of Chicago PMA's secretary-manager Don Geyer, and contains
this startling bit: "There have been many disturbances among the producers in
the last several years, highways have been picketed, milk plants and railroads
have been bombed, barns have been burned, and cattle destroyed. The federal
government had supervision of the market for some time, but was asked to
withdraw by the Pure Milk Association. Politicians and would-be farm leaders

Protesting against low prices in the 1930s, farmers dump milk by the roadside.

had done their best to break up Pure Milk but under Geyer's leadership it has held together in spite of all trials and tribulations."

In at least one case, PMA was the object of direct attack. Their own new PMA co-op plant in Burlington, Wisconsin, was destroyed by a mysterious bombing in 1932, with the night watchman abducted by five men and dumped in a ditch south of town, his hands and feet tied with rope.

Ronald and W.J., so close to all these happenings, cannot be unaware of them. They know that the strength and the muddy history of the organization make PMA a force to be reckoned with. When a letter comes, obviously directed by the PMA, it's best to sit up and take notice.

The ultimatum from the dairy's producers begins abruptly:

> We, the undersigned producers, desire to produce for you a high quality milk in compliance with U.S. Public Health standards. The premiums which we receive for fluid milk are based upon prices paid on other markets in compliance with U.S. Public Health requirements which require 6 hours reduction time or methylene test or 200,000 bacteria count or less per c.c. based upon latest approved standards of the American Public Health Association. If we are to meet the present requirements of 25,000 bacteria per c.c. [*which Dougan's Dairy requires*] a producer should receive a fifty cent premium per hundred weight for total deliveries.

Such plate count shall be made at an approved laboratory.

We believe the present method of penalizing producers for failing to comply with your present requirements will lead to misunderstanding and general dissatisfaction among all of your producers.

We urge the immediate adoption of a pooling plan at your dairy which takes in consideration total sales and total purchases from producers or other sources.

We insist on the immediate installing of a scale and weight tank in order that accurate weights and tests can be determined.

We respectfully request that producers receive statements showing daily weights of milk delivered, these to be furnished producers each month when payment for milk is made.

> Signed,
> Glen Wallace
> Joe Elliot, Swiss Town Farm
> U.S. Walker
> T.R. Higgins
> Roland Higgins
> Emil Punzel
> Cleo Beaver
> Ralf Young
> Phil Holmes
> B. Riese and Clay Davis
> Geo. Holmes
> G. J. Higgins
> Ruby M. Obeck
> Albert E. Marston
> Howard V. Johnson, Mgr., Freeman Farm
> Lois Gates
> Marvin Hefty, Mgr., Blackhawk Farm
> T. Woolsey Jr.

The squeeze is this. These names add up to practically every farmer milking in Turtle Township—including tenant farmers and their farms' owners. There are some astonishing signatures, such as Albert Marston; he and some others must have signed with reluctance. But there are some names missing: primarily, W.J. Dougan himself, who sells the milk of his one-hundred-head herd to the plant—the milkhouse—which is a separate economic entity. His name belongs on the letter as a demander, and on the envelope, along with Ronald's, as the recipient. The other missing names are the instigator of this ultimatum, neighbor Johnny Holmes, who is operating his own small dairy, and behind him and them all, the co-op of milk producers, the Chicago committee of the Pure Milk Association.

Ron's response (and W.J.'s, for the two conferred), sent to each of the signers, is a lengthy one. He ignores specific demands of scales, tanks, and a non-dairy lab for the determination of bacterial count (he, a chemistry grad, has always done the bacterial counts, or someone under his supervision, so it is a slap in the face) and speaks to the larger issues that are implicit.

> To our producers:
> We have thought of our business as almost a partnership.
> 1. Do a good job and put out a fine product at a fair price.
> 2. Return the producer a fair price for his milk.
> 3. Pay a living wage to our employees.
> 4. Make a living ourselves and build up some reserves in the business to take care of reverses.

There should never be a hint of conflicting interest between management and men and producers. In a business this size where all of us should know all about the problems, the difficulties, the advantages and good points, and in which we all contribute to a successful whole, to talk of conflicting interests is silly. Our interests as farmers are as great as those of distributors. The job is all one unit, just as on a one route dairy, the operator thinks of his job as a unit. We think for years the above outlined condition held absolutely true in this business.

We are sorry to say that lately, this has not been entirely the case. We have felt a widening distance coming between ourselves as buyers of your milk and you as farmers. On every other subject you esteem us highly, but as the distributor of your best crop we bear watching.

We don't treat with you directly anymore, but through a committee some of whom we respect and some of whom we do not. Our intimate problems are not treated as they affect you and us only, but a decision that would be fair to you and to us might give another dairy an unfair advantage as a buyer and therefore we are sacrificed.

It doesn't matter to John Knox if we keep the College business or not. If we do not, he suspects Wright & Wagner will get them so his organization will lose no milk. The prestige and profit we accrue from the College business would be lost overnight. Neither you nor we would have very much to say about it.

As we succeed in putting out a good product, we profit. A high bacterial count in milk, even though it isn't enough to spoil a batch, gives every one of us a black eye when it is posted at the Health Office, and talked over at the Hospital.

In the past we have discussed the good of the whole business and have been guided accordingly. From time to time we have discussed plans with you, sometimes as a group, but more often as individuals. We wish it were oftener.

The letter continues, explaining the base-surplus system the dairy introduced which levels out production and keeps down seasonal fluxuation. Ron believes a good business is one where most of the milk is sold in the fluid brackets. He feels that this system allows Dougan's to pay a price well above the average, and that the closest competitor is only close because it is being supported by the PMA. He discusses the uses of surplus milk—that which isn't sold as fluid—going into butter and cream; on these the farm holds even, or loses money.

Much of the rest of the long letter discusses statistics, the Chicago market, the various classes of milk, the difficulties of competing. It goes into the problems with condensary pricing. It is a carefully argued account, and includes that, were the producers to cease with Dougan as their distributor, or if the dairy were to fold, the PMA might well find them other markets where they could sell their milk, for no less than the Chicago market receives. For they are all basically fine farms.

These markets would be guaranteed, for a while. Ron does say, 'During periods of heavy demands for milk, you would have no trouble as private agents getting on as good markets as PMA could offer. In poor times, I question whether they could do better than you could yourselves—their price will be down with everyone else's.'

Then he asks the producers for help in the serious business decision the dairy is facing:

(a) We can not take in the amount of milk we now do and churn as much as we do. Last month the butterfat going into a pound of butter cost us about fifty cents and we sold it for 43 cents. The amount of butterfat we bought from you to make a pound of butter brought you fifty cents and you bought it back nicely packaged for 39 cents. Of course we had the skim milk and some of that was used to good advantage. If we could have bought butterfat for about what we sold it for, the solids would have carried the costs. We could pay more for butterfat for instance than the creamery that is just purchasing cream. But we can not ask it to bridge as wide a gap as we now have. We must decide if we are going to abandon our tight self-sufficient organization capable of handling its entire product through its own outlets.

(b) We can't pay $2.25 or $2.00, or $1.85 for the milk from which we get our churn cream and skim milk.

(c) If we stop churning and have to turn our cream on a still lower market, the urge will be to level out our buying a great deal more. We will put milk and cream back on the routes a second day. We will run very close on cream. We will probably make a dicker with some outfit to supply us with some sweet cream. We may have to use skim milk from returned milk for chocolate. By these practices, some of which aren't to be recommended, we would cut down our business intake and would ask to be relieved of some of our milk.

We would be able to cut plant costs appreciably. We could no doubt get along with less men. We would be crippled in our selling, for butter and cheese are good leaders. Our quality of product would not be quite as good if we had to resort to taking out products a second time.

The upshot is, writes Ron:

Do you want to drop out of the PMA and go back to a closely knit organization looking to us to handle all your products through the lines we are fitted for? What will this do to your price? Very little. In the first place, it won't average below Chicago, because we have always been above. Our method is to run a fluid milk business. In this setup, we will be on our toes to get the best return to you it is possible to get and certainly would not feel we were doing a good job if our price was not better than the Chicago Blended price.

He then gives the alternative:

To continue as at present, but dropping the butter line entirely and cutting our intake to as close our actual sales as it is possible to do. Our own feeling in the matter is for the former policy. We think that month in and month out the business will be more satisfactory for all of us if we keep in our hands the lines we now have. If we in open meeting agree on a price we can agree on as fair. If we can discuss our problems regularly and carry a full knowledge of the business, over the years we will be returning more money to our producers in a happier relationship than if we continue under the P.M.A.

However it is your business as much as ours. Only with your full support can we operate successfully. If you feel that John Knox and his committee can do a better job for you than you can do for yourselves, we will do our best to adjust ourselves to this setup and give you the best market we are able to under the circumstances.

It's obvious from this long and carefully reasoned letter, with its reproachful but respectful start, which then pays more attention to the demands of the times (which the producers seem only narrowly aware of) than to the demands of the producers, that Ronald and W.J. have been feeling increased resentment and frustration during these early years of the forties. The pressures of organized control — federal, the PMA, and labor, are telling on them, as they themselves continue to work themselves to the bone. Ron writes his father, in a discussion about the college business, "All of this is preamble. Their [the PMA's] continual pressure forces us to try to protect ourselves. It puts me on the defensive. It builds up hostility."

Many pages of dialogue pass between Ronald and W.J. during this period. One of Ronald's comments reads:

When we came into PMA, it was with various understandings relative to our particular problems. Over the years new men came into power who knew not Joseph: One by one our prerogatives were clipped as expert bargainers went after us. The last man we have had here from the Dept. of Markets has the attitude that his function is to nose out infractions and sharp practices and stop them. He assumes that the smartest dealer is the one that takes the most, and no man can be condemned for trying a grab. That isn't just the way he says it, but it is the impression he gives me. Instead of farmer, distributor, and customer co-operating to get a good product on the market in a fair way, it is a fight between all three.

A major sore spot is the controversy on the college business, how to continue to supply this fine and prestigious account while meeting the PMA's price, and complying with the wartime Office of Price Administration's restrictions. The two go back and forth, trying to resolve the situation. Finally,

Ron concludes one conversation with:

> So here we are. To get milk for the college, we either have to produce it aw-
> ful cheap, or buy it too dear to sell at 34 cents, and the OPA will not let us
> raise our price. I am not having any fun anymore. The PMA has spoiled our
> buying, etc. It has to be a fight to get quality—and I am sure in many cases
> we aren't getting it. There is no co-operative spirit in the show at all. Many
> of the farmers aren't so interested in giving us the best they can, but rather
> the least they can get by with. Beaver, for instance, hasn't cooled his milk in
> water this winter.
>
> The so called PMA does nothing to police its membership. Its only job is
> to harry the distributor, it seems to me. Very probably they are able to wran-
> gle better prices for the producer—on the other hand supply and demand
> does that and for the most part, all the PMA can do is take credit for trends
> that are bound to occur.

And near the end of several frustrated sheets, still dealing with supply and
price to the College, he writes to his father, "Our plant is loaded with work
anyway, our pasteurizer and boiler are just staggering along with capacity
loads—if we dropped the college it would ease things there and allow us to
handle a little bottled milk expansion." Ronald's last typed line is, "I am sure
the above arrangement would hold water, but I haven't the ambition to do it.
It would be a relief to drop them." His father writes in longhand, "I am more
anxious about you getting the job down where you can handle it efficiently
and happily than about volume. I am worried about your pace and worry."

Evidence of W.J.'s concern about the whole situation is in these lines to a
university friend: "The marketing work of the dairy is becoming somewhat
difficult. The dealer is in the grip of a pincer of which one arm is the organized
labor and the other is the Pure Milk Association or organized producers. This
latter is as greedy and ruthless and short sighted as the organized labor."

One thing the producers do not know, and that Ron and W.J. do not reveal, is that the dairy is quietly changing hands. By the end of 1942 Ron will
have purchased the milk business from his father for about $22,000 which
includes the dairy's debts. He will now officially be a dealer only, and W.J.
the producer. To all outward appearances, the farm will continue to be run
as before.

How does this problem end? The Dougan producers and the farm distributors reach an agreement and decide to keep working together. The realities

of wartime and price fixing make some of the arguments disappear. Butter is a case in point. Its price is so low, with the dairy not able to raise it during the War, that there is no way to produce it at any profit at all, especially if the producers' cooperative won't cooperate. The dairy loses on every pound. The only solution is to cease butter manufacture. Ron chops up the churn, and the space is used for storage. The handsome two-pound and one-pound butter crocks are stacked neatly in the Big House cellar, where they gradually disappear for other uses, and by 2011 are fetching over $250 apiece on eBay.

After he retires from the milk business, in 1967, Daddy briefly explains the PMA in response to a query by Jackie. "It's an organization of farmers producing milk in the Midwest. It developed considerable clout, still has it. A co-op representing the farmers who sold to dealers. The people I bought from were members, our farm was. We contributed a few cents per so many gallons of milk that the farmers would forward to the Pure Milk Association.

"I have files from PMA's monthly reports about prices — base and surplus. Lists of producers and how they were paid. How the prices were arrived at. I kept my own herd in the Association at about $70 a month as dues. They used it for advertising and for maintaining the office. They didn't do any inspection, just represented the farmers in attempting at better prices.

"It was a good association, I sat in on meetings. We'd bicker and bargain and finally decide what this area should be paying for milk. Then we'd have to live with it. I was on both sides as a producer and a dealer! It was always voluntary. Even if a certain farmer didn't belong, he was still governed by what the majority decided.

"They still advertise milk. They have an office in Madison and one in Chicago. There must be groups like this all over the U.S. Ours was just bigger. I would get ideas on advertising, I'd call and discuss with them, and they'd brush me off. After a while I decided I could use the money I gave the PMA and use it to advertise on my own. I quit sending the check from my own herd, but I kept sending it for my farmers."

Daddy doesn't mention the 1942 ultimatum to Jackie. He doesn't mention John Knox, or the hairy history of the organization. In his later years, he's mellowed toward the PMA.

38 ⚹ FATHER OF MY CHILD

The phone rings at the dairy office. Daddy answers it. "Dougan's Dairy, Ronald Dougan speaking."

"Hello, this is Mrs. Whitney Jones," says a voice at the end of the wire. "And I'm calling to thank you."

The name is familiar. It's a customer. But Daddy can't remember ever having done anything particular for Mrs. Jones. "Thank me? What for?" he asks.

"I consider you the father of my baby," says Mrs. Jones.

"Whoa!" exclaims Daddy. "Hold on! What did you say?"

"I consider you the father of my baby," repeats Mrs. Jones. "You perhaps don't remember—"

"I can't say that I do," intersperses Daddy.

"—but my husband and I were out for a drive one Sunday afternoon not quite a year ago, and we stopped at the farm and you showed us through the round barn."

"Yes?" says Daddy, intrigued. He often shows visitors through the round barn.

"And they were feeding the cows while they were being milked," Mrs. Jones goes on. "You said that for many years the cows had been fed yeast, which produced Vitamin D in their milk, but that lately you'd also been giving them large amounts of Vitamin E—"

"Aha," says Daddy, the light beginning to dawn. "That was because Vitamin E has given some evidence of improving cows' conception rates."

"Yes," Mrs. Jones agrees. "That was what you told us. Well, you had no way of knowing this, but my husband and I had been married twelve years and just desperately wanted a child, and we'd been to all the doctors and clinics and tried everything, everything, and nothing helped. But when you said what you were feeding your cows, and why, we figured it couldn't hurt to try—so we stopped at a drug store on the way home and both of us began taking Vitamin E. And within two months I was pregnant, and our baby is now three weeks old. So I'm calling to thank you."

Daddy bursts into laughter, and so does Mrs. Jones.

"Is it a boy? I trust you've named him Ronald?" asks Daddy.

"No, it's a lovely little girl," says Mrs. Jones. "Her name is Elizabeth, after my mother."

"You should have considered Daisy, or Bess, or more appropriately, M-23," says Daddy, explaining how he names his cows. The call ends in much merriment. Daddy congratulates Mr. and Mrs. Jones, and says that when Elizabeth is a little older to take her down to Sharpe's photography studio so that her picture can be in a Dougan baby ad.

Ron at his desk in the dairy office.

"My copy will be discreet," promises Daddy, "although I admit it's a temptation to headline it with an attention-grabber. 'Mother Claims Milkman is Father of her Child.'"

39 ⚔ SODA POP

I t's 1954. The alliance that grew from modest beginnings on the round barn floor in 1933, producing first rabbit feed and then Adams Korn Kurls, has now grown to a large corporation in South Beloit, manufacturing a variety of snack foods sold all over the country and beyond. Daddy still has a few shares in the company, but more than 50 percent is owned by the Adams family, early investors. Its president is Allan Adams, one of several Adams brothers. He and Ron Dougan are old friends, through business, Rotary, the fact that both the Adams and Dougan families have been around Beloit a long time engaging in civic activities (Allen's father was mayor of Beloit when Ron and Allan were in their teens, and the Adams family received milk on the first day of W.J.'s delivery)—and, of course, the unique link between the farm and corporation on account of Korn Kurls. Nevertheless, Daddy's letter to Allen Adams—except for the greeting, is formal.

> Dear Al,
>
> I am writing you relative to the policy that Adams Corporation has ad-opted relative to milk and pop for employees at the plant.
>
> You will remember that I have mentioned this to you previously and told you that I was going to present some arguments in favor of a free choice between dairy products and pop, rather than free pop only.
>
> The reasons for Adams Corporation making milk available on the same basis as pop beverages seem obvious to me. A great deal of evidence has been compiled to show that many workers come to work with inadequate break-fasts and that mid-morning milk is a great pick-up. Then there is the fact that great emphasis is being put on the promotion of dairy products, particularly in this state whose economy is so closely tied to the dairy cow.
>
> Since 1929, when the Wisconsin Manufacturers Association under Riordan coined the phrase, "Farm and Factory Must Prosper Together," we have been interested in promoting milk in shops. As I recall, we started the movement

of milk in factories in Beloit at that time, and I think much of our expansion since that time can be traced to the contacts we made with local workers and management.

We are charging you at present one-half cent per half pint under regular wholesale for the milk that goes into the plant. We believe that if milk is made available at no cost to the worker the consumption of pop will fall off, and while the total cost of beverages will be somewhat higher, it will be offset by the advantages a larger milk consumption will insure. We will be happy to continue the price differential under wholesale as our contribution to an enlarged milk program in your plant. We have recently added to your refrigeration, and we will agree to supply adequate refrigeration equipment in the future to take care of the project.

There is another minor feature which occurs to me and this does not hinge on the free milk angle entirely. I would like to have a picture or two taken in the plant with employees at lunch with milk in evidence to use in our *Daily News* ads. Of course, if you see fit to make milk available as I am suggesting, it will be wonderful to work out an ad or two tying in you and us and employee health benefits and the milk promotion program into one story.

Yours very truly,
R.A. Dougan

This is an adroit letter. It's to a friend who oversees the production of thirst-provoking snacks — salty, fried, cheesy, corn based; all packaged in

Beverley Jorgenson, daughter of a milk-house worker, was not raised on soda pop.

various permutations. This is pioneer junk food, now become the staple of every kid's diet. The workers surely have access to these products at reduced rates. They can reach for a bottle of free pop to wash them down, or for a pint of wholesome milk—for which they must pay. Why? asks Ron, when milk will give the men—especially breakfastless men—a genuine nutritional boost, something that will aid them in their work. So this is a letter subtly against the soft drink industry, which is crowding out milk, Wisconsin's staple. Would Allan Adams really want this?

But the letter isn't accusatory. Ron brings up the history of milk in factories, how he began it in Beloit at the start of the Depression. He implies Allan Adams' service to his employees and the interests of his State. He himself can't afford to supply milk for nothing, but will continue to sell it under wholesale, plus install additional refrigeration if necessary. And he lures further with an afterthought: how about a photo of workers during their lunch break, with milk bottles prominent? Run in the daily paper this would be an ad both for the dairy and the corporation.

Farm records don't indicate whether Allan Adams starts giving free milk along with free soda pop. There is tangible evidence, though, that supports Daddy's letter—a *Daily News* ad of several men drinking milk at their bench, during lunch break. That, and the fact that Daddy and Allan Adams remain friends for the rest of their lives.

40 ❧ CRAIG MOONLIGHTS

Craig has finished his residency and is just starting his medical practice in Beloit. He's only been doctoring a few weeks. He and his family are staying at Chez Nous with Mother and Daddy until they find a place to live.

One evening the phone rings; it's a patient needing a house call. Craig prepares to go.

"Oh, will you deliver a pint of half-and-half to 1842 Highland Avenue?" Daddy calls. "I was going to run it down; the milkman missed them. Mrs. Johnson called a little while ago."

Craig Dougan as a young doctor.

"Sure," says Craig. He stops at the dairy and gets the cream from the cooler. After seeing his patient he goes to Highland Avenue and knocks at 1842. The door opens.

"Why, Dr. Dougan!" exclaims the customer. Craig recognizes Mrs. Johnson; she was one of his very first patients. He saw her only last week.

"They have you delivering milk?" she inquires.

Craig shakes his head ruefully. "Yes," he admits. "We beginning doctors have to moonlight!"

41 ⚔ A STABLE MARKET

In the loft of the round barn, written on the silo, are "The Aims of This Farm." Of the five listed, three, to Jackie, have always seemed attainable. Grampa can cull his animals to achieve "Profitable Livestock." He can have barns, silos, and corncribs up to date and in good repair for "Proper Storage." He can practice, as he always does, "Life as Well as a Living."

The first, though, "Good Crops," is dependent on something Grampa can't control. No matter how good his soil, his seed, his tillage practices, he can't make the weather obey his wishes. There will be a summer when her father will write, "no crop a complete failure, but it makes me sick to think how much we stand to lose because we couldn't have had a little thunder shower about June 1." There really needs to be some directions for God on the silo, too: "Don't forget: A little thunderstorm, June 1."

The other Aim that is almost beyond Grampa's control is "A Stable Market." So many factors drive a market that it cannot be counted on to remain stable for long. Drought and flood affect it, the activities of buyers and sellers, the vagaries of supply and demand, government policies and practices, war, depression, and more, are not under his control. He can only aim.

In 1927, *Hoard's Dairyman* asks Grampa to write a series of articles, to be called overall, "What I Am Trying To Do On My Farm." The third article, appearing in the February 10 issue, is titled, "To Solve My Marketing Problem." Grampa refers to but does not take on the cosmic economic problems of the times. He knows of the depression of the early twenties, and met it; he does not foresee the Great Depression when his own farm will teeter on the brink of bankruptcy. But he writes of what he knows: For a small dairyman to peddle his wares successfully, he must have a standard high quality product, in sufficient quantity to meet the demand, and to advertise it. His words are simple, and speak to what a single farmer can do in the midst of fluctuating markets. He writes:

I do not want to pose as an expert on the great problem of marketing farm products. This subject is engaging some of the brightest minds and shrewdest business experts, still they are baffled and far from a comprehensive solution to this problem.

However there are a few facts bearing on this subject that have become manifest to me in my experiences in trying to dispose of my products at a fair profit.

If one is to market a product he must have a standard quality in sufficient quantity to meet the demand. It must be easily available to the consumer and he must let the consumer know regarding the product. Thus marketing reaches back to production; includes distribution and advertising.

Soon after I had started my dairy business, Dean Henry of the University of Wisconsin gave me this counsel: "Dougan, keep right on producing the quality and let the people know what you are doing." Whatever success I have had in marketing is due to conformity to these principles. When I went onto the farm I had a definite purpose, viz., to produce and distribute to the people of Beloit the best milk to be had anywhere and to get a price for it that would enable me to live in conformity with the standards of the community. Through the years of development, this purpose has remained constant. The development of the business was gradual, both in the improving and standardizing of the quality, and the increase in business and the increase in price.

In quality I was a law unto myself. I fixed my ideals of a good milk and used the knowledge of the university in developing and testing my product, then practiced and still practice eternal vigilance to keep the quality up to standard. One of my greatest difficulties has been to always have the milk to meet the demand. The business has had to produce its own capital. At one time when I was getting four or five cents above the usual price, another milkman wanted to know, "Where in h____ I found people who would give 10 cents per quart for milk." I told him, "I didn't, I found them in Beloit," and I will tell you, I found them by advertising. I have used various means of advertising—newspaper ads, circular letters, store window displays, floats in business parades, demonstrations at fairs, etc. Through all my advertising is a fixed purpose. I never beg nor ever ask for customers. I never hit the other dealers. I never advertise a cut price sale but I aim to give information of how my milk is produced, its great value as food, and its extreme value in saving the babies. I aim to keep my name and methods so completely before the people of our town that if a stranger should ask any man, woman or child, "Who produces the best milk in Beloit," they would answer without hesitation, "Why, Dougan, of course."

Perhaps the uppermost question in your minds is the same as my fellow dairyman asked years ago, "How am I able to get people to pay twenty cents per quart for milk during the last five years?" The question is partly answered in the foregoing, I am producing a quality product that is needed in my town.

In 1921 I was close pressed because prices in every farm product were falling. However, my cost of production was increasing. Moreover, I had been running on too close a margin during the war. I could not reduce price, keep up quality, and remain in business.

I took into counsel some of the businessmen and the doctors. They invariably advised me not to quit or reduce quality. The doctors said, "Beloit needs your product." I give this incident to show how I play above board. I have sought the confidence of the public.

Another factor in holding this confidence is, I play no favorite. I have one price for all. The poorest family in town which sacrifices to get its quart of milk for a sick or young babe gets the same quality of milk and the same service as do the wealthy.

Another reason for my control of price is that I give full value for price received. One lady expressed it this way when I informed her that the price had gone up. "All right," she said, "it is worth it," and pointing to two youngsters remarked, "We consider it a good investment."

What I have worked out in marketing in my little business can and must be done by organized and united farmers in all farm products.

This is Grampa's 1927 answer to marketing. His reasoning is sound, built on his experience and ideals. He can't foresee a market that will shift milk to supermarkets, or advanced refrigeration to the point where ultra-pasteurized cream can squat on the shelf practically forever with no refrigeration at all—though devoid of food value.

He can't foresee other factors that will make retail home delivery—his whole business life—redundant, will make all home delivery collapse, except as it is revived as a luxury in the succeeding century.

For the times, and for many years to come, these standards do serve the farm, embody its Aims, and enrich the area. Ron follows his father's precepts, and adds a brilliance to Grampa's earnest advertising, until the end of the retail milk business.

42 ⚡ THE WATCH

Ron Dougan, often without a watch but rarely lacking a joke.

It's 1956. Daddy has an old friend, Ted Robie, who lives near the college on Harrison Street. He's also a customer. One day when Daddy is filling in on a milk route he stops his truck before Ted's house, delivers the Robie order to the back step, and then instead of going on, starts pacing up and down the front lawn, his hands clasped behind his back, his head down.

It isn't long before Ted notices him and opens the door.

"What are you looking for, Ron?"

"I lost my watch," Daddy says.

Ted, concerned, comes out to help. Together they pace the lawn.

"You're sure it was here?" Ted asks, after a bit.

"Right in front of this house. I was delivering milk."

They search some more. There's no sign of a watch.

"Well," sighs Daddy, "I guess I'll just have to give it up for lost."

"Is it a very valuable one?" asks Ted.

"The first watch I ever had," Daddy says ruefully. "I got it when I was fourteen."

Ted's face expresses quick sympathy, as well as amazement that Daddy has managed to keep an heirloom for so long. "We mowed the grass several days ago," he says anxiously. "You didn't lose it before then, did you?"

"Oh, yes," says Daddy. "I've been looking for it, on and off, ever since."

"Well, it could have got caught in the mower—thrown into the bushes. When did you lose it?"

"About forty years ago," says Daddy.

Books by Jacqueline Jackson

Julie's Secret Sloth, 1953

The Paleface Redskins, 1958

The Taste of Spruce Gum, 1966

Missing Melinda, 1967

Chicken Ten Thousand, 1968

The Ghost Boat, 1969

Spring Song, 1969

The Orchestra Mice, 1970

The Endless Pavement (with William Perlmutter), 1973

Turn Not Pale, Beloved Snail, 1974

Stories from the Round Barn, 1997

More Stories from the Round Barn, 2002

Jacqueline Dougan Jackson (pictured here at about the time she promised she would some day write this book) grew up on a Wisconsin dairy farm amidst extended family and pet goats. Various accounts of her early years are included in this volume, and in two earlier Barn books. She majored in Classics at Beloit College, studying with poet Chad Walsh and artist Franklin Boggs. At the University of Michigan her writing tutor was Hopwood Director Roy Cowden. She began teaching at Kent State University, and continued at Sangamon State (now U of Illinois Springfield) where she was on the founding faculty. She led eight groups of students on hostelling trips to England. Studying children's lit one group climbed Watership Down with Richard Adams; on a mysteries trip, they spent a day with Colin Dexter.

At eight Jackie Jackson won a first in short stories at Beloit's city-wide hobby show; her first novel was serialized in *The Galesburg Post* when she was ten. As an adult she has twelve published books, two self-illustrated, has had plays and musicals performed, and her stories read over Wisconsin Public Radio. *The Taste of Spruce Gum* was the 1968 runner-up for the Newbery Award. For twenty years she hosted "Reading and Writing and Radio," listened to in classrooms throughout Wisconsin's School of the Air, and in central Illinois. Some of the programs are included in her writing book, *Turn Not Pale, Beloved Snail*, and are free on her website for classroom or personal use. She currently has a weekly poem in Springfield's *Illinois Times*.

Jackie Jackson's daughters are Damaris, Megan, Gillian, and Elspeth. She has six grandchildren, all (of course) above average.

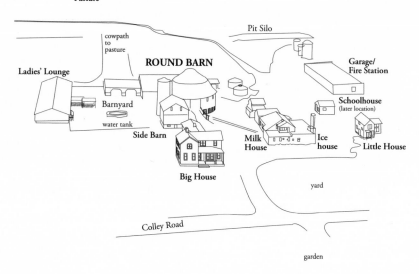

Pasture

Pit Silo

cowpath
to
pasture

ROUND BARN

Garage/
Fire Station

Ladies' Lounge

Schoolhouse
(later location)

Barnyard

water tank

Side Barn

Milk
House

Ice
house

Little House

Big House

yard

Colley Road

garden

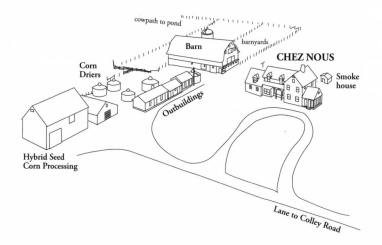

cowpath to pond

Barn

barnyards

CHEZ NOUS

Corn
Driers

Smoke
house

Outbuildings

Hybrid Seed
Corn Processing

Lane to Colley Road